MASTERING

HEBREW

HEAR IT · SPEAK IT · WRITE IT · READ IT

Developed for the
FOREIGN SERVICE INSTITUTE,
DEPARTMENT OF STATE
by Joseph A. Reif
and Hanna Levinson

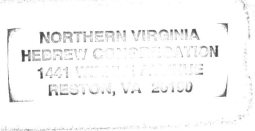
BARRON'S

Cover design by Milton Glaser, Inc.

This course was developed for the Foreign Service Institute,
Department of State, by Joseph A. Reif and Hanna Levinson.

The title of the original course is Hebrew Basic Course

This edition published in 1988 by Barron's Educational Series, Inc.

All inquiries should be addressed to:
Barron's Educational Series, Inc.
250 Wireless Boulevard
Hauppauge, New York, 11788

Paper Edition

International Standard Book No. 0-8120-3990-4

A large part of the text of this book is recorded on the
accompanying tapes as follows:

Unit 1	Tape 1A	Unit 15	Tape 5A, 5B
Unit 2	Tape 1A	Unit 16	Tape 5B, 6A
Unit 3	Tape 1A, 1B	Unit 17	Tape 6A, 6B
Unit 4	Tape 1B	Unit 18	Tape 7A
Unit 5	Tape 1B, 2A	Unit 19	Tape 7B
Unit 6	Tape 2A	Unit 20	Tape 8A
Unit 7	Tape 2B	Unit 21	Tape 8A, 8B, 9A
Unit 8	Tape 2B, 3A	Unit 22	Tape 9A, 9B, 10A
Unit 9	Tape 3A	Unit 23	Tape 10A, 10B
Unit 10	Tape 3B	Unit 24	Tape 11A
Unit 11	Tape 3B	Unit 25	Tape 11A, 11B, 12A
Unit 12	Tape 4A	Unit 26	Tape 12A
Unit 13	Tape 4A, 4B	Unit 27	Tape 12B
Unit 14	Tape 5A		

PRINTED IN THE UNITED STATES OF AMERICA

5   800   987654

Preface

This course in Mastering Hebrew is part of a series being offered by Barron's Educational Series. If you are a serious language student, this course will provide you with the opportunity to become truly fluent in modern Hebrew.

This is one of the famous language courses developed by the Foreign Service Institute of the United States. These courses were designed to train United States Government representatives who need to be able to communicate clearly and accurately in a foreign language.

Mastering Hebrew provides an excellent opportunity for you to learn Hebrew on your own, studying at your own pace. In addition, these tapes are ideal for students who are studying modern Hebrew in a school and would like to supplement their classroom work with additional practice in the spoken language.

TABLE OF CONTENTS

INTRODUCTION

Americans know of Hebrew as the language of the Old Testament. Hebrew had been a living language, that is, it was spoken as a native language by a community of people, at least until the First Century, B.C., and possibly for several centuries after that. But even though it ceased to be a living language in this sense, a large and important body of literature has remained in constant daily use for prayer and study.

During the Middle Ages and into the Renaissance Hebrew served as a lingua franca for Jews throughout the world, and the literature was expanded by scholars and poets. Hebrew thus was kept in continuous familiarity, and in the last century successful efforts were begun to revive it as a modern language.

Today Hebrew is the official language of the State of Israel. It is being taught to immigrants speaking a wide variety of native languages, and the goal is to have all the inhabitants learn to speak it.

To be sure, modern Hebrew is different from the Biblical language. The phonology (sound system) has been symplified, and new syntactic patterns and vocabulary have been developed to express concepts not dreamed of two thousand years ago. But the modern language is unmistakably the descendant of the language of the Psalms and the prophets.

The sounds of modern Hebrew are fairly easy for Americans to learn. Since only a minority of the present population are native speakers of Hebrew, foreign accents can hardly be called rare, and one should not feel the slightest embarrassment in making even halting efforts to speak it.

PURPOSE

It should be stated very clearly at the outset that this book is not intended as an elementary text for the study of the Bible or other Hebrew literature. It is also not intended as a reference grammar of Hebrew. There are a number of good books on the market to fulfill those needs. This book is intended as a training manual, designed to teach a non-speaker of Hebrew to speak and comprehend with some degree of fluency an acceptable form of the modern language. Its relationship to a reference grammar is analogous to the relationship of a program of calisthenics to a textbook on physiology. The student is not supposed to read this book in order to find out about Hebrew; he is supposed to work at the material presented here until he can speak Hebrew, and he will have to work hard.

The goal of this course is performance. One "knows" Hebrew in the same sense that one "knows" how to drive a car. It is not necessary to be an automotive engineer or to know the technical terms for the parts of a car in order to be a good driver. Many excellent drivers even have wrong notions about the mechanical aspects of an automobile. Similarly, it is not necessary to be able to discuss accurately and comprehensively the grammar of a language in order to speak it fluently and correctly. Intensive drilling will produce the proper habits. When the student participates in conversation easily and fluently with a minimum of either "accent" or of conscious effort then he has achieved the goal of the course.

Emphasis on the spoken language does not mean that reading and writing are to be ignored or downgraded in overall importance for the educated speaker. These latter skills are a separate problem which in the initial stages of study are treated as secondary.

Many students who use this book will already be familiar with the Hebrew alphabet and writing system. For those who are not it is suggested that work on reading be postponed until Unit 10 is completed. Classes will of course, vary in their ability to absorb the material, and the instructor should feel free to adjust this schedule.

However, it is felt highly probable, on the basis of a large body of experience with many languages, including Hebrew, that the total competence of the student will be greater if he starts with the spoken language and then adds the written form rather than vice versa. Students who already know how to read will profit greatly if they concentrate exclusively on the spoken language for at least the first ten units.

STYLE OF HEBREW USED

The language presented here as a model for students to imitate is the ordinary informal speech of educated native Israelis. This is different from the Hebrew usually taught outside of Israel, and students who have already learned some Hebrew may have to make some adjustments.

Modern Hebrew is a living language and as such it is changing daily. Slang expression, coinages, variant pronunciations, and grammatical innovations are characteristic of any living language. Furthermore, Hebrew is spoken and written in a variety of styles. These vary from highly formal to highly informal.

Formal spoken style is very similar to the literary style and is more like the Hebrew that is taught traditionally. Formal style is used, as the name implies, for public speaking, official meetings, radio news broadcasts, or other occasions where the speaker would use deferential or deliberate speech.

Informal spoken style is that used by native speakers in ordinary, relaxed conversation. It is often more rapid than the formal style and is the speech which seems most "natural" to native Israelis.

There is a highly informal style which contains much slang, contractions and dropping of sounds, and is fairly rapid. The student should not attempt to learn it until he is fairly fluent in the ordinary informal style.

The informal speech used in this text is tempered with features of more formal speech. These are included because the non-native speaker will be expected to have learned them, and their use will not seem affected.

It is interesting to note that the speakers who provided the material for this book often insisted that one should not use forms or expressions which they, in fact, did. This occasionally led to long discussions about what to include in the book, and sometimes no final decision was reached. Thus, for a example, the forms /birer/ and /otxem/ "you" are included in the material as well as the 'correct' forms /berar/ and /etxem/. In such cases the student will find that either choice will be acceptable in conversation.

METHODS AND PROCEDURE

The Native Speaker

Since the emphasis is on speech throughout the course, an indispensable component is the voice of an instructor whose native language is Hebrew. The student should not attempt to use these materials without either a native instructor or recordings of a native instructor's voice. The method of instruction incorporates <u>guided imitation</u>, <u>repetition</u>, <u>memorization</u>, <u>pattern practice</u>, and <u>conversation</u>.

The instructor performs the following functions:
(a) He serves as a <u>model</u> for imitation and a source for elicitation of material.
In this his ability to repeat without change and his endless patience are most
important.

(b) He <u>corrects</u> mistakes of all kinds: pronunciation, grammar, and vocabulary.
Tape recordings are an extremely useful tool, but they cannot correct the
student.

(c) He <u>drills</u> the student. He conducts, and may himself devise, drills and
exercises designed to fix new language patterns in the habits of the learner.

(d) He <u>converses</u> with the student. He acts out prepared conversations with the
student. It is here that his intelligence, imagination, and skill are most
important.

It is to be noted that <u>explanation</u> is not listed as a normal function
of the instructor. In general, explanation of the language is held to a
minimum. Using the language and talking about it are different things.

The native speaker has under his control the vast array of possible
sentences of the language, knows when to use them, and recognizes and responds
to them when used by others. In this sense only the native speaker really
<u>knows</u> the language. For this reason he is the most satisfactory model, corrector,
and conversation partner.

However, the native speaker is to a great extent unaware of the structural
patterns of his language because he learned them at an early age and has not
thought much about them. The educated man is overtly familiar only with those
patterns of grammar, style, and pronunciation which are emphasized in his
education. These are usually only a small fraction of the total structure of
the language, and by no means the most important for the English-speaking
student. The native speaker's explanations about his language may be satisfactory, or correct but inadequate, or even completely false or misleading. For
these reasons the student should not rely on the native speaker as an explainer.
Normally, the course is conducted under the supervision of a scientific linguist
who provides whatever explanations are necessary.

<u>Intensiveness</u>

Not only is a large total of instructional hours necessary, but concen-
trated study is essential. Experience has shown that greater concentration of
contact hours, especially at the beginning of a language course, yields far
better results than dispersal of the same number of hours of over a long period
of time. The maximum load per day for efficient learning is highly variable,
some students reaching the point of diminishing returns with four contact hours
and others being able to work up to eight or more. At the Foreign Service
Institute students usually have six hours a day five days a week of classroom
contact hours.

The size of the class is another important consideration. As in many
learning situations, the learning of a second language proceeds more thoroughly
and rapidly if it takes place in a small group. This provides greater variety
in drill and conversation, more speaking time for each student per class hour,
and allows the instructor to give more attention to each individual. The
maximum figure for effective learning varies with the personality types of the
students, the skill of the instructor, and other factors, but the number six
serves as a standard, across-the-board maximum.

At the other extreme, a class consisting of a single student is feasible
and may be very successful, but it usually proves better to have several students
for drill and conversation. In the regular intensive courses at the Foreign
Service Institute the norm is about four.

The drill techniques described below assume that the class will have no more than six students.   For larger classes the instructor will have to devise various types of choral drills and responses and to rely more on tape recordings to give the individual student practice in speaking.

An important aspect of the method is OVERLEARNING, that is, learning sentences so thoroughly that they come out automatically.   Any 'thinking in the language' then consists of thinking about what to say and not about how to go about saying it.   This cannot be accomplished unless the student spends a lot of time practicing.

MATERIAL

The material for the spoken Hebrew section of the course is divided into units which consist of the following parts: Basic Conversations, additional vocabulary, vocabulary drills, verb drills, grammar notes and drills, rapid response drills, and review conversations.

Basic Conversations

The Basic Conversation is the core of each unit.   It consists of a set of sentences in dialogue form, which is to be completely memorized by the student.   After having overlearned these sentences the student proceeds to intensive drilling based on the sounds, constructions, and vocabulary contained in the sentences, then to prepared or guided conversations, and finally to free conversation on topics covered in the sentences and expanded by the grammatical points covered in the grammar sections.

The sentence is the natural unit of speech.   All languages have sentences, and sounds and forms of a language normally appear within sentences. It is clear that the student must learn to use sentences readily, no matter how this learning is accomplished.

In learning whole sentences the student acquires words and grammatical patterns simultaneously.   Experience has shown that having the student first learn words and rules and then   produce sentences by combining the words according to the rules is an inefficient way to learn.   For most people a grammatical pattern is learned (in the sense that it is "internalized" and can readily be used) more rapidly by thoroughly learning illustrative sentences which embody it than by having it presented as a rule.

Furthermore, the pronunciation and grammatical form of words or other units of the language may be quite different in isolated citation from what they are in connected speech, and since the connected speech form is far more frequent it normally deserves far more attention and drill than the citation form.

The sentences of the Basic Conversation are presented in three parallel columns.   The column on the right gives the Hebrew sentence in the Hebrew alphabet.   The column on the left gives an English equivalent (not necessarily a literal translation) of the Hebrew sentence.   The middle column is a transcription of the Hebrew sentence.   Since the Hebrew spelling is given without vowel points the student will have to rely on the transcription for rendition of the pronunciation.   The Hebrew in the right hand column is given mainly for the benefit of the instructor who will find it more familiar to read than the transcription, although the student may use it for reading practice later.

After each sentence a "breakdown" of the new words is given.   The English translations of these entries tend to be more literal than those given for the Basic Sentences themselves, and are more like the entries to be found in a dictionary.

The technique for teaching the Basic Sentences is a "build-up" scheme in which each longer sentence or group of sentences is broken up into short pieces, and then each piece is presented <u>last piece first</u> and cumulatively, until the student can speak the entire sentence or group of sentences. When the entire sentence is built up it is repeated by the instructor and student.

The pieces to be presented are printed on separate lines. For example, the group: /todá rabá. šlomí tóv. umá šlomxa?/ "Thank you very much. I'm fine. And how are you?" is written in the book like this:

Thank you very much.	todá rabá.	תודה רבה.
I'm fine.	šlomí tóv.	שלומי טוב.
And how are you?	umá šlomxá?	ומה שלומך?

It is presented to the student as follows:

Instructor or Tape:	umá šlomxá?
Student:	umá šlomxá?
Instructor or Tape:	šlomí tóv. umá šlomxá?
Student:	šlomí tóv. umá šlomxá?
Instructor or Tape:	todá rabá. šlomí tóv. umá šlomxá?
Student:	todá rabá. šlomí tóv. umá šlomxá?
Instructor or Tape:	todá rabá. šlomí tóv. umá šlomxá? (repetition)
Student:	todá rabá. šlomí tóv. umá šlomxá?

A⁴ much as possible the sentences have been divided into natural sounding pieces. However, the instructor will still have to achieve skill in presenting the pieces with the intonation that they have within the entire sentence. The repetitions of these partial sentences should not be dull and mechanical, but should be an accurate model for the student to imitate in a natural conversation.

The instructor's pronunciation may vary somewhat from that indicated by the transcription. The student should imitate the instructor, but the instructor should not try to impose a "bookish" or supposedly "correct" pronunciation if it is not completely natural to him in ordinary, relaxed speech.

For the benefit of the instructor the Basic Sentences are printed in larger type than the vocabulary entries after each sentence. The instructor does not drill the vocabulary entries; they are given for the student's reference.

After acceptable ímitation and accurate pronunciation of the Basic Sentences have been achieved they are assigned for <u>memorization</u> outside of class or repeated in class until memorized. Repetition outside of class, preferably using recorded materials as a guide, must·be continued to the point of over-learning, as mentioned above. As a final step, the students act out the entire Basic Conversation from memory, with the instructor or with other students. Only when the Basic Sentences have been mastered to this extent can they be considered to provide an adequate basis for grammatical drills and for control of the spoken language.

Some Basic Conversations are rather long, and are therefore broken up into sections which cover several units. After the section in each succeeding unit is mastered it may be combined with the sections from preceding units for review and practice of longer conversations.

Additional Vocabulary

Appropriate additional vocabulary is presented in this section which follows the Basic Conversation. New words or expressions are always presented within sentences, and the student is not required to memorize lists of new words as such. Items are included in this section to give material for expanded or varied conversation or to present paradigms to be learned before a grammatical explanation is given.

Vocabulary Drills and Verb Drills

It is not assumed that a student will automatically be able to extend the rules to all new forms encountered. Therefore, further opportunities are presented to practice the manipulations. Whenever, for example, an adjective is introduced in a Basic Sentence or Additional Vocabulary all other forms (masculine, feminine, singular, plural) will be drilled in this section. Whenever a new verb is introduced the entire conjugation is drilled, as far as is practicable. These drills not only reinforce the grammatical patterns, but also give an opportunity to illustrate different meanings and the use of forms in different contexts.

Grammar Notes and Drills

All explanation of the structure of Hebrew - sounds, forms, constructions, or style, - is kept to a minimum in the course. When a grammatical point is to be made clear by a supervising linguist or in a Grammar Note, this is done (a) after examples of the point have appeared in Basic Sentences, (b) by calling attention to these instances and adding other illustrations, and (c) by a simple, clear statement. Then, _most important of all_ , the point is reinforced by drills.

Historical explanations or appeals to "logic" are generally avoided, but contrast with similar or conflicting patterns of English is usually indicated.

It is generally wasteful to spend a great deal of time on grammatical explanations. Even if they explain what IS said, rather than somebody's idea of what SHOULD be said, it is still largely wasted motion in that the student does not participate and does not master the point. The time spent in explaining a point is usually better spent in drilling that point with carefully selected, natural sentences exemplifying it.

On the other hand, the attempt to rule out all explanation and to teach everything by a "direct method" completely in Hebrew also wastes time. Very often a simple point which takes endless repetitions of various sentences before the student gets the hang of it can be explained briefly and effectively in English and then drilled systematically.

The Grammar Notes do not cover all possibilities. The instructor will be sure to find exceptions to each explanation or contexts in which the explanation is contradicted. The Grammar Notes are intended as guides, and the student should not expect them to be comprehensive for all cases.

Some explanations are not given in traditional order. Thus, for example, the first and second person forms of the past tense of verbs are drilled separately from the third person forms, and the complete past tense of verbs is then drilled without regard to binyan, or conjugation. The complete paradigm of each _binyan_ is not presented until Units 21-25, although references are made to them and various verbs are drilled in preceding units. Also, the _pi'el_ is presented before the _kal_ since the former is a simpler conjugation in modern Hebrew and because most new verbs are coined in the _pi'el_.

Terminology

In line with the desire to keep explanations simple, no wild forays into novel terminology are made. All students will recognize such familiar terms as "past tense", "imperative", "gender", etc. Certain other terms which may not be so familiar are "construct state", "radical", and "dual", but these are traditionally used in grammars of Hebrew. Also, some Hebrew grammatical terms are used, such as "<u>lamed hey</u> verb", "<u>pi'el</u>", etc.

Nevertheless, the student may find some of the terms to be strange, especially if he has had no grammatical training embodying the practices of modern scientific linguistics. New terminology has arisen in order to be able to make more objective statements about language, and some of it is used here as a matter of course. Thus, for example, "forms" are said to "occur"; groups of consonants with no intervening vowel are called "consonant clusters"; etc. The most unfamiliar terminology may be the phonetic descriptions of consonants and vowels, such as "affricate", "low central vowel", etc.

The student should keep in mind that he does not have to learn terminology or to talk <u>about</u> Hebrew. It is far better and more pertinent for him to be a good mimic than to know what a voiced velar fricative is.

Rapid Response Drills

In Rapid Response Drills students answer in quick succession questions on the Basic Conversation of the unit. The instructor may vary these questions by having the students take the parts of various actors in the Basic Conversation and asking them direct questions about their parts.

Review Conversations

The Review Conversations give the student opportunity to improvise brief conversations, starting with models given in the text. The sample conversations given in this book may be used both for testing comprehension and for conversation practice. Complete directions for using the Review Conversations for conversation practice are given in Unit 1. Later the instructor and students are left to their own ingenuity in changing and expanding them.

DRILLS

Drills are not tests.

All drills are planned to be easily and rapidly answered. In class they are to be done orally with the students' books closed. Answers are available in the textbook. The drills are not puzzles; they are not to be "figured out" but merely to be spoken for speed and accuracy. They are <u>opportunities</u> to practice new forms or sequences in new contexts. If the student has difficulty this may reflect an inadequate mastery of the Basic Conversations or of previous drills. In any case, it is of no great importance whether or not he can figure them out by himself. The goal is to learn to speak Hebrew <u>accurately</u> and <u>fluently</u>, and this aim can be achieved only by correct repetition of the forms and patterns involved. The instructor should supply the correct response whenever the student hesitates too long or does not answer correctly.

In the earlier units of the course the drills are given in the Hebrew spelling and in transcription so that the student may follow the drills when using the tape recordings. It is assumed, however, that the student will have learned to read Hebrew by the time Unit 20 is completed. After Unit 21, therefore, the transcription is omitted in the drills. <u>Translations</u> are given for the first set of responses in each drill.

The instructor should check to see if the students understand what is going on by stopping at random points in a drill and asking a student to translate the last response. It is best to ask a student other than the one who just responded. The instructor should do this only once in a while so that a maximum amount of time is given to the students to speak Hebrew.

Substitution Drills

The purpose of this type of drill is to present variations in form, such as for gender, number, person, without the student having to do any manipulations at all other than to repeat what the instructor has said and to fit it into the model sentence.

A substitution drill is done as follows: The model sentence is given by the instructor and then repeated by the students. The instructor then gives a form which is to be substituted into the model sentence. The student responds with the entire sentence with the new form substituted. The instructor reinforces the correct response by repeating the student's response.

In the tape recordings of drills a blank interval is left for the student to respond. The correct response is then given. If the student has not responded correctly he will hear something different from what he himself has said. This will serve as a correction from the instructor. If he has responded correctly then the repetition will reinforce the proper habits.

Further instructions for doing substitution drills and substitution-agreement drills are given with examples in Unit 1.

Substitution-Agreement Drills

The purpose of this type of drill is to elicit a variation determined by the cue from the instructor. The instructor gives the student a substitution to make in the model sentence, and this substitution requires the student to make a change elsewhere in the sentence. These subsequent changes are the points being drilled.

A substitution-agreement drill is done in the same way as a simple substitution drill. It will usually require more repetitions for mastery since the student must make more than one change in the model sentence.

Expansion Drills

The purpose of expansion drills is to give the student practice in producing longer utterances while maintaining a certain grammatical context.

The instructor gives the student a model sentence. The student repeats this model sentence and adds another sentence to make a longer utterance. For example:

Instructor: hú gár bemalón dán.

Student: hú gár bemalón dán, vehamišpaxá šeló tagía beód šavúa.

Instructor: He's staying at the Dan Hotel.

Student: He's staying at the Dan Hotel, and his family will arrive in a week.

In this case the reference to the subject of the first sentence is maintained in the added sentence: /hú - šeló/ "he - his".

xxi

The instructor repeats the entire response of the student. After the drill has been done a number of times the instructor may omit this repetition in order to speed up the drill in class.

Transformation Drills

The purpose of transformation drills is to give the student practice in shifting from one tense to another, from one conjugation to another, from singular to plural, etc., or simply to paraphrase. The student must eventually be able to make all grammatical manipulations automatically, and this type of drill is most helpful.

The instructor gives a sentence and the student responds with another sentence, determined by the instructions given for the particular drill. The instructor should give the first reponse so that the student will understand what sort of transformation he is supposed to make.

Response Drills

The purpose of response drills is to simulate a situation which may occur in a real conversation. The question and response is extracted from such a possible conversation in order to concentrate on the grammatical points which must be drilled.

Response drills differ from real conversation in that the student is instructed to give only one possible answer. The instructor should give the first response so that the student will know what his responses to subsequent questions should be.

Translation Drills

The purpose of translation drills is to familiarize the student with the idiom of Hebrew or with characteristic constructions of Hebrew whose literal English translation might be misleading. Translations drills are comparatively few in number in the course, but all drills may be used as translation exercises by asking for spot translations into English as explained above.

TRANSLATIONS

Two kinds of translations are used in this text, literal and free. The latter is often more in the nature of an English equivalent, that is, what would be said in English in an equivalent situation rather than a linguistic translation,

A beginning student often has the impression that the literal meaning is the "true" meaning and that any other meaning is necessarily secondary or wrong. This misunderstanding should be avoided. By comparing literal and free translations, the student will learn how much the translation depends on context. A word, expression, or construction may have several translations, depending on other words in the sentence, the grammatical structure of the two languages involved, and the social situation in which the conversation takes place. For example, the literal translation of /ma šlomxa/ is "What is your peace?" We have translated this as "How are you?", which is what an English speaker says in the same situation. Conversely, though, the literal equivalent of the English, /eyx ata?/, is used in Hebrew but only as a rejoinder to a previous greeting.

In the drills various possible translations are deliberately used to free the student from the idea that there is only one correct translation.

TESTS

The ultimate test is the ability to engage in a conversation in Hebrew and to speak and comprehend accurately, fluently, and easily. Most students, though, will appreciate some measurement of their performance during the course. Certain tests are built into the course material itself, and depend on the instructor's judgment in proceeding to new material. That is, the instructor should not proceed to new material until the students have mastered the old. A decision to proceed is thus a satisfactory mark of performance.

Intensive language training is usually very tedious and the instructor should resist pressure from the students to go on to a new unit if he feels that they need more practice on the old.

The Basic Conversations and Additional Vocabulary must be memorized and overlearned. Any hesitation on the part of a student means that he does not know the material.

The Review Conversations also serve as a test for comprehension and of the ability of the students to use the limited amount of material learned up to that point.

For further testing two other types are suggested below and some examples of each are given in the section on tests.

Interpreter Situations

These require three persons - the instructor, who pretends to know no English, the student, who acts as the interpreter, and a third person who, ideally, knows no Hebrew, but who may be another student pretending to know no Hebrew. The interpreter is the one being tested and his ability to serve in that function with accuracy will be readily apparent. In later stages of the course an error on his part may lead the conversation far off the track or reduce it to an absurdity. Students usually enjoy these interpreter situations once they become familiar with the technique.

Taped Tests

None of the above tests will give the student a number grade. Suggestions for tests which can be marked and a number or percentage grade given are included in the section on tests. These tests require a tape recorder for the student to record his answers. If the school is equipped with a language laboratory, then the entire class may be tested at one time. The tapes are then listened to and marked by the instructor.

The supervising linguist and instructor will, of course, want to devise additional tests which the student will not be able to see beforehand.

The student should not be required on any test to discuss Hebrew grammar per se or to list conjugations or the like. Questions such as "What is the feminine singular imperative of /ba/ 'he came'?" are to be avoided. Instead, the student should be told "Tell that girl to come over here." If he responds with /bói héna/, then he knows the form. Otherwise, he does not.

READINGS

Material for instruction and practice in reading Hebrew is given in a special section at the end of the material for spoken Hebrew. This does not mean that such instruction should wait until the spoken material is completed. Indeed, it is expected that reading will begin about the time Unit 11 is started.

After the explanation of the Hebrew alphabet some simple recognition drills are given. These may be supplemented or replaced by flashcard drills in class. Once the students have learned to recognize all the letters and the most frequent sequences, then they may go back to the earlier units and read the Basic Conversations, drills, and Review Conversations.

Resumés of the Basic Conversations from Unit 11 on are then given in the reading section. These becomes progressively longer and more difficult. Occasionally new vocabulary is supplied in these resumés. The material in the spoken Hebrew does not assume this additional vocabulary, but it may, of course, be used in Review Conversations and the like.

Following the series of resumés is a series of short paragraphs, some of which are based on actual news articles. These are intended to bridge the gap between a fixed written text and free conversation. Progressive stages of different types of questions follow these paragraphs. All of this is in Hebrew, and the student practices reading and free conversation this way.

At the very end are some reading selections taken from newspapers and other periodicals. They are presented as examples of material which the student will see in normal encounters in Israel. The supervising linguist and instructor may prepare additional materials to supplement them and to cover a range of subject matter more pertinent to particular classes or individual students.

SUMMARY

The text provides for the assimilation of all basic forms and patterns of the language by the guided imitation, memorization, and manipulation of a large number of sentences and by practice in confronting several widely occurring everyday situations. Actual living use of the language is a necessary adjunct of the course. The instructor should therefore encourage his students from the start to use Hebrew in every way possible, above and beyond what is provided for in the text. After the first few days of work both students and instructor should avoid the use of English in the classroom. Only by constant use of the skill he is learning can the student hope to master it and retain it as a useful tool.

Transcription

    In addition to the Hebrew spelling the material in this course is
written in a transcription meant to help the student listen. It is an attempt
to put down on paper the sounds that the instructor will say, or that will be
heard on the recordings.   It should be emphasized that the transcription is
just a reminder of what is said and not a substitute for it.

    The transcription is based for the most part directly on spoken Hebrew
and is not a transliteration of ordinary Hebrew spelling.   Thus, for example,
/k/ is used for both כ and ק , and /t/ is used for both ט and ת. Transcriptions
are set off in slash lines / / except in the Basic Conversations and
Additional Vocabulary.   Slash lines are also omitted where they would clutter
the text.

    Some departures are made from a slavish transcription of the spoken
language.   The definite article is spelled /ha-/ even though the /h/ is often
dropped in connected speech.   Root consonants which assimilate to other
consonants in clusters are spelled consistently.   For example, /tisgor/ "you
will close" is spelled with /s/ although /tizgor/ would represent the actual
pronunciation more accurately.   The departures were made <u>ad hoc</u> to eliminate
possible confusion and then only when the normal pronunciation may be easily
read from the varied transcription.

    Students may be familiar with other transcription and transliteration
systems which are in use.   <u>sh</u> is used where we use <u>š</u> and <u>ch</u> or <u>kh</u> where
we use <u>x</u> .   The system used here avoids ambiguities in the use of letters,
and students will have no trouble adopting it.   However, commonly used
transliterations will be found in the English translations: For example, <u>chala</u>,
Moshe, etc.

                        TABLE OF SYMBOLS

<u>Consonants</u>:

Voiceless:	p	t	k	c	č	f	s	š	x		h
Voiced:	b	d	g		j		v	z	ž	r	
Nasal:	m	n
Lateral:	l
Glide:	y
Open juncture:	'

<u>Vowels</u>:   i e a o u

<u>Stress</u>: Strong   ´   Weak   (unmarked)

    The correspondences of these symbols with the letters of the Hebrew
alphabet is given in the section on Readings.

    In the following drills attention will be paid mainly to those Hebrew
sounds or groups of sounds which are very different from their English
counterparts.   The examples in the drills are not to be memorized.   The
English translations are given only for reference.

CONSONANTS

/l/ The articulation represented by this letter differs from the articulations represented by the letter in English, especially at the end of a syllable. The Hebrew articulation is a lateral, with the tongue touching the gum ridge behind the upper teeth. The tongue is somewhat tenser than in English.   The Hebrew articulation is essentially the same at the end as at the beginning of a syllable, whereas in English the tongue is retroflexed with the tip approaching the gum ridge but not making definite contact.

The Hebrew /l/ should be thoroughly learned since substitution of the English or American articulation gives one a "thick" accent to the Israeli ear.

li	"to me"	šalom	"hello"	el	"to"
lo	"to him"	šeli	"mine"	al	"on"
la	"to her"	šelo	"his"	kol	"all"
lánu	"to us"	šelánu	"ours"	gadol	"big"
lev	"heart"	milon	"dictionary"	meíl	"coat"
				kilkul	"malfunction"
				klal	"generalization"
				menahel	"director"
				gidel	"he raised"
				gódel	"size"

/x/ Voiceless velar fricative.

The articulation represented by this letter does not exist in English, and, therefore, may give some difficulty to students. However, it is extremely important that students master it and do not substitute /h/ or /k/ for it.

The tongue is brought back toward the soft palate, but instead of stopping the passage of air, as with /k/, a friction sound is made between the back of the tongue and the soft palate, similar to the noise made in clearing the throat.

Some speakers use an Arabicized pronunciation of /x/ when spelled ח . This pronunciation is affected on the radio, also. However, it is not used in general speech and will not be heard on the accompanying tapes.

xam	"warm"	léxem	"bread"	oréax	"guest"
xalav	"milk"	óxel	"food"	eyx	"how"
xom	"heat"	exad	"one"	šlomex	"(greeting)"
xódeš	"month"	axal	"he ate"	šelax	"yours"
xéci	"half"	šaxav	"he lay"	namux	"short"
xika	"waited"	axim	"brothers"	maclíax	"succeeds"
xuc	"outside"	axot	"sister"	tox	"inside"
xiduš	"renewal"				
xadaš	"new"				
xex	"palate"				
xaxam	"smart"				
šlomxa	"(greeting)"				
xémed	"delight"				
xaval	"pity"				
xut	"thread"				

/r/ Voiced velar fricative.

The articulation of the tongue is similar to that of /x/, but it is accompanied by voicing of the vocal cords. Some speakers use a tongue-tip trill instead of the velar fricative. The trill is also generally used on radio, in the theater etc. Students may use the trill, but for most native Israelis the velar fricative will sound more "natural".

ram	"high"	laruc	"to run"	šoter	"policeman'
rax	"soft"	teruc	"excuse"	xaver	"friend"
rišon	"first"	dérex	"way"	séfer	"book"
rikud	"dance"	érev	"evening"	ir	"city"
réga	"minute"	arox	"long"	sar	"minister"
régel	"foot"	garim	"live"	kar	"cold"
rúax	"wind"	xaverim	"friends"	or	"light"
roš	"head"	šagrirut	"embassy"	barur	"clear"
rak	"only"	šagrir	"ambassador"	lira	"pound"

/p/ Voiceless Bilabial stop.

This consonant is quite similar to the English articulation. It occurs at the end of words only rarely, and these are all loan words or abbreviations used as words. At the end of words the lips are released. Before a stressed vowel it is not as strongly aspirated as the English counterpart.

| po | "here" | bapina | "on the corner" | jip | "jeep" |

/t/ Voiceless alveolar stop.

This sound is also similar to the English, except that at the end of a word it must be released. Before a stressed vowel it is not as strongly aspirated as the English counterpart.

tov	"good"	omédet	"stands"
matay	"when"	menahélet	"directress"
et	"time"	šévet	"tribe"
at	"you"(f.s.)	záit	"olive"
ot	"letter"	báit	"house"
šélet	"sign"	štut	"foolishness"
safot	"languages"	xut	"thread"
kapot	"spoons"	rut	"Ruth"

/k/ Voiceless velar stop.

This consonant, too, is similar to the English articulation except that at the end of a word it must be released. Before a stressed vowel it is not as strongly aspirated as the English counterpart.

kol	"all"	amok	"deep"	dévek	"glue"
sakana	"danger"	xok	"law"	ravak	"bachelor"
rak	"only"	bakbuk	"bottle"	xarak	"insect"
sakik	"small bag"	šotek	"keeps quiet"		
sélek	"beet"	šok	"thigh"	matok	"sweet"
tadlik	"kindle"	šuk	"market"	pihuk	"yawn"
émek	"valley"	porek	"unloads"	xélek	"part"

/c/ Voiceless alveolar affricate.

This consonant is a combination of the articulation /t/ and /s/ functioning as a unit ts. Practice is usually required when /c/ occurs at the beginning of a word or after a consonant.

The single symbol /c/ is used because between vowels the sequence /-ts-/ is broken up into /-t + s-/ when syllabified. /c/, on the other hand, goes with the second syllable as a unit.

/huca/   "he was taken out"   הוצא

/hutsa/   "she was flown"   הוטסה

koc	"thorn"	cav	"turtle"	cafon	"north"
yoec	"advisor"	cava	"army"	cara	"trouble"
ec	"tree"	cédek	"justice"	came	"thirsty"
lauc	"to advise"	céɑef	"shell"	carud	"hoarse"
káic	"summer"	cémed	"pair"	coek	"hollers"
acic	"flowerpot"	céva	"color"	cofe	"scout"
tocéret	"product"	cimuk	"raisin"	coléa	"lame"
kacav	"butcher"	cincénet	"jar"	colélet	"submarine"
tocaa	"result"	cipor	"bird"	cur	"rock"
mecit	"lighter"	cir	"represen- tative"	cuk	"cliff"

/y/ This sound is similar to the English glide and forms diphthongs with preceding vowels.

/iy/   /ey/   /ay/   /oy/   /uy/

The diphthong /iy/ is rare and tends to be reduced to /i/ when it occurs.

/tiyšan/   →   /tišan/   "you will sleep."

At the beginning of a word the sequence /yi/ tends to be reduced to /i/

/yisrael/   →   /israel/

/'/ Open Juncture

The open juncture /'/ has an English counterpart which is not usually written. It is the "catch" that occurs between vowels in the exclamation "oh - oh" or the separation of syllables the second of which begins with a vowel, as in the sequence "an aim" as opposed to "a name", or in "grade A" as opposed to "gray day".

/'/ occurs mainly in slow or deliberate speech. In ordinary conversation it is elided or barely audible.

/'/ is spelled א or ע . The latter has an Arabicized pronunciation which is used by some speakers but which is not heard generally. It does not occur on the accompanying tapes.

The following pairs are given as illustrations. They should not require much practice on the part of the English-speaking student.

/lirot/	"to shoot"	לירות	/lir'ot/	"to see"	לראות
/maca/	"he found"	מצא	/mac'a/	"she found"	מצאה
/nasa/	"he travelled"	נסע	/nas'a/	"she travelled"	נסעה
/mila/	"word"	מלה	/mil'a/	"she filled"	מלאה

For the pronunciation of vowels when the intervening /'/ is elided see the note on vowel clusters.

/h/ This sound is similar to the English counterpart, except that it tends to be dropped in rapid speech. Before stressed vowels it is usually retained.

When /h/ is dropped it is replaced by zero, not /'/.

/lehakir/ ⟶ /leakir/ "to recognize" להכיר (not /le'akir/)

The /h/ is generally kept in the transcription since the student might just as well retain it until he acquires a natural-sounding rapid speech. It will not seem affected or bookish.

The student should be aware in listening to other speakers that the dropping of /'/ and /h/ will produce homonyms.

/gahar/ ⟶ /gaar/ "he crouched" גהר
/ga'ar/ ⟶ /gaar/ "he scolded" גער

The following consonants are infrequent and occur only in loan-words and proper names.

/č/ as the <u>ch</u> in English <u>cheese</u>.

/čizbat/ "tall tale" צ'יזבט

/j/ as in English <u>jeep</u>.

/jip/ "jeep" ג'יפ

/ž/ as the <u>s</u> in English <u>measure</u> or the <u>j</u> in French.

/žaket/ "jacket" ז'קט
/bež/ "beige" בז'

Consonant Clusters

In ordinary speech two adjacent consonants within a word will tend to be either both voiced or both voiceless. If there is a sequence voiced - voiceless, such as / - zk -/, or voiceless-voiced, such as /- sg -/ then the first will assimilate to the second. In slow or very careful speech the distinction may be maintained.

Slow speech voiced-voiceless		Normal speech	
/tizkor/	חזכור	/tiskor/	"you will remember"

voiceless-voiced

/tisgor/	חסגור	/tizgor/	"you will close"

This will often produce homonyms, or forms which in slow speech are distinguishable but in normal speech are not. For example, the singular forms of these verbs are always distinguishable:

/yexapes/ "he will seek" יחפש

/yexabes/ "he will launder" יכבס

The plural forms, though, will usually sound the same:

	/yexapsu/	"they will seek."	יחפשו
(/yexabsu/ →)	/yexapsu/	"they will launder "	יכבסו

English speakers should have no difficulty learning such pronunciations, though in English the second consonant often assimilates to the first rather than the reverse: "observe" is pronounced <u>obzerve</u>, rather than <u>opserve</u>. The student should be aware of the possibilities since the occurrences are quite common, but context usually relieves any ambiguity.

The four consonants which do not have voiceless counterparts /m, n, l, y/ (See chart) as well as /r/ and /v/ do not cause the assimilation of a preceding voiceless consonant.

	/masve/	"veil"	not	*/mazve/
	/nifrad/	"separated"	not	*/nivrad/

/c/ assimilates to a following voiced consonant, also: /hicbía/ "voted" הצביע often sounds like /hidzbía/.

The above examples show medial consonant clusters, that is, clusters between vowels.   Clusters also occur initially (at the beginning of a word) and finally (at the end of a word).   Medial and final clusters should give the English speaker no particular difficulty.

Initial Consonant Clusters

Some initial clusters are similar to their English counterparts and should not present any pronunciation problems,

/pl/	-	/plitim/	"refugees"	פליטים
/tr/	-	/truma/	"contribution"	תרומה
/kl/	-	/klita/	"absorption"	קליטה

Many frequently occurring initial clusters will be unfamiliar and will require practice.   Some examples are given below, but many more will occur in the course material.

The most common error that English speakers make is to insert a vowel between the consonants.

/pt/	-	/ptax/	"open"	פתח
		/ptixa/	"opening"	פתיחה
/pn/	-	/pne/	"turn"	פנה
		/pnim/	"interior"	פנים
/tm/	-	/tmarim/	"dates"	תמרים
		/tmuna/	"picture"	תמונה
/tl/	-	/tluya/	"dependent"	תלויה
		/tlišut/	"detachment"	תלישות
/kt/	-	/któvet/	"address"	כתובת
		/ktana/	"small"	קטנה
/cr/	-	/crixa/	"necessary"	צריכה
		/cror/	"bundle"	צרור
/cf/	-	/cfat/	"Safed"	צפת
		/cfoni/	"northern"	צפוני

/cv/	-	/cvat/	"pliers"	צבת
		/çvai/	"military"	צבאי
/bd/	-	/bdika/	"examination"	בדיקה
		/bdixa/	"joke"	בדיחה
/bg/	-	/bgadim/	"clothes"	בגדים
		/bgida/	"treason"	בגידה
/dl/	-	/dli/	"bucket"	דלי
		/dlatot/	"doors"	דלתות
/dv/	-	/dvaš/	"honey"	דבש
		/dvora/	"bee"	דבורה
/gv/	-	/gvéret/	"Mrs."	גברת
		/gvina/	"cheese"	גבינה
/gd/	-	/gdola/	"big"	גדולה
		/gdud/	"troop"	גדוד

Clusters of Three Consonants

Medial clusters of three consonants are rare. When they occur as a result of grammatical patterning then a vowel (usually /e/) is inserted between the second and third consonants. When clusters of three consonants occur initially the vowel /i/ is usually inserted between the first and second consonants. These insertions are discussed in a number of places in the text.

The clusters of three consonants which do occur are mainly in recent loan-words or proper names:

$$/split/ \qquad \text{"(banana) split"}$$

Non-Permissible Clusters

Some sequences of consonants do not occur in Hebrew. These are called non-permissible clusters. For the most part, restrictions are limited to initial clusters.

When a grammatical pattern would ordinarily produce a cluster, but the cluster is non-permissible, then a vowel is inserted, usually /e/. If the first of the two consonants is /h/, /x/, or /'/ then the inserted vowel is usually /a/.

Examples of non-permissible clusters occurring in a grammatical pattern are:

m.s.		f.s.	
/gadol/	"big"	/gdola/	
/yaxol/	"able"	/yexola/	for */yxola/
/xazak/	"strong"	/xazaka/	for */xzaka/
/'acuv/	"sad"	/'acuva/	for */'cuva/
/na'im/	"pleasant"	/ne'ima/	for */n'ima/

The insertion of such vowels is discussed and drilled for each particular grammatical pattern.

Some non-permissible initial clusters are permissible medially. The addition of a prefix may, therefore, give two possible forms with the same meaning.

/rexov álenbi/   "Allenby Road"
/berexov álenbi/   "On Allenby Road"
    or
/birxov álenbi/

(The shorter form is often the more formal or literary style.)

VOWELS

The vowels of modern Hebrew are harder to master than the consonants. Students who have already learned some Hebrew traditionally may find that they have to un-learn some of the pronunciations.

In stressed syllables the vowels are very similar to the five vowels of Spanish. In unstressed syllables the vowels are generally reduced or centralized. In rapid speech vowels may be dropped entirely.

The student will find that the instructor's pronunciation of vowels will shift when going from deliberate speech to normal speed speech. Often the instructor is unaware of these changes and when asked to repeat or slow down he will produce a somewhat unnatural utterance. The student should be aware of this tendency and imitate the normal speed utterance. Speaking whole sentences at normal speed rather than choppy groupings of individual words will help the student in this regard.

/i/ High front vowel, tenser than the i of English bit

im	"with"	lištot	"to drink"	ani	"I"
iš	"man"	naim	"pleasant"	mi	"who"
iša	"woman"	máim	"water"	bli	"without"
ir	"city"	tikansi	"enter"	kli	"dish"
bišvili	"for me"	adoni	"sir"		

/e/ This symbol represents a vowel which has a range covering several English vowel phonemes. In stressed position followed by a consonant or at the end of a word it is similar to e of English bet.

Students should be very careful not to replace it with /ey/ at the end of a word - /kafe/ does not sound like the English café. The final /e/ is like the e of bet with the t cut off.

bet	"second letter"	bétax	"sure"	nae	"nice"
omed	"stands"	yafe	"pretty"	kafe	"coffee"
oxel	"eats"	et	"time"	roe	"sees"

In primary stress position before a vowel it is slightly higher and followed by a y glide.

yodéa	"knows"	šoméa	"hears"	koréa	"tears"

In other positions it is more centralized, like the e of democracy.

meod	"very"	lamádeti	"I studied"
meot	"hundreds"	dérex	"way"
mevin	"understands"	beséder	"O.K."
késef	"money"	bevakaša	"please"
yéled	"boy"		

/a/ Low central vowel

This vowel is pronounced like the o in American English hot. Before voiced consonants this vowel is shorter than the similar English vowel. At the end of a word it is glottalized, that is, has a "clipped" ending.

In unstressed syllables, especially before a strongly stressed syllable it tends to be centralized, like the e of English below.

at	"you" f.s.	amad	"stood"
rak	"only"	gag	"roof"
šamaš	"custodian"	az	"strong"
mamaš	"really"	kala	"bride"
ahav	"loved"	xala	"twist bread"
ad	"until"	téva	"nature"

/o/ Low-mid back vowel.

This vowel is similar to the ou of cough as pronounced by many Americans. Listen to the tapes or the native instructor to get the exact pronunciation. Be careful not to substitute a diphthong such as the o of note . Before voiced consonants it is shorter that the similar English vowel. At the end of a word it is glottalized.

In unstressed syllables, especially before a strongly stressed syllable it tends to be centralized, like the e of English below.

kof	"monkey"	bóker	"morning"	oto	"him"
tov	"good"	boker	"herdsman"	lo	"no"
sof	"end"	óxel	"food"	o	"or"
xódeš	"month"	oxel	"eats"	šlómo	"Solomon"
yom	"day"	ohev	"loves"		

/u/ High back vowel

This vowel is slightly higher than the oo of shook. Be careful not to substitute a diphthong with a w-off-glide such as the oo of food.

šuk	"market"	yifnu	"they will turn"
šuv	"again"	yištu	"they will drink"
šiput	"jurisdiction"	šávu	"they returned"
sulam	"ladder"	bánu	"in us"
sidur	"arrangement"	banu	"they built"
ud	"firebrand"	kanu	"they bought"
uf	"fly away"	avdu	"they worked"
uc	"advise"	kúmu	"get up"
hu	"he"	úru	"wake up"

Vowel Clusters

All combinations of two vowels occur. The Hebrew spelling may indicate that /'/, /h/, or /y/ should occur between them, and in deliberate speech these consonants will usually be heard. In ordinary speech, however, vowel clusters occur with a smooth transition between them. English speakers will have to practice these vowel clusters in order to achieve a proper Israeli pronunciation.

In the transcriptions these clusters are generally written without the consonants which are indicated by the Hebrew spelling. Appropriate reminders are given at various points in the text.

In pronouncing the following examples for the students to imitate, the instructor should be relaxed and informal in his pronunciation. Otherwise he will tend to insert a consonant and the practice will have lost its point.

Elision of /'/, /h/, and /y/ does not mean that the speech is "sloppy" or "corrupt". In slow or emphatic speech they must occur. But in normal, everyday, "natural" speech they are dropped by native speakers of Hebrew. Maintaining these consonants in this informal style will sound awkward.

paam	"time"
taavor	"you will cross"
laalot	"to go up"
báit	"house"
israel	"Israel"
naim	"pleasant"
menaalim	"directors"
leexol	"to eat"
neíma	"pleasant"
meod	"very"
beemet	"really"
yoec	"counsellor"
yoacim	"counsellors"
bóu,	"come"
šavúa	"week"
batúax	"sure"
šeuit	"beans"
maašaa	"What time is it?"

STRESS AND INTONATION

A complete description of stress and intonation patterns would be very complicated and of little help in the actual learning of them. The instructor should present the sentences as naturally as possible, and the student should do his best to mimic closely.

The following comments will explain the general occurrence of stress on individual words and in connected speech. The learning of the Basic Sentences and the acting out of the conversations constitute the drills on stress and intonation.

In the transcription an accent mark ´ indicates a syllable which may receive strong stress. In words of more than one syllable the placement of stress is meaningful.

In individual words, particularly when pronounced in isolation, the stress is usually on the last syllable or on the next to the last syllable. In most cases the placement of stress is a part of the grammatical pattern, but in others it must be memorized as part of the individual word. For example, the /-ti/ and /-ta/ suffixes of the past tense are never stressed: /amárti/ "I said", /amárta/ "you said". On the other hand the following pairs of words are distinguished from each other by the stress placement.

/oxél/	"(he is) eating"	/óxel/	"food"
/šlomó/	"his peace"	/šlómo/	"Solomon"
/emcá/	"I will find"	/émca/	"middle"
/banú/	"they built"	/bánu/	"in us"

In some words of three or more syllables the stress is on the last syllable but two: /mášehu/ "something",   /míšehu/ "someone"
/ótobus/ "bus"   ,   /amérika/ "America"

(In general, loan-words tend to retain the stress where it was in the language from which it was borrowed.)

Only the main stress of a word is indicated. Of the unstressed (unmarked) syllables some will seem louder than others. English has similar patterns of "secondary" and "tertiary" stresses, and there is no need to drill the pronunciation - provided the main stress is properly placed: /ledabér/ "to speak" and not */lédaber/.

From Unit 18 on the stress mark ´ is placed on a word only when the stress is <u>not</u> on the last syllable.

Reduction of Stress

In ordinary connected speech many words, particularly the prepositions with pronominal suffixes, lose the stress which they have when spoken in isolation: /tagíd li/ "tell me". In effect, these words are pronounced as one word with the stress on the next to last syllable.

Style Differences in Placement of Stress

The placement of stress differs in formal style in some words and grammatical patterns. In general, a stress on the next to last syllable is shifted to the last syllable in these forms. For example:

Informal	Formal	
/šmóne/	/šmoné/	"eight"
/hi báa/	/hi baá/	"she is coming"
/amártem/	/amartém/	"you said"

Intonation Marks

Intonation is indicated only in a very broad way by the use of punctuation marks at the end of a phrase or sentence.

A period indicates a falling intonation. Questions which begin with a question-word (who, what, etc.)generally have a falling intonation at the end and are therefore marked with a period, <u>not</u> with a question mark.

A question mark indicates a rising intonation. Yes-or-no questions and rejoinder questions (And how are you?) generally have a rising intonation at the end.

A comma indicates a possible pause with a relatively sustained intonation. A hyphen indicates a hesitation pause, usually with a sustained or rising intonation.

An exclamation mark indicates an exclamation with increased loudness.

<u>Note</u>: These marks are used in this manner <u>only</u> in the transcription. In the English and Hebrew spellings the standard punctuation is used.

TAPE RECORDINGS

The tape recordings which accompany <u>FSI-Hebrew Basic Course</u> have the following format:

(1) Basic Conversation

(a)   <u>Dialogue for Learning</u>. The first presentation of the Basic Sentences are built up from the partial utterances, as described in the Introduction. Each full sentence is said twice. The student repeats everything he hears at this step. He may follow in his book.

(b)   <u>Dialogue for Fluency</u>. Each complete Basic Sentence is given with space for repetition. The student should not need his book here.

(c)   <u>Dialogue for Comprehension</u>. The Basic Conversation is spoken at normal speed by a group of Hebrew speakers as you might overhear it. The student just listens with his book closed.

(d)   <u>Alternating Drill</u>. The Basic Conversation is presented at normal speed with one speaker's part missing. The Student speaks the missing part. He thus conducts a conversation with the tape recording.

The Basic Conversation is then presented with the other speaker's part missing. The student supplies the part. He thus practices participating in the entire conversation.

In some Basic Conversations a third speaker has a small part. In such cases the entire conversation is not repeated with this small part missing.

(2) Additional Vocabulary

The sentences in the Additional Vocabulary section are presented with build-ups if necessary.

(3) Drills

(a)   <u>Substitution Drills, Substitution-Agreement Drills</u>. The first, or "model" sentence is given with spaces for repetition. Then a substitution cue is given with space for the student to respond with the new sentence. The correct response is then given on the tape. The student may follow in the book.

(b)   <u>Expansion Drills, Transformation Drills, Response Drills</u>. The cue sentence is given with space for the response sentence. The tape then gives the correct response sentence. The student should look in the book to see what his response should be. Only the translation of the first cue-response in given.

Note: In using the tapes the student should not go through an entire tape at one sitting especially when doing the drill sections. Instead he should do a few drills, rewind the tape, and do them again until he can do them perfectly without using the book.

Translation Drills, Rapid Response Drills, and Review Conversations are not recorded.

Occasionally circumstances required the use of a woman's voice to record a man's part and vice versa. This should not disturb the student.

Tape 1A

1.1 Greetings (Two men meet)

MR. WILLIAMS

Hello, Moshe.	šalóm mošé.		שלום, משה.
How are you?	má šlomxá.		מה שלומך?
peace, welfare	šalóm (m)	שלום	
what	má	מה	
the welfare of	šlóm	שלום-	
you, your (m.s.)	-xá (m.s.)	ך-	

MOSHE

Thank you very much.	todá rabá.		תודה רבה.
I'm fine.	šlomí tóv.		שלומי טוב.
And how are you?	umá šlomxá?		ומה שלומך?
thanks	todá (f)	תודה	
much	rabá (f)	רבה	
me, my	-í	י-	
and	u-	ו	

MR. WILLIAMS

Fine.	tóv.		טוב.
How is	má šlóm		מה שלום
the family?	hamišpaxá.		המשפחה?
the	ha-	ה-	
family	mišpaxá (f)	משפחה	

MOSHE

All right.	beséder.		בסדר.
How is	má šlóm		מה שלום
your wife?	ištexá.		אשתך?
in	be-	ב-	
order	séder (m)	סדר	
wife, woman	išá (f)	אשה	

MR. WILLIAMS

She's fine, too.	gám šlomá tóv.		גם שלומה טוב.
Excuse me.	slixá.		סליחה.
I have to	aní muxráx		אני מוכרח
run.	larúc.		לרוץ.
too, also	gám	גם	
her	-á	ה-	
pardon (noun)	slixá (f)	סליחה	
I	aní	אני	
have to, must	muxráx (m.s.)	מוכרח	
to	la-	ל-	
run	rúc	רוץ	

MOSHE

Oh, yes!	ó -- kén!		או -- כן!
It's late already.	kvár meuxár.		כבר מאוחר.
Goodbye.	šalóm.		שלום.
yes	kén	כן	
already	kvár	כבר	
late	meuxár	מאוחר	

MR. WILLIAMS

So long.	šalóm.	שלום.
Be seeing you.	lehitraót.	להתראות.
to see again	lehitraót	להתראות

1.2 Greetings (Two women meet)

MRS. WILLIAMS

Hello, Miriam.	šalóm, miryám.	שלום, מרים.
How are you?	má šloméx.	מה שלומך?
you, your (f.s.)	-éx	ך-

MIRIAM

Thank you very much.	todá rabá.	תודה רבה.
I'm fine.	šlomí tóv.	שלומי טוב.
And how are you?	umá šloméx?	ומה שלומך?

MRS. WILLIAMS

| Fine. | tóv. | טוב. |
| How is the family? | má šlóm hamišpaxá. | מה שלום המשפחה? |

MIRIAM

All right.	beséder.	בסדר.
How is	má šlóm	מה שלום
your husband?	baaléx.	בעלך?
husband	báal (m)	בעל

MRS. WILLIAMS

He's fine, too.	gám šlomó tóv.	גם שלומו טוב.
Excuse me.	slixá.	סליחה.
I have to	aní muxraxá	אני מוכרחה
run.	larúc.	לרוץ.
him, his	-ó	ו-
have to, must	muxraxá (f.s.)	מוכרחה

MIRIAM

| Oh, yes! It's late already. | ó -- kén! kvár meuxár. | או -- כן! כבר מאוחר. |
| So long. | šalóm. | שלום. |

MRS. WILLIAMS

| So long. Be seeing you. | šalóm. lehitraót. | שלום. להתראות. |

1.3 ADDITIONAL VOCABULARY

We are fine.	šloménu tóv.	שלומנו טוב.
How are you? (m.pl.)	má šlomxém.	מה שלומכם?
How are you? (f.pl.)	má šlomxén.	מה שלומכן?
How are they? (m.pl.)	má šlomám.	מה שלומם?
How are they? (f.pl.)	má šlomán.	מה שלומן?

Mr. Carmi	már kármi	מר כרמי
Mr. Carmi (alternate form)	adón kármi	אדון כרמי
Miss or Mrs. Carmi	gvéret kármi	גברת כרמי
It is early.	mukdám.	מוקדם.

1.4 Classroom Expressions

In this section we introduce a few additional Hebrew phrases which will
be used in class. They should be practiced until the pronunciation is learned,
but since they will be used constantly in class they can be memorized without
special effort.

Some of the expressions are given in more than one form, differing in
gender or number. Their use will depend on the make-up of the class, and the
instructor may find it necessary to introduce additional variations not
included here.

1. Close the door.
    (said to a man)   sgór et hadélet.   .סגור את הדלת
    (said to a woman)   sigrí et hadélet.   .סגרי את הדלת

2. Sit down, please.
    (said to a man)   šév, bevakašá.   .שֵב, בבקשה
    (said to a woman)   šví, bevakašá.   .שבי, בבקשה
    (said to men or both) švú, bevakašá.   .שבו, בבקשה

3. Quiet, please.   šéket, bevakašá.   .שקט, בבקשה

4. Open your books.
    (said to men or both) pitxú et hasfarím.   .פתחו את הספרים
    (said to women)   ptáxna et hasfarím.   .פתחנה את הספרים

5. Speak louder.
    (said to a man)   dabér yotér bekól.   .דבר יותר בקול
    (said to a woman)   dabrí yotér bekól.   .דברי יותר בקול

6. All together.   kulám beyáxad.   .כולם ביחד

7. Again.   ód hapáam.   .עוד הפעם

8. Do you understand?
    (said to a man)   atá mevín?   ?אתה מבין
    (said to a woman)   át meviná?   ?את מבינה

9. I don't understand.
    (said by a man)   aní ló mevín.   .אני לא מבין
    (said by a woman)   aní ló meviná.   .אני לא מבינה

10. I don't know.
    (said by a man)   aní ló yodéa.   .אני לא יודע
    (said by a woman)   aní ló yodáat.   .אני לא יודעת

11. Please translate.
    (said to a man)   targém, bevakašá.   .תרגם, בבקשה
    (said to a woman)   targemí, bevakašá.   .תרגמי, בבקשה

12. How do you say   éyx omrím   איך אומרים
    table in Hebrew?   table beivrít.   ?table בעברית

3

GRAMMAR DRILLS

1.5 Masculine and Feminine

Compare the following sets of corresponding sentences from conversations 1.1 and 1.2:

a.	šalóm, mošé. má šlomxá.	Hello, Moshe. How are you?
	šalóm, miryám. má šloméx.	Hello, Miriam. How are you?
b.	má šlóm ištexá.	How is your wife?
	má šlóm baaléx.	How is your husband?

Note that forms differ when a man or woman is being spoken to. It is important that the student learn the corresponding forms at the outset. There are a number of patterns of these corresponding forms, which will be referred to by their traditional names, masculine and feminine. All nouns in Hebrew, whether or not referring to beings with sex, are members of one or the other class. These will be designated (m) or (f) in the vocabulary listings.

Throughout the course the various corresponding forms required by each gender will be drilled.

The following drills should be thoroughly learned. The student should not have to be corrected afterwards on the use of the proper forms. Such errors will produce a reaction similar to that felt by English speakers on hearing the following: "How is your brother?"
"She is fine, thank you."

The cue words in the following drills are names of men and women. Include the name in the response so as to fix firmly the connection of form and sex of person spoken to. The instructor may vary the drill by using the names of members of the class or by introducing other Hebrew names such as /avígdor/ (man) and /xána/ (woman).

The drills are to be done as follows:
Instructor: šalóm mošé má šlomxá.
Student: (repeats) šalóm mošé. má šlomxá.
Instructor: <u>miryám</u>
Student: šalóm miryám. má šloméx.
Instructor: (repeats) šalóm miryám. má šloméx.
                     <u>mar kóhen</u>

A.   šalóm mošé. má šlomxá.   שלום, משה. מה שלומך?

<u>miryám</u>	šalóm miryám. má šloméx.	מרים
<u>már kóhen</u>	šalóm már kóhen. má šlomxá.	מר כהן
<u>gvéret Williams</u>	šalóm gvéret Williams. má šloméx.	גב' ויליאמס
<u>gvéret káspi</u>	šalóm gvéret káspi. má šloméx.	גב' כספי
<u>már Williams</u>	šalóm már Williams. má šlomxá.	מר ויליאמס
<u>avígdor</u>	šalóm avígdor. má šlomxá.	אביגדור
<u>xána</u>	šalóm xána. má šloméx.	חנה
<u>már káspi</u>	šalóm már káspi. má šlomxá.	מר כספי
<u>mošé</u>	šalóm mošé. má šlomxá.	משה

4

B. <u>má šlóm ištexá, már Williams.</u>　　　　　　　מה שלום אשתך, מר וויל`אמס?

　　<u>gvéret Williams</u>　　má šlóm baaléx, gvéret Williams.　　גב' וויליאמס

　　<u>már kóhen</u>　　má šlóm ištexá, már kóhen.　　מר כהן

　　<u>gvéret kármi</u>　　má šlóm baaléx, gvéret kármi.　　גב' כרמי

　　<u>xána</u>　　má šlóm baaléx, xána.　　חנה

　　<u>mošé</u>　　má šlóm ištexá, mošé.　　משה

　　<u>már Williams</u>　　má šlóm ištexá, már Williams.　　מר וויל1אמס

1.6 Pronominal Suffixes - Singular Set

There are several sets of pronouns indicating person, gender, and number. The following occur as suffixes to singular nouns and to certain prepositions. They will be referred to as the singular set.

When suffixed to nouns they are often translated as possessives.

　　má šlomxá.　　(literally) What is <u>your</u> peace?
　　má šlóm ištexá.　　How is <u>your</u> wife?
　　šlomí tóv.　　(literally) <u>My</u> peace is good.

Except for certain stereotyped expressions as these, though, the suffixing of nouns to indicate possession is more formal in style.

When suffixed to prepositions they are usually translated as the objects of the prepositions. This will be discussed later on.

A. Substitution Drill

má šlomxá.	How are you?	מה שלומך?
šloméx		שלומך
šlomxém		שלומכם
šlomám		שלומם
šlomán		שלומן
šlomó		שלומו
šlomxén		שלומכן
šlomá		שלומה

B. Substitution Drill

šlomí tóv.	I'm fine.	שלומי טוב.
šloménu		שלומנו
šlomó		שלומו
šlomán		שלומן
šlomá		שלומה
šlomám		שלומם

C. Response Drill

Instructor:	Student:	
má šlomxá.	šlomí tóv.	מה שלומך?
má šlomxém.	šloménu tóv.	מה שלומכם?
má šlomám.	šlomám tóv.	מה שלומם?
má šlomó.	šlomó tóv.	מה שלומו?
má šlomxén.	šloménu tóv.	מה שלומכן?
má šlomá.	šlomá tóv.	מה שלומה?
má šloméx.	šlomí tóv.	מה שלומך?

D. Response Drill

Instructor:	má šlóm baaléx.	Student:	šlomó tóv.	מה שלום בעלך?
	má šlóm ištexá.		šlomá tóv.	מה שלום אשתך?
	má šlóm hamišpaxá.		šlomá tóv.	מה שלום המשפחה?
	má šlóm baalá.		šlomó tóv.	מה שלום בעלה?
	má šlóm ištó.		šlomá tóv.	מה שלום אשתו?

[Note: In the form /ištexá/ the /-e-/ is inserted for phonological reasons, to break up the three-consonant cluster /-štx-/, which would otherwise result.]

1.7   <u>Alternate forms of nouns before suffixes</u>

Many nouns have an alternate form when occurring with a pronominal suffix.

| šalóm | 'welfare' | ' <u>š</u>lomí | 'my welfare' |
| išá | 'wife' | iští | 'my wife' |

Compare, on the other hand: báal   'husband'   <u>baalí</u>   'my husband'

It is very difficult to predict which nouns will have such alternate forms or what the alternate form will be. The student should simply drill these as they occur in the text until he has mastered them.

When a suffixed noun occurs in a Basic Sentence the independent form of the noun will be given in the vocabulary breakdown, and, as much as possible, drills will be provided.

REVIEW CONVERSATIONS

The purpose of the Review Conversations is to lead the student into free conversation within the range of the vocabulary and grammatical patterns which he has learned. Students should keep their books closed while the instructor follows the procedure suggested here.

1. With the class just listening, the instructor reads the conversation in as natural a manner as possible. The instructor repeats the conversation until the class understands it completely.

2. The instructor rereads the conversation several times with half the class repeating one role and half the other role.

3. The two halves of the class exchange roles and Step 2 is repeated.

4. The instructor takes the first part and acts out the conversation with the class.

5. The class and instructor exchange roles and repeat Step 4.

6. Individual students are assigned the various roles in turn until all have taken both parts in the conversation.

7. Individual students make substitutions freely, including whatever changes may be necessary elsewhere in the conversation. These free conversations should not be prolonged more than four minutes or so. This will give all the students an opportunity to try their hand at the same situation. The instructor should refrain from adding a lot of vocabulary at this point.

A: šalóm, gvéret kóhen. má šloméx.	א: שלום, גברת כהן. מה שלומך?
B: todá. šlomí tóv, umá šlomxá?	ב: תודה. שלומי טוב. ומה שלומך?
A: gám šlomí tóv, todá.	א: גם שלומי טוב, תודה.
B: má šlóm mošé.	ב: מה שלום משה?
A: aní ló yodéa.	א: אני לא יורע.
C: má šlóm ištexá, már kármi.	ג: מה שלום אשתך, מר כרמי?
D: beséder, todá. má šlóm baaléx?	ד: בסדר, תודה. מה שלום בעלך?
C: šlomó tóv. má šlóm hamišpaxá?	ג: שלומו טוב. מה שלום המשפחה?
D: tóv, todá. slixá. meuxár.	ד: טוב, תודה. סליחה. מאוחר.
C: ó, gám aní muxraxá larúc. šalóm.	ג: או, גם אני מוכרחה לרוץ. שלום.
D: šalóm, lehitraót.	ד: שלום, להתראות.

E: šalóm, már Williams.　　　　　　　　　　ה: שלום, מר וויל'אמס.

　　šalóm, gvéret Williams.　má šlomxém.　　שלום, גברת וויל'אמס. מה שלומכם?

F: todá rabá. šloménu tóv.　　　　　　　　ו: תודה רבה. שלומנו טוב.

　　má šloméx, gvéret zahávi.　　　　　　　מה שלומך, גברת זהבי?

E: beséder.　má šlóm hamišpaxá?　　　　　　ה: בסדר. מה שלום המשפחה?

F: slixá. aní ló mevín. ód hapáam,　　　　ו: סליחה. אני לא מבין. עוד הפעם

　　bevakašá.　　　　　　　　　　　　　　　　בבקשה.

E: má šlóm hamišpaxá.　　　　　　　　　　　ה: מה שלום המשפחה?

F: šlomá tóv, todá.　　　　　　　　　　　　ו: שלומה טוב, תודה.

G: šalóm, már kármi.　　　　　　　　　　　　ז: שלום, מר כרמי.

H: o! šalóm, mošé! má šlomxá.　　　　　　ח: או! שלום, משה! מה שלומך?

G: šlomí tóv. má šlóm hamišpaxá.　　　　　ז: שלומי טוב. מה שלום המשפחה?

H: beséder. sgór et hadélet, bevakašá.　ח: בסדר. סגור את הדלת, בבקשה.

G: ken.　slixá.　　　　　　　　　　　　　　ז: כן. סליחה.

I: már Williams, šév, bevakašá.　　　　　ט: מר ווילאמס, שב, בבקשה.

J: ód hapáam, bevakašá. aní ló mevín.　י: עוד הפעם, בבקשה. אני לא מבין.

I: šév, bevakašá.　　　　　　　　　　　　　ט: שב, בבקשה.

J: ó kén. aní mevín. todá.　　　　　　　י: או כן. אני מבין. תודה.

K: slixá, miryám. aní muxráx larúc.　　כ: סליחה, מרים. אני מוכרח לרוץ.

L: ló. šév, bevakašá. mukdám.　　　　　ל: לא. שב, בבקשה. מוקדם.

K: ló, todá. meuxár.　　　　　　　　　　כ: לא, תודה. מאוחר.

L: tóv. lehitraót.　　　　　　　　　　　ל: טוב. להתראות.

M: šéket, bevakašá.　　　　　　　　　　　מ: שקט, בבקשה.

N: slixá. dabér yotér bekól.　　　　　נ: סליחה. דבר יותר בקול.

M: šéket! atá mevín?　　　　　　　　　　מ: שקט! אתה מבין?

N: tóv. aní mevín. slixá.　　　　　　　נ: טוב. אני מבין. סליחה.

2.1   Introductions   (Two men are introduced)

MR. CASPI

Mr. Cohen,	már kóhen,		מר כהן,
please meet	takír bevakašá		תכיר בבקשה
Mr. Williams.	et már Williams.		את מר ווילי אמס.
you will know		takír (m.s.)	תכיר
(preposition indicating object of verb)		et	את

MR. COHEN

I'm very happy	naím li meód		נעים לי מאד
to meet you,	lehakír otxá,		להכיר אותך,
Mr. Williams.	már Williams.		מר ווילי אמס.
pleasant		naím (m.s.)	נעים
to me		lí	לי
very		meód	מאד
to know (a person)		lehakír	להכיר
you (m.s., obj.)		otxá (m.s.)	אותך

MR. WILLIAMS

How do you do,	naím meód,	נעים מאד,
Mr. Cohen.	már kóhen.	מר כהן.

MR. CASPI

Mr. Williams	már Williams		מר ווילי אמס
is Counsellor of	hú yoéc		הוא יועץ
the American Embassy.	hašagrirút		השגרירות
	haamerikáit.		האמדיקאית.
he, it		hú	הוא
counsellor, adviser		yoéc (m)	יועץ
embassy		šagrirút (f)	שגרירות
American		amerikái (m.s.)	אמריקאי

MR. COHEN

Whe..	matáy		מתי
did you arrive	higáta		הגעת
in the country,	laárec,		לארץ,
Mr. Williams?	már Williams.		מר ווילי אמס.
when (interrogative)		matáy	מתי
you arrived (m.s.)		higáta (m.s.)	הגעת
country		érec (f)	ארץ

MR. WILLIAMS

I arrived	higáti		הגעתי
two days ago,	lifnéy yomáim,		לפני יומים,
Mr. Cohen.	már kóhen.		מר כהן.
I arrived		higáti	הגעתי
before, ago		lifnéy	לפני
day		yóm (m)	יום
two days		yomáim	יומים

2.2   Introductions   (Two women are introduced)

MRS. CASPI

Mrs. Cohen,	gvéret kóhen,	, גברת כהן
please meet	takíri bevakašá	תכירי בבקשה
Mrs. Williams.	et gvéret Williams.	.את גברת ויליאמס
you will know (f.s.)	takíri (f.s.	תכירי

MRS. COHEN

I'm very happy	naím lí meód	נעים לי מאד
to meet you,	lehakír otáx,	, להכיר אותך
Mrs. Williams.	gvéret Williams.	.גברת ויליאמס
you (f.s.,obj.)	otáx (f.s.)	אותך

MRS. WILLIAMS

How do you do,	naím meód,	, נעים מאד
Mrs. Cohen.	gvéret kóhen.	.גברת כהן

MRS. CASPI

Mrs. Williams	gvéret Williams	גברת ויליאמס
is the wife	hí ištó	היא אשתו
of the Counsellor	šel yoéc	של יועץ
of the American Embassy.	hašagrirút	השגרירות
	haamerikáit.	.האמריקאית
she, it	hí	היא
of	šél	של

MRS. COHEN

When	matáy	מתי
did you arrive	higát	הגעת
in the country,	laárec,	, לארץ
Mrs. Williams?	gvéret Williams.	?גברת ויליאמס
you arrived (f.s.)	higát (f.s.)	הגעת

MRS. WILLIAMS

I arrived	higáti	הגעתי
two days ago,	lifnéy yomáim,	, לפני יומיים
Mrs. Cohen.	gvéret kóhen.	.גברת כהן

2.3 ADDITIONAL VOCABULARY

I arrived yesterday.	higáti etmól.	.הגעתי אתמול
I arrived the day before yesterday.	higáti šilšóm.	.הגעתי שלשום
I arrived a week ago.	higáti lifnéy šavúa.	.הגעתי לפני שבוע
week	šavúa (m)	שבוע
I arrived two weeks ago.	higáti lifnéy švuáim.	.הגעתי לפני שבועיים
I arrived a month ago.	higáti lifnéy xódeš.	.הגעתי לפני חודש
month	xódeš (m)	חודש
I arrived two months ago.	higáti lifnéy xodšáim.	.הגעתי לפני חודשיים

10

GRAMMAR DRILLS

2.4 Equational Sentences

Compare the following sentences and their English translations:

a. má šlomxá   (literally)   What is your peace?

b. šlomí tóv   (literally)   My peace is good.

c. már Williams hú yoéc   Mr. Williams is the Counsellor
   hašagrirút haamerikáit.   of the American Embassy.

Note that the Hebrew equivalent of the English sentence pattern "A is B" is "A B". The Hebrew equivalent for the English present tense forms <u>am</u>, <u>is</u> and <u>are</u> is the juxtaposition of the two parts of the sentence. Such sentences are called <u>equational sentences</u>.

In Sentence <u>c</u> the form /hú/ 'he' is a pleonastic subject.

Now compare the following sentences and their translations:

d. meuxár.   It is late.

e. naím meód.   It is very pleasant.

In these sentences the English has not only a verb form, but this verb requires a subject, in this case the impersonal pronoun <u>it</u>. The Hebrew sentences are complete as they stand.

A. Substitution Drill

<u>hú</u> amerikái.	He is an American.	הוא אמריקאי.
aní		אני
mošé hú		משה הוא
már Williams		מר ווילימאס
baalá		בעלה

B. Substitution Drill

<u>hí</u> amerikáit.	She is an American.	היא אמריקאית.
aní		אני
iští		אשתי
gvéret Williams		גברת ווילימאס
miryám hí		מרים היא

C. Substitution Drill

<u>hú</u> yoéc hašagrirút.	He is the Counsellor of the Embassy.	הוא יועץ השגרירות.
aní		אני
már Williams hú		מר ווילימאס הוא
baalá		בעלה

D. Substitution Drill

<u>meuxár</u> meód.	It is very late.	מאוחר מאד.
mukdám		מוקדם
naím		נעים

11

2.5 The Direct Object Preposition /et ~ ot-/

The preposition /et/ preceded a direct object of a verb when the object is definite. An object is definite in any of the following cases:
a. It is preceded by the definite article prefix /ha-/ 'the';
b. It has a pronoun suffix, e.g., /iští/ 'my wife';
c. It is a proper name, e.g., /mošé/ 'Moshe';
d. It is the first noun of a noun-noun construction in which the second noun is definite, e.g., /yoéc hašagrirút/ 'the Counsellor of the Embassy'; [The grammar of this last case will be discussed in detail later.]
e. It is an interrogative or demonstrative, e.g. /má/ 'what', /zé/ 'this'.
When the object of the verb is not definite, then the preposition does not occur. Compare: sgór et hadélet.   Close the door.
                      sgór délet.   Close a door.

The sequence /et ha-/ is often contracted in ordinary speech to /ta-/.
            /sgór tadélet./   /pitxú tasfarím./

The singular set of pronominal suffixes is used with this preposition, but the preposition has the alternate form /ot-/ when occuring with a suffix.
    naím li meód lehakír <u>otxá</u>.   naím li meód lehakír <u>otáx</u>.
Some speakers use a regularized form of the latter - /otéx/. The first person plural form is /otánu/ rather than */oténu/. These variants of the pronominal suffixes, /-áx/ and /-ánu/, occur with certain other prepositions.
The second person plural forms are either /otxém, otxén/ or /etxém, etxén/. The latter, however, are considered rather literary and somewhat stilted, though these are the only ones occurring in the classical language.

A. Substitution Drill
                   Please meet Mr. Williams.

takír bevakašá et már Williams.		תכיר בבקשה את מר ווילאמס.
	gvéret Williams	גברת ווילאמס
	mošé	משה
	hayoéc	היועץ
	hamišpaxá	המשפחה
	iští	אשתי
	yoéc hašagrirút	יועץ השגרירות
	baalá	בעלה
	ištó	אשתו
	xána	חנה

B. Substitution Drill

sgór et hadélet.	Close the door.	סגור את הדלת.
hasfarím		הספרים

C. Substitution Drill

pitxú et hadélet.	Open the door.	פתחו את הדלת.
hasfarím		הספרים
hašagrirút		השגרירות

D. Substitution Drill
              I'm very happy to meet you.

naím li meód lehakír otxá.		נעים לי מאד להכיר אותך.
	otáx	אותך
	otó	אותו
	et már Williams	את מר ווילאמס
	et ištó	את אשתו

E. Substitution-Agreement Drill

I'm very happy to meet you, Mr. Williams.

naím li meód lehakír otxá, már Williams.   .נעים לי מאד להכיר אותך, מר וויל'אמס

gvéret kóhen	naím li meód lehakír otáx, gvéret kóhen.	גב' כהן
gvéret Williams	naím li meód lehakír otáx, gvéret Williams.	גב' וויל'אמס
már káspi	naím li meód lehakír otxá, már káspi.	מר כספי
mošé	naím li meód lehakír otxá, mošé.	משה
miryám	naím li meód lehakír otxá, miryám.	מרים
gvéret zahávi	naím li meód lehakír otáx, gvéret zahávi.	גברת זהבי
már óren	naím li meód lehakír otxá, már óren.	מר אורן
xána	naím li meód lehakír otáx, xána.	חנה
avígdor	naím li meód lehakír otxá, avígdor.	אביגדור

נעים לי מאד להכיר אותך...

13

REVIEW CONVERSATIONS

A: šalóm, gevéret Williams.
takíri bevakašá et iští.

א: שלום, גברת וויל"אמס.
תכירי בבקשה את אשתי.

B: naím li meód lehakír otáx
gvéret zahávi. má šloméx.

ב: נעים לי מאד להכיר אותך,
גברת זהבי. מה שלומך?

C: gám lí naím lehakír otáx.

ג: גם לי נעים להכיר אותך.

D: miryám. takíri et baalá šel sára.

ד: מרים. תכירי את בעלה של שרה.

E: naím li meód lehakír otxá, már zahávi.

ה: נעים לי מאד להכיר אותך, מר זהבי.

F: naím meód.

ו: נעים מאד.

G: má šloméx, miryám.
matáy higát lašagrirút.

ז: מה שלומך, מרים?
מתי הגעת לשגרירות?

H: higáti lifnéy yomáim, már Williams.
takír bevakašá et baalí.

ח: הגעתי לפני יומים, מר ווילאמס.
תכיר בבקשה את בעלי.

G: naím li meód lehakír otxá, már kóhen.

ז: נעים לי מאד להכיר אותך, מר כהן.

I: naím meód, már Williams.

ט: נעים מאד, מר ווילאמס.

J: matáy higáta laárec, már Jones.

י: מתי הגעת לארץ, מר ג'ונס?

K: higáti etmól.

כ: הגעתי אתמול.

J: gám aní higáti etmól.

י: גם אני הגעתי אתמול.

L: atára. matáy higát letèl avív.

ל: עטרה. מתי הגעת לתל אביב?

M: higáti lifnéy xódeš.
matáy higáta lašagrirút, davíd.

מ: הגעתי לפני חודש.
מתי הגעת לשגרירות, דוד?

L: higáti šilšóm.

ל: הגעתי שלשום.

N: davíd. sgór et hadélet, bevakašá.

נ: דוד. סגור את הדלת, בבקשה.

O: et má?

ע: את מה?

N: et hadélet.

נ: את הדלת.

O: ó kén. slixá.

ע: או, כן. סליחה.

3.1   Introductions, contd.   (Two men)

MR. COHEN

How did you come?	éx higáta.	איך הגעת?
By plane or	beavirón ó	באורירון או
by ship?	beoniá.	באוניה?
how	éx, éyx	איך
airplane	avirón (m)	אוירון
or	ó	או
ship	oniá (f)	אוניה

MR. WILLIAMS

I came	higáti	הגעתי
by plane	beavirón	באורירון
to Lydda.	lelúd.	ללוד.
Lydda (place name)	lúd, lód	לוד

MR. COHEN

How	éx	איך
were you impressed	hitrašámta	התרשמת
by Lydda?	milúd.	מלוד?
you were impressed	hitrašámta (m.s.)	התרשמת
from, by	mi-, me-	מ-

MR. WILLIAMS

Lydda is	lúd hú	לוד הוא
a beautiful and	nemál teufá	נמל תעופה
modern airport.	yafé	יפה
	vexadíš.	וחדיש.
port	namál, namél (m)	נמל
flight	teufá (f)	תעופה
beautiful, pretty	yafé (m.s.)	יפה
and	ve-	ו-
modern	xadíš (m.s.)	חדיש

MR. COHEN

I hope that	aní mekavé še-	אני מקורה ש-
you like our country.	arcénu	ארצנו
	mócet xén	מוצאת חן
	beeynéxa.	בעיניך.
hope	mekavé (m.s.,pres.)	מקורה
that (conjunction)	še-	ש-
find	mocét (f.s.,pres.)	מוצאת
favor, charm	xén (m)	חן
eye	áin (f)	עין
[two] eyes	eynáim	עיניים
your (m.s.) eyes	eynéxa	עיניך

MR. WILLIAMS

Oh, yes.	ó kén.	או, כן.
The country is	haárec	הארץ
very pretty.	yafá meód.	יפה מאד.
beautiful, pretty	yafá (f.s.)	יפה

3.2 Introductions, contd. (Two women)

MRS. COHEN

How did you come?	éx higát.	?איך הגעת
By plane or	beavirón ó	באוירון או
by ship?	beoniá.	?באוניה

MRS. WILLIAMS

I came	higáti	הגעתי
by plane	beavirón	באוירון
to Lydda.	lelúd.	ללוד.

MRS. COHEN

How	éx	איך
were you impressed	hitrašámt	התרשמת
by Lydda?	milúd.	?מלוד
you were impressed	hitrašámt (f.s.)	התרשמת

MRS. WILLIAMS

Lydda is	lúd hú	לוד הוא
a beautiful and	nemál teufá	נמל תעופה
modern airport.	yafé	יפה
	vexadíš.	וחדיש.

MRS. COHEN

I hope that	aní mekavá še-	–אני מקורה ש
you like our country.	arcénu	ארצנו
	mócet xén	מוצאת חן
	beeynáix.	בעיניך.
hope (present)	mekavá (f.s.,pres.)	מקורה
your (f.s.) eyes	eynáix	עיניך

MRS. WILLIAMS

Oh, yes.	ó kén.	או, כן.
The country is	haárec	הארץ
very pretty.	yafá meód.	יפה מאד.

3.3 ADDITIONAL VOCABULARY

How did you come?		?איך הגעתם
(said to men or both)	éx higátem.	?איך הגעתן
(said to women)	éx higáten.	
We came by plane.	higánu beavirón.	הגענו באוירון.

I like the country.	haárec mócet xén beeynáy.	הארץ מוצאת חן בעיני.
He likes the country.	haárec mócet xén beeynáv.	הארץ מוצאת חן בעיניו.
She likes the country.	haárec mócet xén beeynéha.	הארץ מוצאת חן בעיניה.
We like the country.	haárec mócet xén beeynéynu.	הארץ מוצאת חן בעינינו.
You (m.pl.) like the country.	haárec mócet xén beeyneyxém.	הארץ מוצאת חן בעיניכם.
You (f.pl.) like the country.	haárec mócet xén beeyneyxén.	הארץ מוצאת חן בעיניכן.
They (m) like the country.	haárec mócet xén beeyneyhém.	הארץ מוצאת חן בעיניהם.
They (f) like the country.	haárec mócet xén beeyneyhén.	הארץ מוצאת חן בעיניהן.

End of Tape 1A

16

GRAMMAR DRILLS

3.4 Alternate Forms of Nouns

In Grammar Section 1.6 it was noted that some nouns have an alternate form when occurring with suffixes. Some nouns also have an alternate form when occurring as the first noun in a noun-noun sequence. Some examples of this are:

šalóm	'welfare'	šlóm hamišpaxá	'the welfare of the family'
namál	'port'	nemál teufá	'airport'

Compare, on the other hand:

yoéc　　'counsellor'　　yoéc hašagrirút　'the counsellor of the Embassy'

As with suffixed nouns, it is difficult to predict which nouns will have an alternate form or what the alternate form will be. It may or may not be the same form of the noun which occurs with suffixes (except for stress placement), e.g., /šlomí/ and /šlóm hamišpaxá/.

When a noun occurs in a Basic Sentence as the first noun in such a sequence the independent form will be given in the vocabulary breakdown.

3.5 Dual Number in Nouns

In addition to singular and plural as grammatical numbers Hebrew has a noun suffix, /-áim/, which indicates dual number. Some examples are:

yóm	'day'	yomáim	'two days'
šavúa	'week'	švuáim	'two weeks'
xódeš	'month'	xodšáim	'two months'
áin	'eye'	eynáim	'[two] eyes'

This suffix occurs with a limited number of nouns and in a few other forms. These nouns include parts of the body which come in pairs, doubled numbers and units of time, paired articles of clothing, and a few other items. It is not otherwise used to indicate two of something. Except for this suffix, dual nouns are treated as plurals. Verbs and adjectives used with them have plural forms, and the plural set of pronominal suffixes is also used. (See Section 3.6)

3.6 Pronominal Suffixes - Plural Set

In Section 1.6 the singular set of pronominal suffixes was discussed. Another set of pronominal suffixes occurs with plural (and dual) nouns and with certain prepositions. The form of the noun preceding these suffixes is often a special plural alternate, and this alternation will be drilled later. Often however, the only indication of the number of the noun is the pronominal suffix.

eyní　'my eye'　　　　eynáy　'my eyes'

[Note: As in many other instances, /ey/ is sometimes shortened to /e/. This may cause some confusion in the first and second person plural suffixes of the two sets.]

17

Tape 1B

A. Substitution Drill

haárec mócet xén beeynáy.	I like the country.	הָאָרֶץ מוֹצֵאת חֵן בְּעֵינַי.
beeynéxa		בְּעֵינֶיךָ
beeynáix		בְּעֵינַיִךְ
beeynáv		בְּעֵינָיו
beeynéha		בְּעֵינֶיהָ
beeynéynu		בְּעֵינֵינוּ
beeyneyxém		בְּעֵינֵיכֶם
beeyneyxén		בְּעֵינֵיכֶן
beeyneyhém		בְּעֵינֵיהֶם
beeyneyhén		בְּעֵינֵיהֶן

B. Expansion Drill

The student repeats the question of the instructor and asks the second question.

Instructor: How are you?
Student: How are you? How do you like the country?

		מַה שְׁלוֹמְךָ?
má šlomxá.	éx mócet xén beeynéxa haárec.	
má šlóm ištexá.	éx mócet beeynéha haárec.	
má šlóm hamišpaxá.	éx mócet xén beeynéha haárec.	
má šloméx.	éx mócet xén beeynáix haárec.	
má šlomxém.	ex mócet xén beeyneyxém haárec.	
má šlóm baaléx.	éx mócet xén beeynáv haárec.	
má šlomá.	éx mócet xén beeynéha haárec.	
má šlomxén.	éx mócet xén beeyneyxén haárec.	
má šlóm davíd.	éx mócet xén beeynáv haárec.	
má šlomó.	éx mócet xén beeynáv haárec.	
má šlomám.	éx mócet xén beeyneyhém haárec.	

C. Response Drill

Instructor:	Student:
How are you?	Fine. I like the country.
má šlomxá.	tóv. haárec mócet xén beeynáy.
má šlóm davíd.	tóv. haárec mócet xén beeynáv.
má šlomxém.	tóv. haárec mócet xén beeynéynu.
má šlóm ištexá.	tóv. haárec mócet xén beeynéha.
má šlóm mošé veištó.	tóv. haárec mócet xén beeyneyhém.
má šloméx.	tóv. haárec mócet xén beeynáy.
má šlóm xána umiryám.	tóv. haárec mócet xén beeyneyhén.

D. Transformation Drill - Pronominal Suffixes, singular and Plural Sets

Instructor:	Student:
His country is very beautiful.	He likes the country.
arcó yafá meód.	haárec mócet xén beeynáv.
arcí yafá meód.	haárec mócet xén beeynáy.
arcénu yafá meód.	haárec mócet xén beeynéynu.
arcám yafá meód.	haárec mócet xén beeyneyhém.
arcexá yafá meód.	haárec mócet xén beeynéxa.
arcéx yafá meód.	haárec mócet xén beeynáix.
arcá yafá meód.	haárec mócet xén beeynéha.
arcexém yafá meód.	haárec mócet xén beeyneyxém.

E. Transformation Drill - Repeat Drill D in reverse.

18

F. Substitution-Agreement Drill

In the following drill responses by men should begin with /aní mekavé/ and those of women should begin with /aní mekavá/. The instructor should repeat the correct answer of the particular student.

aní mekavé šearcénu mócet xén <u>beeynéxa</u>, <u>már Williams</u>.

<u>gvéret Williams</u>	aní mekavé šearcénu mócet xén beeynáix, gvéret Williams.	גב' וויל'אמס
<u>már kóhen</u>	aní mekavé šearcénu mócet xén beeynéxa, már kóhen.	מר כהן
<u>gvéret Smith</u>	aní mekavé šearcénu mócet xén beeynáix, gvéret Smith.	גב' סמיט
<u>már Jones</u>	aní mekavé šeárcenu mócet xén beeynéxa, már Jones.	מר ג'ירנס
<u>gvéret Fuller</u>	aní mekavé šearcénu mócet xén beeynaíx, gvéret Fuller.	גב' פולר
<u>gvéret Jones</u>	aní mekavé šearcénu mócet xén beeynáix, gvéret Jones.	גב' ג'ונס
<u>már Williams</u>	aní mekavé šearcénu mócet xén beeynéxa, már Williams.	מר וויל'אמס

אה כן.　　הארץ יפה מאד...

19

REVIEW CONVERSATIONS

A: šalóm, david. matáy higáta laárec.   א: שלום, דוד. מתי הגעת לארץ?

B: higáti etmól beoniá lexáyfa.   ב: הגעתי אתמול באניה לחיפה.

A: éx hitrašámta mehanamál?   א: איך התרשמת מהנמל?

B: hanamál xadíš veyafé.   ב: הנמל חדיש ויפה.

C: matáy higáta lašagrirút, már Jones.   ג: מתי הגעת לשגרירות, מר ג'ונס?

D: higáti lifnéy šavúa, miryám.   ד: הגעתי לפני שבוע, מרים.

C: aní mekavá šehašagrirút mócet xén   ג: אני מקוה שהשגרירות מוצאת חן
   beenéxa.   בעיניך.

D: kén. hašagrirút meód mócet xén beenáy.   ד: כן. השגרירות מאד מוצאת חן בעיני.

E: gvéret kóhen. éyx higát laárec.   ה: גברת כהן, איך הגעת לארץ?

F: higáti beoniá lexáyfa.   ו: הגעתי באניה לחיפה.

E: aní mekavé šehitrašámt mehaoniá.   ה: אני מקוה שהתרשמת מהאניה.

F: ken. haoniá yafá meód.   ו: כן. האניה יפה מאד.

G: már Williams. matáy higáta.   ז: מר וויל''אמס, מתי הגעת?

H: higáti etmól, már kóhen.   ח: הגעתי אתמול, מר כהן.

G: éyx higáta.   ז: איך הגעת?

H: higáti beavirón lelúd.   ח: הגעתי באוירון ללוד.

4.1 Housing Arrangements (Two men speaking)

MR. COHEN

Where	heyxán	היכן
are you staying,	atá gár,	אתה גר,
Mr. Williams?	már Williams.	מר וויליאמס?
where	heyxán	היכן
you	atá (m.s.)	אתה
reside	gár (m.s. pres.)	גר

MR. WILLIAMS

I'm staying	aní gár	אני גר
in the meantime	beynatáim	בינתיים
at the Dan Hotel.	bemalón dán.	במלון דן.
meanwhile	beynatáim	בינתיים
hotel	malón (m)	מלון

MR. COHEN

Very good.	tóv meód.	טוב מאד.
It's close	zé karóv	זה קרוב
to the Embassy.	lašagrirút.	לשגרירות.
it, this, that	zé (m)	זה
near, close	karóv (m.s.)	קרוב

MR. WILLIAMS

Yes, that's right.	kén. naxón.	כן. נכון.
correct	naxón (m.s.)	נכון

MR. COHEN

And where	veeyfó	ואיפה
do you plan	atá mitkonén	אתה מתכונן
to live?	lagúr?	לגור?
where	eyfó, éyfo	איפה
plan	mitkonén (m.s. pres.)	מתכונן
to reside	lagúr	לגור

MR. WILLIAMS

There will be arranged	yesudár	יסודר
for us	avurénu	עבורנו
a house in Ramat Gan.	báit beramát gán.	בית ברמת גן.
will be arranged	yesudar (3.m.s.)	יסודר
for, on behalf of	avúr	עבור
house	báit (m)	בית

MR. COHEN

Have you seen	haím raíta	האם ראית
the house?	et habáit?	את הבית?
(yes-or-no question introducer)	haím	האם
you saw	raíta (m.s.)	ראית

21

MR. WILLIAMS

No. But	ló. áx	לא. אך
I've heard that	šamáti še-	שמעתי ש-
the house is	habáit	הבית
big and beautiful.	gadól veyafé.	גדול ויפה.
but	áx	אך
I heard	šamáti	שמעתי
big, large, great	gadól (m.s.)	גדול

MR. COHEN

When will	matáy tagía	מתי תגיע
your family arrive?	hamišpaxá šelxá.	המשפחה שלך?
will arrive	tagía (3.f.s.)	תגיע
of you, yours	šelxá (m.s.)	שלך

MR. WILLIAMS

My family	hamišpaxá šelí	המשפחה שלי
will arrive in	tagía beód	תגיע בעוד
about a month.	kexódeš yamím.	כחודש ימים.
of me, mine	šelí	שלי
still, yet	ód	עוד
approximately, as	ke-	כ-
days	yamím	ימים
	(pl. of /yóm/)	יום

4.2 __Housing Arrangements__ (Two women speaking)

MRS. COHEN

Where	heyxán	היכן
are you staying,	át gára,	את...גרה,
Mrs. Williams?	gvéret Williams.	גברת וויל$+$אמס?
you (f.s)	át (f.s.)	את
reside (f.s.pres.)	gára (f.s.pres.)	גרה

MRS. WILLIAMS

I'm staying	aní gára	אני גרה
in the meantime	beynatáim	בינתיים
at the Dan Hotel.	bemalón dán.	במלון דן.

MRS. COHEN

Very good.	tóv meód.	טוב מאד.
It's close	zé karóv	זה קרוב
to the Embassy.	lašagrirút.	לשגרירות.

MRS. WILLIAMS

Yes, that's right.	kén. naxón.	כן. נכון.

MRS. COHEN

And where	veeyfó	ואיפה
do you plan	át mitkonénet	את מתכוננת
to live?	lagúr?	לגור?
plan	mitkonénet (f.s.pres.)	מתכוננת

MRS. WILLIAMS

There will be arranged	yesudár	יסודר
for us	avurénu	עבורנו
a house in Ramat Gan.	báit beramát gán.	בית ברמת גן.

MRS. COHEN

Have you seen	haím raít	האם ראית
the house?	et habáit?	את הבית?
you saw	raít (f.s.)	ראית

MRS. WILLIAMS

No. But	ló. áx	לא. אך
I've heard that	šamáti še-	שמעתי ש-
the house is	habáit	הבית
big and beautiful.	gadól veyafé.	גדול ויפה.

MRS. COHEN

When will	matáy tagía	מתי תגיע
the rest of your	yéter hamišpaxá	יתר המשפחה
family arrive?	seláx.	שלך?
rest, remainder	yéter	יתר
of you, yours	seláx (f.s.)	שלך

MRS. WILLIAMS

My family	hamišpaxá šelí	המשפחה שלי
will arrive in	tagía beód	תגיע בעוד
about a month.	kexódeš yamím.	כחורש ימים.

4.3 ADDITIONAL VOCABULARY

His house is very nice.	habáit šeló yafé meód.	הבית שלו יפה מאד.
Her house is very nice.	habáit šelá yafé meód.	הבית שלה יפה מאד.
Our house is very nice.	habáit šelánu yafé meód.	הבית שלנו יפה מאד.
Your (m.pl.) house is very nice.	habáit šelaxém yafé meód.	הבית שלכם יפה מאד.
Your (f.pl.) house is very nice.	habáit šelaxén yafé meód.	הבית שלכן יפה מאד.
Their (m) house is very nice.	habáit šelahém yafé meód.	הבית שלהם יפה מאד.
Their (f) house is very nice.	habáit šelahén yafé meód.	הבית שלהן יפה מאד.
We (m) live in Haifa.	ánu garím bexáyfa.	אנו גרים בחיפה.
You (m.pl.) live in Haifa.	atém garím bexáyfa.	אתם גרים בחיפה.
They (m) live in Haifa.	hém garím bexáyfa.	הם גרים בחיפה.
We (f) live in Haifa.	ánu garót bexáyfa.	אנו גרות בחיפה.
You (f.pl.) live in Haifa.	atén garót bexáyfa.	אתן גרות בחיפה.
They (f) live in Haifa.	hén garót bexáyfa.	הן גרות בחיפה.

GRAMMAR NOTES

4.4 The Preposition /šel/ 'of'

Examine these sentences which have occurred in the text:

hí ištó <u>šel yoéc</u> hašagrirút.   She is the wife of <u>the Counsellor</u> of the
                                            Embassy.
matáy tagía hamišpaxá <u>šelxá</u>.   When will <u>your</u> family arrive?

habáit <u>šeló</u> yafé meód.   <u>His</u> house is very nice.

Note that the preposition /šel/ indicates a genitive or possessive
relationship of the noun following it or pronoun affixed to it with the noun
preceding it.
This is the most frequent construction in spoken Hebrew indicating such a
possessive relationship. The preposition may often be equated to the English
preposition <u>of</u> as in the first example above.
The noun preceding /šel/ is made definite with /ha-/ or with a pronominal
suffix /ištó/. The latter is not used when a pronoun is suffixed to /šel/ itself.
The difference is primarily one of style.

haišá šel már Williams   The wife of Mr. Williams
ištó šel már Williams   The wife of Mr. Williams

The construction with the suffixed preposition is synonymous with the
suffixed noun construction.

habáal šelá naím meód.   Her husband is very pleasant.
baalá naím meód.   Her husband is very pleasant.

When the noun preceding /šel/ is indefinite the usual English equivalent is
a prepositional phrase construction.

avirón šelánu.   An airplane of ours.

The singular set of pronominal suffixes is used with /šel/, with variations
in the feminine second person singular, /šeláx/, and in the plural suffixes.
(compare /otáx/ and /otánu/.)

A. Substitution Drill.

My house is very modern.

habáit šelí xadíš meód.	הבית שלי חדיש מאד.
šelxá	שלך
šeláx	שלך
šeló	שלו
šelá	שלה
šelánu	שלנו
šelaxém	שלכם
šelaxén	שלכן
šelahém	שלהם
šelahén	שלהן

24

B. Transformation Drill

Instructor:	Student:	
Mr. Carmi's plane is in Lydda.	His plane is in Lydda.	

haavirón šel már kármi belúd.	haavirón šeló belúd.	האוירון של מר כרמי בלוד.
haavirón šel xána belúd.	haavirón šelá belúd.	האוירון של חנה בלוד.
haavirón šel mošé veléa belúd.	haavirón šelahém belúd.	האוירון של משה ולאה בלוד.
haavirón šel hayoéc belúd.	haavirón šeló belúd.	האוירון של היועץ בלוד.
haavirón šel hašagrirút belúd.	haavirón šelá belúd.	האוירון של השגרירות בלוד.
haavirón šel baaléx belúd.	haavirón šeló belúd.	האוירון של בעלך בלוד.
haavirón šel iští belúd.	haavirón šelá belúd.	האוירון של אשתי בלוד.

C. Transformation Drill

My wife is very pretty.

Instructor:	Student:	
iští yafá meód.	haišá šelí yafá meód.	אשתי יפה מאד.
ištó yafá meód.	haišá šeló yafá meód.	אשתו יפה מאד.
ištexá yafá meód.	haišá šelxá yafá meód.	אשתך יפה מאד.

D. Transformation Drill - Repeat Drill C in reverse.

E. Transformation Drill

Her husband is staying at the Dan Hotel.

Instructor:	Student:	
baalá gár bemalón dán.	habáal šelá gár bemalón dán.	בעלה גר במלון דן.
baaléx gár bemalón dán.	habáal šeláx gár bemalón dán.	בעלך גר במלון דן.
baalí gár bemalón dán.	habáal šelí gár bemalón dán.	בעלי גר במלון דן.

F. Transformation Drill - Repeat Drill E in reverse.

G. Transformation Drill

Our country is very beautiful.

Instructor:	Student:	
arcénu yafá meód.	haárec šelánu yafá meód.	ארצנו יפה מאד.
arcí yafá meód.	haárec šelí yafá meód.	ארצי יפה מאד.
arcó yafá meód.	haárec šeló yafá meód.	ארצו יפה מאד.
arcám yafá meód.	haárec šelahém yafá meód.	ארצם יפה מאד.
arcán yafá meód.	haárec šelahén yafá meód.	ארצן יפה מאד.
arcexém yafá meód.	haárec šelaxém yafá meód.	ארצכם יפה מאד.
arcexén yafá meód.	haárec šelaxén yafá meód.	ארצכן יפה מאד.
arcá yafá meód.	haárec šelá yafá meód.	ארצה יפה מאד.

H. Transformation Drill - Repeat Drill G in reverse.

I. Transformation Drill

Instructor:	Student:	
He lives in Haifa.	His family lives in Haifa.	

hú gár bexáyfa.	hamišpaxá šeló gára bexáyfa.	.הוא גר בחיפה
hí gára bexáyfa.	hamišpaxá šelá gára bexáyfa.	.היא גרה בחיפה
ánu garím bexáyfa.	hamišpaxá šelánu gára bexáyfa.	.אנו גרים בחיפה
hém garím bexáyfa.	hamišpaxá šelahém gára bexáyfa.	.הם גרים בחיפה
aní gár bexáyfa.	hamišpaxá šelí gára bexáyfa.	.אני גר בחיפה
hén garót bexáyfa.	hamišpaxá šelahén gára bexáyfa.	.הן גרות בחיפה

J. Transformation Drill - Repeat Drill I. in reverse.

K. Expansion Drill

Instructor: He is staying at the Dan Hotel.
Student: He is staying at the Dan Hotel, and his family will arrive in a week.

<u>hú gár bemalón dán</u>.vehamišpaxá šeló tagía beód šavúa.	.הוא גר במלון דן
<u>hém garím bemalón dán</u>.vehamišpaxá šelahém tagía beód šavúa.	.הם גרים במלון דן
<u>aní gár bemalón dán</u>.vehamišpaxá šelí tagía beód šavúa.	.אני גר במלון דן
<u>hí gára bemalón dán</u>.vehamišpaxá šelá tagía beód šavúa.	.היא גרה במלון דן
<u>ánu garím bemalón dán</u>.vehamišpaxá šelánu tagía beód šavúa.	.אנו גרים במלון דן
<u>hayoéc gár bemalón dán</u>.vehamišpaxá šeló tagía beód šavúa.	.היועץ גר במלון דן
<u>hú veištó garím bemalón dán</u>.vehamišpaxá šelahém tagía beód šavúa.	.הוא ואשתו גרים במלון דן

L. Transformation Drill

Instructor:	Student:	
I like the country.	My country is very pretty.	

haárec mócet xén beenáy.	haárec šelí yafá meód.	.הארץ מוצאת חן בעיני
hí gára bexáyfa.	haárec šelxá yafá meód.	.הארץ מוצאת חן בעיניך
haárec mócet xén beenáix.	haárec šeláx yafá meód.	.הארץ מוצאת חן בעיניך
haárec mócet xén beenéynu.	haárec šelánu yafá meód.	.הארץ מוצאת חן בעינינו
haárec mócet xén beeyneyxém.	haárec šelaxém yafá meód.	.הארץ מוצאת חן בעיניכם
haárec mócet xén beenéha.	haárec šelá yafá meód.	.הארץ מוצאת חן בעיניה
haárec mócet xén beeyneyxén.	haárec šelaxén yafá meód.	.הארץ מוצאת חן בעיניכן

M. Response Drill

Instructor:	Student:	
Where is your family staying?	My family is staying at the Dan Hotel.	

heyxán gára hamišpaxá šelxá.	hamišpaxá šelí gára bemalón dán.	?היכן גרה המשפחה שלך
heyxán gára hamišpaxá šeló.	hamišpaxá šeló gára bemalón dán.	?היכן גרה המשפחה שלו
heyxán gára hamišpaxá šelaxém.	hamišpaxá šelánu gára bemalón dán.	?היכן גרה המשפחה שלכם
heyxán gára hamišpaxá šeláx.	hamišpaxá šelí gára bemalón dán.	?היכן גרה המשפחה שלך
heyxán gára hamišpaxá šelahén.	hamišpaxá šelahen gára bemalón dán.	?היכן גרה המשפחה שלהן

4.5 <u>The Preposition /avúr/ 'for', on behalf of'</u>

The preposition /avúr/ is used with the singular set of pronominal suffixes.
yesudár avur<u>é</u>nu báit berámat gán.

A. Substitution Drill

A house will be arranged for me.

yesudár avurí báit.	יסודר עבורי בית.
avurxá	עבורך
avuréx	עבורך
avuró	עבורו
avurá	עבורה
avurénu	עבורנו
avurxém	עבורכם
avurxén	עבורכן
avurám	עבורם
avurán	עבורן

B. Transformation Drill

         Instructor: A house will be arranged for Mr. Williams.
         Student: A house will be arranged for him.

yesudár avúr már Williams báit.	yesudár avuró báit.	יסודר עבור מר ווילי∙אמס בית.
yesudár avúr miryám báit.	yesudár avurá báit.	יסודר עבור מרים בית.
yesudár avúr yaakóv veléa báit.	yesudár avurám báit.	יסודר עבור יעקב ולאה בית.
yesudár avúr hamišpaxá šeló báit.	yesudár avurá báit.	יסודר עבור המשפחה שלו בית.
yesudár avúr hayoéc báit.	yesudár avuró báit.	יסודר עבור היועץ בית.

C. Transformation Drill

         Instructor: His house will be arranged.
         Student: A house will be arranged for him.

habáit šeló yesudár.	yesudár avuró báit.	הבית שלו יסודר.
habáit šelxá yesudár.	yesudár avurxá báit.	הבית שלך יסודר.
habáit šelánu yesudár.	yesudár avurénu báit.	הבית שלנו יסודר.
habáit šelí yesudár.	yesudár avurí báit.	הבית שלי יסודר.
habáit šeláx yesudár.	yesudár avuréx báit.	הבית שלך יסודר.
habáit šelá yesudár.	yesudár avurá báit.	הבית שלה יסודר.
habáit šelahém yesudár.	yesudár avurám báit.	הבית שלהם יסודר.
habáit šelaxém yesudár.	yesudár avurxém báit.	הבית שלכם יסודר.
habáit šel davíd yesudár.	yesudár avúr davíd báit.	הבית של דוד יסודר.

D. Transformation Drill - Repeat Drill C in reverse.

4.6 Contraction of /le- + ha-/ 'to the'

       Examine the underlined forms in the following:
         <u>le</u>lúd   '<u>to</u> Lydda'
         <u>ha</u>šagrirút   '<u>the</u> embassy'
         <u>la</u>šagrirút   '<u>to the</u> embassy'
     Note that the preposition /le-/ and the definite article /ha-/ contract to
/la-/. This is an obligatory contraction.
     When /ha-/ is a verb prefix or is simply the first syllable of a word (but
not the definite article) then the contraction is not made: /lehakír/ 'to know'.
     The preposition has the alternate form /la-/ with certain verb infinitives:
/larúc, lagúr/. However, it is not a contraction of /leha-/ in these cases.

REVIEW CONVERSATIONS

A: heyxán atá gár, már Williams?   ?א: היכן אתה גר, מר וויליאמס

B: aní veiští garím bemalón beynatáim.   .ב: אני ואשתי גרים במלון בינתיים

A: bemalón dán?   ?א: במלון דן

B: kén. zé karóv lašagrirút.   .ב: כן. זה קרוב לשגרירות

A: haím atá mitkonén lagúr betél avív?   ?א: האם אתה מתכונן לגור בתל אביב

B: ló. aní mitkonén lagúr berámat gán.   .ב: לא. אני מתכונן לגור ברמת גן

A: haím yesudár avurxém báit?   ?א: האם יסודר עבורכם בית

B: kén. áx ló raíti otó.   .ב: כן. אך לא ראיתי אותו

C: haím hamišpaxá šelxá betél avív?   ?ג: האם המשפחה שלך בתל אביב

D: ló. hamišpaxá šelí beamérika.   .ד: לא. המשפחה שלי באמריקה

C: matáy tagía hamišpaxá laárec?   ?ג: מתי תגיע המשפחה לארץ

D: beód xódeš.   .ד: בעוד חודש

E: haím raíta et habáit šel már kármi?   ?ה: האם ראית את הבית של מר כרמי

F: kén. vehitrašamtí meód mehabáit.   .ו: כן. והתרשמתי מאד מהבית

E: šamáti šehabáit gadól.   .ה: שמעתי שהבית גדול

F: kén. naxón. habáit gadól vexadíš.   .ו: כן. נכון. הבית גדול וחדיש

G: heyxán át mitkonénet lagúr, atára.   .ז: היכן את מתכוננת לגור, עטרה

H: aní ló yodáat. beynatáim   ח: אני לא יודעת. בינתיים
aní gára bemalón.   .אני גרה במלון

G: ló yesudár avuréx báit?   ?ז: לא יסודר עבורך בית

H: kén. šamáti šeyesudár báit.   .ח: כן. שמעתי שיסודר בית
áx aní ló yodáat eyfó umatáy.   .אך אני לא יודעת איפה ומתי

I: dálya, raít et hayoéc haamerikái?   ?ט: דליה, ראית את היועץ האמריקאי

J: kén. hú naím meód.   .י: כן. הוא נעים מאד

I: éyfo hú gár?   ?ט: איפה הוא גר

J: hú veištó garím bemalón dán.   .י: הוא ואשתו גרים במלון דן

I: raít et ištó?   ?ט: ראית את אשתו

J: ló. áx šamáti šehí yafá meód.   .י: לא. אך שמעתי שהיא יפה מאד

5.1 Speaking Hebrew (Men)

MR. COHEN

Tell me,	emór li	אמור לי,
please.	bevakašá.	בבקשה.
Where did you learn	heyxán lamádeta	היכן למדת
to speak such a	ledabér ivrít	לדבר עברית
beautiful Hebrew?	kol káx yafá.	כל כך יפה?
tell, say	emór (m.s.imv.)	אמור
you learned	lamádeta (m.s.)	למדת
to speak	ledabér	לדבר
all	kól	כל
so, as much	kol káx	כל כך

MR. WILLIAMS

I learned	lamádeti	למדתי
to speak Hebrew	ledabér ivrít	לדבר עברית
in America.	beamérika.	באמריקה.
I learned	lamádeti	למדתי

MR. COHEN

In which	beéyze	באיזה
school	bet séfer	בית ספר
did you study?	lamádeta.	למדת?
which	éyze (m)	איזה
book	séfer (m)	ספר
school	bet séfer	בית ספר

MR. WILLIAMS

In the school	bevét haséfer	בבית הספר
of languages of	lesafót šel	לשפות של
our State Department	misrád haxúc šelánu.	משרד החוץ שלנו.
language	safá (f)	שפה
languages	safót (f.pl.)	שפות
office	misrád (m)	משרד
outside	xúc	חוץ

MR. COHEN

You did well	tóv meód asíta	טוב מאד עשית
to learn Hebrew	šelamádeta ivrít	שלמדת עברית
before	lifnéy še-	לפני ש-
you came here.	báta héna.	באת הנה.
you did	asíta (m.s.)	עשית
you came	báta (m.s.)	באת
[to] here, hither	héna	הנה

You speak	atá medabér	אתה מדבר
Hebrew	ivrít	עברית
just like	mamáš kmó	ממש כמו
an Israeli.	israelí.	ישראלי.
speak	medabér (m.s.pres.)	מדבר
really, just	mamáš	ממש
like	kmó	כמו

MR. WILLIAMS

Don't exaggerate.	ál tagzím.		אל תגזים.
Like an Israeli	kmó israelí		כמו ישראלי
as yet	adáin		עדיין
I don't speak.	eynéni medabér.		אינני מדבר.
don't		ál (neg.part.)	אל
you will exaggerate		tagzím	תגזים
as yet		adáin	עדיין
not		éyn (neg.part.)	אין
I don't		eynéni	אינני

MR. COHEN

You speak	atá medabér	אתה מדבר
very well.	yafé meód.	יפה מאד.

MR. WILLIAMS

I'm happy	aní saméax		אני שמח
with the results.	mehatocaót.		מהתוצאות.
happy		saméax	שמח
result		tocaá (f)	תוצאה
results		tocaót (f.pl.)	תוצאות

5.2　Speaking Hebrew (Women)

MRS. COHEN

Tell me,	imrí li		אמרי לי
Please, please	bevakašá.		בבקשה.
Where did you learn	heyxán lamádet		היכן למדת
to speak such a	ledabér ivrít		לדבר עברית
beautiful Hebrew?	kol káx yafá.		כל כך יפה?
tell, say (imv.)		imrí	אמרי
you learned		lamádet (f.s.)	למדת

MRS. WILLIAMS

I learned	lamádeti	למדתי
to speak Hebrew	ledabér ivrít	לדבר עברית
in America.	beamérika.	באמריקה.

MRS. COHEN

In which	beéyze	באיזה
school	bet séfer	בית ספר
did you study?	lamádet?	למדת?

MRS. WILLIAMS

In the school	bevét haséfer	בבית הספר
of languages of	lesafót šel	לשפות של
our State Department.	misrád haxúc šelánu.	משרד החוץ שלנו.

30

<u>MRS. COHEN</u>

You did well	tóv meód asít	טוב מאד עשית
to learn Hebrew	šelamádet ivrít	שלמדת עברית
before	lifney še-	לפני ש-
you came here.	bát héna.	באת הנה.
you did	asít (f.s.)	עשית
you came	bát (f.s.)	באת

You speak	át medabéret	את מדברת
Hebrew	ivrít	עברית
just like	mamáš kmó	ממש כמו
an Israeli	israelít.	ישראלית.
speak	medabéret (f.s.pres.)	מדברת
Israeli	israelít (f.)	ישראלית

<u>MRS. WILLIAMS</u>

Don't exaggerate.	ál tagzími.	אל תגזימי.
Like an Israeli	kmó israelít	כמו ישראלית
as yet	adáin	עדיין
I don't speak.	eynéni medabéret.	אינני מדברת.
you will exaggerate	tagzími (f.s.)	תגזימי

<u>MRS. COHEN</u>

You speak	at medabéret	את מדברת
very well.	yafé meód.	יפה מאד.

<u>MRS. WILLIAMS</u>

I'm happy	aní smexá	אני שמחה
with the results.	mehatocaót.	מהתוצאות.
happy	smexá (f.s.)	שמחה

<u>End of Tape 1B</u>

31

GRAMMAR NOTES

5.3 Past Tense of Verbs - First and Second Persons

Compare the underlined forms in the following sentences:

1. matáy <u>higáta</u> laárec, már Williams.
   matáy <u>higát</u> laárec, gvéret Williams.

2. heyxán <u>lamádeta</u> ledabér ivrít·kol káx yafá.
   heyxán <u>lamádet</u> ledabér ivrít kol káx yafá.

3. tóv meód <u>asíta</u> šelamádeta ivrít lifnéy šebáta héna.
   tóv meód <u>asít</u> šelamádet ivrít lifnéy šebát héna.

Note that in speaking to a man the forms end in /-ta/, and in speaking to a woman they end in /-t/. Now compare the following forms as spoken by either a man or a woman.

4. <u>higáti</u> lifnéy yomáim.

5. <u>lamádeti</u> ledabér ivrít beamérika.

Note that these forms end in /-ti/. Comparison with some plural verb forms yields three more suffixes.

/-nu/ 'we' <u>higánu</u> lifnéy yomáim.

/-tem/ 'you' (m.pl.) matáy <u>higátem</u> laárec.

/-ten/ 'you' (f.pl.) matáy higáten laárec.

These pronominal suffixes are affixed to the past tense stems of all verbs. Given a past tense form with any of these suffixes, the other five may be derived by substitution.

The third person forms of the past tense will not be drilled until later.

The third person forms involve changes in the stem, whereas the first and second person forms differ only in the suffixes.

The independent pronouns may be used with the first and second person past tense forms for contrast, insistence, etc.

aní higáti héna etmól.   <u>I</u> got here yesterday.
matáy <u>atá</u> higáta.   When did <u>you</u> get here?

A. Substitution Drill

When did you get here?

matáy higáta héna.	מתי הגעת הנה?
higát	הגעת
higátem	הגעתם
higáten	הגעתן

B. Substitution Drill

In which school did you study?

beéyze bet séfer lamádeta.	באיזה בית ספר למדת?
lamádet	למדת
lamádetem	למדתם
lamádeten	למדתן

C. Expansion Drill

Instructor: You came yesterday.
Student: You did well that you came yesterday.

báta etmól.	tóv asíta šebáta etmól.	טוב עשית שבאת אתמול. באת אתמול.
bánu etmól.	tóv asínu šebánu etmól.	טוב עשינו שבאנו אתמול. באנו אתמול.
bát etmól.	tóv asít šebát etmól.	טוב עשית שבאת אתמול. באת אתמול.
báti etmól.	tóv asíti šebáti etmól.	טוב עשיתי שבאתי אתמול. באתי אתמול.
bátem etmól.	tóv asítem šebátem etmól.	טוב עשיתם שבאתם אתמול. באתם אתמול.
báten etmól.	tóv asíten šebáten etmól.	טוב עשיתן שבאתן אתמול. באתן אתמול.

D. Expansion Drill

Instructor: I arrived yesterday.
Student: I arrived yesterday, and I'm
           staying at the Savoy Hotel.

higáti etmól.	veaní gár bemalón savóy.	ואני גר במלון סבוי.	הגעתי אתמול.
higátem etmól.	veatém garím bemalón savóy.	ואתם גרים במלון סבוי.	הגעתם אתמול.
higánu etmól.	veánu garím bemalón savóy.	ואנו גרים במלון סבוי.	הגענו אתמול.
higát etmól.	veát gára bemalón savóy.	ואת גרה במלון סבוי.	הגעת אתמול.
higáten etmól.	veatén garót bemalón savóy.	ואתן גרות במלון סבוי.	הגעתן אתמול.
higáta etmól.	veatá gár bemalón savóy.	ואתה גר במלון סבוי.	הגעת אתמול.

Note: Women students may respond with
      /aní gára/ and /ánu garót/.

E. Expansion Drill

Instructor: Hello, David.
Student: Hello, David. When did you get here?

šalóm davíd.	matáy higáta héna.	שלום, דור. מתי הגעת הנה?
šalóm sára.	matáy higát héna.	שלום, שרה. מתי הגעת הנה?
šalóm, már kármi.	matáy higáta héna.	שלום, מר כרמי. מתי הגעת הנה?
šalóm, xána, šalóm, léa.	matáy higáten héna.	שלום, חנה, שלום,לאה. מתי הגעתן הנה?
šalóm, avígdor.	matáy higáta héna.	שלום, אביגדור. מתי הגעת הנה?
šalóm, mošé, šalóm, dóv.	matáy higátem héna.	שלום, משה. שלום,דב. מתי הגעתם הנה?
šalóm, gvéret kóhen.	matáy higát héna.	שלום, גברת כהן. מתי הגעת הנה?

33

F.   Transformation Drill

Instructor: I was very impressed by the school.
Student: I saw that the school is modern and beautiful.

hitrašámti meód mibét haséfer.	התרשמתי מאד מבית הספר.
raíti šebét haséfer xadíš veyafé.	ראיתי שבית הספר חדיש ויפה.
hitrašámnu meód mibét haséfer.	התרשמנו מאד מבית הספר.
raínu šebét haséfer xadíš veyafé.	ראינו שבית הספר חדיש ויפה.
hitrašámtém meód mibét haséfer.	התרשמתם מאד מבית הספר.
raítem šebét haséfer xadíš veyafé.	ראיתם שבית הספר חדיש ויפה.
hitrašámt meód mibét haséfer.	התרשמת מאד מבית הספר.
raít šebét haséfer xadíš veyafé.	ראית שבית הספר חדיש ויפה.
hitrašámta meód mibét haséfer.	התרשמת מאד מבית הספר.
raíta šebét haséfer xadíš veyafé.	ראית שבית הספר חדיש ויפה.
hitrašámten meód mibét haséfer.	התרשמתן מאד מבית הספר.
raíten šebét haséfer xadíš veyafé.	ראיתן שבית הספר חדיש ויפה.

This drill may be varied by making it an expansion drill.

     Instructor: hitrašámti meód mibét haséfer.
     Student: hitrašámti meód mibét haséfer. raíti šebét haséfer xadíš
                veyafé.

G.   Transformation Drill

Instructor: You live in Tel Aviv.
Student: You have seen the Dan Hotel.

atém garím betél avív.	raítem et malón dán.	אתם גרים בתל אביב.
át gára betél avív.	raít et malón dán.	את גרה בתל אביב.
aní gár betél avív.	raíti et malón dán.	אני גר בתל אביב.
ánu garím betél avív.	raínu et malón dán.	אנו גרים בתל אביב.
atá gár betél avív.	raíta et malón dán.	אתה גר בתל אביב.
atén garót betél avív.	raíten et malón dán.	אתן גרות בתל אביב.

This drill may be varied by making it an expansion drill.

     Instructor: atém garím betél avív.
     Student: atém garím betél avív. raítem et malón dán.

H.   Transformation Drill

Instructor: I learned to speak Hebrew in America.
Student: I studied Hebrew before I came here.

lamádeti ledabér ivrít beamérika.	למדתי לדבר עברית באמריקה.
lamádeti ivrít lifnéy šebáti héna.	למדתי עברית לפני שבאתי הנה.
lamádnu ledabér ivrít beamérika.	למדנו לדבר עברית באמריקה.
lamádnu ivrít lifnéy šebánu héna.	למדנו עברית לפני שבאנו הנה.
lamádeta ledabér ivrít beamérika.	למד לדבר עברית באמריקה.
lamádeta ivrít lifnéy šebáta héna.	למד עברית לפני שבאת הנה.
lamádet ledabér ivrít beamérika.	למד לדבר עברית באמריקה.
lamádet ivrít lifnéy šebát héna.	למד עברית לפני שבאת הנה.
lamádeten ledabér ivrít beamérika.	למדן לדבר עברית באמריקה.
lamádeten ivrít lifnéy šebáten héna.	למדן עברית לפני שבאתן הנה.
lamádetem ledabér ivrít beamérika.	למדתם לדבר עברית באמריקה.
lamádetem ivrít lifnéy šebátem héna.	למדתם עברית לפני שבאתם הנה.

I. Transformation Drill

Instructor: I heard that Haifa is very beautiful.
Student: I haven't seen Haifa.

šamáti šexáyfa yafá meód.	שמעתי שחיפה יפה מאד.
ló raíti et xáyfa.	לא ראיתי את חיפה.
šamátem šexáyfa yafá meód.	שמעתם שחיפה יפה מאד.
ló raítem et xáyfa.	לא ראיתם את חיפה.
šamát šexáyfa yafá meód.	שמעת שחיפה יפה מאד.
ló raít et xáyfa.	לא ראית את חיפה.
šamánu šexáyfa yafá meód.	שמענו שחיפה יפה מאד.
ló raínu et xáyfa.	לא ראינו את חיפה.
šamáta šexáyfa yafá meód.	שמעת שחיפה יפה מאד.
ló raíta et xáyfa.	לא ראית את חיפה.
šamáten šexáyfa yafá meód.	שמעתן שחיפה יפה מאד.
ló raíten et xáyfa.	לא ראיתן את חיפה.

J. Transformation Drill - Repeat Drill I in reverse.

    Drills I and J may be varied by making them expansion drills.

       Instructor: šamáti šexáyfa yafá meód.
       Student: šamáti šexáyfa yafá meód, áx ló raíti otá.

       Instructor: ló raíti et xáyfa.
       Student;   ló raíti et xáyfa, áx šamáti šehí yafá meód.

    In the following drills the instructor supplies the independent pronoun
as a cue, and the student responds with an entire sentence. The instructor
may vary the drills by requiring the students to include the independent
pronoun in the response.

       Instructor: báti héna lifnéy yomáim.
       Student: báti héna lifnéy yomáim.
       Instructor: atá
       Student: báta héna lifnéy yomáim.   (or)   atá báta héna lifnéy
                                                        yomáim.

K. Substitution Drill

    I came here two days ago.

    <u>báti héna lifnéy yomáim.</u>   <u>באתי הנה לפני יומיים.</u>

    atá - ánu - át - atém   אתה - אנו - את - אתם

    atén - ánu - atá - aní   אתן - אנו - אתה - אני

L. Substitution Drill

    You did well to get to Israel a month ago.

    <u>tóv asíta šehigáta laárec lifnéy xódeš.</u>   <u>טוב עשית שהגעת לארץ לפני חודש.</u>

    aní - át - atém - ánu   אני - את - אתם - אנו
    át - atén - aní - atá   את - אתן - אני - אתה

M. Substitution Drill

    We've heard him and we've seen him.

    <u>šamánu otó veraínu otó.</u>   <u>שמענו אותו וראינו אותו.</u>

    aní - át - atá - aní   אני – את – אתה – אני
    atém - atá - atén - ánu   אתם – אתה – אתן – אנו

N. Substitution - Agreement Drill

    When did you arrive in the country, Mr. Williams?

    <u>matáy higáta laárec, már Williams.</u>   ?מתי הגעת לארץ, מר וויליאמס

<u>gvéret fúler</u>	matáy higát laárec, gvéret fúler.	<u>גב' פולר</u>
<u>miryám</u>	matáy higát laárec, miryám.	<u>מרים</u>
<u>avígdor</u>	matáy higáta laárec, avígdor.	<u>אביגדור</u>
<u>gvéret kóhen</u>	matáy higát laárec, gvéret kóhen.	<u>גב' כהן</u>
<u>már óren</u>	matáy higáta laárec, már óren.	<u>מר ארן</u>
<u>gvéret káspi</u>	matáy higát laárec, gvéret káspi.	<u>גב' כספי</u>
<u>már Williams</u>	matáy higáta laárec, már Williams.	<u>מר וויליאמס</u>

5.4 <u>Alternation /mi- ~ me-/ 'from'</u>

    The prefixed preposition /mi-/ 'from' has the alternate form /me-/ when immediately followed by a vowel or by /h/.

                éx hitrašámta <u>mi</u>lúd.
                aní saméax <u>me</u>hatocaót.

    Many speakers, especially in more formal speech, use /me-/ before /x/ and /r/.

                <u>me</u>xáyfa.
                <u>me</u>rámat gán.

5.5 <u>Consonant Alternation /b ~ v/</u>

    The consonant /b/ often alternates with /v/ when not initial in the word.

                <u>bét</u> haséfer   'the school'
                be<u>vét</u> haséfer   'in the school'

    In this particular case the alternation in the second example is optional in informal speech - both /bebét haséfer/ and /bevét haséfer/ are heard. In other cases, particularly in verbs, the alternation is required. The patterns of alternation are rather complicated and are not consistent for all levels of speech nor for all speakers. For the time being the student should simply memorize each particular example as it occurs in the text. [Note: The instructor may insist that students make the optional alternations since it is supposedly 'correct' to do so. Students should interpret 'correct' to mean 'more formal' and not spend much time on this point.]

REVIEW CONVERSATIONS

A.   heyxán lamádeta ledabér ivrít, már Williams.   א: היכן למדת לדבר עברית, מר וויל-יאמס?

B.   lamádeti ivrít beamérika.   ב: למדתי עברית באמריקה.

A.   tóv asíta šelamádeta ivrít.   א: טוב עשׂיתָ שׁלמדת עברית.

B.   kén, aní saméax mehatocaót.   ב: כן, אני שׂמח מהתוצאות.

C.   hitrašámti meód mibét haséfer lesafót.   ג: והתרשׁמתי מאד מבית הסּפר לשׁפות.

D.   kén. zé bét séfer tóv.   ד: כן. זה ביֵן ספר טוב.

C.   gám aní lamádeti ivrít bevét séfer lesafót.   ג: גם אני למדתי עברית בבית סּפר לשׁפות.

D.   ó ? atá ló israelí?   ד: או ! אתה לא ישׂראלי??

C.   ló. báti héna mehungárya.   ג: לא. באוׁי וׁוׁנה מהונגריה.

E.   át medabéret ivrít kmó israelít.   ה: את מדברת עברית כמו ישׂראלית.

F.   ál tagzím. kmó israelít eynéni medabéret.   ו: אל תגזים. כמו ישׂראלית איני מדברת.

E.   át medabéret yafé meód.   ה: את מדברת יפה מאד.

F.   todá rabá.   ו: תודה רבה.

G.   šamáti šehabáit šel mošé gadól veyafé.   ז: שׁמעתי שׁהבית של משׁה גדול ויפה.

H.   ál tagzím. raíti et habáit, vehú ló kól káx gadól.   ח: אל תגזים. ראיתי את הבית, והוא לא כל כך גדול.

I.   haím raítem et habáit šelánu?   ט: האם ראיתם את הבית שלנו?

J.   ló,áx šamánu mimošé šehabáit šelaxém yafé meód.   י: לא. אך שׁמ׳ענו ממשׁה שׁהבית שׁלכם יפה מאד.

I.   matáy raítem et mošé?   ט: מתי ראיתם את משׁה?

J.   raínu otó lifnéy yomáim.   י: ראינו אותו לפני יומים.

I.   eyfó hú gár?   ט: איפה הוא גר?

J.   aní ló yodéa. raínu otó bemisrád haxúc.   י: אני לא יודע. ראינו אותו במשׂרד הרוׁץ.

K. yaakóv. šamáta? hayoéc
    haamerikái medabér ivrít.

כ: יעקב! שמעת? היועץ
   האמריקאי מדבר עברית.

L. kén. šamáti. hú medabér yafé meód.

ל: כן, שמעתי. הוא מדבר יפה מאד.

K. kmó israelí?

כ: כמו ישראלי?

L. 16. 16 kmó israelí.
    áx hú medabér tóv.

ל: לא. לא כמו ישראלי.
   אך הוא מדבר טוב.

M. raínu et habáit šelxá.

מ: ראינו את הבית שלך.

N. éyx hitrašámtem.

נ: איך התרשמתם?

M. hitrašámnu meód. habáit šelxá
    xadíš meód.

מ: התרשמנו מאד. הבית שלך
   חדיש מאד.

N. aní mekavé šegám avurxém
    yesudár báit yafé.

נ: אני מקווה שגם עבורכם
   יסודר בית יפה.

M. gám aní mekavé.

מ: גם אני מקווה.

6.1 Asking Directions (A man asks a man)

MR. WILLIAMS

Tell me, please,	emór lí bevakašá.	אמור לי, בבקשה,
how can I	éx aní yaxól	איך אני יכול
get from here	lehagía mikán	להגיע מכאן
to the main post office?	ladóar hamerkazí.	לדואר המרכזי?
can	yaxól (m.s.) יכול	
to arrive	lehagía להגיע	
here	kán כאן	
mail, post office	dóar (m) דואר	
central	merkazí (m.s.) מרכזי	

PASSERBY

Turn here	pné kán	פנה כאן
at the first corner	bapiná harišoná	בפינה הראשונה
to the right.	yemína.	ימינה.
turn	pné (m.s.imv.) פנה	
corner	piná (f) פינה	
first	rišoná (f.s.) ראשונה	
to the right	yemína ימינה	

MR. WILLIAMS

Yes-	kén-	כן --

PASSERBY

Go	léx	לך
about four blocks,	kearbaá rexovót,	כארבעה רחובות,
and there	vešám	ושם
turn left.	tifné smóla.	תפנה שמאלה.
go	léx (m.s.imv.) לך	
four	arbaá (m) ארבעה	
street	rexóv (m) רחוב	
there	šám שם	
you will turn	tifné (m.s.) תפנה	
to the left	smóla שמאלה	

MR. WILLIAMS

Yes-	kén-	כן --

PASSERBY

Continue straight	tamšíx yašár	תמשיך ישר
to the intersection.	ád lahictalvút.	עד להצטלבות.
you will continue	tamšíx (m.s.) תמשיך	
straight	yašár (m.s.) ישר	
until, up to	ád עד	
intersection	hictalvút (f) הצטלבות	

MR. WILLIAMS

The first	hahictalvút	ההצטלבות
intersection?	harišoná?	הראשונה?

39

PASSERBY

Yes. Go past	kén. avór	כן . עבור
the lights,	et haramzorím,	את הרמזורים,
and continue straight	vehamšéx yašár	והמשך ישר
to the post office building.	ád lebinyán hadóar.	עד לבנין הדואר.
cross, pass	avór (m.s.imv.)	עבור
traffic light	ramzór (m)	רמזור
continue	hamšéx (m.s.imv.)	המשך
building	binyán (m)	בנין

MR. WILLIAMS

Is it	haím zé	האם זה
far from here?	raxók mikán?	רחוק מכאן?
far	raxók (m.s.)	רחוק

PASSERBY

No, it's	ló. zé	לא. זה
not far.	ló raxók.	לא רחוק.

MR. WILLIAMS

Thank you very much,	todá rabá lexá,	תודה רבה לך,
sir.	adoní.	אדוני.
sir	adoní	אדוני

PASSERBY

Don't mention it.	ál ló davár.	על לא דבר.
on	ál	על
thing	davár (m.)	דבר

6.2 <u>Asking Directions</u> (A woman asks a woman)

MRS. WILLIAMS

Tell me, please,	imrí lí bevakašá.	אמרי לי, בבקשה,
how can I	éx aní yexolá	איך אני יכולה
get from here	lehagía mikán	להגיע מכאן
to the main post office?	ladóar hamerkazí.	לדואר המרכזי?
can	yexolá (f.s.)	יכולה

PASSERBY

Turn here	pní kán	פני כאן
at the first corner	bapiná harišoná	בפינה הראשונה
to the right.	yemína.	ימינה.
turn	pní (f.s.imv.)	פני

MRS. WILLIAMS

Yes-	kén-	כן --

PASSERBY

Go	lexí	לכי
about four blocks,	kearbaá rexovót	כארבעה רחובות
and there	vešám	ושם
turn left.	tifní smóla.	תפני שמאלה.
go	lexí (f.s.imv.)	לכי
you will turn	tifní (f.s.)	תפני

MRS. WILLIAMS

Yes-	kén-	-- כן

PASSERBY

Continue straight	tamšíxi yašár	תמשיכי ישר
to the intersection.	ád lahictalvút.	עד להצטלבות.
you will continue	tamšíxi (f.s.)	תמשיכי

MRS. WILLIAMS

The first	hahictalvút	ההצטלבות
intersection?	harišoná?	הראשונה?

PASSERBY

Yes. Go past	kén. ivrí	כן. עברי
the lights	et haramzorím	את הרמזורים
and continue straight	vehamšíxi yašár	והמשיכי ישר
to the post office building.	ád lebinyán hadóar.	עד לבנין הדואר.
cross, pass	ivrí (f.s.imv.)	עברי
continue	hamšíxi (f.s.imv.)	המשיכי

MRS. WILLIAMS

Is it	haím zé	האם זה
far from here?	raxók mikán?	רחוק מכאן?

PASSERBY

No, it's	ló. zé	לא. זה
not far.	ló raxók.	לא רחוק.

MRS. WILLIAMS

Thank you very much,	todá rabí láx,	תודה רבה לך,
ma'am.	gvirtí.	גבירתי.
ma'am	gvirtí	גבירתי

PASSERBY

Don't mention it.	ál ló davár.	על לא דבר.

6.3 ADDITIONAL VOCABULARY

Continue straight.		
(said to men or both)	hamšíxu yašár.	המשיכו ישר.
(said to women)	hamšéxna yašár.	המשכנה ישר.

GRAMMAR NOTES

6.4 Stark Imperatives

Compare the underlined forms in the following sentences:

a. sgór et hadélet.
   sigrí et hadélet.

b. šév, bevakašá.
   šví, bevakašá.

c. dabér, yotér bekól.
   dabrí, yotér bekól.

d. targém, bevakašá.
   targemí, bevakašá.

e. emór lí bevakašá. heyxán lamádeta ledabér ivrít.
   imrí lí bevakašá. heyxán lamádet ledabér ivrít.

f. pné kán bapiná harišoná yemína.
   pní kán bapiná harišoná yeminá.

g. léx kearbá rexovót.
   lexí kearbá rexovót.

h. avór et haramzorím vehamšéx yašár.
   ivrí et haramzorím vehamšíxi yašár.

The underlined words are imperative forms of verbs. They are termed 'stark imperatives' since their only function is as imperatives and to differentiate them from the 'gentle imperative' forms which function also as future tense forms.

There are a number of form classes of verbs in Hebrew, but the imperatives of all of them have certain similar characteristics. The masculine singular does not end in /-i/ and the feminine singular does. In some the /-i/ does not bear the stress /hamšíxi/, and in some it does /imrí, sigrí, pní/.
Examine now the plural forms which have occurred in the text.

i. hamšíxu yašár.
   hamšéxna yašár.

Note that the masculine plural is identical to the feminine singular except for the final vowel, /-u/ instead of /-i/; and that the feminine plural is identical to the masculine singular except for the additional syllable /-na/. This criss-cross patterning occurs with all verbs in the stark imperative. Thus, given both singular forms, both plurals, both masculine forms, or both feminine forms, the other two may be easily derived.
The stress will always be on the corresponding syllable in the feminine singular and masculine plural: /hamšíxi - hamšíxu/ and /sigrí - sigrú/. The feminine plural suffix /-na/ is never stressed.
At this point the student will have to memorize the corresponding pairs. It will be a while before the patterns become sorted out. However, since the pattern of the stark imperative is one of the keys to the identification of a particular verb pattern the student will have lost nothing by memorizing and drilling them thoroughly now.

A. Substitution Drill

    Tell me, please, where is the post office?

emór lí bevakašá. éyfo hadóar.	?אמור לי, בבקשה, איפה הדואר
emórna	אמורנה
imrí	אמרי
imrú	אמרו
emór	אמור

B. Substitution - Agreement Drill

    In the following drill the instructor may vary the substitutions supplied
as cues, alternating between the imperatives and the pronouns.

    Tell me, please, where do you live?

emór lí bevakašá	eyfó atá gár.	?איפה אתה גר, אמור לי, בבקשה
emórna lí bevakašá.	eyfó atén garót.	?איפה אתן גרות, אמורנה לי, בבקשה
imrí lí bevakaší.	eyfó át gára.	?איפה את גרה, אמרי לי, בבקשה
imrú lí bevakašá.	eyfó atém garím.	?איפה אתם גרים, אמרו לי, בבקשה
imrí lí bevakašá.	eyfó át gára.	?איפה את גרה, אמרי לי, בבקשה
emór lí bevakašá.	eyfó atá gár.	?איפה אתה גר, אמור לי, בבקשה
imrú lí bevakašá.	eyfó atém garím.	?איפה אתם גרים, אמרו לי, בבקשה
emórna lí bevakašá.	eyfó atén garót.	?איפה אתן גרות, אמורנה לי, בבקשה
imrí lí bevakašá.	eyfó át gára.	?איפה את גרה, אמרי לי, בבקשה

C. Substitution Drill

    Go past the first intersection.

avór et hahictalvút harišoná.	.עבור את ההצטלבות הראשונה
avórna	עבורנה
ivrí	עברי
ivrú	עברו
avór	עבור
ivrí	עברי
ivrú	עברו

D. Substitution Drill

    Close the door, please.

sigrí et hadélet, bevakašá.	.סגרי את הדלת, בבקשה
sigrú	סגרו
sgór	סגור
sgórna	סגורנה
sigrú	סגרו
sigrí	סגרי
sgór	סגור

E. Substitution Drill

Open the door, please.

pitxú et hadélet bevakašá.	פתחו את הדלת, בבקשה.
pitxí	פתחי
ptáxna	פתחנה
ptáx	פתח
pitxí	פתחי
pitxú	פתחו
ptáx	פתח

F. Substitution Drill

The following drill may be varied by first going through the drill a few times using one verb as substitution cues and then a few times using the other verb as cues. When the forms are mastered the drill may be done by alternating the cues.

Turn left here and go straight.

pné kán yemína	veléx yašár.	ולך ישר.	פנה כאן ימינה
pní kán yemína	velexí yašár.	ולכי ישר.	פני כאן ימינה
pnú kán yemína	velexú yašár.	ולכו ישר.	פנו כאן ימינה
pnéna kán yemína	veléxna yašár.	ולכנה ישר.	פנינה כאן ימינה
pné kán yemína	veléx yašár.	ולך ישר.	פנה כאן ימינה
pnú kán yemína	velexú yašár.	ולכו ישר.	פנו כאן ימינה
pní kán yemína	velexí yašár.	ולכי ישר.	פני כאן ימינה

G. Substitution Drill

Continue straight to the school.

hamšéx yašár ád lebét haséfer.	המשך ישר עד לבית הספר.
hamšíxu	המשיכו
hamšíxi	המשיכי
hamšéxna	המשכנה
hamšéx	המשך
hamšíxi	המשיכי

H. Substitution - Agreement Drill

This drill may be varied by alternating the substitution cues as in Drill F.

Close the door and sit down, please.

sgór et hadélet	vešév bevakašá.	ושב, בבקשה.	סגור את הדלת
sigrú et hadélet	vešvú bevakašá.	ושבו, בבקשה.	סגרו את הדלת
sigrí et hadélet	vešví bevakašá.	ושבי, בבקשה.	סגרי את הדלת
sgórna et hadélet	vešévna bevakašá.	ושבנה, בבקשה.	סגרנה את הדלת
sgór et hadélet	vešév bevakašá.	ושב, בבקשה.	סגור את הדלת
sigrí et hadélet	vešví bevakašá.	ושבי, בבקשה.	סגרי את הדלת
sigrú et hadélet	vešvú bevakašá.	ושבו, בבקשה.	סגרו את הדלת

I. Substitution Drill

Please speak Hebrew.

dabér ivrít, bevakašá.	.דבר עברית, בבקשה
dabrí	דברי
dabrú	דברו
dabérna	דברנה
dabér	דבר

6.5 Gentle Imperatives

Compare the underlined forms in the following sentences:

a. <u>takír</u> bevakašá et már Williams.
    <u>takíri</u> bevakašá et gvéret Williams.

b. šám <u>tifné</u> smóla.
    šám <u>tifní</u> smóla.

c. <u>tamšíx</u> yašár ád lahictalvút.
    <u>tamšíxi</u> yašár ád lahictalvút.

Note that the masculine-feminine alternation is very much the same as in
the stark imperatives. In addition the forms have a prefix beginning with
/t-/. These are identical with the second person future tense forms but are
used as imperatives. They are termed 'gentle imperatives' since they are not
ordinarily used for direct positive commands, and have a gentler connotation.
The stark imperative is used for the whole range of simple request to direct
command.

As with the stark imperatives, the corresponding pairs should be drilled
and memorized. With the exception noted below the same criss-cross derivations
may be made to get the remaining forms.

tifné (m.s.)	tifní (f.s.)
tifnéna (f.pl.)	tifnú (m.pl.)

The exception is with verbs in which the final vowel of the masculine
singular is /-í-/. In most of these verbs the feminine plural has /-é-/, in
the others /-á-/.

tamšíx	—	tamšéxna
takír	—	takérna

(When the feminine plural has /-á-/, this will be especially noted.)

[In the vocabulary breakdown of the basic sentences the gentle
imperatives are translated as future forms. This is a convention adopted for
this text.]

The vowel of the prefix depends on the form class to which the verb
belongs. It may be /i, e, a, o/, but it is the same in all four forms. At
this point the substitution drills should be repeated until the vowel of the
prefix is memorized.

A. Substitution Drill

Turn left at the first corner.

tifné smóla bapiná harišoná.　　　　תפנה שמאלה בפינה הראשונה.
tifní　　　　　　　　　　　　　תפני
tifnú　　　　　　　　　　　　　תפנו
tifnéna　　　　　　　　　　　　תפנינה
tifní　　　　　　　　　　　　　תפני
tifnú　　　　　　　　　　　　　תפנו
tifné　　　　　　　　　　　　　תפנה

B. Substitution Drill

Cross the intersection.

taavór et hahictalvút.　　　　　תעבור את ההצטלבות.
taavrí　　　　　　　　　　　　תעברי
taavrú　　　　　　　　　　　　תעברו
taavórna　　　　　　　　　　　תעבורנה
taavrí　　　　　　　　　　　　תעברי
taavór　　　　　　　　　　　　תעבור
taavrú　　　　　　　　　　　　תעברו

C. Substitution Drill

Keep on speaking.　　　　　I understand.

tamšíx ledabér.　　　aní mevín.　　　תמשיך לדבר. אני מבין.
tamšíxi　　　　　　　　　　　　תמשיכי
tamšíxu　　　　　　　　　　　　תמשיכו
tamšéxna　　　　　　　　　　　תמשכנה
tamšíx　　　　　　　　　　　　תמשיך
tamšíxi　　　　　　　　　　　　תמשיכי

Women students should respond with /aní meviná/.

D. Substitution Drill

Please meet my wife (husband).

takír bevakašá et iští (baalí).　　תכיר בבקשה את אשתי (בעלי).
takíri　　　　　　　　　　　　תכירי
takíru　　　　　　　　　　　　תכירו
takérna　　　　　　　　　　　תכרנה

E. Substitution - Agreement Drill

Moshe, please meet Mr. Oren.

mošé. takír bevakašá et már óren.   משה, תכיר בבקשה את מר אורן.

<u>miryám</u>	miryám. takíri bevakašá et már óren.	מרים
<u>már káspi</u>	már káspi. takír bevakašá et már óren.	מר כספי
<u>már Williams</u>	már Williams. takír bevakaá et már óren.	מר וויל`יאמס
<u>gvéret kóhen</u>	gvéret kóhen. takíri bevakašá et már óren.	גברת כהן
<u>xána</u>	xána. takíri bevakašá et már óren.	חנה
<u>avígdor</u>	avígdor. takír bevakašá et már óren.	אב`יגדור

F. Substitution - Agreement Drill

This drill may be done first as two separate substitution drills, and then
varied by alternating the substitution cues as in Drill F, Section 6.4 above.

Drill 1. <u>tisgór</u> et hadélet.
Drill 2. <u>tešév</u> bešéket.
Drill 3. <u>tisgór</u> et hadélet vetešév bešéket.

Close the door and sit quietly.

<u>tisgór</u> et hadélet	vetešév bešéket.	תסגור את הדלת ותשב בשקט.
<u>tisgerú</u> et hadélet	vetešvú bešéket.	תסגרו את הדלת ותשבו בשקט.
<u>tisgerí</u> et hadélet	vetešví bešéket.	תסגרי את הדלת ותשבי בשקט.
<u>tisgórna</u> et hadélet	vetešévna bešéket.	תסגורנה את הדלת ותשבנה בשקט.
<u>tisgór</u> et hadélet	vetešév bešéket.	תסגור את הדלת ותשב בשקט.
<u>tisgerí</u> et hadélet	vetešví bešéket.	תסגרי את הדלת ותשבי בשקט.
<u>tisgerú</u> et hadélet	vetešvú bešéket.	תסגרו את הדלת ותשבו בשקט.

G. Substitution Drill

Open the office for me.

tiftáx et hamisrád avurí.	תפתח את המשרד עבורי.
tiftexí	תפתחי
tiftexú	תפתחו
tiftáxna	תפתחנה
tiftexí	תפתחי
tiftexú	תפתחו
tiftáx	תפתח

6.6 Negative Imperatives

The negative of both imperatives consists of the construction /ál/ +
gentle imperative.

ál tagzím.   'Don't exaggerate.'

47

A. Substitution Drill

   Don't exaggerate. The house isn't that big.

   ál tagzím. habáit ló kol káx gadól.   .אל תגזים; הבית לא כל כך גדול
       tagzími   תגזימי
       tagzímu   תגזימו
       tagzím   תגזים
       tagzémna   תגזמנה
       tagzími   תגזימי

B. Transformation Drill - Affirmative to Negative

   Instructor: Turn left here.
   Student: Don't turn left here.
                                              :תלמיד   :מורה

   pné smóla.   ál tifné smóla.   .אל תפנה שמאלה   .פנה שמאלה
   pní smóla.   ál tifní smóla.   .אל תפני שמאלה   .פני שמאלה
   pnú smóla.   ál tifnú smóla.   .אל תפנו שמאלה   .פנו שמאלה
   pnéna smóla.   ál tifnéna smóla.   .אל תפנינה שמאלה   .פנינה שמאלה
   pné smóla.   ál tifné smóla.   .אל תפנה שמאלה   .פנה שמאלה

C. Transformation - Expansion Drill

   Repeat Drill B with student adding /pné yemína./ 'Turn right'.

   Instructor: pné smóla.
   Student: ál tifné smóla. pné yemína.

D. Transformation Drill - Affirmative to Negative.

   Instructor: Go to the main post office.
   Student: Don't go to the main post office.

   léx ladóar hamerkazí.   ál teléx ladóar hamerkazí.   .לך לדואר המרכזי
   lexí ladóar hamerkazí.   ál telxí ladóar hamerkazí.   .לכי לדואר המרכזי
   léxna ladóar hamerkazí. ál teléxna ladóar hamerkazí.   .לכנה לדואר המרכזי
   lexú ladóar hamerkazí.   ál telxú ladóar hamerkazí.   .לכו לדואר המרכזי
   lexí ladóar hamerkazí.   ál telxí ladóar hamerkazí.   .לכי לדואר המרכזי
   léx ladóar hamerkazí.   ál teléx ladóar hamerkazí.   .לך לדואר המרכזי

E. Transformation - Expansion Drill

   Repeat Drill D with student adding /léx lašagrirút./ 'Go to the embassy.'

   Instructor: léx ladóar hamerkazí.
   Student: ál teléx ladóar hamerkazí. léx lašagrirút.

F. Transformation Drill - Affirmative to Negative

Instructor: Continue straight to the intersection.
Student: Don't continue straight.

hamšéx yašár ád lahictalvút.	ál tamšíx yašár.	המשך ישר עד להצטלבות.
hamšíxu yašár ád lahictalvút.	ál tamšíxu yašár.	המשיכו ישר עד להצטלבות.
hamšíxi yašár ád lahictalvút.	ál tamšíxi yašár.	המשיכי ישר עד להצטלבות.
hamšéxna yašár ád lahictalvút.	ál tamšéxna yašár.	המשכנה ישר עד להצטלבות.
hamšéx yašár ád lahictalvút.	ál tamšíx yašár.	המשך ישר עד להצטלבות.
hamšíxi yašár ád lahictalvút.	ál tamšíxi yašár.	המשיכי ישר עד להצטלבות.

G. Transformation - Expansion Drill

Repeat Drill F with student adding /pné smóla./ 'Turn left.'

Instructor: hamšéx yašár ád lahictalvút.
Student: ál tamšíx yašár. pné smóla.

H. Transformation Drill - Affirmative to Negative.

Instructor: Cross the lights.
Student: Don't cross the lights.

avór et haramzorím.	ál taavór et haramzorím.	עבור את הרמזורים.
ivrí et haramzorím.	ál taavrí et haramzorím.	עברי את הרמזורים.
avórna et haramzorím.	ál taavórna et haramzorím.	עבורנה את הרמזורים.
avór et haramzorím.	ál taavór et haramzorím.	עבור את הרמזורים.
ivrú et haramzorím.	ál taavrú et haramzorím.	עברו את הרמזורים.
ivrí et haramzorím.	ál taavrí et haramzorím.	עברי את הרמזורים.

I. Transformation Drill - Negative to Affirmative

Instructor: Don't speak loudly.
Student: Speak loudly.

		תלמיד:	מורה:
ál tedabér bekól.	dabér bekól.	דבר בקול.	אל תדבר בקול.
ál tedabrú bekól.	dabrú bekól.	דברו בקול.	אל תדברו בקול.
ál tedabrí bekól.	dabrí bekól.	דברי בקול.	אל תדברי בקול.
ál tedabérna bekól.	dabérna bekól.	דברנה בקול	אל תדברנה בקול.
ál tedaber bekól.	dabér bekól.	דבר בקול.	אל תדבר בקול.
ál tedabrí bekól.	dabrí bekól.	דברי בקול.	אל תדברי בקול.

J. Transformation Drill - Affirmative to Negative

Repeat Drill I in reverse.

K. Transformation - Expansion Drill

Drill I is repeated as follows.

Instructor: dabér bekól.
Student: ál tedabér bekól. dabér bešéket.

L. Substitution Drill

Don't say goodbye.

ál tomár šalóm.	‏אל תאמר שלום.‏
tomrí	‏תאמרי‏
tomárna	‏תאמרנה‏
tomrú	‏תאמרו‏
tomár	‏תאמר‏
tomrí	‏תאמרי‏

M. Expansion Drill

Instructor: <u>Don't say goodbye to me.</u>
Student: Don't say goodbye to me; say 'Be seeing you'.

<u>ál tomár lí šalóm.</u>	emór lí lehitraót.	‏אמור לי להתראות.‏	‏אל תאמר לי שלום.‏
<u>ál tomrí lí šalóm.</u>	imrí lí lehitraót.	‏אמרי לי להתראות.‏	‏אל תאמרי לי שלום.‏
<u>ál tomárna lí šalóm.</u>	emórna lí lehitraót.	‏אמורנה לי להתראות.‏	‏אל תאמרנה לי שלום.‏
<u>ál tomrú lí šalóm.</u>	imrú lí lehitraót.	‏אמרו לי להתראות.‏	‏אל תאמרו לי שלום.‏
<u>ál tomrí lí šalóm.</u>	imrí lí lehitraót.	‏אמרי לי להתראות.‏	‏אל תאמרי לי שלום.‏
<u>ál tomár lí šalóm.</u>	emór lí lehitraót.	‏אמור לי להתראות.‏	‏אל תאמר לי שלום.‏

End of Tape 2A

N. Individual Transformation – Expansion Drill

In this drill the student contradicts the instructor and adds a further instruction.

Instructor: Turn left here.
Student: Don't turn here. Continue straight.

Instructor: pné kán smóla.   ‏מורה: פנה כאן שמאלה.‏
Student: ál tifné kán. hamšéx yašár.   ‏תלמיד: אל תפנה כאן. המשך ישר.‏

léx ladóar hamerkazí.	‏לך לדואר המרכזי.‏
pní bapiná harišoná yemína.	‏פני כפינה הראשונה ימינה.‏
dabér anglít, bevakašá.	‏דבר אנגלית, בבקשה.‏
lexú lemalón dán.	‏לכו למלון דן.‏
avór et hahictalvút.	‏עבור את ההצטלבות.‏
ivrí et haramzorím.	‏עברי את הרמזורים.‏
hamšíxu yašár ád lašagrirút.	‏המשיכו ישר עד לשגרירות.‏
hamšíxi ledabér.	‏המשיכי לדבר.‏
pnú bahictalvút harišoná yemína.	‏פנו כהצטלבות הראשונה ימינה.‏

6.7 <u>Contraction of /be- + ha-/ 'at the, in the'</u>

When the preposition /be-/ is prefixed to a form with the definite article prefix /ha-/, the two syllables are contracted to /ba-/.

hapiná harišoná	'the first corner'
bapiná harišoná	'at the first corner'

This contraction is similar to that of /le- + ha-/ to /la-/, described in Section 4.6, and it is equally obligatory.

6.8   Alternate forms /ve- ~ u-/ 'and'

In formal speech the conjunction /ve-/ has the alternate form /u-/ before the consonants /m, v, f/ and before consonant clusters.

> mošé umiryám.
> léx usqór et hadélet.

In informal speech the form /u-/ is heard occasionally in these cases and in stereotyped expressions, such as /umá šlomxá/ but the form /ve-/ is far more frequently used. With some speakers there is free alternation of these forms, and the student should be prepared for both.

> sigrú et hadélet vešvú bešéket.
> sigrú et hadélet ušvú bešeket.

Since the use of /u-/ in these cases is more formal, 'correct', classical, or what have you, the instructor may insist on the student using it, but the student may safely ignore these strictures in informal conversation.

6.9   Loss of Final Stem Vowel in Verbs

Compare the following pairs of forms:

> dabér   dabrí
> dabérna   dabrú
>
> šév   šví
> šévna   švú
>
> taavór   taavrí
> taavórna   taavrú

Note that the forms in the right-hand column have a suffix beginning with a stressed vowel /-í, -ú/ and that the final vowel of the verb stem is dropped. Now compare the following pairs:

> hamšéx   hamšíxi
> hamšéxna   hamšíxu
>
> takír   takíri
> takérna   takíru

In the forms of the right-hand column the suffix is not stressed, and the final vowel of the stem remains.

When a suffix beginning with a stressed vowel is affixed to a verb, the final vowel of the verb stem is dropped.

This is a general rule in verbs and allows but a few exceptions, which will be stated when they occur.

When the dropping of this stem vowel results in a medial three-consonant cluster, or in a non-permissible initial two-consonant cluster, then /-e-/ is inserted for phonological reasons.

> tiftáx   tiftexí   [for * /tiftxí/]
> targém   targemí   [for * /targmí/]
> léx   lexí   [for * /lxí/]

The latter pair is comparable to /šév~ šví/ except that /šv-/ is a permissible initial cluster and /lx-/ is not. However, in the gentle imperative both verbs are more similar since there are no initial clusters.

tešév	tešví
teléx	telxí

When an initial three-consonant cluster results /-i-/ is usually inserted between the first two.

sgór	sigrí [for * /sgrí/]
ptáx	pitxí [for * /ptxí/]

6.10 <u>Consonant Alternation /p ~ f/ in Related Forms</u>

Examine the following pairs of forms:

ptáx	pné
tiftáx	tifné

In these pairs there is an alternation of the consonants /p/ and /f/. These two consonants often alternate in related forms (such as stark and gentle imperatives.) The patterns of the alternation are regular but somewhat complicated, and at this point the student should simply memorize them by drilling the forms.

REVIEW CONVERSATIONS

A. imrí lí bevakašá. éyx aní yaxól   א: אמרי לי בבקשה, איך אני יכול
     lehagía lemalón dán.   להגיע למלון דן?

B. léx kearbá rexovót, pné smóla,   ב: לך כארבעה רחובות, פנה שמאלה,
     vetamšíx yašár ád lamalón.   ותמשיך ישר עד למלון.

A. haím zé raxók?   א: האם זה רחוק?

B. ló, zé karóv.   ב: לא. זה קרוב.

C. dabér ivrít, bevakašá.   ג: דבר עברית, בבקשה.

D. atá medabér ivrít?   ד: אתה מדבר עברית?

C. kén. lamádeti bevét haséfer.   ג: כן. למדתי בבית הספר.

D. aní eynéni medabér kol káx tóv.   ד: אני אינני מדבר כל כך טוב.

C. léx lebét haséfer.   ג: לך לבית הספר.

D. leéyze bet séfer?   ד: לאיזה בית ספר?

C. lebét haséfer lesafót. kán bapiná.   ג: לבית הספר לשפות. כאן בפינה.

Tape 2B

7.1 Wandering Through Tel Aviv (speaking to man passerby)

MR. WILLIAMS

Pardon me, sir.	tisláx li, adoní.	תסלח לי, אדוני,
I want	aní rocé	אני רוצה
to get	lehagía	להגיע
to the tourist office.	lemisrád hatayarút.	למשרד התיירות.
you will pardon	tisláx (m.s.)	תסלח
want	rocé (m.s.pres.)	רוצה
tourism	tayarút (f)	תיירות

PASSERBY

To the Government	lemisrád hatayarút	למשרד התיירות
tourist office?	hamemšaltí?	הממשלתי?
governmental	memšaltí (m.s.)	ממשלתי

MR. WILLIAMS

Yes. Is it	kén. haím zé	כן. האם זה
far from here?	raxók mikán?	רחוק מכאן?

PASSERBY

No, it's not far.	ló. zé ló raxók.	לא, זה לא רחוק.
you are	atá nimcá	אתה נמצא
now next to	axšáv al yád	עכשיו על יד
the Mugrabi Theater,	kolnóa múgrabi.	קולנוע מוגרבי.
right?	naxón?	נכון?
situated, found	nimcá (m.s.)	נמצא
now	axšáv	עכשיו
next to, alongside	al yád	על יד
movie theater	kolnóa (m)	קולנוע

MR. WILLIAMS

Yes,	kén,	כן,
I think	aní xošév	אני חושב
so.	káx.	כך.
think	xošév (m.s.pres.)	חושב

PASSERBY

What do you mean,	má zot oméret,	מה זאת אומרת,
you think so?	atá xošév káx.	אתה חושב כך?
You don't see	atá ló roé	אתה לא רואה
that this is	šezé	שזה
the Mugrabi Theater?	kolnóa múgrabi?	קולנוע מוגרבי?
it, this	zót (f)	זאת
say	oméret (f.s.pres.)	אומרת
see	roé (m.s.pres.)	רואה

MR. WILLIAMS

Sir,	adoní.	אדוני.
speak a little	dabér kcát	דבר קצת
slower.	yotér leát.	יותר לאט.
a little, some	kcát	קצת

I'm new	aní xadáš		אני חדש
in the country.	baárec.		באָרץ.
new	xadáš (m.s.)	חדש	
I come	aní bá		אני בא
from America.	meamérika.		מאמריקה.
come	bá (m.s.pres.)	בא	

PASSERBY

Oh, you're new in the country.	á- atá xadáš baárec?		אה, אתה חדש בארץ?
That's something else.	zé davár axér.		זה דבר אחר.
other	axér (m.s.)	אחר	
So why didn't	áz láma ló		אז למה לא
you tell me	amárta lí		אמרת לי
before?	kódem?		קודם?
then, so	áz	אז	
why	láma	למה	
you said	amárta (2 m.s.)	אמרת	
before, earlier	kódem	קודם	

MR. WILLIAMS

When before?	matáy kódem.		מתי קודם?
You didn't give me	ló natáta lí		לא נתת לי
a chance to speak.	hizdamnút ledaber.		הזדמנות לדבר.
you gave	natáta (2 m.s.)	נתת	
chance, opportunity	hizdamnút (f)	הזדמנות	

7.2 <u>Wandering through Tel Aviv</u> (speaking to woman passerby)

MRS. WILLIAMS

Excuse me, ma'am.	tislexí li, gvirtí.		תסלחי לי, גברתי,
I want	aní rocá		אני רוצה
to get	lehagía		להגיע
to the tourist office.	lemisrád hatayarút.		למשרד התיירות.
want	rocá (f.s. pres.)	רוצה	

PASSERBY

| To the Government | lemisrád hatayarút | | למשרד התיירות |
| tourist office? | hamemšaltí? | | הממשלתי? |

MRS. WILLIAMS

| Yes. Is it | ken. haím zé | | כן. האם זה |
| far from here? | raxók mikán? | | רחוק מכאן? |

PASSERBY

No, it's not far.	ló. zé ló raxók.		לא. זה לא רחוק.
You are	át nimcét		את נמצאת
now next to	axšáv al yád		עכשיו על יד
the Mugrabi Theater,	kolnóa múgrabi.		קולנוע מוגרבי,
right?	naxón?		נכון?
situated, found	nimcét (f.s.)	נמצאת	

MRS. WILLIAMS

Yes.	kén.	.כן
I think	aní xošévet	אני חושבת
so,	káx.	.כך
think	xošévet (f.s.pres.)	חושבת

PASSERBY

What do you mean,	má zot oméret,	מה זאת אומרת,
you think so?	át xošévet káx.	את חושבת כך?
You don't see	át ló roá	את לא רואה
that this is	šezé	שזה
the Mugrabi Theater?	kolnóa múgrabi?	קולנוע מוגרבי?
see	roá (f.s.pres.)	רואה

MRS. WILLIAMS

Ma'am,	gvirtí.	גברתי,
speak a little	dabrí kcát	דברי קצת
slower.	yotér leát.	יותר לאט.
I'm new	aní xadašá	אני חדשה
in the country	baárec.	בארץ.
new	xadašá (f.s.)	חדשה
I come	aní báa	אני באה
from America.	meamérika.	מאמריקה.
come	báa (f.s.pres.)	באה

PASSERBY

Oh, you're new in the country.	á- át xadašá baárec?	אה, את חדשה בארץ?
That's something else.	zé davár axér.	זה דבר אחר.
So why didn't	áz láma ló	אז למה לא
you tell me	amárt lí	אמרת לי
before?	kódem.	קודם?

MRS. WILLIAMS

When before?	matáy kódem?	מתי קודם?
You didn't give me	ló natát lí	לא נתת לי
a chance to speak.	hizdamnút ledabér.	הזדמנות לדבר.

7.3 Vocabulary Drills

A. Substitution Drill

Excuse me, I don't understand.

tisláx lí. aní ló mevín.	תסלח לי, אני לא מבין.
tislexí	תסלחי
tislexú	תסלחו
tisláxna	תסלחנה

(Women students should substitute /aní ló meviná/.)

B. Substitution - Agreement Drill /tisláx ~tislexí/

Excuse me, Moshe, I have to run.

<u>tisláx li, mošé. aní muxráx larúc.</u>   .תסלח לי משה, אני מוכרח לרוץ

xána - gvirtí - már káspi - miryám   חנה – גברתי – מר כספי – מרים
avígdor - adoní - gvéret kóhen - davíd   אביגדור – אדוני – גברת כהן – דוד

(Women students should substitute /aní muxraxá/.)

C. Substitution - Agreement Drill /amárti/ "I said" אמרתי

The instructor gives the underlined portion of the following sentences, and the student responds with the entire sentence. The instructor may vary the first person sentences, depending on the composition of the class, /aní gára, ánu garót/.

I told Moshe that <u>I live in Tel Aviv.</u>

amárti lemošé <u>šeaní qár</u> betél aviv.   אמרתי למשה שאני גר בתל אביב
amárnu lemošé <u>šeánu qarím</u> betél avív.   אמרנו למשה שאנו גרים בתל אביב
amárt lemošé <u>šeát gára</u> betél avív.   אמרת למשה שאנו גרים בתל אביב
amártem lemošé <u>šeatém qarím</u> betél avív. אמרתם למשה שאנו גרים בתל אביב
    amárta lemošé <u>šeatá qár</u> betél avív.   אמרת למשה שאנו גרים בתל אביב
amárten lemošé <u>šeatén qarót</u> betél avív. אמרתן למשה שאנו גרים בתל אביב

D. Substitution- Agreement Drill

I didn't give David the books.

<u>16 natáti ledavíd et hasfarím.</u>   .לא נתתי לדוד את הספרים

atá - ánu - át - aní   אתה – אנו – את – אני
atém - atén - atá - át   אתם – אתן – אתה – את

GRAMMAR NOTES

7.4 Gender and Number - Present Tense Verbs and Adjectives

Examine the underlined forms in the following sentences:

1. atá <u>medabér</u> ivrít mamáš kmó israelí.   אתה מדבר עברית ממש כמו ישראלי.
   át <u>medabéret</u> ivrít mamáš kmó israelít.   את מדברת עברית ממש כמו ישראלית.

2. aní ló <u>yodéa</u>.   אני לא יודע.
   aní ló <u>yodáat</u>.   אני לא יודעת.

3. atá <u>nimcá</u> axšáv al yád kolnóa múgrabi.   אתה נמצא עכשיו על יד קולנוע מוגרבי.
   át <u>nimcét</u> axšáv al yád kolnóa múgrabi.   את נמצאת עכשיו על יד קולנוע מוגרבי.

4. aní <u>rocé</u> lehagía lemisrád hatayarút.   אני רוצה להגיע למשרד התיירות.
   ani <u>rocá</u> lehagía lemisrád hatayarút.   אני רוצה להגיע למשרד התיירות.

5. aní <u>muxráx</u> larúc.   אני מוכרח לרוץ.
   aní <u>muxraxá</u> larúc.   אני מוכרחה לרוץ.

6. aní <u>gár</u> beynatáim bemalón dán.   אני גר בינתיים במלון דן.
   aní <u>gára</u> beynatáim bemalón dan.   אני גרה בינתיים במלון דן.

7. éyx aní <u>yaxól</u> lehagía ladóar hamerkazí.   איך אני יכול להגיע לדואר המרכזי.
   éyx aní <u>yexolá</u> lehagía ladóar hamerkazí.   איך אני יכולה להגיע לדואר המרכזי.

You will note here that, in contrast to the past tense verb forms, there is
no pronoun suffix to the verb itself. Instead the independent form of the
pronoun is used. Further, the verb form indicates the gender of the subject
with the first person, also. The pattern is similar to the noun-adjective
sentence pattern:

       aní xadáš baárec.   אני חדש בארץ.
       aní xadašá baárec.   אני חדשה בארץ.

The similarity extends to the plurals.

       ánu garím bexáyfa.   אנו גרים בחיפה.
       ánu garót bexáyfa.   אנו גרות בחיפה.

The present tense of verbs has just·these four forms - masculine singular
and plural and feminine singular and plural - and person is indicated by an
independent subject.

Plurals of present tense verb forms and of adjectives are all alike in that
the masculine plural has the suffix /-ím/ and the feminine plural has the suffix
/-ót/.

[Note: Some masculine plural <u>nouns</u> end in /-ót/ and some feminine plural
<u>nouns</u> in /-ím/. The present tense verbs and adjectives for these plurals,
however, end in /-ím/ and /-ót/ respectively.]

The feminine singular forms are of two major types - those that have a
suffix ending in /-t/ and those that have the suffix /-a/. The forms which
have thus far occurred are:

/-t/ feminines	/-a/ feminines
medabéret	muxraxá
oméret	meviná
xošévet	yexolá
mitkonénet	gára
yodáat	rišoná
mocét	báa
nimcét	xadašá
amerikáit	smexá
	mekavá
	rocá
	roá
	yafá

The variations of these two major types will be described and drilled in turn.

7.5 /t/ - Suffix Feminine Forms

a) **Present Tense of Verbs with Stem Pattern /-éC/**

Examine the verb forms in the following sentences:
   atá medabér ivrít.
   át medabéret ivrít.
In this pattern the masculine singular ends in /-éC/. The feminine is the same as the masculine but with an added unstressed /-et/. In the plurals the final stem vowel /-e-/ is dropped, unless a three-consonant cluster would result or two similar consonants would be juxtaposed.
   atém medabrím ivrít.
   atén medabrót ivrít.

   atém mitkonením lagúr berámat gán.
   atén mitkonenót lagúr berámat gán.

The adjective /axér/ is also of this pattern. The forms are:
   m.s. /axér/   m.pl. /axerím/
   f.s. /axéret/   f.pl. /axerót/
There are some other minor variations of this pattern in the plurals, and these will be described as they occur in the text.
The following drills are substitution-agreement drills. The last substitution cue given in each drill will result in the model sentence. Each drill should be done a number of times in continuous succession until correct entire sentences are given without hesitation as responses.
Substitutions for the first person may be masculine or feminine, depending on the class situation.

A. You speak Hebrew very well.

   atá medabér tóv meód ivrít.   .אתה מדבר טוב מאד עברית

   át - hém - már Williams - xána   חנה – מר ווילאמס – הם – אם
   atén - hú - atém - ánu - atá   אתה – אנו – אתם – הוא – אתן

B. Moshe says that it's very late.

mošé omér šekvár meuxár meód.   .משה אומר שכבר מאוחר מאד

    aní - hú - ánu - miryám - hém   אני - הוא - אנו - מרים - הם
    gvéret káspi - hén - atén - mošé   גברת כספי - הן - אתן - משה

C. What do you think — is it far from here?

má atá xošév - zé raxók mikán?   ?מה אתה חושב - זה רחוק מכאן

    hí - atém - át - atén   היא - אתם - את - אתן
    hém - hú - hén - atá   הם - הוא - הן - אתה

D. I plan to live in Savyon.

aní mitkonén lagúr besavyón.   .אני מתכונן לגור בסביון

    hém - avígdor - iští veaní - hí   הם - אביגדור - אשתי ואני - היא
    ánu - hén - hú - atára - aní   אנו - הן - הוא - עטרה - אני

E. In this drill some noun plurals are introduced. The instructor should
   correct the student by giving the correct noun-adjective sequence rather
   than by discussing gender per se.

   He sees something else.

   hú roé davár axér.   .הוא רואה דבר אחר

    oniá - namál - sfarím - báit   אוניה - נמל - ספרים - בית
    melonót - oniót - binyán - délet   מלונות - אוניות - בנין - דלת
    šagrirút - misradím - mišpaxót - davár   שגרירות - משרדים - משפחות - דבר

b) Present Tense of Verbs with Stem Pattern /-éa(x)/

This is the pattern of /yodéa/ 'know'. The four forms are:
    m.s. yodéa   f.s. yodáat   יודעת   יודע
    m.pl. yod'ím   f.pl. yod'ót   יודעות   יודעים
Note that in the plurals an internal open juncture functions as a third
root consonant. Verbs in which the masculine singular ends in /-éax/ have a
similar pattern. The four forms have the following endings:
    m.s. -éax   f.s. -áxat
    m.pl. -xím   f.pl. -xót
[There is a close correspondence with written Hebrew in that all such words
are spelled with ע or ח and not with א or כ .]

F. He knows I'm new in the country.

   hú yodéa šeaní xadáš baárec.   .הוא יודע שאני חדש בארץ

    atá - ištó - hén - gvéret kóhen   אתה - אשתו - הן - גברת כהן
    atén - át - davíd - atém - hú   אתן - את - דוד - אתם - הוא

G. I think he knows how to speak Hebrew.

<u>aní xošév šehú yodéa ledabér ivrít.</u>   . אֲנִי חוֹשֵׁב שֶׁהוּא יוֹדֵעַ לְדַבֵּר עֲבְרִית

     šehí - šeatá - šehém - šeištexá   שהיא – שאתה – שהם – שאשתך
     šebaaléx - šehén - šedóv vemošé - šehú   שכעלך – שהן – שרב ומשה – שהוא

c) <u>Present Tense Pattern /mocé ~mocét/</u>

This pattern is characterized by the singular ending in /-é ~-ét/ and by
an internal open juncture functioning as a third root consonant in the plural
/-'ím ~ -'ót/. The full present of /mocé/ is:
     m.s. mocé   m.pl. moc'ím
     f.s. mocét   f.pl. moc'ót
In the plurals this pattern is similar to that of /yod'ím/ in Section <u>b</u>.
The student should be sure to practice the singulars of any such plural that he
may learn in order not to confuse the two types. There are pairs of verbs
whose only distinction is in this respect. The writing system reflects this
difference in that verbs of the /mocé ~ mocét/ pattern are spelled with א
and not with ע - the reverse of verbs like /yodéa/.

H. I like the country.

<u>haárec mócet xén beeynáy.</u>   . הָאָרֶץ מוּצֵאת חֵן בְּעֵינָי

     habáit - hašagrirút - hasfarím - haavirón   הבית–השגרירות–הספרים–האוירון
     haoniót - hém - atén - harexovót - haárec   האניות–הם–אתן–הרחובות–הארץ

I. He finds that the house is very nice.

<u>hú mocé šehabáit yafé meód.</u>   . הוּא מוֹצֵא שֶׁהַבַּיִת יָפֶה מְאֹד

     aní - már zahávi - ištexá - hém   אני – מר זהבי – אשתך – הם
     atén - ánu - ištó veiští - hú   אתן – אנו – אשתו ואשתי – הוא

d) <u>Present Tense Pattern /nimcá ~ nimcét/</u>

This pattern is a minor variation of a pattern which will be discussed later.
The plural suffixes are added to the masculine singular, and the feminine
singular has the suffix /-t/ with the vowel change. The student should simply
learn this particular verb at this time. The full present is:
     m.s. nimcá   f.s. nimcét
     m.pl. nimcaím
     f.pl. nimcaót
Some speakers use the pronunciation /nimceím, nimceót/ in the plural.
This particular pattern is similar to that of /mocé/ in that such verbs are
always spelled with א. In fact, /mocé/ and /nimcá/ are different conjugations
of the same verb root - /mocé/ 'finds', /nimcá/ 'is found' - but this point
will be discussed in detail further on.

J. The Embassy is located in Tel Aviv.

<u>hašagrirút nimcét betél avív.</u>   . הַשַּׁגְרִירוּת נִמְצֵאת בְּתֵל אֲבִיב

habáit šelí - már Williams - ištó vehú   הבית שלי – מר וויליאמס – אשתו והוא
hén - kulám - ištó - ištexá -xána veléa   הן – כולם – אשתו – אשתך – חנה ולאה
hašagrirút   השגרירות

e. Derived   Adjectives with /-i/

Adjectives are often derived from other parts of speech by the addition
of /-i/, in certain cases with other changes in the form. Examples from our
text so far are:

/memšaltí/ derived from /memšalá/ 'government'
/amerikái/ derived from /amérika/ 'America'
/merkazí/ derived from /merkáz/ 'center'

The endings for these adjectives are of the following pattern:
    m.s. /-í/   f.s. /-ít/
    m.pl. /-iím/   f.pl. /-iót/

In some adjectives the stress is on a non final syllable as in /amerikái,
amerikáit/.

The above pattern occurs in derived <u>adjectives</u>. There are also derived
<u>nouns</u>, which have similar patterns.

For example:
    m.s. yisraeli   f.s. yisraelít
    m.pl. yisraelím   f.pl. yisraeliót

Note that a distinction is made in the following case:

noun: /yisraelím/ 'Israelis'
adjective: /avironím yisraeliím/ 'Israeli airplanes'

K. Where is the Government office?

<u>heyxán hamisrád hamemšaltí.</u>

habinyán - hamisradím - hayoéc
habinyaním - hayoacím - hamísrád

היכן המשרד הממשלתי?
הבניין – המשרדים – היועץ
הבניינים – היועצים – המשרד

L. Where is the American Embassy?

<u>eyfó hašagrirút haamerikáit.</u>

hayoéc - haoniá - habinyaním
haoniót - hakolnóa - hašagrirút

איפה השגרירות האמריקאית?
היועץ – האונייה – הבניינים
האוניות – הקולנוע – השגרירות

REVIEW CONVERSATIONS

A: šalom mošé. láma atá rác.   ‏א. שלום משה. למה אתה רץ?‏

B: šalóm miryám. aní muxráx larúc lemisrád hatayarút.   ‏ב. שלום מרים. אני מוכרח לרוץ‏ ‏למשרד התיירות.‏

A: leéyze misrád tayarút.   ‏א. לאיזה משרד תיירות?‏

B: lemisrád ׳atayarút hamemšaltí.   ‏ב. למשרד התיירות הממשלתי.‏

C: aní nimcá axšáv al yád kolnóa múgrabi. naxón?   ‏ג. אני נמצא עכשיו על יד קולנוע‏ ‏מוגרבי. נכון?‏

D: kén. naxón. veatá rocé lehagía lisfát hayám?   ‏ד. כן. נכון. ואתה רוצה להגיע‏ ‏לשפת הים?‏

C: ken. haim ze raxók mikán?   ‏ג. כן. האם זה רחוק מכאן?‏

D: ló. zé ló raxók . léx yašár berexóv álenbi ád lesfát hayám.   ‏ד. לא.זה לא רחוק. לך ישר‏ ‏ברחוב אלנבי עד לשפת הים.‏

E: adoní. dabér kcat yotér leát.   ‏ה. אדוני, דבר קצת יותר לאט.‏

F: atá ló mevín ivrít?   ‏ו. אתה לא מבין עברית?‏

E: kcát. aní xadáš baárec.   ‏ה. קצת. אני חדש בארץ.‏

F: atá xadáš baárec? zé davár axér.   ‏ו. אתה חדש בארץ? זה דבר אחר.‏

E: aní bá meamérika.   ‏ה. אני בא מאמריקה.‏

8.1 <u>Wandering through Tel Aviv (cont'd.)</u>

PASSERBY

All right.	nú tóv.	נו טוב.
So you say	áz amárta	אז אמרת
you want to get	Seatá rocé lehagía	שאתה רוצה להגיע
to the tourist office,	lemisrád hatayarút.	למשרד התיירות,
right?	naxon?	נכון?

MR. WILLIAMS

Yes, that's right.	kén. naxón.	כן. נכון.

PASSERBY

Listen.	Smá.	שמע.
Are you in a hurry?	atá memahér?	אתה ממהר?
listen, hear	Smá (m.s.imv.)	שמע
hurry (verb)	memahér (m.s.pres.)	ממהר

MR. WILLIAMS

Not really.	ló kol káx.	לא כל כך.
I want to walk around	aní rocé letayél	אני רוצה לטייל
and see the city.	velir'ót et haír.	ולראות את העיר.
to stroll, hike	letayél	לטייל
to see	lir'ót	לראות
city	ír (f)	עיר
cities	arím (f.pl.)	ערים

PASSERBY

If so,	ím káx,	אם כך
go straight	léx yašár	לך ישר
on Allenby Road	berexóv álenbi	ברחוב אלנבי
towards the seashore.	lekivún sfát hayám.	לכיוון שפת הים.
if	ím	אם
direction	kivún (m)	כיוון
shore, language, lip	safá (f)	שפה
sea	yám (m)	ים
seashore	sfát yám	שפת ים

MR. WILLIAMS

In this direction?	bakivún hazé?	בכיוון הזה?

PASSERBY

Yes. You'll pass	kén. taavór et	כן. תעבור את
the Brooklyn Bar.	brúklin bár.	ברוקלין בר.

MR. WILLIAMS

The what?	et má?	את מה?

63

PASSERBY

The Brooklyn Bar.	et brúklin bar.	.אֶת ברוקלין בר
Do you know	atá yodéa	אתה יודע
where the Brooklyn Bar is?	éyfo šebrúklin bar?	?איפה שֶברוקלין בר

MR. WILLIAMS

No, I don't know.	ló.　aní ló yodéa.	.לא. אני לא יודע
Haven't I told you	haréy amárti lexá	הרי אמרתי לך
that I'm new in the country.	šeaní xadáš baárec.	.שאני חדש בארץ
(interjection)	haréy	הרי

End of Tape 2B

Tape 3A

8.2　Wandering through Tel Aviv (cont'd.)

PASSERBY

All right.	nú tóv.	.נו טוב
So you say	áz amárt	אז אמרת
you want to get	šeát rocá lehagía	שאת רוצה להגיע
to the tourist office,	lemisrád hatayarút.	,למשרד התיירות
right?	naxón?	?נכון

MRS. WILLIAMS

| Yes, that's right. | kén.　naxón. | .כן. נכון |

PASSERBY

| Listen. | šim'í. | .שמעי |
| Are you in a hurry? | át memahéret? | ?את ממהרת |

MRS. WILLIAMS

Not really.	ló kol káx.	.לא כל כך
I want to walk around	aní rocá letayél	אני רוצה לטייל
and see the city.	velir'ót et haír.	.ולראות את העיר

PASSERBY

If so,	ím káx,	,אם כך
go straight	lexí yašár	לכי ישר
on Allenby Road	berexóv álenbi	ברחוב אלנבי
towards the seashore.	lekivún sfát hayám.	.לכיוון שפת הים

MRS. WILLIAMS

| In this direction? | bakivún hazé? | ?בכיוון הזה |

PASSERBY

| Yes.　You'll pass | kén.　taavrí et | כן. תעברי את |
| the Brooklyn Bar. | brúklin bár. | .ברוקלין בר |

MRS. WILLIAMS

| The what? | et má? | ?אֶת מה |

PASSERBY

The Brooklyn Bar.	et brúklin bár.	.את ברוקלין בר
Do you know	át yodáat	את יודעת
where the Brooklyn Bar is?	éyfo šebrúklin bár?	?איפה שברוקלין בר

MRS. WILLIAMS

No, I don't know.	16. aní ló yodáat.	.לא. אני לא יודעת
Haven't I told you	haréy amárti láx	הרי אמרתי לך
that I'm new in the country?	šeaní xadašá baárec.	.שאני חרשה בארץ

8.3 Vocabulary Drill

Present tense plurals of verbs in which the middle root consonant is /h/ such as /memahér/ vary slightly from the pattern described in Section 7.5a. The vowel /e/ is replaced by /a/ instead of being dropped. The present tense forms of /memahér/ are:

| m.s. | memahér | m.pl. | memaharím |
| f.s. | memahéret | f.pl. | memaharót |

In normal speech intervocalic /-h-/ is often replaced by a smooth transition between the vowels when the stress does not immediately follow the /h/. Thus, one frequently hears /memaarím/ and /memaarót/.

A. Substitution - Agreement Drill

I'm hurrying to the movies.

<u>aní memahér lakolnóa.</u>   <u>.אני ממהר לקולנוע</u>

| hí - már kóhen - már kóhen veištó | היא – מר כהן – מר כהן ואשתו |
| hén - gvéret Williams - atém - aní | הן – גב' וויליאמס – אתם – אני |

GRAMMAR NOTES

8.4   <u>á-Suffix Feminine Forms</u>

    a.   <u>Present Tense of /lámed héy/ Verbs</u>

        A frequent pattern is illustrated by the following:

        aní <u>rocé</u> lehagía lemisrád hatayarút.
        aní <u>rocá</u> lehagía lemisrád hatayarút.

        In the plurals the suffixes /-ím/ and /-ót/ are substituted.

        hém <u>rocím</u> lehagía lemisrád hatayarút.
        hén <u>rocót</u> lehagía lemisrád hatayarút.

        This pattern occurs in a number of adjectives such as /yafé ~ yafá/.

    [In traditional Hebrew grammars, which deal mainly with the written
language, verbs are classified according to the letters which comprise the
"roots". Verbs of the pattern described in this section are called "/lámed
héy/" verbs since the third letter of the root in the writing system is ה
/héy/. This designation may remain abstruse for the time being until the
student learns to read, but there is little to be gained by coining a new
term for these verbs. All /lámed héy/ verbs exhibit certain similarities
regardless of the conjugation or consonants of the root. With the exception
of one conjugation, this is true of the present tense. The exception will be
described later on.]

    The following drills are substitution-agreement drills and should be done
as the drills in the previous unit.

    A.   He wants to get to the Eden Theater.

        <u>hú rocé lehagía lekolnóa éden.</u>   <u>הוא רוצה להגיע לקולנוע עדן.</u>

        hí - ánu - át - hén - dóv   היא – אנו – את – הן – דב
        atém - sára - aní - hú   אתם – שרה – אני – הוא

    B.   He hopes to speak Hebrew in Israel.

        <u>hú mekavé ledabér ivrít beisraél.</u>   <u>הוא מקווה לדבר עברית בישראל.</u>

        aní - már Williams - gvéret Williams   אני – מר ווילאמס – גב' ווילאמס
        iští veaní - hén - át - ánu - hú   אשתי ואני – הן – את – אנו – הוא

    C.   He sees the office.

        <u>hú roé et hamisrád,</u>   <u>הוא רואה את המשרד.</u>

        hém - atára - aní - xána veléa   הם – עטרה – אני – חנה ולאה
        ánu - hí - hayoéc veištó - hú   אנו – היא – היועץ ואשתו – הוא

D. I heard that the house is very nice.

Šamáti šehabáit yafé meód.   .שמעתי שהבית יפה מאד

Šehaárec - Šemiryám - Šehamisradím   שהארץ - שמרים - שהמשרדים
Šehaoniót - Šehanamál - Šehasfarím   שהאניות - שהנמל - שהספרים
Šesára veatára - Šezé - Šehabáit   שרה ועטרה - שזה - שהבית

b. Common Adjective Pattern

The pattern illustrated in the following pairs of sentences is very frequent in adjectives and occurs in certain conjugations of verbs.

        aní xadáš baárec. (man speaking)
        aní xadašá baárec. (woman speaking)

        aní muxráx larúc. (man speaking)
        aní muxraxá larúc. (woman speaking)

In the plurals the suffixes /-ím/ and /-ót/ are substituted where the feminine singular has /-á/.

        ánu muxraxím larúc.
        ánu muxraxót larúc.

When the masculine singular is a monosyllabic verb then the stress is on the first syllable in the feminine singular.

        aní qára bemalón dán.
        aní báa meamérika.

When the masculine singular form has the consonant-vowel pattern /CaCvC/ e.g. /xadíš, gadól, yašár/, then the pattern of the feminine and plurals is phonologically a bit more complicated.

The /-a-/ of the masculine singular is dropped when the suffixes for the feminine and plurals are added.

m.s.	gadól	karóv
f.s.	gdolá	krová
m.pl.	gdolím	krovím
f.pl.	gdolót	krovót

If a phonologically impossible cluster would result from dropping the /-a-/, then the vowel /e/ occurs between the first two consonants in the patterr /CeCvCá/. Bear in mind that there are many clusters which are quite possible in Hebrew, but which the student will be tempted to break up by inserting a vowel as in /gdolá/ above.

m.s.	raxók	yašár
f.s.	rexoká	yešará
m.pl.	rexokím	yešarím
f.pl.	rexokót	yešarót

If the first consonant is /x/, /'/, or /h/, then the vowel /a/ is inserted
to break up the resulting cluster. The net effect is that the feminine and
plural suffixes are added without change.

			f.s.	xadašá	xadišá
m.s.	xadáš	xadíš	m.pl.	xadaším	xadiším
			f.pl.	xadašót	xadišót

The consonants /h/ and /'/ are often dropped between vowels. Vowels which
break up clusters containing these consonants are retained even when the
consonants are dropped. In this text the transcription usually reflects the
informal spoken pronunciation, especially when /'/ is elided.

			f.s.	neimá	(for /ne'imá/)
m.s.	naím	(for /na'ím/)	m.pl.	neimím	(for /ne'imím/)
			f.pl.	neimót	(for /ne'imót/)

E.   He has to live near the office.

hú muxráx laqúr karóv lamisrád.   .הוא מוכרח לגור קרוב למשרד

át - ánu - hayoéc - hém   אח - אנו - היורע - הם
atén - gvéret kóhen - aní - hú   אתן - גב' כהן - אני - הוא

F.   Moshe lives on Allenby Road.

mošé gár berexóv álenbi.   .משה גר ברחוב אלנבי

hém - aní - atára - ánu   הם - אני - עטרה - אנו
davíd veištó - hén - mošé   דוד ואשתו - הן - משה

G.   I'm coming to see Mr. Zahavi.

aní bá lir'ót et már zahávi.   .אני בא לראות את מר זהבי

ánu - hí - gvéret kármi - hém   אנו - היא - גב' כרמי - הם
atén - avígdor - hén - aní   אתן - אביגדור - הן - אני

H.   The Lydda airport is new and beautiful.

nemál hateufá lúd xadáš veyafé.   .נמל התעופה לוד חדש ויפה

malón dán - haoniót - kolnóa múgrabi   מלון דן - האוניות - קולנוע מוגרבי
haavironím - hašagrirút - nemál hateufá   האוירונים - השגרירות
                                                         נמל התעופה

I.   The tourist office is very large.

misrád hatayarút gadól meód.   .משרד התיירות גדול מאד

malón dán - haoniót - hakolnóa   מלון דן - האוניות - הקולנוע
haavironím - hašagrirút - misrád hatayarút   האוירונים - השגרירות
                                                         משרד התיירות

J.   The ships are very far from the port.

haoniót rexokót meód mehanamál.   .האוניות רחוקות מאד מהנמל

hašagrirút - habatím - misrád hatayarút השגרירות - הבתים - משרד התיירות
haavironím - malón dán - haoniót   האוירונים - מלון דן - האוניות

K. The plane is very close to the port.

haavirón karóv meód lanamál.   .האוירון קרוב מאד לנמל

habatím - haoniót - misrád hatayarút   הבתים - האוניות - משרד התיירות
malón dán - kolnóa múgrabi - haavirón   מלון דן - קולנוע מוגרבי
                                                האוירון

L. Moshe's family is very pleasant.

hamišpaxá šel mošé neimá meód.   .המשפחה של משה נעימה מאד

ištexá - atá - hém - atén - atém   אשתך - אתה - הם - אתן - אתם
gvéret zahávi - már kóhen - hamišpaxá šel mošé   גב' זהבי - מר כהן
                                                המשפחה של משה

M. Mr. Williams is honest and good.

már Williams yašár vetóv.   .מר ווילאמס ישר וטוב

hén - hú - atára - ánu   הן - הוא - עטרה - אנו
mošé - atá vedavíd - már Williams   משה - אתה ודוד - מר ווילאמס

N. You can't see the ship.

atá ló yaxól lir'ót et haoniá.   .אתה לא יכול לראות את האוניה

atém - hén - aní - hú   אתם - הן - אני - הוא
gvéret kármi - ánu - hí - atá   גב' כרמי - אנו - היא - אתה

c. Adjectives ending in /-√ax/

A variation of the above patterns is that of /saméax/ 'happy'. In this
adjective pattern the masculine singular ends in /-√ax/.

      m.s.   saméax   f.s.   smexá
                        m.pl. smexím
                        f.pl. smexót

[There is a close correspondence with written Hebrew in that all such
words are spelled with ח , and not with כ   Compare Section 7.5b.]

o. I'm very happy to see Mr. Carmi.

aní saméax meód lir'ót et már kármi.   .אני שמח מאד לראות את מר כרמי

ánu - hí - atém - sára veléa   אנו - היא - אתם - שרה ולאה
kulám - baalá - ištó - aní   כולם - בעלה - אשתו - אני

REVIEW CONVERSATIONS

A: amárt šeát rocá lehagía
   lemalón dán. naxón?

א: אמרת שאת רוצה להגיע
   למלון דן, נכון?

B: ló. amárti šeaní rocá lehagía
   lemisrád hatayarut.

ב: לא. אמרתי שאני רוצה להגיע
   למשרד התיירות.

A: slixá. ló šamáti otáx.

א: סליחה. לא שמעתי אותך.

C: šim'í. át memahéret?

ג: שמעי, את ממהרת?

D: ló kol káx. veatá?

ד: לא כל כך. ואתה?

C: gám aní ló memahér.

ג: גם אני לא ממהר.

E: át rocá glída?

ה: את רוצה גלידה?

F: ken. éyfo brúklin bar?

ו: כן. איפה ברוקלין בר?

E: berexóv álenbi bekivún sfát hayám.

ה: ברחוב אלנבי בכיוון שפת הים.

F: haglída šám tová meód.

ו: הגלידה שם טובה מאוד.

E: kén, aní yodéa.

ה: כן, אני יודע.

G: atá yodéa éyfo šebrúklin bár?

ז: אתה יודע איפה שברוקלין בר?

H: ló. aní ló yodéa.

ח: לא. אני לא יודע.

G: atá ló tél avívi?

ז: אתה לא תל אביבי?

H: ló. aní xadáš baárec.

ח: לא. אני חדש בארץ.

I: atá rocé laléxet lemisrád hatayarút?

ט: אתה רוצה ללכת למשרד התיירות?

J: kén. lemisrád hatayarút hamemšaltí.

י: כן. למשרד התיירות הממשלתי.

I: im káx, léx yašár birxóv álenbi.

ט: אם כך, לך ישר ברחוב אלנבי.

J: rexóv álenbi hú bakivún hazé?

י: רחוב אלנבי הוא בכיוון הזה?

I: kén.

ט: כן.

K: atá yodéa éyfo nimcét hašagrirút?

כ: אתה יודע איפה נמצאת השגרירות?

L: ló, aní ló yodéa. aní xadáš betél avív.

ל: לא, אני לא יודע. אני חדש בתל אביב.

K: tóv. áz tamšíx yašár barexóv hazé.

כ: טוב. אז תמשיך ישר ברחוב הזה.

L: todá rabá.

ל: תודה רבה.

M: át memahéret, gvirtí?   מ: את ממהרת, גברתי?

N: ló. aní ló memahéret. aní rocá   נ: לא. אני לא ממהרת. אני רוצה

    letayél velir'ót et haír.   לטייל ולראות את העיר.

M: áz lexí lemisrád hatayarút.   מ: אז לכי למשרד התיירות.

N: aní ló yodáat éyfo šemisrád hatayarút.   נ: אני לא יודעת איפה שמשרד התיירות.

M: kán bapiná harišoná.   מ: כאן בפינה הראשונה.

O: láma atá memahér, adoní?   ס: למה אתה ממהר, אדוני?

P: kvár meuxár veaní rocé   ע: כבר מאוחר, ואני רוצה

    lehagía lekolnóa múgrabi.   להגיע לקולנוע מוגרבי.

O: zé ló raxók mikán.   ס: זה לא רחוק מכאן.

P: kén. aní yodéa šezé ló raxók.   ע: כן. אני יודע שזה לא רחוק.

O: áz láma atá memahér?   ס: אז למה אתה ממהר?

P: amárti lexá šekvár meuxár.   ע: אמרתי לך שכבר מאוחר.

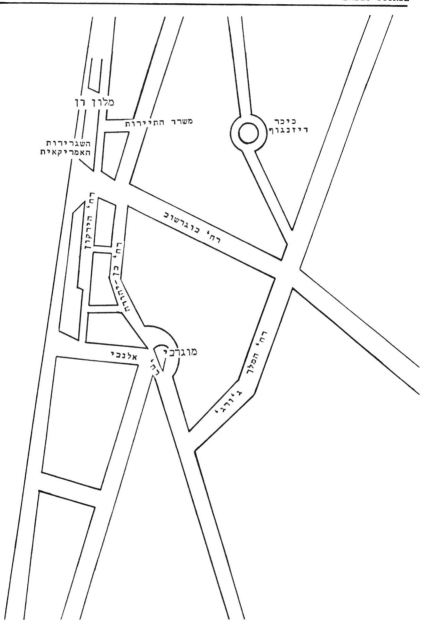

9.1 Wandering through Tel Aviv (cont'd.)

PASSERBY

You can	atá yaxól	אתה יכול
go into the Brooklyn Bar	lehikanés lebrúklin bár	להכנס לברוקלין בר
and eat ice cream.	veleexól glída.	ולאכול גלידה.
to enter	lehikanés	להכנס
to eat	leexól	לאכול
ice cream	glída, glidá (f)	גלידה

MR. WILLIAMS

What kind of ice cream	éyzo glída	איזו גלידה
do they have there?	yéš šám.	יש שם?
which	éyzo (f)	איזו
there is	yéš	יש

PASSERBY

The ice cream there	haglidá šám	הגלידה שם
is very good.	tová meód.	טובה מאד.

MR. WILLIAMS

Really?	beemét?	באמת?
truth	emét (f)	אמת

PASSERBY

They even	hém afílu	הם אפילו
make a banana split	mexiním banána splít	מכינים בננה ספליט
like [with you]	kmó eclexém	כמו אצלכם
in America.	beamérika.	באמריקה.
even	afílu	אפילו
prepare	mexín (m.s.)	מכין
at (French chez)	écel	אצל

MR. WILLIAMS

What do you say!	má atá sáx!	מה אתה שח!
say	sáx (m.s.pres.)	שח

9.2 Wandering through Tel Aviv (cont'd.)

PASSERBY

You can	át yexolá	את יכולה
go into the Brooklyn Bar	lehikanés lebrúklin bár	להכנס לברוקלין בר
and eat ice cream.	veleexól glída.	ולאכול גלידה.

MRS. WILLIAMS

What kind of ice cream	éyzo glída	איזו גלידה
do they have there?	yéš šám.	יש שם?

PASSERBY

The ice cream there is very good.	haglída šám tová meód.	הגלידה שם טובה מאד.

MRS. WILLIAMS

Really?	beemét?	באמת?

PASSERBY

They even make a banana split like [with you] in America.	hém afílu mexiním banána splít kmó eclexém beamérika.	הם אפילו מכינים בננה ספליט כמו אצלכם באמריקה.

MRS. WILLIAMS

What do you say!	má át sáxa!	מה את שחה!

9.3 Vocabulary Drills

A. They are preparing the ice cream.

hém mexiním et haglída.   .הם מכינים את הגלידה

hí - ánu - atén - davíd   היא - אנו - אתן - דוד
atára - xána veiští - hú - hém   עטרה - חנה ואשתי - הוא - הם

The preposition /écel/ is difficult to translate succinctly. It is
roughly comparable to the French chez and means "at the home, place, office
of, by, with", etc.
    The preposition has the alternate form /ecl-/ before pronominal suffixes.
It is used with the singular set.
    Many speakers have the following variant forms with some of the suffixes.

    2 f.s. /eclấx/   for   /ecléx/
    3 m.pl. /eclahém/ for   /eclám/
    3 f.pl. /eclahén/ for   /eclán/

B. Substitution Drill

    The book is at my house.

haséfer nimcá eclí babáit.	.הספר נמצא אצלי כבית
eclexá	אצלך
ecléx	אצלך
ecló	אצלו
eclá	אצלה
eclénu	אצלנו
eclexém	אצלכם
eclexén	אצלכן
eclám	אצלם
eclán	אצלן

GRAMMAR NOTES

9.4   The Construct State of Nouns

     a.   Examine the underlined noun phrases in the following sentences:

        1.   lúd hú <u>nemál teufá</u> yafé vexadíš.
        2.   beéyze <u>bet séfer</u> lamádeta.

In each of these phrases a noun is modified by another noun. In Sentence 1, for example, the noun /namál/ (in the alternate form /nemál/) is modified by /teufá/. This construction is comparable to the English in which one noun modifies another, except that in English the first noun modifies the second, while in Hebrew the reverse is true.

        /namál/   "port"
        /teufá/   "flight"
        /nemál teufá/   (lit.) "flight port"

In sentence 2 the noun /báit/ (in the alternate form /bét/) is modified by /séfer/

        /báit/   "house"
        /séfer/   "book"
        /bet séfer/   "school" (lit.) "book house"

The first noun in such a sequence is said to be in the <u>construct state.</u>

     b.   As noted in Grammar Section 3.4 some nouns have an alternate form when occurring as the first noun in this construction. It is hard to predict the alternate forms, but as patterns occur in this text they will be pointedd out. If not otherwise noted it may be at least temporarily assumed that there is no alternate construct state form.

        (1)   Masculine singular nouns of the pattern /CaCVC/ have a construct form without the /-a-/ unless the first consonant is /x-/.
        /šalóm/ - /šlóm ištexá/
        /namál/ - /nemál teufá/ (with /-e-/ because /nm-/ is a non-permissible initial cluster)
        This pattern is very similar to the pattern of masculine-feminine adjectives described in Grammar Section 8.4b
        (2)   Feminine singular nouns ending in /-á/ have a construct form ending in /-át/, sometimes with other changes.
        /safá/ - /sfát yám/ "seashore"
        (3)   Alternates forms of other nouns in this text so far are:
        /báit/   "house"   -   /bét/ or /béyt/
        /išá/   "wife"   -   /éšet/
        /áin/   "eye"   -   /éyn/
        /mišpaxá/   "family"   -   /mišpáxat/

     c.   The main stress in the comparable noun-noun constructions in English is on the first noun; in Hebrew it is on the second. In this text the primary stress of each word is indicated, but a comparatively louder stress will be heard on the second noun - /nemál teufá/. When the stresses are on contiguous syllables the first may become unstressed - /bet séfer/, but /bét haséfer/.

d. The definite article /ha-/ is prefixed only to the <u>second</u> noun in the construct state sequence. The first noun, however, is still treated as definite.

/yoéc hašagrirút/	"the Embassy counsellor"	יועץ השגרירות
/misrád haxúc/	"the foreign office"	משרד החוץ
/binyán hadóar/	"the post office building"	בנין הדואר
/misrád hatayarút/	"the tourism office"	משרד התיירות

e. Adjectives modifying the first noun of a construct state sequence follow the entire construction.
/nemál teufá yafé vexadíš/ "a beautiful and modern airport"
Note that the adjectives /yafé vexadíš/ modify /nemál/ and are, therefore, masculine.

f. Three nouns may occur in a construct state sequence.
/kivún sfát hayám/ "the direction of the seashore"
Sequences of four nouns occur but they are rare and are often paraphrased.

g. Hebrew construct state sequences are not always translatable as English noun-noun constructions. They are sometimes translated as prepositional phrase constructions, usually with the preposition "of".
/kivún hayám/ "the direction of the sea"
/šagrirút yisraél/ "the Embassy of Israel" or "the Israel Embassy"

Some sequences are translatable as possessives.
/šlóm hamišpaxá/ "the family's welfare"

On the other hand, English noun-noun constructions are not necessarily translated as construct state sequences in Hebrew.
/misrád hatayarút ha<u>memšaltí</u>/ "the <u>government</u> tourist office"
Here the Hebrew has an adjective /memšaltí/ modifying /misrád/ while English has the noun "government" modifying "office".

A. Completion Drill - The instructor gives the sentence and then the noun in parentheses. The student responds by giving the sentence with a construct state sequence using the noun.

Instructor: He is in an office. (the hotel)
Student: He is in the hotel office.

1. hú nimcá bemisrád. (hamalon).
    hú nimcá bemisrád hamalón.

‎.1 הוא נמצא במשרד.(המלון)‎.
   הוא נמצא במשרד המלון.

2. hú nimcá bebinyán. (hašagrirút).
    hú nimcá bebinyán hašagrirút.

‎.2 הוא נמצא בבנין . (השגרירות)‎.
   הוא נמצא בבנין השגרירות.

3. namál nimcá belúd. (teufá).
    nemál teufá nimcá belúd.

‎.3 נמל נמצא בלוד. (תעופה)‎.
   נמל תעופה נמצא בלוד.

4. mišpaxá tagía letél avív. (zahávi).
    mišpáxat zahávi tagía letél avív.

‎.4 משפחה תגיע לתל אביב. (זהבי)‎.
   משפחת זהבי תגיע לתל אביב.

5. raínu báit berexóv álenbi. (kolnóa).
    raínu bét kolnóa berexóv álenbi.

‎.5 ראינו בית ברחוב אלנבי.(קולנוע)‎.
   ראינו בית קולנוע ברחוב אלנבי.

6. hamšéx ád lepiná. (rexóv álenbi).
    hamšéx ád lepinát rexóv álenbi.

‎.6 המשך עד לפינה. (רחוב אלנבי)‎.
   המשך עד לפינת רחוב אלנבי.

B. Transformation Drill - Indefinite to Definite

    Instructor: You saw a movie house.
    Student: You saw the movie house.

1. raítem bét kolnóa.   ראיחם בית קולנוע.
    raítem et bét hakolnóa.   ראיחם את בית הקולנוע.

2. higát etmól lenemál teufá.   הגעת אתמול לנמל תעופה.
    higát etmól lenemál hateufá.   הגעת אתמול לנמל התעופה.

3. már Williams hú yoéc šagrirút.   מר וויל-אמס הוא יועץ שגרירות.
    már Williams hú yoéc hašagrirút.   מר וויל'אמס הוא יועץ השגרירות.

4. lamádeti ivrít bebét séfer.   למדחי עברית בבית ספר.
    lamádeti ivrít bebét haséfer.   למדחי עברית בבית הספר.

5. misrád dóar nimcá kán bapiñá.   משרד דאר נמצא כאן בפינה.
    misrád hadóar nimcá kán bapina.   משרד הדואר נמצא כאן בפינה.

6. hém rocím lir'ót sfát yám.   הם רוצים לראות שפת ים.
    hém rocím lir'ót et sfát hayám.   הם רוצים לראות את שפת הים.

9.5 Definite Article /ha-/ Prefixed to Adjectives

Examine the following underlined forms:

    (1) már Williams hú yoéc <u>hašagrirút haamerikáit</u>.

    (2) pné kán <u>bapiná harišoná yemína</u>.

    (3) <u>bakivún hazé</u>?

Note that both the noun and the adjective modifying it are preceded by the definite article /ha-/. Whenever a noun is definite all adjectives modifying it in the same phrase are preceded by /ha-/. It does not matter how the noun is made definite. (Cf. Grammar Section 2.5)

Examples of nouns made definite in other ways are:

    a. Nouns with a pronoun suffix: /ištó hayafá/ "his pretty wife"
    b. Proper names: /tél avív haxadišá/ "modern Tel Aviv"
    c. The first noun of a definite construct state sequence (see Grammar Section 9.4d): /misrád hatayarút hamemšaltí/

Note that the adjective /memšaltí/ modifies /misrád/ and is, therefore, masculine. On the other hand, in Sentence (1) above, the adjective /amerikáit/ modifies /šagrirút/ and is feminine. Ambiguities may occasionally arise when both nouns are of the same gender and either may reasonably be modified by the adjective, but context or paraphrasing usually settles the matter.

When the adjective is not part of the same noun phrase it is not preceded by /ha-/. Thus, the following contrast may occur:

    (a) /habáit hagadól/ "the big house"
    (b) /habáit gadól/ "The house is big."

In the first example /hagadól/ modifies /habáit/ in the same noun phrase. In the other example /gadól/ modifies /habáit/, but it is in the second half of an equational sentence and, therefore, is not prefixed by /ha-/.

Demonstratives such as /zé/ "this" are prefixed with /ha-/ when they modify nouns as adjectives.

/bakivún hazé/ "in this direction"

In this example, as in Sentences 2 and 3 above, the /ha-/ preceding the noun is contracted into /ba-/. See Grammar Note 6.7.

A. Transformation Drill - Indefinite to Definite

        Instructor: I came in a big airplane.
        Student: I came in the big airplane.

1. báti beavirón gadól   .1 .באתי באוירון גדול
    báti baavirón hagadól.   .באתי באוירון הגדול
2. raínu báit yafé.   .2 .ראינו בית יפה
    raínu et habáit hayafé.   .ראינו את הבית היפה
3. hamšíxi yašár ád rexóv gadól.   .3 .המשיכי ישר עד רחוב גדול
    hamšíxi yašár ád harexóv hagadól.   .המשיכי ישר עד הרחוב הגדול
4. haím zé binyán xadíš?   .4 ?האם זה בנין חדיש
    haím zé habinyán haxadíš?   ?האם זה הבנין החדיש
5. oniá xadašá nimcét banamál.   .5 .אוניה חדשה נמצאת בנמל
    haoniá haxadašá nimcét banamál.   .האוניה החדשה נמצאת בנמל
6. šamáti šezé misrád memšaltí.   .6 .שמעתי שזה משרד ממשלתי
    šamáti šezé hamisrád hamemšaltí.   .שמעתי שזה המשרד הממשלתי

B. Transformation Drill - Definite to Indefinite

        Repeat Drill A in reverse.

C. Transformation Drill - Indefinite to Definite

        Instructor: I was impressed by a new government office.
        Student: I was impressed by the new government office.

1. hitrašámti mimisrád memšaltí xadáš.   .1 .התרשמתי ממשרד ממשלתי חדש
    hitrašámti mehamisrád hamemšaltí haxadáš.   .התרשמתי מהמשרד הממשלתי החדש
2. hí gára bebáit gadól veyafé.   .2 .היא גרה בבית גדול ויפה
    hí gára babáit hagadól vehayafé.   .היא גרה בבית הגדול והיפה
3. hém baím beoniót gdolót vexadišót.   .3 .הם באים באוניות גדולות וחדישות
    hém baím baoniót hagdolót vehaxadišót.   .הם באים באוניות הגדולות והחדישות
4. šamáti šezé malón gadól venaím.   .4 .שמעתי שזה מלון גדול ונעים
    šamáti šezé hamalón hagadól vehanaím.   .שמעתי שזה המלון הגדול והנעים

D. Transformation Drill - Definite to Indefinite

        Repeat Drill C in reverse.

E.   Transformation Drill - Indefinite to Definite

     Instructor: Where is a government tourist office?
     Student: Where is the government tourist office?

1.   éyfo misrád tayarút memšaltí.   ‏1. אֵיפֹה מִשְׂרָד תַּיָּרוּת מֶמְשַׁלְתִּי?‏
     éyfo misrád hatayarút hamemšaltí.   ‏אֵיפֹה מִשְׂרָד הַתַּיָּרוּת הַמֶּמְשַׁלְתִּי?‏
2.   már Williams hú yoéc šagrirút xadáš.   ‏2. מַר וִילְיַאמְס הוּא יוֹעֵץ שַׁגְרִירוּת חָדָשׁ.‏
     már Williams hú yoéc hašagrirút haxadáš.   ‏מַר וִילְיַאמְס הוּא יוֹעֵץ הַשַּׁגְרִירוּת הֶחָדָשׁ.‏
3.   raíti misrád dóar gadól.   ‏3. רָאִיתִי מִשְׂרַד דּוֹאַר גָּדוֹל.‏
     raíti et misrád hadóar hagadól.   ‏רָאִיתִי אֶת מִשְׂרַד הַדּוֹאַר הַגָּדוֹל.‏
4.   zé bet séfer tóv.   ‏4. זֶה בֵּית סֵפֶר טוֹב.‏
     zé bét haséfer hatóv.   ‏זֶה בֵּית הַסֵּפֶר הַטּוֹב.‏
5.   higáta lenemál teufá xadíš.   ‏5. הִגַּעְתָּ לִנְמַל תְּעוּפָה חָדִישׁ.‏
     higáta lenemál hateufá haxadíš.   ‏הִגַּעְתָּ לִנְמַל הַתְּעוּפָה הֶחָדִישׁ.‏
6.   raíti otó bebét kolnóa karóv.   ‏6. רָאִיתִי אוֹתוֹ בְּבֵית קוֹלְנוֹעַ קָרוֹב.‏
     raíti otó bebét hakolnóa hakaróv.   ‏רָאִיתִי אוֹתוֹ בְּבֵית הַקּוֹלְנוֹעַ הַקָּרוֹב.‏
7.   aní roé binyán šagrirút gadól.   ‏7. אֲנִי רוֹאֶה בִּנְיַן שַׁגְרִירוּת גָּדוֹל.‏
     aní roé et binyán hašagrirút hagadól.   ‏אֲנִי רוֹאֶה אֶת בִּנְיַן הַשַּׁגְרִירוּת הַגָּדוֹל.‏

F.   Transformation Drill - Definite to Indefinite

     Repeat Drill E in reverse.

G.   Transformation Drill

     Instructor: I saw his wife. She is pretty.
     Student: I saw his pretty wife.

1.   raíti et ištó. hí yafá.   ‏1. רָאִיתִי אֶת אִשְׁתּוֹ. הִיא יָפָה.‏
     raíti et ištó hayafá.   ‏רָאִיתִי אֶת אִשְׁתּוֹ הַיָּפָה.‏
2.   raíti et baalá. hú báal tóv.   ‏2. רָאִיתִי אֶת בַּעְלָהּ. הוּא בַּעַל טוֹב.‏
     raíti et baalá hatóv.   ‏רָאִיתִי אֶת בַּעְלָהּ הַטּוֹב.‏
3.   raíti et eynéha. hén gdolót.   ‏3. רָאִיתִי אֶת עֵינֶיהָ. הֵן גְּדוֹלוֹת.‏
     raíti et eynéha hagdolót.   ‏רָאִיתִי אֶת עֵינֶיהָ הַגְּדוֹלוֹת.‏
4.   raíti et misradxá. hú xadáš.   ‏4. רָאִיתִי אֶת מִשְׂרָדְךָ. הוּא חָדָשׁ.‏
     raíti et misradxá haxadáš.   ‏רָאִיתִי אֶת מִשְׂרָדְךָ הֶחָדָשׁ.‏
5.   raíti et arcexém. hí yafá.   ‏5. רָאִיתִי אֶת אַרְצְכֶם. הִיא יָפָה.‏
     raíti et arcexém hayafá.   ‏רָאִיתִי אֶת אַרְצְכֶם הַיָּפָה.‏

     The instructor may vary this drill by changing /raíti/ to /aní rocé lir'6t/.

H.   Transformation Drill

     Instructor: We saw Israel. It's modern.
     Student: We saw the modern Israel.

1.   raínu et yisraél. hí xadišá.   ‏1. רָאִינוּ אֶת יִשְׂרָאֵל. הִיא חֲדִישָׁה.‏
     raínu et yisraél haxadišá.   ‏רָאִינוּ אֶת יִשְׂרָאֵל הַחֲדִישָׁה.‏
2.   raínu et atára. hí yafá.   ‏2. רָאִינוּ אֶת עֲטָרָה. הִיא יָפָה.‏
     raínu et atára hayafá.   ‏רָאִינוּ אֶת עֲטָרָה הַיָּפָה.‏
3.   raínu et davíd. hú gadól.   ‏3. רָאִינוּ אֶת דָּוִד. הוּא גָּדוֹל.‏
     raínu et davíd hagadól.   ‏רָאִינוּ אֶת דָּוִד הַגָּדוֹל.‏
4.   raínu et avígdor. hú saméax.   ‏4. רָאִינוּ אֶת אֲבִיגְדּוֹר. הוּא שָׂמֵחַ.‏
     raínu et avígdor hasaméax.   ‏רָאִינוּ אֶת אֲבִיגְדּוֹר הַשָּׂמֵחַ.‏
5.   raínu et dóv. hú tóv.   ‏5. רָאִינוּ אֶת דּוֹב. הוּא טוֹב.‏
     raínu et dóv hatóv.   ‏רָאִינוּ אֶת דּוֹב הַטּוֹב.‏
6.   raínu et sára vexána. hén amerikáiot.   ‏6. רָאִינוּ אֶת שָׂרָה וְחַנָּה. הֵן אֲמֶרִיקָאִיוֹת.‏
     raínu et sára vexána haamerikáiot.   ‏רָאִינוּ אֶת שָׂרָה וְחַנָּה הָאֲמֶרִיקָאִיוֹת.‏

REVIEW CONVERSATIONS

A: éyfo nimcá haséfer.   א : איפה נמצא הספר?

B: haséfer nimcá eclexá babáit.   ב : הספר נמצא אצלך בבית.

A: beemét?   א : באמת?

B: kén. natáti lexá et haséfer habóker.   ב : כן. נתתי לך את הספר הבוקר.

C: atá roé et bét hakolnóa hagadól?   ג : אתה רואה את בית הקולנוע הגדול?

D: ló. éyfo.   ד : לא. איפה?

C: kán bapiná.   ג : כאן בפינה.

D: o, kén.   ד : אה, כן.

E: mexiním banána split bebrúklin bár.   ה : מכינים בננה ספליט בברוקלין בר.

F: má atá sáx !   ו : מה אתה שח !

E: kén. kmó beamérika.   ה : כן. כמו באמריקה.

G: ráinu et misrád hatayarút haxadáš.   ז : ראינו את משרד התיירות החדש.

H: babáit hagadól?   ח : בבית הגדול?

G: kén. babáit hagadól vehaxadíš.   ז : כן. בבית הגדול והחדיש.

I: šamáti šehabáit šel dóv gadól veyafé.   ט : שמעתי שהבית של דב גדול ויפה.

J: kén. raíti et habáit etmól.   י : כן. ראיתי את הבית אתמול.

I: éyfo? berámat gán?   ט : איפה? ברמת גן?

J: ló. hém garím bexulón.   י : לא. הם גרים בחולון.

End of Tape 3A

Tape 3B

10.1 Wandering through Tel Aviv (concluded)

PASSERBY

After	axaréy še-	אחרי ש-
you finish the ice cream	tigmór et haglída	תגמור את הגלידה
continue straight	tamšíx yašár	תמשיך ישר
towards the seashore.	lekivún hayám.	לכיוון הים.
after, behind	axaréy	אחרי
you will finish	tigmór (m.s.)	תגמור

MR. WILLIAMS

| Yes- | ken- | - כן |

PASSERBY

When you get	kšetagía	כשתגיע
to Hayarkon Street	lerexóv hayarkón,	לרחוב הירקון,
turn right	tifné yemína	תפנה ימינה,
and go straight	veteléx yašár	ותלך ישר
to Mendele Street.	ád rexóv méndele.	עד רחוב מנדלי.
when (conjunction)	kšé-	כש-
you will arrive	tagía (m.s.)	תגיע

MR. WILLIAMS

That is to say,	zót oméret še-	זאת אומרת ש-
the tourist office	misrád hatayarút	משרד התיירות
is located on Hayarkon St.	nimcá berexóv hayarkón	נמצא ברחוב הירקון
at the corner of Mendele?	pinát méndele?	פינת מנדלי?

PASSERBY

Not exactly	ló bediyúk	לא בדיוק
on the corner.	bapiná.	בפינה.
exactly	bediyúk	בדיוק

Turn right there	šám tifné yemína	שם תפנה ימינה
and go on to	veteléx ád	ותלך עד
the tourist office.	misrád hatayarút.	משרד התיירות.

MR. WILLIAMS

Is it possible	haím efšár	האם אפשר
to go by way of	laléxet dérex	ללכת דרך
Ben-Yehuda Street?	rexóv bén yehúda?	רחוב בן-יהודה?
possible	efšár	אפשר
to go	laléxet	ללכת
way, path, through	dérex (f)	דרך

PASSERBY

| Yes, of course. | kén. behexlét. | כן. בהחלט. |
| definitely | behexlét | בהחלט |

MR. WILLIAMS

| Thank you, | todá rabá lexá, | תודה רבה לך, |
| Sir. Goodbye. | adoní. šalom. | אדוני, שלום. |

PASSERBY

It was nothing.	al ló davár.	.על לא דבר
Goodbye and good luck.	šalóm uvraxá.	.שלום וברכה
blessing	braxá (f)	ברכה

10.2   Wandering through Tel Aviv (concluded)

PASSERBY

After	axaréy še-	–אחרי ש
you finish the ice cream	tigmerí et haglída	תגמרי את הגלידה
continue straight	tamšíxi yašár	תמשיכי ישר
towards the seashore.	lekivún hayám.	.לכיוון הים

MRS. WILLIAMS

Yes-	kén-	– כן

PASSERBY

When you get	kšetagíi	כשתגיעי
to Hayarkon Street	lerexóv hayarkón	לרחוב הירקון
turn right	tifní yamína	תפני ימינה
and go straight	vetelxí yašár	ותלכי ישר
to Mendele Street.	ád rexóv méndele.	.עד רחוב מנדלי

MRS. WILLIAMS

That is to say,	zót oméret še-	–זאת אומרת ש
that the tourist office	misrád hatayarút	משרד התיירות
is located on Hayarkon St.	nimcá berexóv heyarkón	נמצא ברחוב הירקון
at the corner of Mendele?	pinát méndele?	?פינת מנדלי

PASSERBY

Not exactly	ló bediyúk	לא בדיוק
on the corner.	bapiná.	.בפינה

Turn right there	šám tifní yamína	שם תפני ימינה
and go to	vetelxí ád	ותלכי עד
the tourist office.	misrád hatayarút.	.משרד התיירות

MRS. WILLIAMS

Is it possible	haím efšár	האם אפשר
to go by way of	laléxet dérex	ללכת דרך
Ben-Yehuda street?	rexóv bén yehúda?	?רחוב בן-יהודה

PASSERBY

Yes, of course.	kén. behexlét.	.כן. בהחלט

MRS. WILLIAMS

Thank you,	todá rabá láx	, תודה רבה לך
ma'am. Goodbye.	gvirtí. šalóm.	.גברתי, שלום

PASSERBY

It was nothing.	ál 16 davár.	על לא דבר.
Goodbye and good luck.	šalóm uvraxá.	שלום וברכה.

10.3 Vocabulary Drill

A variation of the stark and gentle imperative is the pattern of /tagía/. In this pattern the masculine singular ends in /-CV̌a/ and the feminine plural ends in /-Cána/. The forms of /tagía/ are:

        m.s. /tagía/   m.pl. /tagíu/
        f.s. /tagíi/   f.pl. /tagána/

[In the Basic Sentences of this unit the verb is used as a second person future.]

A. Substitution-Agreement Drill - Use the underlined words as cues.

When you get to the intersection turn left.

kšetagía lahictalvút <u>tifné</u> smóla.	כשתגיע להצטלבות <u>תפנה</u> שמאלה.
kšetagíu lahictalvút <u>tifnú</u> smóla.	כשתגיעו להצטלבות <u>תפנו</u> שמאלה.
kšetagíi lahictalvút <u>tifní</u> smóla.	כשתגיעי להצטלבות <u>תפני</u> שמאלה.
kšetagána lahictalvút <u>tifnéna</u> smóla.	כשתגענה להצטלבות <u>תפנינה</u> שמאלה.

שם תפנה ימינה...

GRAMMAR NOTES

10.4 The Relative Conjunction /še-/

a)   Whenever an equational sentence, or a declarative sentence containing
a verb, is included within another sentence, but not as a direct quotation,
then it is preceded by the conjunction /še-/.
Examine the following sentences:

1. habáit gadól veyafé.   "The house is big and beautiful."
    šamáti šehabáit gadól veyafé.   "I heard that the house is big
                                          and beautiful!"
2. arcénu mócet xén beeynéxa.   "You like our country."
    aní mekavé šearcénu mócet   "I hope you like our country."
       xén beeynéxa.

     Note that although the conjunction "that" is optional in English the
conjunction /še-/ is required in Hebrew.
b)   /še-/ is used when prepositions precede such included sentences:

3. báta héna.   "You came here."
    lifnéy šebáta hena   "before you came here"
4. tigmór et haglída.   "You will finish the ice cream."
    axaréy šetigmór et   "after you finish the
       haglída   the ice cream"

     The conjunction /kše-/ is a contraction of the prefixed preposition /ke-/
"as" and /še-/.

5. tagía lerexóv hayarkon.   "You will get to Hayarkon Street."
    kšetagía lerexóv hayarkón   "when you get to Hayarkon Street"

c)   When the included sentence is a question beginning with an interrogative,
the /še-/ is optional, but after the interrogative.

6. éyfo brúklin bár.   "Where is the Brooklyn Bar?"
    atá yodéa éyfo   "Do you know where
       šebrúklin bar?   the Brooklyn Bar is?"
(or) atá yodéa éyfo
       brúklin bár?

7. heyxán atá nimca.   "Where are you located?"
    atá ló yodéa heyxán   "You don't know where you are?"
       atá nimca?

d)   A sentence with an included sentence may in turn be included in a still
larger sentence.

8. báta héna.   "You came here."
    lamádeta ivrít lifnéy   "You studied
       šebáta héna.   Hebrew before you came here."

```
        tóv meód asíta                  "You did well
          šelamádeta ivrít lifnéy          to study Hebrew
          šebáta héna.                     before you came here."
```

It cannot be repeated too often that the above description refers to the
Hebrew sentences and <u>not</u> to the English translations. In sentences 4 and 5
the English verb form changes; in sentences 5, 6 and 7 the word order changes;
and in Sentence 8 "you studied" changes to "to study". In the Hebrew,
however, the included sentences remain intact except for intonation patterns.
There are stylistic variations of word order in included sentences in Hebrew,
but these are relatively minor.

    [Note: This conjunction is always written in Hebrew as a prefix to the
following word.   asíta   עשית   lamádeta   למדת   báta   באת
                šeasíta   שעשית   šelamádeta   שלמדת   šebáta   שבאת   ]

The following drills are expansion drills. The instructor gives a
sentence, and the student responds with a larger sentence in which the
instructor's sentence is included.
    Instructor: tigmór et haglidá.   "You will finish the ice cream."
    Student: aní rocé šetigmór   "I want you to
           et haglidá.   finish the ice cream."

A more literal translation would be "I want that you should finish the
ice cream," but this is, of course, awkward English.

Instructor's sentences:

1.	már Williams gár berámat gán.	.1 מר ווילאמס גר ברמת גן.
2.	ištó medabéret ivrít.	.2 אשתו מדברת עברית.
3.	miryám nimcét betél avív.	.3 מרים נמצאת בתל אביב.
4.	lamádeta bevét haséfer lesafót.	.4 למדת נבית הספר לשפות.
5.	hašagrirút nimcét al yád malón dán.	.5 השגרירות נמצאת על יד מלון דן.
6.	habinyán xadíš.	.6 הבנין חדיש.
7.	haárec yafá meód.	.7 הארץ יפה מאד.

Student adds:

A.	aní xošév še-	.א אני חושב ש-
B.	aní mekavé še-	.ב אני מקוה ש-
C.	hú roé še-	.ג הוא רואה ש-
D.	šamánu še-	.ד שמענו ש-
E.	raíti še-	.ה ראיתי ש-

Instructor's Sentences:

8.	lamádeta ivrít.	.8 למדת עברית.
9.	šamáta mimár káspi.	.9 שמעת ממר כספי.
10.	raínu et habáit šeló.	.10 ראינו את הבית שלו.
11.	natáti lemiryám et hasfarím.	.11 נתתי למרים את הספרים.

Student adds:

F.	higáta laárec lifnéy še-	.ו הגעת לארץ לפני ש-
G.	higáta héna axaréy še-	.ז הגעת הנה אחרי ש-

Instructor's Sentences:

12.	natáta ló et haséfer.	.נתח לו את הספר. 12
13.	raíta et hamisrád.	.ראית את המשרד. 13
14.	higáta lamalón.	.הגעת למלון. 14

Student adds:

H.	má amárta ló kše-	ח . מה אמרת לו כש-
I.	má asíta kše-	ט . מה עשית כש-

Additions H and I can be varied by changing /kše-/ to /axaréy še-/ or /lifnéy še-/.

10.5 Adjectives used to Modify Verbs

a. The masculine singular form of adjectives is used to modify verbs.

1. léx yašár berexóv álenbi.   "Go straight on Allenby Street."

2. át medabéret yafé meód.   "You speak very nicely."

3. tóv asíta šelamádeta ivrít.   "You did well to study Hebrew."

The following synonymous sentences illustrate the use of an adjective to modify a noun or a verb.

4. atá medabér ivrít yafá meód.   "You speak a very beautiful Hebrew."

5. atá medabér ivrít yafé meód.   "You speak Hebrew very nicely."

b. When there is no noun antecedent in the context the masculine singular form of the adjective is used.

6. kvár meuxár.   "It's late already."

7. naím lí meod lehakír otxá.   "I am very pleased to meet you."

Although the English translations have pronoun antecedents for "late" and "pleased" the Hebrew does not. In sentence 7 the form is /naím/ even when a woman is speaking. See Section 2.2.

REVIEW CONVERSATIONS

A: axaréy šetigmór leexól et haglída
teléx lemisrád hatayarút?

א: אחרי שתגמור לאכול את הגלידה
תלך למשרד התיירות?

B: ló. lašagrirút haamerikáit.

ב: לא. לשגרירות האמריקאית.

A: áz tamšíx lekivún sfát hayám.

א: אז תמשיך לכיוון שפת הים.

B: kén. aní yodéa.

ב: כן. אני יודע.

C: éyfo nimcá misrád hatayarút.

ג: איפה נמצא משרד התיירות?

D: kán. bapiná harišoná.

ד: כאן. בפינה הראשונה.

C: berexóv bén yehúda?

ג: ברחוב בן יהודה?

D: ló. berexóv méndele.

ד: לא. ברחוב מנדלי.

E: atá medabér ivrít yafé meód.

ה: אתה מדבר עברית יפה מאוד.

F: todá rabá.

ו: תודה רבה.

E: haím lamádeta ivrít lifnéy šebáta héna?

ה: האם למדת עברית לפני שבאת הנה?

F: ló. lamádeti ivrít axaréy šehigáti lekán.

ו: לא. למדתי עברית אחרי שבאתי לכאן.

E: matáy higáta.

ה: מתי הגעת?

F: lifnéy xodšáim.

ו: לפני חודשיים.

E: veatá medabér kvár kmo israelí.
aní xošév šezé tóv meód.

ה: ואתה מדבר כבר כמו ישראלי.
אני חושב שזה טוב מאוד.

G: raíta et habinyán haxadáš
šel misrád hatayarút?

ז: ראית את הבניין החדש
של משרד התיירות?

H: ló. áx šamáti šehú xadíš meód.

ח: לא. אך שמעתי שהוא חדיש מאוד.

G: kén. xadíš vegadól. hú meód móce
xén beeynáy.

ז: כן. חדיש וגדול. הוא מאוד מוצא
חן בעיני.

זו מסורת אצלנו בבית לאכול
כליל שישי דגים ממולאים...

11.1   Dinner Invitation

MR. CASPI

Mr. Williams,	már Williams.		מר וויל יאמס,
what are you doing	má atém osím		מה אתם עושים
Friday evening? *	belél šiší.		בליל שישי?
do		osé (m.s.pres.)	עושה
night		láyla (m)	לילה
sixth		šiší (m.s.)	שישי

MR. WILLIAMS

This Friday evening?	belél šiší hakaróv?	בליל שישי הקרוב?

MR. CASPI

Yes.	kén.	כן.

MR. WILLIAMS

I think that	aní xošév še-		אני חושב ש-
we don't have	éyn lánu		אין לנו
any plans.	kól toxnít.		כל תוכנית.
there is not		éyn	אין
to us		lánu	לנו
plan, program		toxnít (f)	תוכנית

MR. CASPI

We want	ánu rocím		אנו רוצים
to invite you	lehazmín otxém		להזמין אתכם
for dinner.	learuxát érev.		לארוחת ערב.
to invite		lehazmín	להזמין
meal		aruxá (f)	ארוחה
evening		érev (m)	ערב

MR. WILLIAMS

Thank you.	todá rabá.		תודה רבה.
We will be very happy.	nismáx meód.		נשמח מאוד.
we will be happy		nismáx (1 pl. fut.)	נשמח

MR. CASPI

Is	haím		האם
seven-thirty	šéva ušloším		שבע ושלושים
all right?	mat'ím?		מתאים?
seven		šéva	שבע
thirty		šloším	שלושים
is suitable		mat'ím (m.s.pres.)	מתאים

MR. WILLIAMS

Yes. Give me	kén. tén lí		כן. תן לי
your address.	et haktóvet šelaxém.		את הכתובת שלכם.
give		tén (m.s. imv.)	תן
address		któvet (f)	כתובת

[*Many speakers insist that /lél šiší/ is properly <u>Thursday</u> night and that Friday night is /lél šabát/.]

MR. CASPI

We live	ánu garím	אנו גרים
on Mozkin Street,	birxóv móckin	ברחוב מוצקין
number 3.	mispár šalóš.	מספר שלוש.
number	mispár (m)	מספר
three	šalóš	שלוש

MR. WILLIAMS

I think that	aní xošév še-	-אני חושב ש
we will find	nimcá	נמצא
the place	et hamakóm	את המקום
without difficulty.	leló kóši.	ללא קושי.
we will find	nimcá (1 pl. fut.)	נמצא
place	makóm (m)	מקום
difficulty	kóši (m)	קושי

11.2 ADDITIONAL VOCABULARY

What are you doing Sunday?	má atá osé beyóm rišón.	מה אתה עושה ביום ראשון?
What are you doing Monday?	má atá osé beyóm šení.	מה אתה עושה ביום שני?
What are you doing Tuesday?	má atá osé beyóm šliší.	מה אתה עושה ביום שלישי?
What are you doing Wednesday?	má atá osé beyóm revií.	מה אתה עושה ביום רביעי?
What are you doing Thursday?	má atá osé beyóm xamiší.	מה אתה עושה ביום חמישי?
What are you doing Friday?	má atá osé beyóm šiší.	מה אתה עושה ביום שישי?
What are you doing Saturday?	má atá osé bešabát.	מה אתה עושה בשבת?
What are you doing today?	má atá osé hayóm.	מה אתה עושה היום?

What are you doing	má át osá	מה את עושה
...Sunday evening?	..beyóm rišón baérev.	ביום ראשון בערב?
...Monday evening?	..beyóm šení baérev.	ביום שני בערב?
...Tuesday evening?	..beyóm šliší baérev.	ביום שלישי בערב?
...Wednesday evening?	..beyóm revií baérev.	ביום רביעי בערב?
...Thursday evening?	..beyóm xamiší baérev.	ביום חמישי בערב?
...Friday evening?	..beyóm šiší baérev.	ביום שישי בערב?
...Saturday evening?	..bemocaéy šabát.	במוצאי שבת?
...this evening?	..haérev.	הערב?
We have a plan.	yéš lánu toxnít.	יש לנו תוכנית.

I want to eat	aní rocé leexól	אני רוצה לאכול ארוחת בוקר.
breakfast. (morning meal)	aruxát bóker.	
I want to eat	ani rocé leexól	אני רוצה לאכול ארוחת צהריים.
lunch. (noon meal)	aruxát cohoráim.	
I want to eat	aní rocé leexól	אני רוצה לאכול ארוחת עשר.
brunch. (10 a.m. snack)	aruxát éser.	

11.3 Vocabulary Drills

A. Substitution Drill

    Please give me the book.

tén li, bevakašá, et haséfer.	תן לי, בבקשה, את הספר.
tní	תני
tnú	תנו
ténna	תנה

B. <u>Substitution - Agreement Drill</u>   The instructor gives the underlined forms
as cues.

Please give me your telephone number.

תן לי, בבקשה, -

tén li, bevakašá, et mıspár hatélefon <u>šelxá.</u>	אֶת מספר הטלפון <u>שלך.</u>
tnú li, bevakašá, et mıspár hatélefon <u>šelaxém.</u>	תנו אֶת מספר הטלפון <u>שלכם.</u>
tní li, bevakašá, et mıspár hatélefon <u>šeláx.</u>	תני אֶת מספר הטלפון <u>שלך.</u>
tén li, bevakašá, et mıspár hatélefon <u>šelxá,</u>	תן אֶת מספר הטלפון <u>שלך.</u>
ténna li, bevakašá, et mıspár hatélefon <u>šelaxén.</u>	תנה אֶת מספר הטלפון <u>שלכן.</u>
tní li, bevakašá, et mıspár hatélefon <u>šelax.</u>	תני אֶת מספר הטלפון <u>שלך.</u>

C. Substitution Drill

Don't give me any ice cream.

ál titén li glidá.	אל תיתן לי גלידה.
titní	תתני
titnú	תתנו
titénna	תתנה

D. Transformation Drill - Affirmative to Negative

Instructor: Give her the books.
Student: Don't give her the books.

tén lá et hasfarím.	ál titén lá et hasfarím.	אל תיתן לה אֶת הספרים.
tnú lá et hasfarím.	ál titnú lá et hasfarím.	אל תתנו לה אֶת הספרים.
tní lá et hasfarím.	ál titní lá et hasfarím.	אל תתני לה אֶת הספוים.
ténna lá et hasfarím.	ál titénna lá et hasfarím.	אל תתנה לה אֶת הכפרים.
tén lá et hasfarím.	ál titén lá et hasfarím.	אל תיתן לה אֶת הספרים.
tní lá et hasfarím.	ál titní lá et hasfarím.	אל תתני לה אֶת הספרים.
tnú lá et hasfarím.	ál titnú lá et hasfarím.	אל תתנו לה אֶת הספרים.

E. Transformation Drill - Negative to Affirmative

Repeat Drill D in reverse.

F. Substitution Drill

Let me walk around and see the city.

tén lí letayél velir'ót et haír.	תן לי לטייל ולדאות אֶת העיר.
tní	תני
ténna	תנה
tnú	תנו

91

11.4 Cardinal Numbers

a)   The situation with respect to the cardinal numbers can be described as complicated. There are historically two sets of numbers - masculine and feminine. However, the alternation of the forms is the opposite of what one would expect; that is, the masculine appear to be feminine forms, and vice versa.

> For example: šalóš (feminine) šlošá (masculine)
> Compare: karóv (masculine) krová (feminine)

b)   In formal speech masculine numbers (i.e., those with the apparent feminine shape) are used with masculine nouns, and feminine numbers with feminine nouns. This usage is preferable at all levels of speech.

c)   In counting and in reading off numerals the feminine form is used.

> /axát, štáim, šalóš, arbá./   "One, two, three, four."
> /rexóv móckin, mispár šalóš./   "Mozkin Street, number 3."

d)   In informal speech the two sets are often used interchangeably, with the feminine numbers being the more frequent choice. One often hears hybrid forms such as /šnéymesre/ 'twelve' from /šnéymasar/ and /štéymesre/. To complicate matters a bit more, occasional new distinctions have developed in modern Hebrew such as /arbá/ 'four' (masculine) and /árba/ (feminine).

zero (name of numeral only) éfes (m)

	Feminine	Masculine	זכר	נקבה
one	axát	exád	אחד	אחת
two	štáim	šnáim	שנים	שתים
three	šalóš	šlošá	שלושה	שלוש
four	arbá	arbaá	ארבעה	ארבע
five	xaméš	xamišá	חמשה	חמש
six	šéš	šišá	שישה	שש
seven	šéva	šiv'á	שבעה	שבע
eight	šmóne	šmoná	שמונה	שמונה
nine	téša	tiš'á	תשעה	תשע
ten	éser	asará	עשרה	עשר
eleven	axát'esre	axád'asar	אחד-עשר	אחת-עשרה
twelve	štéym'esre	snéym'asar	שנים-עשר	שתים-עשרה
thirteen	šlóš'esre	šlošáasar	שלושה-עשר	שלוש-עשרה
fourteen	arbáesre	arbáasar	ארבעה-עשר	ארבע-עשרה
fifteen	xaméš'esre	xamišáasar	חמשה-עשר	חמש-עשרה
sixteen	šéš'esre	šišáasar	ששה-עשר	שש-עשרה
seventeen	šváesre	šiv'áasar	שבעה-עשר	שבע-עשרה
eighteen	šmonéesre	šmonáasar	שמונה-עשר	שמונה-עשרה
nineteen	tšáesre	tiš'áasar	תשעה-עשר	תשע-עשרה
twenty	esrím	esrím	עשרים	עשרים

A. Count to twenty.

B. Recite the masculine numbers one to twenty.

C. Read off the following numerals.

1. 3 - 0 - 1
2. 5 - 8 - 8
3. 4 - 1 - 8 - 2
4. 2 - 0 - 2
5. 8 - 2 - 9
6. 5 - 3 - 3 - 6
7. 0 - 8 - 15
8. 4 - 7 - 7 - 4
9. 7 - 3 - 7
10. 8 - 7 - 5 - 0
11. 3 - 5 - 1
12. 1 - 1 - 0 -

GRAMMAR NOTES

11.5 <u>Contraction of Initial Syllables</u>

Compare the following underlined forms:

> léx yašár <u>berexóv</u> álenbi.
> ánu garím <u>birxóv</u> móckin.

When the prefix /be-/ precedes a form beginning with the pattern /CeCV-/ (with unstressed /e/) the two syllables may be contracted to /biCCV-/.

This contraction, interestingly enough, is characteristic of the formal style, but it is often heard in informal speech, also.

A similar contraction is made with the prefixes /le-/ 'to' and /ke-/ 'as'.

11.6 <u>/yéš lí/, /éyn lí/</u>

a) A special grammatical construction is used to indicate possession. Examine the following sentence:

> yéš lánu toxnít.   "We have a plan."

b) The construction consists of the form /yéš/ "there is, there are" plus the preposition /le-/ "to". (In the example above the preposition has a pronominal suffix.) This construction translates the present tense forms of the English verb "have" with the meaning "possess".

The negative of this construction consists of /éyn/ plus /le-/.

> éyn lánu toxnít.   "We don't have a plan."

c) Though, strictly speaking, neither /yéš/ nor /éyn/ is a verb, the direct object preposition /et/ is used before definite nouns which are "possessed".

> yéš lánu séfer.   "We have a book."
> yéš lánu et haséfer.   "We have the book."

d) The word order of the construction may be inverted for emphasis or style reasons. This inversion is frequent when a name follows the preposition.

> ledavíd yéš glidá.   "David has ice cream."
> or   yéš ledavíd glidá.

e) The preposition /le-/ occurs with the singular set of pronominal suffixes, with the same variations that occur with /šel/: /láx, lánu, laxém, laxén, lahém, lahén/.

A. Substitution Drill

I have a house in Ramat Gan.

yéš lí báit berámat gán.	‏יש לי בית ברמת גן.‏
lexá	‏לך‏
láx	‏לך‏
ló	‏לו‏
lá	‏לה‏
lánu	‏לנו‏
laxém	‏לכם‏
laxén	‏לכן‏
lahém	‏להם‏
lahén	‏להן‏

B. Substitution Drill - Repeat Drill A in the negative.

      I don't have a house in Ramat Gan.

      éyn lí báit berámat gán.   אין לי בית ברמת גן.

C. Transformation Drill - Affirmative to Negative

      Instructor: I have Miriam's phone number.
      Student: I don't have Miriam's phone number.

yéš li et mispár hatélefon šél miryám.   יש לי את מספר הטלפון של מרים.
  éyn lí ...   אין לי...
yéš lánu et mispár hatélefon šél miryám. יש לנו את מספר הטלפון של מרים.
  éyn lánu ...   אין לנו...
yéš láx et mispár hatélefon šél miryám.   יש לך את מספר הטלפון של מרים.
  éyn láx ...   אין לך...
yéš ló et mispár hatélefon šél miryám.   יש לו את מספר הטלפון של מרים.
  éyn ló ...   אין לו...
yéš laxém et mispár hatélefon šél miryám. יש לכם את מספר הטלפון של מרים.
  éyn laxém ...   אין לכם...
yéš lá et mispár hatélefon šél miryám.   יש לה את מספר הטלפון של מרים.
  éyn lá ...   אין לה...
yéš lexá et mispár hatélefon šél miryám.   יש לך את מספר הטלפון של מרים.
  éyn lexá ...   אין לך...
yéš lahém et mispár hatélefon šél miryám. יש להם את מספר הטלפון של מרים.
  éyn lahém ...   אין להם...

D. Transformation Drill - Negative to Affirmative

      Repeat Drill C in reverse.

E. Response Drill

      Instructor: Student:
      Where do you live?   We have a house in Savyon.

éyfo atém garím.   yeš lánu báit besavyón.   איפה אתם גרים?
éyfo hú gár.   yeš ló báit besavyón.   איפה הוא גר?
éyfo hém garím.   yeš lahém báit besavyón.   איפה הם גרים?
éyfo át gára.   yeš lí báit besavyón.   איפה את גרה?
éyfo gár mošé.   yeš ló báit besavyón.   איפה גר משה?
éyfo atá gár.   yeš lí báit besavyón.   איפה אתה גר?
éyfo gára léa.   yeš lá báit besavyón.   איפה גרה לאה?

F. Transformation Drill

      Instructor: The books are at my place.
      Student: I have the books.

hasfarím nimcaím eclí.   yéš lí et hasfarím.   הספרים נמצאים אצלי.
hasfarím nimcaím ecló.   yéš ló et hasfarím.   הספרים נמצאים אצלו.
hasfarím nimcaím eclá.   yéš lá et hasfarím.   הספרים נמצאים אצלה.
hasfarím nimcaím écel dóv. yéš ledóv et hasfarím. הספרים נמצאים אצל דב.
hasfarím nimcaím eclénu. yéš lánu et hasfarím.   הספרים נמצאים אצלנו.
hasfarím nimcaím eclám.   yéš lahém et hasfarím. הספרים נמצאים אצלם.
hasfarím nimcaím eclexá. yéš lexá et hasfarím.   הספרים נמצאים אצלך.
hasfarím nimcaím ecléx.   yéš láx et hasfarím.   הספרים נמצאים אצלך.
hasfarím nimcaím eclaxém. yéš laxém et hasfarím. הספרים נמצאים אצלכם.

G. Transformation Drill

      Instructor: He doesn't speak Hebrew.
      Student: He doesn't have a chance to speak Hebrew.

hú ló medabér ivrít.	הוא לא מדבר עברית.
éyn ló hizdamnút ledabér ivrít.	אין לו הזדמנות לדבר עברית.
hém ló medabrím ivrít.	הם לא מדברים עברית.
eyn lahém hizdamnút ledabér ivrít.	אין להם הזדמנות לדבר עברית.
aní ló medabér ivrít.	אני לא מדבר עברית.
éyn lí hizdamnút ledabér ivrít.	אין לי הזדמנות לדבר עברית.
atá ló medabér ivrít.	אתה לא מדבר עברית.
éyn lexá hizdamnút ledabér ivrít.	אין לך הזדמנות לדבר עברית.
ánu ló medabrím ivrít.	אנו לא מדברים עברית.
éyn lánu hizdamnút ledabér ivrít.	אין לנו הזדמנות לדבר עברית.
atém ló medabrím ivrít.	אתם לא מדברים עברית.
éyn laxém hizdamnút ledabér ivrít.	אין לכם הזדמנות לדבר עברית.
ištó ló medabéret ivrít.	אשתו לא מדברת עברית.
éyn leištó hizdamnút ledabér ivrít.	אין לאשתו הזדמנות לדבר עברית.
hí ló medabéret ivrít.	היא לא מדברת עברית.
éyn lá hizdamnút ledabér ivrít.	אין לה הזדמנות לדבר עברית.
át ló medabéret ivrít.	את לא מדברת עברית.
éyn láx hizdamnút ledabér ivrít.	אין לך הזדמנות לדבר עברית.
atén ló medabrót ivrít.	אתן לא מדברות עברית.
éyn laxén hizdamnút ledabér ivrít.	אין לכן הזדמנות לדבר עברית.
hén ló medabrót ivrít.	הן לא מדברות עברית.
éyn lahén hizdamnút ledabér ivrít.	אין להן הזדמנות לדבר עברית.

<u>REVIEW CONVERSATIONS</u>

A: má atém osím maxár.   א: מה אתם עושים מחר?

B: aní ló yodéa. aní xošév   ב: אני לא יודע. אני חושב
   šeéyn lánu toxnít.   שאין לנו תוכנית.

A: ánu rocím lehazmín otxém   א: אנו רוצים להזמין אתכם
   lebrúklin bár.   לברוקלין בר.

B: todá rabá. nismáx meód.   ב: תודה רבה. נשמח מאד.

A: haím šéš mat'ím?   א: האם שש מתאים?

B: kén. behexlét.   ב: כן. בהחלט.

C. tén li bevakašá, et hasfarím hagdolím.   ג: תן לי, בבקשה, את הספרים הגדולים.

D: natáti lexá otám etmól.   ד: נתתי לך אותם אתמול.

C: ló. ló natáta et hasfarím lí.   ג: לא. לא נתת את הספרים לי.
   natáta otám lemiryám.   נתת אותם למרים.

D: lemiryám éyn et hasfarím.   ד: למרים אין את הספרים.

C: kén. yéš lá et hasfarím eclá babáit.   ג: כן. יש לה את הספרים אצלה בבית.

E: eyfó atém garím.

ה: איפה אתם גרים?

F: yéš lánu báit betél avív.

ו: יש לנו בית בתל אביב.

E: tnú lí bevakašá, et mispár
hatélefon šelaxém.

ה: תנו לי, בבקשה, את מספר
הטלפון שלכם.

F: éyn lánu adáin télefon.

ו: אין לנו עדיין טלפון.

E: áz tnú lí et haktóvet šelaxém.

ה: אז תנו לי את הכתובת שלכם.

G: atá yodéa éyfo šemisrád hatayarút?

ז: אתה יודע איפה שמשרד התיירות?

H: zé axaréy habinyán hagadól hazé.

ח: זה אחרי הבנין הגדול הזה.

G: todá. aní xošév šenimcá et hamakóm
leló kóši.

ז: תודה. אני חושב שנמצא את המקום
ללא קושי.

I: éyn lánu toxnít lelél šiší.
má atém osím.

ט: אין לנו תוכנית לליל ששי.
מה אתם עושים?

J: ánu rocím laléxet lir'ót
et már Williams.

י: אנו רוצים ללכת לראות
את מר ווילימס.

I: haím már Williams gár adáin
bemalón dán?

ט: האם מר ווילימס גר עדיין
במלון דן?

J: ló. yéš ló báit berámat gán.

י: לא. יש לו בית ברמת גן.

I: atá yodéa et haktóvet šeló?

ט: אתה יודע את הכתובת שלו?

J: kén. yéš lí et haktóvet bamisrád.

י: כן. יש לי את הכתובת במשרד.

End of Tape 3B

96

Tape 4A

12.1 Friday Evening Dinner

MRS. CASPI

Hello, Mrs. Williams.	šalóm gvéret Williams.	שלום, גברת וויליאמס.
Hello, Mr. Williams.	šalóm már Williams.	שלום, מר וויליאמס.
How are you?	má šlomxém.	מה שלומכם?

MR. WILLIAMS

Hello. Good Sabbath.	šalóm. šabát šalóm.	שלום. שבת שלום.
(Greeting used from sunset Friday to sunset Saturday)	šabát šalóm	שבת שלום

MRS. CASPI

I'm very happy	aní smexá meód	אני שמחה מאד
that you came.	šebátem.	שבאתם.

MRS. WILLIAMS

How could we	éyx yaxólnu	איך יכולנו
refuse?	lesarév.	לסרב?
we were able	yaxólnu	יכולנו
to refuse	lesarév	לסרב

MRS. CASPI

Let's go	háva nigáš	הבה ניגש
to the table	lašulxán.	לשולחן.
let's	háva	הבה
we will approach	nigáš (1.pl.fut.)	ניגש
table	šulxán (m)	שולחן

Moshe,	mošé.	משה,
please pour	mezóg bevakašá	מזוג בבקשה
the wine	et hayáin	את היין
for Kiddush.	lekidúš.	לקידוש.
pour	mezóg (m.s.imv.)	מזוג
wine	yáin (m)	יין
(Sabbath ceremony)	kidúš (m)	קידוש

12.2 ADDITIONAL VOCABULARY

Good evening.	érev tóv.	ערב טוב.
Good morning.	bóker tóv.	בוקר טוב.
Good night.	láyla tóv.	לילה טוב.

The above Hebrew expressions are almost identical to the English in usage.
/érev/ 'evening' begins at sunset. In the afternoon /šalóm/ is used.

Happy holiday.	xág saméax.	חג שמח.

This greeting is used on holidays, similarly to /šabát šalóm/.

Happy New Year.	šaná tová.	שנה טובה.
Congratulations.	mazál tóv.	מזל טוב.
luck	mazál (m)	מזל

12.3   <u>Vocabulary Drills</u>

A.   Transformation Drill

        Instructor: We didn't come yesterday.
        Student: We couldn't get here.

lo bánu etmól.	lo yaxólnu lehagía.	לא באנו אתמול.
lo bátem etmól.	lo yaxóltem lehagía.	לא באתם אתמול.
lo báti etmól.	lo yaxólti lehagía.	לא באתי אתמול.
lo báta etmól.	lo yaxólta lehagía.	לא באת אתמול.
lo bát etmól.	lo yaxólt lehagía.	לא באת אתמול.
lo báten etmól.	lo yaxólten lehagía.	לא באתן אתמול.

B.   Substitution Drill

        Please pour the wine.

mezóg bevakašá et hayáin.	מזוג בבקשה את היין.
mizgí	מזגי
mizgú	מזגו
mezógna	מזוגנה

GRAMMAR NOTES

12.4 Cardinal Numbers with Nouns

a)   Note in the following example that the number precedes the noun that is
quantified.

lexí ke<u>arbaá</u> rexovót.   "Go about four blocks."

     With the exception of /exád, axát/ "one" which follow the noun, the
cardinal numbers precede the noun.

/yóm exád/   "one day"
/šlošá yamím/   "three days"

b)   The number /šnáim, štáim/ "two" has the alternate forms /šnéy, štey/
when preceding the quantified noun.

/šnéy avironím/   "two airplanes"
/štéy oniót/   "two ships"

     Compare, on the other hand, the following:

/lí yéš šnéy sfarím,   "I have a book,
vegám ló yéš šnáim./   and he has two, also."

c)   In certain stereotyped expressions the singular form of the noun is
          used after numbers higher than ten.

/éser šaním/   "ten years"
/esrím šaná/   "twenty years"

d)   When the noun is definite the preceding number is treated as a construct
state noun itself. The masculine numbers "three" to "ten" have the alternate
forms listed below.
Compare then:
/
/šlošá batím/   "three houses"
/šlóšet habatím/   "the three houses"

     Some feminine numbers have alternate forms in formal speech, but
otherwise they do not. However, many speakers use the alternate, construct-
state form of the masculine numbers before feminine nouns which are definite.

/šalóš oniót/   "three ships"
/šlóšet haoniót/   "the three ships"

     It should be remembered that there is wide variation in the use of
numbers.

the three...	/šlóšet ha-/
the four...	/arbáat ha-/
the five...	/xaméšet ha-/
the six...	/šéšet ha-/
the seven...	/šiv'át ha-/
the eight...	/šmonát ha-/
the nine...	/tiš'át ha-/
the ten...	/aséret ha-/

In the following drills some new plurals are introduced.
Note that some masculine plural nouns end in /-ót/ and some feminine
plural nouns in /-ím/.

A. Transformation Drill - Student adds one.

       Instructor: I have one table.
       Student: I have two tables.

yéš lí šulxán exád.	yéš lí šnéy šulxanót.	יש לי שולחן אחד.
yéš lí šnéy šulxanót.	yéš lí šlošá šulxanót.	יש לי שני שולחנות.
yéš lí šlošá šulxanót.	yéš lí arbaá šulxanót.	יש לי שלושה שולחנות.
yéš lí arbaá šulxanót.	yéš lí xamišá šulxanót.	יש לי ארבעה שולחנות.
yéš lí xamišá šulxanót.	yéš lí šišá šulxanót.	יש לי חמשה שולחנות.
yéš lí šišá šulxanót.	yéš lí šiv'á šulxanót.	יש לי ששה שולחנות.
yéš lí šiv'á šulxanót.	yéš lí šmoná šulxanót.	יש לי שבעה שולחנות.
yéš lí šmoná šulxanót.	yéš lí tiš'á šulxanót.	יש לי שמונה שולחנות.
yéš lí tiš'á šulxanót.	yéš lí asará šulxanót.	יש לי תשעה שולחנות.

B. Transformation Drill - Repeat Drill A in reverse. Student subtracts one.

       Instructor: yéš lí asará šulxanót.   מורה: יש לי עשרה שולחנות.
       Student: yéš lí tiš'á šulxanót.   תלמיד: יש לי תשעה שולחנות.

The instructor may vary Drills A and B by selecting numbers at random.

C. Transformation Drill - Student adds one.

       Instructor: We want to see one big city.
       Student: We want to see two big cities.

ánu rocím lir'ót ír axát gdolá.	אנו רוצים לראות עיר אחת גדולה.
ánu rocím lir'ót štéy arím gdolót.	
ánu rocím lir'ót štéy arím gdolót.	אנו רוצים לראות שתי ערים גדולות.
ánu rocím lir'ót šalóš arím gdolót.	
ánu rocím lir'ót šalóš arím gdolót.	אנו רוצים לראות שלוש ערים גדולות.
ánu rocím lir'ót árba arím gdolót.	
ánu rocím lir'ót árba arím gdolót.	אנו רוצים לראות ארבע ערים גדולות.
ánu rocím lir'ót xaméš arím gdolót.	
ánu rocím lir'ót xaméš arím gdolót.	אנו רוצים לראות חמש ערים גדולות.
ánu rocím lir'ót šéš arím gdolót.	
ánu rocím lir'ót šéš arím gdolót.	אנו רוצים לראות שש ערים גדולות.
ánu rocím lir'ót šéva arím gdolót.	
ánu rocím lir'ót šéva arím gdolót.	אנו רוצים לראות שבע ערים גדולות.
ánu rocím lir'ót šmóne arím gdolót.	
ánu rocím lir'ót šmóne arím gdolót.	אנו רוצים לראות שמונה ערים גדולות.
ánu rocím lir'ót téša arím gdolót.	
ánu rocím lir'ót téša arím gdolót.	אנו רוצים לראות תשע ערים גדולות.
ánu rocím lir'ót éser arím gdolót.	

D. Transformation Drill - Repeat Drill C in reverse. Student subtracts one.

> Instructor: ánu rocím lir'ót éser arím gdolót.
> Student: ánu rocím lir'ót téša arím gdolót.

The instructor may vary Drills C and D by selecting numbers at random.

E. Transformation Drill - Student totals numbers.

> Instructor: I have four books, and he has seven.
> Student: We have eleven books.

lí yéš arbaá sfarím, veló yéš šiv'á.	לי יש ארבעה ספרים, ולו יש שבעה.
yéš lánu axádasár sfarím.	יש לנו אחד-עשר ספרים.
lí yéš šmoná sfarím, veló yéš arbaá.	לי יש שמונה ספרים, ולו יש ארבעה.
yéš lánu snéymasar sfarím.	יש לנו שנים-עשר ספרים.
lí yéš asará sfarim, veló yéš šlošá.	לי יש עשרה ספרים, ולו יש שלושה.
yéš lánu šlošáasar sfarím.	יש לנו שלושה-עשר ספרים.
lí yéš šmoná sfarím, veló yéš šišá.	לי יש שמונה ספרים, ולו יש ששה.
yéš lánu arbáasar sfarím.	יש לנו ארבעה-עשר ספרים.
lí yéš séfer exád, veló yéš arbáasar.	לי יש ספר אחד, ולו יש ארבעה-עשר.
yéš lánu xamišáasar sfarím.	יש לנו חמשה-עשר ספרים.
lí yéš tiš'á sfarím, veló yéš šiv'á.	לי יש תשעה ספרים, ולו יש שבעה.
yéš lánu šišáasar sfarím.	יש לנו ששה-עשר ספרים.
lí yéš šmoná sfarím, veló yéš tiš'á.	לי יש שמונה ספרים, ולו יש תשעה.
yéš lánu šiváasar sfarím.	יש לנו שבעה-עשר ספרים.
lí yéš asará sfarím, veló yéš šmoná.	לי יש עשרה ספרים, ולו יש שמונה.
yéš lánu šmonáasar sfarím.	יש לנו שמונה-עשר ספרים.
lí yéš axádasar sfarím, veló yéš šmoná.	לי יש אחד-עשר ספרים, ולו יש שמונה.
yéš lánu tišáasar sfarím.	יש לנו תשעה-עשר ספרים.
lí yéš šlošáasár sfarím veló yéš šiv'á.	לי יש שלושה-עשר ספרים, ולו יש שבעה.
yéš lánu esrím sfarím.	יש לנו עשרים ספרים.

F. Transformation Drill - Student total numbers.

> Instructor: I saw four women speaking Hebrew,
>   and you saw seven.
> Student We saw eleven women speaking Hebrew.

aní raíti árba naším medabrót ivrít,	אני ראיתי ארבע נשים מדברות עברית,
veatá raíta šéva.	ואתה ראית שבע.
raínu axát'esre naším medabrót ivrít.	(אחת-עשרה)
aní raíti šmóne naším medabrót ivrit,	אני ראיתי שמונה נשים מדברות עברית,
veatá raíta árba.	ואתה ראית ארבע.
raínu štéym'esre naším medabrót ivrit.	(שתים-עשרה)
aní raíti išá axát medabéret ivrít,	אני ראיתי אשה אחת מדברת עברית,
veatá raíta štéym'esre.	ואתה ראית שתים-עשרה.
raínu šlóš'esre naším medabrót ivrít.	(שלוש-עשרה)
aní raíti xaméš naším medabrót ivrít,	אני ראיתי חמש נשים מדברות עברית,
veatá raíta téša.	ואתה ראית תשע.
raínu arbá'esre naším medabrót ivrít.	(ארבע-עשרה)
aní raíti éser naším medabrót ivrít,	אני ראיתי עשר נשים מדברות עברית,
veatá raíta xaméš.	ואתה ראית חמש.
raínu xaméš'esre naším medabrót ivrít.	(חמש-עשרה)
aní raíti xaméš'esre naším medabrót ivrít,	אני ראיתי חמש-עשרה נשים מדברות עברית,
veatá raíta axát.	ואתה ראית אחת.
raínu šéš'esre naším medabrót ivrít.	(שש-עשרה)

aní raíti téša naším medabrót ivrít,
          veatá raíta šmoné.
raínu švaesre naším medabrót ivrít.
aní raíti šmóne naším medabrót ivrít,
          veatá raíta éser.
raínu šmonáesre naším medabrót ivrít.
aní raíti šlóšesre naším medabrót ivrít,
          veatá raíta šéš.
raínu tšaesre naším medabrót ivrít.
aní raíti švaesré naším medabrót ivrít,
          veatá raíta šalóš.
raínu esrím naším medabrót ivrít.

אני ראיתי תשע נשים מדברות עברית,
ואתה ראית שמונה.
(שבע-עשרה)
אני ראיתי שמונה נשים מדברות עברית,
ואתה ראית עשר.
(שמונה-עשרה)
אני ראיתי שלוש-עשרה נשים מדברות עברית,
ואתה ראית שש.
(תשע-עשרה)
אני ראיתי שבע-עשרה נשים מדברות עברית,
ואתה ראית שלוש.
(עשרים)

G. Transformation Drill

    Instructor: We have two books.
    Student: Give us the two books.

מורה: יש לנו שני ספרים.
תלמיד: תנו לנו את שני הספרים.

yéš lánu šnéy sfarím.
       tnú lánu et šnéy hasfarím.
yéš lánu šlóšá sfarím.
       tnú lánu et šlóšet hasfarím.
yéš lánu arbaá sfarím.
       tnú lánu et arbáat hasfarím.
yéš lánu xamišá sfarím.
       tnú lánu et xaméšet hasfarím.
yéš lánu šišá sfarím.
       tnú lánu et šéšet hasfarím.
yéš lánu šiv'á sfarím.
       tnú lánu et šiv'át hasfarím.
yés lánu šmoná sfarím.
       tnú lánu et šmonát hasfarím.
yéš lánu tiš'á sfarím.
       tnú lánu et tiš'át hasfarím.
yéš lánu asará sfarím.
       tnú lánu et aséret hasfarím.

יש לנו שני ספרים.
תנו לנו את שני הספרים.
יש לנו שלושה ספרים.
תנו לנו את שלושה הספרים.
יש לנו ארבעה ספרים.
תנו לנו את ארבעת הספרים.
יש לנו חמשה ספרים.
תנו לנו את חמשת הספרים.
יש לנו ששה ספרים.
תנו לנו את ששת הספרים.
יש לנו שבעה ספרים.
תנו לנו את שבעת הספרים.
יש לנו שמונה ספרים.
תנו לנו את שמונת הספרים.
יש לנו תשעה ספרים.
תנו לנו את תשעת הספרים.
יש לנו עשרה ספרים.
תנו לנו את עשרת הספרים.

H. Transformation Drill

    Instructor: Yesterday I saw two ships.
    Student: Where did you see the two ships?

etmól raíti štéy oniót.
       éyfo raíta et štéy haoniót.
etmól raíti šalóš oniót.
       éyfo raíta et šlóšet haoniót.
etmól raíti árba oniót.
       éyfo raíta et arbáat haoniót.
etmól raíti xaméš oniót.
       éyfo raíta et xaméšet haoniót.
etmól raíti šéš oniót.
       éyfo raíta et šéšet haoniót.
etmól raíti šéva oniót.
       éyfo raíta et šiv'át haoniót.
etmól raíti šmóne oniót.
       éyfo raíta et šmonát haoniót.
etmól raíti téša oniót.
       éyfo raíta et tiš'át haoniót.
etmól raíti éser oniót.
       éyfo raíta et aséret haoniót.

אתמול ראיתי שתי אוניות.
איפה ראית את שתי האוניות?
אתמול ראיתי שלוש אוניות.
איפה ראית את שלושה האוניות?
אתמול ראיתי ארבע אוניות.
איפה ראית את ארבעת האוניות?
אתמול ראיתי חמש אוניות.
איפה ראית את חמשת האוניות?
אתמול ראיתי שש אוניות.
איפה ראית את ששת האוניות?
אתמול ראיתי שבע אוניות.
איפה ראית את שבעת האוניות?
אתמול ראיתי שמונה אוניות.
איפה ראית את שמונת האוניות?
אתמול ראיתי תשע אוניות.
איפה ראית את תשעת האוניות?
אתמול ראיתי עשר אוניות.
איפה ראית את עשרת האוניות?

12.5 Ordinal Numbers

a) The ordinal numbers are adjectives. The numbers from "second" to "tenth" have forms resembling the corresponding cardinal numbers. Ordinal numbers "eleventh" and higher are identical in form to the corresponding cardinal numbers, but they follow the noun as adjectives.

	Masculine	Feminine	זכר	נקבה
first	rišón	rišoná	ראשון	ראשונה
second	šení	šniá	שני	שניה
third	šliší	šlišít	שלישי	שלישית
fourth	revií	reviít	רביעי	רביעית
fifth	xamiší	xamišít	חמישי	חמישית
sixth	šiší	šišít	שישי	שישית
seventh	švií	šviít	שביעי	שביעית
eighth	šminí	šminít	שמיני	שמינית
ninth	tšií	tšiít	תשיעי	תשיעית
tenth	asirí	asirít	עשירי	עשירית
eleventh	axád'asar	axát'esre	אחד-עשר	אחת עשרה
twelfth	šnéym'asar	štéym'esre	שנים-עשר	שתים עשרה
etc.				

b) The names of the days of the week are proper nouns. Thus, the following distinction is made.

/beyóm rišón/   "on Sunday"
/bayóm harišón/   "on the first day"

The ordinal number may be used with the name of the day.

/beyóm rišón harišón/   "on the first Sunday"

/šabát/ often has the definite article when modified.

/hašabát harišoná/   "the first Saturday"

A. Transformation Drill

       Instructor: Go four blocks.
       Student: Turn right at the fourth street.

léx arbaá rexovót.	barexóv harevií pné yamína.	לך ארבעה רחובות.
léx šnéy rexovót.	barexóv hašení pné yamína.	לך שני רחובות.
léx šlošá rexovót.	barexóv hašliší pné yamína.	לך שלושה רחובות.
léx šišá rexovót.	barexóv hašiší pné yamína.	לך שישה רחובות.
léx šmoná rexovót.	barexóv hašminí pné yamína.	לך שמונה רחובות.
léx asará rexovót.	barexóv haasirí pné yamína.	לך עשרה רחובות.
léx xamišá rexovót.	barexóv haxamiší pné yamína.	לך חמישה רחובות.
léx šiv'á rexovót.	barexóv hašvií pné yamína.	לך שבעה רחובות.
léx tiš'á rexovót.	barexóv hatšií pné yamína.	לך תשעה רחובות.

This drill may be varied by making it an expansion drill.

       Instructor: léx arbaá rexovót.   לך ארבעה רחובות,
       Student: léx arbaá rexovót, ubarexóv   לך ארבעה רחובות וברחוב
               harevií pné yemína.   הרביעי פנה ימינה.

B. Transformation Drill

Instructor: Go four blocks.
Student: Turn left at the fourth corner.

lexí arbaá rexovót.	bapiná hareviít pní smóla.	לכי ארבעה רחובות.
lexí asará rexovót.	bapiná haasirít pní smóla.	לכי עשרה רחובות.
lexí šnéy rexovót.	bapiná hašniá pní smóla.	לכי שני רחובות.
lexí šlošá rexovót.	bapiná hašlišít pní smóla.	לכי שלושה רחובות.
lexí xamišá rexovót.	bapiná haxamišít pní smóla.	לכי חמישה רחובות.
lexí šmoná rexovót.	bapiná hašminít pní smóla.	לכי שמונה רחובות.
lexí šišá rexovót.	bapiná hašišít pní smóla.	לכי שישה רחובות.
lexí šiv'á rexovót.	bapiná hašviít pní smóla.	לכי שבעה רחובות.
lexí tiš'á rexovót.	bapiná hatšiít pní smóla.	לכי תשעה רחובות.

This drill may be varied by may be varied by making it an expansion drill.

Instructor: lexí arbaá rexovót.
Student: lexí arbaá rexovót, ubapiná hareviít
          pní smóla.

C. Transformation Drill

Instructor: He lives eleven blocks from here.
Student: Go up to the eleventh street.

hú gár axád'asar rexovót mikán.	הוא גר אחד-עשר רחובות מכאן.
léx ád harexóv haaxád'asar.	לך עד הרחוב האחד-עשר.
hú gár šnéym'asar rexovót mikán.	הוא גר שנים-עשר רחובות מכאן.
léx ád harexóv hašnéym'asar.	לך עד הרחוב השנים-עשר.
hú gár šlošáasar rexovót mikán.	הוא גר שלושה-עשר רחובות מכאן.
léx ád harexóv hašlošáasar.	לך עד הרחוב השלושה-עשר.
hú gár arbáasar rexovót mikán.	הוא גר ארבעה-עשר רחובות מכאן.
léx ád harexóv haarbáasar.	לך עד הרחוב הארבעה-עשר.
hú gár xamišáasar rexovót mikán.	הוא גר חמישה-עשר רחובות מכאן.
léx ád harexóv haxamišáasar.	לך עד הרחוב החמישה-עשר.
hú gár šišáasar rexovót mikán.	הוא גר שישה-עשר רחובות מכאן.
léx ád harexóv hašišáasar.	לך עד הרחוב השישה-עשר.
hú gár šiváasar rexovót mikán.	הוא גר שבעה-עשר רחובות מכאן.
léx ád harexóv hašiváasar.	לך עד הרחוב השבעה-עשר.
hú gár šmonáasar rexovót mikán.	הוא גר שמונה-עשר רחובות מכאן.
léx ád harexóv hašmonáasar.	לך עד הרחוב השמונה-עשר.
hú gár tišáasar rexovót mikán.	הוא גר תשעה-עשר רחובות מכאן.
léx ád harexóv hatišáasar.	לך עד הרחוב התשיעה-עשר.
hú gár esrím rexovót mikán.	הוא גר עשרים רחובות מכאן.
léx ád harexóv haesrím.	לך עד הרחוב העשרים.

D. Expansion Drill

> Instructor: <u>Yesterday I saw ten ships.</u>
>
> Student: Yesterday I saw ten ships
> and today I saw the eleventh ship.

etmól raíti éser oniót.　　　　　　　　　　　　　1. אתמול ראיתי עשר אוניות.
　vehayóm raíti et haoniá haaxát'esre.　　　　　והיום ראיתי את האוניה האחת-עשרה.
etmól raíti axát'esre oniót.　　　　　　　　　　2. אתמול ראיתי אחת-עשרה אוניות.
　vehayóm raíti et haoniá haštéym'esre.　　　　והיום ראיתי את האוניה השתים-עשרה.
etmól raíti štéym'esre oniót.　　　　　　　　　3. אתמול ראיתי שתים-עשרה אוניות.
　vehayóm raíti et haoniá hašlóš'esre.　　　　　והיום ראיתי את האוניה השלוש-עשרה.
etmól raíti šlóš'esre oniót.　　　　　　　　　　4. אתמול ראיתי שלוש-עשרה אוניות.
　vehayóm raíti et haoniá haarbá'esre.　　　　　והיום ראיתי את האוניה הארבע-עשרה.
etmól raíti arbá'esre oniót.　　　　　　　　　　5. אתמול ראיתי ארבע-עשרה אוניות.
　vehayóm raíti et haoniá haxaméš'esre.　　　　והיום ראיתי את האוניה החמש-עשרה.
etmól raíti xaméš'esre oniót.　　　　　　　　　6. אתמול ראיתי חמש-עשרה אוניות.
　vehayóm raíti et haoniá hašéš'esre.　　　　　והיום ראיתי את האוניה השש-עשרה.
etmól raíti šéš'esre oniót.　　　　　　　　　　7. אתמול ראיתי שש-עשרה אוניות.
　vehayóm raíti et haoniá hašvá'esre.　　　　　והיום ראיתי את האוניה השבע-עשרה.
etmól raíti švá'esre oniót.　　　　　　　　　　8. אתמול ראיתי שבע-עשרה אוניות.
　vehayóm raíti et haoniá hašmóne'esre.　　　　והיום ראיתי את האוניה השמונה-עשרה.
etmól raíti šmóne'esre oniót.　　　　　　　　　9. אתמול ראיתי שמונה-עשרה אוניות.
　vehayóm raíti et haoniá hatšá'esre.　　　　　והיום ראיתי את האוניה התשע-עשרה.
etmól raíti tšá'esre oniót.　　　　　　　　　　10. אתמול ראיתי תשע-עשרה אוניות.
　vehayóm raíti et haoniá haesrím.　　　　　　　והיום ראיתי את האוניה העשרים.

E. Expansion Drill

> Instructor: I live in the second house from
> the corner.
>
> Student: I live in the second house from
> the corner, and Hanna lives in
> the third house.

aní gár babáit hašení mehapiná.　　　　　　　　1. אני גר בבית השני מהפינה.
　vexána gára babáit hašliši.　　　　　　　　　וחנה גרה בבית השלישי.
aní gár babáit harevií mehapiná.　　　　　　　2. אני גר בבית הרביעי מהפינה.
　vexána gára babáit haxamiší.　　　　　　　　וחנה גרה בבית החמישי.
aní gár babáit hašiší mehapiná.　　　　　　　　3. אני גר בבית הששי מהפינה.
　vexána gára babáit hašvií.　　　　　　　　　　וחנה גרה בבית השביעי.
aní gár babáit hašmini mehapiná.　　　　　　　4. אני גר בבית השמיני מהפינה.
　vexána gára babáit hatšií.　　　　　　　　　　וחנה גרה בבית התשיעי.
aní gár babáit haasirí mehapiná.　　　　　　　5. אני גר בבית העשירי מהפינה.
　vexána gára babáit haaxádasar.　　　　　　　וחנה גרה בבית האחד-עשר.

<u>REVIEW CONVERSATIONS</u>

A: šalóm avígdor. matáy higátem letél avív.   א: שלום אביגדור. מתי הגעתם לתל אביב?

B: higánu beyóm rišón.   ב: הגענו ביום ראשון.

A: ánu rocím lehazmín otxém learuxát   א: אנו רוצים להזמין אתכם לארוחת
    cohoráim.   צהריים.

B: nismáx meód. lematáy?   ב: נשמח מאוד. למתי?

A: lehayóm. haím štéymesre mat'ím?   א: להיום. האם שתים-עשרה מתאים?

B: kén. behexlét.   ב: כן, בהחלט.

C: háva nigáš lašulxán.   ג: הבה ניגש לשולחן.

D: ló, todá. kvár meuxár.   ד: לא, תודה. כבר מאוחד.

C: éyx atém yexolím lesarév?   ג: איך אתם יכולים לסרב?

D: slixá. ánu muxraxím larúc.   ד: סליחה, אנו מוכרחים לדוץ.

E: šim'í, miryám. át memahéret?   ה: שמעי, מרים, את ממהרת?

F: ló. ló kol káx.   ו: לא. לא כל כך.

E: háva nigáš lebrúklin bár.   ה: הבה ניגש לברוקלין בר.

F: tóv. haglída šám tová.   ו: טוב. הגלידה שם טובה.

13.1 Friday Evening Dinner (cont'd)

MRS. WILLIAMS

The fish	hadagím	הדגים
is wonderful,	nehedarím.	נהדרים,
and so is the <u>chalah</u>.	vexén haxalá.	וכן החלה.
fish	dág (m)	דג
wonderful	nehedár (m.s.)	נהדר
and so	vexén	וכן
<u>chalah</u> (twist bread)	xalá (f)	חלה

MRS. CASPI

Thank you very much.	todá rabá.	תודה רבה.

MRS. WILLIAMS

Mrs. Caspi,	gvéret káspi,	גברת כספי,
you must	át muxraxá	את מוכרחה
give me	latét lí	לתת לי
the recipe	et hamiršám	את המרשם
for the fish.	ladagím.	לדגים.
to give	latét	לתת
recipe	miršám (m)	מרשם

MRS. CASPI

Gladly.	beracón	ברצון
I'll give you	etén láx	אתן לך
the recipe,	et hamiršám,	את המרשם,
Mrs. Williams.	gvéret Williams.	גברת ווילאמס.
desire,	racón (m)	רצון
willingly	beracón	ברצון
I will give	etén (1 s.)	אתן

It's a tradition	zú masóret	זו מסורת
in our homes	eclénu babáit,	אצלנו בבית
to eat	leexól	לאכול
on Friday evening	belél šiší	בליל שישי
<u>gefilte</u> fish.	dagím memulaím.	דגים ממולאים.
it, this	zú (f)	זו
tradition	masóret (f)	מסורת
filled	memulá	ממולא

MRS. WILLIAMS

Mrs. Caspi,	gvéret káspi.	גברת כספי,
please,	bevakašá	בבקשה
don't give me	ál titní li	אל תתני לי
any more to eat.	yotér óxel.	יותר אוכל.
more	yotér	יותר
food	óxel (m)	אוכל

MRS. CASPI

But	haréy	הרי
you haven't eaten	ló axáltem	לא אכלתם
anything.	klúm.	כלום.

	I ate	axálti	אכלתי
	nothing	ló...klúm	לא...כלום

MRS. WILLIAMS

I'm on a diet.	aní bediéta.	אני בדיאטה.
diet	diéta (f)	דיאטה

The food was	haóxel hayá	האוכל היה
very delicious.	taím meód.	טעים מאד.

	was	hayá (3 m.s.)	היה
	delicious, tasty	taím (m.s.)	טעים

MRS. CASPI

Thank you.	todá rabá.	תודה רבה.

MRS. WILLIAMS

I'll start	atxíl	אתחיל
on my diet	badiéta šelí	בדיאטה שלי
tomorrow.	maxár.	מחר.

	I will begin	atxíl (1 s.)	אתחיל

13.2 ADDITIONAL VOCABULARY

He will give her	hú yitén lá	הוא יתן לה את המירשם.
the recipe.	et hamiršám.	
She will give her	hí titén lá	היא תתן לה את המירשם.
the recipe.	et hamiršám.	
We will give her	nitén lá	ניתן לה את המירשם.
the recipe.	et hamiršám.	
They (m) will give her	hém yitnú lá	הם יתנו לה את המירשם.
the recipe.	et hamiršám.	
They (f) will give here	hén titénna lá	הן תיתנה לה את המירשם.
the recipe.	et hamiršám.	

The meal was	haaruxá haytá	הארוחה היתה טעימה מאד.
very delicious.	teíma meód.	

The fish was	hadagím hayú	הדגים היו טעימים מאד.
very tasty.	teimím meód.	

The chalahs were	haxalót hayú	החלות היו טעימות מאד.
very tasty.	teimót meód.	

13.3 Vocabulary Drills

The adjective /memulá/ is similar to /nimcá/ "is found" in the pattern of its forms.

m.s.	memulá	f.s.	memulét	ממולאת	ממולא
m.pl.	memulaím				ממולאים
f.pl.	memulaót				ממולאות

Note that in the Hebrew spelling the third root consonant is א , as in /nimcá/ נמצא.

The adjective /nehedár/ is also similar to /nimcá/. The feminine singular has a /-t/ suffix with change of vowel.

m.s.	nehedár	f.s.	nehedéret	נהדרת	נהדר
m.pl.	nehedarím				נהדרים
f.pl.	nehedarót				נהדרות

A. Substitution Drill - Masculine Singular

The house is wonderful.

habáit nehedár.	.הבית נהדר
hamalón	המלון
hayám	הים
binyán hadóar	בנין הדואר
atá	אתה
hú	הוא
nemál hateufá	נמל התעופה

B. Substitution Drill - Feminine Singular

The chalah is wonderful.

haxalá nehedéret.	.החלה נהדרת
haárec	הארץ
haglidá	הגלידה
rámat gán	רמת גן
hí	היא
miryám	מרים
dálya	דליה
sfát hayám	שפת הים
haaruxá	הארוחה

C. Substitution Drill - Masculine Plural

The fish is wonderful.

hadagím nehedarím.	.הדגים נהדרים
atém	אתם
harexovót	הרחובות
hayeynót	היינות
habatím	הבתים
hašulxanót	השולחנות
kulám	כולם
hayamím	הימים

D. Substitution Drill - Feminine Plural

The _chalahs_ are wonderful.

haxalót nehedarót.	החלות נהדרות.
hatocaót	התוצאות
atén	אתן
haaracót	הארצות
hanaším	הנשים
hamišpaxót	המשפחות
haglidót	הגלידות

E. Substitution - Agreement Drill - /nehedár/

The country is wonderful.

haárec nehedéret.	הארץ נהדרת.
hamisrád	המשרד
haxalá	החלה
hadagím	הדגים
hayáin	היין
atém	אתם
hatocaót	התוצאות
hamišpaxá	המשפחה
haanaším	האנשים
hamisradím	המשרדים
habatím	הבתים
haoniót	האוניות
hamlonót	המלונות
haaruxót	הארוחות

F. Substitution - Agreement Drill - /axálti/ "I ate"

I haven't eaten breakfast yet.

adáin ló axálti aruxát bóker.	עדיין לא אכלתי ארוחת בוקר.
áta - át - ánu - atém	אתה - את - אנו - אתם
aní veiští - atén - aní	אני ואשתי - אתן - אני

End of Tape 4A

GRAMMAR NOTES

13.4 Consonant Alternation /k ~ x/

The consonant /k/ often alternates with /x/ when not initial in the
word.

/kén/   'so, yes'
/vexén/   'and so'

This alternation occurs in a number of forms and is characteristic of roots
in certain verb patterns. In other cases it is optional, with the /x/-form
usually the more formal in style.

/lekán ~ lexán/   "to here"

This alternation is similar to that of /b ~ v/ described in Grammar Note
5.6. The alternation is always spelled in Hebrew with the ambiguous letter
כ , and not with ק and ח .

13.5 Formation of the Future Tense

As has been noted in the description of the gentle imperative, Grammar
Section 6.5, the second person future forms of verbs have a prefix of the
pattern /tV-/.

Examples are:

/tifné/ "you will turn   /teléx/ "you will go"
/tigmór/ "you will finish"   /tedabér/ "you will speak"

/tamšíx/ "you will continue"/tomár/ "you will say"
/taavór/ "you will pass"

(Some verbs have /u/ as the prefix vowel, though none have occurred in
this text so far.)

Compare now the first person plural forms which have occurred so far:
nimcá et hamakóm leló kóši.
háva niqáš lašulxán.
nitén lá et hamiršám.

Note that these all begin with a prefix of the pattern /nV-/. (By
coincidence the vowel of the prefix in the three examples is /-i-/.) Thus it
may be seen that the future tense of verbs consists of a stem plus prefixes
to distinguish person, gender, and number. Some of the forms have suffixes,
also.

/titén/   "you (m.s.) will give"
/titní/   "you (f.s.) will give
/titnú/   "you (m.pl.) will give"
/titénna/ "you (f.pl.) will give"

These second person forms have been described in the section on the
gentle imperatives. The forms of the entire future tense of this verb are
shown in the following table:

111

1 s.	etén	1 pl.	nitén
2 m.s.	titén	2 m.pl.	titnú
2 f.s.	titní	2 f.pl.	titénna
3 m.s.	yitén	3 m.pl.	yitnú
3 f.s.	titén	3 f.pl.	titénna

Extracting the stem /tén/, the pattern of prefixes and suffixes in the future tense is as follows:

[Note: The stem appears as /-tn-/ before the suffixes /-í, -ú/. See Grammar Note 6.9.]

1.s.	e____	1 pl.	ni____
2 m.s.	ti____	2 m.pl.	ti____ú
2 f.s.	ti___í	2 f.pl.	ti____na
3 m.s.	yi____	3 m.pl.	yi____ú
3 f.s.	ti____	3 f.pl.	ti___na

The following observations may be made which are characteristic of the future tense of all verbs:

a. There is no gender distinction in the first person. (This is true of the past tense forms, also. See Grammar Note 5.4)

b. The 2 m.s. and the 3 f.s. are identical in form.

c. The 2 f.pl. and the 3 f.pl. are identical in form. In some patterns these two forms have a different stem vowel from that in the other future tense forms - /tamšíxi, tamšéxna/; /tagíi, tagána/. See Vocabulary Drill, Section 10.3.

The following are general comments about the future tense:

d. The first person singular prefix is simply a vowel. In some verb patterns it is the same vowel as in the other prefixes. This is always so when the vowel is /o/ or /u/.
In other verb patterns the vowel of the first person singular is different from that of the other prefixes. At this point the student will have to drill the verbs in order to memorize which ones have a different vowel. Verbs showing possible alternations have occurred in the text. Examples are:

Alternation	1 s.	2 m.s.
/e- ~ ti-/	egmór	tigmór
/ee- ~ taa-/	eevór	taavór
/a- ~ te-/	adabér	tedabér

Nevertheless, one frequently hears these first person singular forms with the same prefix vowel as in the rest of the future tense - e.g., /edabér/ as well as /adabér/.

When the first person singular prefix has a different vowel it will be noted in the drills.

e. The suffixes /-i, -u/ are not stressed in the following cases:
   1. When the stem vowel is /-í/: /tamšíxi, tamšíxu, yamšíxu/
   2. When the stem has the pattern /CúC/: /taqúri, taqúru, yaqúru/ "will reside"
   3. In a small list of other verbs. Example: /tavói, tavóu, yavóu/ "will come"

f. Verbs such as /nimcá/ "we will find" have an internal open juncture as a third root consonant. At the end of a word it is, of course, not pronounced. Before the suffixes /-í, -ú/ it creates a three-consonant cluster which is broken up by the insertion of /-e-/.

/timcá/   "you (m.s.) will find"
/timce'í/   "you (f.s.) will find"
/timce'ú/   "you (m.pl.) will find"
/yimce'ú/   "they (m) will find"

The juncture is usually replaced by a smooth transition in ordinary speech. /timceí/, etc.

g. Some verbs have a more complicated future tense pattern, but these have been described generally in the note on the gentle imperative. The full set of future tense forms may be derived from the gentle imperative by substitution of prefixes.

Example:
From 2 m.s. /tagía/ the following may be derived /agía, yagía, nagía/.
The 3 f.s. /tagía/ is identical in form with the 2 m.s.
From 2 m.pl. /tagíu/ the 3 m.pl. /yagíu/ may be derived.
The 3 f.pl. /tagána/ is identical to the 2 f.pl., as in all verbs.

13.6 Use of the Future Tense

a. The future tense is used to indicate an occurrence later in time than the present moment. This often corresponds to the English construction "will_____".

   1. hamišpaxá šelí <u>taqía</u>   "My family <u>will arrive</u>
      beód kexódeš yamím.   in about a month."

In an included sentence it often corresponds to the simple English verb.

   2. axaréy <u>šetiqmór</u> et haglidá, "After <u>you finish</u> the ice cream
      tamšíx yašar lekivún hayám.   continue towards the sea."

Other sentences which illustrate its use and the corresponding English are:

   3. amárta lí <u>šeatxíl</u> maxár.   "You said that <u>I would begin</u>
                               tomorrow."

4.   amárnu ló šeyedabér   "We told him that <u>he should speak</u>
      ivrít beisraél.   Hebrew in Israel."

b.   The third person forms generally occur with an independent subject
    unless one is stated in a closely preceding context.

    hú yitén lá et hamiršám.
    amartí <u>ló</u> šeyitén lá et hamiršám.

    Independent pronoun subjects may be used with the first and second person
forms for emphasis, contrast, etc. Compare this with the similar use of
independent pronouns with past tense forms. See Grammar Note 5.4.

    aní eléx maxár,   "I'll go tomorrow,
    veatá teléx beyóm šení.   and you'll go on Monday."

c.   The negative of the future tense is formed by using /ló/ before the
    verb. In the second person this will contrast with the negative
    imperative in which /ál/ is used.

    ló telxí hayóm.   "You won't go today."
    ál telxí hayóm.   "Don't go today."

Tape 4B

A.   Substitution Drill - /e- ~ ti-/

    I'll give the recipe to Miriam.

aní etén et hamiršám lemiryám.	.אני אתן את המירשם למרים
atá titén	אתה תיתן
át titní	את תיתני
dóv yitén	דוב יתן
léa titén	לאה תיתן
ánu nitén	אנו ניתן
atém titnú	אתם תיתנו
atén titénna	אתן תיתנה
hém yitnú	הם יתנו
hén titénna	הן תיתנה

B.   Substitution - Agreement Drill

    I won't let him speak English.

<u>aní ló etén ló ledabér anglít.</u>   .<u>אני לא אתן לו לדבר אנגלית</u>

atá – ánu – yoéc hašagrirút – hí	אתה – אנו – יועץ השגרירות – היא
hén – atén – yaakóv vedóv – atém	הן – אתן – יעקב ודוב – אתם
iští veaní – át – aní	אשתי ואני – את – אני

C.   Substitution Drill - /e- ~ ti-/

    I will finish the meal.

ani egmór et haaruxá.	.אני אגמור את הארוחה
atá tigmór	אתה תגמור
át tigmerí	את תגמרי
hú yigmór	הוא יגמור
hí tigmór	היא תגמור
ánu nigmór	אנו נגמור
atém tigmerú	אתם תגמרו
atén tigmórna	אתן תגמורנה
hém yigmerú	הם יגמרו
hén tigmórna	הן תגמורנה

D.   Substitution - Agreement Drill

I'll finish the book by tomorrow.

<u>eqmór et haséfer ád maxár.</u>   <u>אגמור את הספר עד מחר.</u>

atém - már kóhen - ánu - hí	אתם - מר כהן - אנו - היא
atén - hém - át - hén	אתן - הם - את - הן
ištexá - atá - baaléx - aní	אשתך - אתה - בעלך - אני

E.   Substitution Drill - /e- ~ ti-/

I'll find the place without difficulty.

emcá et hamakóm leló kóši.	אמצא את המקום ללא קושי.
timcá	תמצא
timceí	תמצאי
hú yimcá	הוא ימצא
hí timcá	היא תמצא
nimcá	נמצא
timceú	תמצאו
timcána	תמצאנה
hém yimceú	הם ימצאו
hén timcána	הן תמצאנה

F. Substitution-Agreement Drill

You'll find Moshe in the office.

<u>timcá et mošé bamisrád.</u>   <u>תמצא את משה במשרד.</u>

át - hém - atém - hú	את - הם - אתם - הוא
aní - ánu - atén - hén	אני - אנו - אתן - הן
hí - át - atém - atá	היא - את - אתם - אתה

G.   Substitution Drill - /e- ~ ti-/

I'll go to the Brooklyn Bar to have ice cream.

egáš lebrúklin bár leexól glidá.	אגש לברוקלין בר לאכול גלידה.
tigáš	תיגש
tigší	תיגשי
davíd yigáš	דוד יגש
atára tigáš	עטרה תיגש
nigáš	ניגש
tigšú	תגשו
tigášna	תגשנה
hém yigšú	הם יגשו
hanaším tigášna	הנשים תגשנה

H. Substitution Agreement Drill

We'll go see Mr. Williams.

nigáš lir'6t et már Williams.   .ניגש לראות את מר וויליאמס

aní - át - atén - mošé		אני - את - אתן - משה
baaléx - ištó - atá - hén		בעלך - אשתו - אתה - הן
atém - dóv veištó - ánu		אתם - דוב ואשתו - אנו

I. Substitution Drill - /e- ~ ti-/

I'll be very happy to see them.

esmáx meód lir'6t otám.	.אשמח מאוד לראות אותם
tismáx	תשמח
tismexí	תשמחי
hú yismáx	הוא ישמח
hí tismáx	היא תשמח
nismáx	נשמח
tismexú	תשמחו
tismáxna	תשמחנה
hém yismexú	הם ישמחו
hén tismáxna	הן תשמחנה

J. Substitution - Agreement Drill

She'll be happy to live there.

hí tismáx lagúr šám.   .היא תשמח לגור שם

atá - ánu - hayoéc haxadáš		אתה - אנו - היועץ החדש
atém - hú veištó - atén - át		אתם - הוא ואשתו - אתן - את
aní - hamišpaxá - hén - hí		אני - המשפחה - הן - היא

K. Substitution Drill - /e- ~ ti-/

I'll turn at this corner.

aní efné bapiná hazót.	.אני אפנה בפינה הזאת
atá tifné	אתה תפנה
át tifní	את תפני
hú yifné	הוא יפנה
hí tifné	היא תפנה
ánu nifné	אנו נפנה
atém tifnú	אתם תפנו
atén tifnéna	אתן תפנינה
hém yifnú	הם יפנו
hén tifnéna	הן תפנינה

L. Substitution - Agreement Drill

We'll address Mr. Cohen in Hebrew.

nifné lemár kóhen beivrít.

נפנה למר כהן בעברית.

hú - aní - atén - gvéret kármi

הוא – אני – אתן – גברת כרמי

atém - hém - hén - atá

אתם – הם – הן – אתה

már Williams - át - ánu

מר ויליאמס – את – אנו

M. Substitution Drill - /e- ~ ti-/

I'll open the door.

eftáx et hadélet.   אפתח את הדלת.
tiftáx   תפתח
tiftexí   תפתחי
dóv yiftáx   דוב יפתח
xána tiftáx   חנה תפתח
niftáx   נפתח
atém tiftexú   אתם תפתחו
atén tiftáxna   אתן תפתחנה
hém yiftexú   הם יפתחו
hén tiftáxna   הן תפתחנה

N. Substitution - Agreement Drill

Mr. Zahavi will open the office this morning.

már zahávi yiftáx et hamisrád habóker.

מר זהבי יפתח את המשרד הבוקר.

aní - miryám vedóv - gvéret kóhen.

אני – מרים ודוב – גברת כהן

atém - sára veléa - atén - ánu

אתם – שרה ולאה – אתן – אנו

át - atá - már zahávi

את – אתה – מר זהבי

O. Substitution Drill - /e- ~ ti-/

I'll close the door.

aní esgór et hadélet.   אני אסגור את הדלת.
atá tisgór   אתה תסגור
át tisgerí   את תסגרי
dóv yisgór   דוב יסגור
léa tisgór   לאה תסגור
ánu nisgór   אנו נסגור
atém tisgerú   אתם תסגרו
atén tisgórna   אתן תסגורנה
hém yisgerú   הם יסגרו
hén tisgóina   הן תסגורנה

P. Substitution - Agreement Drill

I'll close the office this evening.

aní esgór et hamisrád haérev.

אני אסגור את המשרד הערב.

david - atá - atára - át

דוד – אתה – עטרה – את

atém - mošé veaní - hén

אתם – משה ואני – הן

hém - atén - aní

הם – אתן – אני

Q.   Substitution Drill - /ee- ~ taa-/

I'll pass the embassy.

eevór et hašagrirút.	.אעבור את השגרירות
taavór	תעבור
taavrí	תעברי
hú yaavór	הוא יעבור
hí taavór	היא תעבור
naavór	נעבור
taavrú	תעברו
taavórna	תעבורנה
hém yaavrú	הם יעברו
hén taavórna	הן תעבורנה

R.   Substitution - Agreement Drill

We'll go past their house.

<u>naavór al yád habáit šelahém.</u>   <u>.נעבור על יד הבית שלהם</u>

mošé - sára - atá veištexá - aní	משה - שרה - אתה ואשתך - אני
atén - át - hí veiští - hí vebaalá	אתן - את - היא ואשתי - היא ובעלה
atá - ánu	אתה - אנו

S.   Substitution Drill - /a- ~ te-/

I'll speak Hebrew, too.

gám aní adabér ivrít.	.גם אני אדבר עברית
atá tedabér	אתה תדבר
át tedabrí	את תדברי
hú yedabér	הוא ידבר
hi tedabér	היא תדבר
ánu nedabér	אנו נדבר
atém tedabrú	אתם תדברו
atén tedabérna	אתן תדברנה
hém yedabrú	הם ידברו
hén tedabérna	הן תדברנה

T.   Substitution - Agreement Drill

I think you'll speak Hebrew on the phone.

<u>aní xošév šeatá tedabér ivrít batélefon.</u>   <u>.אני חושב שאתה תדבר עברית בטלפון</u>

šehém - šehayoéc haxadáš - šeaní	שהם - שהיועץ החדש - שאני
šehí - šeatém - šehén - šeánu	שהיא - שאתם - שהן - שאנו
šeát vemiryám - šeát - šeatá	שאת ומרים - שאת - שאתה

118

U. Substitution Drill

I'll go to the Eden Theater this evening.

eléx lekolnóa éden haérev.	.אלך לקולנוע עדן הערב
teléx	תלך
telxí	תלכי
mošé yeléx	משה ילך
sára teléx	שרה תלך
ánu neléx	אנו נלך
telxú	תלכו
teléxna	תלכנה
kulám yelxú	כולם ילכו
hén teléxna	הן תלכנה

V. Substitution - Agreement Drill

I'll go as far as the hotel and no further.

eléx ád lamalón veló yotér.   .אלך עד למלון ולא יותר

ánu - hú - hí - atá	אנו – הוא – היא – אתה
át - atém - hém - hén	את – אתם – הם – הן
atén - aní	אתן – אני

W. Substitution Drill

I'll sit in the office until 5:00.

ešév bamisrád ád xaméš.	.אשב במשרד עד חמש
tešév	תשב
tešví	תשבי
hú yešév	הוא ישב
sára tešév	שרה תשב
nešév	נשב
tešvú	תשבו
tešévna	תשבנה
hém yešvú	הם ישבו
hén tešévna	הן תשבנה

X. Substitution - Agreement Drill

We'll sit here until he arrives.

nešév kán ád šehú yagía.   .נשב כאן עד שהוא יגיע

aní - atá - át - ištó	אני – אתה – את – אשתו
kulám - hén - ánu - atén	כולם – הן – אנו – אתן
avígdor - atém - ánu	אביגדור – אתם – אנו

119

Y. Substitution Drill

What shall I say to Moshe?

má omár lemošé.	?מה אומר למשה
tomár	תאמר
tomrí	תאמרי
hú yomár	הוא יאמר
hí tomár	היא תאמר
nomár	נאמר
tomrú	תאמרו
tomárna	תאמרנה
hém yomrú	הם יאמרו
hén tomárna	הן תאמרנה

Z. Substitution - Agreement Drill

She won't tell Moshe anything.

<u>hí ló tomár klúm lemošé.</u>   <u>היא לא תאמר כלום למשה.</u>

aní - xána - ánu - atá	אני - חנה - אנו - אתה
baaléx - atém - hém - aní	בעלך - אתם - הם - אני
atén - davíd - hén - hi	אתן - דוד - הן - היא

AA. Substitution Drill

I'll start eating before 6:00.

	atxíl leexól lifnéy šéš.	אתחיל לאכול לפני שש.
	tatxíl	תתחיל
	tatxíli	תתחילי
moše	yatxíl	משה יתחיל
xána	tatxíl	חנה תתחיל
	natxíl	נתחיל
	tatxílu	תתחילו
atén	tatxélna	אתן תתחלנה
hú veištó	yatxilu	הוא ואשתו יתחילו
hén	tatxélna	הן תתחלנה

BB. Substitution - Agreement Drill

I'll start strolling after lunch.

<u>atxíl letayél axaréy aruxát hacohoráim.</u>   <u>אתחיל לטייל אחרי ארוחת הצהריים.</u>

ánu - atá - kulám - davíd	אנו - אתה - כולם - דוד
gvéret alón - át - atén - hén	גברת אלון - את - אתן - הן
atém - iští veaní - sára - aní	אתם - אשתי ואני - שרה - אני

CC. Substitution Drill

I'll arrive in Haifa on Tuesday.

agía lexáyfa beyóm šliší.   .אגיע לחיפה ביום שלישי
tagía   חגיע
tagíi   תגיעי
már Williams yagía   מר ורילייאמס יגיע
ištó tagía   אשתו תגיע
nagía   נגיע
tagíu   תגיעו
atén tagána   אתן תגענה
hém yagíu   הם יגיעו
hén tagána   הן תגענה

DD. Substitution - Agreement Drill

I'll arrive in Tel Aviv tomorrow.

<u>agía maxár letél avív.</u>   <u>.אגיע מחר לתל אביב</u>

már kóhen - atá - hamišpaxá   מר כהן - אתה - המשפחה
át - át vebaaléx - hú veaní   את - את ובעלך - הוא ואני
hém - gverét zahávi - atén - hén - aní   הם - גברת זהבי - אתן - הן - אני

EE. Substitution Drill

I'll continue straight on this street.

amšíx yašár barexóv hazé.   .אמשיך ישר ברחוב הזה
tamšíx   תמשיך
tamšíxi   תמשיכי
hú yamšíx   הוא ימשיך
hí tamšíx   היא תמשיך
namšíx   נמשיך
tamšíxu   תמשיכו
tamšéxna   תמשכנה
hém yamšíxu   הם ימשיכו
hén tamšéxna   הן תמשכנה

FF. Substitution - Agreement Drill

We'll keep going towards the harbor.

<u>namšíx laléxet lekivún hanamál.</u>   <u>.נמשיך ללכת לכיוון הנמל</u>

aní - át - hén - hú   אני - את - הן - הוא
hém - atá - hí - atém   הם - אתה - היא - אתם
atén - ánu   אתן - אנו

REVIEW CONVERSATIONS

A: haóxel hayá taím meód.　　　　　　　　　א: האוכל היה טעים מאוד.

B: todá rabá. ló axált klúm.　　　　　　　ב: תודה רבה. לא אכלת כלום.

A: aní bediéta.　　　　　　　　　　　　　א: אני בדיאטה.

B: zé davár axér.　　　　　　　　　　　　ב: זה דבר אחר.

C: zú masóret eclénu leexól　　　　　　　ג: זו מסורת אצלנו לאכול
   belél šiší dagím memulaím.　　　　　　　בליל שישי דגים ממולאים.

D: hadagím teimím meód.　　　　　　　　ד: הדגים טעימים מאוד.

C: át rocá et hamiršám?　　　　　　　　　ג: את רוצה את המירשם?

D: kén. tní li bevakašá et hamiršám.　　ד: כן. תני לי בבקשה את המידשם.

C: beracón.　　　　　　　　　　　　　　　ג: ברצון.

E: bevakašá. ál titní lánu yotér óxel.　ה: בבקשה. אל תתני לנו יותר אוכל.

F: láma? atém bediéta?　　　　　　　　　ו: למה? אתם בדיאטה?

E: kén.　　　　　　　　　　　　　　　　　ה: כן.

F: tatxílu badiéta maxár.　　　　　　　　ו: תתחילו בדיאטה מחר.

G: atém rocím glidá?　　　　　　　　　　ז: אתם רוצים גלידה?

H: ló todá. ánu rocím yáin.　　　　　　　ח: לא תודה. אנו רוצים יין.

G: mošé. mezóg bevakašá yáin.　　　　　ז: משה. מזוג בבקשה יין.

H: mizgí át, miryám. hayáin al yadéx.　ח: מזגי את, מרים. היין על ידך.

I: dóv rocé lehazmín et már alón　　　　ט: דוב רוצה להזמין את מר אלון
   learuxát érev. matáy hú yagía.　　　　לארוחת ערב. מתי הוא יגיע?

J: hú yagía haérev.　　　　　　　　　　　י: הוא יגיע הערב.

I: gám gvéret alón tagía?　　　　　　　　ט: גם גברת אלון תגיע?

J: ken. aní xošév káx.　　　　　　　　　י: כן. אני חושב כך.

K:　háva nigáš lir'ót et miryám.　　　　　　כ: הבה ניגש לראות את מרים.

L:　yéš láx et haktóvet šelá?　　　　　　　ל: יש לך את הכתובת שלה?

K:　ló. tén lí et mispár hatélefon šelá.　　כ: לא. תן לי את מספר הטלפון שלה.

L:　éyn lí et mispár hatélefon.　　　　　　ל: אין לי את מספר הטלפון.

K:　aní xošévet šeemcá et hamakóm.　　　　כ: אני חושבת שאמצא את המקום.

M:　xána. matáy telxí letayél.　　　　　　מ: חנה, מתי תלכי לטייל?

N:　axaréy šeegmór et haaruxá.　　　　　　נ: אחרי שאגמור את הארוחה.

M:　aní xošév šegám aní eléx.　　　　　　מ: אני חושב שגם אני אלך.

N:　tóv. neléx yáxad.　　　　　　　　　　נ: טוב. נלך יחד.

O:　miryám tigáš lir'ót et mošé haérev.　　ס: מרים תיגש לראות את משה הערב.

P:　beemét? mošé yismáx meód lir'ót otá.　ע: באמת? משה ישמח מאוד לראות אותה.

O:　hém yismexú meód lehitraót.　　　　　ס: הם ישמחו מאוד להתראות.

Q:　zú masóret eclénu leexól xalót belél šiší.　　פ: זו מסורת אצלנו לאכול חלות בליל שישי.

R:　zú masóret yafá meód. haxalót teimót.　צ: זו מסורת יפה מאד. החלות טעימות.

Q:　todá rabá. atá rocé dagím?　　　　　פ: תודה רבה. אתה רוצה דגים?

R:　kén. éyx aní yaxól lesarév.　　　　　צ: כן. איך אני יכול לסרב?

Q:　amárta šeatá bediéta.　　　　　　　פ: אמרת שאתה בדיאטה.

R:　adáin ló. atxíl maxár.　　　　　　　צ: עדיין לא. אתחיל מחר.

End of Tape 4B

123

לא, תודה. זה הכל...

Tape 5A

14.1 At the Grocery Store /bexanút makólet/   .בחנות מכולת

STOREKEEPER /xenvaní/

Good morning, Mrs. Zahavi.	bóker tóv, gvéret zahávi.	בוקר טוב, גברת זהבי,
What can I	má aní yaxól	מה אני יכול
do for you?	laasót bišviléx.	לעשות בשבילך?
to do	laasót	לעשות
for	bišvíl	בשביל

MRS. ZAHAVI

Please give me	tén li bevakašá,	תן לי בבקשה,
200 grams	matáim grám	מאתיים גרם
of cheese.	gviná.	גבינה.
two hundred	matáim	מאתיים
gram	grám (m)	גרם
cheese	gviná (f)	גבינה

STOREKEEPER

Yellow cheese or	gviná cehubá, ó	גבינה צהובה או
white cheese?	gviná levaná.	גבינה לבנה?
yellow	cahóv (m.s.)	צהוב
white	laván (m.s.)	לבן

MRS. ZAHAVI

Yellow cheese.	gviná cehubá.	גבינה צהובה.
Are the eggs fresh?	habeycím triót?	הביצים טריות?
egg	beycá (f)	ביצה
fresh	tarí (m.s.)	טרי

STOREKEEPER

Yes.	kén.	כן.
I received them	kibálti otán	קיבלתי אותן
this morning.	habóker.	הבוקר.
I received	kibálti	קבלתי

MRS. ZAHAVI

Then give me	áz tén li	אז תן לי
a dozen.	treysár.	תריסר.
dozen	treysár (m)	תריסר

STOREKEEPER

Do you need	át crixá	את צריכה
any vegetables?	yerakót?	ירקות?
Fruits?	peyrót?	פירות?
need, must, have to	caríx (m.s.)	צריך
vegetable	yérek (m)	ירק
fruit	prí (m)	פרי

125

MRS. ZAHAVI

No, thank you.	ló, todá.		לא, תודה.
That's all.	zé hakól.		זה הכל.
How much do I	káma aní		כמה אני
owe you?	xayévet lexá.		חייבת לך?
everything	hakól	הכל	
how much, how many	káma	כמה	
owe	xayáv (m.s.)	חייב	

STOREKEEPER

That will cost you	zé yaalé láx		זה יעלה לך
eighty-three	šmoním vešalóš		שמונים ושלוש
agorot.	agorót.		אגורות.
will cost, go up	yaalé (3 m.s.)	יעלה	
eighty	šmoním	שמונים	
agora (1/100 lira)	agorá (f)	אגורה	

MRS. ZAHAVI

Give me	tén li		תן לי
change from a lira.	ódef milíra.		עודף מלירה.
surplus	ódef (m)	עודף	
Israeli pound	líra (f)	לירה	

14.2 ADDITIONAL VOCABULARY

The vegetables are	hayerakót		הירקות
cheap today.	zolím hayóm.		זולים היום.
cheap	zól (m.s.)	זול	
The vegetables are	hayerakót		הירקות
expensive today.	yekarím hayóm.		יקרים היום.
expensive, dear	yakár (m.s.)	יקר	

[The names of vegetables and fruits in the following list are given in the singular or plural depending on how one asks for them in the question /bekáma.../ "How much is/are..."]

How much are the beans?	bekáma hašuít.		בכמה השעועית?
beans	šeuít (f)	שעועית	
beet	sélek (m)	סלק	
cabbage	krúv (m)	כרוב	
carrot	gézer (m)	גזר	
cauliflower	kruvít (f)	כרובית	
corn	tíras (m)	תירס	
cucumbers	melafefoním (m.pl.)	מלפפונים	
dill	šamír (m)	שמיר	
eggplants	xacilím (m.pl.)	חצילים	
garlic	šúm (m)	שום	
kohlrabi	kolerábi (m)	קולרבי	
lettuce	xása (f)	חסה	
olives	zeytím (m.pl.)	זיתים	
onion	bacál (m)	בצל	
parsley	petruzília (f)	פטרוזיליה	
peas	afuná (f)	אפונה	
potatoes	tapuxéy adamá (m.pl.)	תפוחי אדמה	

126

radishes	cnoniót (f.pl.)	צנוניות
scallion	bacál yarók (m)	בצל ירוק
spinach	téred (m)	תרד
squash	kišuím (m.pl.)	קשואים
tomatoes	agvaniót (f.pl.)	עגבניות
turnip	cnón (m)	צנון

I want	aní rocá	אני רוצה
to buy fruit.	liknót peyrót.	לקנות פירות.
to buy	liknót	לקנות

How much are the apples?	bekáma hatapuxím.	בכמה התפוחים?
apple	tapúax (m)	תפוח

bananas	banánot (f.pl.)	בננות
canteloupe	milón (m)	מילון
cherries	duvdevaním (m.pl.)	דובדבנים
dates	tmarím (m.pl.)	תמרים
figs	teením (f.pl.)	תאנים
fig	teená (f)	תאנה
grapefruits	eškoliót (f.pl.)	אשכוליות
grapes	anavím (m.pl.)	ענבים
lemons	limoním (m.pl.)	לימונים
oranges	tapuzím (m.pl.)	תפוזים
peaches	afarsekím (m.pl.)	אפרסקים
pears	agasím (m.pl.)	אגסים
plums	šezifím (m.pl.)	שזיפים
pomegranates	rimoním (m.pl.)	רימונים
watermelons	avatixím (m.pl.)	אבטיחים
watermelon	avatíax (m)	אבטיח

Give me two kilos	tén lí šnéy kílo	תן לי שני קילו
of flour.	kémax.	קמח.
flour	kémax (m)	קמח
salt	mélax (m)	מלח
sugar	sukár (m)	סוכר

How much is	káma olé	כמה עולה
a bottle of milk?	bakbúk xaláv.	בקבוק חלב?
cost	olé (m.s.pres.)	עולה
bottle	bakbúk (m)	בקבוק
milk	xaláv (m)	חלב
oil	šémen (m)	שמן
orange juice	míc tapuzím	מיץ תפוזים
juice	míc (m)	מיץ

How much is	káma olá	כמה עולה
a can of sardines?	kufsát sardínim.	קופסת סרדינים?
can, box	kufsá (f)	קופסה
cans, boxes	kufsaót (f.pl.)	קופסאות

How much is	káma olá	כמה עולה
a package of butter?	xavilát xem'á.	חבילת חמאה?
package	xavilá (f)	חבילה
butter	xem'á (f)	חמאה

How much is	káma olá		כמה עולה
a jar of sour cream?	cincénet šaménet.		צנצנת שמנת?
jar	cincénet (f)	צנצנת	
sour cream	šaménet (f)	שמנת	
jelly	ribá (f)		ריבה
mustard	xardál (m)		חרדל

Give me half a	tén lí xací		תן לי חצי
kilo of grapes.	kílo anavím.		קילו ענבים.
half	xéci (m)	חצי	
half of	xací (construct)	חצי	

14.3   Vocabulary Drills

A.   Transformation Drill - /bišvíl/ "for"

> Instructor: I want ice cream.
> Student: I'll have ice cream. (lit. For me ice cream.)

aní rocé glida.	bišvili glidá.	כשבילי גלידה.	אני רוצה גלידה.
atá rocé yáin.	bišvilxá yáin.	כשבילך יין.	אתה רוצה יין.
át rocá xaláv.	bišviléx xaláv.	כשבילך חלב.	את רוצה חלב.
hú rocé míc.	bišviló míc.	כשבילו מיץ.	הוא רוצה מיץ.
hí rocá ribá.	bišvilá ribá.	כשבילה ריבה.	היא רוצה ריבה.
ánu rocím tapuzím.	bišvilénu tapuzím.	כשבילנו תפוזים.	אנו רוצים תפוזים.
atém rocím dagím.	bišvilxém dagím.	כשבילכם דגים.	אתם רוצים דגים.
atén rocót gviná.	bišvilxén gviná.	כשבילכן גבינה.	אתן רוצות גבינה.
hém rocím šaménet.	bišvilám šaménet.	כשבילם שמנת.	הם רוצים שמנת.
hén rocót kémax.	bišvilán kémax.	כשבילן קמח.	הן רוצות קמח.

B.   Substitution - Agreement Drill /tarí/ "fresh"

Is the milk fresh?

| haím haxaláv tarí? | | האם החלב   טרי? |

haagvaniót - haagvaniá - hasélek	העגבניות - העגבניה - הסלק
hapeyrót - hayerakót - haxása	הפרות - הירקות - החסה
hateením - habeycím - haxaláv	התאנים - הביצים - החלב

C.   Substitution - Agreement Drill - /caríx/ "have to, need"

I have to buy chalahs for the Sabbath.

| aní caríx liknót xalót lešabát. | אני צריך לקנות חלות לשבת. |

| iští - hén - baalá - hí | אשתי - הן - בעלה - היא |
| ánu - hú - atém - aní | אנו - הוא - אתם - אני |

D.   Substitution - Agreement Drill - /kibálti/ "I received"

I received a bottle of wine from Dov.

kibálti bakbúk yáin midóv.   קבלתי בקבוק יין מדוב.

atém - át - ánu   אתם – את – אנו
atá - atén - aní   אתה – אתן – אני

E.   Substitution Drill - /ee- ~ taa-/ Endings are similar to /tifné/.

I'll go up to the Embassy this morning.

eelé lašagrirút habóker.   אעלה לשגרירות הבוקר.
   taalé   תעלה
   taalí   תעלי
   hú yaalé   הוא יעלה
   hi taalé   היא תעלה
   naalé   נעלה
   atém taalú   אתם תעלו
   atén taaléna   אתן תעלינה
   hém yaalú   הם יעלו
   hén taaléna   הן תעלינה

F.   Substitution - Agreement Drill

Let's go up to Miriam's this evening.

háva naalé lemiryám haérev.   הבה נעלה למרים הערב.

át - dóv veištó - atá veištexá   את – דוב ואשתו – אתה ואשתך
aní - atá - xána - atén   אני – אתה – חנה – אתן
avígdor - hén - háva   אביגדור – הן – הבה

14.4   Cardinal Numbers, 20 - 1000

Numbers which are multiples of 10 do not show gender distinction.

20	esrím	עשרים
30	šloším	שלושים
40	arbaím	ארבעים
50	xamiším	חמישים
60	šiším	שישים
70	šiv'ím	שבעים
80	šmoním	שמונים
90	tiš'ím	תשעים

The numbers 'one' to 'nine' follow the multiples of ten and are preceded by /ve-/. These numbers show gender distinction.

/šmoním vešalóš agorót/   "83 agorot"   שמונים ושלוש אגורות
/esrím vexamišá sfarím/   "25 books"   עשרים וחמשה ספרים

The form /meá/ "hundred" and its multiples are also used before both masculine and feminine nouns.

100	meá	מאה
200	matáim	מאתיים

300	šlóš meót	שלוש מאות
400	arbá meót	ארבע מאות
500	xaméš meót	חמש מאות
600	šéš meót	שש מאות
700	švá meót	שבע מאות
800	šmóne meót	שמונה מאות
900	tšá meót	תשע מאות
1000	élef	אלף

Numbers are given with the highest digit first, as in English.

1965   /élef tšámeot šiším vexaméš/

A. Read off the following numbers. Do not read the individual numerals.

1.	82	13.	217
2.	73	14.	458
3.	64	15.	336
4.	55	16.	789
5.	46	17.	265
6.	37	18.	924
7.	28	19.	593
8.	19	20.	847
9.	90	21.	670
10.	101	22.	1040

B. The instructor asks each student for the year of his/her birth.

In which year	beéyze šaná		באיזה שנה
were you born?	noládeta		נולדת?
you were born		noládeta	נולדת

I was born	noládeti		נולדתי
in (the year)	bišnát		בשנת
1948.	élef tšá meót		אלף תשע מאות
	arbaím vešmóne.		ארבעים ושמונה.

C. Conversational Response Drill

      Instructor: How much are beets?
      Student: 30 agorot a kilo.
      Instructor: Give me one and a half kilos.
      Student: That will be 45 agorot.

Instructor: bekáma hasélek.	המורה: כמה הסלק?
Student: šloším agorót hakílo.	תלמיד: שלושים אגורות הקילו.
Instructor: tén lí kílo vaxéci.	המורה: תן לי קילו וחצי.
Student: zé yaalé lexá arbaím vexaméš agorót.	תלמיד: זה יעלה לך ארבעים וחמש אגורות.

The instructor and students may substitute other items, prices, and quantities.

14.5 <u>Colors</u>   /cvaím/   צבעים

What is the color	má hacéva	מה הצבע
of the table?	šél hašulxán.	של השולחן?
color	céva (m)	צבע

The table is black.	hašulxán šaxór.	השולחן שחור.
The box is black.	hakufsá šxorá.	הקופסה שחורה.

The apple is red.	hatapúax adóm.	התפוח אדום.
The cherries are red.	haduvdevaním adumím.	הדובדבנים אדומים.

The carrot is orange.	hagézer katóm.	הגזר כתום.
The package is orange.	haxavilá ktumá.	החבילה כתומה.

The corn is yellow.	hatíras cahóv.	התירס צהוב.
The bananas are yellow.	habanánot cehubót.	הבננות צהובות.

The pear is green.	haagás yarók.	האגס ירוק.
The olives are green.	hazeytím yerukím.	הזיתים ירוקים.

The book is blue.	haséfer kaxól.	הספר כחול.
The sky is blue.	hašamáim kxulím.	השמים כחולים.
sky, heaven	šamáim (m.pl.)	שמים

The eggplant is purple.	haxacíl segól.	החציל סגול.
The grapes are purple.	haanavím sgulím.	הענבים סגולים.

The date is brown.	hatamár xúm.	התמר חום.
The figs are brown.	hateením xumót.	התאנים חומות.

GRAMMAR NOTES

14.6 /o ~ u/ Alternation in Related Forms

Examine the following set of related forms:

m.s.	/yarók/	"green"	ירוק
f.s.	/yeruká/		ירוקה
m.pl.	/yerukím/		ירוקים
f.pl.	/yerukót/		ירוקות

This pattern is similar to the pattern of /raxók ~ rexoká/ except that
in the suffixed forms the vowel /u/ occurs instead of /o/. This alternation
occurs in a limited but fairly frequently used set of forms. The student
will have to memorize them since there are sets of related forms which have
/o/ when suffixed, as /rexoká, gdolá/, and sets which have /u/ whether
suffixed or not, as /xúm, xumá/ "brown".
Now compare the following pair of forms.

m.s.	/cahóv/	"yellow"	צהוב
f.s.	/cehubá/		צהובה

Forms which have this /o ~ u/ alternation will also have the /v ~ b/
alternation, with the /b/ occurring before the suffixes.
Similarly, the alternation /f ~ p/ occurs in such forms, with /p/
occurring before the suffixes.
The alternation /x ~ k/ may occur in related forms with the /o ~ u/
alternation, with /k/ occurring in the suffixed forms.

m.s.	/aróx/	"long"	ארוך
f.s.	/aruká/		ארוכה

However, some forms have /k/ throughout, as /yarók/ "green". These
latter forms are spelled with ק, while those which alternate /x ~ k/ are
spelled with כ ~ ך.

A. Substitution - Agreement Drill

The apples are red.

<u>hatapuxím adumím.</u>   .הַתַפּוּחִים אֲדוּמִים

haxavilót - hakufsá - haséfer   החבילות – הקופסה – הספר
habatím - hayáin - hacincénet   הבתים – היין – הצנצנת
hatapuxím   התפוחים

B. Progressive Substitution Drill

In this drill the instructor gives a substitution first from one column and then from the other.

The wine is red.

hayáin adóm.		היין אדום.
haagvaniá		העגבניה
	yeruká	ירוקה
hatapúax		התפוח
	cahóv	צהוב
habanánot		הבננות
	xumót	חומות
haséfer		הספר
	katóm	כתום
habakbukím		הבקבוקים
	levaním	לבנים
habinyán		הבנין
	adóm	אדום
hayáin		היין

C. Progressive Substitution Drill

The sky is blue.

hašamáim kxulím.		השמים כחולים.
hašezíf		השזיף
	segól	סגול
haxacilím		החצילים
	gdolím	גדולים
hacincénet		הצנצנת
	xumá	חומה
habakbúk		הבקבוק
	yarók	ירוק
hazáit		הזית
	šaxór	שחור
hakufsaót		הקופסאות
	kxulót	כחולות
hašamáim		השמים

14.7 Review of Negative Sentences

a. /ló/ precedes past, present, and future verb forms.

axálti et haglída.   "I ate the ice cream."
ló axálti et haglída.   "I didn't eat the ice cream."

hí rocá liknót perót. "She wants to buy fruit."
hí ló rocá liknót   "She doesn't want to buy fruit."
  perót.

hú yagía maxár.   "He'll arrive tomorrow."
hú ló yagía maxár.   "He won't arrive tomorrow."

This corresponds to the negative, usually with -n't, of the verb auxiliary in English.

133

b. /ló/ occurs between the main elements of an equational sentence.

| hú amerikái. | "He's an American." | .הוא אמריקאי |
| hú ló amerikái. | "He's not an American." | .הוא לא אמריקאי |

c. /éyn/, usually with a pronoun suffix, may negate a present tense verb form or an equational sentence. The use of /éyn/ instead of /ló/ in these cases is more formal in style.

| aní medabér ivrít. | "I speak Hebrew." | .אני מדבר עברית |
| eynéni medabér ivrít. | "I don't speak Hebrew." | .אינני מדבר עברית |

| aní xadáš baárec. | "I'm new in the country." | .אני חדש בארץ |
| eynéni xadáš baárec. | "I'm not new in the country." | .אינני חדש בארץ |

Comparison of style:

| aní ló yodéa. | (casual, informal) | .אני לא יודע |
| eynéni yodéa. | (less casual, formal) | .אינני יודע |

The suffixed, or contracted forms of /éyn/ + the pronouns are:

éyn aní	eynéni	איני	אין אני
éyn atá	eynxá	אינך	אין אתה
éyn át	eynéx	אינך	אין את
éyn hú	eynénu, eynó	אינו, איננו	אין הוא
éyn hí	eynéna, eyná	אינה, איננה	אין היא
éyn ánu	eynénu	איננו	אין אנו
éyn atém	eynxém	אינכם	אין אתם
éyn atén	eynxén	אינכן	אין אתן
éyn hém	eynám	אינם	אין הם
éyn hén	eynán	אינן	אין הן

/éyn ánu/ is usually not contracted. The other sequences may be used in the uncontracted form, but this generally results in a very formal or stiff expression.

| eynéni yodéa. | (less casual, formal) | .אינני יודע |
| éyn aní yodéa. | (formal, stiff) | .אין אני יודע |

d. /éyn/ is the negative of /yéš/ "there is."

| yéš li gviná levaná. | "I have white cheese." | .יש לי גבינה לבנה |
| éyn li gviná levaná. | "I don't have white cheese." | .אין לי גבינה לבנה |

e. /ál/ negates the imperative.

| tifné smóla. | "Turn left." | .תפנה שמאלה |
| ál tifné smóla. | "Don't turn left." | .אל תפנה שמאלה |

A. Transformation Drill - Affirmative to Negative

       Instructor: I was very impressed by the house.
       Student: I wasn't very impressed by the house.

1. (ló) hitrašámti meód mehabáit.   1. (לא) התרשמוני מאוד מהבית.
2. (ló) axáltem et haxalá.   2. (לא) אכלתם את החלה.
3. (ló) yaxólti lehagía bešéva.   3. (לא) יכולתי להגיע בשבע.
4. (ló) kibálti et hapeyrót.   4. (לא) קבלתי את הפירות.
5. (ló) natáta lí hizdamnút ledabér.   5. (לא) נתת לי הזדמנות לדבר.
6. (ló) šamáti et hakól.   6. (לא) שמעתי את הקול.
7. atá (ló) raíta et hamisrád šelánu.   7. אתה (לא) ראית את המשרד שלנו.
8. hadagím (ló) hayú teimím.   8. הדגים (לא) היו טעימים.

B. Transformation Drill - Negative to Affirmative

       Repeat Drill A in reverse.

C. Transformation Drill - Affirmative to Negative

       Instructor: I know where the Brooklyn Bar is.
       Student: I don't know where the Brooklyn Bar is.

1. aní (ló) yodéa éyfo   brúklin bar.   1. אני (לא) יודע איפה ברוקלין בר.
2. gvéret zahávi (ló) gára betél avív.   2. גברת זהבי (לא) גרה בתל אביב.
3. hén (ló) medabrót ivrít.   3. הן (לא) מדברות עבריו.
4. hí (ló) mexiná dagím memulaím.   4. היא (לא) מכינה דגים ממולאים.
5. haím haárec (ló) mócet xén beeynéxa?   5. האם הארץ (לא) מוצאת חן בעיניך?
6. hú (ló) rocé lehagía ladóar hamerkazí.   6. הוא (לא) רוצה להגיע לדואר דמרכזי.
7. ánu (ló) medabrím ivrít.   7. אנו (לא) מדברים עברית.
8. aní (ló) caríx et hašulxán.   8. אני (לא) צריך את השולחן.

D. Transformation Drill - Negative to Affirmative

       Repeat Drill D in reverse.

E. Transformation Drill - Affirmative to Negative

       Instructor: We'll go to the movies tonight.
       Student: We won't go to the movies tonight.

1. (ló) neléx lakolnóa haérev.   1. (לא) נלך לקולנוע הערב.
2. (ló) nigáš lexána hayóm.   2. (לא) ניגש לחנה היום.
3. hú (ló) yaavór al yád habáit šelánu.   3. הוא (לא) יעבור על יד הבית שלנו.
4. hém (ló) yisgerú et haxanút bešéš.   4. הם (לא) יסגרו את החנות בשש.
5. gvéret kármi (ló) tiftáx et hamisrád.   5. גברת כרמי (לא) תפתח את המשרד.
6. sára vexána (ló) tagána maxár.   6. שרה וחנה (לא) תגענה מחר.
7. ánu (ló) natxíl leexól lifnéy šéš.   7. אנו (לא) נתחיל לאכול לפני שש.
8. (ló) emcá otó bemisradó.   8. (לא) אמצא אותו במשרדו.

F. Transformation Drill - Negative to Affirmative

       Repeat Drill E in reverse.

G. Transformation Drill - Affirmative to Negative.

      Instructor: They're new in the country.
      Student: They're not new in the country.

1.	hém (ló) xadaším baárec.	.הם (לא) חדשים בארץ. 1
2.	iští (ló) amerikáit.	.אשתי (לא) אמריקאית. 2
3.	habáit šelahém (ló) yafé.	.הבית שלהם (לא) יפה. 3
4.	haglidá šehí mexiná (ló) tová.	.הגלידה שהיא מכינה (לא) טובה. 4
5.	nemál hateufá (ló) raxók mehaír.	.נמל התעופה (לא) רחוק מהעיר. 5
6.	haóxel (ló) hayá taím.	.האוכל (לא) היה טעים. 6

H. Transformation Drill - Affirmative to Negative

    In this drill the sentences are negated by /éyn/.

1.	aní (eynéni) yodéa et haktóvet šelá.	.אני (אינני) יודע את הכתובת שלה. 1
2.	atá (eynxá) gár karóv lašagrirút.	.אתה (אינך) גר קרוב לשגרירות. 2
3.	át (eynéx) yodáat ledabér ivrít.	.את (אינך) יודעת לדבר עברית. 3
4.	hú (eynénu) rocé lehazmín et miryám.	.הוא (איננו) רוצה להזמין את מרים. 4
5.	hí (eynéna) rocá lehazmín otó.	.היא (איננה) רוצה להזמין אותו. 5
6.	(éyn) ánu yod'ím éyfo šehém garím.	.(אין) אנו יודעים איפה שהם גרים. 6
7.	atém (eynxém) xadaším baárec.	.אתם (אינכם) חדשים בארץ. 7
8.	láma atén (eynxén) bediéta.	?למה אתן (אינכן) בדיאטה. 8
9.	hém (eynám) xošvím šemeuxár.	.הם (אינם) חושבים שמאוחר. 9
10.	hén (eynán) crixót liknót dagím.	.הן (אינן) צריכות לקנות דגים. 10

I. Transformation Drill - Negative to Affirmative

    Repeat Drill H in reverse.

REVIEW CONVERSATIONS

A:	má aní yaxól laasót bišviléx.	?א: מה אני יכול לעשות בשבילך
B:	tén li bevakašá, gviná.	.ב: תן לי, בבקשה, גבינה
A:	éyze gviná át rocá.	?א: איזה גבינה את רוצה
B:	gviná levaná.	.ב: גבינה לבנה
C:	habeycím triót?	?ג: הביצים טריות
D:	kén, gvirtí. triót meód.	.ד: כן, גברתי, טריות מאוד
C:	káma olé treysár?	?ג: כמה עולה תריסר
D:	šiším agorót.	.ד: שישים אגורות
C:	áz tén li šnéy treysár.	.ג: אז תן לי שני תריסר

136

E: át crixá yerakót, gvirtí?   ה: את צריכה ירקות, גברתי?

F: kén. aní crixá melafefoním.   ו: כן. אני צריכה מלפפונים.

E: hamelafefoním zolím hayóm.   ה: המלפפונים זולים היום.

F: tóv meód. tén li kílo.   ו: טוב מאוד. תן לי קילו.

G: adoní, atá xayáv lí kílo agvaniót.   ז: אדוני, אתה חייב לי קילו עגבניות.

H: natáti láx et haagvaniót etmól.   ח: נתתי לך את העגבניות אתמול.

G: kén. áx hén ló hayú tovót.   ז: כן. אך הן לא היו טובות.

H: zé davár axér. etén láx axerót.   ח: זה דבר אחר. אתן לך אחרות.

I: matáy kibálta et hazeytím.   ט: מתי קבלת את הזיתים?

J: kibálti otám etmól. át rocá zeytím?   י: קבלתי אותם אתמול. את רוצה זיתים?

I: hém teimím?   ט: הם טעימים?

J: kén. teimím meód.   י: כן. טעימים מאוד.

I: áz tén lí arbá meót grám.   ט: אז תן לי ארבע מאות גרם.

K: bekáma hakolerábi.   כ: בכמה הקולרבי?

L: esrím agorót hakílo.   ל: עשרים אגורות הקילו.

K: zé yakár meód.   כ: זה יקר מאוד.

L: zé ló yakár. zé zól.   ל: זה לא יקר. זה זול.

M: bekáma hasélek.   מ: בכמה הסלק?

N: xamiším agorót hakílo.   נ: חמישים אגורות הקילו.

M: tén lí šlošá kílo.   מ: תן לי שלושה קילו.

N: zé yaalé láx líra vaxéci.   נ: זה יעלה לך לירה וחצי.

     Substitute other foods, prices, etc.

אתם רוצים עוגרות?...

15.1 At a Coffee House /bebét kafé/

ATARA

Hello, David.	šalóm davíd.	.שלום, דוד
What's new?	má nišmá.	?מה נשמע
is heard	nišmá (m.s.) נשמע	

DAVID

Let's get	bói lištót	בואי לשתות
a cup of coffee,	kós kafé.	,כוס קפה
and I'll tell you	veasapér láx	ואספר לך
everything.	et hakól.	.את הכל
come	bó (m.s.imv.) בוא	
to drink	lištót לשתות	
drinking glass	kós (f) כוס	
coffee	kafé (m) קפה	
I will tell	asapér (1 s.fut.) אספר	

ATARA

Good idea.	rayón tóv.	.רעיון טוב
Where's the coffee house?	éyfo bét hakafé.	?איפה בית הקפה
idea	rayón (m) רעיון	

DAVID

Here on the corner.	pó bapiná.	.פה בפינה
here	pó פה	

(In the coffee house)

DAVID

Waiter,	melcár –	,מלצר
two	paamáim	פעמים
coffees, please.	kafé bevakašá.	.קפה, בבקשה
waiter	melcár (m) מלצר	
waitress	melcarít (f) מלצרית	
time (occurrence)	páam (f) פעם	

WAITER

With or without milk?	ím o blí xaláv.	?עם או בלי חלב
with	ím עם	
or	ó או	
without	blí בלי	

ATARA

I'll have	bišvilí	בשבילי
espresso with milk.	espréso ím xaláv.	.אספרסו עם חלב

DAVID

And I'll have	vebišvilí	ובשבילי
café au lait.	kafé hafúx.	.קפה הפוך
reversed, inverted	hafúx (m.s.) הפוך	

WAITER

| Do you want cakes? | atém rocím ugót? | ?אתם רוצים עוגות |
| cake | ugá (f) | עוגה |

ATARA

| What kind of cake | éyze ugót | איזה עוגות |
| do you have? | yéš laxém. | ?יש לכם |

WAITER

We have	yéš lánu	יש לנו
apple cake	ugát tapuxím	עוגת תפוחים
and cheese cake.	veugát gviná.	ועוגת גבינה.

ATARA

| Apple cake, please. | ugát tapuxím, bevakašá. | עוגת תפוחים, בבקשה. |

DAVID

| For me, too. | gám bišvilí. | גם בשבילי. |

ATARA

The coffee is hot.	hakafé xám.	הקפה חם.
Be careful.	hizahér.	הזהר.
hot, warm	xam (m.s.)	חם
be careful	hizahér (m.s.imv.)	הזהר

DAVID

I'll wait a bit,	axaké kcát,	אחכה קצת,
and the coffee	vehakafé	והקפה
will cool down.	yitkarér.	יתקרר.
I will wait	axaké (1.s.fut.)	אחכה
it will cool	yitkarer (3 m.s.fut.)	יתקרר

15.2 ADDITIONAL VOCABULARY

Give me a glass of water.	tén li kós máim.	תן לי כוס מים.
water	máim (m.pl.)	מים
Give me a glass of seltzer.	tén li kós sóda.	תן לי כוס סודה.
club soda	sóda (f)	סודה

| The tea is hot. | hatéy xám. | התה חם. |
| The tea is cold. | hatéy kár. | התה קר. |

| The milk is sour. | haxaláv xamúc. | החלב חמוץ. |

| The coffee is bitter. | hakafé már. | הקפה מר. |

| The tea is sweet. | hatéy matók. | התה מתוק. |
| The cake is sweet. | haugá metuká. | העוגה מתוקה. |

| Let's go to a restaurant. | bó neléx lemis'adá. | בוא נלך למסעדה. |
| restaurant | mis'adá (f) | מסעדה |

End of Tape 5A

Tape 5B

15.3 Vocabulary Drills

A. Substitution Drill - /bó/ "come"

Come see our house.

bói lir'ót et habáit šelánu.	בואי לראות את הבית שלנו.
bóu	בואו
bó	בוא
bóna	בואנה

B. Substitution Drill - /ál tavó/ "don't come"

Don't come in the afternoon.

ál tavó axaréy hacohoráim.	אל תבוא אחרי הצהריים.
tavói	תבואי
tavóu	תבואו
tavóna	תבואנה

C. Transformation Drill - Affirmative to Negative

Instructor: Come with Tamar.
Student: Don't come with Tamar.

bó im tamár.	ál tavó im tamár.	בוא עם תמר. אל תבוא עם תמר.
bóu im tamár.	ál tavóu im tamár.	בואו עם תמר. אל תבואו עם תמר.
bói im tamár.	ál tavói im tamár.	בואי עם תמר. אל תבואי עם תמר.
bóna im tamár.	ál tavóna im tamár.	בואנה עם תמר. אל תבואנה עם תמר.

D. Transformation Drill - Negative to Affirmative

Repeat Drill C in reverse.

E. Substitution Drill - /avó/ "I will come"

I'll come to her office tomorrow.

avó lemisradá maxár.	אבוא למשרדה מחר.
tavó	תבוא
tavói	תבואי
davíd yavó	דוד יבוא
sára tavó	שרה תבוא
navó	נבוא
atém tavóu	אתם תבואו
atén tavóna	אתן תבואנה
kulám yavóu	כולם יבואו
hén tavóna	הן תבואנה

F. Substitution - Agreement Drill

He'll come for dinner.

hú yavó learuxát érev.	הוא יבוא לארוחת ערב.
aní - hagvéret umár Williams	אני - הגברת ומר ווילאמס
át veatára - hén - atém - ánu	את ועטרה - הן - אתם - אנו
atá - ištó šel dóv - át - hú	אתה - אשתו של דוב - את - הוא

141

G. Substitution Drill - /a- ~ te-/

I'll tell Atara everything.

asapér leatára et hakól.	אספר לעטרה את הכל.
tesapér	תספר
tesaprí	תספרי
davíd yesapér	דוד יספר
sára tesapér	שרה תספר
aní veiští nesapér	אני ואשתי נספר
atém tesaprú	אתם תספרו
atén tesapérna	אתן תספרנה
hém yesaprú	הם יספרו
hén tesapérna	הן תספרנה

H. Substitution - Agreement Drill - /asapér/ "I will tell"

We'll tell them the good news.

<u>nesapér lahém et haxadašót hatovót.</u>   <u>נספר להם את החדשות הטובות.</u>

atém - atára vedavíd - hén - hú	אתם - עטרה ודוד - הן - הוא
aní - atén - sára - át	אני - אתן - שרה - את
atá - avígdor - hú - ánu	אתה - אביגדור - הוא - אנו

I. Substitution Drill - /a- ~ te-/

I'll wait for Moshe till 5:00.

axaké lemošé ád xaméš.	אחכה למשה עד חמש.
texaké	תחכה
texakí	תחכי
dóv yexaké	דב יחכה
hí texaké	היא תחכה
ánu nexaké	אנו נחכה
atém texakú	אתם תחכו
atén texakéna	אתן תחכינה
hém yexakú	הם יחכו
hén texakéna	הן תחכינה

J. Substitution - Agreement Drill - /axaké/ "I will wait"

(Use the forms of the verb /ešév/"sit" as cues.)

I'll sit in the hotel and wait for him.

ešév bamalón veaxaké ló.		אצא במלון ואחכה לו.
nešév	(venexaké)	נשב (ונחכה)
tešvú	(vetexakú)	תשבו (ותחכו)
yešév	(veyexaké)	ישב (ויחכה)
tešév	(vetexaké)	תשב (ותחכה)
léa tešév	(vetexaké)	לאה תשב (ותחכה)
yešvú	(veyexakú)	ישבו (ויחכו)
hén tešévna	(vetexakéna)	הן תשבנה (ותחכינה)
tešví	(vetexakí)	תשבי (ותחכי)
atén tešévna	(vetexakéna)	אתן תשבנה (ותחכינה)

K. Substitution Drill - /hizahér/ "be careful"

Be careful; the cup is hot.

hizahér. hakós xamá.	.הזהר, הכוס חמה
hizaharí	הזהרי
hizaharú	הזהרו
hizahérna	הזהרנה

In Grammar Section 6.9 it was pointed out that the final stem vowel is dropped in verb forms beginning with a stressed vowel. However, when the second root consonant is h . as in /hizahér/, the sequence /-hr-/ results, and the vowel /a/ is inserted.⎺ The /-h-/ is often replaced by a smooth transition in ordinary speech - /hizaarí, hizaarú/. Compare the forms of /memahér/ "hurry" in Section 8.3.

In the following drills L to P the instructor supplies the verb form with the noun substitution.

L. Substitution - Agreement Drill - /xám/ "hot"

The water was hot.

<u>hamáim hayú xamím.</u>   <u>.המים היו חמים</u>

haxalá haytá - haóxel hayá	החלה היתה – האוכל היה
habeycím hayú - haugá haytá	הביצים היו – העוגה היתה
hakafé hayá - hayerakót hayú	הקפה היה – הירקות היו
haagvaniót hayú - hamáim hayú	העגבניות היו – המים היו

M. Substitution - Agreement Drill - /kár/ "cold"

The milk was cold.

<u>haxaláv hayá kár.</u>   <u>.החלב היה קר</u>

haglída haytá - hadagím hayú	הגלידה היתה – הדגים היו
haeškoliót hayú - hamíc hayá	האשכוליות היו – המיץ היה
hagvinót hayú - haavatixím hayú	הגבינות היו – האבטיחים היו
hašaménet haytá - haxaláv hayá	השמנת היתה – החלב היה

N. Substitution - Agreement Drill - /már/ "bitter"

The coffee was bitter.

<u>hakafé hayá már.</u>   <u>.הקפה היה מר</u>

hateením hayú - hatéy hayá	התאנים היו – התה היה
hayeynót hayú - haribá haytá	היינות היו – הריבה היתה
haeškolít haytá - haanavím hayú	האשכולית היתה – הענבים היו
hagvinót hayú - hakafé hayá	הגבינות היו – הקפה היה

O. Substitution - Agreement Drill - /xamúc/ "sour"

The grapes were sour.

<u>haanavím hayú xamucím.</u>   .העןבים היו חמוצים

haxaláv hayá - hašaménet haytá   החלב היה – השמנת היתה
hadagím hayú - hagviná haytá   הדגים היו – הגבינה היתה
hayáin hayá - hateením hayú   היין היה – התאנים היו
haugót hayú - haanavím hayú   העוגות היו – העןבים היו

P. Substitution - Agreement Drill - /matók/ "sweet"

The plums were sweet.

<u>hašezifím hayú metukím.</u>   .השזיפים היו מתוקים

hayáin hayá - haavatixím hayú   היין היה – האבטיחים היו
haribá haytá - haeškoliót hayú   הריבה היתה – האשכוליות היו
haxalót hayú - harimón hayá   החלות היו – הרימון היה
haxalá haytá - hašezifím hayú   החלה היתה – השזיפים היו

The instructor may vary the above drills by supplying only the noun
substitution, with the student making the necessary changes in the verb
/hayá, haytá, hayú/.

GRAMMAR NOTES

15.4 Roots

Examine the following sets of related forms and note that in each set
there is a sequence of consonants which recurs in all the forms:

1. /ledabér/   "to speak"   לדבר
    /dabér/   "speak"   דבר
    /adabér/   "I will speak"   אדבר
    /medabér/   "speaks"   מדבר

2. /saméax/   "happy"   שמח
    /nismáx/   "we will be happy"   נשמח

3. /slixá/   "pardon" (noun)   סליחה
    /tisláx/   "you will pardon"   תסלח

4. /séder/   "arrangement, order"   סדר
    /yesudár/   "it will be arranged"   יסודר

In group 1 the sequence /d-b-r/ recurs, with the basic meaning "speak";
in group 2 the sequence /s-m-x/ recurs, with the basic meaning "happy";
in group 3 the sequence /s-l-x/ recurs, with the basic meaning "pardon"; and
in group 4 the sequence /s-d-r/ recurs, with the basic meaning "arrange".
Such sequences, called <u>roots</u>, have been hinted at in the preceding units.
Hebrew roots generally consist of three consonants. Roots of four consonants,
such as /t-r-g-m/ in /targém/ "translate", are fairly common. Roots with only
one or two consonants, such as /b/ in /bá/ "come" and /r-c/ in /larúc/ "to run",
are less frequent. Roots of five consonants also occur, but infrequently, and
they are generally technical, or slang coinages, such as /letalgréf/ "to
telegraph".

These root consonants are often called <u>radicals</u>, and dictionaries list
verbs according to these radicals. Roots of less than three radicals are
"supplied" with additional radicals to make three for purposes of listing.
The particular consonant supplied is usually based on the Hebrew spelling of
one of the forms. The patterns are rather regular but complicated, and they
will be discussed as the opportunity presents itself.

15.5 Patterns Occurring with Roots

Examine the following groups of forms and note that in each group there is
a recurring sequence of vowels, and, in some of the groups, of consonants also:

5. /xošév/   "thinks"   חושב
    /omér/   "says"   אומר
    /mocé/   "finds"   מוצא
    /rocé/   "wants"   רוצה
    /olé/   "costs"   עולה
    /osé/   "does"   עושה
    /roé/   "sees"   רואה

6. /medabér/   "speaks"   מדבר
    /memahér/   "hurries"   ממהר
    /mekavé/   "hopes"   מקוה

7.   /lamádeti/   "I studied"   למדתי
       /amárti/   "I said"   אמרתי
       /axálti/   "I ate"   אכלתי
       /šamáti/   "I heard"   שמעתי
       /natáti/   "I gave"   נתתי

8.   /natxíl/   "we will begin"   נחחיל
       /namšíx/   "we will continue"   נמשיך

In group 5 the sequence /-o-é-/ indicates the present tense, while in
group 6 the sequence /me-a-é-/ carries this meaning.
    In group 7 the sequence /-a-á-ti/ carries the general meaning "I _____
(past tense), with the root consonants indicating the basic verb meaning.
    In group 8 the sequence /na--í-/ carries the meaning "we will _____",
and the radicals /t-x-l/ and /m-š-x/ indicate the basic verb meanings.

    Thus it may be seen that the roots carry the basic meanings, and the
patterns of vowels, prefixes, and suffixes indicate the precise meanings of the
forms as they occur in sentences, such as present tense, etc.

    Up to this point the emphasis in the grammatical drills has been on
prefixing, suffixing, and other changes which occur regardless of the pattern
occurring with the root. For example, the present tense verbs /xošév/ and
/medabér/ show similar changes for the feminine and plurals.

m.s.	/xošév/	/medabér/	מדבר	חושב
f.s.	/xošévet/	/medabéret/	מדברת	חושבת
m.pl.	/xošvím/	/medabrím/	מדברים	חושבים
f.pl.	/xošvót/	/medabrót/	מדברות	חושבות

    However, though the /-o-é-/ and /me-a-é-/ patterns both indicate present
tense they are of different verb patterns and the other tenses will show
differences, also. The future tense forms of these verbs are, for example,
/taxšóv/ and /tedabér/.
    If the student learns the various patterns with a few representative roots,
he will be able to derive all the forms of a new root by analogy from one or
two forms. For example, the following forms of the verb "to speak" have
occurred:

infinitive:	/ledabér/	"to speak"	לדבר
m.s.imv.	/dabér/	"speak"	דבר
f.s.imv.	/dabrí/	"speak"	דברי
1 s.fut.	/adabér/	"I will speak"	אדבר
3 m.pl.fut.	/yedabrú/	"they will speak"	ידברו
m.s.pres.	/medabér/	"speaks"	מדבר

    Forms of two other roots with the same pattern have occurred so far:
/asapér/ "I will tell" and /letayél/ "to walk about". From these the matching
forms may be derived: (The derived forms are listed to the right.)

infinitive		/lesapér/	/letayél/
m.s.imv.		/sapér/	/tayél/
f.s.imv.		/saprí/	/taylí/
1 s.fut.	/asapér/		/atayél/
3 m.pl.fut.	/yesaprú/		/yetaylú/
m.s.pres.		/mesapér/	/metayél/

As a further illustration, the root of /xošév/, x̱šv, occurs with the
pattern of /dabér/ with the somewhat different meaning "to calculate" instead
of "to think". The corresponding forms are:

infinitive	/lexašév/	"to calculate"	לחשב
m.s.imv.	/xašév/	"calculate"	חשב
f.s.imv.	/xašví/	"calculate"	חשבי
1 s.fut.	/axašév/	"I will calculate"	אחשב
3 m.pl.fut.	/yexašvú/	"they will calculate"	יחשבו
m.s.pres.	/mexašév/	"calculates"	מחשב

It is not all so simple as the above illustrations might make it appear.
For one thing, even the simplest pattern with an unvarying root may have
over twenty different forms of which the student must have automatic control.
This requires a tremendous amount of drill, and the student should not be
lulled into a feeling of confidence simply because he finds it easy to "encode"
the correct form with some reflection.
    Second, there are quite a few different verb patterns alone, not
counting variations for phonological reasons. Mastery of these represents the
major task for the beginning Hebrew student. In the following units a great
deal of attention will be paid to it in the drills.

15.6 Alternating Radicals

Compare the related forms in the following groups:

1.	/pné/	"turn"	פנה
	/tifné/	"you will turn!'"	תפנה
2.	/ptáx/	"open"	פתח
	/tiftáx/	"you will open"	תפתח
3.	/bó/	"come"	בוא
	/tavó/	"you will come"	תבוא

The first member of each group has a root varying slightly from the
apparent root of the second member. In the first two groups /p/ alternates
with /f/, and in the third /b/ alternates with /v/. In addition, some roots
have /k/ alternating with /x/ as one of the radicals.
    These alternations have been mentioned before, and they are quite frequent
in verbs. The patterns of alternation often depend on the pattern occurring
with the root, but a few generalizations may be made at this point.

a) At the beginning of a word the alternants /p/, /b/, and /k/ occur:

	/pné/	"turn"	פנה
	/bó/	"come"	בוא
	/kén/	"yes, so"	כן

b) At the end of a word the alternants /f/, /v/, and /x/ occur:

	/cahóv/	"yellow"	צהוב
	/dérex/	"way"	דרך

c) After a stressed vowel the alternants /f/, /v/, and /x/ occur:

	/séfer/	"book"	ספר
	/šéva/	"seven"	שבע
	/óxel/	"food"	אוכל

d) As the second consonant of an initial two-consonant cluster the
alternants /f/, /v/, and /x/ occur:

/sfarím/	"books"	ספרים
/švií/	"seventh"	שביעי

There is a close correspondence in the Hebrew spelling of radicals that
alternate and those which do not:

/k/ alternating with /x/ is spelled   כ .
/k/ not alternating with /x/ is spelled   ק .
/x/ not alternating with /k/ is spelled   ח .

Thus, for example, initial /x/ will be spelled always with   ח .
/xošév/   חושב
    Final /k/ will be spelled with   ק .   /yarók/   ירוק

/v/ alternating with /b/ is spelled   ב .
/v/ not alternating with /b/ is spelled   ו .

In listing the roots p, b, and k will be used for the alternating radicals.
The student should learn these roots by drilling the forms. Attention to the
Hebrew spelling will be of help in roots with /k/ and /x/.
    Thus, the root of /séfer/ "book" will be listed as spr, the same as
for /sapér/ "tell".

15.7   Alternating Patterns

Patterns alternate in a number of ways, and some of these have been described
already. Alternations such as the /a/ in /memaharím/ m.pl.pres. "hurry"
depend on the particular consonants which comprise the root. Other pattern
alternations are the result of historical or phonological changes in Hebrew
which leave forms similar in one part of a pattern and different in other
parts. For example, the future of the roots /p-t-x/ "open" and /s-m-x/ "be
happy" are very similar - /eftáx/ "I will open" and /esmáx/ "I will be happy".
However, the present tense of the former is /potéax/ and the corresponding
form of the latter is /saméax/, which has been treated as an adjective.
    The student should not try to memorize a huge series of rules, but he
should drill the patterns as they occur and use the descriptions in the notes
as an aid. Summaries will be provided from time to time for further assistance.

15.8   Designation of Patterns

In previous units we have discussed patterns by using the symbols C for
"consonant" and V for "vowel". For ease in discussing patterns we will
designate them by using the arbitrary root p'l. The choice of this root is
dictated by Hebrew grammatical tradition. Other roots which are often used by
grammarians for this purpose are q t l and š m r.
    The choice of p'l has the disadvantage that the internal open juncture
/'/ is usually replaced by a smooth transition. The roots q t l (q is often
used as a symbol for the /k/ which never alternates with /x/) and šmr do not
have this disadvantage; their consonants do not vary. However, the use of
p'l will allow the student to be a bit conversant in the traditional Hebrew
description of Hebrew as taught in Israeli schools.

An advantage in using p'l is that the p will occur as /f/ in the patterns where it is called for and give the student an additional aid in deriving forms.

Thus, for example, the form /kibél/ will be said to be a pi'él form (pronounced /pi'él/ or /piél/). The form /slixá/ will be said to be a p'ilá form (pronounced /pe'ilá/ or /peilá/ since /p'/ is a non-permissible initial cluster).

NOTE: This section and the following one are not grammatical explanations. They are explanations of grammatical terms used in this text.

15.9 Designation of Radicals

The root p'l consists, in the Hebrew spelling, of the letters פ /péy/, ע /áin/, and ל /lámed/   Since most Hebrew roots consist of three consonants or can be spelled with three letters when they consist of less, the radicals are named after these letters. The first radical is called the "/péy/" of the root, the second is called the "/áin/", and the third is called the "/lámed/". We will use these traditional designations as well as C with subscript numerals in discussion of roots and patterns.

In Grammar Note 8.4a the term /lámed héy/ was used. This means that some forms of these roots are spelled in Hebrew with the letter ה /héy/ as the third consonant. Actually, there is no third consonant in their pronunciation. The root consists of two consonants with the second always followed by a vowel. The /héy/ is an instance of a third "consonant" being added to regularize the designation.

More specifically, the dictionary listing of the root is usually the third person masculine singular past tense form of the verb. The verb "to be" would be listed under the root hyh since the 3 m.s. past is /hayá/ היה . This verb, also, is a lámed héy verb.

Below is a partial list of the roots which have occurred in the text and some representative forms illustrating the root. Note that the internal open juncture /'/ may function as a radical.

Verbs listed with h as the third radical may be assumed to be lámed héy verbs. Verb roots in which the final radical is the consonantal aspirate /h/ are very few in number and will be specifically designated when they occur. They are listed in dictionaries in their normal alphabetical order.

The student need not memorize the following list. It is included here only for illustration of the grammatical points discussed in this unit.

Root

dbr	דבר	/dabér/ "speak"	/davár/ "thing"		
mc'	מצא	/moc'ím/ "find"	/nimca'ím/ "are found"		
šm'	שמע	/šim'í/ "hear" (f.s. imv.) /nišmá/ "is heard"	/šamáti/ "I heard"		
mšx	משך	/hamšéx/ "continue"	/tamšíx/ "you will continue"		
r'h	ראה	/lir'ót/ "to see"	/roé/ "sees"	/raíti/ "I saw"	
'sh	עשה	/laasót/ "to do"	/osé/ "does"	/asíti/ "I did"	
'kl	אכל	/leexól/ "to eat"	/axálti/ "I ate"	/óxel/ "food"	
sgr	סגר	/sgór/ "close"	/esgór/ "I will close"		
ptx	פתח	/ptáx/ "open"	/eftáx/ "I will open"		

<u>gzm</u>	/tagzím/ "you will exaggerate"	
<u>gdl</u>	/gadól/ "big"	
<u>sdr</u>	/yesudár/ "it will be arranged"	/séder/ "order"
<u>zhr</u>	/hizahér/ "be careful"	
<u>kns</u>	/lehikanés/ "to enter"	

[Note: In this text abstracted root consonants are indicated by underlining. Transcriptions of spoken forms are indicated by slash lines. Thus, for example, the statement "<u>b</u> occurs as /v/" would mean that a radical <u>b</u>, which alternates between /b/ and /v/, occurs as /v/ in the particular form being discussed.
Root <u>šbr</u> -- 3 m.s. past /šavar/ "he broke" שבר]

RAPID RESPONSE DRILL

איפה היה בית הקפה?

מה הזמינו לעזרת?

איזה קפה רצתה עטדה?

איזה עוגות יש נגבית היה?

באיזו עוגה בחרה עטדה?

באיזו עוגה בחר דוד?

מדוע דוד אינו יכול עדיין לשתות את הקפה?

REVIEW CONVERSATIONS

A: bó nigáš lištót kós kafé.

א: בוא ניגש לשתות כוס קפה.

B: éyfo bét hakafé.

ב: איפה בית הקפה?

A: šám bapiná.

א: שם בפינה.

B: esmáx meód.

ב: אשמח מאוד.

C: hatéy xám. hizaharí.

ג: התה חם. הזהרי.

D: hú ló xám. hú kvár kár.

ד: הוא לא חם. הוא כבר קר.

C: át rocá xaláv latéy?

ג: את רוצה חלב לתה?

D: ló. aní rocá limón vesukár.

ד: לא. אני רוצה לימון וסוכר.

E: melcarít. tní li kós máim karím, bevakašá.

ה: מלצרית, תני לי כוס מים קרים, בבקשה.

F: atá rocé ód mášehu?

ו: אתה רוצה עוד משהו?

E: kén. banána splít.

ה: כן. בננה ספליט.

F: tóv adoní. beracón.

ו: טוב אדוני. ברצון.

G: matáy tavó lir'ót otánu.

ז: מתי תבוא לראות אותנו?

H: avó haérev, ím atém rocím.

ח: אבוא הערב אם אתם רוצים.

G: tov. bó im hamišpaxá.

ז: טוב. בוא עם המשפחה.

H: rayón tóv. lehitraót haérev.

ח: רעיון טוב. להתראות הערב.

151

I: sapér li. heyxán raíta et xána.

ט: ספר לי, היכן ראית את חנה?

J: raíti otá birxóv álenbi.

י: ראיתי אותה ברחוב אלנבי.

I: má hí osá betél avív.

ט: מה היא עושה בתל אביב?

J: hí báa lekán kól šavúa.

י: היא באה לכאן כל שבוע.

I: im kén, caríx lehazmín otá
learuxát érev.

ט: אם כן, צריך להזמין אותה
לארוחת ערב.

K: haím mošé yavó héna hayóm?

כ: האם משה יבוא הנה היום?

L: aní xošév šeyavó bexaméš.

ל: אני חושב שיבוא בחמש.

K: tóv. nexaké ló kán ád šeyagía.

כ: טוב. נחכה לו כאן עד שיגיע.

16.1 <u>Conversation in the Coffee House</u> /sixá bebét hakafé/   .שיחה בבית הקפה

DAVID

I met	pagášti	פגשתי
Moshe this morning.	et mošé habóker.	את משה הבוקר.
I met	pagášti	פגשתי

ATARA

Really?	beemét?	באמת?
What did he	má hú	מה הוא
say to you?	sipér lexá.	סיפר לך?
he told	sipér (3 m.s.past)	סיפר

DAVID

He told me	hú sipér li	הוא סיפר לי
that he got	šehú kibél	שהוא קיבל
a letter	mixtáv	מכתב
from Mr. Williams.	mimár Williams.	ממר ויליאמס.
he received	kibél (3.m.s.past)	קיבל
letter	mixtáv (m)	מכתב

ATARA

From where	meáin	מאין
did he send	hú šaláx	הוא שלח
the letter?	et hamixtáv,	את המכתב?
From the U.S.?	meamérika?	מאמריקה?
he sent	šaláx(3 m.s.past)	שלח

DAVID

No. From Tel Aviv.	ló. mitél avív.	לא. מתל אביב.

ATARA

From Tel Aviv?	mitél avív?	מתל אביב?
What is he doing there?	má hú osé šám.	מה הוא עושה שם?

DAVID

He was appointed	hú nitmaná	הוא נתמנה
Counsellor of	leyoéc	ליועץ
the American Embassy.	hašagrirút haamerikáit.	השגרירות האמריקאית.
he was appointed	nitmaná (3 m.s.past)	נתמנה

ATARA

When	matáy	מתי
did he arrive?	hú higía.	הוא הגיע?
he arrived	higía (3 m.s.past)	הגיע

DAVID

Last week.	bešavúa šeavár.	בשבוע שעבר
he passed	avár (3 m.s.past)	עבר

153

Moshe went	mošé nasá	מֹשֶׁה נֹסֹע
to Tel Aviv	letél avív	לתל אביב,
and saw him.	veraá otó.	וראה אותו.
he travelled	nasá (3 m.s.past)	נֹסֹע
he saw	raá (3 m.s.past)	ראה

ATARA

How does he look?	éyx hú nir'é.	איך הוא נראה?
is seen, appears	nir'é (m.s.pres.)	נראה

DAVID

Moshe said that	mošé amár šé –	מֹשֶׁה אמר ש–
he looks good.	hú nir'é tóv.	הוא נראה טוב.
he said	amár (3 m.s.past)	אמר

ATARA

Does he still	hú ód	הוא עוד
speak Hebrew?	medabér ivrít?	מדנר עברית?

DAVID

Yes. He spoke	kén. hú dibér	כן. הוא דינר
Hebrew with Moshe.	ivrít im mošé.	עברית עם מֹשֶׁה.
he spoke	dibér (3 m.s.past)	דינר

16.2 ADDITIONAL VOCABULARY

She received a letter.	hí kiblá mixtáv.	היא קנלה מכתב.
They (m) received a letter.	hém kiblú mixtáv.	הם קנלו מכתב.
They (f) received a letter.	hén kiblú mixtáv.	הן קנלו מכתב.
She sent a letter.	hí šalxá mixtáv.	היא שלחה מכתב.
They sent a letter.	hém šalxú mixtáv.	הם שלחו מכתב.
What did she say?	má hí amrá.	מה היא אמרה?
What did they say?	má hén amrú.	מה הן אמרו?
She went to Haifa.	hí nas'á lexáyfa.	היא נסעה לחיפה.
They went to Haifa.	hém nas'ú lexáyfa.	הם נסעו לחיפה.
She arrived yesterday.	hí higía etmól.	היא הגיעה אתמול.
They arrived yesterday.	hén higíu etmól.	הן הגיעו אתמול.
She saw him.	hí raatá otó.	היא ראתה אותו.
They saw him.	hém raú otó.	הם ראו אותו.
He arrived here	hú higía héna	הוא הגיע הנה
last year.	bešaná šeavrá.	בשנה שענרה.

16.3 Vocabulary Drills

A. Response Drill - /pagášti/ "I met"

Instructor: When did you meet Atara?
Student: I met her this morning.

matáy pagášta et atára.	pagášti otá habóker.	?מתי פגשת את עטרה
matáy pagaštém et atára.	pagášnu otá habóker.	?מתי פגשתם את עטרה
matáy pagášten et atára.	pagášnu otá habóker.	?מתי פגשתן את עטרה
matáy pagášt et atára.	pagášti otá habóker.	?מתי פגשת את עטרה

B. Substitution Drill - /nir'é/ "appears"

When the present tense pattern has a /ni-/ prefix the feminine singular ends
in /-t/, even with lamed hey verbs. This is the exception to the general
lámed héy present tense pattern.with /-á/ feminine mentioned in the note to
Grammar Section 8.4a.

He looks well.

hú nir'é tóv.	.הוא נראה טוב
nir'ét	נראית
nir'ím	נראים
nir'ót	נראות

C. Substitution - Agreement Drill

How does Moshe look?

éyx nir'é mošé.	?איך נראה משה
habáit šel dóv - gvéret zahávi	הבית של דוב - גברת זהבי
haoniót haxadašót - hamalón	האוניות החדשות - המלון
hatapuxím - hayerakót - hašagrirút	התפוחים - הירקות - השגרירות
haugót - mišpáxat kármi - mošé	העוגות - משפחת כרמי - משה

D. Individual Response Drill

Instructor: How does the new hotel look?
Student: It's very beautiful.

éyx nir'é hamalón haxadáš.	.איך נראה המלון החדש
hú yafé meód.	.הוא יפה מאוד
éyx nir'ét ištó šel davíd.	.איך נראית אשתו של דוד
éyx nir'ím harexovót.	.איך נראים הרחובות
éyx nir'é habáit šel xána.	.איך נראה הבית של חנה
éyx nir'ót haagvaniót.	.איך נראות העגבניות
éyx nir'ét sfát hayám.	.איך נראית שפת הים
éyx nir'é bét hakafé.	.איך נראה בית הקפה

GRAMMAR NOTES

16.4   Third Person Past Tense Verb Forms

Examine the following verb forms:

hú <u>kibél</u>	"he received"
hí <u>kiblá</u>	"she received"
hém <u>kiblú</u>	"they (m) received"
hén <u>kiblú</u>	"they (f) received"
hú <u>šaláx</u>	"he sent"
hí <u>šalxá</u>	"she sent"
hém <u>šalxú</u>	"they (m) sent"
hén <u>šalxú</u>	"they (f) sent"
hú <u>amár</u>	"he said"
hí <u>amrá</u>	"she said"
hém <u>amrú</u>	"they (m) said"
hén <u>amrú</u>	"they (f) said"

Note, first of all, that the third person plural forms are the same for both genders. This is true of all past tense verbs, regardless of conjugation.

Note further that the feminine singular has the suffix /-á/, and the plural has suffix /-ú/. The preceding vowel is dropped as with the /-í/ and /-ú/ suffixes in the future.

In addition to these characteristics there are variations depending on the type of root. Some of these variations will be illustrated in the following drills. After the third person forms are drilled the corresponding first and second person forms will be described and drilled.

In the following drills the instructor gives a sentence with a 3 m.s. past tense verb. The students repeat the sentence. The instructor then gives the substitution cues, and the students give the sentence with the necessary changes.

Some of the verbs have not occurred in the third person past tense previously, but the student should have no trouble recognizing them.

    a.   Ordinary Roots

These are roots whose final two radicals do not require any additional variations. The consonants which may require variations in the third person pattern are /'/, /h/, and /x/. The possibilities of these variations will be described as they occur.

A.   Substitution - Agreement Drill - /kibél/   "received"

He received a letter from Mr. Cohen.

<u>hú kibél mixtáv mimár kóhen.</u>   .הוא קיבל מכתב מימר כהן

xána - hém - mošé - hén   חנה - הם - משה - הן
már kármi - hú veištó - hí - hú   מר כרמי - הוא ואשתו - היא - הוא

B. Substitution - Agreement Drill - /sipér/ "told"

He told Miriam the news.

hú sipér lemiryám et haxadašót.   הוא ספר למרים את החדשות.

sára - davíd - hén - gvéret kóhen   שרה - דוד - הן - גברת כהן
hí vebaalá - dóv - mošé vedóv - hú   היא ובעלה - דוב - משה ודוב - הוא

C. Substitution - Agreement Drill - /dibér/ "spoke"

He spoke Hebrew in the office.

hú dibér ivrít bamisrád.   הוא דבר עברית במשרד.

hén - xána - davíd - hém   הן - חנה - דוד - הם
sára veléa - gvéret Williams - hú   שרה ולאה - גברת ווילאמס - הוא

D. Substitution - Agreement Drill - /šaláx/ "sent"

He sent a package to America.

hú šaláx xavilá leamérika.   הוא שלח חבילה לאמריקה.

mošé veištó - miryám - hém   משה ואשתו - מרים - הם
dóv - hén - atára - hú   דוב - הן - עטרה - הוא

E. Substitution - Agreement Drill - /saláx/ "forgave"

He forgave Miriam for the letter.

hú saláx lemiryám al hamixtáv.   הוא סלח למרים על המכתב.

xána - kulám - mošé - hí   חנה - כולם - משה - היא
már káspi - hén - hú   מר כספי - הן - הוא

F. Substitution - Agreement Drill - /amár/ "said"

He said it was cold yesterday.

hú amár šehayá kár etmól.   הוא אמר שהיה קר אתמול.

hém - sára - davíd - hén   הם - שרה - דוד - הן
gvéret kármi - hí - hú   גברת כרמי - היא - הוא

G. Substitution - Agreement Drill - /avár/ "passed"

He passed by the office this morning.

hú avár al yád hamisrád habóker.   הוא עבר על יד המשרד הבוקר.

hém - avígdor - atára - hén   הם - אביגדור - עטרה - הן
mošé - hí - dóv veištó - hú   משה - היא - דוב ואשתו - הוא

157

H.   Substitution - Agreement Drill   /xašáv/   "thought"

     He thought that today was Friday.

     <u>hú xašáv šehayóm yóm šiší.</u>   .<u>הוא חשב שהיום יום שי</u>

     hí - hém -gvéret kóhen   היא – הם – גברת כהן
     hén - yoséf - sára - hú   הן – יוסף – שרה – הוא

I.   Substitution - Agreement Drill - /patáx/   "opened"

     He opened the door.

     <u>hú patáx et hadélet.</u>   .<u>הוא פתח את הדלת</u>

     hí - mošé vedóv - hén   היא – משה ודב – הן
     sára - már kóhen - hém - hú   שרה – מר כהן – הם – הוא

J.   Substitution - Agreement Drill - /sagár/   "opened"

     He closed the door.

     <u>hú sagár et hadélet.</u>   .<u>הוא סגר את הדלת</u>

     hén - davíd veatára - hí   הן – דוד ועטרה – היא
     már kármi - hém - sára - hú   מר כרמי – הם – שרה – הוא

K.   Substitution - Agreement Drill - /axál/   "ate"

     He ate watermelon.

     <u>hú axál avatíax.</u>   .<u>הוא אכל אבטיח</u>

     hém - hí - sára vexána   הם – היא – שרה וחנה
     avígdor - gvéret káspi - hú   אביגדור – גברת כספי – הוא

L.   Substitution - Agreement Drill   /natán/   "gave"

     He gave me all the food.

     <u>hú natán li et kól haóxel.</u>   .<u>הוא נתן לי את כל האוכל</u>

     ištó šel haxenvaní - hamelcár   אשתו של החנוני – המלצר
     hém - mošé - ištexá - hú   הם – משה – אשתך – הוא

M.   Substitution - Agreement Drill   /pagáš/   "met"

     He met her in America.

     <u>hú pagáš otá beamérika.</u>   .<u>הוא פגש אותה באמריקה</u>

     atára - hén - már zahávi   עטרה – הן – מר זהבי
     gvéret zahávi - hém - hú   גברת זהבי – הם – הוא

                                               <u>End of Tape 5B</u>

Tape 6A

N. Substitution - Agreement Drill /hitrašém/   "was impressed"

He was impressed by the new building.

<u>hú hitrašém mehabinyán haxadáš.</u>   .הוא התרשם מהבנין החדש

   gvéret Williams - hém - atára   גברת ויליאמס – הם – עטרה
   baalá - hén - hí - hú   בעלה – הן – היא – הוא

O. Substitution - Agreement Drill - /lamád/   "studied"

He studied in this school.

<u>hú lamád bebét haséfer hazé.</u>   .הוא למד בבית הספר הזה

   xána vebaalá - baaléx - léa   חנה ובעלה – בעלך – לאה
   hém - davíd - hí - hú   הם – דוד – היא – הוא

   b.   <u>Verbs with Third Radical ' or x</u>

   There are two sub-classes of verbs whose third radical is ' or x. The '
and x of one sub-class are spelled in Hebrew with א and כ, respectively, and
the ' and x of the other sub-class are spelled with ע and ח.

   The first sub-class has the same general pattern as ordinary verbs.
Examples are: /macá/ "he found" מצא /mocé/ "finds" מוצא ,
   /himšíx/ "he continued" המשיך.

   In verbs of the latter sub-class the vowel /a/ must immediately precede the
third radical when it is final in the word. This is true even in the case of '
which is spelled but not pronounced, as in /yodéa/ "knows" יודע.
   If the vowel /a/ precedes it anyway, then there is no problem. Examples are:
/yadá/ "he knew" ידע ,/patáx/ "he opened" פתח ,/šaláx/ "he sent" שלח.
   When the conjugation pattern calls for another vowel, then an unstressed /a/
is inserted. /saméax/ "happy" שמח   but /nismáx/ "we will be happy" נשמח
         /šoméa/ "hears" שומע   but /šmá/ "hear" (imv.) שמע
   (pi'el) /šiléax/ "he sent away" שילח   but /šaláx/ "he sent" שלח.

P. Substitution - Agreement Drill - /nasá/   "traveled"

He went to see Haifa.

<u>hú nasá lir'ót et xáyfa.</u>   .הוא נסע לראות את חיפה

   hí - hém - mošé - sára   היא – הם – משה – שרה
   dóv vemiryám - hén - hú   דוב ומרים – הן – הוא

Q. Substitution - Agreement Drill - /yadá/   "knew"

He didn't know that Miriam is in Tel Aviv.

<u>hú ló yadá šemiryám betél avív.</u>   .הוא לא ידע שמרים בתל אביב

   gvéret kóhen - mošé - iští   גברת כהן – משה – אשתי
   hém - sára - hén - hú   הם – שרה – הן – הוא

R.   Substitution - Agreement Drill - /macá/   "found"

He didn't find the bottle.

<u>hú ló macá et habakbúk.</u>   .הוא לא מצא את הבקבוק

gvéret kóhen - mošé - iští - hén   גברת כהן - משה - אשתי - הן
hém - yaakóv - hí - hú   הם - יעקב - היא - הוא

S.   Substitution - Agreement Drill - /šamá/   "heard"

He didn't hear the news this evening.

<u>hú ló šamá et haxadašót haérev.</u>   .הוא לא שמע את החדשות הערב

ištó - dóv - hém - yaakóv   אשתו - דוב - הם - יעקב
hén - gvéret óren - hú   הן - גברת אורן - הוא

c.   lamed hey Verbs

Examine the pattern of the following forms:

/hayá/	"he was"	היה
/haytá/	"she was"	היתה
/hayú/	"they were"	היו

The pattern of the third person endings is:
    3 m.s. /-á/
    3 f.s. /-tá/
    3 pl. /-ú/

These endings follow the second radical regardless of the conjugation of the verb. The third radical is listed as <u>h</u>, but this is only a spelling convention.
    The 3 m.s. ending may be confusing at first since it resembles the 3 f.s. of ordinary verbs in pronunciation and spelling. It is also similar in pronunciation to verbs with third radical <u>'</u>.

T.   Substitution - Agreement Drill /hayá/ "was"

He was in Jerusalem yesterday.

<u>hú hayá beyerušaláim etmól.</u>   .הוא היה בירושלים אתמול

ištó šel davíd - mošé vedóv - hén   אשתו של דוד - משה ודוב - הן
yaakóv - hí - hém - léa - hú   יעקב - היא - הם - לאה - הוא

U.   Substitution - Agreement Drill - /asá/ "did"

What did he do in Jerusalém?

<u>má hú asá beyerušaláim.</u>   ?מה הוא עשה בירושלים

hí - hém - ištexá - hén   היא - הם - אשתך - הן
gvéret óren - baaléx - hú   גברת אורן - בעלך - הוא

V. Substitution - Agreement Drill - /paná/ "turned"

He turned left at the intersection.

<u>hú paná smóla bahictalvút.</u>   <u>הוא פנה שמאלה בהצטלבות.</u>

haišá - hanaším - mošé veraxél   האשה – הנשים – משה ורחל
hí - avígdor - hém - hú   היא – אביגדור – הם – הוא

W. Substitution - Agreement Drill - /kivá/ "hoped"

He hoped for a good result.

<u>hú kivá letocaá tová.</u>   <u>הוא קיווה לתוצאה טובה.</u>

gvéret zahávi - yoséf - hém   גברת זהבי – יוסף – הם
ištó šel dóv - miryám veléa - hú   אשתו של דוב – מרים ולאה – הוא

X. Substitution - Agreement Drill - /racá/ "wanted"

He didn't want to eat so early.

<u>hú 16 racá leexól kol káx mukdám.</u>   <u>הוא לא רצה לאכול כל כך מוקדם.</u>

hém - sára - davíd veatára   הם – שרה – דוד ועטרה
avígdor - hanaším - hí - hú   אביגדור – הנשים – היא – הוא

d. <u>Verbs with Second Radical ' or h</u>

Whenever the conjugation pattern or other v   attern would result in a second radical /'/ or /h/ occurring immediately before a consonant, the vowel /a/ is inserted between them. Other examples of this have been drilled previously, such as /memahér ~memaharím/ and /hizahér ~hizaharí/.

The root of the verb "to see" is <u>r'h</u>, a <u>lamed hey</u> verb. Accordingly the third person past tense would be:

        3 m.s. /ra'á/ "he saw"
        3 f.s. */ra'tá/ "she saw"
        3 pl. /ra'ú/ "they saw"

In the 3 f.s. the second radical /'/ occurs before a consonant - the suffix /tá/. The form is then /ra'atá/.

In ordinary speech the /'/ is replaced by a smooth transition, and the forms are:

        3 m.s. /raá/ "he saw"
        3 f.s. /raatá/ "she saw"
        3 pl. /raú/ "the saw"

Y. Substitution - Agreement Drill - /raá/ "saw"

He saw the new house.

<u>hú raá et habáit haxadáš.</u>   <u>הוא ראה את הבית החדש.</u>

iští - hanaším šelánu - davíd   אשתי – הנשים שלנו – דוד
hém - gvéret kóhen - hú   הם – גברת כהן – הוא

e. Verbs with Unstressed Third Person Suffixes

The 3 f.s. and the 3 pl. endings /-a, -u/ are unstressed in the following cases:

1) When the 3 m.s. is one syllable and the vowel is /á/.
   /rác/ "he ran"
   /ráca/ "she ran"
   /rácu/ "they ran"

2) When the final vowel of the conjugation pattern is /í/.
   /himšíx/ "he continued"
   /himšíxa/ "she continued"
   /himšíxu/ "they continued"

This latter conjugation is traditionally called the   hif'íl

Z. Substitution - Agreement Drill - /rác/ "ran"

He ran after the bus.

hú rác axaréy haótobus.   .הוא רץ אחרי האוטובוס

   hí - hém - mošé - raxél   היא – הם – משה – רחל
   yoséf veištó - hén - hú   יוסף ואשתו – הן – הוא

AA. Substitution - Agreement Drill - /bá/ "came"

He came to see the house.

hú bá lir'ót et habáit.   .הוא בא לראות את הבית

   gvéret zahávi - yicxák - hí   גברת זהבי – יצחק – היא
   hém - léa - hén - hú   הם – לאה – הן – הוא

BB. Substitution - Agreement Drill - /himšíx/ "continued"

He continued seeing her every day.

hú himšíx lir'ót otá kól yóm.   .הוא המשיך לראות אותה כל יום

   már kármi - sára - dóv - hén   מר כרמי – שרה – דוב – הן
   iští - hém - gvéret óren - hú   אשתי – הם – גברת אורן – הוא

CC. Substitution - Agreement Drill - /hitxíl/ "began"

He began the diet this morning.

hú hitxíl badiéta habóker.   .הוא התחיל בדיאטה הבוקר

   gvéret kóhen - mošé - iští   גברת כהן – משה – אשתי
   sára veyoséf - hí - hén - hú   שרה ויוסף – היא – הן – הוא

DD. Substitution - Agreement Drill - /hizmín/ "invited"

He invited them for dinner.

hú hizmín otám learuxát érev.   .הוא הזמין אותם לארוחת ערב

hí - dóv veištó - xána - hén   היא – דוב ואשתו – חנה – הן

yaakóv - yaakóv vemiryám - hú   יעקב – יעקב ומרים – הוא

The root of the verb /higía/ "arrived" is listed as nq'. The vowel /a/ precedes the third radical ' whenever it is final in the word. See Section 16.4b above. The third person past tense forms are:

3 m.s. /higía/ for */higí'/ הגיע

3 f.s. /higía/ for /higí'a/ הגיעה

3 pl. /higíu/ for /higí'u/ הגיעו

By coincidence, therefore, the 3 m.s. and 3 f.s. are identical in ordinary speech.

EE. Substitution - Agreement Drill

He arrived in Israel last week.

hú higía leisraél bešavúa šeavár.   .הוא הגיע לישראל בשבוע שעבר

hí - hém - iští - hanaším   היא – הם – אשתי – הנשים

davíd - hamišpaxá šeló - hú   דוד – המשפחה שלו – הוא

RAPID RESPONSE DRILL

The following questions are based on the conversation of this unit.

1. matáy pagáš davíd et mošé.   ?מתי פגש דוד את משה .1

2. má sipér mošé ledavíd.   ?מה ספר משה לדוד .2

3. mimí kibél mošé mixtáv.   ?ממי קבל משה מכתב .3

4. meáin šaláx már Williams et hamixtáv.   ?מאין שלח מר וויליאמס את המכתב .4

5. má osé már Williams betél avív.   ?מה עושה מר וויליאמס בתל אביב .5

6. matáy higía már Williams leisraél.   ?מתי הגיע מר וויליאמס לישראל .6

7. leán nasá mošé.   ?לאן נסע משה .7

8. heyxán raá mošé et már Williams.   ?היכן ראה משה את מר וויליאמס .8

9. éyx nir'é már Williams.   ?איך נראה מר וויליאמס .9

10. beéyze safá hém dibrú.   ?באיזה שפה הם דברו .10

REVIEW CONVERSATIONS

A. pagášti et yaakóv.   .פגשתי את יעקב א.

B. éyfo pagášta otó.   ?איפה פגשת אותו ב.

A. pagášti otó barexóv.   .פגשתי אותו ברחוב א.

B. má hú sipér lexá.   ?מה הוא סיפר לך ב.

A. hú sipér li šehú sagár et hamisrád šeló.   .הוא ספר לי שהוא סגר את המשדר שלו א.

C. šamáti šemiryám gára betél avív.   .שמעתי שמרים גרה בתל אביב ג.

D. mimí šamát.   ?ממי שמעת ד.

C. mimošé. hú šamá et zót midóv.   .ממשה. הוא שמע את זאת מדוב ג.

D. hú natán láx et haktóvet šelá?   ?הוא נתן לך את הכתובת שלה ד.

C. 16. áx hú yitén li et haktóvet maxár.   .לא. אך הוא יתן לי את הכתובת מחר ג.

E. axálti glidá bebrúklin bár.   .אכלתי גלידה בברוקלין בר ה.

F. éyx haglidá šám.   ?איך הגלידה שם ו.

E. tová veteimá.   .טובה וטעימה ה.

F. gám iští axlá šám veamrá šehaglidá tová.   .גם אשתי אכלה שם ואמרה שהגלידה טובה ו.

G. dóv raá et menaxém habóker.   .דוב ראה את מנחם הבוקר ז.

H. eyfó hú raá otó.   ?איפה הוא ראה אותו ח.

G. kšehú veištó tiyelú birxóv álenbi hém pagšú otó al yád hašagrirút.   כשהוא ואשתו טיילו ברחוב אלנבי הם פגשו אותו על יד השגרירות. ז.

I. avíva hizmína otánu learuxát érev leyóm šiší.   אביבה הזמינה אותנו לארוחת ערב ליום ששי. ט.

J. beemét? hí amrá šehí tazmín gám et yaakóv.   באמת? היא אמרה שהיא תזמין גם את יעקב. י.

I. nismáx meód lir'ót otó. matáy hú higía lexáyfa.   נשמח מאוד לראות אותו. מתי הוא הגיע לחיפה? ט.

J. hú ód ló higía. hú yagía maxár.   .הוא עוד לא הגיע. הוא יגיע מחר י.

K.   xána vebaalá avrú al yád   כ. חנה ובעלה עברו על יד
     habáit šelánu habóker.   הבית שלנו הבוקר.

L.   beemét? má hém amrú lexá.   ל. באמת? מה הם אמרו לך?

K.   hém siprú li šedibrú im sára.   כ. הם ספרו לי שדברו עם שרה.

L.   éyfo nimcét sára?   ל. איפה נמצאת שרה?

K.   bexáyfa. hém natnú li et   כ. בחיפה. הם נתנו לי את
     mispár hatélefon šelá.   מספר הטלפון שלה.

M.   atára hitrašmá meód mehabáit   מ. עטרה התרשמה מאוד מהבית
     haxadáš šel yoséf.   החדש של יוסף.

N.   gám aní hitrašámti.   נ. גם אני התרשמתי.
     habáit gadól vexadíš.   הבית גדול וחדיש.

M.   matáy raít et habáit.   מ. מתי ראית את הבית?

N.   raíti et habáit šilšóm.   נ. ראיתי את הבית שלשום.

M.   gám atára raatá et habáit šilšóm.   מ. גם עטרה ראתה את הבית שלשום.

O.   lamádnu ivrít bebét haséfer lesafót.   ס. למדנו עברית בבית הספר לשפות.

P.   gám dálya lamdá šám.   ע. גם דליה למדה שם.

O.   matáy hí lamdá šám.   ס. מתי היא למדה שם?

P.   aní xošévet šelifnéy šaná.   ע. אני חושבת שלפני שנה.

Q.   haínu hašavúa benatánya.   פ. היינו השבוע בנתניה.

R.   beéyze yóm haítem šám.   צ. באיזה יום הייתם שם?

Q.   aní haíti beyóm šení veyéter   פ. אני הייתי ביום שני ויתר
     hamišpaxá haytá beyóm šliší.   המשפחה היתה ביום שלישי.

S.   davíd nasá leamérika.   ק. דוד נסע לאמריקה.

T.   matáy.   ר. מתי?

S.   lifnéy šavúa.   ק. לפני שבוע.

T.   haím ištó gám ken nas'á?   ר. האם אשתו גם כן נסעה?

S.   kén. hém nas'ú yáxad.   ק. כן. הם נסעו יחד.

אני רוצה לשלוח את המכתב הזה
לאמריקה...

17.1 At the Post Office

MR. WILLIAMS

I want	aní rocé	אני רוצה
to send	lišlóax et	לשלוח את
this letter	hamixtáv hazé	המכתב הזה
to the United States.	leamérika.	לאמריקה.
to send	lišlóax	לשלוח
letter	mixtáv (m)	מכתב

CLERK

By regular mail	bedóar ragíl	בדואר רגיל
or by air mail?	o bedóar avír.	או בדואר אוויר?
usual, habitual	ragíl (m.s.)	רגיל
air	avír (m)	אוויר

MR. WILLIAMS

By air mail.	bedóar avír.	בדואר אוויר.

CLERK

It will cost you	zé yaalé lexá	זה יעלה לך
thirty-five	šloším vexaméš	שלושים וחמש
agorot.	agorót.	אגורות.
agora (IL 0.01)	agorá (f)	אגורה

MR. WILLIAMS

How long	káma zmán	כמה זמן
will it take?	zé yikáx.	זה יקח?
time (duration)	zmán (m)	זמן
it will take	yikáx (3 m.s. fut.)	יקח
he took	lakáx	לקח

CLERK

I don't know.	aní ló yodéa.	אני לא יודע.
Maybe a week.	uláy šavúa.	אולי שבוע.
maybe, perhaps	uláy	אולי

MR. WILLIAMS

A week?	šavúa?	שבוע?
That's a long time.	zé harbé zmán.	זה הרבה זמן.
much, many	harbé	הרבה

CLERK

If it's	beím ze	באם זה
so urgent,	kol káx daxúf,	כל כך דחוף,
send a telegram.	šláx mivrák.	שלח מברק.
if	beím	באם
urgent	daxúf (m.s.)	דחוף
send	šláx (m.s. imv.)	שלח
telegram	mivrák (m)	מברק

MR. WILLIAMS

That's a good idea.	ze rayón tóv.	זה רעיון טוב.
Where is	heyxán	היכן
the telegraph office?	hamivraká.	המברקה?
idea	rayón (m)	רעיון
telegraph office	mivraká (f)	מברקה

167

CLERK

Here.	kán.	.כאן
On the second floor.	bakomá hašniá.	.בקומה השניה
story	komá (f)	קומה

MR. WILLIAMS

| Thank you very much. | todá rabá. | .תודה רבה |

17.2 ADDITIONAL VOCABULARY

| Give me five postal cards. | tén li xaméš gluyót. | תן לי חמש גלויות. |
| postal card | gluyá (f) | גלויה |

| Give me five envelopes. | tén li xaméš maatafót. | תן לי חמש מעטפות. |
| envelope | maatafá (f) | מעטפה |

| Give me five air letters. | tén li xaméš igrót avír. | תן לי חמש אגרות אויר. |
| letter | igéret (f) | אגרת |

| Give me five ten-agora stamps. | tén li xamišá bulím šel éser agorót. | תן לי חמישה בולים של עשר אגורות. |
| stamp | búl (m) | בול |

| Send the letter special delivery. | šláx et hamixtáv eksprés. | שלח את המכתב אקספרס. |

| Send the letter by registered mail. | šláx et hamixtáv bedóar rašúm. | שלח את המכתב בדואר רשום. |
| recorded, listed | rašúm (m.s.) | רשום |

17.3 Vocabulary Drills

A. Substitution-Agreement Drill - /ragíl/ "habitual"

He is used to eating on time.

hú ragíl leexól bazmán.
xána - mošé - kulám
sára veatára - aní - hú

הוא רגיל לאכול בזמן.
– חנה – משה – כולם –
שרה ועטרה – אני – הוא

B. Substitution Drill   /e - ~ti -/

I'll take the package.

ekáx et haxavilá.
atá tikáx
át tikxí
hú yikáx
hí tikáx
ánu nikáx
atém tikxú
atén tikáxna
hém yikxú
hén tikáxna

אקח את החבילה.
אתה תקח
את תקחי
הוא יקח
היא תקח
אנו נקח
אתם תקחו
אתן תקחנה
הם יקחו
הן תקחנה

C. Substitution-Agreement Drill

We'll take Miriam as far as Haifa.

nikáx et miryám ád xáyfa.   ‏נֵיקַח את מרים עד חיפה.‏

már óren - aní - hém - atén   ‏מר אורן – אני – הם – אתן‏
raxél - hén - atém - át   ‏רחל – הן – אתם – את‏
gvéret kóhen - atá - ánu   ‏גברת כהן – אתה – אנו‏

D. Substitution Drill /šláx/ "send"

Send him a post card.

šláx ló gluyá.   ‏שלח לו גלויה.‏

šilxí   ‏שלחי‏
šilxú   ‏שלחו‏
šláxna   ‏שלחנה‏

GRAMMAR NOTES

17.4 Past Tense of pi'el

The complete past tense pattern of ordinary <u>pi'el</u> verbs with three-consonant roots is as follows: (dashes indicate root consonants).

		spr				spr
1 s.	/-i-á-ti/	sipárti	1 pl.	/-i-á-nu /	sipárnu
2 m.s.	/-i-á-ta/	sipárta	2 m.pl.	/-i-á-tem/	sipartém
2 f.s.	/-i-á-t /	sipárt	2 f.pl.	/-i-á-ten/	sipartén
3 m.s.	/-i-é- ,	sipér	3 pl.	/-i--ú /	siprú
3 f.s.	/-i-- á /	siprá			

Note that the 3 m.s. has the vowels /-i-é-/ and the first and second person forms have the vowels /-i-á-/.

A. Substitution-Agreement Drill /sipér/ "told"

He told me about the dinner.

<u>hú sipér li ál aruxát haérev.</u>　　　　　.הוא סיפר לי על ארוחת הערב

xána - atém - mošé vedóv　　　　　　　חנה - אתם - משה ורוב
át - atá - sára - hú　　　　　　　　　　את - אתה - שרה - הוא

B. Substitution-Agreement Drill - /kibél/ "received"

I received a telegram this morning.

<u>kibálti mivrák habóker.</u>　　　　　　.קבלתי מברק הבוקר

hém - atém - davíd　　　　　　　　　　הם - אתם - דוד
ánu - gvéret kármi - aní　　　　　　　אנו - גברת כרמי - אני

C. Substitution-Agreement Drill /mihér/ "hurried"

She hurried to the telegraph office.

<u>hí mihará lamivraká.</u>　　　　　　.היא מיהרה למברקה

aní - atá - iští vegvéret káspi　　　אני - אתה - אשתי וגברת כספי
ánu - atém - yehudá - hí　　　　　　　אנו - אתם - יהודה - היא

D. Substitution-Agreement Drill /tiyél/ "strolled"

We took a walk on Allenby Road.

<u>tiyálnu berexóv álenbi.</u>　　　　　.טיילנו ברחוב אלנבי

atén - avígdor veatára - aní　　　　אתן - אביגדור ועטרה - אני
át vedóv - atá - ánu　　　　　　　　　את ורוב - אתה - אנו

End of Tape 6A

17.5 Past Tense of kal (pa'al)

The complete past tense pattern of ordinary <u>kal</u> verbs with three-consonant roots is as follows:

		šlx				šlx
1 s.	/-a-á-ti/	šaláxti	1 pl.	/-a-á-nu /	šaláxnu
2 m.s.	/-a-á-ta/	šaláxta	2 m. pl.	/-a-á-tem/	šaláxtem
2 f.s.	/-a-á-t /	šaláxt	2 f. pl.	/-a-á-ten/	šaláxten
3 m.s.	/-a-á- /	šaláx	3 pl.	/-a--ú /	šalxú
3 f.s.	/-a--á /	šalxá			

Tape 6B

E. Substitution-Agreement Drill /šaláx/ "sent"

When did they sent the package?

<u>matáy hém šalxú et haxavilá.</u>   ?מתי הם שלחו את החבילה

atém - haxenvaní - át - xána   אתם – החנווני – את – חנה
heń - atá - már káspi - hém   הן – אתה – מר כספי – הם

F. Substitution-Agreement Drill /mazág/ "poured"

I poured the wine into the glasses.

<u>mazágti et hayáin lakosót.</u>   .מזגתי את היין לכוסות

iští - át - atá - mošé   אשתי – את – אתה – משה
ánu - baaléx - hén - aní   אנו – בעלך – הן – אני

G. Substitution-Agreement Drill /macá/ "found"

She found the package on the third floor.

<u>hí mac'á et haxavilá bakomá hašlišít.</u>   .היא מצאה את החבילה בקומה השלישית

aní - hém - atá - avígdor   אני – הם – אתה – אביגדור
át - ištó - hú - hí   את – אשתו – הוא – היא

Verbs such as /rác/ "ran" are traditionally listed as pa'al conjugations. They resemble the ordinary pa'al verbs in the past tense in that the same vowel /a/ occurs in all forms:

1 s.	/rácti/	"I ran"	1 pl.	/rácnu/	"we ran"
2 m.s.	/rácta/	"you ran"	2 m. pl.	/ráctem/	"you ran"
2 f.s.	/ráct/	"you ran"	2 f. pl.	/rácten/	"you ran"
3 m.s.	/rác/	"he ran"	3 pl.	/rácu/	"they ran"
3 f.s.	/ráca/	"she ran"			

Note that the stress remains on the infixed /á/ in the 3 f.s. and the 3 pl.:

/ráca/ "she ran"   /rácu/ "they ran"

Verbs such as /rác/ have only two consonants in the root, but are listed in dictionaries with vav (ו) or yud (י) as the second root consonant. Thus, /rác/ רץ will be listed alphabetically under רוץ

The verb /bá/ "he came" is listed under בוא . Its pattern is similar to /rác/ except that it has only one consonant. All forms, though, are spelled with א .

H.   Substitution-Agreement Drill /rác/ "ran"

Dov ran to the office this morning.

dóv rác habóker lamisrád .   .דוב רץ הבוקר למשרד

aní - atá - már káspı - át   את - כספי מר - אתה - אחה - אני
ánu - raxél - raxél vesára - dóv   דוב - ושרה רחל - רחל - אנו

I.   Substitution-Agreement Drill /ba/ "came"

David came to the office yesterday.

davíd bá etmól lamisrád.   .דוד בא אתמול למשרד

atá - át - hanaším - aní   אני - הנשים - את - אחה
hém - ánu - atém - hí - davíd   דוד - היא - אתם - אנו - הם

17.6 Past Tense of hitpa'el

The hitpa'el is characterized by a prefix of the pattern /Cit-/. The first consonant of the prefix is usually /h/ in the past tense.

The hitpa'el resembles the pi'el in that the second stem vowel is /e/ in the 3 m.s. and /a/ in the first and second person in verbs with three root consonants.

/hitrašámti/   " I was impressed"
/hitrašém/   " he was impressed"

The first stem vowel is either /a/ or /o/.

/hitrašém/   " he was impressed"
/hitkonén/   " he planned"

The complete past tense pattern of the <u>hitpa'el</u> is as follows:

1 s.	/hit-a-á-ti/	hitrašámti		1 pl.	/hit-a-á-nu/	hitrašámnu
2 m.s.	/hit-a-á-ta/	hitrašámta		2 m.pl.	/hit-a-á-tem/	hitrašámtem
2 f.s.	/hit-a-á-t /	hitrašámt		2 f.pl.	/hit-a-á-ten/	hitrašámten
3 m.s.	/hit-a-é- /	hitrašém		3 pl.	/hit-a--ú/	hitrašmú
3 f.s.	/hit-a--á /	hitrašmá				

J. Substitution-Agreement Drill /hitrašém/ "was impressed"

We were impressed by the new stamps.

<u>hitrašámnu mehabulím haxadaším.</u>   .התרשמנו מהבולים החדשים

haamerikáim - atém - aní - iští   האמריקאים - אתם - אני - אשתי
át - baalá - atá - gvéret kóhen   אתְ - בעלה - אתה - גברת כהן

K.   Substitution-Agreement Drill /hitkonén/ "got ready"

He got ready to move to a new house.

<u>hú hitkonén laavór lebáit xadáš.</u>   .הוא התכונן לעבור לבית חדש

áta - ánu - mišpáxat zahávi   אתה - אנו - משפחת זהבי
hayoéc haxadáš - aní - hém - át   היועץ החדש - אני - הם - אתְ

17.7 <u>Past Tense of hif'il.</u>

The <u>hif'il</u> conjugation is characterized in the past tense by the prefix /hi-/, /he-/, or /ho-/.

Verbs whose first root consonant is <u>x</u> (spelled with ח , but not <u>x</u> when spelled with כ) or <u>'</u> will have the prefix /he-/.

           /hexlít/ "he decided" - root <u>xlt</u>   חלט
           /he'evír/ "he brought over" - root <u>'vr</u>   עבר

The prefix /he-/ also occurs with some verbs whose first root consonant is <u>r</u>.

      Verbs with only two root consonants also have the prefix /he-/. These verbs are listed in the dictionary with <u>vav</u> (ו) or <u>yud</u> (') as the second root consonant.

           /heríc/ "he caused to run" - root <u>r-c</u>   רוץ
           /hekím/ "he set up" - root <u>k-m</u>   קום

      Roots listed with <u>yud</u> (') as the first consonant will have the prefix /ho-/, with a <u>vav</u> replacing the <u>yud</u> of the root.

           /hodía/ "he informed"   - root <u>yd'</u>   ידע
           /hošív/ "he seated"   - root <u>yšv</u>   ישב

      The root <u>hlx</u> "go" also has the prefix /ho-/ in the <u>hif'il</u>, with the <u>vav</u> replacing the <u>h</u> of the root.

           /holíx/ "he led"   - root <u>hlx</u>   הלך

All other verbs have the prefix /hi-/.

/himšíx/	"he continued"	- root m̱š̱x̱	משך
/hizmín/	"he invited"	- root ẕm̱ṉ	זמן
/higzím/	"he exaggerated"	- root g̱ẕm̱	גזם

If the first of the three consonants is n, then the n will be dropped in the hif'il conjugation.

/hikír/	"he recognized"	- root ṉḵṟ	נכר
/higía/	"he arrived"	- root ṉg̱'	נגע

The full pattern of the past tense is as follows: (The prefix /hi-/ is used as an example).

		mš̱x				mš̱x
1 s.	/hi--á-ti/	himš̱áxti		1 pl.	/hi-á-nu/	himš̱áxnu
2 m.s.	/hi--á-ta/	himš̱áxta		2 m.pl.	/hi--á-tem/	himš̱áxtem
2 f.s.	/hi--á-t/	himš̱áxt		2 f.pl.	/hi--á-ten/	himš̱áxten
3 m.s.	/hi--í- /	himš̱íx		3 pl.	/hi--í-u/	himš̱íxu
3 f.s.	/hi--í-a/	himš̱íxa				

Note that the stress remains on the infixed vowel in the third person forms:

/himš̱íxa/ "she continued"
/himš̱íxu/ "they continued"

L. Substitution-Agreement Drill /himš̱íx/ "continued".

He continued studying in Israel.

hú himš̱íx lilmód baárec.   .הוא המשיך ללמוד בארץ

gvéret Smith - yónatan - hém   גברת סמית – יונתן – הם
aní - át - ánu - kulám - atém   אני – את – אנו – כולם – אתם
iští veaní - atá - hú   אשתי ואני – אתה – הוא

M. Substitution-Agreement Drill /hitxíl/ "began"

Yosef started eating an hour ago.

yoséf hitxíl leexól lifnéy š̱aá.   .יוסף החחיל לאכול לפני שעה

raxél - moš̱é - aní - atá   רחל – משה – אני – אתה
ánu - atém - hém - xána   אנו – אתם – הם – חנה
hén - atén - át - yoséf   הן – אתן – את – יוסף

N. Substitution-Agreement Drill /hizmín/ "invited"

Mr. Zahavi invited them for dinner.

már zahávi hizmín otám learuxát érev. .מר זהבי הזמין אוחם לארוחת ערב

hén - ánu - ištó - aní   הן – אנו – אשתו – אני
yaakóv - atém - át - hí   יעקב – אתם – את – היא
atén - atá - hém - már zahávi   אתן – אתה – הם – מר זהבי

O. Substitution-Agreement Drill /hikír/ "recognized, knew"

He was introduced to her in the Brooklyn Bar.

hú hikír otá bebrúklin bár.   הוא הכיר אותה בברוקלין בר.

xána – át – atá – ánu   חנה – את – אתה – אנו
dóv – aní – hén – hú   דוב – אני – הן – הוא

P. Substitution-Agreement Drill /higía/ "arrived"

The counsellor arrived in Tel Aviv this morning.

hayoéc higía letél avív habóker.   היועץ הגיע לתל אביב הבוקר.

ánu – atém – sára veyoséf   אנו – אתם – שרה ויוסף
hí – atá – hém – át – hayoéc   היא – אתה – הם – את – היועץ

Q. Substitution-Agreement Drill /higzím/ "exaggerated"

He exaggerated his story.

hú higzím basipúr šeló.   הוא הגזים בסיפור שלו.

hém – atá – aní – át   הם – אתה – אני – את
menaxém – atára – atém – hú   מנחם – עטרה – אתם – הוא

R. Substitution-Agreement Drill /hexlít/ "decided"

(Note: In the first and second person forms an /e/ is inserted before the
suffix – /hexláteti/.)

He decided not to go by ship.

hú hexlít ló linsóa beoniá.   הוא החליט לא לנסוע באוניה.

atém – aní – haxenyaní – hí   אתם – אני – החנווני – היא
atá – hém – ánu – át – hú   אתה – הם – אנו – את – הוא

S. Substitution-Agreement Drill /heríc/ "caused to run"

He had us running the whole morning.

hú heríc otánu kol habóker.   הוא הריץ אותנו כל הבוקר.

hí – atém – át – yónatan   היא – אתם – את – יונתן
atá – hém – atára – hú   אתה – הם – עטרה – הוא

T. Substitution-Agreement Drill /hodía/ "informed"

He told Yonatan that he didn't get the telegram.

hú hodía leyónatan šeló kibél et hamivrák.   הוא הודיע ליונתן שלא קבל את המברק.

aní – atára – atém – át   אני – עטרה – אתם – את
sára veaní – hém – atá – hú   שרה ואני – הם – אתה – הוא

17.8 Past Tense of lamed h.ey verbs

Regardless of the conjugation (<u>binyan</u>) these verbs have the following similarities:

a) The vowel before the 1st and 2nd person suffixes is /-í-/ or /-é-/. In the <u>kal</u> and <u>pi'el</u> the vowel is /-í-/. In the other <u>binyanim</u> it is /-é-/.

b) The 3rd person forms are as described in Grammar Section 16.4c.

  3 m.s. -á
  3 f.s. -tá
  3 pl. -ú

  A complete past tense is as follows:
  (The verb illustrated is /xiká/ חכה "waited")

1 s.	/-V-íti/	xikíti	חכיתי	1 pl.	/-V ínu/	xikínu	חכינו
2 m.s.	/-V-íta/	xikíta	חכית	2 m.pl.	/-V-ítem/	xikítem	חכיתם
2 f.s.	/-V-ít/	xikít	חכית	2 f.pl.	/-V-íten/	xikíten	חכיתן
3 m.s.	/-V-á/	xiká	חכה	3 pl.	/-V-ú/	xikú	חכו
3 f.s.	/-V-tá/	xiktá	חכתה				

U. Substitution-Agreement Drill /kivá/ "hoped"

  I hoped to go to Haifa.

  <u>kivíti linsóa lexáyfa.</u>   <u>קוויתי לנסוע לחיפה.</u>

  yónatan - raxél - hén - át   יונתן - רחל - הן - את
  ánu - atá - atén - aní   אנו - אתה - אתן - אני

V. Substitution-Agreement Drill /xiká/ "waited"

  I waited and waited for Friday to come.

  <u>xikíti vexikíti leyóm šiší šeyavó.</u> <u>חכיתי וחכיתי ליום שישי שיבוא.</u>

  ánu - atá - hém - hí   אנו - אתה - הם - היא
  mošé - át - atén - sára   משה - את - אתן - שרה
  atém - dóv vexána - aní   אתם - דוב וחנה - אני

W. Substitution-Agreement Drill /racá/ "wanted"

  I wanted to go to the tourist office.

  <u>racíti laléxet lemisrád hatayarút.</u> <u>רציתי ללכת למשרד התיירות.</u>

  atén - át - iští veaní - mí אתן - את - אשתי ואני - מי
  atá - avígdor - atára - hém אתה - אביגדור - עטרה - הם
  már Williams - atém - aní מר ווילליאמס - אתם - אני

X. Substitution-Agreement Drill /asá/ "made, did"

  I did well to get here early.

  <u>tóv asíti šehigáti mukdám</u> . <u>טוב עשיתי שהגעתי מוקדם.</u>

  át - davíd - atá - léa   את - דוד - אתה - לאה
  ánu - hém - atén - aní   אנו - הם - אתן - אני

Y. Substitution-Agreement Drill /kaná/ "bought".　　　קנה

He bought a new house.

hú kaná báit xadáš.　　　　　　　　　　　　　　הוא קנה בית חדש.

ánu - xána vebaalá - aní　　　　　　　　　אנו – חנה ובעלה – אני
gvéret kóhen - atém - hí　　　　　　　　　גברת כהן – אתם – היא
atá - yoséf - hém - hú　　　　　　　　　　　אתה – יוסף – הם – הוא

Z. Substitution-Agreement Drill / raá/ "saw"　　　ראה

He saw her this morning.

hú raá otá habóker.　　　　　　　　　　　　　הוא ראה אותה הבוקר.

aní - át - hí - ánu　　　　　　　　　　　　　אני – את – היא – אנו
atén - hén - yónatan　　　　　　　　　　　　אתן – הן – יונתן
atá - ištó - hú　　　　　　　　　　　　　　　אתה – אשתו – הוא

AA. Substitution-Agreement Drill /paná/ "turned"　　　פנה

He addressed him in English.

hú paná eláv beanglít.　　　　　　　　　　　הוא פנה אליו באנגלית.

át - hayoéc haxadáš - atá　　　　　　　את – היועץ החדש – אתה
aní -gvéret káspi - hém - hú　　　　　אני – גברת כספי – הם – הוא

BB. Substitution-Agreement Drill /šatá/ "drank"　　　שתה

I didn't drink the water.

ló šatíti et hamáim.　　　　　　　　　　　　לא שתיתי את המים.

ánu - atém - hém - dóv　　　　　　　　　אנו – אתם – הם – דב
avíva - hén - sára - atá　　　　　　　אביבה – הן – שרה – אתה
haamerikáim - át - aní　　　　　　　　האמריקאים – את – אני

CC. Substitution-Agreement Drill /alá/ "went up"　　　עלה

We went up to the third floor.

alínu lakomá hašlišít.　　　　　　　　　　עלינו לקומה השלישית.

aní - kulám - atém - át　　　　　　　אני – כולם – אתם – את
már alón - ištexá - hém　　　　　　　מר אלון – אשתך – הם
atá - atén - hú - ánu　　　　　　　　אתה – אתן – הוא – אנו

DD. Substitution-Agreement Drill /nitmaná/ "was appointed"　　　נתמנה

We were appointed as advisers in the foreign office.

nitmanénu keyoacím bemisrád haxúc.　　　　נתמנינו כיועצים במשרד החרץ.

atém - hém - már kóhen - aní　　　　אתם – הם – מר כהן – אני
hén - hí - át - ánu　　　　　　　　　הן – היא – את – אנו

177

EE. Substitution-Agreement Drill /hayá/ "was"

The verb /hayá/ poses problems other than the <u>lamed hey</u> pattern. In ordinary speech the /h/ is often dropped, and the /y/ is often a very slight glide between the surrounding vowels. A spelling consistent with other <u>lamed hey</u> verbs would be as in the left-hand column.

Transcriptions of frequently heard pronunciations are in the middle and right hand columns.

1 s.	hayíti	/haíti/ or	/aíti/
2 m.s.	hayíta	/haíta/ or	/aíta/
2 f.s.	hayít	/haít/ or	/aít/
3 m.s.	hayá		/ayá/
3 f.s.	haytá		/aytá/
1 pl.	hayínu	/haínu/ or	/aínu/
2 m.pl.	hayítem	/haítem/ or	/aítem/
2 f.pl.	hayíten	/haíten/ or	/aíten/
3 pl.	hayú		/ayú/

In previous units the transcriptions in the middle column have been used since they represent the most generally acceptable pronunciation.

I was in Haifa a week ago.

<u>haíti bexáyfa lifnéy šavúa.</u>   הייתי בחיפה לפני שבוע.

hém - baalá - mošé - ánu	הם - בעלה - משה - אנו
atén - xána - atá - át	אתן - חנה - אתה - את
hí - hén - dóv - aní	היא - הן - דוב - אני

FF. Substitution-Agreement Drill /nir'á/ "seemed, was seen"

This <u>binyan</u>, <u>nif'al</u>, will be discussed in detail in Unit 19. However, the forms of /nir'á/ may be drilled here as an example of a <u>lamed hey</u> verb. The prefix /ni-/ is the same in all forms.

You looked well yesterday.

nir'ét tóv etmól.   נראית טוב אתמול.

atá sára - hú - aní	אתה - שרה - הוא - אני
ánu - xána vemošé - hí	אנו - חנה ומשה - היא
davíd - atém - hém - át	דוד - אתם - הם - את

RAPID RESPONSE DRILL

1. má rocé már Williams lišlóax.	1. מה רוצה מר ווילאמס לשלוח ?
2. leán hú rocé lišlóax et hamixtáv.	2. לאן הוא רוצה לשלוח את המכתב ?
3. haím hú yišláx et hamixtáv bedóar avír o bedóar ragíl.	3. האם הוא ישלח את המכתב בדואר אוויר או בדואר רגיל ?
4. káma yaalé lo lišlóax et hamixtáv.	4. כמה יעלה לו לשלוח את המכתב ?
5. káma zmán yikáx lamixtáv lehagía leamérika.	5. כמה זמן יקח למכתב להגיע לאמריקה ?
6. haím hamixtáv daxúf?	6. הם המכתב דחוף?
7. haím mar Williams yišláx mivrák?	7. האם מר ווילאמס ישלח מברק?
8. heyxán nimcét hamivraká.	8. היכן נמצאת המברקה?

REVIEW CONVERSATIONS

A: aní rocé lišlóax et haxavilá hazót letél avív.

א: אני רוצה לשלוח את החבילה הזאת לתל אביב.

B: éyx atá rocé lišlóax otá. ragíl o exprés.

ב: איך אתה רוצה לשלוח אותה, רגיל או אקספרס?

A: káma zmán yikáx bedóar ragíl, vekáma beeksprés.

א: כמה זמן יקח בדואר רגיל, וכמה באקספרס?

B: ragíl yikáx xamišá yamím, beeksprés yomáim.

ב: רגיל יקח חמישה ימים, באקספרס יומיים.

A: im káx, šláx et haxavilá ragíl. zé ló kol káx daxúf.

א: אם כך, שלח את החבילה רגיל. זה לא כל כך דחוף.

C: tén li bevakašá, xaméš, igrót avír.

ג: תן לי בבקשה, חמש אגרות אויר.

D: kén. bevakašá.

ד: כן. בבקשה.

C: káma zé olé.

ג: כמה זה עולה?

D: šlosím vexaméš agorót kol axát. yáxad líra vešiv'ím vexaméš agorót.

ד: שלושים וחמש אגורות כל אחת. יחד לירה שבעים וחמש אגורות.

E: kibálnu habóker gluyá mimišpáxat zahávi.

ה: קבלנו הבוקר גלויה ממשפחת זהבי.

F: má hém kotvím.

ו: מה הם כותבים?

E: hém kotvím šeyavóu lir'ót otánu bekaróv.

ה: הם כותבים שיבואו לראות אותנו בקרוב.

F: tóv méod. hém katvú matáy šehém yavóu?

ו: טוב מאוד. הם כתבו מתי שהם יבואו?

E: ló. ax hém yišlexú mivrák lifnéy šeyagiú.

ה: לא. אך הם ישלחו מברק לפני שיגיעו.

G: aní caríx bulím. éyfo aní yaxól liknót otám.

ז: אני צריך בולים. איפה אני יכול לקנות אותם?

H: bulím efšar liknót badóar.

ח: בולים אפשר לקנות בדואר.

G: éyfo hadóar?

ז: איפה הדואר?

H: hadóar nimcá birxóv álenbi, lo raxók mikán.

ח: הדואר נמצא ברחוב אלנבי, לא רחוק מכאן.

G: ad éyze šaá hadóar patúax.

ז: עד איזה שעה הדואר פתוח?

H: ad xaméš.

ח: עד חמש.

End of Tape 6B

NOTE ON TRANSCRIPTION

In the remainder of the book the stress mark ´ is used only when a syllable other than the last ‾ in a a word is stressed.

היית רוצה להגיע חצי שעה לפני הזמן...

Tape 7A

18.1 Telling Time

DOV

What time is it?	ma hašaa.		?מה השעה
hour	šaa (f)	שעה	

AVIVA

It's	hašaa		השעה
a quarter to seven.	réva lešéva.		.רבע לשבע
quarter	réva (m)	רבע	

DOV

When are (your) parents	matay omdim		מתי עומדים
supposed to arrive?	hahorim lehagía.		?ההורים להגיע
he stood	amad	עמד	
parents	horim (m.pl)	הורים	

AVIVA

I don't know	ani lo yodáat		אני לא יודעת
exactly.	bediyuk.		.בדיוק
It seems to me	nidme li		נדמה לי
at eight thirty.	šebešmóne vaxéci.		.שבשמונה וחצי
seems	nidme (m.s. pres.)	נדמה	

DOV

Please check	bidki bevakaša,		בידקי בבקשה
when	matay		מתי
the plane will arrive.	šehamatos yagía.		.שהמטוס יגיע
I'd like	hayíti roce		הייתי רוצה
to get (there)	lehagía		להגיע
a half hour	xaci šaa		חצי שעה
ahead of time.	lifney hazman.		.לפני הזמן
he examined	badak	בדק	
airplane	matos (m)	מטוס	

AVIVA

All right.	beracon.		.ברצון
I want	gam ani roca		גם אני רוצה
to go with you, too.	linsóa itxa.		.לנסוע אתך
to travel	linsóa	לנסוע	
he traveled	nasa	נסע	
with me	iti	אתי	

DOV

Good, I'll take you.	tov, ekax otax.		.טוב. אקח אותך
We'll have to	nictarex		נצטרך
wait	lexakot		לחכות
until they clear	ad šehem yaavru		עד שהם יעברו
customs.	et haméxes.		.את המכס
he needed, had to	hictarex	הצטרך	
customs	méxes (m)	מכס	

181

AVIVA

We have	yeš lánu		יש לנו
enough time.	maspik zman.		מספיק זמן.
enough		maspik	מספיק
he made it in time		hispik	הספיק

DOV

I hope so.	ani mekave kax.		אני מקווה כך.
Call up right away.	hitkašri miyad.		התקשרי מיד.
he got in touch		hitkašer	התקשר
immediately		miyad	מיד

18.2 ADDITIONAL VOCABULARY

The following are several of the expressions for telling time. The feminine numbers are used with /dakot/ "minutes", and the masculine numbers with /regaim/ "minutes".

/hašaa/ may be omitted in the reply.

What time do you have?	ma hašaa eclexa?		?מה השעה אצלך
The time is	hašaa		השעה
ten minutes	éser dakot		עשר דקות
before seven.	lifney šéva.		לפני שבע.
minute	daka (f)	דקה	
The time is	hašaa		השעה
ten to seven.	asara lešéva.		עשרה לשבע.
The time is	hašaa		השעה
ten to seven.	šéva paxot asara.		שבע פחות עשרה.
less	paxot	פחות	
The time is	hašaa		השעה
ten minutes	éser dakot		עשר דקות
after seven.	axarey šéva.		אחרי שבע.
The time is	hašaa		השעה שבע ועשרה.
7:10.	šéva veasara.		
The time is	hašaa		השעה שבע ורבע.
7:15.	šéva varéva.		
I'll meet her	efgoš ota		אפגוש אותה
at 9:00 A.M.	betéša babóker.		בתשע בבוקר.
I'll meet her	efgoš ota		אפגוש אותה
at 3:00 P.M.	bešalóš axarey hacohoráim.		בשלוש אחרי הצהריים.
I'll meet her	efgoš ota		אפגוש אותה
at 8:00 P.M.	bešmóne baérev.		בשמונה בערב.
I'll arrive at midnight.	agía bexacot.		אגיע בחצות.
midnight	xacot	חצות	
It'll take us	yikax lánu		יקח לנו
24 hours to get there.	yemama lehagía.		ימה להגיע.
24 hour period	yemama (f)	ימה	
Wait a minute.	xake réga.		חכה רגע.
minute, moment	réga	רגע	

My watch	hašaon šeli	השעון שלי
is slow.	mefager.	מפגר.
retarded	mefager (m.s. pres) מפגר	

| My watch is fast. | hašaon šeli memaher. | השעון שלי ממהר. |

The big hand	hamaxog hagadol	המחוג הגדול
is on the five,	al xameš,	על חמש,
and the little hand	vehamaxog hakatan	והמחוג הקטן
is on the three.	al šaloš.	על שלוש.
dial hand	maxog	מחוג
(plural)	mexugim	מחוגים

18.3 Vocabulary Drills

A. Substitution-Agreement Drill /omed/ "stand" (pres.)

He is standing next to the movie.

<u>hu omed al yad hakolnóa.</u>   <u>הוא עומד על יד הקולנוע.</u>

    at - hem - sára vebaala - hi   את – הם – שרה ובעלה – היא
    ani - hanašim - ata - hu   אני – הנשים – אתה – הוא

B. Substitution-Agreement Drill /amad/ "stood" (past)

He stood on the corner all morning.

<u>hu amad bapina kol habóker.</u>   <u>הוא עמד בפינה כל הבוקר.</u>

    hem - ani - átem - at   הם – אני – אתם – את
    hi - moše - ánu - hu   היא – משה – אנו – הוא

C. Substitution Drill /bdok/ "examine" (imv.)

Check all the doors.

    bdok et kol hadlatot.   בדוק את כל הדלתות.
    bidki   בדקי
    bidku   בדקו
    bdókna   בדוקנה

D. Transformation Drill - Negative to Affirmative
   (The first column may be done as a substitution drill first.)

Don't examine the packages.

  al tivdok et haxavilot. bdok et haxavilot.   אל תבדוק את החבילות.
  al tivdeki et haxavilot. bidki et haxavilot.   אל תבדקי את החבילות.
  al tivdeku et haxavilot. bidku et haxavilot.   אל תבדקו את החבילות.
  al tivdókna et haxavilot.bdókna et haxavilot. אל תבדוקנה את החבילות.

E. Transformation Drill - Affirmative to Negative

Do Drill D in reverse.

F. Substitution Drill /e - ~ti -/

I'll check his phone number.

evdok et mispar hatélefon šelo.   אבדוק את מספר הטלפון שלו.
  ata tivdok   אתה תבדוק
  at tivdeki   את תבדקי
  dov yivdok   דוב יבדוק
  hi tivdok   היא תבדוק
     nivdok   נבדוק
     tivdeku   תבדקו
     tivdókna   תבדוקנה
  hem yivdeku   הם יבדקו
  hen tivdókna   הן תבדוקנה

G. Substitution-Agreement Drill

David will check the mail.

<u>david yivdok et hadóar.</u>   <u>דוד יבדוק את הדואר.</u>

ani - xána - hem - ata   אני – חנה – הם – אתה
ánu - at - atem - mi   אנו – את – אתם – מי
aten - hen - hi - david   אתן – הן – היא – דוד

H. Substitution-Agreement Drill   /badak/ "examined"

He checked the address in the phone book.

<u>hu badak et haktóvet beséfer hatelefónim.</u>   <u>הוא בדק את הכתובת בספר הטלפונים.</u>

hi - ata - ánu - ani   היא – אתה – אנו – אני
hem - yosef - at - hu   הם – יוסף – את – הוא

I. Substitution Drill /e - ~ti -/

I'll have to get to Lydda by five o'clock.

ectarex lehagiá lelud ad xameš.   אצטרך להגיע ללוד עד חמש.
     tictarex   תצטרך
  at tictarxi   את תצטרכי
  hu yictarex   הוא יצטרך
  hi tictarex   היא תצטרך
     nictarex   נצטרך
  atem tictarxu   אתם תצטרכו
  aten tictaréxna   אתן תצטרכנה
  hem yictarxu   הם יצטרכו
  hen tictaréxna   הן תצטרכנה

J. Substitution-Agreement Drill

He'll have to send the letter special delivery.

<u>hu yictarex lišlóax et hamixtav ekspres.</u>   <u>הוא יצטרך לשלוח את המכתב אקספרס.</u>

ánu - aten - raxel - hem   אנו – אתן – רחל – הם
at - ata - ani - hen - hi   את – אתה – אני – הן – היא
atem - mar káspi - hi - hu   אתם – מר כספי – היא – הוא

K. Substitution-Agreement Drill /hispik/ "he had the time to"

Dov didn't have time to eat breakfast.

<u>dov lo hispik leexol aruxat bóker.</u>   .דוב לא הספיק לאכול ארוחת בוקר

    ani - ata - išto - baala   אני - אתה - אשתו - בעלה
    hem - ánu - at - dov   הם - אנו - את - דוב

L. Substitution Drill

I won't get a chance to see the whole city.

     lo aspik lir'ot et kol hair.   .לא אספיק לראות את כל העיר
     lo taspik   לא תספיק
     lo taspíki   לא תספיקי
hu   lo yaspik   הוא לא יספיק
hi   lo taspik   היא לא תספיק
     lo naspik   לא נספיק
     lo taspíku   לא תספיקו
aten lo taspékna   אתן לא תספקנה
hem   lo yaspíku   הם לא יספיקו
hen   lo taspékna   הן לא תספקנה

M. Expansion Drill

    Instructor: I didn't get a chance to see him.
    Student   : I didn't get a chance to see him,
            I'll have to come tomorrow.

lo hispákti lir'ot oto.   .לא הספקתי לראות אותו
       ectarex lavo maxar.   .אצטרך לבוא מחר

lo hispáknu lir'ot oto.   .לא הספקנו לראות אותו
       nictarex lavo maxar.   .נצטרך לבוא מחר

xána lo hispíka lir'ot oto.   .חנה לא הספיקה לראות אותו
       hi tictarex lavo maxar.   .היא תצטרך לבוא מחר

ata lo hispákta lir'ot oto.   .אתה לא הספקת לראות אותו
       tictarex lavo maxar.   .תצטרך לבוא מחר

hem lo hispíku lir'ot oto.   .הם לא הספיקו לראות אותו
       yictarxu lavo maxar.   .יצטרכו לבוא מחר

lo hispákta lir'ot oto.   .לא הספקת לראות אותו
       tictarex lavo maxar.   .תצטרך לבוא מחר

aten lo hispákten lir'ot oto.   .אתן לא הספקתן לראות אותו
       tictaréxna lavo maxar.   .תצטרכנה לבוא מחר

hen lo hispíku lir'ot oto.   .הן לא הספיקו לראות אותו
       tictaréxna lavo maxar.   .תצטרכנה לבוא מחר

at lo hispakt lir'ot oto.   .את לא הספקת לראות אותו
       tictarxi lavo maxar.   .תצטרכי לבוא מחר

N. Substitution Drill

Call right away; it's urgent.

hitkašer miyad. ze daxuf.	.התקשר מיד. זה דחוף
hitkašri	התקשרי
hitkašru	התקשרו
hitkašérna	התקשרנה

O. Substitution Drill   /e- ~ ti - /

I'll get in touch with Mr. Caspi.

ani etkašer im mar káspi.	.אני אתקשר עם·מר כספי
ata titkašer	אתה תתקשר
at titkašri	את תתקשרי
hu yitkašer	הוא יתקשר
hi titkašer	היא תתקשר
ánu nitkašer	אנו נתקשר
atem titkašru	אתם תתקשרו
aten titkašérna	אתן תתקשרנה
hem yitkašru	הם יתקשרו
hen titkašérna	הן תתקשרנה

P. Substitution-Agreement Drill

I'll call them this week.

<u>etkašer itam hašavúa.</u>   .<u>אתקשר אתם השבוע</u>

moše veišto - dov - sára	משה ואשתו - דוב - שרה
ata - aten - ánu - hi	אתה - אתן - אנו - היא
at - hen - atem - ani	את - הן - אתם - אני

R. Substitution-Agreement Drill /hitkašer/ "he contacted"

He got in touch with Mrs. Cohen this morning.

<u>hu hitkašer im gvéret kóhen habóker.</u>   .<u>הוא התקשר עם גברת כהן הבוקר</u>

ani - at - hem - sára	אני - את - הם - שרה
ata - atem - išto - hi	אתה - אתם - אשתו - היא
ánu - yosef - hen - hu	אנו - יוסף - הן - הוא

S. Expansion Drill   /iti /   "with me"

Instructor: I'll go to school.
Student: I'll go to school, and Moshe
           will go with me.

ani elex lebet haséfer, vemoše yelex iti.		.אני אלך לבית הספר ומשה ילך אתי
ata telex	itxa.	.אתה תלך אתך
dov yelex	ito.	.דוב ילך אתו
xána telex	ita.	.חנה תלך אתה
ánu nelex	itánu.	.אנו נלך אתנו
hem yelxu	itam.	.הם ילכו אתם
atem telxu	itxem.	.אתם תלכו אתכם
at telxi	itax.	.את תלכי אתך
aten teléxna	itxen.	.אתן תלכנה אתכן
hen teléxna	itan.	.הן תלכנה אתן

The unsuffixed form of this preposition is /et/, identical to the preposition /et/ indicating a direct object. The unsuffixed form /et/ is used with the meaning "with" only in special literary styles. In ordinary Hebrew the preposition /im/ is used, and /et/ is used for the direct object. With the pronominal suffixes all three are in common use: /oti/ "me", /iti/, /imi/ "with me".

T. Substitution Drill   /iti ~ imi/

The student repeats the sentence, substituting the preposition /im-/. The drill may then be done in reverse.

Yonatan will go with me this evening.

yónatan yelex iti haérev.	יונתן ילך אתי הערב.
yónatan yelex imi haérev.	יונתן ילך עמי הערב.
axálti ito aruxat cohoráim.	אכלתי אתו ארוחת צהריים.
(imo)	(עמו)
mi hitkašer itxa habóker.	מי התקשר אתך הבוקר?
(imxa)	(עמך)
šaláxnu et haxavila itam.	שלחנו את החבילה אתם.
(imam)	(עמם)
hu roce linsóa itánu lexáyfa.	הוא רוצה לנסוע אתנו לחיפה.
(imánu)	(עמנו)
išti telex ita lakolnóa.	אשתי תלך אתה לקולנוע.
(ima)	(עמה)
tikxu et moše itxem.	תקחו את משה אתכם.
(imaxem)	(עמכם)
hen lo tikáxna et hasfarim itan.	הן לא תקחנה את הספרים אתן.
(iman)	(עמן)
haim hem lamdu itax bebet haséfer?	האם הם למדו אתך בבית הספר?
(imax)	(עמך)
haim hen garot itxen bebáit exad?	האם הן גרות אתכם בבית אחד?
(imaxen)	(עמכן)

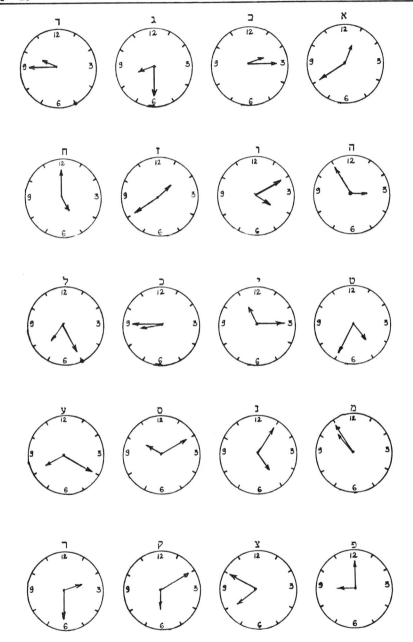

18.4 Clock Drills

A. The students cover this page, and the instructor asks at random for the time on the clocks.

What time is it on clock_____.

ma hašaa al šaon ____.   •_____ מה השעה על שעון

א	hašaa esrim dakot lifney axat.	השעה עשרים דקות לפני אחת. א
ב	hašaa štáim varéva.	השעה שתיים ורבע. ב
ג	hašaa šmóne vaxéci.	השעה שמונה וחצי. ג
ד	hašaa réva leéser.	השעה רבע לעשר. ד
ה	hašaa xaméš dakot lifnéy šaloš.	השעה חמש דקות לפני שלוש. ה
ו	hašaa éser dakot axarey árba.	השעה עשר דקות אחרי ארבע. ו
ז	hašaa esrim dakot lifney štáim.	השעה עשרים דקות לפני שתיים. ז
ח	hašaa xameš (bediyuk).	השעה חמש (בדיוק). ח
ט	hašaa esrim vexameš dakot lifney xaméš.	השעה עשרים וחמש דקות לפני חמש. ט
י	hašaa axát'esre varéva.	השעה אחת עשרה ורבע. י
כ	hašaa réva letéša.	השעה רבע לתשע. כ
ל	hašaa esrim vexameš dakot axarey šéva.	השעה עשרים וחמש דקות אחרי שבע. ל
מ	hašaa xameš dakot leaxát'esre.	השעה חמש דקות לאחת עשרה. מ
נ	hašaa xameš vexamiša.	השעה חמש וחמישה. נ
ס	hašaa éser veasara.	השעה עשר ועשרה. ס
ע	hašaa šmóne veesrim.	השעה שמונה ועשרים. ע
פ	hašaa téša.	השעה תשע. פ
צ	hašaa asara lešmóne.	השעה עשרה .לשמונה. צ
ק	hašaa éser dakot axarey šeš.	השעה עשר דקות אחרי שש. ק
ר	hašaa štáim vaxéci.	השעה שתיים וחצי. ר

GRAMMAR NOTES

18.5 The Expected Future

Note the following sentence from the Basic Conversation of this unit:

matay omdim hahorim lehagia. "when are your parents supposed to arrive?"

The construction /omdim lehagía/ (literally "stand to arrive") may also be translated "expect to arrive". It is a paraphrase of the future with the added meaning of expectation. The first verb, "stand" may occur in the past tense /amad/ in this construction. It then may be translated "was supposed to have", and usually implies that the second verb did not occur.   hem amdu liknot báit. (velo kanu). "They were supposed to have bought a house.(but didn't)" With the present tense it may mean "about to".
/hu omed lehagía./   "He is about to arrive."

A. Substitution-Agreement Drill

He's supposed to go to America.

hu omed linsóa leamérika.	.הוא עומד לנסוע לאמריקה
gvéret zahávi - ánu - hen	גברת זהבי - אנו - הן
ani - dov - xána - hu	אני - דוב - חנה - הוא

B. Transformation Drill

Instructor: She'll receive a letter today.
Student: She's supposed to received a letter today.

hi tekabel mixtav hayom.	.היא תקבל מכתב היום
hi omédet lekabel mixtav hayom.	.היא עומדת לקבל מכתב היום
moše veišto yiknu báit.	.משה ואשתו יקנו בית
moše veišto omdim liknot báit.	.משה ואשתו עומדים לקנות בית
hamišpaxa tagía beod xódeš.	.המשפחה תגיע בעוד חודש
hamišpaxa omédet lehagia beod xódeš.	.המשפחה עומדת להגיע בעוד חודש
mar Williams yišlax et haxavila.	.מר ויליאמס ישלח את החבילה
mar Williams omed lišlóax et haxavila.	.מר ויליאמס עומד לשלוח את החבילה
hanašim tagána lifney xameš.	.הנשים תגענה לפני חמש
hanašim omdot lehagía lifney xameš.	.הנשים עומדות להגיע לפני חמש

C. Transformation Drill

Instructor: I sent him a telegram.
Student: I was supposed to have sent him
          a telegram, but I didn't.

šaláxti lo mivrak.	.שלחתי לו מברק
amádeti lišlóax lo mivrak, velo šaláxti.	.עמדתי לשלוח לו מברק ולא שלחתי
kibálti et hagluya.	.קבלתי את הגלויה
amádeti lekabel et hagluya, velo kibálti.	.עמדתי לקבל את הגלויה ולא קבלתי
hu kibel xavila habóker.	.הוא קבל חבילה הבוקר
hu amad lekabel xavila habóker, velo kibel.	.הוא עמד לקבל חבילה הבוקר ולא קבל
kanínu báit benatánya.	.קנינו בית בנתניה
amádnu liknot báit benatánya, velo kanínu.	.עמדנו לקנות בית בנתניה ולא קנינו
hem higíu lelud etmol.	.הם הגיעו ללוד אתמול
hem amdu lehagiá lelud etmol, velo higíu.	.הם עמדו להגיע ללוד אתמול ולא הגיעו
sára avra lebáit xadaš.	.שרה עברה לבית חדש
sára amda laavor lebáit xadaš, velo avra.	.שרה עמדה לעבור לבית חדש ולא עברה
david axal itánu haérev.	.דוד אכל אתנו הערב
david amad leexol itánu haérev, velo axal.	.דוד עמד לאכול אתנו הערב ולא אכל

18.6 /matay še-/

Compare the following sentences:

/matay yagía hamatos./ "when will the plane arrive?"

/bidki matay šehamatos yagía/ "check [as to] when the plane will arrive."

This is another example of an included sentence. [See Grammar Note 10.4] in this case the included sentence is a question beginning with the interrogative /matay/ "when". When the subject is an independent noun, as /hamatos/ in the example above, the word order in the included sentence, may differ from that of the original sentence.

/matay tagía hamišpaxa šelxa./ "When will your family arrive?"

or /emor li matay šetagía hamišpaxa šelxa./ /emor li matay šehamišpaxa šelxa tagía./ "Tell me when your family will arrive."

A. Transformation Drill /matay ~ matay še - /

In the following drill the instructor will ask a question beginning with /matáy/ "When?". The student will respond by paraphrasing the same question with a sentence beginning with /emor li matáy še-/ "Tell me when..."

Example: Instructor: matáy tagia hamišpaxa šelxá. "When will your family arrive?"
Student: emor li matáy šetagia hamišpaxá šelxá. "Tell me when your family will arrive".

The instructor may vary this drill by having the students respond with the feminine form /imri/ or with a plural form /imru/ or /emórna/.

1. matay tavo. | מתי תבוא?
אמור לי מתי שתבוא. | .1
2. matay nigaš lemoše. | מתי ניגש למשה?
אמור לי מתי שניגש למשה. | .2
3. matay nelex lir'ot et haxanut haxadaša. | מתי נלך לראות את החנות החדשה?
אמור לי מתי שנלך לראות את החנות החדשה. | .3
4. matay lamadeta ledaber ivrit. | מתי למדת לדבר עברית?
אמור לי מתי שלמדת לדבר עברית. | .4
5. matay tatxil bedieta. | מתי תתחיל בדיאטה?
אמור לי מתי שתתחיל בדיאטה. | .5
6. matay raita et miryam. | מתי ראית את מרים?
אמור לי מתי שראית את מרים. | .6
7. matay ata roce lišloax mivrak. | מתי אתה רוצה לשלוח מברק?
אמור לי מתי שאתה רוצה לשלוח מברק. | .7

RAPID RESPONSE DRILL

1. matay omdim hahorim šel avíva lehagía. | מתי עומרים ההורים של אביבה להגיע? | .1
2. ma crixa avíva livdok. | מה צריכה אביבה לבדוק? | .2
3. káma zman lifney šehamatos yagía roce dov lehagía lelud. | כמה זמן לפני שהמטוס יגיע רוצה דוב להגיע ללוד? | .3
4. lean roca avíva linsóa. | לאן רוצה אביבה לנסוע? | .4
5. haim dov yikax ota ito? | האם דוב יקח אותה אתו? | .5
6. lema hem yictarxu lexakot. | למה הם יצטרכו לחכות? | .6
7. haim hem yagíu bazman? | האם הם יגיעו בזמן? | .7
8. im mi avíva crixa lehitkašer. | עם מי אביבה צריכה להתקשר? | .8

REVIEW CONVERSATIONS

A: ma hašaa.   א : מה השעה?

B: hašaa šeš bediyuk.   ב : השעה שש בדיוק.

A: toda raba.   א : תודה רבה.

C: matay hahorim šelxa omdim lehagía.   ג : מתי ההורים שלך עומרים להגיע?

D: beod yomáim.   ד : בעוד יומיים.

C: hem hitkašru itxa telefónit?   ג : הם התקשרו אתך טלפונית?

D: lo, hem šalxu mixtav.   ד : לא. הם שלחו מכתב.

E: ani roca linsóa itxa lexáyfa.   ה : אני רוצה לנסוע אתך לחיפה.

F: tov. beracon.   ו : טוב. ברצון.

E: beéyze šaa tisa.   ה : באיזה שעה תיסע.

F: bešéva varéva.   ו : בשבע ורבע.

G: matay carix moše lehagía.   ז : מתי צריך משה להגיע?

H: ani lo yodáat bediyuk.   ח : אני לא יודעת בדיוק.

G: hu lo hitkašer itax?   ז : הוא לא התקשר אתך?

H: lo, hu amar šeyišlax mivrak.   ח : לא. הוא אמר שישלח מברק.

I: ata noséa lelud habóker?   ט : אתה נוסע ללוד הבוקר?

J: ken.   י : כן.

I: beéyze šaa ata noséa.   ט : באיזה שעה אתה נוסע?

J: bešmóne.   י : בשמונה.

I: yeš lexa maspik zman.   ט : יש לך מספיק זמן.

K: ani mekave šelo nictarex   כ : אני מקוה שלא נצטרך
   lexakot harbe zman.   לחכות הרבה זמן.

L: gam ani mekava kax.   ל : גם אני מקוה כך.

K: káma zman yikax lahem   כ : כמה זמן יקח להם
   laavor et haméxes.   לעבור את המכס?

L: kexaci šaa.   ל : כחצי שעה.

K: xaci šaa? ze lo harbe zman.   כ : חצי שעה? זה לא הרבה זמן.

M: bidki matay šehamatos omed lehagía.   מ: בדקי מתי שהמטוס עומד להגיע.

N: ken. etkašer miyad.   נ: כן. אתקשר מיד.

M: ani xošev šebešaa šeš.   מ: אני חושב שבשעה שש.

N: gam ani xošévet kax.   נ: גם אני חושבת כך.

O: matay omédet hamišpaxa šelxa lehagía.   ס: מתי עומדת המשפחה שלך להגיע.

P: hamišpaxa šeli tagía beod   xódeš yamim.   ע: המשפחה שלי תגיע בעוד חודש ימים.

O: heyxan tagúru?   ס: היכן תגורו?

P: yesudar avurénu báit berámat gan.   ע: יסודר עבורנו בית ברמת גן.

O: rámat gan hi ir yafa meod.   ס: רמת גן היא עיר יפה מאוד.

Q: ma at xošévet? yikax lemoše harbe   פ: מה את חושבת? יקח למשה הרבה
   zman laavor et haméxes?   זמן לעבור את המכס?

R: ken. ki yeš lo harbe xavilot.   צ: כן. כי יש לו הרבה חבילות.

Q: O ken. naxon. ad šeyivdeku et kol   פ: אה, כן. נכון. עד שיבדקו את כל
   haxavilot yikax šaa, šaatáim.   החבילות יקח שעה – שעתיים.

End of Tape 7A

הלו, היפה שתיים שבע שש ארבע אפס?
תל אביב קוראת. דברו בבקשה...

Tape 7B

19.1 Calling Long Distance

YONATAN

Atara, do you know	atára. at yodáat	עטרה, את יודעת
the telephone number	et mispar hatélefon	את מספר הטלפון
of Uncle Reuven?	šel hadod reuven?	של הדוד ראובן?
uncle	dod (m)	דוד
aunt	doda (f)	דודה

ATARA

No. Call	lo. hitkašer im	לא. התקשר עם
information.	modiin.	מודיעין.
Dial "zero".	xayeg éfes.	חייג אפס.
information(service)	modiin (m.s.)	מודיעין
he dialed	xiyeg	חייג
zero	éfes	אפס

YONATAN

Hello, information?	halo. modiin?	הלו. מודיעין?
Please give me	tni li bevakaša	תני לי בבקשה
a number in Haifa.	mispar bexáyfa.	מספר בחיפה.
The name is	hašem hu	השם הוא
Reuven Duvdevani,	reuven duvdeváni.	ראובן דובדבני,
Jaffa Street 76.	rexov yáfo šiv'im vešeš.	רחוב יפו שבעים ושש.
name	šem (m)	שם
names	šemot (m.pl.)	שמות

INFORMATION

The number is	hamispar hu	המספר הוא
27640.	štáim šéva šeš árba éfes.	שתיים שבע שש ארבע אפס.
You can dial	ata yaxol	אתה יכול
direct or	lexayeg yeširot	לחייג ישירות
through long distance,	o dérex sixot xuc	או דרך שיחות-חוץ,
number 19.	mispar tšá'esre.	מספר תשע-עשרה.
direct	yašir (m.s.)	ישיר
conversation	sixa (f)	שיחה

YONATAN

Thank you.	toda raba.	תודה רבה.
I'll make the call	azmin et hasixa	אזמין את השיחה
through number 19.	bemispar tšá'esre.	במספר תשע-עשרה.

LONG DISTANCE

Long distance. Hello.	sixot xuc. šalom.	שיחות חוץ. שלום.

YONATAN

Please give me	tni li bevakaša	תני לי בבקשה
Haifa 27640.	xáyfa štáim šéva šeš	חיפה שתיים שבע שש
	árba éfes.	ארבע אפס.

LONG DISTANCE

What is your number?	ma hamispar šelxa?	מה המספר שלך?

YONATAN

60783.		
	šeš éfes šéva šmóne	שש אפס שבע שמונה
	šaloš.	שלוש.

LONG DISTANCE

One moment.	xake réga.		חכה רגע.
The line is busy.	hakav tafus.		הקו תפוס.
	line	kav (m)	קו
	occupied	tafus (m.s.)	תפוס

Hello, Haifa	haló - xáyfa		הלו, חיפה
27640?	štaim ševa šeš árba éfes?	שתיים שבע שש ארבע אפס?	
Tel Aviv calling.	tel aviv koret.		תל אביב קוראת.
Go ahead please.	dabru bevakaša.		דברו בבקשה.
calls, reads	kore (m.s. pres.)		קורא

19.2   ADDITIONAL VOCABULARY

A call from a phone booth	sixa mita télefon		שיחה מתא טלפון
costs 20 "grush".	ola esrim gruš.		עולה עשרים גרוש.
	booth	ta (m)	תא
(old name for agora)	gruš (m)		גרוש

Tokens	asimonim		אסימונים
are sold	nimkarim		נמכרים
in every post office.	bexol misrad dóar.		בכל משרד דואר.
	token	asimon (m)	אסימון
	is sold	nimkar (m.s.)	נמכר
	he sold	maxar	מכר

In order to find out	kedey levarer		כדי לברר
what time it is	ma hašaa		מה השעה
dial 15.	xayeg xaméš'esre.		חייג חמש-עשרה.
	in order to	kedey	כדי
	he found out	birer	בירר

When the phone is out of	kšehatélefon mekulkal		כשהטלפון מקולקל
order dial 16.	xayeg šéš'esre.		חייג שש-עשרה.
	out of order	mekulkal (m.s.)	מקולקל
	he damaged	kilkel	קלקל

To call	lehitkašer im		להתקשר עם
outside the country	xuc laárec		חוץ לארץ
dial 18.	xayeg šmóne'esre.		חייג שמונה-עשרה.

19.3   Vocabulary Drills

A. Substitution-Agreement Drill

    This drill may be done as a substitution drill using either verb as a cue and also as an expansion drill.

Dial 15 and check the time.

xayeg xaméš'esre ubdok ma hašaa.	חייג חמש-עשרה ובדוק מה השעה.
xaygi vebidki	חייגי חמש-עשרה ובדקי מה השעה.
xaygu vebidku	חייגו חמש-עשרה ובדקו מה השעה.
xayegna ubdókna	חייגנה חמש-עשרה ובדוקנה מה השעה.

    (Both /u-/ and /ve-/ have been used to illustrate possible variations).

B. Substitution Drill   / a - ~ te - /

I'll dial direct to Rehovot.

	axayeg yeširot lerexóvot.	אחייג ישירות לרחובות.	
	texayeg	תחייג	
at	texaygi	תחייגי	את
hu	yexayeg	יחייג	הוא
hi	texayeg	תחייג	היא
	nexayeg	נחייג	
atem	texaygu	תחייגו	אתם
aten	texayégna	תחייגנה	אתן
hem	yexaygu	יחייגו	הם
hen	texayégna	תחייגנה	הן

C. Substitution-Agreement Drill   /xiyeg/ "he dialed"

He didn't dial the right number.

hu lo xiyeg et hamispar hanaxon.   הוא לא חייג את המספר הנכון.
hi - ani - at - hu   היא – אני – את – הוא
hem - ánu - ata - hi   הם – אנו – אתה – היא
atem - hen - hu   אתם – הן – הוא

D. Substitution-Agreement Drill   /kore/ "calls"

The root of this verb is kr' קרא , and it is conjugated like mc' מצא "find".

Miriam is calling us. Hurry.

miryam koret lánu. maharu.   מרים קוראת לנו. מהרו.

dov - hem - hi - hen   דוב – הם – היא – הן
moše veišto - hu - miryam   משה ואשתו – הוא – מרים

E. Substitution-Agreement Drill   /birer/ "he found out"

We found out Mrs. Zahavi's address.

birárnu et haktóvet šel gvéret zahávi.   בררנו את הכתובת של גברת זהבי.

atem - at - hu - hi   אתם – את – הוא – היא
hem - ani - moše - ata   הם – אני – משה – אתה
xana - hen - ánu   חנה – הן – אנו

F. Substitution Drill   /a - ~ te -/

I'll find out if the bus goes to Lydda.

	avarer im haótobus noséa lelud.	אברר אם האוטובוס נוסע ללוד.	
	tevarer	תברר	
	tevareri	תבררי	
hu	yevarer	יברר	הוא
hi	tevarer	תברר	היא
	nevarer	נברר	
atem	tevareru	תבררו	אתם
aten	tevarérna	תבררנה	אתן
hem	yevareru	יבררו	הם
hen	tevarérna	תבררנה	הן

G. Substitution-Agreement Drill

She'll find out if Miriam is going.

<u>hi tevarer im miryam nosáat.</u>   .היא תברר אם מרים נוסעת

ani - ánu - hen - hu   אני – אנו – הן – הוא
ata - at - hem - hi   אתה – את – הם – היא

H. Substitution-Agreement Drill

Moshe is checking when the plane arrives.

<u>mo</u>še mevarer maṭay šehamatos megía.   .משה מברר מתי שהמטוס מגיע
<u>sára</u> mevaréret   שרה מבררת
<u>ánu</u> mevarerim   אנו מבררים
<u>hen</u> mevarerot   הן מבררות

GRAMMAR NOTES

19.4 Adverbs

  Adverbs or adverbial phrases are of several types.

(a)   The masculine singular form of the adjective is often used.
/at medabéret yafe./ "You speak beautifully."
/tov asíta./ "You did well."

  This was discussed earlier in Grammar Note 10.5.

(b)   The /t/ feminine singular of some adjectives ending in / - i / is used.
This is so with the ordinal numbers.

/šenit/ "secondly"
/šlišit/ "thirdly"

  Note that the feminine singular form of the adjective "second" is /šnia/.
There are some adverbs of this type which have no corresponding masculine
singular form.

/rešit/ "first" (cf. /rišon/)

(c)   The feminine plural adjective is sometimes used.

/xayeg yeširot./ "Dial directly."

(d)   Some adverbs have unique forms, though with recognizable roots.
/kódem/ "early, preceding" (cf. /mukdám/)
/heytev/ "well" (/cf. /tov/)

(e)   The preposition /be-/ is often used with a corresponding noun.

/bekol/ "loudly"
/beemet/ "really"
/bediyuk/ "exactly"
/beracon/ "willingly"
/behexlet/ "decidedly"
/bekarov/ "shortly"

(f)   Other prepositions are sometimes used.

/miyad/ "immediately"

199

19.5 The nif'al Conjugation - Present and Past Tenses

Compare the following forms.

/moxer/	"sells"	/nimkar/	"is sold"
/moce/	"find"	/nimca/	"is found"
/roe/	"sees"	/nir'e/	"is seen, seems"

Note that the meaning of the forms on the right is the passive or intransitive of the verbs on the left.

Most nif'al verbs have a counterpart in the pa'al with the corresponding active meaning. A few have active counterparts in the pi'el or hif'il. The correspondence of form is sometimes remote in the English translations, but the Hebrew speaker has a definite feeling for the basic meaning of the root.

1. Prefix of the nif'al:

The present and past tenses of the nif'al have a prefix to the root. The prefix is / ni - / except in the following cases:

(a) If the first consonant of the root is / x / (ח) then the prefix is /ne-/.

/nexšav/   "is considered"   נחשב

(b) If the first consonant of the root is / ' / (א or ע) then the form begins /ne'e-/ with the /'/ usually replaced by a smooth transition.

/ne'exal/ or /neexal/   "eaten"   נאכל

(c) If the first consonant is /'/ represented by ע , the form may begin /na'a-/ or, with smooth transition, /naa-/.

/naase/   "done, made"   נעשה

(d) If the first consonant of the root is /h/ then the form begins /nehe-/.

/nehedar/   "wonderful"   נהדר

(e) If the first consonant of the root is y, then the prefix and the y coalesce to /no-/, spelled נו . Compare this with the comment on /hodia/ "he informed" in Grammar Note 17.7.

/yada/	"he knew"	ידע	/yalda/	"she gave birth"	ילדה
/noda/	"known"	נודע	/nolda/	"she was born"	נולדה

2. Alternation of root consonants in the nif'al:

(a) If the first radical is n , then it is dropped in the present and past tenses.

/natan/ "he gave"
/nitan/ "was given" for */nintan/

(b) If the first radical is <u>b</u> or <u>p</u> , then it occurs as /v/ or /f/, respectively.

/badak/ "he checked"   בדק
/nivdak/ "was checked"   נבדק

/patax/ "he opened"   פתח
/niftax/ "was opened"   נפתח

[Note the designation /nif'al/ itself.]

(c) If the first radical is <u>k</u>, spelled כ, then it occurs as /x/. However, the prefix is /ni-/, not /ne-/ as with /x/ spelled ח .

/nixnas/ "he entered"   נכנס

but   /nexšav/ "is considered"   נחשב

(d) If the <u>second</u> radical is <u>b</u> or <u>p</u> , then it occurs as /b/ or /p/, respectively.

/nišbar/ "was broken"   נשבר
/nišpax/ "was spilled"   נשפך

(e) If the second radical is <u>k</u>, spelled כ , then it occurs as /k/.

/nimkar/ "is sold"   נמכר

There is an exception to rules (d) and (e). If the second radical is preceded by /nee/ or /no/ then the variants /v/, /f/, and /x/ occur.

/neevad/ "lost"   נאבד
/neefe/   "baked"   נאפה
/neexal/ "eaten"   נאכל

There are other relatively minor features of the present and past tense forms of the <u>nif'al</u> which should be learned by the student as they are met, but which need not be discussed here. A more complete description of the consonant alternations is given in Unit 23.

19.6 The Present Tense of the nif'al

The pattern of the present tense is as follows: (The prefix is given as /ni-/ since this is the most frequent form.)

m.s.   /ni - - a - / nimkar   נמכר
f.s.   /ni - - é - et/ nimkéret   נמכרת
m.pl. /ni - - a - im/ nimkarim   נמכרים
f.pl. /ni - - a - ot/ nimkarot   נמכרות

The feminine singular always ends in /-t/, even in <u>lamed hey</u> verbs.

m.s.   /nir'e / "seems"   נראה
f.s.   /nir'et/   נראית

This is the exception to the f.s. /-a/ endings mentioned in Grammar Note 8.4a and section 16.3, Drill B. It avoids confusion with the 3 m.s. past tense form /nir'a/ "he seemed".

When the third root consonant is <u>'</u> (ע) or <u>x</u> (ח) the feminine singular has the suffix / - at/. Cf. m.s. /šoméa/ f.s. /šomáat/ "hears"
                 m.s. /nišma/ "is heared"   נשמע
                 f.s. /nišmáat/   נשמעת

When the third root consonant is ' (א) the feminine singular ends in /-et/.

m.s. /nimca/   "is located"   נמצא
f.s. /nimcet/   נמצאת

A. Substitution-Agreement Drill   /nimkar/ "is sold"   נמכר

Tokens are sold in the post office.

asimonim nimkarim badóar.   אסימונים נמכרים בדואר.

bulim - gluyot - igrot avir   בולים – גלויות – אגרות אויר
maatafa - bul - gluya - asimonim   מעטפה – בול – גלויה – אסימונים

B. Substitution-Agreement Drill   /neexal/ " is eaten"   נאכל

Chala is eaten on the Sabbath.

xala neexélet bešabat.   חלה נאכלת בשבת.

dagim memulaim - ugot - basar   דגים ממולאים – עוגות – בשר
beycim - melafefonim - xala   ביצים – מלפפונים – חלה

C. Substitution-Agreement Drill   /nišma/ "is heard"   נשמע

He is heard well over the phone.

hu nišma tov batélefon.   הוא נשמע טוב בטלפון.

išti - hem - ata - aten   אשתי – הם – אחה – אתן
yónatan - sára - atem - hu   יונתן – שרה – אתם – הוא

D. Substitution-Agreement Drill   /nexšav/   "is considered"   נחשב

She is considered a good teacher.

hi nexšévet lemora tova.   היא נחשבת למורה טובה.

ata - kulam - sára veatára   אתה – כולם – שרה ועטרה
ištexa - ánu - hu - hi   אשתך – אנו – הוא – היא

E. Substitution-Agreement Drill   /nir'e/   "seems"   נראה

They don't look well today.

hem lo nir'im tov hayom.   הם לא נראים טוב היום.

at - sára vexána - ata   את – שרה וחנה – אתה
baalex - hi - aten - hem   בעלך – היא – אתן – הם

F. Substitution-Agreement Drill   /nimca/   "is located"

The books are in my house.

<u>hasfarim nimcaim bebeyti.</u>   <u>הספרים נמצאים בביתי.</u>

haóxel – hašulxanot – haxala – habakbuk   הבקבוק – החלה – השולחנות – האוכל

hateenim – hakufsa – haxavilot – hasfarim   הספרים – החבילות – הקופסה – התאנים

The following drills require the student to transform a sentence with the verb
in the <u>kal</u> (<u>pa'al</u>) conjugation into a more-or-less equivalent sentence with the
verb in the <u>nif'al</u> conjugation. The drills should also be done in reverse.

The native English speaker is often stunned when the Hebrew speaker assumes,
for example, that the meaning of   /histadárnu tov./   "we got along well"
should be clear from /séder/ "order".   The astonishment is increased when he
adds, "You know /yesudar/ 'will be arranged', don't you?" The point is that the
Hebrew speaker is primarily aware of the consonant sequence <u>s-d-r</u>, and the English
speaker is not.

English has only a few comparable patterns (<u>sing</u> – <u>sang</u> – <u>sung</u> – <u>song</u>), but
each of these is unique. (There is the pattern <u>ring-rang-rung</u>, but not <u>rong</u>.)
Similarities of spelling train the English speaker to be unaware of others, such
as <u>democrat</u> – <u>democracy</u>, which do not share a single vowel in pronunciation in
corresponding syllables.

It cannot be emphasized too strongly that the student must learn to handle the
roots, conjugations, and paradigms with great ease. Most students will learn to
"encode" the forms without much trouble, but drilling should be continued until
correct forms and sentences are produced rapidly and automatically.

G. Transformation Drill

Instructor: [They] sell tokens at the post office.

Student: Tokens are sold at the post office.

1. moxrim asimonim badóar.   .1   מוכרים אסימונים בדואר.
    asimonim nimkarim badóar.   אסימונים נמכרים בדואר.

2. moxrim gluyot badóar.   .2   מוכרים גלויות בדואר.
    gluyot nimkarot badóar.   גלויות נמכרות בדואר.

3. moxrim igrot avir badóar.   .3   מוכרים אגרות אויר בדואר.
    igrot avir nimkarot badóar.   אגרות אויר נמכרות בדואר.

4. moxrim maatafa badóar.   .4   מוכרים מעטפה בדואר.
    maatafa nimkéret badóar.   מעטפה נמכרת בדואר.

5. moxrim bul badóar.   .5   מוכרים בול בדואר.
    bul nimkar badóar.   בול נמכר בדואר.

6. moxrim gluya badóar.   .6   מוכרים גלויה בדואר.
    gluya nimkéret badóar.   גלויה נמכרת בדואר.

7. moxrim bulim badóar.   .7   מוכרים בולים בדואר.
    bulim nimkarim badóar.   בולים נמכרים בדואר.

H. Transformation Drill

    Instructor: We eat <u>chala</u> on the Sabbath.
    Student: <u>chala</u> is eaten on the Sabbath.

1. ánu oxlim xala bešabat.   .אנו אוכלים חלה בשׁבת 1.
     xala neexélet bešabat.   .חלה נאכלת בשבת

2. ánu oxlim basar bešabat.   .אנו אוכלים בשׂר בשׁבת 2.
     basar neexal bešabat.   .בשר נאכל בשבת

3. ánu oxlim dagim memulaim bešabat.   .אנו אוכלים דגים ממולאים בשׁבת 3.
     dagim memulaim neexalim bešabat.   .דגים ממולאים נאכלים בשבת

4. ánu oxlim ugot bešabat.   .אנו אוכלים עוגות בשׁבת 4.
     ugot neexalot bešabat.   .עוגות נאכלות בשבת

5. ánu oxlim perot bešabat.   .אנו אוכלים פירות בשׁבת 5.
     perot neexalim bešabat.   .פירות נאכלים בשבת

6. ánu oxlim beycim bešabat.   .אנו אוכלים ביצים בשׁבת 6.
     beycim neexalot bešabat.   .ביצים נאכלות בשבת

19.7 <u>The Past Tense of the nif'al</u>

    The pattern of the past tense is as follows:

                           šlx

1. s.	/ni--á-ti/	nišláxti	"I was sent"
2. m.s.	/ni--á-ta/	nišláxta	"you were sent"
2. f.s.	/ni--á-t /	nišláxt	"you were sent"
3. m.s.	/ni--a- /	nišlax	"he was sent"
3. f.s.	/ni---a /	nišlexa	"she was sent"
1. pl.	/ni--á-nu/	nišláxnu	"we were sent"
2. m.pl.	/ni--á-tem/	nišláxtem	"you were sent"
2. f.pl.	/ni--á-ten/	nišláxten	"you were sent"
3.pl.	/ni---u/	nišlexu	"they were sent.

    There are no surprises at all in the above chart. The first and second person
forms differ only in the suffixes, as described back in Grammar Note 5.4. The
pattern of the third person forms is quite regular, as described in Grammar Note
6.9 and 16.4. The / - e - / in 3 f.s. and 3 pl. /nišlexa , nišlexu/ is
introduced to break up the three-consonant cluster which results in these forms.

    The past tense of <u>lamed hey</u> verbs has the vowel / e / before the suffix.

               /nir'éti/   "I was seen"

A. Substitution-Agreement Drill   /nišlax/ "was sent"   נשלח

    I was sent to the grocery store.

    <u>nišláxti lexanut hamakólet.</u>   .נשלחתי לחנות המכולת

    hem - moše - dálya - ánu   אנו – דליה – משה – הם
    ata - at - atára - ani   אני – עטרה – את – אתה

B. Substitution-Agreement Drill /nifgaš/ "met" נפגש

We got together with Dov this morning.

nifgášnu im dov habóker. ‏.נפגשנו עם דוב הבוקר

ani - avíva - baali - hen ‏אני – אביבה – בעלי – הן
ata - atem - hem - ánu ‏אתה – אתם – הם – אנו

C. Substitution-Agreement Drill /nigaš/ "approached" ניגש

(This verb is irregular in that in the present and past tenses it is
conjugated in the nif'al, but in the imperative and future it is conjugated
in the pa'al. The future was drilled in Grammar Section 13.6, Drills G & H.)

I went to the main post office.

nigášti ladóar hamerkazi. ‏.נגשתי לדואר המרכזי

hi - dov - atem - ánu ‏היא – דוב – אתם – אנו
at - david veyónatan - ani ‏את – דוד ויונתן – אני

The following drills should be done in reverse, also.

D. Transformation Drill /nišlax/ "was sent" נשלח

Instructor: They sent me to the store.
Student: I was sent to the store.

šalxu oti laxanut.	‏.שלח אותי לחנות
nišláxti laxanut.	‏.נשלחתי לחנות
šalxu otxa laxanut.	‏.שלח אותך לחנות
nišláxta laxanut.	‏.נשלחת לחנות
šalxu et moše laxanut.	‏.שלח את משה לחנות
moše nišlax laxanut.	‏.משה נשלח לחנות
šalxu otánu laxanut.	‏.שלח אותנו לחנות
nišláxnu laxanut.	‏.נשלחנו לחנות
šalxu otxem laxanut.	‏.שלח אתכם לחנות
nišláxtem laxanut.	‏.נשלחתם לחנות
šalxu et léa laxanut.	‏.שלח את לאה לחנות
léa nišlexa laxanut.	‏.לאה נשלחה לחנות
šalxu otax laxanut.	‏.שלח אותך לחנות
nišlaxt laxanut.	‏.נשלחת לחנות
šalxu otan laxanut.	‏.שלח אותן לחנות
hen nišlexu laxanut.	‏.הן נשלחו לחנות
šalxu otam laxanut.	‏.שלח אותם לחנות
hem nišlexu laxanut.	‏.הם נשלחו לחנות
šalxu otxen laxanut.	‏.שלח אתכן לחנות
nišláxten laxanut.	‏.נשלחתן לחנות
šalxu oti laxanut.	‏.שלח אותי לחנות
nišláxti laxanut.	‏.נשלחתי לחנות

E. Transformation Drill   /nifgaš/   "met"   נפגש

Instructor: I met Yael the day before yesterday.

Student: I got together with Yael the day before yesterday.

pagášti et yael šilšom.	פגשתי את יעל שלשום.
nifgašti im yael šilšom.	נפגשתי עם יעל שלשום.
išti pagša et yael šilšom.	אשתי פגשה את יעל שלשום.
išti nifgeša im yael šilšom.	אשתי נפגשה עם יעל שלשום.
hu pagaš et yael šilšom.	הוא פגש את יעל שלשום.
hu nifgaš im yael šilšom.	הוא נפגש עם יעל שלשום.
pagášta et yael šilšom.	פגשת את יעל שלשום.
nifgašta im yael šilšom.	נפגשת עם יעל שלשום.
atem pagáštem et yael šilšom.	אתם פגשתם את יעל שלשום.
atem nifgáštem im yael šilšom.	אתם נפגשתם עם יעל שלשום.
pagášnu et yael šilšom.	פגשנו את יעל שלשום.
nifgášnu im yael šilšom.	נפגשנו עם יעל שלשום.
pagašt et yael šilšom.	פגשת את יעל שלשום.
nifgašt im yael šilšom.	נפגשת עם יעל שלשום.
mi pagaš et yael šilšom.	מי פגש את יעל שלשום?
mi nifgaš im yael šilšom.	מי נפגש עם יעל שלשום?
hem pagšu et yael šilšom.	הם פגשו את יעל שלשום.
hem nifgešu im yael šilšom.	הם נפגשו עם יעל שלשום.
pagášten et yael šilšom.	פגשתן את יעל שלשום.
nifgášten im yael šilšom.	נפגשתן עם יעל שלשום.
pagášti et yael šilšom.	פגשתי את יעל שלשום.
nifgášti im yael šilšom.	נפגשתי עם יעל שלשום.

F. Transformation Drill   /nišma/   "was heard"   נשמע

Instructor: We heard well over the phone.
Student: We were heard well over the phone.

šamánu tov batélefon.	שמענו טוב בטלפון.
nišmánu tov batélefon.	נשמענו טוב בטלפון.
šamátem tov batélefon.	שמעתם טוב בטלפון.
nišmátem tov batélefon.	נשמעתם טוב בטלפון.
šamáti tov batélefon.	שמעתי טוב בטלפון.
nišmáti tov batélefon.	נשמעתי טוב בטלפון.
moše šama tov batélefon.	משה שמע טוב בטלפון.
moše nišma tov batélefon.	משה נשמע טוב בטלפון.
hem šam'u tov batélefon.	הם שמעו טוב בטלפון.
hem nišme'u tov batélefon.	הם נשמעו טוב בטלפון.
šamat tov batélefon.	שמעת טוב בטלפון.
nišmat tov batélefon.	נשמעת טוב בטלפון.
ištexa šam'a tov batélefon.	אשתך שמעה טוב בטלפון.
ištexa nišme'a tov batélefon.	אשתך נשמעה טוב בטלפון.
šamáten tov batélefon.	שמעתן טוב בטלפון.
nišmáten tov batélefon.	נשמעתן טוב בטלפון.
šamáta tov batélefon.	שמעת טוב בטלפון.
nišmáta tov batélefon.	נשמעת טוב בטלפון.

G. Transformation Drill   /nir'a/   "was seen"   נראה

Instructor: He saw me in the Dan Hotel.
Student: I was seen in the Dan Hotel.

hu raa oti bemalon dan.   הוא ראה אותי במלון דן.
    nir'éti bemalon dan.   נראיתי במלון דן.

hu raa otxá bemalon dan.   הוא ראה אותך במלון דן.
    nir'éta bemalon dan.   נראית במלון דן.

hu raa otánu bemalon dan.   הוא ראה אותנו במלון דן.
    nir'énu bemalon dan.   נראינו במלון דן.

hu raa otax bemalon dan.   הוא ראה אותך במלון דן.
    nir'et bemalon dan.   נראית במלון דן.

hu raa et moše bemalon dan.   הוא ראה את משה במלון דן.
    moše nir'a bemalon dan.   משה נראה במלון דן.

hu raa otan bemalon dan.   הוא ראה אותן במלון דן.
    hen nir'u bemalon dan.   הן נראו במלון דן.

hu raa et sára bemalon dan.   הוא ראה את שרה במלון דן.
    sára nir'ata bemalon dan.   שרה נראתה במלון דן.

hu raa otxem bemalon dan.   הוא ראה אתכם במלון דן.
    nir'étem bemalon dan.   נראיתם במלון דן.

hu raa otxen bemalon dan.   הוא ראה אתכן במלון דן.
    nir'éten bemalon dan.   נראיתן במלון דן.

hu raa otam bemalon dan.   הוא ראה אותם במלון דן.
    hem nir'u bemalon dan.   הם נראו במלון דן.

H. Transformation Drill   /nivdak/   "was checked"   ניברק

Instructor: The doctor examined us.
Student: We were examined by the doctor.

harofe badak otánu.   הרופא בדק אותנו.
    nivdáknu al yedey harofe.   נבדקנו על ידי הרופא.
harofe badak et baalex.   הרופא בדק את בעלך.
    baalex nivdak al yedey harofe.   בעלך נבדק על ידי הרופא.
harofe badak otxem.   הרופא בדק אתכם.
    nivdáktem al yedey harofe.   נבדקתם על ידי הרופא.
harofe badak oti.   הרופא בדק אותי.
    nivdákti al yedey harofe.   נבדקתי על ידי הרופא.
harofe badak otax.   הרופא בדק אותך.
    nivdakt al yedey harofe.   נבדקת על ידי הרופא.
harofe badak otxa.   הרופא בדק אותך.
    nivdákta al yedey harofe.   נבדקת על ידי הרופא.
harofe badak et kulam.   הרופא בדק את כולם.
    kulam nivdeku al yedey harofe.   כולם נבדקו על ידי הרופא.
harofe badak et išto.   הרופא בדק את אשתו.
    išto nivdeka al yedey harofe.   אשתו נבדקה על ידי הרופא.
harofe badak otxen.   הרופא בדק אתכן.
    nivdákten al yedey harofe.   נבדקתן על ידי הרופא.
harofe badak otan.   הרופא בדק אותן.
    hen nivdeku al yedey harofe.   הן נבדקו על ידי הרופא.

I. Transformation Drill   /nisgar/ "was closed"   נסגר

    Instructor: They locked me in the office.
    Student: I was locked in the office.

sagru oti bamisrad.	סגרו אותי במשרד.
nisgárti bamisrad.	נסגרתי במשרד.
sagru otxa veet dov bamisrad.	סגרו אותך ואת דוב במשרד.
dov veata nisgártem bamisrad.	דוב ואתה נסגרתם במשרד.
sagru et baala šel xána bamisrad.	סגרו את בעלה של חנה במשרד.
baala šel xána nisgar bamisrad.	בעלה של חנה נסגר במשרד.
sagru otánu bamisrad.	סגרו אותנו במשרד.
nisgárnu bamisrad.	נסגרנו במשרד.
sagru otax bamisrad.	סגרו אותך במשרד.
nisgart bamisrad.	נסגרת במשרד.
sagru otxen bamisrad.	סגרו אתכן במשרד.
nisgárten bamisrad.	נסגרתן במשרד.
sagru et moše veet david bamisrad.	סגרו את משה ואת דוד במשרד.
moše vedavid nisgeru bamisrad.	משה ודוד נסגרו במשרד.
sagru ota bamisrad.	סגרו אותה במשרד.
hi nisgera bamisrad.	היא נסגרה במשרד.
sagru oto bamisrad.	סגרו אותו במשרד.
hu nisgar bamisrad.	הוא נסגר במשרד.

J. Transformation Drill   /nexšav/ "was considered"   נחשב

    Instructor: They considered you a good teacher.
    Student: You were considered a good teacher.

xašvu otxa lemore tov.	חשבו אותך למורה טוב.
nexšavta lemore tov.	נחשבת למורה טוב.
xašvu otax lemora tova.	חשבו אותך למורה טובה.
nexšavt lemora tova.	נחשבת למורה טובה.
xašvu otam lemorim tovim.	חשבו אותם למורים טובים.
hem nexševu lemorim tovim.	הם נחשבו למורים טובים.
xašvu otxen lemorot tovot.	חשבו אתכן למורות טובות.
nexšávten lemorot tovot.	נחשבתן למורות טובות.
xašvu otxem lemorim tovim.	חשבו אתכם למורים טובים.
nexšávtem lemorim tovim.	נחשבתם למורים טובים.
xašvu otánu lemorim tovim.	חשבו אותנו למורים טובים.
nexšávnu lemorim tovim.	נחשבנו למורים טובים.
xašvu oto lemore tov.	חשבו אותו למורה טוב.
hu nexšav lemore tov.	הוא נחשב למורה טוב.
xašvu et išti lemora tova.	חשבו את אשתי למורה טובה.
išti nexševa lemora tova.	אשתי נחשבה למורה טובה.
xašvu et sára veet raxel lemorot tovot.	חשבו את שרה ואת רחל למורות טובות.
sára veraxel nexševu lemorot tovot.	שרה ורחל נחשבו למורות טובות.
xašvu oti lemore tov.	חשבו אותי למורה טוב.
nexšávti lemore tov.	נחשבתי למורה טוב.

REVIEW CONVERSATIONS

A: at yodáat et mispar hatélefon šel david?   ?א: את יודעת את מספר הטלפון של דוד

B: lo. kax asimon vehitkašer im modiin.   ב: לא. קח אסימון והתקשר עם מודיעין.

A: eyn kan séfer telefónim?   א: אין כאן ספר טלפונים?

B: ani lo roa séfer telefónim.   ב: אני לא רואה ספר טלפונים.

C: ma hašaa.   ג: מה השעה?

D: ani xošévet šešeš.   ד: אני חושבת שש.

C: xayegi xaméš'esre vebidki.   ג: חייגי חמש-עשרה ובדקי.

D: amárti lax šehašaa šeš.   ד: אמרתי לך שהשעה שש.

E: hatélefon mekulkal.   ה: הטלפון מקולקל.

F: hitkašri im šéš'esre.   ו: התקשרי עם שש-עשרה.

E: hitkašárti aval hakav tafus.   ה: התקשרתי אבל הקו תפוס.

F: xaygi od hapáam.   ו: חייגי עוד הפעם.

G: hizmánti sixa lexéyfa.   ז: הזמנתי שיחה לחיפה.

H: láma lo hitkašárta yeširot?   ח: למה לא התקשרת ישירות.

G: efšar lehitkašer yeširot lexéyfa?   ז: אפשר להתקשר ישירות לחיפה?

H: ken, behexlet.   ח: כן. בהחלט.

I: lean ata holex?   ט: לאן אתה הולך?

J: nišláxti lexanut hamakólet.   י: נשלחתי לחנות המכולת.

I: mi šalax otxa?   ט: מי שלח אותך?

J: nišláxti al yedey moše liknot xalav.   י: נשלחתי על ידי משה לקנות חלב.

K: ma asíta habóker?   כ: מה עשית הבוקר?

L: nifgášti im david.   ל: נפגשתי עם דוד.

K: eyfo nifgášta ito?   כ: איפה נפגשת אתו?

L: nifgášti ito bekafe atára.   ל: נפגשתי אתו בקפה עטרה.

M: hitkašárnu etmol im xáyfa.   מ: התקשרנו אתמול עם חיפה.

N: eyx hem nišmeu?   נ: איך הם נשמעו?

M: šamánu otam heytev.   מ: שמענו אותם היטב.

N: im mi dibártem?   נ: עם מי דברתם?

M: dibárnu im kol hamišpaxa.   מ: דברנו עם כל המשפחה.

O: noda lánu šeat nimcet betel aviv.   ס: נודע לנו שאת נמצאת בתל אביב.

P: meáin noda laxem?   ע: מאין נודע לכם?

O: nir'et bemalon dan.   ס: נראית במלון דן.

P: ken. ani gára šam.   ע: כן. אני גרה שם.

Q: éyfo háita etmol baláyla.   פ: איפה היית אתמול בלילה?

R: nisgárti bamisrad.   צ: נסגרתי במשרד.

Q: eyx ze kara?   פ: איך זה קרה?

R: hadélet nisgera velo yaxólti liftóax ota.   צ: הדלת נסגרה ולא יכולתי לפתוח אותה.

S: nexšávti lemore tov.   ק: נחשבתי למורה טוב.

T: éyfo? betel aviv?   ר: איפה? בתל אביב?

S: ken. gam betel aviv xašvu oti.   ק: כן. גם בתל אביב חשבו אותי.

T: vekan?   ר: וכאן?

S: gam kan ani nexšav lemore tov.   ק: גם כאן אני נחשב למורה טוב.

End of Tape 7B

Tape 8A

20.1   Hot weather

<u>DAVID</u>

What a hot day !	éyze xom !	! איזה חום
heat	xom (m)	חום

<u>YONATAN</u>

Yes.	ken.	כן.
It's for sure	ze lavétax	זה לבטח
a <u>chamsin</u>.	xamsín.	חמסין.
sure	bétax	בטח
for sure	lavétax	לבטח
desert heat wave	xamsin (m)	חמסין

<u>DAVID</u>

Come let's go	bo nelex	בוא נלך
bathing	lehitraxec	להתרחץ
in the ocean.	bayam.	בים.
he bathed	hitraxec	התרחץ

<u>YONATAN</u>

That's an excellent	ze raayon	זה רעיון
idea.	mecuyan.	מצוין.
idea	raayon (m)	רעיון
excellent	mecuyan (m.s.)	מצוין

<u>DAVID</u>

Do you know how	ata yodéa	אתה יודע
to swim?	lisxot?	לשחות?
to swim	lisxot	לשחות
he swam	saxa	שחה

<u>YONATAN</u>

Yes. A little.	ken. kcat.	כן. קצת.
And you?	veata?	ואתה?

<u>DAVID</u>

Yes. I'm	ken, ani	כן. אני
a good swimmer.	saxyan tov.	שחיין טוב.
swimmer	saxyan (m)	שחיין
swimmer	saxyanit (f)	שחיינית

<u>YONATAN</u>

What do you think	ma daatxa	מה דעתך
about going	šenisa	שניסע
to Herzliyah?	lehercelíya?	להרצליה?
opinion	dea (f)	דעה
your opinion	daatxa	דעתך
we will go (by vehicle)	nisa	ניסע

<u>DAVID</u>

Fine.	beracon.	ברצון.
The beach there	haxof šam	החוף שם
is very nice.	yafé meod.	יפה מאוד.
beach, shore, coast	xof (m)	חוף
beaches, shores, etc.	xupim (m.pl)	חופים

211

20.2 <u>Cold weather</u>

<u>RUTH</u>

It's cold today.   kar hayom.   .קר היום

<u>YOSEF</u>

Yes.	ken.		.כן
Winter	haxóref		החורף
is already here.	kvar higía.		.כבר הגיע
winter	xóref (m)	חורף	

<u>RUTH</u>

Does snow fall	haim yored		האם יורד
here?	kan šéleg?		?כאן שלג
he descended	yarad	ירד	
snow	šéleg (m)	שלג	

<u>YOSEF</u>

At times.	leitim.		.לעתים
When it's very cold.	kšekar meod.		.כשקר מאוד
time	et (f)	עת	
times	itim	עתים	
at times	leitim	לעתים	

<u>RUTH</u>

I like snow	ani meod		אני מאוד
very much.	ohévet šéleg.		.אוהבת שלג
he liked, loved	ahav	אהב	

<u>YOSEF</u>

Yes.	ken.		.כן
It's a beautiful	ze mar'e		זה מראה
sight.	nexmad.		.נחמד
sight, vision	mar'e	מראה	
lovely, nice	nexmad	נחמד	

<u>RUTH</u>

Have you ever seen	haim raíta		האם ראית
snow?	šéleg?		?שלג

<u>YOSEF</u>

Sure.	bétax.	.בטח
Once.	páam axat.	.פעם אחת
In Jerusalem.	beyerušaláim.	.בירושלים

212

20.3 ADDITIONAL VOCABULARY

The sun is shining.	hašémeš zoráxat.	.השמש זורחת
sun	šémeš (f)	שמש
it shined	zarax	זרח
The wind is blowing.	harúax nošévet.	הרוח נושבת.
wind	rúax (f)	רוח
(it) blew	našva (3f.s.)	נשבה
The sky is clouding up.	hašamáim mit'anenim.	.השמים מתעננים
The sky is cloudy.	hašamáim meunanim.	.השמים מעוננים
The clouds are gray.	haananim afurim.	.העננים אפורים
cloud	anan (m)	ענן
gray	afor (m.s.)	אפור
In a little while	od meat	עוד מעט
it will rain.	yered géšem.	.ירד גשם
a little, few	meat	מעט
rain	géšem (m)	גשם
It's bitter cold.	kor klavim.	.קור כלבים
cold	kor (m)	קור
dog	kélev (m)	כלב
The weather is strange.	mézeg haavir mešune.	.מזג האויר משונה
temperament	mézeg (m)	מזג
weather	mézeg avir	מזג אויר
odd, strange	mešune (m.s.)	משונה
It's very hot here	kan xam meod	כאן חם מאוד
in the summer.	bakáic.	.בקיץ
summer	káic (m)	קיץ

213

20.4   VOCABULARY DRILLS

In the following drills verbs are presented in tenses other than those of the Basic Sentences. The student should learn to assimilate consonantal root patterns. A resumé of the tenses of each <u>binyan</u> will be given later. In the meantime the student should thoroughly drill the verbs as they occur.

(a)   /hitraxec/ "he bathed"   התרחץ

The root of this verb is <u>rxc</u> רחץ , and in the <u>kal</u> it means "to wash something". In the <u>hitpa'el</u> it is reflexive and means "to wash oneself, bathe, etc.," In ordinary speech it is completely regular. In deliberate speech some forms have an inserted /a/:
                    /hitraxci ~ hitrax<u>a</u>ci/ (f.s. imv.)

A. Substitution Drill

   Get washed. It's late!

   hitraxec. ha\u0161aa meux\u00e9ret!   !התרחץ. השעה מאוחרת
   hitraxci   התרחצי
   hitraxcu   התרחצו
   hitrax\u00e9cna   התרחצנה

B. Substitution Drill   /e - ~ ti - /

   I'll bathe in the ocean tomorrow.

   etraxec bayam maxar.   .אתרחץ בים מחר
   titraxec   תתרחץ
   titraxci   תתרחצי
   hu yitraxec   הוא יתרחץ
   hi titraxec   היא תתרחץ
   nitraxec   נתרחץ
   atem titraxcu   אתם תתרחצו
   aten titrax\u00e9cna   אתן תתרחצנה
   hem yitraxcu   הם יתרחצו
   hen titrax\u00e9cna   הן תתרחצנה

C. Substitution-Agreement Drill

   I bathe in cold water every day.

   <u>ani mitraxec bem\u00e1im karim kol b\u00f3ker.</u>   .אני מתרחץ במים קרים כל בוקר

   hem - av\u00edva - kol hami\u0161paxa   הם – אביבה – כל המשפחה
   s\u00e1ra veraxel - hu - ani   שרה ורחל – הוא – אני

D. Substitution-Agreement Drill

   We bathed in the ocean when we were in Herzliah.

   <u>hitrax\u00e1cnu bayam k\u0161ehay\u00ednu bahercel\u00eda.</u>   .התרחצנו בים כשהיינו בהרצליה

   k\u0161ehai\u0301ti - k\u0161ehu haya - k\u0161ehait   כשהייתי – כשהוא היה – כשהיית
   k\u0161ehai\u0301ta - k\u0161ehayta - k\u0161ehayu   כשהיית – כשהיתה – כשהיו
   k\u0161ehai\u0301ten - k\u0161ehai\u0301tem - k\u0161ehai\u0301nu   כשהייתן – כשהייתם – כשהיינו

E. Substitution-Agreement Drill   /mecuyan/ "excellent" מצוין

The food there is excellent.

haóxel šam mecuyan.   <u>האוכל שם מצוין.</u>

haglída – hadagim – haugot   הגלידה – הדגים – העוגות
haxala – haavir – haxof   החלה – האויר – החוף

F. Substitution-Agreement Drill   /nexmad/ "nice" נחמד

Miriam's husband is very nice.

habáal šel miryam nexmad meod.   <u>הבעל של מרים נחמד מאוד.</u>

išto – kulam – kol hanašim   אשתו – כולם – כל הנשים
hayoec haxadaš – hadod šelax   היועץ החדש – הדוד שלך

G. Substitution-Agreement Drill   /afor/ "gray" אפור

The building is gray.

habinyan afor.   <u>הבנין אפור.</u>

hašamáim – haonia – hamaatafot   השמים – האוניה – המעטפות
habulim – habáit šela – hakélev   הבולים – הבית שלה – הכלב

H. Transformation Drill

Instructor: What do you think of the weather?
Student: What is your opinion about the weather?

1. ma ata xošev al mézeg haavir.   מה אתה חושב על מזג האויר? .1
      ma daatxa al mézeg haavir.   מה דעתך על מזג האויר ?

2. ma hem xošvim al mézeg haavir.   מה הם חושבים על מזג האויר? .2
      ma daatam al mézeg haavir.   מה דעתם על מזג האויר?

3. ma hi xošévet al mézeg haavir.   מה היא חושבת על מזג האויר? .3
      ma daata al mézeg haavir.   מה דעתה על מזג האויר?

4. ma aten xošvot al mézeg haavir.   מה אתן חושבות על מזג האויר? .4
      ma daatxen al mézeg haavir.   מה דעתכן על מזג האויר?

5. ma hen xošvot al mézeg haavir.   מה הן חושבות על מזג האויר? .5
      ma daatan al mézeg haavir.   מה דעתן על מזג האויר?

6. ma at xošévet al mézeg haavir.   מה את חושבת על מזג האויר? .6
      ma daatex al mézeg haavir.   מה דעתך על מזג האויר?

7. ma atem xošvim al mézeg haavir.   מה אתם חושבים על מזג האויר? .7
      ma daatxem al mézeg haavir.   מה דעתכם על מזג האויר?

8. ma hu xošev al mézeg haavir.   מה הוא חושב על מזג האויר? .8
      ma daato al mézeg haavir.   מה דעתו על מזג האויר?

9. ma xošévet ištexa al mézeg haavir.   מה חושבת אשתך על מזג האויר? .9
      ma daat ištexa al mézeg haavir?   מה דעת אשתך על מזג האויר?

GRAMMAR NOTES

20.5 Further Remarks on lamed hey Verbs

It has been noted in previous units that <u>lamed hey</u> verbs have many features in common regardless of the <u>binyan</u>. The following are other characteristics of this type of verb.

(a) Infinitives
    Compare these two columns:

<u>kal</u>	/ligmor/ "to finish"	לגמור	/lir'ot/ "to see"	לראות
<u>pi'el</u>	/ledaber/ "to speak"	לדבר	/lexakot/ "to wait"	לחכות
<u>hif'il</u>	/lehazmin/ "to invite"	להזמין	/lehar'ot/ "to show"	להראות
<u>hitpa'el</u>	/lehitraxec/ "to bathe"	להתרחץ	/lehitmanot/ "to be appointed"	להתמנות

Note that the <u>lamed hey</u> verb infinitives on the right resemble other infinitives of the same <u>binyan</u> except that they have the ending /-ot/ after the second root consonant.

A. Transformation Drill

    Instructor: He sees the building.
    Student: He wants to see the building.

1. hu roe et habinyan.
    hu roce lir'ot et habinyan.
       .1 הוא רואה את הבנין.
       הוא רוצה לראות את הבנין.

2. hu pone elav beivrit.
    hu roce lifnot elav beivrit.
       .2 הוא פונה אליו בעברית.
       הוא רוצה לפנות אליו בעברית.

3. ani nitmanéti lašagrirut betel aviv.
    ani roce lehitmanot lašagrirut betel aviv.
       .3 אני נתמניתי לשגרירות בתל אביב.
       אני רוצה להתמנות לשגרירות בתל אביב.

4. hem soxim bayam hayom.
    hem rocim lisxot bayam hayom.
       .4 הם שוחים בים היום.
       הם רוצים לשחות בים היום.

5. alínu laárec hašána.
    anu rocim laalot laárec hašana.
       .5 עלינו לארץ השנה.
       אנו רוצים לעלות לארץ השנה.

6. hu her'a li et haséfer haxadaš.
    hu roce lehar'ot li et haséfer haxadaš.
       .6 הוא הראה לי את הספר החדש.
       הוא רוצה להראות לי את הספר החדש.

7. ani lo axake ad šehem yagíu.
    ani lo roce lexakot ad šehem yagíu.
       .7 אני לא אחכה עד שהם יגיעו.
       אני לא רוצה לחכות עד שהם יגיעו.

8. ánu nitrae maxar beštáim.
    ánu rocim lehitraot maxar beštáim.
       .8 אנו נתראה מחר בשתיים.
       אנו רוצים להתראות מחר בשתיים.

9. ma at kona?
    ma at roca liknot?
       .9 מה את קונה?
       מה את רוצה לקנות?

(b) <u>y</u> as third radical of <u>lamed hey</u> verbs.

    In earlier grammar notes <u>lamed hey</u> verbs were treated as verbs with only two root consonants. Since the 3 m.s. past tense form of these verbs always ends in <u>hey</u> (ה) traditional Hebrew grammar treats it as the third radical. However, note the following pair of forms:

/saxa/	"he swam"	שחה
/saxyan/	"swimmer"	שחיין

    The latter form has a third consonant /y/ before the suffix /-an/. In derived forms of <u>lamed hey</u> verb roots the consonant /y/ is often used as a third radical.

    The first and second person past tense forms are spelled with a <u>yud</u> (י), though it represents a vowel in pronunciation, e.g., /kaníti/ קניתי.

B. Transformation Drill

    Instructor: He swims well.
    Student: He is a good swimmer.

1. hu soxe tov.   .הוא שוחה טוב .1
   hu saxyan tov.   .הוא שחיין טוב

2. haim at soxa tov?   ?האם את שוחה טוב .2
   haim at saxyanit tova?   ?האם את שחיינית טובה

3. atem soxim tov meod.   .אתם שוחים טוב מאוד .3
   atem saxyanim tovim meod.   .אתם שחיינים טובים מאוד

4. atára vexána soxot tov meod.   .עטרה וחנה שוחות טוב מאוד .4
   atára vexána saxyaniot tovot meod. .עטרה וחנה שחייניות טובות מאוד

20.6 Verbs with Initial Radical y

    Some of the verbs whose first root consonant is y have irregular charac-
teristics in the infinitive, imperative and future tense of the kal.   In these
forms the y does not occur, and the prefix and stem vowels are /e/.

                /yered géšem./ (literally) "Rain will come down".

    (The /y/ in this example is the 3 masc. prefix, not part of the root.)

    The stark imperative of this verb is simply:

                        m.s. /red/
                        f.s. /redi/
                        m.pl. /redu/
                        f.pl. /rédna/

    The infinitive of these verbs has this pattern:

            la C₂é C₃et /larédet/ "to go down"

    The rest of the kal conjugation is regular:
                        present: /yored/
                        past :   /yarad/

    Other verbs of this type which have occurred so far are:

            yšv "sit " – infinitive: /lašévet/

            yld "give birth" – infinitive: /lalédet/

    The verb hlx "go" is similar to these, except that in the present and
past tenses the first radical is h, rather than y : Infinitive /laléxet/

    The verb yd' "know" is similar to these, also, except that the stem
vowel is /a/ because of the third radical ', which is spelled with y .

        Imperative: /da/   רד   Infinitive: /ladáat/ לרעת

[Remember – these verbs have vav (ו) in other binyanim :]

                    /nolad/ "was born"   נולד
                    /horid/ "brought down"   הוריד
                    /hošiv/ "caused to sit"   הושיב
                    /holix/ "led, brought"   הוליך
                    /hodía/ "informed"   הודיע

A. Substitution Drill

    Go down there, and don't come up.

    red šáma, veal taale.   רד שמה, ואל תעלה.
    redi   (taali)   (תעלי) רדי
    redu   (taalu)   (תעלו) רדו
    rédna   (taaléna)   (תעלינה) רדנה

218

B. Response Drill

Instructor: Come down with me.
Student: I don't want to go down with you.

red iti.
    ani lo roce larédet itxa.   .רד אתי
      אני לא רוצה לרדת אתך.
redi iti.
    ani lo roca larédet itxa.   .רדי אתי
      אני לא רוצה לרדת אתך.
redu iti.
    ánu lo rocim larédet itxa.   .רדו אתי
      אנו לא רוצים לרדת אתך.
rédna iti.
    ánu lo rocot larédet itxa.   .רדנה אתי
      אנו לא רוצות לרדת אתך.

C. Response Drill

Instructor: Where will you sit?
Student: I like to sit near the door.

éyfo tešev.
    ani ohev lašévet al yad hadélet.   ?איפה תשב
      אני אוהב לשבת על יד הדלת.
eyfo tešvi.
    ani ohévet lašévet al yad hadélet.   ?איפה תשבי
      אני אוהבת לשבת על יד הדלת.
eyfo tešvu.
    ánu ohavim lašévet al yad hadélet.   ?איפה תשבו
      אנו אוהבים לשבת על יד הדלת.
eyfo tešévna.
    ánu ohavot lašévet al yad hadélet.   ?איפה תשבנה
      אנו אוהבות לשבת על יד הדלת.

D. Response Drill

Instructor: When are they going?
Student: They have to go right now.

matay hem holxim.
    hem crixim laléxet miyad.   ? מתי הם הולכים
      הם צריכים ללכת מיד.
matay hi holéxet.
    hi crixa laléxet miyad.   ? מתי היא הולכת
      היא צריכה ללכת מיד.
matay ata holex.
    ani carix laléxet miyad.   ? מתי אתה הולך
      אני צריך ללכת מיד.
matay hen holxot.
    hen crixot laléxet miyad.   ?.מתי הן הולכות
      הן צריכות ללכת מיד.

E. Substitution Drill

Know before whom you are standing.

da lifney mi ata omed.   .דע לפני מי אתה עומד
de'i   (at omédet)   (את עומדת)   דעי
de'u   (atem omdim)   (אתם עומדים)   דעו
dána   (aten omdot)   (אתן עומדות)   דענה

F. Substitution-Agreement Drill

I'll know the results tomorrow.

ani eda et hatocaot maxar.   .אני אדע את התוצאות מחר
ata - hu - at - kulam   אתה — הוא — את — כולם
ánu - aten - atem - hen   אנו — אתן — אתם — הן
hayoec - išto šel dov - ani   היועץ — אשתו של דוב — אני

20.7 Loss of n before Consonants

Compare these two columns:

/natan/ "he gave"   /yiten/ "he will give"
/nasánu/ "we travelled" /nisa/   "we will travel"

The forms on the right illustrate a frequent occurrence - namely the loss of n immediately before another consonant. The rule may be formulated thus:

$$*-VnCV- \longrightarrow -VCV-$$

This loss of n most frequently occurs in verbs whose first root consonant is n. For example, the forms on the right might have been expected to be */yinten/ and */ninsa/.

(In the first and second person past tense forms of /natan/, the third radical n is lost: /natáti/, instead of */natánti/. However, this is the only verb in which a third radical n is dropped before a suffix. In the infinitive /latet/ both n's have been lost.)

This loss does not generally occur in the infinitive of these verbs:/linsóa/ "to travel" and it does not occur if the second root consonant is h or ' : /yinhag/ "he will drive".

The n is missing in the stark imperative of some of these verbs:

m.s.   /sa/   "travel"
f.s.   /se'i/
m.pl. /se'u/
f.pl. /sána/

[This loss of n has been noted earlier. In Grammar Note 17.7 it was noted for hif'il forms: /hikir/ "he recognized",from the root nkr. In Grammar Note 19.5 it was noted for nif'al forms: /nitan/ "was given", instead of */nintan/.]

A. Substitution-Agreement Drill

We'll go to Safed if the weather will be hot.

nisa licfat im mézeg haavir yihye xam.   .ניסע לצפת אם מזג האויר יהיה חם

ani - atem - hem - gvéret kóhen   אני – אתם – הם – גברת כהן
aten - at - hem - hen   אתן – את – הם – הן
hu - dov veišto - hi - ánu   הוא – דוב ואשתו – היא – אנו

B. Substitution Drill

Go to Safed. The air there is excellent.

sa licfat. haavir šam mecuyan.   .סע לצפת. האויר שם מצוין
se'i   סעי
se'u   סעו
sána   סענה

RAPID RESPONSE DRILL

1. ma amar yónatan al mezeg haavir?   ?מה אמר יונתן על מזג האויר .1

2. lean roce david lalexet?   ?לאן רוצה דוד ללכת .2

3. ma xošev yónatan al ze?   ?מה חושב יונתן על זה .3

4. haim yónatan yodéa lisxot?   ?האם יונתן יודע לשחות .4

5. haim gam david yodéa lisxot?   ?האם גם דוד יודע לשחות .5

6. haim haxof beherceliya hu yafe?   ?האם החוף בהרצליה הוא יפה .6

7. matay yored šéleg?   ?מתי יורד שלג .7

8. láma ohev yosef et hašéleg?   ?למה אוהב יוסף את השלג .8

9. káma peamim raa yosef šéleg?   ?כמה פעמים ראה יוסף שלג .9

10. heyxan hu raa et hašéleg?   ?היכן הוא ראה את השלג .10

REVIEW CONVERSATIONS

א: חם מאד היום.

ב: כן. אני מקווה לגשם.

א: גם אני. אם ירד גשם אז מזג האוויר יתקרר קצת.

ב: יהיה חם גם מחר.

א: אך מחר אנו נוסעים להרצליה לשחות בים.

ב: רעיון טוב. החוף שם יפה מאד.

ג: דוד, מהר. אנו רוצים לטייל קצת והשמים כבר מתעננים.

ד: חכו רגע, עוד לא התרחצתי.

ג: כמה זמן יקח לך להתרחץ?

ד: חמש דקות.

ג: טוב. נחכה לך.

ה: האם את יודעת לשחות?

ו: כן, אני שחיינית טובה. אני מאד אוהבת לשחות.

ה: גם אני אוהב לשחות אך אני לא שחיין טוב.

ז: האם יורד כאן שלג?

ח: כן. בחורף.

ז: תודה. האם יורד שלג לעתים קרובות בחורף?

ח: לא. לעתים רחוקות כי לא כל כך קר כאן בחורף.

ט: ירושלים היא עיר יפה.

י: כן. כשיורד שלג היא עיר יפה מאד.

ט: הייתי בירושלים בחורף אך לא ירד שלג.

י: לא היה מספיק קר בחורף שעבר.

מ: השמים מתעננים עכשיו.

נ: השמים לא היו מעוננים כל היום?

מ: לא, רק זרחה השמש, ועכשיו התחילו להתענן.

נ: עוד מעט ירד גשם ויתקרר קצת.

מ: אתה יודע, מזג האויר כאן משונה מאד.

21.1 Going to the Theater

YONATAN

Hello, Atara	šalom atára,	שלום עטרה,
Hello David.	šalom david.	שלום דוד.
How are you?	ma šlomxem.	מה שלומכם?

DAVID

Thank you.	toda raba.	תודה רבה.
We're fine.	šloménu tov.	שלומנו טוב.
How are you?	ma šlomxa ?	מה שלומך?

YONATAN

Fine, thanks. What are	tov toda. ma	טוב תודה. מה
your plans	hatoxniyot šelaxem	התוכניות שלכם
for Saturday night?	lemocaey šabat?	למוצאי שבת?

DAVID

I think	ani xošev	אני חושב
we'll go	šenelex	שנלך
to the Mugrabi Theater.	lekolnóa múgrabi.	לקולנוע מוגרבי.
They're showing	mecigim	מציגים
a good film there.	šam séret tov.	שם סרט טוב.
show	mecig (m.s.pres.)	מציג
he showed	hicig	הציג
film, ribbon	séret (m)	סרט

ATARA

I	ani	אני
just want	dávka roca	דווקא רוצה
to see a show.	lir'ot hacaga.	לראות הצגה.
just, it so happens	dávka	דווקא
show, presentation	hacaga (f)	הצגה

YONATAN

You'll decide	taxlítu	תחליטו
and let me know	vetodíu li	ותודיעו לי
where you're going	lean telxu,	לאן תלכו,
because I want	ki ani roce	כי אני רוצה
to go along.	lehictaref.	להצטרף.
he decided	hexlit	החליט
he informed	hodía	הודיע
because, that	ki	כי
he joined	hictaref	הצטרף

DAVID

Gladly.	beracón.	ברצון.

ATARA

I think	ani xošévet	אני חושבת
we'll go	šenelex	שנלך
to the Habima.	lebet habíma.	לבית הבימה.

| Habima (Tel Aviv theater) | habíma | הבימה |

YONATAN

Come past	ivru	עברו
my house	al yad beyti	על יד ביתי
and call for me.	vekir'u li.	וקראו לי.
he called, read	kara	קרא

DAVID

Fine. Will do.	tov. beséder.	טוב. בסדר.

YONATAN

What time	béeyze šaa	באיזה שעה
approximately	beérex	בערך
will you pass	taavru	תעברו
by my house?	al yad beyti.	על יד ביתי?
hour	šaa (f)	שעה
value	érex (m)	ערך
approximately	beérex	בערך

DAVID

At eight.	bešaa šmóne.	בשעה שמונה.

YONATAN

See you	lehitraot	להתראות
Saturday night.	bemocaey šabat.	במוצאי שבת.

DAVID

Don't forget –	al tiškax,	אל תשכח,
Saturday night	mocaey šabat,	מוצאי שבת
at eight,	bešaa šmóne	בשעה שמונה
or so.	beérex.	בערך.
he forget	šaxax	שכח

21.2 VOCABULARY DRILLS

Explanatory notes are included in the following drills to point out to the students various features of the verbs. However, the student should not try to memorize these notes, but to drill the verbs until he does not need the explanation.

(a)   /kara/ "he called, read" קרא

The root of this verb is <u>kr'</u> קרא , and it is conjugated like <u>mc'</u> מצא "find".

A. Substitution Drill   /kra/   "read, call"   קרא

Read the new book.

kir'u et haséfer haxadaš.   קראו את הספר החדש.
kir'i   קראי
kra   קרא
krána   קראנה

B. Substitution Drill   /e - ~ ti ~/

I'll read the letter this evening.

ekra et hamixtav haérev.   אקרא את המכתב הערב.
tikra   תקרא
tikre'i   תקראי
hu yikra   הוא יקרא
hi tikra   היא תקרא
ánu nikra   אנו נקרא
tikre'u   תקראו
aten tikrána   אתן תקראנה
hem yikre'u   הם יקראו
hen tikrána   הן תקראנה
(Some speakers say /tikréna/ for 2 and 3 f.pl.)

C. Expansion Drill

Instructor: I'll go past his house.
Student: I'll go past his house and call him.

eevor al yad beyto, veekra lo.   אעבור על יד ביתו,   ואקרא לו.
taavor al yad beyto, vetikra lo.   תעבור על יד ביתו,   ותקרא לו.
taavri al yad beyto, vetikre'i lo.   תעברי על יד ביתו,   ותקראי לו.
moše yaavor al yad beyto, veyikra lo.   משה יעבור על יד ביתו,   ויקרא לו.
sára taavor al yad beyto, vetikra lo.   שרה תעבור על יד ביתו,   ותקרא לו.
ánu naavor al yad beyto, venikra lo.   אנו נעבור על יד ביתו,   ונקרא לו.
taavru al yad beyto, vetikre'u lo.   תעברו על יד ביתו,   ותקראו לו.
taavórna al yad beyto, vetikrána lo.   תעבורנה על יד ביתו,   ותקראנה לו.
hem yaavru al yad beyto, veyikre'u lo. הם יעברו על יד ביתו,   ויקראו לו.
hen taavórna al yad beyto, vetikrána lo. הן תעבורנה על יד ביתו,ותקראנה לו.

In the above drill the imperative forms may be used in the second person
substitutions.
                    taavor al yad beyto vekra lo.

                                                        End of Tape 8A

Tape 8B

D. Substitution-Agreement Drill   /kore/ "reads" קורא

He reads Hebrew like he speaks Hebrew - with difficulty.

<u>hu kore ivrit kmo šehu medaber ivrit. bekóši.</u>

hi - ánu - hen - ani
kulam - šteyhen - at - hu

                    הוא קורא עברית כמו שהוא מדבר עברית. בקושי.

                    היא - אנו - הן - אני
                    כולם - שתיהן - את - הוא

                              225

E. Substitution-Agreement Drill   /kara/   "he read, called"   קרא

He read Moshe's telegram.

hu kara et hamivrak mimoše.   .הוא קרא את המברק ממשה

ani - atem - išti - at   את – אשתי – אתם – אני
ánu - ata - hem - dov   אנו – אתה – הם – דוב
aten - kulam - hi - hu   אתן – כולם – היא – הוא

(b)   /šaxax/   "he forgot"   שכח

The root of this verb is **škx** שכח, Three things should be noted about it at
this point:
 (1) The second radical, **k** כ , has the k/x alternation in the various tenses.
In the future it is /k/; in the present and past it is /x/; and in the stark
imperative it varies in some of the forms.

 (2) The third radical is **x** ח . Therefore, the vowel /a/ must precede it when
the **x** is at the end of the word. See Grammar Note 16.4b. In the infinitive
/liškóax/ לשכוח and the m.s. pres. /šoxéax/ שוכח an unstressed /a/ is
inserted. Similar verbs are /patax/ "open", /salax/ "forgive", and /šalax/ "send".

 (3) Whenever the sequence /-xx-/ would otherwise occur in the conjugation
the vowel /e/ is inserted to break up the cluster, e.g., /šaxexa/ "she forgot".

F. Substitution Drill

Forget what he said.

šxax ma šehu amar.   .שכח מה שהוא אמר
šixexi   שכחי
šixexu   שכחו
škáxna   שכחנה

(/škax/ and /škáxna/ are often heard for the m.s. and f.pl.)

G. Transformation Drill - Affirmative to Negative.

Instructor: Forget what you heard.
Student: Don't forget what you heard.

šxax ma šešamáta.   al tiškax ma šešamáta.   .אל תשכח מה ששמעת   .שכח מה ששמעת
šixexi ma šešamat.   al tiškexi ma šešamat.   .אל תשכחי מה ששמעת   .שכחי מה ששמעת
šixexu ma šešamátem. al tiškexu ma šešamátem.   .אל תשכחו מה ששמעתם .שכחו מה ששמעתם
škáxna ma šešamáten. al tiškáxna ma šešamáten. .אל תשכחנה מה ששמעתן .שכחנה מה ששמעתן

The drill should also be done in reverse.

H. Substitution Drill   /e - ~ ti -/

I won't forget the Hebrew that I learned.

ani lo eškax et haivrit šelamádeti.		.אני לא אשכח את העברית שלמדתי
ata lo tiškax	(šelamádeta)	(שלמדת) אתה לא תשכח
at lo tiškexi	(šelamádet)	(שלמדת) את לא תשכחי
hu lo yiškax	(šelamad)	(שלמד) הוא לא ישכח
hi lo tiškax	(šelamda)	(שלמדה) היא לא תשכח
lo niškax	(šelamádnu)	(שלמדנו) לא נשכח
lo tiškexu	(šelamádetem)	(שלמדתם) לא תשכחו
lo tiškáxna	(šelamádeten)	(שלמדתן) לא תשכחנה
hem lo yiškexu	(šelamdu)	(שלמדו) הם לא ישכחו
hen lo tiškáxna	(šelamdu)	(שלמדו) הן לא תשכחנה

I. Substitution-Agreement Drill

We won't forget to come tomorrow.

<u>lo niškax lavo maxar.</u>   .לא נשכח לבוא מחר

ata - hem - ani - david	אתה – הם – אני – דוד
hen - atára - at - atem	הן – עטרה – את – אתם
hu - aten - ánu	הוא – אתן – אנו

J. Substitution Drill

He forgets what he is told.

hu šoxéax ma šeomrim lo.		.הוא שוכח מה שאומרים לו
hi šoxáxat	(la).	(לה) היא שוכחת
hem šoxexim	(lahem)	(להם) הם שוכחים
hen šoxexot	(lahen)	(להן) הן שוכחות

K. Substitution-Agreement Drill

I forgot to read the book.

<u>šaxáxti likro et haséfer.</u>   .שכחתי לקרוא את הספר

ata - ánu - atem - at	אתה – אנו – אתם – את
moše - sára - hatalmidim	משה – שרה – החלמידים
aten - hu - hi - ani	אתן – הוא – היא – אני

(c)   /hodía/   "he informed"

The root of this verb is <u>yd'</u> יד' "know". In the <u>hif'il</u> it means "to cause to know", i.e., "to inform, tell, etc." Two things should be noted here:

(1) The first radical y is replaced in the <u>hif'il</u> with <u>vav</u> ו and is pronounced /o/ throughout the <u>binyan</u>. See Grammar Note 17.7

(2) The third radical is ' y . This is never pronounced when the pattern calls for it to be at the end of the verb form, but nevertheless the vowel /a/ will occur after the stem vowel /í/ in such cases, e.g. /hodía/ for /hodí'/. This verb will, therefore, be similar to /higía/ "arrived". For example:

Future:	2 m.s.	/tagía/	/todía/
	2 f.s.	/tagíi/	/todíi/
	2 f.pl.	/tagána/	/todána/
Past:	1 s.	/higáti/	/hodáti/
	3 m.s.	/higía/	/hodía/
	3 f.s.	/higía/	/hodía/

The student will now realize more fully the need to master completely and automatically the verb paradigms which have occurred so far in the course. If there is any hesitation on the part of the student in responding with the correct form, the instructor should not hesitate to go back to earlier units and to do the pertinent drills again.

L. Substitution-Agreement Drill

I'll tell Dov the new address.

<u>odía ledov et haktóvet haxadaša.</u>   .אוריע לדוב את הכתובת החדשה

ata - sára - yónatan - at   אתה - שרה - יונתן - את
atem - ánu - hen - hem   אתם - אנו - הן - הם
aten - david - hi - ani   אתן - דוד - היא - אני

M. Substitution-Agreement Drill

He told Mr. Alon that he got the letter.

<u>hu hodía lemar alon šekibel et hamixtav.</u>   .הוא הודיע למר אלון שקבל את המכתב

hem - hi - ánu - ata   הם - היא - אנו - אתה
at - moše - ani - raxel   את - משה - אני - רחל
atem - hen - aten - hu   אתם - הן - אתן - הוא

(The verb /kibel/ should also be changed.)

GRAMMAR NOTES

21. 3   <u>Generalizations</u>

Study the following sentences:

/eyx omrim <u>table</u> beivrit./
         "How do you say 'table' in Hebrew?"

/moxrim asimonim badóar./
         "Tokens are sold in the post office."

/mecigim šam séret tov./
         "They're showing a good film there."

In these sentences the subject is not expressed and the verb is in the masculine plural present tense. This is the most frequent way in which generalized statements and questions are made in Hebrew.

The English translations are varied in structure.

In the first sentence the English has an unstressed 'you' as the subject.

In the second sentence the Hebrew is translated as a passive.

In the third sentence the English has an unstressed 'they' as the subject.

There are other ways of expressing generalizations in English, and the student should be aware of the alternate possibilities in translating. For example the first sentence may also be translated as "How does one say 'table' in Hebrew?" or "How do they say 'table' in Hebrew?" (with unstressed 'they').

The inclusion of a pronoun subject in the Hebrew will often be taken to mean that a particular statement is being made rather than a generalized one.

medabrim anglit beisrael.   "English is spoken in Israel."

hem medabrim anglit beisrael. "They (in particular) speak English in Israel."

A. Translation Drill

The English translations given here are intended as examples. The instructor should accept alternate possibilities as described above. When doing the drill in reverse, i.e., from English to Hebrew, the instructor should be careful not to stress the pronoun subjects of the verbs.

1. English is spoken throughout the country.   .1 מדברים אנגלית בכל הארץ.

2. Cheese is sold in grocery stores.   .2 מוכרים גבינה בחנות מכולת.

3. What time do they start to perform?   .3 באיזה שעה מתחילים להציג?

4. One doesn't swim when it's raining.   .4 לא שוחים כשיורד גשם.

5. People stroll a lot along the beach.   .5 מטיילים הרבה על שפת הים.

6. There is no traveling on Saturday.   .6 אין נוסעים בשבת.

7. They eat big lunches in Israel.   .7 אוכלים ארוחת צהריים גדולה בארץ.

8. They're sending me to Haifa.   .8 שולחים אותי לחיפה.

9. You forget the language if you don't speak it.   .9 שוכחים את השפה אם לא מדברים.

21.4   The pi'el Conjugation

[In this section and in following units a resumé of the <u>binyanim</u> will be given. The examples will illustrate the major types of verbs, and irregular but frequently occurring verbs will also be included. In order to test the student's mechanical control of the conjugations new roots will be included in drills. The student need not memorize their meanings at this point, though there is no objection to this, since the verbs occur in later units.

The order of forms will be as follows: infinitive, stark imperative, future, present and past tenses. Various ways are used to indicate the root consonants with the patterns of prefixes, infixes and suffixes. If there is any question as to which root consonant is meant, then the designation $C_1C_2C_3$ will be used. Occasionally traditional grammatical terms will be introduced, e.g., lamed hey ה"ל].

(a)   The <u>pi'el</u> is traditionally listed as the third <u>binyan</u> after the <u>kal</u> and <u>nif'al</u>. It is drilled first here because in modern Hebrew there are fewer consonant alternations in the tenses of this <u>binyan</u>. The vowel patterns are also simpler to memorize. Except for the past tense the infixed stem vowels are /-a-e-/.   Remember that the /e/ is dropped before certain suffixes. If the sequence /-hC₃-/ or /-'C₃-/ would result, then /a/ is inserted: /mahari/.

In order to illustrate the pattern of the <u>pi'el</u> the stems in the following chart are printed in capital letters and the prefixes and suffixes are separated.

				Forms with vowel suffix	
Infinitive:		le DABER			
Imperative:	m.s.	DABER		f.s.	DABR i
				m.pl.	DABR u
	f.pl.	DABÉR na			
Future:	1 s.	a DABER			
	2 m.s.	te DABER		2 f.s.	te DABR i
	3 m.s.	ye DABER			
	f.s.	te DABER			
	1 pl.	ne DABER		2 m.pl.	te DABR u
	2 f.pl.	te DABÉR na			
	3 f.pl.	te DABÉR na		3 m.pl.	ye DABR u
Present:	m.s.	me DABER			
	f.s.	me DABER et		m.pl.	me DABR im
				f.pl.	me DABR ot

In the past tense the distinguishing feature is the stem vowel /i/.

	1 s.	DIBÁR ti			
	2 m.s.	DIBÁR ta			
	2 f.s.	DIBÁR t			
	3 m.s.	DIBER		3 f.s.	DIBR a
	1 pl.	DIBÁR nu			
	2 m.pl.	DIBÁR tem			
	2 f.pl.	DIBÁR ten		3 pl.	DIBR u

In the following drills the instructor will give a sentence containing a time word such as /maxar/ "tomorrow", /axšav/ "now", /etmol/ "yesterday".

The class repeats this sentence. The instructor then supplies either a substitution for the time-word or for the subject. When the instructor supplies a time-word, the student then changes the verb to the suitable tense form.

Example: Instructor: moše kibel mixtav etmol.   "Moshe got a letter yesterday"
       Student: moše kibel mixtav etmol.

       Instructor: maxar.   "tomorrow"
       Student: moše yekabel mixtav maxar."Moshe will get a letter tomorrow".

When the instructor supplies a new subject the student responds by changing the verb form to the correct person while maintaining the tense.

Example: Instructor: moše yekabel mixtav maxar."Moshe will get a letter tomorrow"
       Student: moše yekabel mixtav maxar.

       Instructor: miryam.   "Miriam".
       Student: miryam tekabel mixtav maxar."Miriam will get a letter
                                  tomorrow".

These drills require the students to pay very close attention because the shifts are quick. If the student gives correct sentence but not the response called for by the cue, then the instructor should give the cue again without discussion. This will keep the drills moving rapidly. The entire responses of some drills are given below in Hebrew. These sentences may be used as a reading drill, also.

A. hu medaber axšav im haxenvani.   "He's speaking with the storekeeper now."

הוא מדבר עכשיו עם החנווני.

1.	raxel	רחל מדברת עכשיו עם החנווני.	רחל .1
2.	etmol	רחל דברה אתמול עם החנווני.	אתמול .2
3.	aten	אתן דברתן אתמול עם החנווני.	אתן .3
4.	axšav	אתן מדברות עכשיו עם החנווני.	עכשיו .4
5.	hem	הם מדברים עכשיו עם החנווני.	הם .5
6.	maxar	הם ידברו מחר עם החנווני.	מחר .6
7.	hen	הן תדברנה מחר עם החנווני.	הן .7
8.	etmol	הן דברו אתמול עם החנווני.	אתמול .8
9.	hu	הוא דבר אתמול עם החנווני.	הוא .9
10.	maxar	הוא ידבר מחר עם החנווני.	מחר .10
11.	ánu	אנו נדבר מחר עם החנווני.	אנו .11
12.	axšav	אנו מדברים עכשיו עם החנווני.	עכשיו .12
13.	dálya	דליה מדברת עכשיו עם החנווני.	דליה .13
14.	etmol	דליה דברה אתמול עם החנווני.	אתמול .14
15.	atem	אתם דברתם אתמול עם החנווני.	אתם. .15
16.	axšav	אתם מדברים עכשיו אם החנווני.	עכשיו .16
17.	mar káspi	מר כספי מדבר עכשיו עם החנווני.	מר כספי .17
18.	etmol	מר כספי דיבר אתמול עם החנווני.	אתמול .18
19.	xána	חנה דברה אתמול עם החנווני.	חנה .19
20.	maxar	חנה תדבר מחר עם החנווני.	מחר .20
21.	hem	הם ידברו מחר עם החנווני.	הם .21
22.	axšav	הם מדברים עכשיו עם החנווני.	עכשיו .22
23.	hi	היא מדברת עכשיו עם החנווני.	היא .23
24.	etmol	היא דברה אתמול עם החנווני.	אתמול .24
25.	ata vemoše	אתה ומשה דברתם אתמול עם החנווני.	אתה ומשה .25
26.	maxar	אתה ומשה תדברו מחר עם החנווני.	מחר .26
27.	hu veišto	הוא ואשתו ידברו מחר עם החנווני.	הוא ואשתו .27
28.	axšav	הוא ואשתו מדברים עכשיו עם החנווני.	עכשיו .28
29.	ánu	אנו מדברים עכשיו עם החנווני.	אנו .29

[Note: /axšav/ occurs with the future and past tenses, also, but with a change of meaning. /dibárti ito axšav./ "I have just spoken with him."
        /adaber ito axšav. / "I'll speak with him now."
However, in these drills /axšav/ is used only as a cue for the present tense.]

B. hu mešalem lo axšav et hakésef.　"He's paying him the money now."

הוא משלם לו עכשיו את הכסף.

1.	sára	שרה משלמת לו עכשיו את הכסף.	שרה 1.
2.	etmol	שרה שלמה לו אתמול את הכסף.	אתמול 2.
3.	yaakov	יעקב שלם לו אתמול את הכסף.	יעקב 3.
4.	axšav	יעקב משלם לו עכשיו את הכסף.	עכשיו 4.
5.	hen	הן משלמות לו עכשיו את הכסף.	הן 5.
6.	maxar babóker	הן תשלמנה לו מחר בבוקר את הכסף.	מחר בבוקר 6.
7.	ánu	אנו נשלם לו מחר בבוקר את הכסף.	אנו 7.
8.	bašavúa šeavar	אנו שלמנו לו בשבוע שעבר את הכסף.	בשבוע שעבר 8.
9.	ani	אני שלמתי לו בשבוע שעבר את הכסף.	אני 9.
10.	axšav	אני משלם לו עכשיו את הכסף.	עכשיו 10.
11.	hem	הם משלמים לו עכשיו את הכסף.	הם 11.
12.	beod xódeš	הם ישלמו לו בעוד חורש את הכסף.	בעוד חורש 12.
13.	at	את תשלמי לו בעוד חורש את הכסף.	את 13.
14.	lifney yomáim	את שלמת לו לפני יומיים את הכסף.	לפני יומיים 14.
15.	hu	הוא שלם לו לפני יומיים את הכסף.	הוא 15.
16.	axšav	הוא משלם לו עכשיו את הכסף.	עכשיו 16.
17.	aten	אתן משלמות לו עכשיו את הכסף.	אתן 17.
18.	bašavúa haba	אתן תשלמנה לו בשבוע הבא את הכסף.	בשבוע הבא 18.
19.	ata	אתה תשלם לו בשבוע הבא את הכסף.	אתה 19.
20.	lifney šaa	אתה שלמת לו לפני שעה את הכסף.	לפני שעה 20.
21.	ani	אני שלמתי לו לפני שעה את הכסף.	אני 21.
22.	beréga ze	אני משלם לו ברגע זה את הכסף.	ברגע זה 22.
23.	raxél	רחל משלמת לו ברגע זה את הכסף.	רחל 23.
24.	beod šaa	רחל תשלם לו בעוד שעה את הכסף.	בעוד שעה 24.
25.	mišpáxat zahávi	משפחת זהבי תשלם לו בעוד שעה את הכסף.	משפחת זהבי 25.
26.	šilšom	משפחת זהבי שלמה לו שלשום את הכסף.	שלשום 26.
27.	yael	יעל שלמה לו שלשום את הכסף.	יעל 27.
28.	axšav	יעל משלמת לו עכשיו את הכסף.	עכשיו 28.

C. hu mekabel et haxavila axšav.　"He's receiving the package now."

הוא מקבל את החבילה עכשיו.

1.	hi	היא מקבלת את החבילה עכשיו.	היא 1.
2.	bašana šeavra	היא קבלה את החבילה בשנה שעברה.	בשנה שעברה 2.
3.	at	את קבלת את החבילה בשנה שעברה.	את 3.
4.	axšav	את מקבלת את החבילה עכשיו.	עכשיו 4.
5.	hem	הם מקבלים את החבילה עכשיו.	הם 5.
6.	beod xódeš	הם יקבלו את החבילה בעוד חורש.	בעוד חורש 6.
7.	hen	הן תקבלנה את החבילה בעוד חורש.	הן 7.
8.	lifney šavúa	הן קבלו את החבילה לפני שבוע.	לפני שבוע 8.
9.	moše	משה קבל את החבילה לפני שבוע.	משה 9.
10.	axšav	משה מקבל את החבילה עכשיו.	עכשיו 10.
11.	léa	לאה מקבלת את החבילה עכשיו.	לאה 11.
12.	maxar	לאה תקבל את החבילה מחר.	מחר 12.
13.	ata	אתה תקבל את החבילה מחר.	אתה 13.
14.	lifney xódeš	אתה קבלת את החבילה לפני חורש.	לפני חורש 14.
15.	atem	אתם קבלתם את החבילה לפני חורש.	אתם 15.
16.	axšav	אתם מקבלים את החבילה עכשיו.	עכשיו 16.
17.	ani	אני אקבל את החבילה בקרוב.	אני 17.
18.	bekarov	אני אקבל את החבילה בקרוב.	בקרוב 18.
19.	aten	אתן תקבלנה את החבילה בקרוב.	אתן 19.
20.	lifney yomáim	אתן קבלתן את החבילה לפני יומיים.	לפני יומיים 20.
21.	yaakov	יעקב קבל את החבילה לפני יומיים.	יעקב 21.
22.	axšav	יעקב מקבל את החבילה עכשיו.	עכשיו 22.
23.	miryam	מרים מקבלת את החבילה עכשיו.	מרים 23.
24.	beod yomáim	מרים תקבל את החבילה בעוד יומים.	בעוד יומים 24.
25.	gvéret Jones	גב' ג'ונס תקבל את החבילה בעוד יומים.	גב' ג'ונס 25.
26.	etmol	גב' ג'ונס קבלה את החבילה אתמול.	אתמול 26.
27.	ata	אתה קבלת את החבילה אתמול.	אתה 27.

(b) Alternating first radicals

When the first root consonant is <u>b</u>, <u>p</u>, or <u>k</u> (spelled כ) the consonant
will vary. In prefixed forms the consonant is /v/,/f/, and /x/ respectively.
In other forms it is /b/, /p/, and /k/.   The chart below illustrates this
alternation.

Prefixed forms

Infinitive: le Vakeš

	Imperative:
	Bakeš etc.
Future: a Vakeš te Vakeš etc.	
Present: me Vakeš etc.	
	Past: Bikášti Bikášta etc.

Some roots have /v/ (spelled ו) throughout the conjugation:/viter/
"he conceded" ויתר. There are not many of these verbs, and no verbs have /b/
throughout.

Some slang verbs have /f/ throughout the conjugation: /fisfes/ "he missed
(the target)".

The k/x alternation poses a problem, although once the student has learned
to read he can use the spelling to help fix the alternation, or lack of it, in
his speech habits.

Some verbs have /k/ in all forms of the <u>binyan</u>. /lekabel/ "to receive".
These are spelled with ק .   Some have /x/ in all forms: /xilek/ "he
distributed". These are spelled with ח

(c) Verbs with four radicals

Verbs with four root consonants occur in the <u>pi'el</u>. The pattern is
similar to the regular verbs but with the <u>two middle</u> consonants taking the place
of the second consonant of the three-consonant verb roots.

m.s. imv. / ta rg em/ "translate"
          / da b er/ "speak"

In one respect these four-consonant verbs are simpler than the three-
consonant verbs. In the forms with a vowel suffix the dropping of the preceding
vowel would cause a three-consonant cluster to result. The /e/ would then occur
anyway. Thus, the stems of these verbs are constant throughout the tenses.

2 m.s. /tetargem/ "you will translate"
2 f.s. /tetargemi/

[In the following drill the time word is put first in order to avoid an ambiguity.]

D. axšav hu mevakeš midavid lavo bazman. "Now he's asking David to come on time."

עכשיו הוא מבקש מדוד לבוא בזמן.

1.	raxel	עכשיו רחל מבקשת מדוד לבוא בזמן.	רחל 1.
2.	etmol	אתמול רחל ביקשה מדוד לבוא בזמן.	אתמול 2.
3.	atem	אתמול אתם ביקשתם מדוד לבוא בזמן.	אתם 3.
4.	axšav	עכשיו אתם מבקשים מדוד לבוא בזמן.	עכשיו 4.
5.	hem	עכשיו הם מבקשים מדוד לבוא בזמן.	הם 5.
6.	maxar	מחר הם יבקשו מדוד לבוא בזמן.	מחר 6.
7.	hen	מחר הן תבקשנה מדוד לבוא בזמן.	הן 7.
8.	etmol	אתמול הן ביקשו מדוד לבוא בזמן.	אתמול 8.
9.	hu	אתמול הוא ביקש מדוד לבוא בזמן.	הוא 9.
10.	maxar	מחר הוא יבקש מדוד לבוא בזמן.	מחר 10.
11.	anu	מחר אנו נבקש מדוד לבוא בזמן.	אנו 11.
12.	axšav	עכשיו אנו מבקשים מדוד לבוא בזמן.	עכשיו 12.
13.	dálya	עכשיו דליה מבקשת מדוד לבוא בזמן.	דליה 13.
14.	etmol	אתמול דליה בקשה מדוד לבוא בזמן.	אתמול 14.
15.	aten	אתמול אתן בקשתן מדוד לבוא בזמן.	אתן 15.
16.	axšav	עכשיו אתן מבקשות מדוד לבוא בזמן.	עכשיו 16.
17.	mar káspi	עכשיו מר כספי מבקש מדוד לבוא בזמן.	מר כספי 17.
18.	etmol	אתמול מר כספי ביקש מדוד לבוא בזמן.	אתמול 18.
19.	šošána	אתמול שושנה ביקשה מדוד לבוא בזמן.	שושנה 19.
20.	maxar	מחר שושנה תבקש מדוד לבוא בזמן.	מחר 20.
21.	hem	מחר הם יבקשו מדוד לבוא בזמן.	הם 21.
22.	axšav	עכשיו הם מבקשים מדוד לבוא בזמן.	עכשיו 22.
23.	mišpaxat alon	עכשיו משפחת אלון מבקשת מדוד לבוא בזמן.	משפחת אלון 23.
24.	etmol	אתמול משפחת אלון ביקשה מדוד לבוא בזמן.	אתמול 24.
25.	ata vemoše	אתמול אתה ומשה ביקשתם מדוד לבוא בזמן.	אתה ומשה 25.
26.	maxar	מחר אתה ומשה תבקשו מדוד לבוא בזמן.	מחר 26.
27.	haxayalim	מחר החיילים יבקשו מדוד לבוא בזמן.	החיילים 27.
28.	axšav	עכשיו החיילים מבקשים מדוד לבוא בזמן.	עכשיו 28.

E. maxar hu yefahek bakita. "Tomorrow he'll be yawning in class."

מחר הוא יפהק בכיתה.

1.	sára	מחר שרה תפהק בכיתה.	שרה 1.
2.	etmol	אתמול שרה פיהקה בכיתה.	אתמול 2.
3.	yaakov	אתמול יעקב פיהק בכיתה.	יעקב 3.
4.	axšav	עכשיו יעקב מפהק בכיתה.	עכשיו 4.
5.	hen	עכשיו הן מפהקות בכיתה.	הן 5.
6.	maxar babóker	מחר בבוקר הן תפהקנה בכיתה.	מחר בבוקר 6.
7.	ánu	מחר בבוקר אנו נפהק בכיתה.	אנו 7.
8.	etmol baérev	אתמול בערב אנו פיהקנו בכיתה.	אתמול בערב 8.
9.	ani	אתמול בערב אני פיהקתי בכיתה.	אני 9.
10.	axšav	עכשיו אני מפהק בכיתה.	עכשיו 10.
11.	hem	עכשיו הם מפהקים בכיתה.	הם 11.
12.	maxar	מחר הם יפהקו בכיתה.	מחר 12.
13.	at	מחר את תפהקי בכיתה.	את 13.
14.	lifney yomáim	לפני יומים את פיהקת בכיתה.	לפני יומים 14.
15.	hu	לפני יומים הוא פיהק בכיתה.	הוא 15.
16.	axšav	עכשיו הוא מפהק בכיתה.	עכשיו 16.
17.	aten	עכשיו אתן מפהקות בכיתה.	אתן 17.
18.	maxar	מחר אתן תפהקנה בכיתה.	מחר 18.
19.	ata	מחר אתה תפהק בכיתה.	אתה 19.
20.	lifney šaa	לפני שעה אתה פיהקת בכיתה.	לפני שעה 20.
21.	anu	לפני שעה אנו פיהקנו בכיתה.	אנו 21.
22.	beréga ze	ברגע זה אנו מפהקים בכיתה.	ברגע זה 22.
23.	raxel	ברגע זה רחל מפהקת בכיתה.	רחל 23.
24.	beod šaa	בעוד שעה רחל תפהק בכיתה.	בעוד שעה 24.
25.	hi	בעוד שעה היא תפהק בכיתה.	היא 25.
26.	šilšom	שלשום היא פיהקה בכיתה.	שלשום 26.
27.	yael	שלשום יעל פיהקה בכיתה.	יעל 27.
28.	axšav	עכשיו יעל מפהקת בכיתה.	עכשיו 28.

The following is a list of substitutions to be used in drilling the
sentences below. The instructor may vary the substitutions by reading only one
or two columns at a time, by reading the cues from bottom to top, etc.

Some of the substitutions will produce sentences which may seem strange out
of context. It should be remembered that the translations of the three Hebrew
tenses need not be simple and rigid. Thus, the sentence /lifney šavúa hu gidel
perot banégev/ may be translated "A week ago he was growing fruit in the Negev.
[This week he's working in an office in the city]", rather than the awkward "A
week ago he grew fruit in the Negev." In any case, the goal is to control
automatically and with ease all the forms of the binyan with any root.

עכשיו	אתה	אתמול	אני
אתמול	אתם	מחר	דוד
מחר	הן	עכשיו	אשתו
עכשיו	אנו	אתמול	אתן
לפני יומיים	הוא	בעוד חודש	הם
בעוד יומיים	את	ברגע זה	הן
כרגע	אתן	לפני שבוע	דב ואתה
אתמול	כולם	מחר	אנו
בקרוב	היא	עכשיו	את
עכשיו	אני	שלשום	אתה

A. He is setting the clocks.   .הוא מכוון את השעונים .א
B. He's ruining the program.   .הוא מקלקל את התוכנית .ב

C. He refused to eat the meal.   .הוא סירב לאכול את הארוחה .ג
D. He passed up the ice cream.   .הוא ויתר על הגלידה .ד

E. He's wiping the glasses.   .הוא מנגב את הכוסות .ה
F. He's straightening the house.   .הוא מסדר את הבית .ו

G. He telephoned Mr. Caspi.   .הוא טלפן למר כספי .ז
H. He told him the truth.   .הוא סיפר לו את האמת .ח

                                              End of Tape 8B

Tape 9A

I. He embarrassed Moshe.   .הוא בייש את משה .ט
J. He didn't visit his house.   .הוא לא ביקר בביתו .י

K. He's strolling on the beach.   .הוא מטייל על החוף .כ
L. He's not hurrying to the office. .הוא לא ממהר למשרד .ל

M. He translates from English to Hebrew. .הוא מתרגם מאנגלית לעברית .מ
N. He broadcasts the news on the radio.   .הוא משדר את החדשות ברדיו .נ

O. He grows fruit in the Negev.   .הוא מגדל פירות בנגב .ס
P. He runs the school.   .הוא מנהל את בית הספר .ע

Q. He folds the letters.   .הוא מקפל את המכתבים .פ
R. He distributes the mail.   .הוא מחלק את הדואר .צ

For further drill the instructor should combine sentences to make an expansion
drill. For example:
              Instructor: hu nigev et hakosot.
              Student: hu nigev et hakosot vesider et habáit.
              Instructor: hi nigva et hakosot.
              Student: hi nigva et hakosot vesidra et habáit.
Other suggestions for combinations are:
            הוא לא כיוון את השעונים. הוא קלקל אותם.
      הוא סירב לאכול את הארוחה אבל הוא לא ויתר על הגלידה.

21.5 lamed hey verbs in the pi'el conjugation

The following chart illustrates the conjugation of a lamed hey verb in the pi'el. Note that the stem is / xak/ in all forms except in the past where it is /xik-/. To these stems are added the regular prefixes (if any) and the endings characteristic of all lamed hey verbs.

Infinitive:			le xak OT			
Imperative:	m.s.		xak E	m.pl.		xak U
	f.s.		xak I	f.pl.		xak ÉNA
Future:	1 s.	a	xak E	1 pl.	ne	xak E
	2 m.s.	te	xak E	2 m.pl.	te	xak U
	2 f.s.	te	xak I	2 f.pl.	te	xak ÉNA
	3 m.s.	ye	xak E	3 m.pl.	ye	xak U
	3 f.s.	te	xak E	3 f.pl.	te	xak ÉNA
Present:	m.s.	me	xak E	m.pl.	me	xak IM
	f.s.	ne	xak A	f.pl.	me	xak OT
Past:	1 s.		xik ÍTI	1 pl.		xik ÍNU
	2 m.s.		xik ÍTA	2 m.pl.		xik ÍTEM
	2 f.s.		xik IT	2 f.pl.		xik ÍTEN
	3 m.s.		xik A	3 pl.		xik U
	3 f.s.		xik TA			

The list of substitutions from the preceding page should be used with the following drill sentences:

A. He's waiting for a letter from the government.   הוא מחכה למכתב מהממשלה.
B. He's hoping for good news.   הוא מקווה לחדשות טובות.
C. He changed his mind.   הוא שינה את. דעתו.

This last drill may be varied by having /daato/ changed to agree with the subject or not.

/ani šiníti et daati/   " I changed my mind."
/ani šiníti et daato/   " I changed his opinion."

21.6 Stem Vowel Variations in the pi'el

a)   In the past tense of some pi'el verbs whose <u>second</u> root consonant is '
or <u>r</u> the first stem vowel is /e/ rather than /i/, and the 3 m.s. stem has the
vowels /-e-a-/ instead of /-i-e-/.

/berárti/   "I found out"
/berar/   "he found out"

This usage is more like classical Hebrew, and some instructors will
insist on it as more "correct" than the regularized form /birer/. The latter,
however, is commonly used and has been cited in this text.

b)   Some <u>pi'el</u> verbs have /o/ as the first stem vowel throughout the <u>binyan</u>.
These verbs are listed under roots with second radical <u>vav</u> (ו) or <u>yud</u> (י) or
under roots whose second and third radicals are the same.

/komem/ "he re-established"   root <u>kvm</u>
/šorer/ "he sang"   root <u>šyr</u>
/sovev/ "he circled"   root <u>sbb</u>

Some roots have two <u>pi'el</u> types with different meanings:
The root <u>kvm</u> קום has the <u>pi'el</u> form /kiyem/ "he fulfilled" קיים as well
as /komem/ קומם "he re-established".

The root <u>kvn</u> כון has the <u>pi'el</u> form /konen/ כונן "he established" as well
as /kiven/ כיון "he directed".

The list of substitutions in section 21.4 should be used with the following
sentences:

A. He circled the building.   א. הוא סובב את הבנין.

B. He sang in the show.   ב. הוא שורר בהצגה.

C. He encouraged the students.   ג. הוא עודד את התלמידים.

c)   When the third radical is <u>'</u> (spelled א) the /'/ is dropped at the end of
a word or before a consonant. The first and second person past tense forms have
the stem vowels /-i-e-/.

Imperative:	m.s.	male	מלא		m.pl.	mal'u	מלאו
	f.s.	mal'i	מלאי		f.pl.	maléna	מלאנה
Past:	1 s.	miléti	מלאתי		1 pl.	milénu	מלאנו
	2 m.s.	miléta	מלאת		2 m.pl.	milétem	מלאתם
	2 f.s.	milét	מלאת		2 f.pl.	miléten	מלאתן
	3 m.s.	mile	מילא				
	3 f.s.	mil'a	מילאה		3 pl.	mil'u	מילאו

D. He filled the bottles.   ד. הוא מילא את הבקבוקים.

E. He made sure of the address.   ה. הוא וידא את הכתובת.

21.7 Verbal Nouns of the pi'el

A noun may be derived from pi'el verbs in one of two patterns, or both.

$C_1iC_2uC_3$ -	/kivun/	"direction"	כוון
	/sipur/	"story"	ספור
	/kibul/	"capacity"	קבול
$C_1aC_2aC_3a$	/kavana/	"intention"	כוונה
	/bakaša/	"request"	בקשה
	/kabala/	"reception"	קבלה

The first type is masculine, and the second is feminine.

It cannot be predicted for a particular verb which of these types will occur, nor can the exact meaning be predicted. Compare the derived nouns of these verbs:

/kiven/	"he directed"	כיון
/kivun/	"direction"	כיוון
/kavana/	"intention, aim"	כוונה
/kibel/	"he received"	קיבל
/kibul/	"capacity"	קבול
/kabala/	"reception"	קבלה
/bikeš/	"he requested"	ביקש
/bikuš/	"demand"　(opp. of supply)	ביקוש
/bakaša/	"request"	בקשה

In trying to form (guess) a verbal noun, the student should try the pattern $C_1iC_2uC_3$ first. There are more verbal nouns of this type than of the $C_1aC_2aC_3a$ type.

In lamed hey verbs /y/ is used as the third consonant. See Grammar Note 20.5b.

| /šinuy/ | "change" | שינוי |

In verbs whose second radical is ' (spelled א) or r the first type has the vowels /-e-u-/. Cf. Grammar Note 21.6a.

| /šerut/ | "service" | שרות |

A. Transformation Drill

Instructor: He visited Haifa.
Student: The visit was yesterday.

.1 הוא ביקר בחיפה.
הביקור היה אתמול.

.2 הוא שידר את החדשות.
השידור היה אתמול.

.3 הוא שינה את התוכנית.
השינוי היה אתמול.

.4 האוטובוס איחר לבוא.
האיחור היה אתמול.

21.8 The pu'al Conjugation

Compare the forms in the following pairs:

/yesader/	"he will arrange"	יסדר
/yesudar/	"it will be arranged"	יוסדר
/mekalkel/	"damages"	מקלקל
/mekulkal/	"damaged"	מקולקל

Note that the second form of each pair has the stem vowel pattern /-u-a-/ where the other form has the pattern /-a-e-/ which has been drilled in the previous sections of this unit. Note further that the second form is the passive of the first.

These passive forms are part of a conjugation traditionally called the pu'al (since the 3 m.s. past has that pattern.) The pu'al is very simple in structure. It is exactly like the corresponding pi'el except that the vowels /-u-a-/ occur throughout in place of the pi'el stem vowels. The /-a-/ will be dropped before suffixes beginning with a stressed vowel: /yesudru avurénu batim/ "Houses will be arranged for us".

The f.s. present has the pattern: $C_1uC_2éC_3et$ - /mesudéret/ "arranged"

The pu'al, however, is comparatively restricted in use. Not all pi'el verbs are so easily transformed into passives. In theory they could be, but idiomatically other constructions or conjugations are often used, for example, hitpa'el: /lehitkabel/ "to be received"; the generalized statement:/medabrim ivrit kan/ "Hebrew is spoken here"; etc.

With some verbs only third person or impersonal subjects make sense in the pu'al: /dubar/ "it was said".

The present tense forms of certain verbs are in very frequent use, and these forms are often treated as adjectives. Examples from the units so far are:

/meuxar/	"late"	מאוחר
/mecuyan/	"excellent"	מצוין
/mekulkal/	"damaged"	מקולקל
/me'unan/	"cloudy"	מעונן
/mešune/	"strange"	משונה

When the second radical is spelled ' (spelled א) or r, the stem vowels are /-o-a/. These roots were discussed in Grammar Note 21.6a.

/mefo'ar/	"luxurious"	מפואר

The following drills should be done in reverse, also.

A. Transformation Drill

Instructor: He will arrange a house for us.
Student: A house will be arranged for us.

1. הוא יסדר עבורנו בית.
               יסודר עבורנו בית.
2. הוא יקפל את המעטפות.
               המעטפות תקופלנה.
3. הוא יחלק את המכתבים.
               המכתבים יחולקו.
4. הוא ישנה את הסדר.
               הסדר ישונה.
5. הוא ינגב את הכוס.
               הכוס תנוגב.
6. הוא ישדר את החדשות.
               החדשות תשודרנה.

B. **Transformation Drill**

Instructor: He set up the house.
Student: The house was set.

1. ‏הוא סידר את הבית.‏
   ‏הבית סודר.‏

2. ‏הוא קיפל את המעטפות.‏
   ‏המעטפות קופלו.‏

3. ‏הוא חילק את המכתבים.‏
   ‏המכתבים חולקו.‏

4. ‏הוא שינה את הסדר.‏
   ‏הסדר שונה.‏

5. ‏הוא ניגב את הכוס.‏
   ‏הכוס נוגבה.‏

6. ‏הוא שידר את החדשות.‏
   ‏החדשות שודרו.‏

C. **Transformation Drill**

Instructor: He is straightening up the house.
Student: The house is in order.

1. ‏הוא מסדר את הבית.‏
   ‏הבית מסודר.‏

2. ‏הוא מקפל את המעטפות.‏
   ‏המעטפות מקופלות.‏

3. ‏הוא מחלק את המכתבים.‏
   ‏המכתבים מחולקים.‏

4. ‏הוא מנגב את הכוס.‏
   ‏הכוס מנוגבת.‏

5. ‏הוא משדר את החדשות.‏
   ‏החדשות משודרות.‏

RAPID RESPONSE DRILL

1. ‏מה מתכנן דוד לעשות במוצאי שבת?‏

2. ‏למה הוא רוצה ללכת לקולנוע מוגרבי?‏

3. ‏מה רוצה עטרה לעשות?‏

4. ‏מי החליט לאן ילכו?‏

5. ‏איך יודיעו ליונתן על התוכנית?‏

6. ‏באיזה שעה יעברו על יד ביתו?‏

REVIEW CONVERSATIONS

א: משה, אנו הולכים לקולנוע הערב. אתה רוצה להצטרף?

ב: לא, תודה. אני הולך לראות הצגה.

א: למה אתה מסרב להצטרף אלינו?

ב: אני לא מסרב. דווקא הערב אני רוצה ללכת לי"הבכימה".

א: ואתמול? אתמול סרבת ללכת אתנו, וגם שלשום.

ב: נו, דווקא השבוע לא יכולתי ללכת אתכם.

ג: יעקב, האם שמעת שגבי כהן נוסעת לחיפה?

ד: לא. לא ידעתי. למה לא הודעת לי קודם?

ג: עברתי על יד ביתך כדי להודיע לך אבל לא היית בבית.

ד: באיזה שעה עברת?

ג: בערך בשש, שש וחצי.

ד: אתה יודע שאני במשרד עד רבע לשבע.

ג: אה כן. שכחתי.

ה: האם החלטתם לאן תסעו הקיץ?

ו: עוד לא. אני מקווה לראות את הנמל החדש באילת, אבל אשתי רוצה לנסוע לצפת.

ה: אז כנראה שתסעו לצפת.

ו: מה אתה שח? היא נותנת לי להחליט.

ז: אני לא אוהב מה שאהרן עושה.

ח: מה הוא עושה?

ז: כל יום הוא משנה את הסדר במשרד ואנו לא יודעים היכן להתחיל והיכן לגמור.

ח: אולי אתם צריכים בשינויים?

ז: כן. קצת. אבל כל יום?!

ח: זה באמת משונה.

ט: אדוני, בכמה האבטיח?

י: חצי לירה האבטיח.

ט: חצי לירה?! למה זה כל כך יקר?

י: כי הביקוש הוא גדול.

ט: הביקוש? מי מבקש?

י: מה זאת אומרת מי מבקש? אנשים מבקשים, ואנשים משלמים.

מקרמות טורכים, בבקשה...

22.1 <u>At the Box Office</u> /bakupa/   בקופה

DAVID

Sir.	adoni	אדוני,
Please give me	ten li bevakaša	תן לי בבקשה
three tickets	šloša kartisim	שלושה כרטיסים
for tomorrow.	lemaxar.	למחר.
ticket, card	kartis (m)	כרטיס
Good seats,	mekomot tovim	מקומות טובים
please.	bevakaša.	בבקשה.

CASHIER /kupai/   קופאי

I have	yeš li	יש לי
three tickets	šloša kartisim	שלושה כרטיסים
in the balcony.	bayacia.	ביציע.
balcony	yacia (m)	יציע

DAVID

In the center?	baémca?	באמצע?
middle, center	émca (m)	אמצע

CASHIER

A bit on the side,	kcat bacad,	קצת בצד.
but it's possible	aval efšar	אבל אפשר
to see well.	lir'ot tov.	לראות טוב.
side	cad (m)	צד
but	aval	אבל
possible	efšar	אפשר

DAVID

In which row?	beéyze šura?	באיזה שורה?
row	šura (f)	שורה

CASHIER

Are you interested	ata meunyan	אתה מעונין
in the seventh row?	bašura hašviit?	בשורה השביעית?
interested	meunyan (m.s.)	מעונין

DAVID

These are	élu	אלו
the last tickets?	hakartisim	הכרטיסים
	haaxaronim?	האחרונים?
these	élu	אלו
last	axaron	אחרון

CASHIER

| Yes, sir. | ken, adoni. | כן, אדוני. |
| Do you want them? | ata roce otam? | אתה רוצה אותם? |

DAVID

All right.	tov.	טוב.
I have no choice.	eyn li brera.	אין לי ברירה.
I'll take them.	ekax otam.	אקח אותם.
How much do I	káma ani	כמה אני
owe you?	xayav lexa?	חייב לך?
choice	brera (f)	ברירה

CASHIER

| Eighteen liras. | šmóne'esre lírot. | שמונה-עשרה לירות. |

22.2 ADDITIONAL VOCABULARY

Give me three	ten li šloša	תן לי שלושה
seats in the orchestra.	kartisim baulam.	כרטיסים באולם.
hall, orchestra	ulam (m)	אולם
I'm interested	ani meunyan	אני מעונין
in good seats	bemekomot tovim	במקומות טובים
on the aisle.	al yad hamaavar.	על יד המעבר.
aisle	maavar (m)	מעבר
There are seats	yeš mekomot	יש מקומות
on the left or	bacad hasmali o	בצד השמאלי או
on the right.	bacad hayemini.	בצד הימיני.
left	smali (m.s.)	שמאלי
right	yemini (m.s.)	ימיני
The seats are near	hamekomot krovim	המקומות קרובים
the stage.	labama.	לבמה.
stage, platform	bama (f)	במה
The seats are near	hamekomot krovim	המקומות קרובים
the entrance.	laknisa.	לכניסה.
entrance	knisa (f)	כניסה
The seats are near	hamekomot krovim	המקומות קרובים
the exit.	layecia.	ליציאה.
exit	yecia (f)	יציאה
There is a parking place.	yeš mekom xanaya.	יש מקום חנייה.
parking	xanaya (f)	חנייה
They charge for parking.	haxanaya betašlum.	החנייה בתשלום.
fee, payment	tašlum (m)	תשלום
The parking is free.	haxanaya xofšit.	החנייה חופשית.
free	xofši (m.s.)	חופשי

22.3   The kal (pa'al) Conjugation

Though its name means "easy" this conjugation requires more drill to master than the _pi'el_ because there are more stem patterns for the tenses and more consonant alternations. However, if the student has thoroughly learned the Basic Sentences and verb drills of the preceding units he will find that he has already mastered the most frequent variations and that the following charts will merely diagram this knowledge.

At this point the student should review the phonological rules discussed in Grammar Note 6.9. In the following charts the stems are indicated in capital letters, but the euphonic vowels which break up the three-consonant clusters are in lower-case letters.

A completely regular verb will be given first, and the variations will be introduced one by one afterwards.

(a)   Regular verb pattern

			Forms with vowel suffix		
Infinitive:		li GMOR			
Imperative:	m.s.	GMOR			
			f.s.	GiMR i	
			m.pl.	GiMR u	
	f.pl.	GMÓR na			
Future:	1 s.	e GMOR			
	2 m.s.	ti GMOR			
			2 f.s.	ti GMeR i	
	3 m.s.	yi GMOR			
	3 f.s.	ti GMOR			
	1 pl.	ni GMOR			
			2 m.pl.	ti GMeR u	
	2 f.pl.	ti GMÓR na			
	3 f.pl.	ti GMÓR na	3 m.pl.	yi GMeR u	
Present:	m.s.	GOMER	m.pl.	GOMR im	
	f.s.	GOMÉR et	f.pl.	GOMR ot	
Past:	1 s.	GAMÁR ti			
	2 m.s.	GAMAR ta			
	2 f.s.	GAMAR t			
	3 m.s.	GAMAR			
			3 f.s.	GAMR a	
	1 pl.	GAMÁR nu			
	2 m.pl.	GAMÁR tem			
	2 f.pl.	GAMÁR ten			
			3 pl.	GAMR u	

A. hu yigmor et hahaxanot maxar.   "He'll finish the preparations tomorrow."

הוא יגמור את ההכנות מחר.

1.	ani	אני אגמור את ההכנות מחר.	אני .1
2.	etmol	אני גמרתי את ההכנות אתמול.	אתמול .2
3.	ata	אתה גמרת את ההכנות אתמול.	אתה .3
4.	axšav	אתה גומר את ההכנות עכשיו.	עכשיו .4
5.	david	דוד גומר את ההכנות עכשיו.	דוד .5
6.	maxar	דוד יגמור את ההכנות מחר.	מחר .6
7.	atem	אתם תגמרו את ההכנות מחר.	אתם .7
8.	etmol	אתם גמרתם את ההכנות אתמול.	אתמול .8
9.	išto	אשתו גמרה את ההכנות אתמול.	אשתו .9
10.	axšav	אשתו גומרת את ההכנות עכשיו.	עכשיו .10
11.	hen	הן גומרות את ההכנות עכשיו.	הן .11
12.	maxar	הן תגמורנה את ההכנות מחר.	מחר .12
13.	aten	אתן תגמורנה את ההכנות מחר.	אתן .13
14.	etmol	אתן גמרתן את ההכנות אתמול.	אתמול .14
15.	ánu	אנו גמרנו את ההכנות אתמול.	אנו .15
16.	axšav	אנו גומרים את ההכנות עכשיו.	עכשיו .16
17.	hem	הם גומרים את ההכנות עכשיו.	הם .17
18.	beod xódeš	הם יגמרו את ההכנות בעוד חודש.	בעוד חודש .18
19.	at	את תגמרי את ההכנות בעוד חודש.	את .19

B. hu sagar et haxanut etmol.   "He closed the store yesterday."

הוא סגר את החנות אתמול.

1.	at	את סגרת את החנות אתמול.	את .1
2.	beod xódeš	את תסגרי את החנות בעוד חודש.	בעוד חודש .2
3.	hem	הם יסגרו את החנות בעוד חודש.	הם .3
4.	axšav	הם סוגרים את החנות עכשיו.	עכשיו .4
5.	ánu	אנו סוגרים את החנות עכשיו.	אנו .5
6.	etmol	אנו סגרנו את החנות אתמול.	אתמול .6
7.	aten	אתן סגרתן את החנות אתמול.	אתן .7
8.	maxar	אתן תסגורנה את החנות מחר.	מחר .8
9.	hen	הן תסגורנה את החנות מחר.	הן .9
10.	axšav	הן סוגרות את החנות עכשיו.	עכשיו .10
11.	išto	אשתו סוגרת את החנות עכשיו.	אשתו .11
12.	etmol	אשתו סגרה את החנות אתמול.	אתמול .12
13.	atem	אתם סגרתם את החנות אתמול.	אתם .13
14.	bekarov	אתם תסגרו את החנות בקרוב.	בקרוב .14
15.	mar kóhen	מר כהן יסגור את החנות בקרוב.	מר כהן .15
16.	axšav	מר כהן סוגר את החנות עכשיו.	עכשיו .16
17.	ata	אתה סוגר את החנות עכשיו.	אתה .17
18.	šilšom	אתה סגרת את החנות שלשום.	שלשום .18
19.	ani	אני סגרתי את החנות שלשום.	אני .19

b) <u>Verbs with future stem vowel /a/</u>

Verbs whose third root consonant is <u>'</u> or <u>x</u> (spelled ח , not כ) and
certain other verbs have /a/ as a stem vowel in the imperative and future,
instead of /o/. The student is reminded that the vowel /a/ must precede /x/ (ח)
or <u>'</u> (ע) when these are at the end of the word: /šoléax/ "sends" שולח

Infinitive: li šlóax

Imperative:	m.s.	ŠLAX	
	f.pl.	ŠLAX na	
Future:	1 s.	e ŠLAX	
	2 m.s.	ti ŠLAX	etc.

The following is a list of substitutions to be used in drilling the
sentences below. The substitutions may be varied similarly to the list in
Unit 21.

אתמול	אתה	עכשיו	אני
עכשיו	את	בקרוב	היא
מחר	אנו	אתמול	משה ודב
לפני יומיים	רחל ואתה	כרגע	אתן
ברגע זה	רחל ולאה	בעוד שבוע	את
בעוד שבועיים	הם	לפני חודש	הוא
שלשום	אתן	עכשיו	אנו
עכשיו	היא	מחר	הן
מחר	מר זהבי	אתמול	אתם
אתמול	אני	עכשיו	אתה

C. Yesterday he sent the package
   by air mail.

ג. הוא שלח את החבילה
בדואר אויר אתמול.

End of Tape 9A

Tape 9B

D. Yesterday he found the post office
   without any trouble.

ד. אתמול הוא מצא את הדואר
ללא קושי.

E. He's listening to the broadcast now.

ה. הוא שומע את השידורים עכשיו.

F. She's washing the bottles now.

ו. היא רוחצת את הבקבוקים עכשיו.

G. Now she reads Hebrew easily.

ז. עכשיו היא קוראת עברית בקלות.

H. Tomorrow I'll learn how to make ice cream.

ח. מחר אלמד להכין גלידה.

247

c) Alternating first radicals

In Grammar Note 21.4b we saw that the consonants /b/,/p/ and /k/(spelled כ) alternated with /v/, /f/ and /x/ when they were the first root consonant of the verb.

The same rules apply in the <u>kal</u> as in the <u>pi'el</u>: In prefixed forms the consonant is /v/, /f/ and /x/ respectively. In other forms it is /b/, /p/ and /k/.

In some respects the alternations in the <u>kal</u> are simpler to remember. First of all, there are no roots with <u>v</u> (ו) as the first radical. Thus, all /v/ is the result of the b/v alternation.

Second, the prefix before /x/ (spelled כ) is /ti-, yi- / etc., and the prefix before /x/ (spelled ח) is /ta-, ya- / etc.

/tixtov/ "you will write" תכתוב
/taxšov/ "you will think" תחשוב

	Prefixed forms			
Infinitive:	liVdok			
		Imperative:	m.s.	Bdok
			f.s.	Bidki etc.,
Future: 1 s.	eVdok			
2 m.s.	tiVdok			
2 f.s.	tiVdeki etc.			
		Present:	m.s.	Bodek
			f.s.	Bodéket etc.,
		Past:	1 s.	Badákti
			2 m.s.	Badákta etc.,

I. We checked the program yesterday.

ט. בדקנו את התוכנית אתמול.

J. Moshe opened the new store a week ago.

י. משה פתח את החנות החדשה לפני שבוע.

K. Atara will write to her tomorrow.

כ. עטרה תכתוב לה מחר.

·L. I'll think about it tomorrow.

ל. אחשוב על כך מחר.

M. They tied up the packages yesterday.

מ. הם קשרו אתמול את החבילות.

N. Transformation Drill - Affirmative to Negative

Instructor: Check the boxes right now.
Student: Don't check the boxes now, wait till tomorrow.

אל תבדוק את הקופסאות עכשיו, חכה עד מחר.   בדוק את הקופסאות מיד.

אל תבדקי את הקופסאות עכשיו, חכי עד מחר.   בדקי את הקופסאות מיד.

אל תבדקו את הקופסאות עכשיו, חכו עד מחר.   בדקו את הקופסאות מיד.

אל תבדרוקנה את הקופסאות עכשיו, חכינה עד מחר.   בדוקנה את הקופסאות מיד.

O. Transformation Drill - Negative to Affirmative

Instructor: Don't open the windows. It's cold outside.
Student: Open the windows. It's hot in the house.

פתח את החלונות. חם בבית.   אל תפתח את החלונות. קר בחוץ.

פתחי את החלונות. חם בבית.   אל תפתחי את החלונות. קר בחוץ.

פתחו את החלונות. חם בבית.   אל תפתחו את החלונות. קר בחוץ.

פתחנה את החלונות. חם בבית.   אל תפתחנה את החלונות. קר בחוץ.

P. Transformation Drill - Affirmative to Negative

Instructor: Write him a letter.
Student: Don't write him a letter. Phone him.

אל תכחוב אליו מכחב. התקשר אתו בטלפון.   כתוב אליו מכתב.

אל תכחבי אליו מכחב. התקשרי אתו בטלפון.   כתבי אליו מכתב.

אל תכחבו אליו מכחב. התקשרו אתו בטלפון.   כתבו אליו מכתב.

אל תכחובנה אליו מכחב. התקשרנה אתו בטלפון.   כוובנה אליו מכחב.

Q. Transformation Drill - Negative to Affirmative

Instructor: Don't work right now. It's still early.
Student: Get to work right away. Otherwise the time will pass.

פעל מיד. אחרת יעבור הזמן.   אל תפעל מיד. עוד מוקדם.

פעלי מיד. אחרת יעבור הזמן.   אל תפעלי מיד. עוד מוקדם.

פעלו מיד. אחרת יעבור הזמן.   אל תפעלו מיד. עוד מוקדם.

פעלנה מיד. אחרת יעבור הזמן.   אל תפעלנה מיד. עוד מוקדם.

The above drills should also be done in reverse.

(d) Alternating second radicals

To complicate things a bit more, the three consonants b, p and k (‏כ‎)
alternate when they are the second radical of the verb. In prefixed forms
the second root consonant is /b/, /p/ and /k/, and in the unprefixed forms
they are /v/, /f/ and /x/. This is the reverse of the pattern described
in the predecing section for the alternating first radical.

	Prefixed forms				
Infinitive:		lisPor			
			Imperative:	m.s.	sFor
				f.s.	siFri
				m.pl.	siFru
				f.pl.	sFórna
Future:	1 s.	esPor			
	2 m.s.	tisPor			
	3 m.s.	yisPor			
	3 f.s.	tisPor			
	1 pl.	nisPor			
	2 m.pl.	tisPeru			
	2 f.pl.	tisPórna			
	3 m.pl.	yisPeru			
	3 f.pl.	tisPórna			
			Present:	m.s.	soFer
				f.s.	soFéret
				m.pl.	soFrim
				f.pl.	soFrot
			Past:	1 s.	saFárti
				2 m.s.	saFárta
				2 f.s.	saFárt
				3 m.s.	saFár
				3 f.s.	saFra
				1 pl.	saFárnu
				2 m.pl.	saFártem
				2 f.pl.	saFárten
				3 pl.	saFru

In the stark imperative of some verbs the student may hear vacillation
between forms, for example, /šxax ~ škax/ "forget". (See section 21.2, Drill F)
This can result when the speaker drops the /ti-/ of the gentle imperative /tiškax/
to make a regularized stark imperative /škax/. Similarly one might hear /šikxi/
as the feminine singular instead of /šixexi/.

Such regularizations are not surprising, but they are often deplored by
educated speakers.

The division of the conjugation into prefixed forms and unprefixed forms is
merely a handy device to help the student in doing the drills of these verbs.
The general rules for the b/v, p/f and k/x alternations in verbs are complex
and are no benefit to the student at this point.

In any event, the student should not try to memorize rules but must keep
drilling the correct forms until, for example, /timkor/ and /moxer/ just sound
right, and the incorrect forms */timxor/ and */moker/ jar his ears.

R. He counted the jars the day before yesterday.

הוא ספר את הצנצנות שלשום.

הן .1	הן ספרו את הצנצנות שלשום.
ברגע זה .2	הן סופרות את הצנצנות ברגע זה.
את .3	את סופרת את הצנצנת ברגע זה.
בעוד יומיים .4	את תספרי את הצנצנות בעוד יומיים.
רב ואתה .5	רב ואתה תספרו את הצנצנות בעוד יומיים.
לפני שבוע .6	רב ואתה ספרתם את הצנצנות לפני שבוע.
אתן .7	אתן ספרתן את הצנצנות לפני שבוע.
כרגע .8	אתן סופרות את הצנצנות כרגע.
אנו .9	אנו סופרים את הצנצנות כרגע.
מחר .10	אנו נספור מחר את הצנצנות.
כולם .11	כולם יספרו מחר את הצנצנות.
אתמול .12	כולם ספרו אתמול את הצנצנות.
את .13	את ספרת אתמול את הצנצנות.
עכשיו .14	את סופרת את הצנצנות עכשיו.
היא .15	היא סופרת את הצנצנות עכשיו.
בקרוב .16	היא תספור את הצנצנות בקרוב.
אתה .17	אתה תספור את הצנצנות בקרוב.
שלשום .18	אתה ספרת את הצנצנות שלשום.
אני .19	אני ספרתי את הצנצנות שלשום.
עכשיו .20	אני סופר את הצנצנות עכשיו.

S. He broke some of the jars yesterday morning.

הוא שבר כמה מהצנצנות אתמול בבוקר.

עוד מעט .1	עוד מעט הוא ישבור כמה מהצנצנות.
הם .2	עוד מעט הם ישברו כמה מהצנצנות.
עכשיו .3	הם שוברים עכשיו כמה מהצנצנות.
אנו .4	אנו שוברים עכשיו כמה מהצנצנות.
אתמול .5	אתמול אנו שברנו כמה מהצנצנות.
אתן .6	אתן שברתן אתמול כמה מהצנצנות.
מחר .7	אתן תשברנה מחר כמה מהצנצנות.
הן .8	הן תשברנה מחר כמה מהצנצנות.
עכשיו .9	הן שוברות עכשיו כמה מהצנצנות.
אשתך .10	אשתך שוברת עכשיו כמה מהצנצנות.
אתמול .11	אשתך שברה אתמול כמה מהצנצנות.
אתם .12	אתם שברתם אתמול כמה מהצנצנות.
מחר .13	מחר אתם תשברו כמה מהצנצנות.
דוד .14	דוד ישבור מחר כמה מהצנצנות.
עכשיו .15	דוד שובר עכשיו כמה מהצנצנות.
אתה .16	אתה שובר עכשיו כמה מהצנצנות.
אתמול .17	אתה שברת אתמול כמה מהצנצנות.
אני .18	אני שברתי אתמול כמה מהצנצנות.

T. He sold the tickets yesterday evening.

הוא מכר את הכרטיסים אתמול בערב.

אתה .1	אתה מכרת את הכרטיסים אתמול בערב.
עכשיו .2	אתה מוכר את הכרטיסים עכשיו.
אתם .3	אתם מוכרים את הכרטיסים עכשיו.
אתמול .4	אתם מכרתם את הכרטיסים אתמול.
הן .5	הן מכרו את הכרטיסים אתמול.
מחר .6	הן תמכורנה מחר את הכרטיסים.
אנו .7	אנו נמכור מחר את הכרטיסים.
עכשיו .8	אנו מוכרים עכשיו את הכרטיסים.
הקופאי .9	הקופאי מוכר עכשיו את הכרטיסים.
לפני יומיים .10	הקופאי מכר את הכרטיסים לפני יומיים.
את .11	את מכרת את הכרטיסים לפני יומיים.
בעוד יומיים .12	את תמכרי את הכרטיסים בעוד יומיים.
אתן .13	אתן תמכורנה את הכרטיסים בעוד יומיים.
כרגע .14	אתן מוכרות את הכרטיסים כרגע.
הם .15	הם מוכרים את הכרטיסים כרגע.
אתמול .16	הם מכרו את הכרטיסים אתמול.
הקופאית .17	הקופאית מכרה את הכרטיסים אתמול.
בקרוב .18	הקופאית תמכור את הכרטיסים בקרוב.

U. Transformation Drill - Affirmative to Negative

Instructor: Please count the nuts for me.
Student: Don't count the nuts. I already know how many there are.

אל תספור את האגוזים. אני כבר יודע כמה שיש.   בבקשה, ספור את האגוזים בשבילי.

אל תספרי את האגוזים. אני כבר יודע כמה שיש.   בבקשה, ספרי את האגוזים בשבילי.

אל תספרו את האגוזים. אני כבר יודע כמה שיש.   בבקשה, ספרו את האגוזים בשבילי.

אל תספורנה את האגוזים. אני כבר יודע כמה שיש.   בבקשה, ספורנה את האגוזים בשבילי.

V. Transformation Drill - Negative to Affirmative

Instructor: Don't sell the house.
Student: Sell the house.

מכור את הבית.   אל תמכור את הבית.

מכרי את הבית.   אל תמכרי את הבית.

מכרו את הבית.   אל תמכרו את הבית.

מכורנה את הבית.   אל תמכורנה את הבית.

W. Substitution Drill

Break something else but not the glass.

שבור משהו אחר, אבל לא את הכוס.

שברי

שברו

שבורנה

(e) Verbs with first radical '

[The following remarks pertain to most, not all, verbs whose first radical
is ' . Verbs different from those described in this section are not too
frequent, and the student can learn them as he meets them.]

A distinction must be made between verbs whose first radical is ' (א) and
those whose first radical is ' (ע). The charts below illustrate the patterns
of two such verbs.

In the present and past tenses there is no distinction, and both types have
the regular vowel patterns of the kal in these tenses.

If the second radical is b, p or k (כ) then only the alternants /v/,/f/ and
/x/ occur. The rules described in the preceding section (d) do not apply. The
examples chosen for the charts illustrate this.

The main feature to observe in the following charts is the prefix of each
type. The future stem vowel of the first type is /a/: /toxal/ "you will eat",
and the future stem vowel of the second type is /o/:/taavor/ "you will pass".

	אכל	עבר
Infinitive:	LEExol	LAAvor

Imperative:		
m.s.	Exol	Avor
f.s.	ixli	ivri
m.pl.	ixlu	ivru
f.pl.	Exólna	Avórna

Future:		
1 s.	Oxal	EEvor
2 m.s.	TOxal	TAAvor
2 f.s.	TOxli	TAAvor
3 m.s.	YOxal	YAAvor
3 f.s.	TOxal	TAAvor
1 pl.	NOxal	NAAvor
2 m.pl.	TOxlu	TAAvru
2 f.pl.	TOxálna	TAAvórna
3 m.pl.	YOxlu	YAAvru
3 f.pl.	TOxálna	TAAvórna

Present:		
m.s.	oxel	over
f.s.	oxélet	overet
m.pl.	oxlim	ovrim
f.pl.	oxlot	ovrot

Past:		
1 s.	axálti	avárti
2 m.s.	axálta	avárta
2 f.s.	axalt	avart
3 m.s.	axal	avar
3 f.s.	axla	avra
1 pl.	axálnu	avárnu
2 m.pl.	axáltem	avártem
2 f.pl.	axálten	avárten
3 pl.	axlu	avru

(The infinitive of /amar/ is /lomar/ "to say", spelled לומר)

Use the list of substitution cues given in section 22.3(b).

X. I told him not to wait for me. אמרתי לו לא לחכות לי.

Y. I ate it all because it's good. אכלתי את הכל כי זה טעים.

Tape 10A End of Tape 9B

Z. I liked to stroll in the evening. אהבתי לטייל בערב.

AA. I passed by the cafe. עברתי על יד בית הקפה.

253

(f) <u>lamed hey verbs in the kal</u>

<u>lamed hey</u> verbs in the <u>kal</u> have the features common to all such verbs, and the student should find them quite familiar. In the past tense of the <u>kal</u> the stem vowels are /-a-i/ in the first and second person: /kaníti/ "I bought".

In addition to the features of <u>lamed hey</u> verbs, the first and second root consonants may cause the alternations described in Sections (c) to (e). For example:

pnh   פנה "turn" has the first radical alternation described in Section (c): /pne/ ~ /tifne/.

'lh   עלה "go up, cost" has the features of a first radical ʿ (ע) described in Section /(e): /eele/ ~ /taale/

bkh   בכה "cry" combines the alternations of Sections (c) and (d): /yivke/ ~ /baxa/.

Infinitive:		liknOT			
Imperative:	m.s.	kne	m. pl.	knu	
	f.s.	kni	f. pl.	knéna	
Future:	1 s.	ekne	1 pl.	nikne	
	2 m.s.	tikne	2 m.pl.	tiknu	
	2 f.s.	tikni	2 f.pl.	tiknéna	
	3 m.s.	yikne	3 m.pl.	yiknu	
	3 f.s.	tikne	3 f.pl.	tiknéna	
Present:	m.s.	kone	m.pl.	konim	
	f.s.	kona	f.pl.	konót	
Past:	1 s.	kaníti	1 pl.	kanínu	
	2 m.s.	kaníta	2 m.pl.	kanítem	
	2 f.s.	kanit	2 f.pl.	kaníten	
	3 m.s.	kana	3 pl.	kanu	
	3 f.s.	kanta			

Use the list of substitution cues given in Section 22.3 (b):

BB.	She turned at the second intersection.	.היא פנתה בהצטלבות השניה
CC.	She saw the storekeeper outside the store.	.היא ראתה את החנווני מחוץ לחנות
DD.	She bought flour and sugar.	.היא קנתה קמח וסוכר
EE.	She went up to the house and set things up.	.היא עלתה לבית ועשתה סדר
FF.	He wanted to swim.	.הוא רצה לשחות
GG.	He swam in the new pool.	.הוא שחה בבריכה החדשה
HH.	He cried when he heard the news.	.הוא בכה כששמע את החדשות

(g) <u>ayin vav</u> (ע"ו) <u>verbs</u>

A frequently occurring type of verb is the <u>ayin vav</u> verb, whose second radical is listed as <u>vav</u> (ו) in the dictionaries (hence the term <u>ayin vav</u>), although it does not represent the consonant /v/ but rather the vowel /u/.

The chart below illustrates what is traditionally called the <u>kal</u> conjugation of these verbs. This classification as <u>kal</u> is based on historical reasons and the fact that it is the simplest conjugation of this type of verb.

Some verbs resemble the <u>ayin vav</u> verbs in all respects except that they have <u>yud</u>, representing /i/, instead of the <u>vav</u>. These verbs are called, appropriately, <u>ayin yud</u> (ע"י) <u>verbs</u>.

Infinitive:		la kum			
Imperative: m.s.		kum		m.pl.	kúm u
f.s.		kúm i		f.pl.	kúm na
Future: 1 s.		a kum		1 pl.	na kum
2 m.s.		ta kum		2 m.pl.	ta kúm u
2 f.s.		ta kúm i		2 f.pl.	ta kúm na
3 m.s.		ya kum		3 m.pl.	ya kúm u
3 f.s.		ta kum		3 f.pl.	ta kúm na
Present: m.s.		kam		m.pl.	kam im
f.s.		kám a		f.pl.	kam ot
Past: 1 s.		kám ti		1 pl.	kám nu
2 m.s.		kám ta		2 m.pl.	kám tem
2 f.s.		kam t		2 f.pl.	kám ten
3 m.s.		kam			
3 f.s.		káma		3 pl.	kám u

A frequently heard variant of the 2 and 3 f.pl. forms is /takómna/ in the <u>ayin vav</u> verbs and /tašérna/ in the <u>ayin yud</u> verbs.

The verb /lavo/ "to come" is an <u>ayin vav</u> verb, but with /o/ as a stem vowel. It is listed in the dictionaries under בוא . The first radical alternates between /b/ and /v/ as described in Section (c).

Use the substitution cues given in Section 22.3 (b).

II. I stayed at the Savoy Hotel yesterday.   .גרתי במלון סבוי אתמול

JJ. I got up early yesterday.   .קמתי מוקדם אתמול

KK. I ran to the bus yesterday.   .רצתי לאוטובוס אתמול

LL. I came to the theater yesterday.   .באתי לתיאטרון אתמול

MM. I sang in the show yesterday.   .שרתי בהצגה אתמול

22.4 Verbal Noun of the kal

The verbal noun of the <u>kal</u> has the following pattern:　/$C_1C_2iC_3a$/

These nouns are feminine and have the plural pattern:　/$C_1C_2iC_3ot$/

Examples which have occurred in the text are:

/slixa/	"pardon"	סליחה	<u>slx</u>
/knisa/	"entrance"	כניסה	<u>kns</u>
/yeci'a/	"exit"	יציאה	<u>yc'</u>

(In the third example the /e/ breaks up the beginning cluster /yc-/.)

As with verbal nouns of all conjugations it is hard to predict the exact shade of meaning which it might have. The translations, therefore, may cover a wide range.

The root <u>kns</u> occurs in the <u>nif'al</u> with the meaning "to enter", but the verbal noun is still in the <u>kal</u>.

The verbal nouns of <u>lamed hey</u> verbs have <u>y</u> as the third root consonant. Cf. Grammar Note 21.7. However, since the glide from the vowel /i/ to the vowel /a/ produces the /y/ anyway, the nouns are transcribed without the /y/:
　　　　　/knia/ "purchase"　קניה　　<u>knh</u> (kny)　קנה

In ordinary speech verbal nouns of roots whose third consonant is <u>'</u> are often pronounced with a smooth glide: /yecia/ as well as /yeci'a/.

When the first root consonant is <u>'</u>, <u>h</u> or <u>x</u>, then the pattern is: /$C_1aC_2iC_3a$/
　　　　　/'axila/ "eating"　אכילה

A. Translation Drill
(The instructor reads both parts of the sentence before the student translates)

1. The doctor examined him,
and the examination was quick.
　　　　　1. הרופא בדק אותו,
　　　　　והבדיקה היתה מהירה.

2. He went to Eilat,
and the trip was long.
　　　　　2. הוא נסע לאילת,
　　　　　והנסיעה היתה ארוכה.

3. He opened the store,
and the opening was beautiful.
　　　　　3. הוא פתח את החנות,
　　　　　והפתיחה היתה יפה.

4. He walked six kilometers,
but the walk was easy.
　　　　　4. הוא הלך ששה קילומטרים,
　　　　　אבל ההליכה היתה קלה.

5. They went to eat,
because it came time to eat.
　　　　　5. הם הלכו לאכול,
　　　　　כי שעת האכילה הגיעה.

6. He wrote one letter,
and it took a long time to write.
　　　　　6. הוא כתב מכתב אחד,
　　　　　והכתיבה לקחה הרבה זמן.

7. We swim every day,
because we like to swim.
　　　　　7. אנו שוחים כל יום,
　　　　　כי אנו אוהבים את השחיה.

8. They went to Israel
in the last immigration.
　　　　　8. הם עלו לארץ
　　　　　בעליה האחרונה.

9. He sold the jelly.
The jelly was on sale.
　　　　　9. הוא מכר את הריבה.
　　　　　הריבה היתה במכירה.

10. I'm going to meet Miriam,
and we'll meet in a cafe.
　　　　　10. אני אפגוש את מרים,
　　　　　והפגישה תהיה כבית קפה.

RAPID RESPONSE DRILL

1. כמה כרטיסים רצה דוד לקנות?

2. האם המקומות היו באולם?

3. האם המקומות היו באמצע?

4. באיזו שורה היו המקומות?

5. למה לא סרב דוד לקחת את הכרטיסים?

6. כמה שילם בעד הכרטיסים?

REVIEW CONVERSATIONS

א: משה, מה אתה עושה הערב?

ב: אין לי תוכנית. מה אתם עושים?

א: יש לנו כרטיסים להצגה ב"הבימה".

ר: טוב מאד.

א: לא כל כך טוב. אשתי לא יכולה ללכת.

ב: מכור לי את הכרטיסים ואני אלך.

א: ברצון. אמכור לך את הכרטיסים.

ב: האם המקומות טובים?

א: לא רעים. קצת בצד. הם עולים 6 לירות לכרטיס.

ב: תודה רבה.

ג: מדים בכתה בהצגה.

ד: מדוע?

ג: היא קראה את הספר וההצגה היתה מצויינת.

ד: איך היא נהנתה ממדים נרקיס?

ג: היא אוהבת אותה מאד.

ד: גם לדעתי היא שחקנית גדולה.

ה: היינו בפתיחה של החנות החדשה.

ו: גם אנו היינו. היתה לנו פגישה עם המנהל.

ה: מכירת הפתיחה היתה יפה מאד.

ו: כן. היו שם הרבה דברים יפים.

ה: קניתם משהו?

ו: כן. קנינו שולחן יפה ובזול.

ז: רחל לא מצאה את הבית של דב.

ח: איך זה? היא לא בדקה את הכתובת בספר הטלפונים?

ז: נתתי לה את הכתובת כשהיא עברה על יד ביתנו.

ח: אולי במקום ללכת ימינה היא הלכה שמאלה.

ט: גמרנו את הלימודים והלכנו לשחות.

י: איך היו המים?

ט: המים היו נהדרים והשחייה היתה מצויינת.

י: עליתם לאכול במזנון?

ט: כן. האוכל שם טעים מאד.

23.1 Before The Play

<u>YONATAN</u>

Atara,	atára,	עטרה,
I see that	ani roe še-	אני רואה ש-
you have won again.	šuv nicaxt.	שוב ניצחת.
again	šúv	שוב
he won	nicéax	ניצח

<u>ATARA</u>

I	ani	אני
generally	bedérex klal	בדרך כלל
win	menacáxat,	מנצחת
because I have	ki yeš li	כי יש לי
a good husband.	báal tov.	בעל טוב.
generalization	klál (m)	כלל

<u>DAVID</u>

Do you want	atem rocim	אתם רוצים
to drink anything?	lištot mášehu?	לשתות משהו?
he drank	šata	שתה
something	mášehu (m)	משהו
chocolate	šokolad (m)	שוקולד

<u>ATARA</u>

No, thanks.	lo toda.	לא תודה.
I'm not thirsty.	ani lo cmea.	אני לא צמאה.
Oh – the bell	o – hapaamon	אה – הפעמון
is ringing.	mecalcel.	מצלצל.
thirsty	cama	צמא
bell	paamon (m)	פעמון
rang	cilcel	צלצל

<u>YONATAN</u>

Let's go	bóu nigaš	בואו ניגש
to our seats.	lamekomot šelánu.	למקומות שלנו.

<u>DAVID</u>

We're sitting	ánu yošvim	אנו יושבים
in the balcony.	bayacía.	ביציע.

<u>ATARA</u>

The seats	hamekomot	המקומות
are pretty good.	day tovim.	די טובים.
enough	day	די

259

DAVID

What do you want	ma at roca	מה את רוצה
for six liras?	bešeš lírot,	בשש לירות?
To sit	lašévet	לשבת
in the front row?	bašura harišona?	בשורה הראשונה?

ATARA

Quiet.	šéket.		שֶׁקֶט
Don't disturb.	al tafría.		אל תַפְרִיע.
he disturbed		hifría	הפריע

23.2 ADDITIONAL VOCABULARY

The curtain's going up.	hamasax ole.		המסך עולה.
curtain		masax (m)	מסך
The first act	hamaaraxa harišona		המערכה הראשונה
is over.	nigmera.		נגמרה.
act		maaraxa (f)	מערכה
There's an intermission	yeš hafsaka		יש הפסקה
for ten minutes.	leéser dakot.		לעשֶׂר רקות.
interruption		hafsaka (f)	הפסקה
he interrupted		hifsik	הפסיק
You're not allowed to	asur leašen		אסור לעשן
smoke inside.	bifnim.		בפנים.
forbidden		asur (m.s.)	אסור
he smoked		išen	עישן
interior		pnim (m)	פנים
Smoking is permitted	mutar leašen		מותר לעשן
in the lobby.	bamisderon.		במסדרון.
lobby		misderon (m)	מסדרון
Use the ashtray.	hištameš bamaafera.		השתמש במאפרה.
ashtray		maafera (f)	מאפרה
Where's the snack bar?	éyfo hamiznon?		איפה המזנון ?
luncheonette		miznon (m)	מזנון
I'm hungry.	ani raev.		אני רעב.
hungry		raev (m.s.)	רעב

23.3 VOCABULARY DRILLS

A. Substitution-Agreement Drill   /raev/ "hungry"   /came/ "thirsty"

   He's not hungry; he's thirsty.

<u>הוא לא רעב. הוא צמא.</u>

הם – היא – הן – אני

B. Substitution Drill   /hištameš/   "use"

   Use the exit on the right.

השתמש ביציאה מימין.
השתמשי
השתמשו
השתמשנה

Tape 10B

23.4 VERB DRILLS

The student may soon begin to feel overwhelmed at the large number of different forms that a verb root may have in the various conjugations. He will be required to conjugate fully almost every new verb that occurs. A shift in tense, person, gender, or number - and the form learned in the Basic Sentence is incorrect in the new sentence.

However, the task is not nearly so difficult as it may seem at this point. The student will find that the regularities of the system are very great and that a few patterns take care of the large majority of verbs which actually occur in ordinary speech. Conscientious overlearning of these drills will bring an increasing measure of confidence.

In previous units the different forms of new words have been drilled in the Vocabulary Drill sections. In this and following units new verbs will be drilled in special Verb Drill sections. These will serve as a constant review of the binyanim and verb types. Pertinent comments for individual verbs will be made from time to time.

(a)./nicéax/ "he won"   נצח

The third root consonant of this verb is x (ח), and the vowel /a/ must precede it at the end of a word.

A. Substitution-Agreement Drill - Past Tense

I'm happy that I've won again.   אני שמח ששוב ניצחתי.

אתה – אנו – יו.נתן – עטרה – את
הם – אתם – הן – אתן – אנו – אני

(This drill may be varied by varying /saméax/ to agree with the alternations of /nicáxti/: /ata saméax šešuv nicáxta/, /ánu smexim šešuv nicáxnu/, etc.)

B. Substitution-Agreement Drill - Present Tense

I generally win.   אני בדרך כלל מנצח.

את – אשתי – הם – הנשים – דוד – אני

C. Substitution-Agreement Drill - Future Tense

I hope you'll win tomorrow.   אני מקורה שתנצח מחר.

שמשה – שאת – שהם – שאנו – שאתם
שהיא – שאתן – שאתה – שאני

D. Substitution-Agreement Drill - All Tenses

We win every time.   אנו מנצחים כל פעם.
We won yesterday,   ניצחנו אתמול
and we'll win today.   ונַנצח היום.

אתה – אתם – הם – הנשים שלנו – היא
בעלך – אני – אתה – אתן – את – אנו

(b) /cilcel/ "rang" צלצל

This verb is conjugated exactly like /kilkel/ "he damaged". The pi'el is used in both the transitive meaning /cilcálti bapaamon/ "I rang the bell" and the intransitive meaning /hapaamon cilcel/ "the bell rang".

E. Substitution-Agreement Drill - Past Tense

We rang the bell on time.   .צלצלנו בפעמון בזמן

המורה - המנהלת - אני - אתם - התלמידים
אתה - את - והוא - אתן - אנו

F. Substitution-Agreement Drill - Present Tense

We ring the bells at noon.   .אנו מצלצלים בפעמונים בצהריים

אני - את - הוא - הן - אנו

G. Substitution-Agreement Drill - Future Tense

When will he ring the bell?   ?מתי הוא יצלצל בפעמון

אתה - אתן - אתם - היא
את - הן - הם - הוא

(c) /išen/ "he smoked" עישן

H. Substitution-Agreement Drill - Past Tense

She smoked all morning.   .היא עישנה כל הבוקר

אני - הם - הן - המורה - אתה
אתם - אנו - את - אתן - היא

I. Substitution-Agreement Drill - Present Tense

I smoke in my free time.   .אני מעשן בזמני החורשי

הם - אנו - הן - את
הוא - היא - אתם - אני

J. Substitution-Agreement Drill - Future Tense

We'll smoke during the second intermission.   .אנו נעשן בהפסקה השניה

אני - אתה - הם - את - הן
אתן - הוא - אתם - היא - אנו

(d) /šata/ "he drank" שתה

This is a <u>lamed hey</u> verb of the <u>kal</u>. It is conjugated exactly like /kana/ "he bought" קנה . The 3 f.s. past tense is /šateta/ שתחה.

K. Transformation Drill - Affirmative to Negative

Instructor: Drink tea.
Student: Don't drink tea. Drink coffee.

שתה קפה.	אל תשתה תה.	שתה תה.
שתי קפה.	אל תשתי תה.	שתי תה.
שתו קפה.	אל תשתו תה.	שתו תה.
שתינה קפה.	אל תשתינה תה.	שתינה תה.

L. Transformation Drill - Past to Future

Instructor: I drank the milk.
Student: I'll drink the milk.

אשתה את החלב.	שתיתי את החלב.
תשתו את החלב.	שתיתם את החלב.
תשתי את החלב.	את שתית את החלב.
הוא ישתה את החלב.	הוא שתה את החלב.
נשתה את החלב.	שתינו את החלב.
היא תשתה את החלב.	היא שתתה את החלב.
תשתינה את החלב.	שתיתן את החלב.
הם ישתו את החלב.	הם שתו את החלב.
אתה תשתה את החלב.	אתה שתית את החלב.
הן תשתינה את החלב.	הן שתו את החלב.

This drill should be done in reverse, also.

M. Substitution-Agreement Drill - Present Tense

Do you drink plain water?   <u>האם אתה שותה מים רגילים?</u>

אתה – הוא – הם – אתן – אתה

End of Tape 10A

263

23.5 The nif'al Conjugation

The present and past tenses of the nif'al were drilled in Unit 19 and should be quite familiar to the student. The future tense is simple in structure, but in verbs whose first or second radical is b, p, or k (כ), the alternation of consonants may be confusing at first. Care should also be taken not to confuse the future tense pattern of the nif'al with that of the pi'el.

In the charts below, the vowel of the prefix in the imperative and future is separated from the consonant of the prefix in order to point out more clearly the differences from the pi'el. Euphonic vowels are in lower case when they occur within a capitalized pattern.

The following charts will have some forms which would make sense only in rather contrived contexts: For example, the imperative /hisager/ "be locked in". However, they are included in order to illustrate the complete conjugation.

As with the pu'al (See Grammar Note 21.8) some forms make sense only in the third person. No general rules can be given to predict these, but the student can usually rely on his own judgment, though English idiom can be misleading. For example, "I will be finished" meaning "I will finish" is rendered in Hebrew in the kal: /egmor/. The nif'al form /egamer/ would be a slang innovation.

(a) Pattern with unchanging root consonants:

			Forms with vowel suffix	
Infinitive:		le h ISAGER		
Imperative:	m.s.	h ISAGER	f.s.	h ISAGR i
	f.pl.	h ISAGÉR na	m.pl.	h ISAGR u
Future:	1 s.	ESAGER		
	2 m.s.	t ISAGER	2 f.s.	t ISAGR i
	3 m.s.	y ISAGER		
	3 f.s.	t ISAGER		
	1 pl.	n ISAGER	2 m.pl.	t ISAGR u
	2 f.pl.	t ISAGÉR na		
	3 f.pl.	t ISAGÉR na	3 m.pl.	y ISAGR u
Present:	m.s.	ni SGAR		
	f.s.	ni SGÉR et		
	m.pl.	ni SGAR im		
	f.pl.	ni SGAR ot		
Past:	1 s.	ni SGÁR ti		
	2.m.s.	ni SGÁR ta		
	2 f.s.	ni SGAR t		
	3 m.s.	ni SGAR	3 f.s.	ni SGeR a
	1 pl.	ni SGÁR nu		
	2 m.pl.	ni SGÁR tem		
	2 f.pl.	ni SGÁR ten	3 pl.	ni SGeR u

Tape 10B

A. Expansion Drill

Instructor: I will hurry.
Student: If I don't hurry I will be locked in the building.

אם לא אמהר, אסגר בבניין.	אני אמהר.
אם לא תמהר, אתה תסגר בבניין.	אתה תמהר.
אם לא תמהרי, את תסגרי בבניין.	את תמהרי.
אם לא ימהר, הוא יסגר בבניין.	הוא ימהר.
אם לא תמהר, היא תסגר בבניין.	היא תמהר.
אם לא נמהר, אנו נסגר בבניין.	אנו נמהר.
אם לא תמהרו, אתם תסגרו בבניין.	אתם תמהרו.
אם לא תמהרנה, אתן תסגרנה בבניין.	אתן תמהרנה.
אם לא ימהרו, הם יסגרו בבניין.	הם ימהרו.
אם לא תמהרנה, הן תסגרנה בבניין.	הן תמהרנה.

B. Transformation Drill – Future to Past

Instructor: He will be locked in the building.
Student: He was locked in the building yesterday.

הוא נסגר אתמול בבניין.	הוא יסגר בבניין.
היא נסגרה אתמול בבניין.	היא תיסגר בבניין.
הם נסגרו אתמול בבניין.	הם יסגרו בבניין.
הן נסגרו אתמול בבניין.	הן תיסגרנה בבניין.
את נסגרת אתמול בבניין.	את תיסגרי בבניין.
נסגרתם אתמול בבניין.	אתם תיסגרו בבניין.
נסגרנו אתמול בבניין.	אנו ניסגר בבניין.
אתה נסגרת אתמול בבניין.	אתה תיסגר בבניין.
נסגרתי אתמול בבניין.	אני אסגר בבניין.

The drill should be done in reverse, also.

(b) Alternating root consonants b, p, k (כ)

The pattern of root consonant alternations in the <u>nif'al</u> is different from that in the <u>kal</u>. In the <u>nif'al</u> all forms have a prefix, and therefore, the handy rule about prefixed and unprefixed forms would not be applicable.

However, if the /ni-/ of the present and past tenses is disregarded, then the rule for the alternations is exactly the reverse of the <u>kal</u>. The following charts will illustrate this more clearly.

(1) <u>Alternating first radicals</u>

	kal		nif'al	
	Prefixed	Unprefixed	Prefixed	Unprefixed (disregard /ni-/)
<u>b/v</u> Future: Past:	yiVdok	Badak	yiBadek	ni Vdak
<u>p/f</u> Future: Past:	yiFtax	Patax	yiPatax *	ni Ftax
<u>k/x</u> Future: Past:	yiXtov	Katav	yiKatev	ni Xtav

*When a third radical <u>'</u> (y) or <u>x</u> (ח) is at the end of a <u>nif'al</u> form, then just the vowel /a/ precedes it: /yipatax/ instead of /yipatéax/.

C. Substitution-Agreement Drill

You will be examined tomorrow morning.　　　　　.אתה תיבדק מחר בבוקר

אני – אתם – הוא – העולים – הן
את – אתן – היא – אנו – אתה

D. Transformation Drill – Past to Future

Instructor: The building was examined yesterday.
Student: The building will be examined tomorrow.

.הבניין ייבדק מחר	.הבניין נבדק אתמול
.אני אבדק מחר	.אני נבדקתי אתמול
.התלמידות תיבדקנה מחר	.התלמידה נבדקה אתמול
.אתה תיבדק מחר	.אתה נבדקת אתמול
.את תיבדקי מחר	.את נבדקת אתמול
.העולים החדשים ייבדקו מחר	.העולים החדשים נבדקו אתמול
.אתם תיבדקו מחר	.אתם נבדקתם אתמול
.אנו ניבדק מחר	.אנו נבדקנו אתמול
.המשפחה תיבדק מחר	.המשפחה ניבדקה אתמול
.אתן תיבדקנה מחר	.אתן נבדקתן אתמול

Do this drill in reverse, also.

E. Transformation Drill – Past to Future

Instructor: The door was opened an hour ago.
Student: The door will be opened in an hour.

.הדלת תיפתח בעוד שעה	.הדלת נפתחה לפני שעה
.המשרד ייפתח בעוד שעה	.המשרד נפתח לפני שעה
.הדלתות תיפתחנה בעוד שעה	.הדלתות ניפתחו לפני שעה
.הדואר ייפתח בעוד שעה	.הדואר נפתח לפני שעה
.משרד התיירות ייפתח בעוד שעה	.משרד התיירות נפתח לפני שעה
.המלונות ייפתחו בעוד שעה	.המלונות נפתחו לפני שעה
.בתי הספר ייפתחו בעוד שעה	.בתי הספר נפתחו לפני שעה

Do this drill in reverse, also.

F. Substitution Drill

The following greetings are used on the Hebrew New Year, Rosh Hashana. The verb forms are Classical Hebrew and are slightly different from the ordinary modern Hebrew forms.

May you be inscribed for a good year.

lešana tova tikatev.　　　　　　　　　　.לשנה טובה תכתב
　　　　　tikatévi　　　　　　　　　　　　תכתבי
　　　　　tikatévu　　　　　　　　　　　　תכתבו
　　　　　tikatávna　　　　　　　　　　　תכתבנה

G. Substitution Drill

Come into the office, please.　　　　　　　.הכנס למשרד, בבקשה
　　　　　　　　　　　　　　　　　　　　　היכנסי
　　　　　　　　　　　　　　　　　　　　　היכנסו
　　　　　　　　　　　　　　　　　　　　　היכנסנה

(In ordinary speech the shortened forms /kanes, kansi/ etc., will often be heard.)

H. Substitution-Agreement Drill

The following drill can be varied by leaving off the phrase /lakáxat et hamixtavim/.

I will go into his office tomorrow to get the letters.

אכנס מחר למשׂרדו לקחת את המכתבים.

1.	sára	שרה תיכנס מחר למשרדו לקחת את המכתבים.	שרה .1
2.	etmol	שרה נכנסה אתמול למשרדו לקחת את המכתבים.	אתמול .2
3.	yaakov	יעקב נכנס אתמול למשרדו לקחת את המכתבים.	יעקב .3
4.	axšav	יעקב נכנס עכשיו למשרדו לקחת את המכתבים.	עכשיו .4
5.	hen	הן נכנסות עכשיו למשרדו לקחת את המכתבים.	הן .5
6.	maxar babóker	הן תיכנסנה מחר בבקר למשרדו לקחת את המכתב	מחר בבקר .6
7.	ánu	אנו ניכנס מחר בבקר למשרדו לקחת את המכתבים.	אנו .7
8.	bašavúa šeavar	נכנסנו בשבוע שעבר למשרדו לקחת את המכתבים.	בשבוע שעבר .8
9.	ani	נכנסתי בשבוע שעבר למשרדו לקחת את המכתבים.	אני .9
10.	hayom	אני נכנס היום למשרדו לקחת את המכתבים.	היום .10
11.	hem	הם נכנסים היום למשרדו לקחת את המכתבים.	הם .11
12.	beod xódeš	הם יכנסו בעוד חודש למשרדו לקחת את המכתבים.	בעוד חודש .12
13.	at	את תכנסי בעוד חודש למשרדו לקחת את המכתבים.	את .13
14.	lifney yomáim.	את נכנסת לפני יומיים למשרדו לקחת את המכתבים.	לפני יומיים .14
15.	hu	הוא נכנס לפני יומיים למשרדו לקחת את המכתבים.	הוא .15
16.	axšav	הוא נכנס עכשיו למשרדו לקחת את המכתבים.	עכשיו .16
17.	aten	אתן נכנסות עכשיו למשרדו לקחת את המכתבים.	אתן .17
18.	bašavúa haba	תכנסנה בשבוע הבא למשרדו לקחת את המכתבים.	בשבוע הבא .18
19.	ata	תיכנס בשבוע הבא למשרדו לקחת את המכתבים.	אתה .19
20.	lifney šaa	נכנסת לפני שעה למשרדו לקחת את המכתבים.	לפני שעה .20
21.	ánu	נכנסנו לפני שעה למשרדו לקחת את המכתבים.	אנו .21
22.	beréga ze	אנו נכנסים ברגע זה למשרדו לקחת את המכתבים.	ברגע זה .22
23.	raxel	רחל נכנסה ברגע זה למשרדו לקחת את המכתבים.	רחל .23
24.	beod šaa	רחל תיכנס בעוד שעה למשרדו לקחת את המכתבים.	בעוד שעה .24
25.	mišpáxat zahávi	משפחת זהבי תיכנס בעוד שעה למשרדו...	משפחת זהבי .25
26.	šilšom	משפחת זהבי נכנסה שלשום למשרדו לקחת את המכתבים.	שלשום .26
27.	yael	יעל נכנסה שלשום למשרדו לקחת את המכתבים.	יעל .27
28.	hayom	יעל נכנסת היום למשרדו לקחת את המכתבים.	היום .28

I. Transformation Drill - Affirmative to Negative

Instructor: Come in, please.
Student: Don't come in. I'll come out.

אל תיכנס. אני אצא.	היכנס בבקשה.
אל תיכנסו. אני אצא.	היכנסו בבקשה.
אל תיכנסי. אני אצא.	היכנסי בבקשה.
אל תיכנסנה. אני אצא.	היכנסנה בבקשה.

J. Expansion Drill (Keep the tense the same in both parts of the response)

Instructor: He went into the house.
Student: He went into the house, but he came right out.

אבל הוא יצא מיד.	הוא נכנס לבית.
אבל יצאנו מיד.	נכנסנו לבית.
אבל אצא מיד.	אכנס לבית.
אבל היא תצא מיד.	היא תיכנס לבית.
אבל יצאתם מיד.	נכנסתם לבית.
אבל יצאו מיד.	הם ייכנסו לבית.
אבל היא יצאה מיד.	היא נכנסה לבית.
אבל הוא יצא מיד.	הוא ייכנס לבית.

K. Expansion Drill (Reverse of Drill J)

Instructor: He came out of the house.
Student: He came out of the house, but he went right back in.

אבל הוא נכנס מיד.	הוא יצא מהבית.
אבל נכנסנו מיד.	יצאנו מהבית.
אבל אכנס מיד.	אצא מהבית.
אבל היא תיכנס מיד.	היא יצאה מהבית.
אבל נכנסתם מיד.	יצאתם מהבית.
אבל הם יכנסו מיד.	הם יצאו מהבית.
אבל נכנסה מיד.	היא יצאה מהבית.
אבל הוא ייכנס מיד.	הוא יצא מהבית.

L. Substitution-Agreement Drill

He'll get together with David this evening.

הוא ייפגש עם דוד הערב.

עטרה – אחה – הם – את – אנו
אתם – אני – אתן – הן – יונתן

M. Transformation Drill

Instructor: He'll meet David this evening.
Student: He'll get together with David this evening.

הוא ייפגש עם דוד הערב.		הוא יפגוש את דוד הערב.
אני אפגש עם דוד הערב.		אני אפגוש את דוד הערב.
שרה תיפגש עם דוד הערב.		שרה תפגוש את דוד הערב.
אנו ניפגש עם דוד הערב.		אנו נפגוש את דוד הערב.
אתה תיפגש עם דוד הערב.		אתה תפגוש את דוד הערב.
הם ייפגשו עם דוד הערב.		הם יפגשו את דוד הערב.
את תיפגשי עם דוד הערב.		את תפגשי את דוד הערב.
מר וויליאמס ייפגש עם דוד הערב.		מר וויליאמס יפגוש את דוד הערב.

N. Transformation Drill – Future to Past

Instructor: We'll get together with Atara in the cafe.
Student: We got together with Atara in the cafe.

נפגשנו עם עטרה בבית הקפה.	אנו ניפגש עם עטרה בבית הקפה.
דוד נפגש עם עטרה בבית הקפה.	דוד ייפגש עם עטרה בבית הקפה.
שרה נפגשה עם עטרה בבית הקפה.	שרה תיפגש עם עטרה בבית הקפה.
הם נפגשו עם עטרה בבית הקפה.	הם ייפגשו עם עטרה בבית הקפה.
אשתי נפגשה עם עטרה בבית הקפה.	אשתי תיפגש עם עטרה בבית הקפה.
הן נפגשו עם עטרה בבית הקפה.	הן תיפגשנה עם עטרה בבית הקפה.

Do this drill in reverse, also.

(2) <u>Alternating second radicals</u>

	<u>kal</u>			nif'al	
	Prefixed	Unprefixed		Prefixed	Unprefixed
					(disregard /ni-/)
<u>b/v</u>					
Future:	yišBor			yišaVer	
Past:		šaVar			ni šBar
<u>p/f</u>					
Future:	yišPox			yišaFex	
Past:		šaFax			ni šPax
<u>k/x</u>					
Future:	yimKor			yimaXer	
		maXar			ni mKar

Some exceptions to the pattern in the column on right ("unprefixed") have already been noted. In Grammar Note 19.5 it was noted that the second radical is /v/, /f/, or /x/ if the prefix is /nee-/ or /no-/. For example:
/neexal/ "eaten" נאכל

O. Substitution-Agreement Drill

The glass will break.   .הכוס תישבר

הבקבוק – הכוסות – הצנצנות
השולחן – הבקבוקים – הצנצנת

P. Substitution-Agreement Drill

The glass broke.   .הכוס נשברה

הבקבוק – הכוסות – הצנצנות
השולחן – הבקבוקים – צנצנת אחת

Q. Transformation Drill – Future to Past

Instructor: The glass will break.
Student: The glass broke.

הכוס נשברה.	הכוס תישבר.
הבקבוקים נשברו.	הבקבוקים יישברו.
השולחנות נשברו.	השולחנות יישברו.
הכוסות נשברו.	הכוסות יתשברנה.
צנצנת אחת נשברה.	צנצנת אחת תישבר.
השולחן הקטן נשבר.	השולחן הקטן יישבר.
הדלת נשברה.	הדלת תישבר.
החלון נשבר.	החלון יישבר.

Do this drill in reverse, also.

R. Transformation Drill

Instructor: Be careful that you don't break the glass.
Student: Be careful that the glass doesn't get broken.

היזהר שהכוס לא תישבר.	היזהר שלא תשבור את הכוס.
היזהר שהבקבוק לא ישבר.	היזהר שלא תשבור את הבקבוק.
היזהר שהכוסות לא תשברנה.	היזהר שלא תשבור את הכוסות.
היזהר שהשולחנות לא ישברו.	היזהר שלא תשבור את השולחנות.

This drill may be varied by putting the first part in the feminine or plural:

היזהרי שלא תשברי את הכוס.

S. Substitution-Agreement Drill

The house will be sold by tomorrow.　　　　　<u>הבית יימכר עד מחר.</u>

התפוחים – החלות – החבילה – הבתים
הספר – הכרטיסים – השולחן – הקופסאות

T. Substitution-Agreement Drill

The house was sold before I got there.　　<u>הבית נמכר לפני שהגעתי לשם.</u>

החלות – הכרטיסים – הספר – הפירות
כל החסה – שתי קופסאות – האשכולית – הלחם

U. Transformation Drill - Future to Past

Instructor: The tickets will be sold today.
Student: The tickets have already been sold.

הכרטיסים נמכרו כבר.	הכרטיסים יימכרו היום.
הספר נמכר כבר.	הספר יימכר היום.
הפירות נמכרו כבר.	הפירות יימכרו היום.
האשכוליות נמכרו כבר.	האשכוליות תימכרנה היום.

Do this drill in reverse, also.

V. Transformation Drill

Instructor: They have sold the vegetables already.
Student: The vegetables have already been sold.

הירקות כבר נמכרו.	כבר מכרו את הירקות.
הגלידה כבר נמכרה.	כבר מכרו את הגלידה.
המקומות הטובים כבר נמכרו.	כבר מכרו את המקומות הטובים.
הבית שרצינו כבר נמכר.	כבר מכרו את הבית שרצינו.
התאנים כבר נמכרו.	כבר מכרו את התאנים.
הכרטיסים הזולים כבר נמכרו.	כבר מכרו את הכרטיסים הזולים.
החלה כבר נמכרה.	כבר מכרו את החלה.

W. Transformation Drill

Instructor: He will sell his house.
Student: His house will be sold.

הבית שלו יימכר.	הוא ימכור את הבית שלו.
הספרים שלו יימכרו.	הוא ימכור את הספרים שלו.
החבילה הגדולה תימכר.	הוא ימכור את החבילה הגדולה.
הכוסות היפות תימכרנה.	הוא ימכור את הכוסות היפות.

(c) Verbs with first radical r, x, (ח), ' or h

If the first root consonant of the verb is r,x (ח), ', or h then the vowel
of the prefix in the infinitive, imperative and future is /e/, rather than
/i/. Examples are:

r
/leherašem/	"to be recorded"	להרשם
/yerašem/	"it will be recorded"	יירשם
/lehera'ot/	"to be seen"	להיראות
/yera'e/	"he will be seen"	ייראה

x
| /lehexašev/ | "to be considered" | לוהחשב |
| /yexašev/ | "he will be considered" | ייחשב |

'
| /lehe'axel/ | "to be eaten" | להאכל |
| /ye'axel/ | "it will be eaten" | ייאכל |

| /lehe'asot/ | "to be done" | להיעשות |
| /ye'ase/ | "it will be done" | ייעשה |

h
| /lehehanot/ | "to enjoy" | להיהנות |
| /yehane/ | "he will enjoy" | ייהנה |

(See 24.4(c), p.282)

In Grammar Note 19.5 it was noted that the present and past tense prefix
of the last three types is /ne-/, rather than /ni-/.

X. Substitution-Agreement Drill

The bread will be eaten first.   הלחם ייאכל תחילה.

הגבינה – הפירות – העוגות – הבשר
הדגים הממולאים – התאנים – החלה

Y. Substitution-Agreement Drill

The cheese was eaten first.   הגבינה נאכלה תחילה.

העוגות – הבשר – הדגים הממולאים
הלחם – הפירות – התאנים – החלה

Z. Transformation Drill - Future to Past

Instructor: The <u>chala</u> will be eaten first.
Student: The <u>chala</u> was eaten first.

.החלה נאכלה תחילה	החלה תיאכל תחילה.
.הבשר נאכל תחילה	הבשר ייאכל תחילה.
.הלחם נאכל תחילה	הלחם ייאכל תחילה.
.הפירות נאכלו תחילה	הפירות ייאכלו תחילה.
.הדגים נאכלו תחילה	הדגים ייאכלו תחילה.
.הגבינות נאכלו תחילה	הגבינות תיאכלנה תחילה.

Do this drill in reverse, also.

AA. Substitution-Agreement Drill

He will be considered a good boss.

הוא ייחשב למנהל טוב.

אני – אתה – את – גב' כספי – אתם
הם – אתן – אנו – הן – מר וויליאמס

BB. Transformation Drill

Instructor: They will consider him a good boss.
Student: He will be considered a good boss.

הוא ייחשב למנהל טוב.	יחשבו אותו למנהל טוב.
אתה תיחשב למנהל טוב.	יחשבו אותך למנהל טוב.
אנו ניחשב למנהלים טובים.	יחשבו אותנו למנהלים טובים.
אני אחשב למנהל טוב.	יחשבו אותי למנהל טוב.
אתם תיחשבו למנהלים טובים.	יחשבו אתכם למנהלים טובים.
הם ייחשבו למנהלים טובים.	יחשבו אותם למנהלים טובים.
היא תיחשב למנהלת טובה.	יחשבו אותה למנהלת טובה.
הן תיחשבנה למנהלות טובות.	יחשבו אותן למנהלות טובות.
אתן תיחשבנה למנהלות טובות.	יחשבו אתכן למנהלות טובות.
את תיחשבי למנהלת טובה.	יחשבו אותך למנהלת טובה.

Do this drill in reverse, also.

(d) <u>lamed hey verbs in the nif'al</u>

The pattern of <u>lamed hey</u> verbs in the <u>nif'al</u> is like all such verbs except that the f.s. present ends in /-t/ rather than /-a/. This was noted in Grammar Note 19.6.

/nir'et/ "is seen, seems"   נראית

It is thus not confused with the 3 m.s. past: /nir'a/ "he was seen" נראה

CC. Substitution-Agreement Drill

You'll look better after the vacation.

אתה תיראה יותר טוב אחרי החופש.

אני – את – אתם – מר כספי – היא
אתן – הם – אנו – הן – אתה

DD. Transformation Drill - Future to Past

    Instructor: You'll look better after the vacation.
    Student: You looked better before the vacation.

אתה תיראה יותר טוב אחרי החופש.

נראית יותר טוב לפני החופש.

היא תיראה יותר טוב אחרי החופש.

היא נראתה יותר טוב לפני החופש.

מר כהן ייראה יותר טוב אחרי החופש.

מר כהן נראה יותר טוב לפני החופש.

אתם תיראו יותר טוב אחרי החופש.

אתם נראיתם יותר טוב לפני החופש.

הן תיראינה יותר טוב אחרי החופש.

הן נראו יותר טוב לפני החופש.

אנו ניראה יותר טוב אחרי החופש.

נראינו יותר טוב לפני החופש.

הם ייראו יותר טוב אחרי החופש.

הם נראו יותר טוב לפני החופש.

אתן תיראינה יותר טוב אחרי החופש.

נראיתן יותר טוב לפני החופש.

אני איראה יותר טוב אחרי החופש.

נראיתי יותר טוב לפני החופש.

את תיראי יותר טוב אחרי החופש.

נראית יותר טוב לפני החופש.

Do this drill in reverse, also.

(e) Verbs with first radical y

    If the first root consonant (as listed for the kal) is y, then it occurs as v (spelled ו) in the nif'al. In the present and past tenses the forms begin with /no-/. See Grammar Note 19.5, part 1(e): /nolad/ "born" נולד

    In the infinitive, imperative, and future this root consonant is pronounced /v/ and the vowel pattern is the same as with regular verbs. For example:

        /yivaled/ "it will be born"   יוולד   root yld   ילד
        /yivada/ "it will be known"   יוודע   root yd'   ידע

    (The future tense of these verbs will not be drilled here, but the drills on the past tense in Unit 19 may be reviewed.)

    The following are drills on the nif'al of various verbs which have occurred in the text.

EE. Expansion Drill

    Instructor: Speak louder.
    Student: Speak louder; then you'll be heard better.

אז תישמע יותר טוב.   דבר בקול.

אז תישמעי יותר טוב.   דברי בקול.

אז תישמעו יותר טוב.   דברו בקול.

אז תישמענה יותר טוב.   דברנה בקול.

FF. Transformation Drill - past to Future

Instructor: What time was the play over?
Student: What time will the play be over?

באיזה שעה ההצגה תיגמר?	באיזה שעה נגמרה ההצגה?
באיזה שעה המכירות תיגמרנה?	באיזה שעה נגמרו המכירות?
באיזה שעה השידור ייגמר?	באיזה שעה נגמר השידור?
באיזה שעה הלימודים ייגמרו?	באיזה שעה נגמרו הלימודים?

GG. Substitution-Agreement Drill

Moshe is being careful not to break the glasses.

משה נזהר לא לשבור את הכוסות.

1. raxel	רחל נזהרת לא לשבור את הכוסות.	1. רחל
2. etmol	רחל נזהרה אתמול לא לשבור את הכוסות.	2. אתמול
3. atem	אתם נזהרים אתמול לא לשבור את הכוסות.	3. אתם
4. axšav	אתם נזהרים עכשיו לא לשבור את הכוסות.	4. עכשיו
5. hem	הם נזהרים עכשיו לא לשבור את הכוסות.	5. הם '
6. maxar	הם ייזהרו מחר לא לשבור את הכוסות.	6. מחר
7. hen	הן תיזהרנה מחר לא לשבור את הכוסות.	7. הן
8. etmol	הן נזהרו אתמול לא לשבור את הכוסות.	8. אתמול
9. hu	הוא נזהר אתמול לא לשבור את הכוסות.	9. הוא
10. maxar	הוא ייזהר מחר לא לשבור את הכוסות.	10. מחר
11. ánu	אנו נזהרים היום לא לשבור את הכוסות.	11. אנו
12. hayom	אנו נזהרים היום לא לשבור את הכוסות.	12. היום
13. dálya	דליה נזהרת היום לא לשבור את הכוסות.	13. דליה
14. etmol	דליה נזהרה אתמול לא לשבור את הכוסות.	14. אתמול
15. aten	אתן נזהרות אתמול לא לשבור את הכוסות.	15. אתן
16. hayom	אתן נזהרות היום לא לשבור את הכוסות.	16. היום
17. mar káspi	מר כספי ניזהר היום לא לשבור את הכוסות.	17. מר כספי
18. etmol	מר כספי ניזהר אתמול לא לשבור את הכוסות.	18. אתמול
19. šošána	שושנה ניזהרה אתמול לא לשבור את הכוסות.	19. שושנה
20. maxar	שושנה תיזהר מחר לא לשבור את הכוסות.	20. מחר
21. hem	הם נזהרים היום לא לשבור את הכוסות.	21. הם
22. hayom	הם נזהרים היום לא לשבור את הכוסות.	22. היום
23. mišpáxat alon	משפחת אלון נזהרת היום לא לשבור את הכוסות.	23. משפחת אלון
24. etmol	משפחת אלון נזהרה אתמול לא לשבור את הכוסות.	24. אתמול
25. ata umoše	אתה ומשה נזהרתם אתמול לא לשבור את הכוסות.	25. אתה ומשה
26. maxar	אתה ומשה תזהרו מחר לא לשבור את הכוסות.	26. מחר
27. haxayalim	החיילים יזהרו מחר לא לשבור את הכוסות.	27. החיילים
28. hayom	החיילים ניזהרים היום לא לשבור את הכוסות.	28. היום

HH. Substitution-Agreement Drill

I will be sent to Israel next year.

אשלח לישראל בשנה הבאה.

עכשיו	את	בשנה שעברה	היא
לפני שבוע	הן	בעוד חודש	הם
מחר	לאה	עכשיו	משה
עכשיו	אתם	לפני חודש	אתה
לפני יומיים	אתן	בקרוב	אני
בעוד יומיים	מרים	עכשיו	יעקב
עכשיו	את	אתמול	גברת כהן

<u>End of Tape 10B</u>

RAPID RESPONSE DRILL

1. למה עטרה מנצחת בדרך כלל?
2. האם הם רצו לשתות משהו?
3. מדוע הם ניגשר למקומות?
4. היכן ישבו, ביציע או באולם?
5. האם המקומות מצאו חן בעיני עטרה?
6. מה אמרה עטרה לדוד?

REVIEW CONVERSATIONS

א: אני רואה עטרה, שנצחת שוב.
ב: זה לא דבר חדש. אני תמיד מנצחת.
א: גם אני אוהבת לנצח, אבל לא הולך לי.
ב: לי יש מזל טוב, לכן אני מנצחת.

ג: בואו ניגש למזנון לשתות משהו.
ד: לא תודה. אני לא צמאה.
ג: אני רוצה לקנות שוקולד.
ד: או ! הפעמון מצלצל. צריך להכנס.
ג: טוב. נלך למזנון בהפסקה.

ה: אתה מעשן?
ו: כן. ואתה?
ה: אני הפסקתי לעשן לפני שבוע.
ו: מצויין! אני לא יכול להפסיק.

ז : איך המקומות?

ח : טובים מאד. אתה רואה טוב?

ז : כן. אני רואה מצויין.

ח : המערכה הראשונה נגמרה.

ז : נצא לעשן סיגריה.

ט : אדוני, שקט בבקשה. אל תפריע.

י : אני מדבר בשקט.

ט : כן. אבל אתה מפריע לנו לשמוע.

י : סליחה. אפסיק לדבר.

כ : גמור לשתות את המיץ.

ל : מה את ממהרת? הפעמון עוד לא צלצל.

כ : כן, אבל הרא יצלצל בעוד כמה דקות.

ל : אם כך, בואי ניגש למקומות שלנו.

מ : משפחת זהבי מכרה את הבית.

נ : למי נמכר הבית?

מ : הבית נמכר למשפחת כהן.

Tape 11A

24.1 Discussing the Show

ATARA

Come, let's go	bóu nigaš	בואו ניגש
to the Kasit	lekasit	ל"כסית"
and get a cup of coffee.	venište kos kafe.	ונשתה כוס קפה.
(name of a coffee shop)	kasit	כסית

DAVID

Good idea.	raayon tov.	רעיון טוב.
We'll see the	nir'e šam	נראה שם
actors there.	et hasaxkanim.	את השחקנים.
player, actor	saxkan (m)	שחקן
player, actress	saxkanit (f)	שחקנית

YONATAN

Atara,	atára,	עטרה,
how did you enjoy	ex nehenet	איך נהנית
the performance?	mehahacaga?	מהההצגה?
he enjoyed, derived benefit	nehena	נהנה

ATARA

I had a very good time.	ani meod neheneti.	אני מאד נהניתי.
The stage setting	hatif'ora	התפאורה
was wonderful,	hayta maksima,	היתה מקסימה,
and the actors	vehasaxkanim	והשחקנים
were good.	hayu tovim.	היו טובים.
stage setting	tif'ora (f)	תפאורה
wonderful, fascinating	maksim (m.s.)	מקסים

YONATAN

I enjoyed it, too.	gam ani neheneti	גם אני נהניתי
especially	bifrat	בפרט
Miriam Narkis.	mimiryam narkis.	ממרים נרקיס.
detail	prat (m)	פרט
especially	bifrat	בפרט

DAVID

I'm not crazy	ani lo mištagéa	אני לא משתגע
about her.	axaréha.	אחריה.
She's old,	hi zkena	היא זקנה
and her voice	vehakol šela	והקול שלה
is (too) low.	namux.	נמוך.
he went crazy	hištagéa	השתגע
after me	axaray	אחרי
old	zaken (m.s.)	זקן
low, short (height)	namux (m.s.)	נמוך

ATARA

You're sorry	ata mitxaret	אתה מתחרט
that you went?	šehaláxta?	שהלכת?
he regretted	hitxaret	התחרט

277

DAVID

No,	lo.	לא.
But I would have	ax haíti	אך הייתי
enjoyed better	nehene yoter	נהנה יותר
a good movie.	miséret tov.	מסרט טוב.
I would have enjoyed	haíti nehene	הייתי נהנה

ATARA

Yonatan,	yónatan,	יונתן,
I'm sure	ani btuxa	אני בטוחה
that your parents	šehahorim šelxa	שההורים שלך
would have enjoyed	hayu nehenim	היו נהנים
the show very much.	meod mehahacaga.	מאד מההצגה.
sure, certain	batúax (m.s.)	בטוח

YONATAN

Yes, it's too bad that	ken, xaval	כן. חבל
this was	šezu hayta	שזו היתה
the last performance.	hahacaga haaxrona.	ההצגה האחרונה.
it's too bad that	xaval še-	חבל ש-
this	zu (f)	זו

24.2 ADDITIONAL VOCABULARY

The show was	hahacaga hayta	ההצגה היתה
boring.	mešaamémet.	משעממת.
he bored (s.o.)	šiamém	שיעמם
I was bored	hištaamámti	השתעממתי
to death.	ad mávet.	עד מות.
he became bored	hištaamem	השתעמם
death	mávet (m)	מות
They didn't put any	lo natnu	לא נתנו
life into the play.	xayim lahacaga.	חיים להצגה.
life	xayim (m.pl.)	חיים
I got interested	hit'anyánti	התעניינתי
in the stage setting.	batif'ora.	בתפאורה.
he became interested	hit'anyen	התעניין
Let's go away	bo nitraxek	בוא נתרחק
from the snack bar.	mehamiznon.	מהמזנון.
he withdrew	hitraxek	התרחק
Let's go near	bo nitkarev	בוא נתקרב
the stage.	labama.	לבמה.
he approached	hitkarev	התקרב
stage	bama (f)	במה

24.3 VOCABULARY DRILL

A. Substitution-Agreement Drill   /zaken/   "aged"   זקן

(In the feminine and plural forms the initial cluster /zk-/ is pronounced /sk-/)

He's not so old.

הוא לא כל כך זקן.

גב׳ כהן – המנהל ואשתו
השחקניות בסרט – בעלה של גב׳ כהן

B. Substitution-Agreement Drill   /namux/   "short, low"   נמוך

The table is low.

השולחן נמוך.

הבתים ברמת-גן – אשתו של יוסף
העוגות שאפתה – החלון במשרד שלי

C. Substitution-Agreement Drill

I'm sure it's all right.

אני בטוח שזה בסדר.

את – המנהל החדש – אנו
הן – אתם – מי – הוא

D. Expansion Drill

Instructor: The Dan Hotel is on Hayarkon Street.
Student: I'm certain that the Dan Hotel is on Hayarkon Street.

1. אני בטוח ש מלון דן נמצא ברחוב הירקון.

2. אני בטוח ש נשמח מאד.

3. אני בטוח ש שבע ושלושים מתאים.

4. אני בטוח ש רמת גן תמצא חן בעיניך.

5. אני בטוח ש אתה שחיין טוב.

6. אני בטוח ש נהנה מאד.

7. אני בטוח ש בקולנוע "מוגרבי" מציגים סרט טוב.

8. אני בטוח ש אשתו מדברת עברית.

9. אני בטוח ש כבר מאוחר מאד.

The instructor may vary this drill further by having the students respond with plural forms /ánu btuxim/ or /ánu btuxot/, or by varying the subject in the response sentence. For example: /xána btuxa šemalon dan nimca birxov hayarkon./

E. Substitution Drill   /axarey/   "after"   אחרי

They arrived after me.

הם הגיעו אחרי.
אחריך
אחריך
אחריו
אחריה
אחרינו
אחריכם
אחריכן
אחריהם
אחריהן

F. Expansion Drill

Instructor: I arrived first.
Student: I arrived first and they came after me.

אני הגעתי קודם.	והם באו אחרי.
אתה הגעת קודם.	והם באו אחריך.
מרים הגיעה קודם.	והם באו אחריה.
הנשים הגיעו קודם.	והם באו אחריהן.
אנו הגענו קודם.	והם באו אחרינו.
את הגעת קודם.	והם באו אחריך.
אתם הגעתם קודם.	והם באו אחריכם.
דוד הגיע קודם.	והם באו אחריו.
אתן הגעתן קודם.	והם באו אחריכן.
התלמידים הגיעו קודם.	והם באו אחריהם.

24.4 VERB DRILLS

(a) /nigaš/ "he approached"   נגש

This verb is unusual in that it is conjugated in the <u>kal</u> in the infinitive imperative, and future, and in the <u>nif'al</u> in the present and past tenses. The infinitive is /lagéšet/   לגשת.

A. Substitution Drill

Come to the window.   גש אל החלון.
                                                         גשי
(Some speakers say / geš, géšna /)   גשו
                                                         גשנה

B. Transformation Drill - Future to Past

Instructor: He'll come to the embassy.
Student: He came to the embassy.

הוא ניגש אל השגרירות.	הוא יגש אל השגרירות.
אתה ניגשת אל השגרירות.	אתה תיגש אל השגרירות.
אתם ניגשתם אל השגרירות.	אתם תיגשו אל השגרירות.
אנו ניגשנו אל השגרירות.	אנו ניגש אל השגרירות.
את ניגשת אל השגרירות.	את תיגשי אל השגרירות.
הם ניגשו אל השגרירות.	הם ייגשו אל השגרירות.
אני ניגשתי אל השגרירות.	אני אגש אל השגרירות.
הן ניגשו אל השגרירות.	הן תיגשנה אל השגרירות.
היא ניגשה אל השגרירות.	היא תיגש אל השגרירות.
אתן ניגשתן אל השגרירות.	אתן תיגשנה אל השגרירות.

Do this drill in reverse, also.

C. Substitution-Agreement Drill

She is coming to the window.   <u>היא ניגשת אל החלון.</u>

הם – אנו – הנשים – דודו
דודתי – התלמידים – אשתך

(b) /ši'amem/ "he bored (some one)"   שיעמם

The root of this verb has four consonants š'mm.   All forms of this verb have the consonant sequence / -'m-/, and therefore the /a/ is inserted. The juncture /'/ is often replaced by a smooth transition: /šiamem/ as well as /ši'amem/.

D. Substitution Drill

Don't bore us so much.   אל תשעמם אותנו כל כך.
                                                         תשעממי
                                                         תשעממו
                                                         תשעממנה

E. Substitution-Agreement Drill

If you continue this way,
you'll bore them to death.

אם תמשיך כך, תשעמם אותם עד מות.

נמשיך   (נשעמם)
תמשיכי   (תשעממי)
תמשכנה   (תשעממנה)
ימשיך   (ישעמם)
תמשיכו   (תשעממו)
ימשיכו   (ישעממו)
אמשיך   (אשעמם)

F. Substitution-Agreement Drill

He's very boring.

הוא משעמם מאד.

היא – הם – הן – הוא

G. Substitution-Agreement Drill

I think you bored them.

אני חושב שאתה שעממת אותם.

שאת – שאתם – שהשחקנים – שהוא – שאתן
שהשחקניות החדשות – שאנו – שאני – שאתה

(c) /nehena/ "he enjoyed"   נהנה

Most speakers conjugate the infinitive and future tense of /nehena/ in the
<u>kal</u> instead of in the <u>nif'al</u>. The difference is mainly in the vowel of the
unstressed syllable.

	kal	nif'al
Infinitive:	lehenot	lehehanot
Future: 1 s.	ehene	ehane
2 m.s.	tehene$_{etc.,}$	tehane$_{etc.,}$

H. Substitution-Agreement Drill

You'll enjoy the hike very much.

תהנה מאד מהטיול.

התלמידים – בעלך – אתם – את – אני
אתן – היא – אנו – הן – אתה

I. Substitution-Agreement Drill

I enjoy films in Hebrew.

אני נהנה מסרטים בעברית.

אשתי – התלמידים – הנשים – המורה

J. Response Drill

Instructor: How did you enjoy the movie?
Student: I enjoyed the movie very much.

נהניתי מאד מהסרט.   איך נהנית מהסרט?
נהנינו מאד מהסרט.   איך נהניתם מהסרט?
אשתי נהנתה מאד מהסרט.   איך נהנתה אשתך מהסרט?
משה נהנה מאד מהסרט.   איך נהנה משה מהסרט?
התלמידים נהנו מאד מהסרט.   איך נהנו התלמידים מהסרט?

24.5 The hitpa'el Conjugation

In English the distinction between transitive and intransitive verbs, between active, passive, and reflexive verbs is often made by changing the structure of the sentence rather than the form of the verb. For example, in the sentences "He cooled the coffee" and "The coffee cooled" the verb forms are identical, but in the first sentence there is a subject-verb-object construction, and in the second sentence just a subject-verb construction. The verb in the first sentence is usually said to be "transitive", that is, having a direct object; and the verb in the second is said to be "intransitive".

Sometimes the verb forms are quite different and without any obvious relationship. For example, "to bring (something) near" and "to approach" do not show any overt relationship, though the latter may be paraphrased as "to bring oneself near". This latter construction is said to be "reflexive."

In Hebrew the intransitive, reflexive and passive counterparts of verbs are often conjugated in the hitpa'el.

/kibel/	"he accepted"
/hitkabel/	"he was accepted"
/ciref/	"he joined (two things together)"
/hictaref/	"he joined (himself to other people)"
/šina/	"he changed (something)"
/hištana/	"he changed, became different"

The characteristic feature of this binyan is the prefix /hit-/. In the future and present tenses the /h-/ is dropped after other prefixes.

There are no root consonant alternations in the hitpa'el .

(a) Conjugation of a regular verb

Infinitive:		le hit kašer	Forms with vowel suffix	
Future:	1 s.	et kašer		
	2 m.s.	t it kašer		
			2 f.s.	t it kašr i
	3 m.s.	y it kašer		
	3 f.s.	t it kašer		
	1 pl.	n it kašer		
	2 f.pl.	t it kašér na	2 m.pl.	t it kašr u
	3 f.pl.	t it kašér na	3 m.pl.	y it kašr u
Present:	m.s.	m it kašer	m.pl.	m it kašr im
	f.s.	m it kašér et	f.pl.	m it kašr ot
Past:	1 s.	hit kašár ti		
	2 m.s.	hit kašár ta		
	2 f.s.	hit kašár t		
	3 m.s.	hit kašer		
			3 f.s.	hit kašr a
	1 pl.	hit kašár nu		
	2 m.pl.	hit kašár tem		
	2 f.pl.	hit kašár ten		
			3 pl.	hit kašr u

(In the future 1 s. some speakers use the prefix /a-/: /atkašer/.)

Some verbs have the prefix /nit-/ in the past tense. These verbs are more clearly the passive counterparts of pi'el verbs, but there is no general rule for predicting which verbs will have /nit-/ instead of /hit-/.

/mina/   "he appointed"   מינה
/nitmana/   "he was appointed"   נתמנה

Some verbs have either possibility, depending on the context:
/hitkabel/   "he was received"   התקבל
/nitkabel/   "he was received"   נתקבל

/hitkabel/ is usually followed by a prepositional phrase such as "at the university, for an interview, etc.," and /nitkabel/ is usually followed by /al yedey/ "by" : /hu nitkabel al yedey hamenahel/ "he was received by the director."

Verbs which have the stem vowels /-o-e-/ in the pi'el will have /-o-e-/ in the hitpa'el, also.

/konen/   "he established"   כונן
/hitkonen/   "he set himself up (to do something)"   התכונן

The /t/ of the prefix coalesces with a first radical t or d.

(b) Verbs with first radical s, š, c, z

When the first root consonant is s, š or c, then the /t/ of the hitpa'el prefix follows it:

/his tader/	"he got along"	הסתדר	sdr	סדר
/hiš tagéa/	"he went crazy"	השתגע	šg'	שגע
/hic taref/	"he joined"	הצטרף	crf	צרף

[Note that the /t/ of the prefix is spelled ט when preceded by /c/ צ].

When the first root consonant is z then the /t/ of the prefix not only follows the /z/ but becomes /d/:

/hiz damen/   "he had the opportunity"   הזדמן
/hiz daken/   "he grew old"   הזדקן

A. Substitution-Agreement Drill

I was impressed by their program of studies.   .התפעלתי מתוכנית הלימודים שלהם

ánu	אנו התפעלנו מתוכנית הלימודים שלהם.	אנו .1
hu	הוא התפעל מתוכנית הלימודים שלהם.	הוא .2
ata	אתה התפעלת מתוכנית הלימודים שלהם.	אתה .3
atára	עטרה התפעלה מתוכנית הלימודים שלהם.	עטרה .4
išti veani	אשתי ואני התפעלנו מתוכנית הלימודים שלהם.	אשתי ואני .5
hayoec	היורעץ התפעל מתוכנית הלימודים שלהם.	היורעץ .6
hatalmidim	התלמידים התפעלו מתוכנית הלימודים שלהם.	התלמידים .7
hamenahel veata	המנהל ואתה התפעלתם מתוכנית הלימודים שלהם.	המנהל ואתה .8
at vedálya	את ודליה התפעלתן מתוכנית הלימודים שלהם.	את ודליה .9
ani	אני התפעלתי מתוכנית הלימודים שלהם.	אני .10
hem	הם התפעלו מתוכנית הלימודים שלהם.	הם .11
at	את התפעלת מתוכנית הלימודים שלהם.	את .12
atem	אתם התפעלתם מתוכנית הלימודים שלהם.	אתם .13

B. Substitution-Agreement Drill

(Use the underlined words as cues.)

I think you'll regret it if you don't go.

אני חושב שתחחרט	אם	‫לא תלך.‬
אני חושב שנתחרט	אם	‫לא נלך.‬
אני חושב שיתחרט	אם	‫לא ילך.‬
אני חושב שיתחרטו	אם	‫לא ילכו.‬
אני חושב שתחחרטנה	אם	‫לא תלכנה.‬
אני חושב שאתחרט	אם	‫לא אלך.‬
אני חושב שתתחרטו	אם	‫לא תלכו.‬
אני חושב שתתחרטי	אם	‫לא תלכי.‬

C. Expansion Drill

Instructor: Tell him when you're going.
Student: Tell him when you're going, and he'll join you.

אמור לו מתי תלך	‫והוא יצטרף אליך.‬
אמור לנו מתי תלך	‫ונצטרף אליך.‬
אמור להם מתי תלך	‫ויצטרפו אליך.‬
אמור לה מתי תלך	‫ותצטרף אליך.‬
אמור להן מתי תלך	‫ותצטרפנה אליך.‬
אמור לי מתי תלך	‫ואצטרף אליך.‬

D. Substitution-Agreement Drill

He calls his family every evening.   ‫הוא מתקשר עם המשפחה כל ערב.‬

‫התלמידים בבית הספר – שרה – שרה ולאה – הוא‬

(c) lamed hey verbs in the hitpa'el

In the past tense the first and second person forms have the vowel /e/
before the pronoun suffixes:

/hištanéti/ "I changed" ‫השתניתי‬

Infinitive:		lehištanot	
Future:	1 s.	eštane	
	2 m.s.	tištane, etc.	
Present:	m.s.	mištane	
	f.s.	mištana, etc. (Many speakers use the f.s. form /mištanet/)	
Past:	1 s.	hištanéti, etc.	
	3 m.s.	hištana	
	3 f.s.	hištanta	
	3 pl.	hištanu	

E. Substitution-Agreement Drill

You haven't changed a bit.

אתה לא השתנית בכלל.

בעלך – אתם – אשתך – הם
שרה ועטרה – אתן – את – אתה

F. Substitution-Agreement Drill

They will be appointed to the Embassy in Tel Aviv.

הם יתמנו לשגרירות בתל אביב.

מר ויליאמס – גב' ג'ונס – אחה
הן – את – אני – אתן – הם

G. Transformation Drill – <u>pi'el</u> to <u>hitpa'el</u>

Instructor: The program didn't interest me.
Student: I wasn't interested in the program.

לא התענייני בתוכנית.	התוכנית לא עניינה אותי.
לא התענייננו בתוכנית.	התוכנית לא עניינה אותם.
לא התענייננו בתוכנית.	התוכנית לא עניינה אותנו.
לא התענייניה בתוכנית.	התוכנית לא עניינה אותה.
לא התעניינו בתוכנית.	התוכנית לא עניינה אותך.
לא התענייין בתוכנית.	התוכנית לא עניינה אותו.

Do this drill in reverse, also.

H. Transformation Drill

Instructor: I was cold outside.
Student: I caught cold outside.

התקררתי בחוץ.	היה לי קר בחוץ.
התקררנו בחוץ.	היה לנו קר בחוץ.
התקררו בחוץ.	היה להן קר בחוץ.
התקרר בחוץ.	היה לו קר בחוץ.
התקררו בחוץ.	היה להם קר בחוץ.
התקררה בחוץ.	היה לה קר בחוץ.
התקררת בחוץ.	היה לך קר בחוץ.
התקררתם בחוץ.	היה לכם קר בחוץ.

I. Transformation Drill

Instructor: We were tired from the hike.
Student: We got tired hiking.

התעייפנו בטיול.	היינו עייפים מהטיול.
הוא התעייף בטיול.	הוא היה עייף מהטיול.
שרה התעייפה בטיול.	שרה היתה עייפה מהטיול.
התעייפתם בטיול.	הייתם עייפים מהטיול.
התעייפתי בטיול.	הייתי עייף מהטיול.
הן התעייפו בטיול.	הן היו עייפות מהטיול.

J. Transformation Drill

Instructor: The director will receive him tomorrow.
Student: He will be received tomorrow.

הוא יתקבל מחר.	המנהל יקבל אותו מחר.
אנו נתקבל מחר.	המנהל יקבל אותנו מחר.
אתה תתקבל מחר.	המנהל יקבל אותך מחר.
אתם תתקבלו מחר.	המנהל יקבל אתכם מחר.
התלמידים יתקבלו מחר.	המנהל יקבל את התלמידים מחר.
אני אתקבל מחר.	המנהל יקבל אותי מחר.
הן תתקבלנה מחר.	המנהל יקבל אותן מחר.
את תתקבלי מחר.	המנהל יקבל אותך מחר.
אתן תתקבלנה מחר.	המנהל יקבל אתכן מחר.
היא תתקבל מחר.	המנהל יקבל אותה מחר.

K. Transformation Drill - <u>pi'el to hitpa'el</u>

Instructor: School bores me.
Student: I get bored in school.

אני משתעמם בבית הספר.	בית הספר משעמם אותי.
היא משתעממת בבית הספר.	בית הספר משעמם אותה.
אנו משתעממים בבית הספר.	בית הספר משעמם אותנו.
התלמידות משתעממות בבית הספר.	בית הספר משעמם את התלמידות.

Do this drill in reverse, also.

L. Substitution Drill

Go away from the window.

התרחק מהחלון.
התרחקי
התרחקו
התרחקנה

M. Expansion Drill

Instructor: I'm going out for a walk.
Student: I'm going out for a walk, but I won't go far from the house.

אבל לא אתרחק מהבית.	אני אצא לטייל,
אבל לא יתרחק מהבית.	הוא ייצא לטייל,
אבל לא תתרחקנה מהבית.	הן תצאנה לטייל,
אבל לא יתרחקו מהבית.	משה ומרים יצאו לטייל,
אבל לא נתרחק מהבית.	אנו נצא לטייל,
אבל היא לא תתרחק מהבית.	רבקה תצא לטייל,

N. Expansion Drill

Instructor: I don't let him go out.
Student: I don't let him go out because he goes far from the house.

כי הוא מתרחק מהבית.	אני לא נותן לו לצאת
כי הם מתרחקים מהבית.	אני לא נותן להם לצאת
כי היא מתרחקת מהבית.	אני לא נותן לה לצאת
כי הן מתרחקות מהבית.	אני לא נותן להן לצאת
כי אתה מתרחק מהבית.	אני לא נותן לך לצאת
כי אתם מתרחקים מהבית.	אני לא נותן לכם לצאת

O. Expansion Drill

Instructor: We didn't see the ship.
Student: We didn't see the ship until we came close to the port.

לא ראינו את האוניה   עד שהתקרבנו לנמל.
הוא לא ראה את האוניה   עד שהתקרב לנמל.
הם לא ראו את האוניה   עד שהתקרבו לנמל.
לא ראיתי את האוניה   עד שהתקרבתי לנמל.
היא לא ראתה את האוניה עד שהתקרבה לנמל.

24.6 Verbal Noun of the hitpa'el

The verbal noun of the hitpa'el has the pattern $/hitC_1aC_2C_3ut/$.

/hitrašmut/	"being impressed"	התרשמות
/hitkarvut/	"approaching"	התקרבות
/hitraxakut/	"estrangement"	התרחקות

These nouns are feminine and have the plural pattern $/hitC_1aC_2C_3uyot/$.

/hitkašruyot/	"relations, connections"	התקשרויות
/hitrašmuyot/	"impressions"	התרשמויות

When the first root consonant is s, š, c, or z the /t/ (or /d/) of the prefix follows.

/hictalvut/	"intersection"	הצטלבות
/hizdamnut/	"opportunity"	הזדמנות

RAPID RESPONSE DRILL

1. לאן רצתה עטרה לגשת אחרי ההצגה?

2. את מי הם ראו שם?

3. איך נהנתה עטרה מההצגה?

4. ממה בפרט נהנתה עטרה?

5. ממי נהנה יונתן?

6. למה דוד לא אוהב את מרים נרקיס?

7. האם דוד מתחרט שהלך להצגה?

8. מי היה נהנה מאד מההצגה, לדעתה של עטרה?

9. מדוע ההורים של יונתן אינם יכולים ליהנות מההצגה?

REVIEW CONVERSATIONS

א: בואו ניגש לכסית.

ב: למה לכסית?

א: נשתה כוס קפה ונראה את השחקנים.

ב: הרי שתית קפה במזנון.

א: אז נשתה עוד כוס קפה.

ג: איך נהנית מהההצגה, רחל?

ד: אני לא נהניתי.

ג: מדוע?

ד: אני לא אוהבת את מרים נרקיס.

ג: אומרים שהיא שחקנית טובה מאד.

ד: כן. היא היתה פעם. כשהיא היתה צעירה.

ג: גם אני לא מתפעל ממנה.

ה: התפאורה נהדרת.

ו: כן. יפה מאד.

ה: אבל ההצגה משעממת.

ו: למה? אני דווקא נהנה מאד.

ז: משה ומרים נראים עייפים מאד.

ח: הם עייפים כי ההצגה משעממת.

ז: אל תגזים. ההצגה לא רעה.

ח: היא לא רעה אך גם לא טובה.

ט: ראינו את יעקב צור.

י: איפה הוא יושב? אני לא רואה אותו.

ט: שם, בשורה השניה.

י: איפה? בצד השמאלי?

ט: כן. התקרבו קצת, אז תראו אותו.

כ: בוא אתנו מחר לקולנוע.

ל: לא תודה. אני לא חושב שאהנה מהסרט.

כ: בוא, אודד כך תתחרט שלא הלכת.

ל: אני לא אתחרט.

מ: הקפה שלך כבר התקרד.

נ: כן. עד שהספקתי לשתות אותו הוא כבר היה קר.

מ: אמור למלצר שיתן לך כוס קפה אחרת.

נ: לא. אני עייף. אשתה קפה בבית.

25.1 Leaving the Cafe

ATARA

David,	david,	דוד
Let's go home.	bo nelex habáyta.	בוא נלך הביתה.
It's late.	kvar meuxar.	כבר מאוחר.
(to) home	habáyta	הביתה

DAVID

Wait a while.	xaki réga.	חכי רגע.
I want to drink	ani roce lištot	אני רוצה לשתות
another cup of coffee.	od kos kafe.	עוד כוס קפה.

ATARA

No. Come.	lo. bo.	לא. בוא.
We have to get up	carix lakum	צריך לקום
early tomorrow.	maxar mukdam.	מחר מוקדם.

YONATAN

You're leaving already?	atem kvar holxim?	אתם כבר הולכים?
It's still early.	od mukdam.	עוד מוקדם.

ATARA

What do you mean 'early' !	ma mukdam!	מה מוקדם?!
It's midnight.	kvar xacot.	כבר חצות.
midnight	xacot	חצות

YONATAN

I'm going to stay	ani ešaer	אני אשאר
a while longer.	od kcat.	עוד קצת.
Maybe I'll meet	ulay efgoš	אולי אפגוש
some friends.	xaverim.	חברים.
he stayed	niš'ar	נשאר
friend	xaver (m)	חבר

DAVID

As you wish.	kirconxa.	כרצונך.
How much is the bill?	ma haxešbon.	מה החשבון?
bill, account	xešbon (m)	חשבון

YONATAN

Don't worry.	al tid'ag	אל תדאג.
It's on my bill.	ze al xešboni.	זה על חשבוני.
he worried	da'ag	דאג

DAVID

Thank you very much.	toda raba.	.תודה רבה
So long, Yonatan.	šalom yónatan.	.שלום יונתן
Sleep well.	leyl menuxa.	.ליל מנוחה
rest	menuxa (f)	מנוחה

YONATAN

Good night.	láyla tov laxem.	.לילה טוב לכם
Thanks for the	toda avur	תודה עבור
pleasant company.	haxevra haneima.	.החברה הנעימה
night	láyla (m)	לילה
company	xevra (f)	חברה

End of Tape 11A

Tape 11B

25.2 ADDITIONAL VOCABULARY

It's 3 o'clock	hašaa šaloš	השעה שלוש
in the morning.	lifnot bóker.	.לפנות בוקר
near, before	lifnot	לפנות
I'm tired.	ani ayef.	.אני עייף
tired	ayef (m.s.)	עייף
I want to sleep.	ani roce lišon.	.אני רוצה לישון
he slept	yašan	ישן
I'm falling asleep.	ani nirdam.	.אני נרדם
he fell asleep	nirdam	נרדם
I'm dozing.	ani menamnem.	.אני מנמנם
he dozed	nimnem	נמנם
I wake up	ani mit'orer	אני מתעורר
at dawn.	im šáxar.	.עם שחר
he woke up	hit'orer	התעורר
dawn	šáxar (m)	שחר
Pleasant dreams.	xalomot neimim.	.חלומות נעימים
dream	xalom (m)	חלום

25.3 VOCABULARY DRILLS

A. Substitution-Agreement Drill /xaver/ "friend" חבר

He's a good friend of ours.

הוא חבר טוב שלנו.

היא – הם – השחקניות בהצגה החדשה   הן – הוא

B. Substitution-Agreement Drill /ayef/ "tired" עייף

Are you tired?

האם אתה עייף?

אתם – אתן – את – הוא

292

25.4 VERB DRILLS

(a) /niš'ar/   "he remained"   נשאר

The vowel /a/ is inserted in forms which would otherwise have the sequence
/-'r-/: For example: f.s. imv. /hiša'ari/.

A. Substitution Drill

Stay here. I'll go.   .השאר כאן. אני אלך
                                                      השארי
                                                      השארו
                                                      השארנה

B. Substitution-Agreement Drill

How much longer will we stay?   ?עוד כמה זמן נישאר

                                    הם – אתה – הרופא – את – הן
                                    היא – אתם – אתן – אנו

C. Substitution-Agreement Drill

She stays late every Monday and Thursday.   .היא נשארת מאוחר כל שני וחמישי

                                    אני – המנהל – התלמידים – הן – היא

D. Transformation Drill - Future to Past

Instructor: I'll stay a little while longer.
Student: I stayed a while longer and then I left.

.נשארתי עוד קצת ואז יצאתי   .אני אשאר עוד קצת
.הם נשארו עוד קצת ואז יצאו   .הם ישארו עוד קצת
.אנו נשארנו עוד קצת ואז יצאנו   .אנו נישאר עוד קצת
.אתם נשארתם עוד קצת ואז יצאתם   .אתם תישארו עוד קצת
.הן נישארו עוד קצת ואז יצאו   .הן תישארנה עוד קצת
.את נשארת עוד קצת ואז יצאת   .את תישארי עוד קצת
.היא נשארה עוד קצת ואז יצאה   .היא תישאר עוד קצת
.הוא נשאר עוד קצת ואז יצא   .הוא ישאר עוד קצת

(b) /da'ag/ "he worried"   דאג

The second root consonant of this verb is ', also. The future stem vowel
is /a/ - /tid'ag/. The infinitive is /lid'og/.

E. Substitution Drill

Don't worry about us.   .אל תדאג לנו
                                                    תדאגי
                                                    תדאגו
                                                    תדאגנה

F. Substitution-Agreement Drill

He worries about each and every student.   .הוא דואג לכל תלמיד ותלמיד

                                    הם – המנהלת – הן – המורה

293

G. Transformation Drill - Future to Past

     Instructor: I'll see about getting the tickets.
     Student: I took care of getting the tickets.

אני דאגתי לקנות את הכרטיסים.	אני אדאג לקנות את הכרטיסים.
את דאגת לקנות את הכרטיסים.	את תדאגי לקנות את הכרטיסים.
אנו דאגנו לקנות את הכרטיסים.	אנו נדאג לקנות את הכרטיסים.
הן דאגו לקנות את הכרטיסים.	הן תדאגנה לקנות את הכרטיסים.
אתה דאגת לקנות את הכרטיסים.	אתה תדאג לקנות את הכרטיסים.
חנה דאגה לקנות את הכרטיסים.	חנה תדאג לקנות את הכרטיסים.
הם דאגו לקנות את הכרטיסים.	הם ידאגו לקנות את הכרטיסים.
מי דאג לקנות את הכרטיסים?	מי ידאג לקנות את הכרטיסים?

(c) /yašan/ "he slept"   ישן

     The future of this verb has the stem vowel /a/ and is regular except for
a couple of minor features: The prefix and first root consonant sometimes
coalesce: /tiyšan → tišan/. This difference is hard for an English speaker
to hear and is unimportant, anyway. The first person singular is /iyšan/ "I
will sleep".

     The present tense is /yašen/, and the feminine is /yešena/. This is
similar to /saméax ~ smexa/, which has been treated as an adjective. Many
speakers, however, use the present tense forms /yošen ~ yošénet/ based on analogy
with other kal verbs.

H. Substitution-Agreement Drill

     He will sleep at the Zahavis'.   <u>הוא יישן אצל הזהבים.</u>

אני – אתם – משפחתי – את – הן
אנו – אתן – אתה – הם – הוא

I. Substitution-Agreement Drill

     How many hours do you usually sleep?   <u>כמה שעות אתה ישן בדרך כלל?</u>

אתם – הן – את – הוא

J. Substitution-Agreement Drill

     She slept all night.   <u>היא ישנה כל הלילה.</u>

אני – הם – אתה – הוא – את

(d)   /nirdam/ "he fell asleep"   נירדם

K. Expansion Drill

     Instructor: Give him some rest.
     Student: Give him some rest; he'll fall asleep right away.

הוא ירדם מיד.	תן לו מנוחה.
אני ארדם מיד.	תן לי מנוחה.
הם ירדמו מיד.	תן להם מנוחה.
היא תרדם מיד.	תן לה מנוחה.
הן תרדמנה מיד.	תן להן מנוחה.
אנו נרדם מיד.	תן לנו מנוחה.

L. Expansion Drill

Instructor: He studies the whole night.
Student: He studies the whole night, and in the morning he falls asleep
in class.

ובבוקר הוא נרדם בכתה.	הוא לומד כל הלילה
ובבוקר היא נרדמת בכתה.	היא לומדת כל הלילה
ובבוקר הם נרדמים בכתה.	התלמידים לומדים כל הלילה
ובבוקר הן נרדמות בכתה.	הן לומרות כל הלילה

M. Expansion Drill

Instructor: I was bored.
Student: I was bored and fell asleep.

ונרדמתי.	השתעממתי
ונרדמנו.	השתעממנו
ונרדם.	הוא השתעמם
ונרדמה.	היא השתעממה
ונרדמו.	כולם השתעממו

(e) /hit'orer/ "he woke up"   התעורר

N. Substitution Drill

Wake up, it's late !

התעורר, השעה מאוחרת !
התעוררי
התעוררו
התעוררנה

O. Expansion Drill

Instructor: I don't have an alarm clock.
Student: I don't have an alarm clock, but I get up early anyway.

אבל אני בכל זאת מתעורר מוקדם.	אין לי שעון מעורר
אבל אנו בכל זאת מתעוררים מוקדם.	אין לנו שעון מעורר
אבל היא בכל זאת מתעוררת מוקדם.	אין לה שעון מעורר
אבל הן בכל זאת מתעוררות מוקדם.	אין להן שעון מעורר

P. Response Drill

Instructor: When did you get up this morning?
Student: I got up at dawn.

התעוררתי עם שחר.	מתי התעוררת הבוקר?
התעוררנו עם שחר.	מתי התעוררתם הבוקר?
הוא התעורר עם שחר.	מתי התעורר בעלך הבוקר?
היא התעוררה עם שחר.	מתי התעוררה אשתך הבוקר?

25.5 The hif'il Conjugation

The hif'il conjugation has the basic meaning "to cause (whatever the root means) to happen". This is evident to an English speaker in many cases:

/pa'al/	"he worked"	פעל
/hif'il/	"he caused to work, put into operation, etc."	הפעיל
/yada/	"he knew"	ידע
/hodia/	"he informed (caused to know)"	הודיע
/gadal/	"he grew"	גדל
/higdil/	"he enlarged"	הגדיל
/katav/	"he wrote"	כתב
/hixtiv/	"he dictated"	הכתיב
/axal/	"he ate"	אכל
/he'exil/	"he fed"	האכיל
/rac/	"he ran"	רץ
/heric/	"he caused to run"	הריץ

In other cases, however, the causative meaning is not apparent either because the English translations of the roots in various conjugations are so different or because the causative meaning has changed in Hebrew itself.

The pattern of the hif'il is comparatively simple. The characteristic feature is a prefix of the form /h-/ or the infixed vowel /i/ or both, as in the name /hif'il/ itself.

In the past tense the prefix is /hi-/, /he-/, or /ho-/ depending on the consonants of the root. These prefixes were described in Grammar Note 17.7, and the student should review them at this point.

In the infinitive, imperative, future, and present the vowel of the prefix is /a/, except for pey yud verbs, such as yd', in which case the prefix vowel becomes /o/ : /yodia/ "he will inform."

The stem vowel /i/ is not dropped in any of the suffixed forms of the hif'il. Except for the present tense, the suffixes are not stressed.

(a) General pattern of the hif'il
(Note the stem vowel /e/ in the underlined forms.)

Infinitive:		le hamšix			
Imperative:	m.s.	hamšex		m.pl.	hamšíx u
	f.s.	hamšíx i		f.pl.	hamšéx na
Future:	1 s.	amšix		1 pl.	n amšix
	2 m.s.	t amšix		2 m.pl.	t amšíx u
	2 f.s.	t amšíx i		2 f.pl.	t amšéx na
	3 m.s.	y amšix		3 m.pl.	y amšíx u
	3 f.s.	t amšix		3 f.pl.	t amšéx na
Present:	m.s.	m amšix		m.pl.	m amšix im
	f.s.	m amšix a		f.pl.	m amšix ot
Past:	1 s.	himšáx ti		1 pl.	himšáx nu
	2 m.s.	himšáx ta		2 m.pl.	himšáx tem
	2 f.s.	himšáx t		2 f.pl.	himšáx ten
	3 m.s.	himšix		3 pl.	himšíx u
	3 f.s.	himšix a			

If the first radical is <u>n</u>, then the <u>n</u> is dropped in the <u>hif'il</u>. (similar dropping of a radical <u>n</u> was noted for the <u>nif'al</u>).

/yakir/ "he will recognize" - root <u>nkr</u>   נכר
/yagía/ "he will arrive"   - root <u>ng'</u>   נגע

Occasional variations from the above pattern will be heard, for example, /mekir/ "knows" as well as the regular /makir/.

A. Substitution Drill

°tart speaking. Everybody is waiting.   התחל לדבר. כולם מחכים.
                                                                 התחילי
                                                                 התחילו
                                                                 התחלנה

B. Substitution-Agreement Drill

I'll start speaking Hebrew when I get there.   <u>אני אתחיל לדבר עברית כשאגיע לשם.</u>

אתה – הוא – רחל – אתם – הם
רחל ומשה – אנו – היא – את
הן – אתן – מר וויל'אמס – אני

C. Transformation Drill - Future to Past

Instructor: I'll start working as soon as I get there.
Student: I started working as soon as I got here.

אתחיל לעבוד מיד אחרי שאגיע לשם.
התחלתי לעבוד מיד אחרי שהגעתי לכאן.

הוא יתחיל לעבוד מיד אחרי שיגיע לשם.
הוא התחיל לעבוד מיד אחרי שהגיע לכאן.

אשתי תתחיל לעבוד מיד אחרי שתגיע לשם.
אשתי התחילה לעבוד מיד אחרי שהגיעה לכאן.

את תתחילי לעבוד מיד אחרי שתגיעי לשם.
את התחלת לעבוד מיד אחרי שהגעת לכאן.

הן תתחלנה לעבוד מיד אחרי שתגענה לשם.
הן התחילו לעבוד מיד אחרי שהגיעו לכאן.

Do this drill in reverse, also.

D. Substitution-Agreement Drill.

He starts working at 9:00 A.M.   <u>הוא מתחיל לעבוד בתשע בבוקר.</u>

הם – גב' כהן – הנשים – המנהל

E. Substitution-Agreement Drill

We'll move up the meeting to 3:00.   <u>נקדים את הפגישה לשלוש.</u>

אתה – אני – את – המנהל – המורים
אתן – המנהלת – הן – אתם – אנו

F. Transformation Drill

    Instructor: He comes early every day.
    Student: Every day he comes earlier (than the day before).

הוא מקדים לבוא כל יום.	הוא בא מוקדם כל יום.
את מקדימה לבוא כל יום.	את באה מוקדם כל יום.
התלמידים מקדימים לבוא כל יום.	התלמידים באים מוקדם כל יום.
הן מקדימות לבוא כל יום.	הן באות מוקדם כל יום.

G. Transformation Drill – Future to Past

    Instructor: I'll go to the office early this morning.
    Student: I got to the office early this morning.

הקדמתי לבוא למשרד הבוקר.	אקדים לבוא למשרד הבוקר.
הקדמת לבוא למשרד הבוקר.	תקדימי לבוא למשרד הבוקר.
הנשים הקדימו לבוא למשרד הבוקר.	הנשים תקדמנה לבוא למשרד הבוקר.
המנהל הקדים לבוא למשרד הבוקר.	המנהל יקדים לבוא למשרד הבוקר.
הקדמנו לבוא למשרד הבוקר.	נקדים לבוא למשרד הבוקר.
היא הקדימה לבוא למשרד הבוקר.	היא תקדים לבוא למשרד הבוקר.

Do this drill in reverse, also.

H. Transformation Drill – Future to Past

    Instructor: I'll decide when to go.
    Student: I haven't yet decided when to go.

עוד לא החלטתי מתי לנסוע.	אני אחליט מתי לנסוע.
הוא עוד לא החליט מתי לנסוע.	הוא יחליט מתי לנסוע.
אשתו עוד לא החליטה מתי לנסוע.	אשתו תחליט מתי לנסוע.
עוד לא החלטנו מתי לנסוע.	אנו נחליט מתי לנסוע.
עוד לא החלטתם מתי לנסוע.	אתם תחליטו מתי לנסוע.
עוד לא החלטת מתי לנסוע.	אתה תחליט מתי לנסוע.

Do this drill in reverse, also.

(b) <u>Verbs with first radical '</u>

    In the past tense the forms of these verbs begin with /he'e-/; For example:
                    /he'exil/ "he fed"

    In the other tenses the forms begin with /ha'a-/ or /-a'a-/ if there is a
pronoun prefix. For example, /ha'axel/ "feed" (m.s. imv.)
                           /ya'axil/ "he will feed."

There is no difference between verbs spelled with א or ע in this respect.

Infinitive:		le ha'axil			
Imperative:	m.s.	ha'axel	f.s.	ha'axíl i	etc.
Future:	1 s.	a'axil			
	2 m.s.	t a'axil	2 f.s.	t a'axíl i	etc.
Present:	m.s.	m a'axil	etc.		
Past:	1 s.	he 'exál ti etc.			
	3 m.s.	he 'exil			
	3 f.s.	he 'exíl a			
	3 pl.	he 'exíl u			

I. Substitution Drill

Feed the children. They're hungry.

האכל את הילדים. הם רעבים.
האכילי
האכילו
האכלנה

J. Transformation Drill - Future to Past

Instructor: She'll feed the children.
Student: She fed the children.

היא האכילה את הילדים.   היא תאכיל את הילדים.
הנשים האכילו את הילדים.   הנשים תאכלנה את הילדים.
אני האכלתי את הילדים.   אני אאכיל את הילדים.
את האכלת את הילדים.   את תאכילי את הילדים.
הוא האכיל את הילדים.   הוא יאכיל את הילדים.
הם האכילו את הילדים.   הם יאכילו את הילדים.

Do this drill in reverse, also.

K. Transformation Drill

Instructor: He eats at my house.
Student: I give him to eat.

אני מאכיל אותו.   הוא אוכל אצלי.
מרים מאכילה אותו.   הוא אוכל אצל מרים.
אנו מאכילים אותו.   הוא אוכל אצלנו.
הן מאכילות אותו.   הוא אוכל אצלן.

L. Substitution Drill

Put the table over here.

העמד את השולחן כאן.
העמידי
העמידו
העמדנה

M. Substitution-Agreement Drill

He'll put the table near the window.

הוא יעמיד את השולחן על יד החלון.

אני – אתה – התלמידים – אנו
היא – אתם – את – הן – הוא

N. Transformation Drill - Future to Past

Instructor: Where will you put the coffee?
Student: Where did you put the coffee?

איפה העמדת את הקפה?   איפה תעמיד את הקפה?
איפה העמדתם את הקפה?   איפה תעמידו את הקפה?
איפה היא העמידה את הקפה?   איפה היא תעמיד את הקפה?
איפה הוא העמיד את הקפה?   איפה הוא יעמיד את הקפה?
איפה הן העמידו את הקפה?   איפה הן תעמרנה את הקפה?

Do this drill in reverse, also.

(c) Verbs with first radical b, p, k, (כ)

If the first radical is b, p, or k (כ) then it occurs as /v/, /f/, or /x/ throughout the hif'il conjugation.

/hivdil/	"he distinguished"	הבדיל
/hif'il/	"he caused to operate"	הפעיל
/hixtiv/	"he dictated"	הכתיב

O. Transformation Drill

Instructor: My clock isn't working.
Student: I'll start the clock.

אני אפעיל את השעון.	השעון שלי לא פועל.
אתה תפעיל את השעון.	השעון שלך לא פועל.
הוא יפעיל את השעון.	השעון שלו לא פועל.
הם יפעילו את השעון.	השעון שלהם לא פועל.
היא תפעיל את השעון.	השעון שלה לא פועל.
אתן תפעלנה את השעון.	השעון שלכן לא פועל.

Do this drill in reverse, also.

P. Transformation Drill

Instructor: My clock is working now.
Student: I started the clock.

הפעלתי את השעון.	השעון שלי פועל עכשיו.
הפעלתן את השעון.	השעון שלכן פועל עכשיו.
היא הפעילה את השעון.	השעון שלו פועל עכשיו.
הוא הפעיל את השעון.	השעון שלו פועל עכשיו.
הם הפעילו את השעון.	השעון שלהם פועל עכשיו.
אתה הפעלת את השעון.	השעון שלך פועל עכשיו.

Do this drill in reverse, also.

Q. Transformation Drill

Instructor: I'll write a letter for him.
Student: He'll dictate a letter to me.

הוא יכתיב לי מכתב.	אני אכתוב מכתב בשבילו.
אתה תכתיב לי מכתב.	אני אכתוב מכתב בשבילך.
אתם תכתיבו לי מכתב.	אני אכתוב מכתב בשבילכם.
הן תכתבנה לי מכתב.	אני אכתוב מכתב בשבילן.
את תכתיבי לי מכתב.	אני אכתוב מכתב בשבילך.
הם יכתיבו לי מכתב.	אני אכתוב מכתב בשבילם.
היא תכתיב לי מכתב.	אני אכתוב מכתב בשבילה.

Do this drill in reverse, also.

R. Transformation Drill

    Instructor: I wrote a letter for him.
    Student: He dictated a letter to me.

הוא הכתיב לי מכתב.	כתבתי מכתב בשבילו.
היא הכתיבה לי מכתב.	כתבתי מכתב בשבילה.
הם הכתיבו לי מכתב.	כתבתי מכתב בשבילם.
את הכתבת לי מכתב.	כתבתי מכתב בשבילך.
אתם הכתבתם לי מכתב.	כתבתי מכתב בשבילכם.
אתה הכתבת לי מכתב.	כתבתי מכתב בשבילך.
הן הכתיבו לי מכתב.	כתבתי מכתב בשבילן.

Do this drill in reverse, also.

S. Response Drill

    Instructor: Do you write letters?
    Student: No, I dictate them.

לא, אני מכתיב אותם.	האם אתה כותב מכתבים?
לא, הם מכתיבים אותם.	האם הם כותבים מכתבים?
לא, אני מכתיבה אותם.	האם את כותבת מכתבים?
לא, אנו מכתיבות אותם.	האם אתן כותבות מכתבים?

(d) Verbs with second radical b, p, k (כ)

    If the second radical is b, p, or k (כ) then it occurs as /b/, /p/, or /k/ throughout the hif'il conjugation.

/hisbir/	"he explained"	הסביר
/hispik/	"he had an opportunity"	הספיק
/hizkir/	"he reminded"	הזכיר

    However, if the first radical is ' or y (spelled ה in the hif'il) then the second radical occurs as /v/, /f/, or /x/.

/he'evir/	"he brought over"	העביר
/he'efil/	"he darkened"	האפיל
/he'exil/	"he fed"	האכיל
/hovil/	"he transported"	הוביל
/hofia/	"he appeared"	הופיע
/hoxiax/	"he proved"	הוכיח

T. Substitution Drill

    (The sequence /-sb-/ is assimilated to /-zb-/).

    Explain it to me, please.

הסבר לי את זה, בבקשה.
הסבירי
הסבירו
הסברנה

U. Transformation Drill

Instructor: He knows about it.
Student: He'll explain it to us.

הרא יסכיר לנו את זה.	הוא יודע על כך.
אתה תסכיר לנו את זה.	אתה יודע על כך.
גב' כהן תסכיר לנו את זה.	גב' כהן יודעת על כך.
הם יסכירו לנו את זה.	הם יודעים על כך.
את תסכירי לנו את זה.	את יודעת על כך.
הן תסכרנה לנו את זה.	הן יודעות על כך.
אתם תסכירו לנו את זה.	אתם יודעים על כך.

V. Expansion Drill

Instructor: I read the story.
Student: I read the story and explained it to them.

והסכרתי אותו להם.	קראתי את הספור
והסכיר אותו להם.	משה קרא את הספור
והסכירה אותו להם.	אשׁזי ראה את הספור
והסכרנו אותו להם.	אשׁזי ואני קראנו את הספור
והסכירו אותו להם.	התלמידים קראו את הספור

W. Substitution-Agreement Drill

I'll bring over the books.
אני אעביר את הספרים.

הוא – אתם – התלמידים – שרה – מי
הן – אתה – את – אנו – אני

X. Substitution-Agreement Drill

David brought over the books.
דוד העביר את הספרים.

אני – הן – אחה – אתם – מי
את – אנו – עטרה – התלמידים

(e) lamed hey verbs in the hif'il.

In the past tense of <u>lamed hey</u> verbs the vowel preceding the pronoun suffixes
is /e/: /hifnéti/ "I turned" הפניתי . The rest of the conjugation has the
typical pattern of such verbs.

Infinitive:		le hafnot				
Imperative:	m.s.	hafne		f.s.	hafni	etc.
Future:	1 s. 2 m.s.	afne tafne		2 f.s.	tafni	etc.
Present:	m.s.	mafne		f.s.	mafna	etc.
Past:	1 s.	hifnéti	etc.			
	3 m.s.	hifna		3 f.s.	hifnetá	
	3 pl.	hifnu				

Y. Substitution Drill

Turn your face to the audience.

הפנה את פניך אל הקהל.
הפני   (פנייך)
הפנו   (פניכם)
הפנינה (פניכן)

Z. Substitution Drill

Show me your hands.

הראה לי את הידיים שלך.
הראי   (שלך)
הראו   (שלכם)
הראינה (שלכן)

AA. Substitution Drill

Bring up the books to the third floor.

העלה את הספרים לקומה השלישית.
העלי
העלו
העלינה

BB. Substitution-Agreement Drill

I'll show him the way.

<u>אני אראה לו את הדרך.</u>

אתה – אביגדור – אשתי – אנו – מי
הן – אתם – את – אתן – הם – אני

CC. Transformation Drill - Future to Past

Instructor: I'll show him the way.
Student: I showed him the way.

הראיתי לו את הדרך.	אני אראה לו את הדרך.
דוד הראה לו את הדרך.	דוד יראה לו את הדרך.
הם הראו לו את הדרך.	הם יראו לו את הדרך.
רחל הראתה לו את הדרך.	רחל תראה לו את הדרך.
אתה הראית לו את הדרך.	אתה תראה לו את הדרך.
אתם הראיתם לו את הדרך.	אתם תראו לו את הדרך.
את הראית לו את הדרך.	את תראי לו את הדרך.
אנו הראינו לו את הדרך.	אנו נראה לו את הדרך.

DD. Expansion Drill

Instructor: The tourists come to him.
Student: The tourists come to him, and he shows them the city.

והוא מראה להם את העיר.	התיירים באים אליו
ואנו מראים להם את העיר.	התיירים באים אלינו
והיא מראה להם את העיר.	התיירים באים אליה
והן מראות להם את העיר.	התיירים באים אליהן

(f) ayin vav verbs in the hif'il

In previous units these verbs have been described as having only radicals, with a _vav_ (ו) or _yud_ (י) supplied to make three radicals for dictionary listings.

In the hif'il the pattern of these verbs is the same as verbs with three radicals except that in the present and past tenses the prefix vowel is /e/.

If the first radical is _b, p,_ or _k_ (כ), then it occurs as /v/, /f/, or /x/ just as with verbs with three radicals.

/hevin/	"he understood"	הכין
/hefic/	"he spread"	הפיץ
/hexin/	"he prepared"	הכין

Root בין

Infinitive:		le havin			
Imperative:	m.s.	haven	m.pl.	havin u	
	f.s.	havin i	f.pl.	haven na	
Future:	1 s.	avin	1 pl.	n avin	
	2 m.s.	t avin	2 m.pl.	t avin u	
	2 f.s.	t avin i	2 f.pl.	t aven na	
	3 m.s.	y avin	3 m.pl.	y avin u	
	3 f.s.	t avin	3 f.pl.	t aven na	
Present:	m.s.	m evin	m.pl.	m evin im	
	f.s.	m evin a	f.pl.	m evin ot	
Past:	1 s.	hevan ti	1 pl.	hevan nu	
	2 m.s.	hevan ta	2 m.pl.	hevan tem	
	2 f.s.	hevan t	2 f.pl.	hevan ten	
	3 m.s.	hevin			
	3 f.s.	hevin a	3 pl.	hevin u	

EE. Expansion Drill

Instructor: Explain it to him.

Student: If you explain it to him well, I'm sure he'll understand.

היטב אני בטוח שיבין.	תסביר לו את זה אם
היטב אני בטוח שנבין.	תסביר לנו את זה אם
היטב אני בטוח שתבין.	תסביר לה את זה אם
היטב אני בטוח שיבינו.	תסביר להם את זה אם
היטב אני בטוח שאבין.	תסביר לי את זה אם
היטב אני בטוח שתבנה.	תסביר להן את זה אם

FF. Expansion Drill

Instructor: You explained it to him very well.

Student: You explained it to him very well but he still didn't understand.

אבל בכל זאת הוא לא הבין.	הסברת לו יפה מאד
אבל בכל זאת לא הבנתי.	הסברת לי יפה מאד
אבל בכל זאת לא הבינו.	הסברת להם יפה מאד
אבל בכל זאת היא לא הבינה.	הסברת לה יפה מאד
אבל בכל זאת הן לא הבינו.	הסברת להן יפה מאד
אבל בכל זאת לא הבנו.	הסברת לנו יפה מאד

GG. Substitution Drill

    Prepare the food, we're starved.

הכן את האוכל, אנו רעבים.
הכיני
הכינו
הכנה

HH. Substitution-Agreement Drill

    Who will prepare the meal?

מי יכין את הארוחה?

את – אנו – הנשים – אשתי – אתם
עטרה ודוד – אני – אתה – אתן – הוא

II. Substitution-Agreement Drill

    They prepared a banana split
    exactly as in America.

הם הכינו בננה ספליט בדיוק כמו באמריקה.

המלצר – אני – את – המלצרית
אתן – אנו – אתה – הם

End of Tape 11B

Tape 12A

JJ. Substitution-Agreement Drill

    I put up the house.

אני הקמתי את הבית.

מר כספי – אנו – גב' כהן – הם
המשפחה שלו – אתם – את – מי

KK. Transformation Drill - Past to Future

    Instructor: I put up the house.
    Student: I will put up the house.

אני אקים את הבית.	אני הקמתי את הבית.
מי יקים את הבית?	מי הקים את הבית?
את תקימי את הבית.	את הקמת את הבית.
הם יקימו את הבית.	הם הקימו את הבית.
אתם תקימו את הבית.	אתם הקמתם את הבית.
אשתו תקים את הבית.	אשתו הקימה את הבית.
אנו נקים את הבית.	אנו הקמנו את הבית.

Do this drill in reverse, also.

LL. Transformation Drill - Past to Future
    (The vowel preceding the suffix in the first and second person forms is /e/:
    /hevéti/ "I brought". הבאתי   Cf. /miléti/ "I filled" מלאתי . Grammar
    Note 21.6c)

    Instructor: I brought the <u>chalas</u> for Shabbat.
    Student: I'll bring the <u>chalas</u> for Shabbat.

אכיא את החלות לשבת.	הבאתי את החלות לשבת.
הנשים תבאנה את החלות לשבת.	הנשים הביאו את החלות לשבת.
את תביאי את החלות לשבת.	את הבאת את החלות לשבת.
אתה תביא את החלות לשבת.	אתה הבאת את החלות לשבת.
אתם תביאו את החלות לשבת.	אתם הבאתם את החלות לשבת.
אנו נביא את החלות לשבת.	אנו הבאנו את החלות לשבת.
הם יביאו את החלות לשבת.	הם הביאו את החלות לשבת.
יונתן יביא את החלות לשבת.	יונתן הביא את החלות לשבת.
אשתי תביא את החלות לשבת.	אשתי הביאה את החלות לשבת.

305

25.6 Verbal Nouns of the hif'il

There are two verbal noun patterns of the hif'il:

(a) $heC_1C_2eC_3$ - /hesber/ "explanation"   הסבר
                              /hemšex/ "continuation"   המשך
These nouns are masculine, and their plurals end in /-im/:
                              /hesberim/ "explanations"   הסברים

(b) $haC_1C_2aC_3a$ - /hatxala/ "beginning"   התחלה
                              /hazmana/ "invitation"   הזמנה
                              /hagzama/ "exaggeration"   הגזמה
                              /haxlata/ "decision"   החלטה
                              /hakdama/ "introduction"   הקדמה
                              /hoda'a/ "announcement"   הודעה
                              /havana/ "understanding"   הבנה
                              /haxana/ "preparation"   הכנה

These nouns are feminine and their plurals end in /-ot/:
                              /hatxalot/ "beginnings"   התחלות

Some verbs have nouns of both types:
                              /heker/   "indication"   הכר
                              /hakara/ "recognition"   הכרה

As with the verbal nouns of the other binyanim it is difficult to predict which type will occur or what its precise meaning will be.

Some of these verbal nouns occur only in stereotyped expressions:

                           /behexlet/ "certainly"   בהחלט
                           /behekdem/ "as soon as possible"   בהקדם

The verbal nouns of lamed hey verbs usually have /'/ (א) as the third radical:

                           /ha'ala'a/ "promotion"   העלאה

A. Transformation Drill

Instructor: He began yesterday.
Student: The beginning was yesterday.

הוא התחיל אתמול.	ההתחלה היתה אתמול.
הוא הזמין אותי אתמול.	ההזמנה היתה אתמול.
הוא החליט לנסוע אתמול.	ההחלטה היתה אתמול.
הוא הודיע לנו אתמול.	ההודעה היתה אתמול.
המנהל העלה אותו אתמול.	ההעלאה היתה אתמול.
היא הכינה את האוכל אתמול. ההכנה היתה אתמול.	
הכרנו אותה אתמול.	ההכרה היתה אתמול.
העמדתי את השולחן אתמול.	ההעמדה היתה אתמול.

B. Transformation Drill

Instructor: He explained it yesterday.
Student: I didn't like the explanation.

הוא הסביר את זה אתמול.	ההסבר לא מצא חן בעיני.
הוא המשיך לכתוב את הספר.	ההמשך לא מצא חן בעיני.

25.7 <u>The hof'al Conjugation</u>

The passive of the <u>hif'il</u> is the <u>hof'al</u> conjugation. This conjugation is traditionally considered a separate <u>binyan</u>, but it is a simple change of the <u>hif'il</u> and does not have an infinitive or imperative.

The prefix and stem vowels /-u--a-/ occur throughout the conjugation in place of the <u>hif'il</u> vowels. All rules about root consonants, <u>lamed hey</u> verbs, <u>ayin vav</u> verbs, etc., are the same as for the <u>hif'il</u>.

The vowels suffixes are stressed in the future and past tenses.

Future:	1 s.	uzman	1 pl.	n uzman
	2 m.s.	t uzman	2 m.pl.	t uzmen u
	2 f.s.	t uzmen i	2 f.pl.	t uzmán na
	3 m.s.	y uzman	3 m.pl.	y uzmen u
	3 f.s.	t uzman	3 f.pl.	t uzmán na
Present:	m.s.	m uzman	m.pl.	m uzman im
	f.s.	m uzman a	f.pl.	m uzman ot

[With some verbs the present tense has a /-t/ feminine: /mukdémet/. With some verbs both types are in use /muzménet/ as well as /muzmana/.]

Past:	1 s.	huzmán ti	1 pl.	huzmán nu
	2 m.s.	huzmán ta	2 m.pl.	huzmán tem
	2 f.s.	huzman t	2 f.pl.	huzmán ten
	3 m.s.	huzman		
	3 f.s.	huzmen a	3 pl.	huzmen u

With some verbs the prefix vowel is /o/: /hor'a/ "it was shown" הוראה . In modern Hebrew many of these have been regularized to the /-u--a-/ pattern. For example, though the name of the <u>binyan</u> has the /o/ vowel, <u>hof'al</u>, the passive of the verb /hif'il/ "he caused to operate" is /huf'al/ "it was put into operation."

In theory all <u>hif'il</u> verbs have a passive counterpart in the <u>hof'al</u>. However, in ordinary speech the <u>hof'al</u> is not in frequent use, and the active construction is used. The <u>hof'al</u> is more frequent in written Hebrew such as newspaper style, etc.

The present tense forms of certain verbs are in very frequent use, and these forms are often treated as adjectives, nouns, or verb auxiliaries.

/mukdam/	"early"	מוקדם
/muxan/	"prepared, ready"	מוכן
/muvan/	"understood"	מובן
/muxlat/	"decided, definite"	מוחלט
/mu'amad/	"candidate"	מועמד
/muxrax/	"must"	מוכרח

[Compare the description of the <u>hof'al</u> with the description of the <u>pu'al</u> conjugation in Grammar Note 21.8.]

A. Transformation Drill - Active to Passive

Instructor: He moved up the meeting.
Student: The meeting was moved up.

הפגישה הוקדמה.	הוא הקדים את הפגישה.
הפגישות הוקדמו.	הוא הקדים את הפגישות.
המכתב הוכתב.	הוא הכתיב את המכתב.
המכתבים הוכתבו.	הוא הכתיב את המכתבים.
הקופסה הוכנסה.	הוא הכניס את הקופסה.
הספר הוכנס.	הוא הכניס את הספר.
החבילות הוכנסו.	הוא הכניס את החבילות.
הקפה הוגש.	הוא הגיש את הקפה.
הארוחה הוגשה.	הוא הגיש את הארוחה.
הבית הוקם.	הוא הקים את הבית.
הבתים הוקמו.	הוא הקים את הבתים.

B. Transformation Drill - Active to Passive

Instructor: I prepared the ice cream.
Student: The ice cream is ready.

הגלידה מוכנה.	הכנתי את הגלידה.
היין מוכן.	הכנתי את היין.
הרשימות מוכנות.	הכנתי את הרשימות.
התלמידים מוכנים.	הכנתי את התלמידים.

C. Transformation Drill - Active to Passive

Instructor: I'll dictate the letter.
Student: The letter will be dictated.

המכתב יוכתב.	אכתיב את המכתב.
המברקים יוכתבו.	אכתיב את המברקים.
הארוחה תוכן.	אכין את הארוחה.
התוכניות תוכנה.	אכין את התוכניות.

D. Substitution-Agreement Drill

We were invited to the embassy.

<u>הוזמנו לשגרירות.</u>

אתה – אני – אתם – בעלה של מרים
את – הם – שרה – אתן – אנו

E. Transformation Drill - Future to Past

Instructor: The food will be prepared by five o'clock.
Student: The food was prepared by five o'clock.

האוכל הוכן עד חמש.	האוכל יוכן עד חמש.
המכתב הוכתב עד שלוש.	המכתב יוכתב עד שלוש.
אתה הוזמנת לביתו של היועץ.	אתה תוזמן לביתו של היועץ.
הקופסאות הוכנסו למשרד.	הקופסאות תוכנסנה למשרד.
הפגישה הוקדמה להיום.	הפגישה תוקדם להיום.
הבית הוקם על ידי בעלה.	הבית יוקם על ידי בעלה.

RAPID RESPONSE DRILL

1. ‫למה רצתה עטרה ללכת הביתה?‬

2. ‫למה רצה דוד להישאר עוד קצת?‬

3. ‫מה היתה השעה?‬

4. ‫למה רצה יונתן להישאר בבית הקפה?‬

5. ‫מי שילם את החשבון?‬

6. ‫עבור מה הודה יונתן לעטרה ודוד?‬

REVIEW CONVERSATIONS

א: ‫בואו נלך הביתה.‬

ב: ‫למה? עוד מוקדם.‬

א: ‫מה מוקדם?! כבר אחרי חצות.‬

ב: ‫אז מה?‬

א: ‫אז בואו הביתה.‬

ג: ‫אתה עייף?‬

ד: ‫לא. לא כל כך, ואת?‬

ג: ‫אני עייפה מאד, מיד אלך לישון.‬

ד: ‫אני רואה שאת כבר מנמנמת.‬

ג: ‫כן. אני כבר נרדמת.‬

ה: ‫אתם הולכים?‬

ו: ‫כן, ואתה?‬

ה: ‫אני אשאר עוד קצת. אולי יבואו חברים שלי.‬

ו: ‫טוב, כרצונך. לילה טוב.‬

ה: ‫לילה טוב. להתראות.‬

ז : מה אתם רוצים לאכול?

ח: אנו נאכל גלידה עם פירות.

ז : ומה תשתו?

ח : קפה קר.

ז : הזמינו מה שאתם רוצים. אני מזמין.

ט : איך תקום מחר?

י : אל תדאג. אקום. השעון יעורר אותי.

ט : באיזה שעה אתה מתעורר?

י : בערך בשבע.

ט : בשבע? זה מוקדם.

י : כן. אני צריך להכין ארוחת בוקר למשפחה.

כ : משה נסע לצרפת.

ל : כן, אני יודע על כך.

כ : אני באמת צריך לכתוב לו.

ל : כשהכתוב תודיע לי. אני צריך להעביר לו מכתב.

כ : בסדר. אתקשר אתך.

26.1 <u>Military Service</u>

MR. WILLIAMS

Hello, Avigdor.	šalom avígdor.	שלום אביגדור.
It's been a long time	ze harbe zman	זה הרבה זמן
since I've seen you.	šelo raíti otxa.	שלא ראיתי אותך.
Where are you hiding?	éyfo ata mitxabe.	איפה אתה מתחבא?
he hid (himself)	mitxabe מתחבא	

AVIGDOR

I've been serving	ani mešaret	אני משרת
in the army	bacava	בצבא
a year already.	kvar šana.	כבר שנה.
he served	šeret שרת	
military services	cava (m) צבא	

MR. WILLIAMS

In which branch	beéyze xáil	באיזה חיל
are you serving?	ata mešaret?	אתה משרת?
branch of service	xail (m) חיל	

AVIGDOR

I'm serving	ani mešaret	אני משרת
in the air force.	bexeyl haavir.	בחיל האויר.

MR. WILLIAMS

And how is	uma šlom	ומה שלום
your sister Miriam?	axotxa miryam?	אחותך מרים?
sister	axot (f) אחות	

AVIGDOR

She's fine.	šloma tov.	שלומה טוב.
She finished	hi gamra	היא גמרה
high school	et hagimnásia	את הגמנסיה
this summer,	hakáic.	הקיץ,
high school	gimnásia (f) גמנסיה	
and she's waiting	vehi mexaka	והיא מחכה
for her draft notice.	lecav giyus.	לצו גירס.
order	cav (m) צו	
conscription	giyus (m) גירס	

MR. WILLIAMS

Wonderful.	yófi.	יופי.
The whole family	kol hamišpaxa	כל המשפחה
will be in service.	tihye bacava.	תהיה בצבא.
beauty	yófi (m) יופי	
How much time	káma zman	כמה זמן
do you have to	ata carix	אתה צריך
serve yet?	od lešaret.	עוד לשרת?

AVIGDOR

Another year and a half.	od šana vaxéci.	עוד שנה וחצי.

311

MR. WILLIAMS

And how long	vemiryam	ומרים
does Miriam	káma zman	כמה זמן
have to serve?	crixa lešaret?	צריכה לשרת?

AVIGDOR

Miriam will serve	miryam tešaret	מרים תשרת
a year and a half.	šana vaxéci.	שנה וחצי.
Girls serve less.	banot mešartot paxot.	בנות משרתות פחות.

daughter	bat (f)	בת
girls, daughters	banot (f.pl.)	בנות
less, fewer	paxot	פחות

26.2 ADDITIONAL VOCABULARY

He's a soldier.	hu xayal.	הוא חייל.
She's a soldier.	hi xayélet.	היא חיילת.
He's serving in the navy.	hu mešaret bexeyl hayam.	הוא משרת בחיל הים.

He's serving
in the army.
  dry land, continent
	hu mešaret
	bexeyl hayabaša.
	  yabaša (f)
		הוא משרת
		בחיל היבשה.
		יבשה

He's a parachutist.	hu canxan.	הוא צנחן.
He's an officer.	hu kacin.	הוא קצין.
He's only a private.	hu rak turai.	הוא רק טוראי.
only	rak	רק
private	turai (m)	טוראי
We'll be discharged next year.	anáxnuništaxrer bašana habaa.	אנחנו נשתחרר בשנה הבאה.
we	anáxnu	אנחנו
he was freed	hištaxrer	השתחרר

26.3 VOCABULARY DRILL

A. Substitution-Agreement Drill /xayal/   "soldier"   חייל

Moshe is a good soldier.   <u>משה הוא חייל טוב.</u>

אחותי – דוד ויונתן – הכנות האלה – דב

B. Substitution-Agreement Drill /kacin/   "officer"   קצין

He's an officer in the air force.   <u>הוא קצין בחיל האוויר.</u>

גב' כספי – מרים ולאה – הם

דוד – אנחנו

26.4 VERB DRILLS

(a) /hitxabe/ "he hid himself" התחבא

The third radical of this verb is ׳ (א׳). In the first and second person forms of the past tense the stem vowel before the suffix is /e/: /hitxabéti/ " I hid myself". This pattern is similar to that of /miléti/ " I filled" מלאתי See Grammar Note 21.6(c).

A. Substitution-Agreement Drill

David is hiding behind the house.   דוד מתחבא מאַחורי הבית.

רחל - אביגדור ומשה - הבנות - ירונתן

B. Transformation Drill - Past to Future

Instructor: I was hiding on the other side of the building.
Student: I'll hide on the other side of the building.

אתחבא בצד השני של הבנין.	התחבאתי בצד השני של הבנין.
הוא יתחבא בצד השני של הבנין.	הוא התחבא בצד השני של הבנין.
הבנות תתחבאנה בצד השני של הבנין.	הבנות התחבאו בצד השני של הבנין.
אתה תתחבא בצד השני של הבנין.	אתה התחבאת בצד השני של הבנין.
את תתחבאי בצד השני של הבנין.	את התחבאת בצד השני של הבנין.
מרים תתחבא בצד השני של הבנין.	מרים התחבאה בצד השני של הבנין.
נתחבא בצד השני של הבנין.	התחבאנו בצד השני של הבנין.
תתחבאו בצד השני של הבנין.	התחבאתם בצד השני של הבנין.

Do this drill in reverse, also.

(b) /šeret/ "he served" שרת

The first and second person forms are spelled with only one ת - שרתי etc. In ordinary speech /šeráteti/ is heard more frequently than /šerátti/. Some speakers have regularized the past tense to /širet/ etc. See Grammar Note 21.6(a).

C. Transformation Drill - Future to Past

Instructor: We'll serve in the navy.
Student: We served in the navy.

שרתנו בחיל הים.	נשרת בחיל הים.
שרתי בחיל הים.	אשרת בחיל הים.
שרתם בחיל הים.	אתם תשרתו בחיל הים.
אחותי שרתה בחיל הים.	אחותי תשרת בחיל הים.
יעקב שרת בחיל הים.	יעקב ישרת בחיל הים.
הם שרתו בחיל הים.	הם ישרתו בחיל הים.
שרת בחיל הים.	את תשרתי בחיל הים.
הן שרתו בחיל הים.	הן תשרתנה בחיל הים.
אתה שרת בחיל הים.	אתה תשרת בחיל הים.

Do this drill in reverse, also.

D. Substitution-Agreement Drill

In which branch are you serving?   באיזה חיל אתה משרת?

אתן – הוא – את – הם – אתה

(c) /guyas/ "he was drafted" גויס

This is the pu'al of /giyes/.

E. Substitution-Agreement Drill

I was drafted a month ago.   גויסתי לפני חודש.

הוא – רחל – אנו – הם – אתה – הן

F. Transformation Drill - Past to Future

Instructor: I was drafted a month ago.
Student: I'll be drafted next month.

אגויס בחורש הבא.	גויסתי לפני חודש.
לאה תגויס בחודש הבא.	לאה גויסה לפני חודש.
הם יגויסו בחורש הבא.	הם גויסו לפני חודש.
אתה תגויס בחורש הבא.	אתה גויסת לפני חודש.
הן תגויסנה בחורש הבא.	הן גויסו לפני חודש.
דוד יגויס בחורש הבא.	דוד גויס לפני חודש.
נגויס בחורש הבא.	גויסנו לפני חודש.

Do this drill in reverse, also.

G. Transformation Drill

Instructor: I'm waiting for a draft notice.
Student: I'll be drafted soon.

אגויס בקרוב.	אני מחכה לצו גיוס.
דוד ואני נגויס בקרוב.	דוד ואני מחכים לצו גיוס.
אחותו תגויס בקרוב.	אחותו מחכה לצו גיוס.
הכנות תגויסנה בקרוב.	הבנות מחכות לצו גיוס.

(d) /hitgayes/ "he registered for the draft" התגייס

H. Substitution-Agreement Drill

He registered for the draft yesterday.   הוא התגייס אתמול.

אני – כולם – אחותו של משה – אנו
משה – אתם – התלמידים בכית הספר

(e)   /hištaxrer/   "he was freed"   השתחרר

The root of this verb has four consonants, <u>šxrr</u> . In the <u>hitpà'el</u>, the /t/ of the prefix follows the <u>š</u>. As with four-consonant roots in the <u>pi'el</u> the second and third radicals take the place of the middle radical of three-consonant roots:

/hicta r ef/   "he joined"   הצטרף
/hišta xr er/   "he was freed"   השתחרר

I. Substitution-Agreement Drill

We will be discharged next year.   <u>אנחנו נשתחרר בשנה הבאה.</u>

אני – אתה – החיילים האלה – אחותו

את – הם – אתם – הן – אנחנו

J. Substitution-Agreement Drill

I was discharged just the day before yesterday.   <u>השתחררתי רק שלשום.</u>

דוד ואני – אביגדור – חנה – הם

אתם – אנחנו – את – אני

K. Transformation Drill – <u>pi'el</u> to <u>hitpa'el</u>

Instructor: They'll discharge me next week.
Student: I'll be discharged next week.

אשתחרר בשבוע הבא.	ישחררו אותי בשבוע הבא.
תשתחרר בשבוע הבא.	ישחררו אותך בשבוע הבא.
משה ישתחרר בשבוע הבא.	ישחררו את משה בשבוע הבא.
אתן תשתחררנה בשבוע הבא.	ישחררו אתכן בשבוע הבא.
היא תשתחרר בשבוע הבא.	ישחררו אותה בשבוע הבא.
את תשתחררי בשבוע הבא.	ישחררו אותך בשבוע הבא.
הם ישתחררו בשבוע הבא.	ישחררו אותם בשבוע הבא.
נשתחרר בשבוע הבא.	ישחררו אותנו בשבוע הבא.

Do this drill in reverse, also.

L. Transformation Drill – <u>pi'el</u> to <u>hitpa'el</u>

Instructor: They discharged me a year ago.
Student: I was discharged a year ago.

השתחררתי לפני שנה.	שיחררו אותי לפני שנה.
השתחררנו לפני שנה.	שיחררו אותנו לפני שנה.
השתחררת לפני שנה.	שיחררו אותך לפני שנה.
אחותך השתחררה לפני שנה.	שיחררו את אחותך לפני שנה.
הם השתחררו לפני שנה.	שיחררו אותם לפני שנה.
השתחררתם לפני שנה.	שיחררו אתכם לפני שנה.
הוא השתחרר לפני שנה.	שיחררו אותו לפני שנה.

Do this drill in reverse, also.

26.5   Members of the Family

(a)   Parents and children   /horim veyeladim/   הורים וילדים

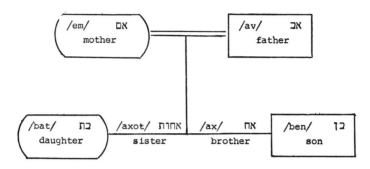

(b)   Grandparents and grandchildren

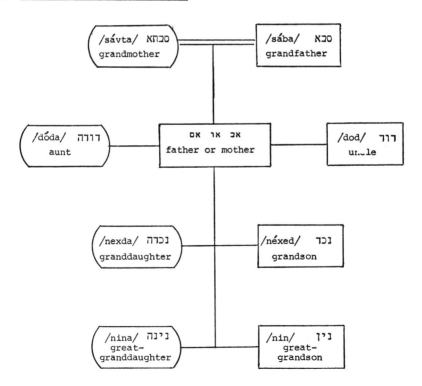

The plurals of the nouns in the preceding charts are:

fathers	/avot/		אבות
mothers	/imahot/		אמהות
sons	/banim/		בנים
daughters	/banot/		בנות
brothers	/axim/		אחים
sisters	/axayot/		אחיות
grandfathers	/sabim, savim/		סכים, סבים
grandmothers	/sabtot, savot/		סבתות, סבות
grandsons	/nexadim/		נכדים
granddaughters	/nexadot/		נכדות
great-grandsons	/ninim/		נינים
great-granddaughters	/ninot/		נינות

The suffixed forms of /av/ "father" are as follows:

my father	/aví/	אבי
your (m.s.) father	/avíxa/	אביך
your (f.s.) father	/avíx/	אביך
his father	/avív/	אביו
her father	/avíha/	אביה
our father	/avínu/	אבינו
your (m.pl.) father	/avíxem/	אביכם
your (f.pl.) father	/avíxen/	אביכן
their (m.pl.) father	/avíhem/	אביהם
their (f.pl.) father	/avíhen/	אביהן

The suffixed forms of /ax/ "brother" are similar to those of /av/:

my brother	/axí/	אחי
your (m.s.) brother	/axíxa/	אחיך
your (f.s.) brother	/axíx/	אחיך
his brother	/axív/	אחיו
her brother	/axíha/	אחיה
our brother	/axínu/	אחינו
your (m.s.) brother	/axíxem/	אחיכם
your (f.s.) brother	/axíxen/	אחיכן
their (m.pl.) brother	/axíhem/	אחיהם
their (f.pl.) brother	/axíhen/	אחיהן

The forms /em/, /bat/ and /ben/ have the variants /im-/, /bit-/, and /bn-/, respectively, before the singular set of pronominal suffixes:

my mother	/imi/		אמי
your (m.s.) mother	/imxa/	etc.	אמך
my daughter	/biti/		בתי
your (m.s.) daughter	/bitxa/	etc.	בתך
my son	/bni/		בני
your (m.s.) son	/binxa/ *		בנך
his son	/bno/		בנו
her son	/bna/		בנה
our son	/bnénu/		בננו
your (pl.) son	/binxem/ *		בנכם
their son	/bnam/		בנם

*[These forms have an inserted /i/ to break up the beginning three-consonant cluster /bnx-/.]

The forms /ába/ אבא and /íma/אמא are used to address one's parents.
In ordinary conversation they are used before the preposition /šel/ instead of
/haav/ and /haem/, e.g. /ába šelxa/ "your father", /íma šelxa/ "your mother".

A. Response Drill

Instructor: How is your father?
Student: He's fine.

שלומו טוב.	מה שלום אבא שלך?
שלומה טוב.	מה שלום אמא שלך?
שלומו טוב.	מה שלום אחיך?
שלומה טוב.	מה שלום אחותך?
שלומו טוב.	מה שלום אביך?
שלומה טוב.	מה שלום אמך?
שלומן טוב.	מה שלום האחיות שלך?
שלומם טוב.	מה שלום ההורים שלך?

B. Transformation Drill

My father is a good teacher.

תלמיד:　　　　　　　　　　　　　　　　　מורה:

תלמיד	מורה
אבא שלי הוא מורה טוב.	אבי הוא מורה טוב.
אבא שלך הוא מורה טוב.	אביך הוא מורה טוב.
אבא שלך הוא מורה טוב.	אביך הוא מורה טוב.
אבא שלו הוא מורה טוב.	אביו הוא מורה טוב.
אבא שלה הוא מורה טוב.	אביה הוא מורה טוב.
אבא שלנו הוא מורה טוב.	אבינו הוא מורה טוב.
אבא שלכם הוא מורה טוב.	אביכם הוא מורה טוב.
אבא שלכן הוא מורה טוב.	אביכן הוא מורה טוב.
אבא שלהם הוא מורה טוב.	אביהם הוא מורה טוב.
אבא שלהן הוא מורה טוב.	אביהן הוא מורה טוב.

Do this drill in reverse, also.

C. Transformation Drill

My brother is a good student.

תלמיד:　　　　　　　　　　　　　　　　　מורה:

תלמיד	מורה
האח שלי הוא תלמיד טוב.	אחי הוא תלמיד טוב.
האח שלך הוא תלמיד טוב.	אחיך הוא תלמיד טוב.
האח שלו הוא תלמיד טוב.	אחיו הוא תלמיד טוב.
האח שלה הוא תלמיד טוב.	אחיה הוא תלמיד טוב.
האח שלך הוא תלמיד טוב.	אחיך הוא תלמיד טוב.
האח שלנו הוא תלמיד טוב.	אחינו הוא תלמיד טוב.
האח שלכם הוא תלמיד טוב.	אחיכם הוא תלמיד טוב.
האח שלכן הוא תלמיד טוב.	אחיכן הוא תלמיד טוב.
האח שלהם הוא תלמיד טוב.	אחיהם הוא תלמיד טוב.
האח שלהן הוא תלמיד טוב.	אחיהן הוא תלמיד טוב.

Do this drill in reverse, also.

D. Transformation Drill

My mother likes to bake.

תלמיד:　　　　　　　　　　　　　　　　　מורה:

תלמיד	מורה
אמא שלי אוהבת לאפות.	אמי אוהבת לאפות.
אמא שלך אוהבת לאפות.	אמך אוהבת לאפות.
אמא שלה אוהבת לאפות.	אמה אוהבת לאפות.
אמא שלנו אוהבת לאפות.	אמנו אוהבת לאפות.
אמא שלהם אוהבת לאפות.	אמם אוהבת לאפות.

Do this drill in reverse, also.

E. Transformation Drill

His daughter is a big girl.

מורה:	תלמיד:
בִּתוֹ ילדה גדולה.	הבת שלו ילדה גדולה.
בִּתִי ילדה גדולה.	הבת שלי ילדה גדולה.
בִּתֵך ילדה גדולה.	הבת שלך ילדה גדולה.
בִּתכם ילדה גדולה.	הבת שלכם ילדה גדולה.
בִּתֵנוּ ילדה גדולה.	הבת שלנו ילדה גדולה.

Do this drill in reverse, also.

F. Transformation Drill

My son is studying Hebrew.

מורה:	תלמיד:
בְּנִי לומד עברית.	הבן שלי לומד עברית.
בִּנך לומד עברית.	הבן שלך לומד עברית.
בְּננוּ לומד עברית.	הבן שלנו לומד עברית.
בִּנכם לומד עברית.	הבן שלכם לומד עברית.
בְּנוֹ לומד עברית.	הבן שלו לומד עברית.
בְּנה לומד עברית.	הבן שלה לומד עברית.

G. Conversational Exercise

The instructor asks each student the following questions, and the student gives the correct answer pertaining to himself.

How many brother do you have?	?כמה אחים יש לך
I have _____ brothers.	אחים. _____ יש לי
How many sisters do you have?	?כמה אחיות יש לך
I have _____ sisters.	אחיות. _____ יש לי
How many children do you have?	?כמה ילדים יש לך
I have _____ children.	ילדים. _____ יש לי
How many sons do you have?	?כמה בנים יש לך
I have _____ sons.	בנים. _____ יש לי
How many daughters do you have?	?כמה בנות יש לך
I have _____ daughters.	בנות _____ יש לי
How many grandchildren do your parents have?	?כמה נכדים יש להורים שלך
My parents have _____ grandchildren.	נכדים. _____ להורים שלי
How many grandchildren does your grandfather have?	?כמה נכדים יש לסבא שלך
My father's father has _____ grandchildren,	נכדים, _____ לאבא של אבי
and my mother's father has _____ grandchildren.	נכדים. _____ לאבא של אמי
How many great-grandchildren does your grandfather have?	?כמה נינים יש לסבא שלך
My grandfather has _____ great-grandchildren.	נינים. _____ לסבא שלי יש

H. Transformation Drill

My parents live outside the city.

מורה:

הורי גרים מחוץ לעיר.
הוריך גרים מחוץ לעיר.
הוריך גרים מחוץ לעיר.
הורֿיו גרים מחוץ לעיר.
הוריה גרים מחוץ לעיר.
הורינו גרים מחוץ לעיר.
הוריכם גרים מחוץ לעיר.
הוריכן גרים מחוץ לעיר.
הוריהם גרים מחוץ לעיר.
הוריהן גרים מחוץ לעיר.

תלמיד:

ההורים שלי גרים מחוץ לעיר.
ההורים שלך גרים מחוץ לעיר.
ההורים שלך גרים מחוץ לעיר.
ההורים שלו גרים מחוץ לעיר.
ההורים שלה גרים מחוץ לעיר.
ההורים שלנו גרים מחוץ לעיר.
ההורים שלכם גרים מחוץ לעיר.
ההורים שלכן גרים מחוץ לעיר.
ההורים שלהם גרים מחוץ לעיר.
ההורים שלהן גרים מחוץ לעיר.

Do this drill in reverse, also.

I. Transformation Drill

(Note the form /exav/ "his brothers".)

My brothers are serving in the navy.

מורה:

אחי משרתים בחיל הים.
אחיך משרתים בחיל הים.
אחיך משרתים בחיל הים.
אחיו משרתים בחיל הים.
אחיה משרתים בחיל הים.
אחינו משרתים בחיל הים.
אחיכם משרתים בחיל הים.
אחיכן משרתים בחיל הים.
אחיהם משרתים בחיל הים.
אחיהן משרתים בחיל הים.

תלמיד:

האחים שלי משרתים בחיל הים.
האחים שלך משרתים בחיל הים.
האחים שלך משרתים בחיל הים.
האחים שלו משרתים בחיל הים.
האחים שלה משרתים בחיל הים.
האחים שלנו משרתים בחיל הים.
האחים שלכם משרתים בחיל הים.
האחים שלכן משרתים בחיל הים.
האחים שלהם משרתים בחיל הים.
האחים שלהן משרתים בחיל הים.

Do this drill in reverse, also.

J. Transformation Drill

(Note the variant /axyot-/ before pronominal suffixes.)

My sisters finished high school.

מורה:

אחיותי גמרו את הגמנסיה.
אחיותיך גמרו את הגמנסיה.
אחיותיך גמרו את הגמנסיה.
אחיותיו גמרו את הגמנסיה.
אחיותיה גמרו את הגמנסיה.
אחיותינו גמרו את הגמנסיה.
אחיותיכם גמרו את הגמנסיה.
אחיותיכן גמרו את הגמנסיה.
אחיותיהם גמרו את הגמנסיה.
אחיותיהן גמרו את הגמנסיה.

תלמיד:

האחיות שלי גמרו את הגמנסיה.
האחיות שלך גמרו את הגמנסיה.
האחיות שלו גמרו את הגמנסיה.
האחיות שלה גמרו את הגמנסיה.
האחיות שלנו גמרו את הגמנסיה.
האחיות שלכם גמרו את הגמנסיה.
האחיות שלכן גמרו את הגמנסיה.
האחיות שלהם גמרו את הגמנסיה.
האחיות שלהן גמרו את הגמנסיה.

Do this drill in reverse, also.

K. Transformation Drill

(Note the variant /bn-/ before the second and third person plural suffixes.)

My sons received their draft notice.

תלמיד:	מורה:
הבנים שלי קבלו צו גיוס.	בני קבלו צו גיוס.
הבנים שלו קבלו צו גיוס.	בניו קבלו צו גיוס.
הבנים שלה קבלו צו גיוס.	בניה קבלו צו גיוס.
הבנים שלנו קבלו צו גיוס.	בנינו קבלו צו גיוס.
הבנים שלכם קבלו צו גיוס.	בניכם קבלו צו גיוס.
הבנים שלכן קבלו צו גיוס.	בניכן קבלו צו גיוס.
הבנים שלהם קבלו צו גיוס.	בניהם קבלו צו גיוס.
הבנים שלהן קבלו צו גיוס.	בניהן קבלו צו גיוס.

(c) <u>In-laws</u>   /mexutanim/   מחותנים

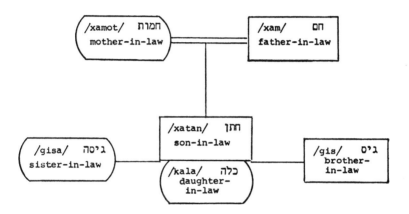

In addition to the above terms Hebrew has two additional terms which must be paraphrased in English:

/mexutan/   "son's (or daughter's) father-in-law"
/mexuténet/   "son's (or daughter's) mother-in-law"

Some speakers use /xoten/ "father-in-law"

The plural of /xamot/ is /xamayot/

L. Completion Drill

Instructor: My wife's father is _____.
Student: My wife's father is
       my father-in-law.

חמי.	האבא של אשתי הוא
חמותי.	האמא של אשתי היא
גיסי.	האח של אשתי הוא
גיסתי.	האחות של אשתי היא
גיסי.	בעלה של אחותי הוא
גיסתי.	אשתו של אחי היא
חתני.	בעלה של בתי הוא
כלתי.	אשתו של בני היא

The instructor may vary this drill by changing
the pronoun suffix: האח של אשתך הוא גיסך.

<u>End of Tape 12A</u>

RAPID RESPONSE DRILL

1. ‏מה עושה אביגדור?‏

2. ‏כמה זמן כבר משרת אביגדור בצבא?‏

3. ‏באיזה חיל הוא משרת?‏

4. ‏היכן למדה אחותו של אביגדור.‏

5. ‏למה מחכה מרים?‏

6. ‏כמה זמן משרתים בנים בצבא?‏

7. ‏כמה זמן משרתות בנות בצבא?‏

REVIEW CONVERSATIONS

‏א: איפה הבן שלך?‏

‏ב: הבן שלי משרת בצבא.‏

‏א: בצבא? הוא כבר בן 18 ?‏

‏ג: הוא כבר בן 19.‏

‏א: הזמן עובר מהר.‏

‏ב: מה לעשות? מזדקנים!‏

‏ג: אמור לי משה, מי האיש הזה?‏

‏ד: זה גיטי. אחיה של מרים.‏

‏ג: באמת? לא ידעתי שלמרים יש אח.‏

‏ד: למרים יש שני אחים ואחות.‏

‏ג: ידעתי שיש לה אחות אבל לא ידעתי שיש לה אחים.‏

‏ד: אז עכשיו אתה יודע.‏

‏ה: באיזה חיל משרתת מרים?‏

‏ו: מרים משרתת בחיל האויר.‏

‏ה: מתי היא גוייסה?‏

‏ו: לפני כשנה.‏

‏ה: גם אחותי משרתת בחיל האויר.‏

ז: מה אתה עושה בעיר, דב?

ח: אני מטייל. גמרתי את הגמנסיה ואני מחכה לצו גיוס.

ז: באיזה גמנסיה למדת?

ח: למדתי בגימנסיה הרצליה.

ז: ומתי אתה חושב להתחיל בשירות הצבאי?

ח: אני מקוה שבעוד שבועיים.

ט: מה שלום ההורים שלך, יוסף?

י: תודה רבה. שלומם טוב.

ט: הם עוד גרים ברמת גן?

י: כן, הם עוד גרים ברמת גן.

ט: אמר עוד אופה עוגות טובות?

י: אני רואה שאתה אוהב את העוגות של אמי.

ט: כן. העוגות של אמר היו טעימות מאד.

כ: מה אתם עושים במוצאי שבת?

ל: אנו נוסעים לחיפה לראות את הילדים.

כ: גם אנו נוסעים השבוע לראות את הילדים שלנו.

ל: כמה נכדים יש לכם?

כ: לנו יש שתי נכדות. ולכם?

ל: לנו יש נכד אחד ונכדה אחת.

כ: שכן ירבו.

מ: אמור לי, האם יעקב הוא גיסך?

נ: לא בדיוק. הוא גיסה של אשתי.

מ: איך זה?

נ: הוא בעלה של אחות אשתי.

איזה תספורת אתה רוצה?...

Tape 12B

27.1 <u>At the Barbershop</u> /bamaspera/ במספרה

BARBER   /sapar/   ספר

Hello, sir. What can I do for you.	Šalom adoni. ma ani yaxol laasot bišvilxa.	שלום אדוני. מה אני יכול לעשות בשבילך?

<u>MR. WILLIAMS</u>

I'd like a haircut and a shave.	ani roce lehistaper velehitgaléax.	אני רוצה להסתפר ולהתגלח.
he got a haircut he shaved (himself), got a shave	histaper hitgaléax	הסתפר התגלח

<u>BARBER</u>

Please sit down. I'll be free right away.	šev bevakaša, ani miyad mitpane eléxa.	שב בבקשה. אני מיד מתפנה אליך.
he became unoccupied	hitpana	התפנה
What kind of haircut do you want? hairdo	éyze tispóret ata roce. tispóret (f)	איזה תספורת אתה רוצה? תספורת

<u>MR. WILLIAMS</u>

A short haircut. short	tispóret kcara. kacar (m.s.)	תספורת קצרה. קצר

<u>BARBER</u>

Do you want a shampoo? shampoo	ata roce xafifa? xafifa (f)	אתה רוצה חפיפה? חפיפה

<u>MR. WILLIAMS</u>

No, but
trim the mustache.
      he shortened
      mustache
	lo. aval
	kacer li et hasafam.
	kicer
	safam (m)
		לא. אבל
		קצר לי את השפם.
		קיצר
		שפם

<u>BARBER</u>

I hope you're satisfied, Sir. satisfied	ani mekave šeata sva racon adoni. sva racon (m.s.)	אני מקוה שאתה שבע רצון, אדוני. שבע רצון

<u>MR. WILLIAMS</u>

Yes. Thank you. How much do I owe you?	ken. toda. káma ani xayav lexa.	כן. תודה. כמה אני חייב לך?

<u>BARBER</u>

Two liras for the haircut and one lira for the shave. shave	štey lírot hatispóret, velíra axat hagilúax. gilúax (m)	שתי לירות התספורת ולירה אחת הגילוח. גילוח

325

27.2 ADDITIONAL VOCABULARY

I want a shampoo and set.	ani roca xafifa vesidur.	אני רוצה חפיפה וסידור.

I want to dye my gray hair.	ani roca licbóa et saarot haseva šeli.	אני רוצה לצבוע את שערות השיבה שלי.
he dyed	cava	צבע
hair	sear (m.s.)	שער
a hair	seara (f.s.)	שערה
hair, hairs	searot	שערות
gray	séva (f)	שיבה

How much is a hair-do?	káma ola tisróket.	כמה עולה תסרוקת?
hair-do	tisróket (f)	תסרוקת

I want a permanent.	ani roca pérmanent.	אני רוצה פרמננט.

How much is a permanent wave?	káma ole silsul tmidi.	כמה עולה סלסול תמידי?
curling	silsul (m)	סלסול
permanent	tmidi (m.s.)	תמידי

I want a manicure.	ani roca manikyur.	אני רוצה מניקיור.

27.3 VOCABULARY DRILL

A. Substitution-Agreement Drill /kacar/ "short"   קצר

    The day is short.   <u>היום קצר.</u>

ההצגה – הרחובות – שתי המערכות האחרונות – הדרך
השער שלו – השערות שלו – החורף – הקיץ – הלילה

B. Substitution Drill   /sva racon/ "satisfied"   שבע רצון

    I'm satisfied with the service.

אני	<i>שבע-רצון</i> מהשרות.
היא	שבעת-רצון
אנחנו	שבעי-רצון
הן	שבעות-רצון

C. Substitution-Agreement Drill

    Are you pleased with the food?   <u>האם אתה שבע-רצון מהאוכל?</u>

אתך – מר ווילאמס – העולים – האחית שלך – את

27.4 VERB DRILLS

A. Substitution-Agreement Drill   /histaper/   "he got a haircut"   הִסְתַּפֵּר

I'll get a haircut on Friday.

אני אסתפר ביום ששי.

הוא – אתה – אתם – את – אנחנו
החיילים – הן – בתי – הילדים – אני

B. Substitution-Agreement Drill

I get a haircut every two weeks.

אני מסתפר כל שבועיים.

אחותו – אתם – הנשים – אחיה

C. Substitution-Agreement Drill

I got a haircut only last week.

הסתפרתי רק בשבוע שעבר.

הילדים – אתה – את – דוד
הן – אתם – אנו – אשתי – אני

D. Substitution-Agreement Drill   /hitgaléax/   "he shaved"   התגלח

I'll shave just before Shabbat.

אתגלח לפני כניסת השבת.

אתה – הוא – הם – אנו – אתם – אני

E. Substitution-Agreement Drill

Sometimes I shave twice in one day.

לפעמים אני מתגלח פעמיים ביום אחד.

אחי – הם – אנו – אני

F. Substitution-Agreement Drill

I shaved last night.

התגלחתי אתמול בערב.

אתה – אתם – אנחנו – החיילים – הוא – אני

G. Transformation Drill - <u>hitpa'el</u> to <u>pi'el</u>

Instructor: I got shave at the barber's.
Student: The barber shaved me.

הספר גילח אותי.	התגלחתי אצל הספר.
הספר גילח אותנו.	התגלחנו אצל הספר.
הספר גילח אותם.	הם התגלחו אצל הספר.
הספר גילח את משה.	משה התגלח אצל הספר.
הספר גילח אותך.	התגלחת אצל הספר.

Do this drill in reverse, also.

H. Expansion Drill

Instructor: I'm waiting.
Student: I'm waiting until the barber is ready for me.

עד שהספר יתפנה אלי.	אני מחכה
עד שהספר יתפנה אליך.	אתה מחכה
עד שהספר יתפנה אליו.	משה מחכה
עד שהספר יתפנה אלינו.	אנו מחכים
עד שהספר יתפנה אליכם.	אתם מחכים
עד שהספר יתפנה אליהם.	הם מחכים

I. Substitution-Agreement Drill

Just today I got some free time to write letters.

רק היום התפניתי לכתוב מכתבים.

אנו – אשתי – אחי – החיילים
אתה – את – בני – התלמידות – אני

J. Substitution Drill   /cava/   "he painted, dyed" צבע

Paint the house.

צבע את הבית.
צבעי
צבעו
צבענה

K. Transformation Drill - Negative to Affirmative

Instructor: Don't paint the house.
Student: Paint the house.

צבע את הבית.	אל תצבע את הבית.
צבעי את הבית.	אל תצבעי את הבית.
צבעו את הבית.	אל תצבעו את הבית.
צבענה את הבית.	אל תצבענה את הבית.

Do this drill in reverse, also.

L. Substitution-Agreement Drill

I paint the house every three years.

אני צובע את הבית כל שלוש שנים.

אנו – גב' כספי – הם – הן – אבי

M. Substitution-Agreement Drill

When did she dye her hair?

מתי היא צבעה את השער?

את – אתן – הן – אחותך

328

N. Substitution Drill   /kícer/   "he shortened"   קצר

  Shorten the way. Go straight.

קצר את הדרך . לך ישר .
קצרי   (לכי)
קצרו   (לכו)
קצרנה   (לכנה)

O. Expansion Drill

  Instructor: I'll go straight.
  Student: If I go straight, I'll shorten the way.

אם אלך ישר, אקצר את הדרך.
אם תלכי ישר, תקצרי את הדרך.
אם תלכנה ישר, תקצרנה את הדרך.
אם ילך ישר, יקצר את הדרך.
אם נלך ישר, נקצר את הדרך.
אם תלך ישר, תקצר את הדרך.
אם תלכו ישר, תקצרו את הדרך.
אם ילכו ישר, יקצרו את הדרך.

P. Substitution-Agreement Drill

  He writes briefly.

הוא מקצר בכתיבה.

חמותי – התלמידרות – החיילים – גיסי

Q. Substitution-Agreement Drill

  I shortened the letter.

קצרתי את המכתב.

אחן – אחיו – אנחנו – אתם – את
האחות שלך – הן – אתה – הם – אני

R. Transformation Drill   -   Future to Past.

  Instructor: I'll cut my hair short.
  Student: I cut my hair short.

אקצר את השער.   קצרתי את השער.
תקצרי את השער.   קצרת את השער.
נקצר את השער.   קצרנו את השער.
תקצר את השער.   קצרת את השער.
יקצר את השער.   יקצר את השער.
יקצרו את השער.   קצרו את השער.
תקצרנה את השער.   קצרתן את השער.
תקצרו את השער.   קצרתם את השער.

  Do this drill in reverse, also.

329

GRAMMAR NOTES

27.5 /haya/ " he was" היה

The pronunciation of the forms of /lihyot/ "to be" will vary, depending on the rate of speech. In slow, deliberate speech the vowel /i/ or /e/ may be inserted between the /h/ and a following consonant: /tihiye/ "you will be". In more rapid speech the /h/ will be dropped: /tiye/.

In the past tense a definite y- glide is heard only in very careful speech. There is always some glide from the /a/ to the /i/ but in ordinary speech it is rather weak: /hajti/. See Grammar Note 17.8, Drill EE.

/haya/ is a lamed hey verb conjugated in the kal. In the following chart the root consonants hy are shown throughout as though it were a regular verb. The student should note the instructor's pronunciation of the forms and also be aware that in pronouncing the forms carefully the instructor will tend to say, for example, /eheye/ "I will be" rather than /eye/.

Infinitive:		lihyot		
Imperative:	m.s.	heye	m.pl.	heyu
	f.s.	heyi	f.pl.	heyéna
Future:	1 s.	ehye	1 pl.	nihye
	2 m.s.	tihye	2 m.pl.	tihyu
	2 f.s.	tihyi	2 f.pl.	tihyéna
	3 m.s.	yihye	3 m.pl.	yihyu
	3 f.s.	tihye	3 f.pl.	tihyéna
Present:	See below			
Past:	1 s.	hayíti	1 pl.	hayínu
	2 m.s.	hayíta	2 m.pl.	hayítem
	2 f.s.	hayit	2 f.pl.	hayíten
	3 m.s.	haya	3 pl.	hayu
	3 f.s.	hayta		

In poetry the form /hove/ הווה is sometimes used as a present tense form meaning "exists". Otherwise, there is no present tense of this verb. See Grammar Note 2.4 Equational Sentences.

The word /hove/ הווה is also the grammatical term for "present tense"

A. Substitution Drill

Be at school at 8:00.

היה בבית הספר בשמונה.
היי
היו
היינה

B. Expansion Drill

Instructor: Don't be there at 9:00.
Student: Don't be there at 9:00; be there at 8:00.

אל תהיה שם בתשע.	היה שם בשמונה.
אל תהיי שם בתשע.	היי שם בשמונה.
אל תהיו שם בתשע.	היו שם בשמונה.
אל תהיינה שם בתשע	היינה שם בשמונה.

Do this drill in reverse, also.

330

C. Substitution Drill

(The instructor supplies only the verb form. The student should make the
necessary changes in /muxan/.)

I'll be ready at 7:00.   .אהיה מוכן בשבע

תהיה (מוכן)
תהיי (מוכנה)
אבא יהיה (מוכן)
אמא תהיה (מוכנה)
נהיה (מוכנים)
אתם תהיו (מוכנים)
אתן תהיינה (מוכנות)
הם יהיו (מוכנים)
הן תהיינה (מוכנות)

D. Substitution-Agreement Drill

Rachel will be at home this evening.   .רחל תהיה בבית הערב

אני – אתה – הם – אנחנו – את – אחיותי
אנו – אתם – אחי – אמי – אתן – רחל

E. Substitution-Agreement Drill

Yaakov was a student in the language school.   יעקב היה תלמיד בבית הספר לשפות

אני – אתה – היא – אנו – אתם
הם – היא – את – הם – הן

F. Transformation Drill   – Future to Past

Instructor: Rachel will be at our house next week.
Student: Rachel was at our house last week.

רחל תהיה אצלנו בשבוע הבא.   רחל היתה אצלנו בשבוע שעבר.
אתה תהיה אצלנו בשבוע הבא.   אתה היית אצלנו בשבוע שעבר.
איך יהיה אצלנו בשבוע הבא.   אכיך היה אצלנו בשבוע שעבר.
הנכדים שלנו יהיו אצלנו בשבוע הבא.   הנכדים שלנו היו אצלנו בשבוע שעבר.
הבנות שלנו תהיינה אצלנו בשבוע הבא.   הבנות שלנו היו אצלנו בשבוע שעבר.
אתם תהיו אצלנו בשבוע הבא.   אתם הייתם אצלנו בשבוע שעבר.
את תהיי אצלנו בשבוע הבא.   את היית אצלנו בשבוע שעבר.
אתן תהיינה אצלנו בשבוע הבא.   אתן הייתן אצלנו בשבוע שעבר.
חמותי תהיה אצלנו בשבוע הבא.   חמותי היתה אצלנו בשבוע שעבר.

Do this drill in reverse, also.

331

27.6   " I had" , "I will have"

In Grammar Note 11.6 the construction /yeš li/ " I have" was described.
In the past and future tenses the verb /haya/ replaces /yeš/. The negative
/eyn/ is replaced by /lo haya/, etc.

The forms of /haya/ must agree in gender and number with the objects possessed.

/haya li séfer/	"I had a book"	היה לי ספר
/hayta li eškolit/	"I had a grapefruit"	היתה לי אשכולית
/hayu li sfarim/	"I had books"	היו לי ספרים

Though the object possessed is the grammatical <u>subject</u> of the Hebrew
construction the preposition /et/ is used by many speakers when this object is
definite:

/haya li et haséfer/ "I had the book"   היה לי את הספר

A. Transformation Drill - Present to Past, Masculine Singular

Instructor: I have a book.
Student: I had a book.

מורה: יש לי _____•   תלמיד: היה לי _____•

ספר – טלפון – אוכל – קפה – בית – מנהל טוב – יין
שוקולד – חבר – מברק – דוד באמריקה – מרשם לעוגה

B. Transformation Drill   - Present to Past, Feminine Singular

Instructor: I have a <u>lira</u>.
Student: I had a <u>lira</u>.

מורה: יש לי _____•   תלמיד: היתה לי_____•

לירה – עוגה – גבינה – חברה בשגרירות
חלה – אשכולית – צנצנת שמנת – מורה טובה

C. Transformation Drill - Present to Past, Plural

Instructor: I have two telegrams.
Student: I had two telegrams.

מורה: י_ לי _____•   תלמיד: היו לי _____•

שני מברקים – רגים ממולאים – כוסות – מקומות טובים – עוגות
גבינות – חברים בכית – תאנים – כרטיסים לקולנוע

D. Transformation Drill - Present to Past

Instructor: I have a good boss.
Student: I used to have a good boss.

מורה: יש לי _____•   תלמיד: היה לי _____•

מנהל טוב – מרשם לעוגה – הרבה ספרים – גלידה – חלות
חברה במשרד התיירות – שערות ארוכות – בית כרמת גן

Drills A to D should be varied by changing the sentences to negative sentences:
Instructor: I don't have a house.   אין לי בית.
Student: I didn't have a house.   לא היה לי בית.

E. Expansion Drill

Instructor: I bought a house.
Student: I bought a house because I didn't have a house.

כי לא היה לי בית.	קניתי בית,
כי לא היתה לי עוגה.	קניתי עוגה,
כי לא היה לי קפה.	קניתי קפה,
כי לא היתה לי גלידה.	קניתי גלידה,
כי לא היתה לי גבינה.	קניתי גבינה,
כי לא היו לי ספרים.	קניתי ספרים,
כי לא היה לי לחם.	קניתי לחם,
כי לא היה לי יין.	קניתי יין,
כי לא היו לי דגים.	קניתי דגים,
כי לא היו לי עוגות.	קניתי עוגות,
כי לא היה לי ספר.	קניתי ספר,
כי לא היו לי חלות.	קניתי חלות,

Note: This drill may be varied by changing the subject of the verb /kaníti/:
Instructor: Moshe bought a house.
Student: Moshe bought a house because he didn't have a house.

כי לא היה לו בית.	משה קנה בית,

F. Expansion Drill

Instructor: She bought fruit.
Student: She bought fruit.because she didn't have any.

כי לא היו לה.	היא קנתה פירות
כי לא היו לך.	את קנית פירות
כי לא היו לנו.	אנו קנינו פירות
כי לא היו להם.	הם קנו פירות
כי לא היו לכם.	אתם קניתם פירות
כי לא היו להן.	הנשים קנו פירות
כי לא היו לו.	הוא קנה פירות
כי לא היו לי.	אני קניתי פירות

G. Transformation Drill - Present to Future, Masculine Singular

Instructor: I have a book.
Student: I'll have a book.

מורה: יש לי _____.   תלמיד: יחיה לי _____.

ספר – טלפון – אוכל – קפה – בית – מנהל טוב – יין
שוקולד – חבר – מברק – דוד באמריקה – מרשם לעוגה

H. Transformation Drill - Present to Future, Feminine Singular

Instructor: I have an appointment.
Student: I'll have an appointment.

מורה: יש לי _____.   תלמיד: תהיה לי _____.

פגישה – עוגה – גבינה – חברה בשגרירות
חלה – אשכולית – צנצנת שמנת – מורה טובה

I. Transformation Drill - Present to Future, Masculine Plural

Instructor: I have two telegrams.
Student: I'll have two telegrams.

מורה: יש לי _____.   תלמיד: יהיו לי _____.

שני מברקים – דגים ממולאים – מקומות טובים –
חברים בבית – ירקות ירוקים – כרטיסים לסרט – בולים

J. Transformation Drill - Present to Future, Feminine Plural

Instructor: I have good news.
Student: I'll have good news.

מורה: יש לי _____.   תלמיד: תהיינה לי _____.

חדשות טובות – תאנים – ביצים טריות –
מעטפות למכתבים – גלויות – גבינות לבנות וצהובות

K. Transformation Drill - Present to Future

Instructor: I have three tickets.
Student: I'll have three tickets.

מורה: יש לי _____.   תלמיד: יהיו לי _____.

שלושה כרטיסים – טלפון בבית – ספר מעניין – קופסת צבע – שער שיבה
חלות נהדרות – שני אחים בצבא – זמן להסתפר – פגישה רחופה – ארוחה חמה
כוסות חדשות – אגרת אויר – עוגות דובדבנים – תפוחי אדמה

L. Transformation Drill - Past to Future

Instructor: I had a parking place.
Student: I'll have a parking place.

יהיה לי מקום חניה.	היה לי מקום חניה.
יהיה לי טלפון בבית.	היה לי טלפון בבית.
יהיו לי כרטיסים לקולנוע.	היו לי כרטיסים לקולנוע.
תהיה לי קופסת שוקולד.	היתה לי קופסת שוקולד.
תהיה לי חבילה בדואר.	היתה לי חבילה בדואר.
תהיינה לי גבינות טעימות.	היו לי גבינות טעימות.
יהיו לי ירקות טריים.	היו לי ירקות טריים.
תהיינה לי ביצים טריות.	היו לי ביצים טריות.
יהיה לי מכתב מהמשפחה.	היה לי מכתב מהמשפחה.
תהיה לי פגישה עם חבר.	היתה לי פגישה עם חבר.
יהיו לי ספרים מעניינים.	היו לי ספרים מעניינים.
תהיינה לי חלות חמות.	היו לי חלות חמות.

Do this drill in reverse, also.

End of Tape 12B

RAPID RESPONSE DRILL

1. מה רצה מר ווייליאמס לעשות במספרה?
2. האם היה הספר מוכן לקבל אותו מיד?
3. איזה תספורת רצה מר ווייליאמס?
4. האם הספר חפף לו את הראש?
5. מה ביקש מר ווייליאמס לעשות לשפם?
6. כמה עלתה התספורת?
7. כמה עלה הגילוח?

REVIEW CONVERSATIONS

א: מׂשה, תראה את חנה, היא בלונדינית.
ב: בלונדינית? מתי היא צבעה את השער?
א: לפני שבוע. היא נראית יפה, נכון?
ב: כן היא נראית מצוּיין. הצבע באמת יפה.

ג: לאן את רצה מרים?
ד: אני ממהרת למספרה. אני צריכה להיות שם בעׂשר.
ג: מה את הולכת לעשות?
ד: אני הולכת לעשות פרמננט.

ה: דב, אתה צריך להסתפר.
ו: מה את שׂחה חנה, הרי הסתפרתי רק לפני שבועיים.
ה: כן, אבל הגיע הזמן להסתפר שוב.
ו: טוב. אם את חוׂשבת כך, אגש להסתפר הערב.

335

ז: אדוני, שב בבקשה. אני מיד מתפנה אליך.

ח: אין לי הרבה זמן. אני ממהר.

ז: חכה רגע. אני כבר בא.

ח: אני לא יכול לחכות. אבוא מחר.

ז: כרצונך.

ט: גברתי, אני מקוה שאת שבעת רצון מהסדור.

י: כן. אבל הצבע לא כל כך יפה.

ט: הצבע יפה מאד, גברתי. לא רואים את שערות השיבה.

י: נראה כמה זמן הצבע יהיה טוב.

כ: כמה כסף יש לך, מרים?

ל: יש לי חמש לירות.

כ: חמש לירות? זה הכל?

ל: קניתי ירקות והלכתי למספרה והכסף הלך.

כ: כן. מה לעשות.

מ: מה אתם עושים?

נ: אנו עומדים לצבוע את הבית.

מ: את כל הבית?

נ: רק מבחוץ. צבענו את פנים הבית בשנה שעברה.

מ: באיזה צבע תצבעו?

נ: בצבע לבן.

28.1 <u>At the Cleaner's</u>   /bamaxbesa/   במכבסה

MRS. WILLIAMS

Ma'am, I want	gvirti, ani roca	גברתי, אני רוצה
to put in these clothes	limsor et habgadim	למסור את הבגדים
for cleaning.	lenikuy.	לניקוי.
he delivered	masar	מסר
garment	béged (m)	בגד
he cleaned	nika	ניקה

CLERK /pkida/   פקידה

Fine, let's see	beséder. nir'e	בסדר. נראה
how many pieces	káma xatixot yeš.	כמה חתיכות יש.
there are.		
piece	xatixa (f)	חתיכה

MRS. WILLIAMS

Two suits	štey xalifot	שתי חליפות
and two	vešney	ושני
pairs of pants.	zugot mixnasáim.	זוגות מכנסיים.
suit	xalifa (f)	חליפה
pair	zug (m)	זוג
trousers, slacks	mixnasáim (m.du.)	מכנסיים

CLERK

Yes. I see .	ken, ani roa.	כן. אני רואה.

MRS. WILLIAMS

Pay attention	sími lev	שימי לב
to the stains.	laktamim.	לכתמים.
he put	sam	שם
heart	lev (m)	לב
stain, spot	kétem (m)	כתם

CLERK

Do you know	at yodáat	את יודעת
what the stains are from?	mima haktamim?	ממה הכתמים?

MRS. WILLIAMS

I think	ani xošévet	אני חושבת
that the stains	šehaktamim	שהכתמים
on the trousers	al hamixnasáim	על המכנסיים
are from grease.	hem mišuman.	הם משומן.
grease	šuman (m)	שומן

CLERK

And the stains on the jacket?	vehaktamim al haẑaket?		והכתמים על הז'קט?
jacket	ẑaket (m)	ז'קט	

MRS. WILLIAMS

Oh, they're from pomegranate juice.	o - hem mimic rimon.	או – הם ממיץ רימון.

CLERK

Do you know that pomegranate juice doesn't come out easily?	at yodáat ẑemic rimon lo yored bekalut.		את יודעת שמיץ רימון לא יורד בקלות?
ease	kalut (f)	קלות	

MRS. WILLIAMS

Yes, but try to get them out as best as you can.	ken. aval nasi lehoridam kemeytav yexoltex.		כן. אבל נסי להורידם כמיטב יכולתך.
he tried	nisa	ניסה	
he brought down	horid	הוריד	
the best	meytav	מיטב	
ability	yexólet (f)	יכולת	

CLERK

We'll try to get it clean.	niẑtadel ẑeyihye naki.		נשתדל שיהיה נקי.
he strove	hiẑtadel	השתדל	
clean	naki (m.s.)	נקי	
When do you need the clothes?	lematay at crixa et habgadim?		למתי את צריכה את הבגדים?

MRS. WILLIAMS

For the week end. Will they be ready?	lesof haẑavúa. hem yihyu muxanim?		לסוף השבוע. הם יהיו מוכנים?
end	sof (m)	סוף	

CLERK

Yes. They'll be ready.	ken. hem yihyu muxanim.	כן. הם יהיו מוכנים.

338

28.2 ADDITIONAL VOCABULARY

I took the dress in to be dry cleaned.	masárti et hasimla lenikuy yaveš.	מסרתי את השמלה לניקוי יבש.
dress	simla (f)	שמלה
dry	yaveš	יבש

I brought in the skirt with the pleats to be pressed.	hevéti et haxacait im hakfalim legihuc.	הבאתי את החצאית עם הקפלים לגיהוץ.
skirt	xacait (f)	חצאית
pleat	kéfel (m)	קפל
he pressed	gihec	גיהץ

I brought in the "linen" to the laundry.	masárti et halvanim lekvisa.	מסרתי את הלבנים לכביסה.
sheets, underwear, etc.	levanim (m,pl.)	לבנים
laundry	kvisa (f)	כביסה

It's possible to wash this with soap.	efšar lexabes et ze besabon.	אפשר לכבס את זה בסבון.
he laundered	kibes	כיבס
soap	sabon (m)	סבון

28.3 VOCABULARY DRILLS

A. Substitution-Agreement Drill   /naki/ "clean" נקי

The table is clean.

השולחן נקי.

המים – הכביסה – הפירות – החנויות
הבית שלה – הרחובות – המזנון – השמלה

B. Substitution-Agreement Drill /yaveš/ "dry"   יבש

The weather is dry.

מזג האויר יבש.

הכוסות – הבקבוקים – החצאית – הכגדים
השמלות – האויר – העוגה – הלחם

28.4 VERB DRILLS

(a) /masar/ "he delivered, transmitted"   מסר

A. Substitution Drill

Take the clothes to the cleaners.

מסור את הבגדים למכבסה.
מסרי
מסרו
מסורנה

339

B. Substitution-Agreement Drill

My brother will get the books to the teacher.   <u>אחי ימסור את הספרים למורה.</u>

אתה – אחותך – את – אנו – התלמידות
אתם – הבנים שלו – אתן – אני – הוא

C. Transformation Drill – Future to Past

Instructor: Who will take in the laundry?
Student: Who took in the laundry?

מי מסר את הכביסה?   מי ימסור את הכביסה?
אשתי מסרה את הכביסה.   אשתי תמסור את הכביסה.
אני מסרתי את הכביסה.   אני אמסור את הכביסה.
אתם מסרתם את הכביסה.   אתם תמסרו את הכביסה.
הבנות מסרו את הכביסה.   הבנות תמסורנה את הכביסה.
אנו מסרנו את הכביסה.   אנו נמסור את הכביסה.
אתה מסרת את הכביסה.   אתה תמסור את הכביסה.
את מסרת את הכביסה.   את תמסרי את הכביסה.

Do this drill in reverse, also.

D. Substitution-Agreement Drill

He's delivering the message.   <u>הוא מוסר את ההודעה.</u>

הן – החברים שלי – אחותה – אני

(b) /nika/ "he cleaned"   ניקה

E. Substitution Drill

Clean the windows.   נקה את החלונות.
נקי
נקו
נקינה

F. Substitution-Agreement Drill

We'll clean the tables.   <u>אנחנו ננקה את השולחנות.</u>

אני – את – אחיך – הנשים – אתה
אתם – בתכם – אתן – הם – מי

G. Substitution-Agreement Drill

I clean the house every day.   <u>אני מנקה את הבית כל יום.</u>

אשתו – החיילים – הבנות שלהם – בני

H. Transformation Drill - Future to Past

Instructor: She will clean the clothes.
Student: She cleaned the clothes.

היא נקתה את הבגדים.	היא תנקה את הבגדים.
הן ניקו את הבגדים.	הן תנקינה את הבגדים.
אנו ניקינו את הבגדים.	אנו נ נקה את הבגדים.
את ניקית את הבגדים.	את תנקי את הבגדים.
בעל המכבסה ניקה את הבגדים.	בעל המכבסה ינקה את הבגדים.
אתם ניקיתם את הבגדים.	אתם תנקו את הבגדים.
אני ניקיתי את הבגדים.	אני אנקה את הגדים.

Do this drill in reverse, also.

(c) /sam/ "he put"   שם

This is an <u>ayin yud</u> verb and is conjugated like /šar/ "he sang".

I. Substitution Drill

Pay attention, please.

שים לב, בבקשה.
שימי
שימו
שמנה

J. Substitution-Agreement Drill

I'll put the fruit on the table.

אני אשים את הפירות על השולחן

את – הבן שלי – אתה – הן
אנחנו – אתם – אתן – הילדים

K. Substitution-Agreement Drill

He puts everything in its place.

הוא שם את הכל במקום.

חמותי – הילדות – הם – אני

L. Expansion Drill

Instructor: I didn't hear.
Student: I didn't hear because I wasn't paying attention.

כי לא שמחי לב.	לא שמעתי
כי לא שמחם לב.	לא שמעתם
כי לא שמנו לב.	לא שמענו
כי הוא לא שם לב.	הוא לא שמע
כי היא לא שמה לב.	היא לא שמעה
כי הן לא שמו לב.	התלמידות לא שמער
כי לא שמת לב.	לא שמעת

341

(d) /nisa/ "he attempted" ניסה

M. Substitution Drill

Try your best.

נסה כמיטב יכולתך.

נסי	(יכולתך)
נסו	(יכולתכם)
נסינה	(יכולתכן)

N. Substitution-Agreement Drill

He'll try to finish on time.

<u>הוא ינסה לגמור בזמן</u>.

אני – הפועלים – אנחנו – אתה – המנהלת
את – אתם – הן – כולם

O. Substitution-Agreement Drill
(Change the form /yexolti/, also)

I try my best.

<u>אני מנסה כמיטב יכולתי</u>.

אנחנו – אתה – היא – הילדים
הן – אתן – את – אני

P. Expansion Drill .

Instructor: I didn't go.
Student: I didn't go nor did I even try to go.

לא הלכתי	ובכלל לא ניסיתי ללכת.
הם לא הלכו	ובכלל לא ניסו ללכת.
לא הלכנו	ובכלל לא ניסינו ללכת.
לא הלכת	ובכלל לא ניסית ללכת.
היא לא הלכה	ובכלל לא ניסתה ללכת.
לא הלכת	ובכלל לא ניסית ללכת.

(e) /horid/ "he brought down" הוריד

This is the <u>hif'il</u> of /yarad/ "he descended" ירד

Q. Substitution Drill

Take the men down to the first floor.

הורד את האנשים לקומה הראשונה.
הורידי
הורידו
הורדנה

R. Substitution-Agreement Drill

I'll get the spots out.

<u>אוריד את הכתמים</u>.

אני – את – הוא – האשה – הם – הן

S. Expansion Drill

Instructor: I brought up the box.
Student: I brought up the box and took down the bottles.

העליתי את הקופסה.	והורדתי את הבקבוקים.
העלינו את הקופסה	והורדנו את הבקבוקים.
העליתם את הקופסה	והורדתם את הבקבוקים.
הוא העלה את הקופסה	והוריד את הבקבוקים.
היא העלתה את הקופסה	והורידה את הבקבוקים.
העלית את הקופסה	והורדת את הבקבוקים.
הם העלו את הקופסה	והורידו את הבקבוקים.

(f) /hištadel/ "he strove" השתדל

T. Substitution Drill

Try to come early.

השתדל לבוא מוקדם.
השתדלי
השתדלו
השתדלנה

U. Substitution-Agreement Drill

I'll try to visit him today.

<u>אשתדל לבקר אותו עוד היום.</u>

הם – אתה – אתם – אנחנו – את – אני
היא – יונתן – אתן – הילדים – הן

V. Substitution-Agreement Drill

We try harder.

<u>אנו משתדלים יותר.</u>

היא – אני – אתן – הם – הוא

W. Substitution-Agreement Drill
(Change the form /yaxolti/, also.)

I tried to understand you, but I couldn't. <u>השתדלתי להבין אותך, אבל לא יכולתי.</u>

אנו – אבא שלי – אמי – התלמידים – אני

X. Transformation Drill - <u>pi'el</u> to <u>hitpa'el</u>

Instructor: He persuaded me to study Hebrew.
Student: I tried to learn Hebrew.

הוא שידל אותי ללמוד עברית.	השתדלתי ללמוד עברית.
הוא שידל אותנו ללמוד עברית.	השתדלנו ללמוד עברית.
הוא שידל את אחיו ללמוד עברית.	אחיו השתדל ללמוד עברית.
הוא שידל את בתו ללמוד עברית.	בתו השתדלה ללמוד עברית.
הוא שידל את נכדיו ללמוד עברית.	נכדיו השתדלו ללמוד עברית.

343

(g) /gihec/ "he pressed"   גיהץ

Y. Substitution Drill

Press all the dresses.

גהץ את כל השׂמלות.
גהצי
גהצו
גהצנה

Z. Expansion Drill

Instructor: I'll clean the suits.
Student: I'll clean and press the suits.

ואגהץ את החליפות.	אנקה
וגגהץ את החליפות.	ננקה
ויגהצו את החליפות.	הם ינקו
ותגהצי את החליפות.	את תנקי
ותגהץ את החליפות.	היא תנקה
ותגהצו את החליפות.	אתם תנקו
ותגהצנה את החליפות.	הן תנקינה
ותגהץ את החליפות.	אתה תנקה
ויגהץ את החליפות.	הוא ינקה

AA. Substitution-Agreement Drill

They press very nicely.

הם מגהצים יפה מאד.

היא – הפועלים במכבסה – אני – הן

BB. Expansion Drill

Instructor: He cleaned the skirts.
Student: He pressed the skirts that he cleaned.

הוא גיהץ את החצאירות שניקה.	הוא ניקה את החצאירות.
גיהצתי את החצאירות שניקיתי.	ניקיתי את החצאירות.
הם גיהצו את החצאירות שניקו.	הם ניקו את החצאירות.
גיהצת את החצאירות שניקית.	ניקית את החצאירות.
גיהצנו את החצאירות שניקינו.	ניקינו את החצאירות.
אשתי גיהצה את החצאירות שניקתה.	אשתי ניקתה את החצאירות.

(h) /kibes/ "he laundered"   כיבס

    The first root consonant alternates <u>k</u>/<u>x</u>.

CC. Substitution Drill

    Wash the laundry.

כבס את הכביסה.

כבסי

כבסו

כבסנה

DD. Expansion Drill - Negative to Affirmative

    Instructor: Don't wash the clothes in hot water.
    Student: Don't wash the clothes in hot water, wash them in cold water.

כבס אותם במים קרים.	אל תכבס את הבגדים במים חמים.
כבסי אותם במים קרים.	אל תכבסי את הבגדים במים חמים.
כבסנה אותם במים קרים.	אל תכבסנה את הבגדים במים חמים.
כבסו אותם במים קרים.	אל תכבסו את הבגדים במים חמים.

EE. Substitution-Agreement Drill

    We'll wash the laundry with soap.

<u>נכבס את הלבנים בסבון.</u>

אני – את – היא – אתם – אתן
הוא – אתה – הם – הן – אנחנו

FF. Substitution-Agreement Drill

    My wife does the laundry once a week.

<u>אשתי מכבסת פעם בשבוע.</u>

הוא – הנשים – אנו – הם – היא

DD. Transformation Drill - Future to Past

    Instructor: When will you do the laundry?
    Student: When did you do the laundry?

מתי כיבסת את הכביסה?	מתי תכבסי את הכביסה?
מתי כיבסתם את הכביסה?	מתי תכבסו את הכביסה?
מתי היא כיבסה את הכביסה?	מתי היא תכבס את הכביסה?
מתי הם כיבסו את הכביסה?	מתי הם יכבסו את הכביסה?
מתי הן כיבסו את הכביסה?	מתי הן תכבסנה את הכביסה?
מתי כיבסת את הכביסה?	מתי אתה תכבס את הכביסה?

Do this drill in reverse, also.

28.5 Object Suffixes of Verbs

Examine the following sentence from the Basic Conversation:

/nasi lehoridam kemeytav yexoltex./   "Try to get them out as best as you can".

Compare this sentence with the following paraphrase:

/nasi lehorid otam kemeytav yexoltex./

Note that the form /lehoridam/ is a contraction of /lehorid otam/. Such contractions are made with a verb form plus the following suffixes: (Except for the first person singular they are the singular set of pronominal suffixes.)

1 s.	/oti/	- -	/ - éni/	
2 m.s.	/otxa/	- -	/ - xa /	
2 f.s.	/otax/	- -	/ - ex /	
3 m.s.	/oto/	- -	/ - o /	or / -éhu/
3 f.s.	/ota/	- -	/ - a /	or / -éna/
1 pl.	/otánu/	- -	/ - énu/	
2 m.pl.	/etxem/	- -	/ - xem/	
2 f.pl.	/etxen/	- -	/ - xen/	
3 m.pl.	/otam/	- -	/ - am/	
3 f.pl.	/otan/	- -	/ - an/	

If the verb form has a vowel suffix then the object suffixes are as follows:

1 s.	/ - ni/	-	/yekablúni/	"they will receive me"	יקבלוני
2 m.s.	/ - xa/	-	/yekablúxa/	"they will receive you"	יקבלוך
2 f.s.	/ - x /	-	/yekablux/	"they will receive you"	יקבלוך
3 m.s.	/ - hu/	-	/yekablúhu/	"they will receive him"	יקבלוהו
3 f.s.	/ - ha/	-	/yekablúha/	"they will receive her"	יקבלוה
1 pl.	/ - nu/	-	/yekablúnu/	"they will receive us"	יקבלונו
2 m.pl.	/ -xem/	-	/yekablúxem/	"they will receive you"	יקבלוכם
2 f.pl.	/ -xen/	-	/yekablúxen/	"they will receive you"	יקבלוכן
3 m.pl.	/ - m /	-	/yekablúm/	"they will receive them"	יקבלום
3 f.pl.	/ - n /	-	/yekablún/	"they will receive them"	יקבלון

After the 1 singular past tense the suffix / - o/ has the variant / - v/:

/kibaltiv/   " I received him."

Note that the stress remains on the vowel suffix. However, the stress will generally be on the suffix if there is no vowel suffix to the original verb form.

The verb forms will be changed under certain conditions, and these changes complicate the patterns.

In the pi'el, the stem vowel /e/ will be dropped for all object suffixes:

/yekabel otxa/ -- /yekablexa/   "he will receive you"
(The /e/in the contraction breaks up the resulting /-blx-/ cluster).

In the infinitive of the kal the /o/ shifts back to precede the second root consonant:

/ligmor oto/ -- /legomro/   "to finish it"

Other changes in the verb form will occasionally occur:

/lakáxti otxa/   --   /<u>lek</u>axtíxa/   "I took you"

Other forms of some of the object suffixes exist, but the student can learn them as he meets them.

Such contractions are characteristic of the literary or formal styles of Hebrew, but they are used in informal speech, also. The uncontracted forms (with /ot-/) are correct in all styles, but the student should be acquainted with the contracted forms, too.

The following drills will familiarize the student with the more frequent types of contractions. It should be remembered that the differences are stylistic and that some contractions are never made because of the awkwardness of the resulting forms.

Each of the following drills are to be done in three ways. First, as a substitution drill in which the student repeats the contracted forms. Second, as a transformation drill in which the instructor gives the contracted form and the student responds with the full paraphrase. Third, the reverse of the second way, in which the instructor gives the uncontracted forms and the student responds with the contraction. The instructor may further vary the drills by selecting sentences randomly.

A. Substitution - Transformation Drill

He will receive me right away.

.הוא יקבל אותי מיד	.הוא יקבלני מיד
.הוא יקבל אותך מיד	.הוא יקבלך מיד
.הוא יקבל אותך מיד	.הוא יקבלך מיד
.הוא יקבל אותו מיד	.הוא יקבלו מיד
.הוא יקבל אותה מיד	.הוא יקבלה מיד
.הוא יקבל אותנו מיד	.הוא יקבלנו מיד
.הוא יקבל אתכם מיד	.הוא יקבלכם מיד
.הוא יקבל אתכן מיד	.הוא יקבלכן מיד
.הוא יקבל אותם מיד	.הוא יקבלם מיד
.הוא יקבל אותן מיד	.הוא יקבלן מיד

B. Substitution - Transformation Drill

I received you yesterday.

.קבלתי אותך אתמול	.קבלתיך אתמול
.קבלתי אותך אתמול	.קבלתיך אתמול
.קבלתי אותו אתמול	.קבלתיו אתמול
.קבלתי אותה אתמול	.קבלתיה אתמול
.קבלתי אתכם אתמול	.קבלתיכם אתמול
.קבלתי אתכן אתמול	.קבלתיכן אתמול
.קבלתי אותם אתמול	.קבלתים אתמול
.קבלתי אותן אתמול	.קבלתין אתמול

C. Substitution – Transformation Drill

They will count me in class.

הם יספרו אותי בכתה.	הם יספרוני בכתה.
הם יספרו אותך בכתה.	הם יספרוך בכתה.
הם יספרו אותך בכתה.	הם יספרוך בכתה.
הם יספרו אותו בכתה.	הם יספרוהו בכתה.
הם יספרו אותה בכתה.	הם יספרוה בכתה.
הם יספרו אותנו בכתה.	הם יספרונו בכתה.
הם יספרו אתכם בכתה.	הם יספרוכם בכתה.
הם יספרו אתכן בכתה.	הם יספרוכן בכתה.
הם יספרו אותם בכתה.	הם יספרום בכתה.
הם יספרו אותן בכתה.	הם יספרון בכתה.

D. Substitution – Transformation Drill

They counted me in class.

ספרו אותי בכתה.	ספרוני בכתה.
ספרו אותך בכתה.	ספרוך בכתה.
ספרו אותך בכתה.	ספרוך בכתה.
ספרו אותו בכתה.	ספרוהו בכתה.
ספרו אותה בכתה.	ספרוה בכתה.
ספרו אותנו בכתה.	ספרונו בכתה.
ספרו אתכם בכתה.	ספרוכם בכתה.
ספרו אתכן בכתה.	ספרוכן בכתה.
ספרו אותם בכתה.	ספרום בכתה.
ספרו אותן בכתה.	ספרון בכתה.

E. Substitution – Transformation Drill

He'll take me down to the first floor.

הוא יוריד אותי לקומה הראשונה.	הוא יורידני לקומה הראשונה.
הוא יוריד אותך לקומה הראשונה.	הוא יורידך לקומה הראשונה.
הוא יוריד אותך לקומה הראשונה.	הוא יורידך לקומה הראשונה.
הוא יוריד אותו לקומה הראשונה.	הוא יורידו לקומה הראשונה.
הוא יוריד אותה לקומה הראשונה.	הוא יורידה לקומה הראשונה.
הוא יוריד אותנו לקומה הראשונה.	הוא יורידנו לקומה הראשונה.
הוא יוריד אתכם לקומה הראשונה.	הוא יורידכם לקומה הראשונה.
הוא יוריד אתכן לקומה הראשונה.	הוא יורידכן לקומה הראשונה.
הוא יוריד אותם לקומה הראשונה.	הוא יורידם לקומה הראשונה.
הוא יוריד אותן לקומה הראשונה.	הוא יורידן לקומה הראשונה.

348

F. Substitution – Transformation Drill

I recognized you right away.

הכרתי אותך מיד.	הכרתיך מיד.
הכרתי אותך מיד.	הכרתיך מיד.
הכרתי אותו מיד.	הכרתיו מיד.
הכרתי אותה מיד.	הכרתיה מיד.
הכרתי אתכם מיד.	הכרתיכם מיד.
הכרתי אתכן מיד.	הכרתיכן מיד.
הכרתי אותם מיד.	הכרתים מיד.
הכרתי אותן מיד.	הכרתין מיד.

RAPID RESPONSE DRILL

‎1. מה הביאה גב' וויל``יאמס למכבסה?

‎2. כמה חתיכות היו לה?

‎3. מה היו על הבגדים?

‎4. ממה היו הכתמים על המכנסיים?

‎5. ממה היו הכתמים על הז'קט?

‎6. האם כתמים ממיץ רימונים יורדים בקלות או בקושי?

‎7. למתי הצטרכה גב' וויל``יאמס את הבגדים?

REVIEW CONVERSATIONS

‎א: גברתי, אני רוצה למסור את הבגדים לניקוי.

‎ב: לניקוי יבש?

‎א: את החליפות לניקוי יבש ואת השמלות לכיבוס.

‎ב: יש הרבה כתמים על החליפה.

‎א: כן, אני יודעת. נסי להוציא אותם.

‎ב: נשתדל.

349

ג : שוב יש כתמים על הבגדים. אתה לא יכול להזהר?

ד : כוס תה התהפכה עלי.

ג : התה היה מתוק?

ד : כן, אני חושב כך. למה את שואלת?

ג : אני שואלת כי סוכר קשה להוריד בכביסה.

ה : שימי לב לז'קט.

ו : כן אני רואה את הכתמים. ממה הם?

ה : אני חושבת שמשמן.

ו : טוב. אשתדל להוציא את הכתמים.

ה : הז'קט הוא חדש.

ו : אל תדאגי. הכל יצא בכביסה.

ז : מה עם הכביסה הזאת?

ח : צריך להביא אותה למכבסה.

ז : למכבסה? אפשר לכבס אותה בבית, נכון?

ח : לכבס אפשר אבל מי יגהץ?

ז : מה זאת אומרת מי? את.

ט : מה עושה רחל?

י : היא מנקה את הבית.

ט : למה דווקא היום?

י : כי הבית הצורך מאתמול.

כ : היועץ החדש יגיע מחר.

ל : מי יקבל אותו בנמל התעופה?

כ : אם משה לא יכול, אני מוכן.

29.1 <u>At the Shoemaker's</u> /basandlaria/   כסנדלריה

MR. WILLIAMS

Hello. I want to give in these shoes to be fixed.	šalom. ani roce limsor et hanaaláim letikun.	שלום. אני רוצה למסור את הנעליים לתיקון.
shoe	náal (f)	נעל
he repaired	tiken	תיקן

SHOEMAKER /sandlar/ סנדלר

what has to be fixed?	ma carix letaken.	מה צריך לתקן ?

MR. WILLIAMS

New soles for the black shoes and heels for the sandals.	suliot xadašot lanaaláim hašxorot veakevim lasandalim.	סוליות חדשות לנעליים השחורות ועקבים לסנדלים.
sole	sulia (f)	סוליה
heel	akev (m)	עקב
sandal	sandal (m)	סנדל

SHOEMAKER

What kind of heels do you want - rubber or leather?	éyze akevim ata roce - gúmi o or.	איזה עקבים אתה רוצה – גומי או עור ?
rubber	gúmi (m)	גומי
leather, skin	or (m)	עור

MR. WILLIAMS

Rubber heels. How much will it be?	akevey gúmi. káma ze yaale li.	עקבי גומי. כמה זה יעלה לי?

SHOEMAKER

Six <u>liras</u> all together.	šeš lírot beyáxad.	שש לירות ביחד.

MR. WILLIAMS

That's a lot of money.	ze harbe késef.	זה הרבה כסף.
money, silver	késef (m)	כסף

SHOEMAKER

Sir, I have a uniform price. This is the price.	adoni. ecli mexir axid. zéhu hamexir.	אדוני, אצלי מחיר אחיד. זהו המחיר.
price	mexir (m)	מחיר
uniform	axid (m.s.)	אחיד

351

MR. WILLIAMS

Well, all right.	nu méyle.	נו מילא,
Fix them,	taken otam.	תקן אותם.
and take out the nail	vetoci et hamasmer	ותוציא את המסמר
for the same money.	beoto hakésef.	באותו הכסף.
so be it	méyle	מילא
he took out	hoci	הוציא
nail	masmer (m)	מסמר

29.2 ADDITIONAL VOCABULARY

Sew the strap.	tfor et harecua.	תפור את הרצועה.
he sewed	tafar	תפר
strap	recua (f)	רצועה
Polish the shoes.	caxcéax et hanaaláim.	צחצח את הנעליים.
he polished	cixcéax	צחצח
I need new laces.	ani carix sroxim xadašim.	אני צריך שרוכים חדשים.
lace	srox (m)	שרוך
I need shoe polish.	ani carix mišxat naaláim.	אני צריך משחת נעליים.
ointment	mišxa (f)	משחה

29.3 VERB DRILLS

(a) /tiken/ "he repaired" חיקן

A. Substitution Drill

Repair the clothes.   תקן את הבגדים.
            תקני
            תקנו
            תקנה

B. Substitution-Agreement Drill

I'll repair it before the day is over.   אתקן אותו עוד היום.

אנו – הסנדלר – אתה – היא – הם
את – אתן – אתם – אני

C. Substitution-Agreement Drill

Her husband repairs what the children break.   בעלה מתקן מה שהילדים שוברים.

אשתי – אנחנו – האמהות – הוא

D. Substitution-Agreement Drill

Who fixed the clock?

מי תִיקֵן את השעון?

את – שלי – אמא – אחי – אני – אתה
מי – זהבי 'גב – הם – אתם

(b) /hoci/ "he took out" הוציא

In the first and second person forms of the past tense the stem vowel is /e/:
/hocéti/   "I brought out".

E. Substitution Drill

Take the children outside.

הוצא את הילדים החוצה.
הוציאי
הוציאו
הוצאנה

F. Expansion Drill

Instructor: I'll bring the children in now.
Student: I'll bring the children in now and
I'll take them out after they eat.

ואוציא אותם אחרי האוכל.
ותוציא אותם אחרי האוכל.
ויוציא אותם אחרי האוכל.
ונוציא אותם אחרי האוכל.
ותוציאי אותם אחרי האוכל.
ויוציאו אותם אחרי האוכל.
ותוצאנה אותם אחרי האוכל.

אכניס את הילדים עכשיו
הַנָתָא תכניס את הילדים עכשיו
הוא יכניס את הילדים עכשיו
אנו נכניס את הילדים עכשיו
את תכניסי את הילדים עכשיו
הם יכניסו את הילדים עכשיו
אתן תכנסנה את הילדים עכשיו

G. Substitution-Agreement Drill

I took the money out of the bank.

הוצאתי את הכסף מהבנק.

אנו – אתה – אשתי – את – בעלך
הבנים שלו – אתם – מי – אני

(c) /tafar/ "he sewed" תפר

The second root consonant of this verb alternates p/f. Some speakers use /f/
throughout the conjugation, e.g., /yitfor/ instead of /yitpor/ "he will sew".

H. Substitution Drill

Sew the dresses.

תפור את השמלות.
תפרי
תפרו
תפורנה

I. Substitution-Agreement Drill

I'll sew the clothes.

אני אתפור את הבגדים.

הוא – אחותי – אתה – אנו – הן
אתם – הם – את – שרה – אני

J. Substitution-Agreement Drill

He sewed the straps.

הוא תפר את הרצועות.

אני – אתה – הסנדלר – אשתו של הסנדלר
הם – את – אמי – הוא

(d) /cixcéax/ "he polished"   צחצח

This is a <u>pi'el</u> verb with four root consonants.

K. Substitution Drill

Shine your shoes before you go out.

צחצח את הנעליים לפני שתצא.
צחצחי   (שתצאי)
צחצחו   (שתצאו)
צחצחנה   (שתצאנה)

L. Substitution-Agreement Drill

He'll shine the shoes for us.

הוא יצחצח לנו את הנעליים.

אתה – הם – אתם – את – היא – מצחצח הנעליים

M. Substitution-Agreement Drill

You haven't shined your shoes yet?

עוד לא צחצחת את הנעליים?

הוא – הם – את – אתם – היא

GRAMMAR NOTES

29.4   /oto ha- /   "The same"- אותו ה-

Examine the following sentence from the Basic Conversation.

/toci et hamasmer be<u>oto</u> ha<u>késef</u>/   "Take out the nail for the same money."

Note that the English expression "the same" is translated by the construction /oto ha-/. When the following noun is feminine singular the construction is /ota ha-/, and before masculine and feminine plurals the forms are /otam ha-/ and /otan ha-/.

m.s. /oto haiš/   "the same man " אותו האיש

f.s. /ota haiša/   "the same woman " אותה האשה

m.pl. /otam hamiršamim/   "The same recipes." אותם המרשמים

f.pl. /otan hamišpaxot/   "The same families." אותן המשפחות

This construction may be preceded by any preposition, independent or prefixed, including the direct object indicator /et/. Some speakers omit /et/ before this construction.

/ani gar beoto harexov/   "I live on the same street."

/raíti et ota hahacaga/   "I saw the same show."

In a construct state noun sequence the /ha-/ is omitted:

/nigášnu leoto bet kafe/   "We went to the same coffee house."

A. Transformation Drill

Instructor: He lives on Mozkin Street.
Student: I live on the same street.

הוא גר ברחוב מוצקין.	אני גר כאותו הרחוב.
הוא נוסע למלון "דן".	אני נוסע לאותו המלון.
הוא ראה סרט טוב.	אני ראיתי את אותו הסרט.
הוא ניגש לבית קפה.	אני ניגשתי לאותו בית קפה.
הוא ראה את הזירירון החדש.	אני ראיתי את אותו האירירון.
הוא משרת בחיל הים.	אני משרת באותו החיל.
הוא קורא ספר מעניין.	אני קורא את אותו הספר.
הוא מוזג יין טעים.	אני מוזג את אותו היין.
הוא הולך לרחוב אלנבי.	אני הולך לאותו הרחוב.
הוא מגיע היום למשרד שלה.	אני מגיע היום לאותו המשרד.
הוא אוהב שוקולד מתוק.	אני אוהב את אותו השוקולד.
הוא נהנה מהסרט.	אני נהניתי מאותו הסרט.

355

B. Transformation Drill

Instructor: He saw the new show.
Student: I saw the same show.

אני ראיתי את אותה ההצגה.	הוא ראה את ההצגה החדשה.
אני אוהב את אותה העוגה.	הוא אוהב עוגת גבינה.
אני לומד את אותה השפה.	הוא לומד שפה חדשה.
אני קניתי את אותה הגלידה.	הוא קנה גלידה.
אני מכין את אותה הגלידה.	הוא מכין גלידה טובה.
אני פגשתי את אותה האשה.	הוא פגש אשה יפה.
אני נוסע באותה הדרך.	הוא נוסע בדרך ישרה.
אני עובד באותה השגרירות.	הוא עובד בשגרירות.
אני אוהב את אותה הגבינה.	הוא אוהב גבינה צהובה.
אני מכין את אותה העוגה.	הוא מכין עוגת תפוחים.

C. Transformation Drill

Instructor: He spoke to some soldiers.
Student: I spoke to the same soldiers.

אני דברתי עם אותם החיילים.	הוא דיבר עם כמה חיילים.
אני אוהב את אותם הדגים.	הוא אוהב דגים ממולאים.
אני קורא את אותם הספרים.	הוא קורא ספרים טובים.
אני קונה את אותם הפירות.	הוא קונה פירות יפים.
אני קבלתי את אותם המכתבים.	הוא קבל מכתנים מהממשלה.
אני נהנה מאותם הסרטים.	הוא נהנה מסרטים טובים.
אני ראיתי את אותם האוירונים.	הוא ראה אוירונים גדולים.
אני דברתי עם אותם הצנחנים.	הוא דיבר עם צנחנים.

D. Transformation Drill

Instructor: He speaks five languages.
Student: I speak the same languages.

אני מדבר את אותן השפות.	הוא מדבר חמש שפות.
אני דברתי עם אותן החיילות.	הוא דיבר עם חיילות.
אני נוסע באותן האוניות.	הוא נוסע באוניות ישראליות.
אני אוהב את אותן העוגות.	הוא אוהב עוגות גבינה.
אני אוכל את אותן הבננות.	הוא אוכל בננות ירוקות.
אני נהנה מאותן ההצגות.	הוא נהנה מהצגות טובות.
אני אוכל את אותן הארוחות.	הוא אוכל שלוש ארוחות.
אני מכיר את אותן המשפחות.	הוא מכיר שלוש משפחות.
אני מכין את אותן העוגות.	הוא מכין עוגות תפוחים.

E. Transformation Drill

Instructor: He's staying at the Savoy Hotel.
Student: I'm staying at the same hotel.

אני גר באותו המלון.   הוא גר במלון סבוי.

אני קורא את אותם הספרים.   הוא קורא ספרים טובים.

אני אוכל את אותן הגלידות.   הוא אוכל גלידות מתוקות.

אני ראיתי את אותה ההצגה.   הוא ראה את ההצגה היפה.

אני קונה את אותם הפירות.   הוא קונה פירות יפים.

אני דברתי עם אותן החיילות.   הוא דיבר עם חיילות.

אני אוהב את אותה העוגה.   הוא אוהב עוגת גבינה.

אני נהנה מאותם הדברים.   הוא נהנה מדברים יפים.

אני נוסע באותן האוניות.   הוא נוסע באוניות גדולות.

אני לומד את אותה השפה.   הוא לומד שפה חדשה.

אני ראיתי את אותו הסרט.   הוא ראה סרט טוב.

אני קבלתי את אותו המכתב.   הוא קבל מכתב מהמשרד.

אני אוהב את אותן העוגות.   הוא אוהב עוגות גבינה.

אני קניתי את אותה הגלידה.   הוא קנה גלידת שוקולד.

אני ניגשתי לאותו בית קפה.   הוא ניגש לבית קפה.

אני נהנה מאותם הסרטים.   הוא נהנה מסרטים טובים.

RAPID RESPONSE DRILL

1. למה בא מר ווילאמס לסנדלריה?

2. מה צריך היה לתקן?

3. איזה עקבים רצה מר ווילאמס?

4. כמה עלה לו לתקן את הנעליים?

5. האם זה היה מעט כסף?

6. למה לא הוריד הסנדלר את המחיר?

7. כמה שילם מר ווילאמס בשביל להוציא את המסמר?

357

REVIEW CONVERSATIONS

א: אני רוצה למכור את הנעליים לתיקון.

ב: כן. מה צריך לתקן?

א: סוליות ועקבים חדשים נ.נעליים השחורות.

ב: ומה עוד?

א: ראה אותו הדבר בנעליים החומות.

ג: איזה סוליות אתה רוצה?

ד: סוליות עור.

ג: ואיזה עקבים?

ד: עקני גומי שיהיה יורד טוב.

ג: אני חושב שעקבי עור יותר חזקים.

ד: טוב. אם אתה חושב כך.

ה: את יודעת מרים, הסנדלר יקר מאד.

ו: כן אני יודעת.

ה: אז למה את נותנת לו נעליים לתיקון?

ו: אני נותנת לו כי הוא עובד יפה מאד.

ה: מה זאת אומרת עונד יפה מאוד? תיקון נעליים הוא תיקון נעליים.

ז: מתי צחצחת את הנעליים שלך?

ח: הבוקר, למה את שואלת?

ז: הן נראות כמו נעליים חדשות.

ח: קניתי משחת נעליים חדשה והיא מצויינת.

ז: תן לי את המשחה ואני אצחצח את הנעליים שלי.

ח: ברצון.

ט: אדוני, אתה יכול לתקן את הנעליים עוד היום?

י: כן. אני אתקן אותם בעוד שעה.

ט: שים שרוכים חדשים וצחצח את הנעליים.

י: בסדר,אדוני. הן תהיינה מוכנות בעוד שעתיים.

ט: תודה רבה.

כ: נהניתי מאד מההצגה.

ל: איפה הייתם? בבית הבימה?

כ: כן.

ל: גם אנו ראינו את אותה ההצגה ונהנינו מאד.

מ: קבלתי מכתב ממשה.

נ: מה הוא כותב?

מ: שהוא יהיה בתל אביב ביום ג'.

נ: גם אני קבלתי מכתב ממנו.

מ: ומה הוא כתב לך?

נ: הוא כתב את אותו הדבר.

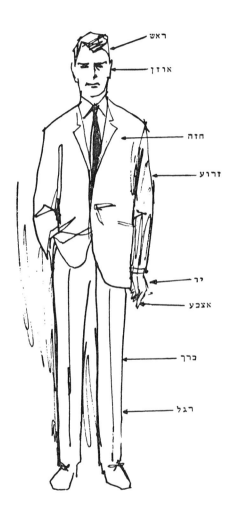

ראש

אוזן

חזה

זרוע

יד

אצבע

ברך

רגל

כל הגוף. הרגליים, הידיים, הראש –

30.1 <u>Aches and Pains</u>

<u>MOSHE CASPI</u>

| Hello, Miriam. | šalom miryam, | שלום מרים, |
| How are you? | ma šlomex. | מה שלומך? |

<u>MIRIAM ZAHAVI</u>

Not good.	lo tov.	לא טוב.
I'm sick.	ani xola.	אני חולה.
he got sick	xala	חלה

<u>MOSHE CASPI</u>

| What hurts you? | ma koev lax? | מה כואב לך? |
| it hurt | ka'av | |

<u>MIRIAM ZAHAVI</u>

My whole body.	kol haguf.	כל הגוף.
My legs, my hands,	haraglaim, hayadaim,	הרגליים, הידיים,
my head –	haroš –	הראש –
body	guf (m)	גוף
leg	régel (f)	רגל
hand	yad (f)	יד
head	roš (m)	ראש

<u>MOSHE CASPI</u>

Have you been	hayit écel	היית אצל
to the doctor?	harofe?	הרופא?
doctor	rofe (m)	רופא

<u>MIRIAM ZAHAVI</u>

Yes. He said	ken. hu amar	כן. הוא אמר
that I have the flu	šeyeš li šapáat	שיש לי שפעת
without fever.	bli xom.	בלי חום.
influenza, grippe	šapáat (f)	שפעת

<u>MOSHE CASPI</u>

| That's not so bad. | lo nora. | לא נורא. |
| terrible | nora (m) | נורא |

<u>MIRIAM ZAHAVI</u>

What's with you?	uma itxa?	ומה אתך?
How do you feel?	eyx ata margiš?	איך אתה מרגיש?
he felt	hirgiš	הרגיש

361

MOSHE CASPI

I'll tell you	omar lax	אומר לך
the truth,	et haemet,	את האמת,
I don't feel	gam ani lo	גם אני לא
well either.	margiš tov.	מרגיש טוב.

MIRIAM ZAHAVI

What's the matter with you?	ma yeš lexa ?	מה יש לך?

MOSHE CASPI

I have strong	yeš li	יש לי
stomach pains	keevey béten xazakim	כאבי בטן חזקים
and my ears hurt.	vekoavot li haoznáim.	וכואבות לי האוזניים.
pain	keev (m)	כאב
stomach, abdomen	béten (f)	בטן
strong	xazak (m.s.)	חזק
ear	ozen (f.s.)	אוזן

MIRIAM ZAHAVI

Oho !	oho !	אהה!
We'll have to open	nictarex kvar liftóax	נצטרך כבר לפתוח
a hospital already.	bet xolim.	בית חולים.

30.2 ADDITIONAL VOCABULARY

Dov has a cold.	ledov yeš nazélet.	לדב יש נזלת.
head cold	nazélet (f)	נזלת
I caught it from him.	nidbákti miménu.	נדבקתי ממנו.
he was attached	davak	דבק
from him	miménu	ממנו
I've been sneezing	ani mit'atéš	אני מתעטש
and coughing all day.	umišta'el kol hayom.	ומשתעל כל היום.
he sneezed	hit'atéš	התעטש
he coughed	hišta'el	השתעל
What does the thermometer show?	ma mar'e hamadxom.	מה מראה המדחום?
thermometer	madxom (m)	מדחום
The thermometer shows	hamadxom mar'e	המדחום מראה
thirty eight degrees.	šlošim vešmóne maalot.	שלושים ושמונה מעלות.
degree, a virtue	maala (f)	מעלה

| My throat hurts. | koev li hagaron. | |
| throat | garon (m) | גרון |

כואב לי הגרון.

| My chest hurts. | koev li haxaze. | |
| chest | xaze (m) | חזה |

כואב לי החזה.

| My heart hurts. | koev li halev. | |

כואב לי הלב.

| My tooth aches. | koévet li hašen. | |
| tooth | šen (f) | שן |

כואבת לי השן.

| My knee hurts. | koévet li habérex. | |
| knee | bérex (f) | ברך |

כואבת לי הברך.

| My finger hurts. | koévet li haécba. | |
| finger | écba (f) | אצבע |

כואבת לי האצבע.

| My legs hurt. | koavot li haragláim. | |

כואבות לי הרגליים.

| My hands hurt. | koavot li hayadáim. | |

כואבות לי הידיים.

| My ears hurt. | koavot li haoznáim. | |

כואבות לי האוזניים.

| My eyes hurt. | koavot li haeynáim. | |

כואבות לי העיניים.

| My teeth hurt. | koavot li hašináim. | |

כואבות לי השיניים.

| My knees hurt. | koavot li habirkáim. | |

כואבות לי הברכיים.

The doctor prescribed a medicine.	harofe rašam refua.	
he listed	rašam	רשם
medicine	refua (f)	רפואה

הרופא רשם רפואה.

| The drugstore is across (the street). | bet hamerkáxat nimca mimul. | |
| opposite | mul | מול |

בית המרקחת נמצא ממול.

| Get well. | tihye bari. | |
| healthy | bari (m.s.) | בריא |

תהיה בריא.

Health is the main thing.	haikar habriut.	
principle	ikar (m)	עיקר
health	briut (f)	בריאות

העיקר הבריאות.

30.3 VOCABULARY DRILLS

A. Substitution-Agreement Drill

My brother is very strong.

אחי חזק מאד.

האנשים – החיילות – השמש – השולחן

B. Substitution-Agreement Drill

Get well

תהיה בריא.

תהיי – תהיו – תהיינה

363

30.4 VERB DRILLS

(a) /xala/   "he got sick"   חלה

A. Substitution-Agreement Drill

   Mr. Cohen is sick today.

מר כהן חולה היום.

גב' כספי – שלושת החיילים – אני – אנו
הרופאה – הכנות – הוא

B. Substitution-Agreement Drill

   Yaakov came down with the flu.

יעקב חלה בשפעת.

אשתי – אתה – התלמידים – אנו – את
אתם – הן – אני – יעקב

(b) /ka'av/   "it hurt"   כאב

   The future stem vowel of this verb is /a/:   /yix'av/   "it will hurt"

C. Substitution-Agreement Drill

   Your feet will hurt.

תכאבנה לך הרגליים.

הבטן – הראש – האוזניים – הגרון – העיניים

D. Substitution-Agreement Drill

   My throat hurt.

כאב לי הגרון.

הבטן – הראש – הידיים – האוזן – השיניים
העין השמאלית – החזה – האצבעות

(c) /hirgiš/   "he felt"   הרגיש

E. Expansion Drill

   Instructor: Take the medicine.
   Student: If you take the medicine you'll feel better.

תרגיש יותר טוב.	אם זקח את הרופאה
ארגיש יותר טוב.	אם אקח את הרפואה
תרגישי יותר טוב.	אם תקחי את הרפואה
תרגישו יותר טוב.	אם תקחו את הרפואה
נרגיש יותר טוב.	אם נקח את הרפואה
הוא ירגיש יותר טוב.	אם הוא יקח את הרפואה
בתך תרגיש יותר טוב.	אם בתך תקח את הרפואה
הן תרגשנה יותר טוב.	אם הן תקחנה את הרפואה
הם ירגישו יותר טוב.	אם הם יקחו את הרפואה
אתן תרגשנה יותר טוב.	אם אתן תקחנה את הרפואה

F. Substitution-Agreement Drill

How do you feel?　　　　　　　　　　　　　　　　?איך אתה מרגיש

את – היא – אתם – הם – אתן

G. Expansion Drill

Instructor: I took the medicine.
Student: After I took the medicine I felt better.

הרגשתי יותר טוב.	אחרי שלקחתי את הרפואה
הרגשנו יותר טוב.	אחרי שלקחנו את הרפואה
הרגישה יותר טוב.	אחרי שלקחה את הרפואה
הרגישו יותר טוב.	אחרי שלקחו את הרפואה
הרגשתם יותר טוב.	אחרי שלקחתם את הרפואה
הרגשת יותר טוב.	אחרי שלקחת את הרפואה
הוא הרגיש יותר טוב.	אחרי שאהי לקח את הרפואה

(d)　/davak/　"he was attached"　דבק

This verb will be drilled here in the nif'al. Some speakers use /b/
instead of /v/ in the future. /yidabek/ ∼ /yidavek/.

H. Substitution-Agreement Drill

You'll catch (a cold) from him.　　　　　　　　תידבק ממנו.

אני – את – הילדים – הבנות – אתם
אנו – הם – אתן – הוא – אתה

I. Substitution-Agreement Drill

I picked it up from Dov.　　　　　　　　　　נדבקתי מדב.

אתה – התלמידים – אתם – אנו – את
הן – אתן – אכיבה – הוא – אני

(e)　/hit'ateš/　"he sneezed"　התעטש

J. Substitution-Agreement Drill

He's been sneezing all day.　　　　　　הוא מזעטש כל היום.

היא – אנו – הילר – הילדות – הם

(f)　/hišta'el/　"he coughed"　השתעל

K. Substitution-Agreement Drill

He coughed all night without a let-up.　　הוא השתעל כל הלילה ולי הפסק.

אני – אחותי – אנהנו – הילדים
אתה – אתם – הן – הוא

365

30.5   The Preposition /mi-/ "from"

The preposition /mi-/ "from" has the following suffixed forms:

1 s.	/miméni/	"from me"	ממני
2 m.s.	/mimxa/	"from you"	ממך
2 f.s.	/mimex/	"from you"	ממך
3 m.s.	/miménu/	"from him"	ממנו
3 f.s.	/miména/	"from her"	ממנה
1 pl.	/meitánu/	"from us"	מאתנו
2 m.pl.	/mimxem/	"from you"	ממכם
2 f.pl.	/mimxen/	"from you"	ממכן
3 m.pl.	/mehem/	"from them"	מהם
3 f.pl.	/mehen/	"from them"	מהן

The second person plural has the alternate forms /mikem/ מכם and /miken/ מכן .

There is a literary form /miménu/ "from <u>us</u>", identical with /miménu/ "from him", but it has been replaced in modern Hebrew by /meitánu/. The other forms of this type: /meiti/ "from me", /meitxa/ "from you", etc., are also used, but are more formal in style.

An independent form of the preposition /min/ מן will also be heard. For the alteration /mi- ~ me-/. See Grammar Note 5.5 .

A. Substitution Drill

I got an invitation from you.   קבלתי ממך הזמנה.

ממך
ממנו
ממנה
ממכם
ממכן
מהם
מהן

B. Substitution Drill

Buy the book from me.   קנה את הספר ממני.

ממנו
ממנה
מאתנו
מהם
מהן

C. Expansion Drill

Instructor: I had the flu.
Student: I had the flu and he caught it from me.

והוא נדבק ממני.	היתה לי שפעת
והוא נדבק ממך.	היתה לך שפעת
והוא נדבק מאתנו.	היתה לנו שפעת
והוא נדבק מהם.	היתה להם שפעת
והוא נדבק מכם.	היתה לכם שפעת
והוא נדבק ממנה.	היתה לרחל שפעת
והוא נדבק ממנו.	היתה ליצחק שפעת
והוא נדבק מכן.	היתה לכן שפעת
והוא נדבק מהן.	היתה להן שפעת

D. Expansion Drill

Instructor: He lives in Savyon.
Student: He lives in Savyon and I live not far from him.

הוא גר בסביון	ואני גר לא רחוק ממנו.	
אתה גר בסביון	ואני גר לא רחוק ממך.	
עטרה גרה בסביון	ואני גר לא רחוק ממנה.	
הוריה גרים בסביון	ואני גר לא רחוק מהם.	
בנותיו גרות בסביון	ואני גר לא רחוק מהן.	
את גרה בסביון	ואני גר לא רחוק ממך.	
אתם גרים בסביון	ואני גר לא רחוק מכם.	

E. Transformation Drill

Instructor: I gave him the order.
Student: He took the order from me.

נתתי לו את ההזמנה.	הוא לקח את ההזמנה ממני.	
נתת לו את ההזמנה.	הוא לקח את ההזמנה ממך.	
נתנו לו את ההזמנה.	הוא לקח את ההזמנה מאתנו.	
היא נתנה לו את ההזמנה.	הוא לקח את ההזמנה ממנה.	
נתתם לו את ההזמנה.	הוא לקח את ההזמנה מכם.	
הוא נתן לו את ההזמנה.	הוא לקח את ההזמנה ממנו.	
הבנים נתנו לו את ההזמנה.	הוא לקח את ההזמנה מהן.	

30.6 Comparatives and Superlatives

(a) Comparatives

The comparative construction is formed by the word /yoter/ "more" preceding the adjective and the preposition /mi-/ following it:

/dov yoter xazak mimoše./   "Dov is stronger than Moshe."

/sára yoter yafa meraxel./   "Sara is more beautiful than Rachel."

A reversed construction may be made by using /paxot/ "less".

/moše paxot xazak midov./   "Moshe is less strong than Dov."

/raxel paxot yafa misára./   "Rachel is less beautiful than Sarah."

Constructions using /paxot/ are more idiomatically translated into English as "not as...as" -

"Moshe is not as strong as Dov."
"Rachel is not as beautiful as Sarah."

In formal style /yoter/ may be omitted:

/ata xazak miménu/   "You are stronger than he is."

/yoter/ and /paxot/ are also used with verbs and adverbs:

/sélek ole yoter mitapuxey adama/   "Beets cost more than potatoes."

/tapuxey adama olim paxot misélek/ "Potatoes cost less than beets."

/daber kcat yoter leat/   "Speak a little slower."

When /mi-/ "than" does not immediately precede a noun in the Hebrew
it is usually replaced by /meašer/ "than" מאשר .

/batim olim yoter betel aviv <u>meašer</u> berexóvot./　"Houses cost more in
Tel Aviv than they do in Rehovot."

In the above example /meašer/ immediately precedes the preposition /be-/ "in".

A. Expansion Drill

Instructor: I am a good swimmer.
Student: I am a good swimmer but David is a better swimmer than I am.

אבל דוד שחיין יותר טוב ממני.	אני שחיין טוב
אבל דוד שחיין יותר טוב ממך.	אתה שחיין טוב
אבל דוד שחיין יותר טוב ממנו.	אחי שחיין טוב
אבל דוד שחיין יותר טוב ממנה.	מרים שחיינית טובה
אבל דוד שחיין יותר טוב מאתנו.	אנו שחיינים טובים
אבל דוד שחיין יותר טוב ממך.	את שחיינית טובה
אבל דוד שחיין יותר טוב מהם.	הבנים שלי שחיינים טובים
אבל דוד שחיין יותר טוב מכן.	אתן שחייניות טובות
אבל דוד שחיין יותר טוב מהן.	הן שחייניות טובות

B. Expansion Drill

Instructor: I don't have much money.
Student: I don't have much money, and Moshe has even less than I do.

ולמשה יש עוד פחות מאשר לי.	אין לי הרבה כסף
ולמשה יש עוד פחות מאשר לנו.	אין לנו הרבה כסף
ולמשה יש עוד פחות מאשר לכם.	אין לכם הרבה כסף
ולמשה יש עוד פחות מאשר לה.	לאחותי אין הרבה כסף
ולמשה יש עוד פחות מאשר להם.	לחיילים אין הרבה כסף
ולמשה יש עוד פחות מאשר לך.	אין לך הרבה כסף
ולמשה יש עוד פחות מאשר להן.	לנשים אין הרבה כסף
ולמשה יש עוד פחות מאשר לכן.	לכן אין הרבה כסף
ולמשה יש עוד פחות מאשר לו.	לדב אין הרבה כסף

C. Expansion Drill

Instructor: I speak Hebrew.
Student: I speak Hebrew but Miriam speaks better than I do.

אבל מרים מדברת יותר טוב ממני.	אני מדבר עברית
אבל מרים מדברת יותר טוב ממנה.	אני מדברת עברית
אבל מרים מדברת יותר טוב מאתנו.	אנחנו מדברים עברית
אבל מרים מדברת יותר טוב מכם.	אתם מדברים עברית
אבל מרים מדברת יותר טוב מהם.	התלמידים מדברים עברית
אבל מרים מדברת יותר טוב ממנו.	מר ויליאמס מדבר עברית
אבל מרים מדברת יותר טוב מהן.	הן מדברות עברית
אבל מרים מדברת יותר טוב ממך.	את מדברת עברית
אבל מרים מדברת יותר טוב ממך.	אתה מדבר עברית

D. Transformation Drill

 Instructor: He is healthier than you.
 Student: You are not as healthy as he is.

אתה פחות בריא ממנו.	הוא יותר בריא ממך.
המורה שלכם פחות טוב מהמורה שלנו.	המורה שלנו יותר טוב מהמורה שלכם.
האניה הזאת פחות גדולה מהאניה החדשה.	האניה החדשה, יותר גדולה מהאניה הזאת.
הבתים בחולון פחות יקרים מהבתים כאן.	הבתים כאן יותר יקרים מהבתים בחולון.
שבע מתאים פחות משבע ושלושים.	שבע ושלושים מתאים יותר משבע.
הסרט פחות ארוך מהההצגה בהכימה.	ההצגה בהכימה יותר ארוכה מהסרט.
הקצינים עובדים פחות מהטוראים.	הטוראים עובדים יותר מהקצינים.
מלון דן פחות חדיש מהמלון הזה.	המלון הזה יותר חדיש ממלון דן.
תל-אביב פחות שקטה מירושלים.	ירושלים יותר שקטה מתל-אביב.
כוס תה עולה פחות מכוס קפה.	כוס קפה עולה יותר מכוס תה.

Do this drill in reverse, also.

E. Transformation Drill

 Instructor: The weather is hot.
 Student: The weather is hotter today than it was yesterday.

מזג האויר יותר חם היום מאשר היה אתמול.	מזג האויר חם.
טיילתי היום יותר מאשר טיילתי אתמול.	טיילתי היום הרבה.
יש לי היום יותר כסף מאשר היה לי אתמול.	יש לי הרבה כסף.
הירקות יותר יקרים היום מאשר היו אתמול.	הירקות יקרים.
קניתי יותר אוכל היום מאשר קניתי אתמול.	קניתי אוכל.
הוא שתה יותר קפה היום מאשר שתה אתמול.	הוא שתה קפה.
היום כואבת לו הבטן יותר מאשר כאבה לו אתמול.	כואבת לו הבטן.

The instructor may vary this drill by substituting /paxot/ for /yoter/.

(b) Superlatives

 The superlative construction is formed by the word /beyoter/ following the adjective or adverb:

 /tel aviv hair hagdola beyoter baárec./ "Tel Aviv is the biggest city in the country."

As in English, paraphrases may be used:

 /hu hatalmid hatov beyoter bevet haséfer./ "He is the best student in the school."

 /hu talmid yoter tov mikol hatalmidim./ "He is a better student than all the [other] students."

An alternative construction is formed by preceding the adjective with /haxi/ הכי. The definite article is omitted before the adjective when /haxi/ is used.

 /ze habinyan haxi gadol bair./ "This is the biggest building in the city."

369

F. Transformation Drill　/beyoter/　　ביותר

Instructor: His house is big.
Student: His house is the biggest in the city.

הבית שלו הגדול ביותר בעיר.	הבית שלו גדול.
הרחוב הזה הארוך ביותר בעיר.	הרחוב הזה ארוך.
בנין השגרירות החריש ביותר בעיר.	בנין השגרירות חדיש מאד.
המלון החדש היפה ביותר בעיר.	המלון החדש יפה מאד.
מר כהן האיש הנמוך ביותר בעיר.	מר כהן איש נמוך.
הם התלמידים הטובים ביותר בעיר.	הם תלמידים טובים.
הביצים הן הטריות ביותר בעיר.	הביצים טריות.
העוגות הן המחוקות ביותר בעיר.	העוגות מתוקות.

G. Transformation Drill　/haxi/　　הכי

Instructor: His house is big.
Student: His house is the biggest in the city.

הבית שלו הכי גדול בעיר.	הבית שלו גדול.
הרחוב הזה הכי ארוך בעיר.	הרחוב הזה ארוך.
בנין השגרירות הכי חדיש בעיר.	בנין השגרירות חדיש מאד.
המלון החדש הכי יפה בעיר.	המלון החדש יפה מאד.
מר כהן האיש הכי נמוך בעיר.	מר כהן איש נמוך.
הם התלמידים הכי טובים בעיר.	הם תלמידים טובים.
הביצים הן הכי טריות בעיר.	הביצים טריות.
העוגות הן הכי מתוקות בעיר.	העוגות מתוקות.

RAPID RESPONSE DRILL

1. מה קרא למרים?
2. האם היתה אצל הרופא?
3. מה אמר לה הרופא?
4. האם משה דואג לה?
5. איך מרגיש משה?
6. איזה כאבים יש למשה?
7. האם יצטרכו לפתוח בית-החולים או מרים מגזימה?

370

REVIEW CONVERSATIONS

א: מה שלומך משה?
ב: לא כל כך טוב. אני מצונן.
א: ואיך מרים?
ב: גם היא מצוננת.
א: היא בטח נדבקה ממך.

ג: לאן את ממהרת, אביבה?
ד: אני ממהרת לרופא.
ג: מה, את חולה?
ד: לא. אני רצה לרופא שיניים.
ג: זה לא נורא.

ה: או, אני עייפה מאד.
ו: ממה?
ה: לא ישנתי כל הלילה.
ו: את מרגישה לא טוב?
ה: לא אני. דב השתעל בלי הפסק ולא נתן לי לישון.

ז: ליעקב יש חום גבוה.
ח: כמה חום יש לו?
ז: 40 מעלות.
ח: זה באמת חום גבוה.
ז: טלפנתי לרופא והוא יבוא מיד.
ח: שיהיה בריא.
ז: תודה.

ט: הרופא רשם רפואה לדב?
י: כן. הוא רשם לו אספירין וסירדוף לשיעול.
ט: אני מקווה שהוא ירגיש יותר טוב.
י: גם לי הוא רשם אותו הדבר.
ט: גם את חולה?
י: כן. נדבקתי ממנו.

371

כ: אחרי שלקחתי את הרפואה הרגשתי יותר טוב.

ל: באיזה בית מרקחת קנית את הרפואה?

כ: כאן. ממול.

ל: גם אני צריכה לקנות רפואה.

כ: גשי לשם. יש להם את כל הרפואות.

מ: היתה לי שפעת בשבוע שעבר.

נ: ואיך את מרגישה היום?

מ: לא רע.

נ: היה לך חום?

מ: כן. היה לי חום גבוה.

ס: אין לי הרבה כסף.

ע: לא נורא. לדוד יש עוד פחות מאשר לך.

ס: אל תגזים.

ע: אני לא מגזים. אין לו כלום.

פ: אני מדבר עברית.

צ: כן, אבל דב מדבר עברית יותר טוב ממך.

פ: אני יודע. הוא לימד אותי.

צ: איפה? בבית הספר לשפות?

פ: כן.

ק: מרים מכינה גלידה טובה.

ר: אמי מכינה את הגלידה הטובה ביותר בתל אביב.

ק: לא אכלתי את הגלידה של אמך.

ר: טוב. נזמין אותך בשבוע הבא.

31.1 <u>Friends Meet at an Office</u>   /pgišat xaverim/   פגישת חברים

MENAHEM

Hello, Dov. What are you doing here?	šalom dov, ma ata ose kan.	שלום דב, מה אתה עושה כאן?

<u>DOV</u>

Oh, hello Menahem, What are <u>you</u> doing here?	o - šalom, menáxem. ma ata ose kan.	או – שלום מנחם. מה אתה עושה כאן?

MENAHEM

Very simple. I work here.	pašut meod. ani oved kan.	פשוט מאד. אני עובד כאן.
simple he worked	pašut (m.s.) avad	פשוט עבד

<u>DOV</u>

Really? How long?	beemet? káma zman?	באמת? כמה זמן?

MENAHEM

About a year now. almost, approximately	kvar kim'at šana. kim'at	כבר כמעט שנה. כמעט

<u>DOV</u>

In which section do you work? section, class department, division	beéyze maxlaka ata oved? maxlaka (f)	באיזה מחלקה אתה עובד? מחלקה

MENAHEM

I work in the economic section. economic	ani oved bamaxlaka hakalkalit. kalkali (m.s.)	אני עובד נמחלקה הכלכלית. כלכלי

<u>DOV</u>

How is the work? Interesting? work, job	ex haavoda. meanyénet? avoda (f)	איך העבודה? מעניינת?

MENAHEM

Yes, quite interesting. I'm satisfied.	ken. day meanyénet. ani sva racon.	כן. די מעניינת. אני שבע רצון.

373

31.2 ADDITIONAL VOCABULARY

| I work in the administrative section. | ani oved bemaxléket hamanganon. | אני עובד במחלקת המנגנון. |
| administration | manganon (m) | מנגנון |

I work in the agricultural section.	ani oved bamaxlaka haxaklait.	אני עובד במחלקה החקלאית.
agricultural	xaklai (m.s.)	חקלאי
agriculture	xaklaut (f)	חקלאות

| I work in the commercial section. | ani oved bamaxlaka hamisxarit. | אני עובד במחלקה המסחרית. |
| commercial | misxari (m.s.) | מסחרי |

I work in the consular section.	ani oved bamaxlaka hakonsulárit.	אני עובד במחלקה הקונסולרית.
consul	konsul (m)	קונסול
consular	konsulári (m.s.)	קונסולרי

| I work in the financial section. | ani oved bamaxlaka hakaspit. | אני עובד במחלקה הכספית. |
| financial | kaspi (m.s.) | כספי |

| I work in the information service. | ani oved bešerut hahasbara. | אני עובד בשרות ההסברה. |
| information | hasbara (f) | הסברה |

| I work in the political section. | ani oved bamaxlaka hamedinit. | אני עובד במחלקה המדינית. |
| political | medini (m.s.) | מדיני |

I work in the press section.	ani oved bemaxléket haitonut.	אני עובד במחלקת העתונות.
newspaper	iton (m)	עתון
press	itonut (f)	עתונות

31.3 VOCABULARY DRILLS

A. Substitution-Agreement Drill   /pašut/   "simple"   פשוט

Miriam's job is very simple.   העבודה של מרים פשוטה מאד.

הספרים – הנעלים – המרשם – העוגות – האוכל
הבגדים – החליפה – הסנדלים – התסרוקת

B. Expansion Drill   /kim'at/   "almost"   כמעט

Instructor: Moshe has been working here two years.
Student: Moshe has been working here almost two years.

משה עובד כאן כמעט שנתיים.	1. משה עובד כאן שנתיים.
הלכנו כמעט עד שפת הים.	2. הלכנו עד שפת הים.
אנו גרים כמעט באותו הרחוב.	3. אנו גרים באותו הרחוב.
היא מדברת עברית כמעט כמו ישראלית.	4. היא מדברת עברית כמו ישראלית.
אנו גרים בתל אביב כמעט חודשיים.	5. אנו גרים בתל אביב חודשיים.
ספרתי להם כמעט את הכל.	6. ספרתי להם את הכל.
יעקב הוא כמעט מנהל המחלקה.	7. יעקב הוא מנהל המחלקה.
הוא הגיע הנה כמעט לפני שבוע.	8. הוא הגיע הנה לפני שבוע.

31.4 VERB DRILLS

/avad/ "he worked"   עבד

A.   Substitution Drill

Work till 5 o'clock.

עבוד עד שעה חמש.
עברי
עברו
עבורנה

B.   Substitution-Agreement Drill

He will work in the economic section.

<u>הוא יעבוד במחלקה הכלכלית.</u>

הם – אנו – אתם – הן
אתן – אשתו – אני – הוא

C.   Substitution-Agreement Drill

Miriam works in a movie theater.

<u>מרים עובדת בקולנוע.</u>

אנו – אתם – את – בעלה – **היא**
הם – אתן – אני – אביה – מרים

D.   Substitution-Agreement Drill

Yonatan worked in the American Embassy.

<u>יונתן עבד בשגרירות האמריקאית.</u>

אנו – אתם – את – אשתו – הוא
בעלה – הן – אני – היא – הם

E.   Transformation Drill - Past to future

Instructor: We worked in a government office.
Student: We will work in a government office.

נעבור במשרד ממשלתי.	עברנו במשרד ממשלתי.
תעבור במשרד ממשלתי.	עברת במשרד ממשלתי.
הם יעברו במשרד ממשלתי.	הם עברו במשרד ממשלתי.
אעבור במשרד ממשלתי.	עברתי במשרד ממשלתי.
אחיך יעבור במשרד ממשלתי.	אחיו עבר במשרד ממשלתי.
גיסתי תעבור במשרד ממשלתי.	גיסתי עברה במשרד ממשלתי.
הבנות תעבורנה במשרד ממשלתי.	הבנות עברו במשרד ממשלתי.
תעברו במשרד ממשלתי.	עברתם במשרד ממשלתי.
תעברי במשרד ממשלתי.	עברת במשרד ממשלתי.

Do this drill in reverse, also.

GRAMMAR NOTES

31.5   Too much

The excessive degree, "too, too much", is rendered by the phrase
/yoter miday/ "more than enough" יותר מדי .

/habáit yoter miday gadól bišvilénu./ "The house is too big for us."

/yoter/ may be omitted, in which case /miday/ usually follows the modifier.
This is more formal in style.

/habáit gadol miday bišvilénu./ "The house is too big for us."

A.   Transformation Drill   /yoter miday/   יותר מדי

Instructor: The trip is very long.
Student: The trip is too long for us.

הנסיעה יותר מדי ארוכה בשבילנו.	1. הנסיעה ארוכה מאד.
התה יותר מדי מתוק בשבילנו.	2. התה מתוק מאד.
מזג האויר יותר מדי חם בשבילנו.	3. מזג האויר חם מאד.
הבגדים יותר מדי פשוטים בשבילנו.	4. הבגדים פשוטים מאד.
הכיצים יותר מדי יקרות בשבילנו.	5. הביצים יקרות מאד.
המים יותר מדי קרים בשבילנו.	6. המים קרים מאד.
הערוגה יותר מדי יבשה בשבילנו.	7. הערוגה יבשה מאד.
השולחנות יותר מדי נמוכים בשבילנו.	8. השולחנות נמוכים מאד.
המשכורות יותר מדי קטנות בשבילנו.	9. המשכורות קטנות מאד.
הז'קטים יותר מדי קצרים בשבילנו.	10. הז'קטים קצרים מאד.

B.   Transformation Drill   /miday/   מדי

Instructor: The hotel is very expensive
Student: The hotel is too expensive for us.

המלון יקר מדי בשבילנו.	1. המלון יקר מאד.
הקפה מר מדי בשבילנו.	2. הקפה מר מאד.
הגלידה מתוקה מדי בשבילנו.	3. הגלידה מתוקה מאד.
השעה מוקדמת מדי בשבילנו.	4. השעה מוקדמת מאד.
הוא קרוב מדי בשבילנו.	5. הוא קרוב מאד.
הבית גדול מדי בשבילנו.	6. הבית גדול מאד.
הלימורים פשוטים מדי בשבילנו.	7. הלימודים פשוטים מאד.
המשרד רחוק מדי בשבילנו.	8. המשרד רחוק מאד.

C.   Transformation Drill

Instructor: He ate a lot.
Student: He ate too much.

הוא אכל יותר מדי.	1. הוא אכל הרבה.
היא מעשנת יותר מדי.	2. היא מעשנת הרבה.
הם עבדו יותר מדי.	3. הם עבדו הרבה.
אתה עושה יותר מדי.	4. אתה עושה הרבה.
היא קנתה יותר מדי.	5. היא קנתה הרבה.
הן כותבות יותר מדי.	6. הן כותבות הרבה.
אנחנו רצים יותר מדי.	7. אנחנו רצים הרבה.
היא מדברת יותר מדי.	8. היא מדברת הרבה.

31.6 The Passive Participle

(a) A passive participle is formed with many roots in the pattern $C_1aC_2uC_3$.
These participles are used as adjectives and are inflected for gender and
number.

The English translations of most of these participles are past participles:
"opened", "closed", etc. Others are translated as adjectives: "simple",
"certain", etc.

Examples which have occurred so far are:

/pašut/	"simple"	פשוט
/batúax/	"certain"	בטוח
/namux/	"short"	נמוך

(b) The third consonant of <u>lamed hey</u> verbs is /y/ in this pattern:

/panuy/	"vacant"	פנוי
/asuy/	"made, done"	עשוי
/ra'uy/	"suitable"	ראוי

(c) When the third radical is ' (א but <u>not</u> ע) then the third consonant
of the participle varies. In some verbs it is /'/; in others it is /y/;
in still others it is /y/ in the masculine singular but /'/ in the feminine
and plurals.

m.s.	/karu, karuy/	"called"	קרוי ,קרוא
f.s.	/kru'a, kruya/		קרויה, קרואה
m.s.	/macuy/	"available"	מצוי
f.s.	/mecuya/		מצויה
m.s.	/nasuy/	"married"	נשוי
f.s.	/nesu'a/		נשואה

377

A.   Transformation Drill   /sagur/   "closed"   סגור

Instructor: He closed the window.
Student: The window is closed.

החלון סגור.	הוא סגר את החלון.
הדלת סגורה.	הוא סגר את הדלת.
המשרדים סגורים.	הוא סגר את המשרדים.
החנויות סגורות.	הוא סגר את החנויות.

B.   Transformation Drill   /patúax/   "open"   פתוח

Instructor: They opened the office.
Student: The office is open.

המשרד פתוח.	פתחו את המשרד.
החנות פתוחה.	פתחו את החנות.
החלונות פתוחים.	פתחו את החלונות.
הדלתות פתוחות.	פתחו את הדלתות.

C.   Transformation Drill   /panuy/   "vacant"   פנוי

Instructor: They cleared the house.
Student: The house is vacant.

הבית פנוי.	פינו את הבית.
החנות פנויה.	פינו את החנות.
הרחובות פנויים.	פינו את הרחובות.
הדרכים פנויות.	פינו את הדרכים.

D.   Transformation Drill   /asuy/   "made, done"   עשוי

Instructor: He did a good repair job.
Student: The repair job was done well.

התיקון עשוי טוב.	הוא עשה תיקון טוב.
העבודה עשויה טוב.	הוא עשה עבודה טובה.
הסרטים עשויים טוב.	הוא עשה סרטים טובים.
החסרוקות עשויות יפה.	הוא עשה להן תסרוקות יפות.

RAPID RESPONSE DRILL

1. מי ומי נפגשו במשרד?

2. מי עובד במשרד שבו נפגשו?

3. כמה זמן עובד מנחם באותו המשרד?

4. באיזה מחלקה עובד מנחם?

5. איך העבודה מוצאת חן בעיני מנחם?

REVIEW CONVERSATIONS

א: אני עובד במחלקת המנגנון, ואתה?

ב: אני עובד במחלקה הכלכלית.

א: איך העבודה שלך, מעניינת?

ב: לא יותר מדי מעניינת.

א: חבל. העבודה במחלקה שלי מעניינת מאד.

ג: כמה שעות אתה עובד?

ד: אני עובד יותר מדי שעות.

ג: מה זה יותר מדי שעות?

ד: עשר שעות ליום. זה יותר מדי.

ג: כן. זה באמת הרבה.

ה: איך העבודה במשרד החקלאות?

ו: פשוטה מאד.

ה: מה עושים שם?

ו: עובדים שם כמו בכל משרד אחר.

ה: יש לכם הרבה פקידים?

ו: כן. די הרבה.

379

ז: עד איזה שעה אתה עובד?

ח: בדרך כלל עד שעה חמש.

ז: והיום?

ח: היום אעבוד עד שתיים.

ז: מדוע?

ח: כי היום יום שישי ועובדים חצי יום.

כ: מנחם עובד הרבה מאד.

ל: מדוע?

כ: הוא עובד במקום חדש.

ל: איך המנהל שלו?

כ: לא רע. אתה מכיר אותו. זה מר ארן.

מ: התקשרת עם אשתך?

נ: לא. הטלפון תפוס.

מ: מי מדבר?

נ: יעקב. הוא מדבר כבר חצי שעה.

מ: מעניין. אומרים שנשים מדברות יותר מדי.

ס: בואו ניגש ל"כסית".

ע: "כסית" כבר סגור. כבר מאוחר.

ס: באיזה שעה סוגרים שם?

ע: בשתיים לפנות בוקר.

ס: מה, כבר כל כך מאוחר?

ע: כן. כבר רבע לשלוש.

פ: באיזה שעה פותחים את החנויות?

צ: החנויות פתוחות מ-8 עד 1, ומ-3 עד 7.

פ: והן סגורות מ-1 עד 3?

צ: כן. פרט ליום שישי שבו סוגרים ב-4.

380

32.1 Friends meet at an office (contd.)

MENAHEM

What's with you, Dov?	ma itxa, dov.	?מה אתך, דב
Do you still work	ata od oved	אתה עוד עובד
at the electric company?	bexevrat haxašmal?	?בחברת החשמל
electricity	xašmal (m)	חשמל

DOV

No, I changed	lo, hexláfti	לא. החלפתי
my job,	et mekom haavoda,	את מקום העבודה
and I work	veani oved	ואני עובד
in a commercial firm.	bexevra misxarit.	.בחברה מסחרית
he exchanged	hexlif	החליף

MENAHEM

In the same work?	beoto hatafkid?	?באותו התפקיד
As a bookkeeper?	kemenahel pinkasim?	?כמנהל פנקסים
duty, function	tafkid (m)	תפקיד
notebook, ledger	pinkas	פנקס

DOV

No.	lo.	.לא
I'm a certified public	ani roe xešbon	אני רואה חשבון
accountant.	musmax.	.מוסמך
accountant	roe xešbon (m)	רואה חשבון
certified, ordained	musmax (m.s.)	מוסמך
authorized, plenipotientiary		

MENAHEM

Finally, you finished	sof sof siyámta	סוף סוף סיימת
your studies.	et halimudim.	.את הלימודים
end	sof (m)	סוף
he finished	siyem	סיים

DOV

Yes. Barely.	ken. bekóši.	.כן. בקושי
About six months ago.	lifney kexaci šana.	.לפני כחצי שנה

32.2 ADDITIONAL VOCABULARY

| She is a secretary. | hi mazkira. | .היא מזכירה |
| secretary | mazkir (m) | מזכיר |

| She works as a secretary. | hi ovédet kemazkira. | .היא עובדת כמזכירה |

| She works as a secretary. | hi ovédet betor mazkira. | .היא עובדת בתור מזכירה |
| line, turn | tor (m) | תור |

| She works like a horse. | hi ovédet kmo sus. | .היא עובדת כמו סוס |
| horse | sus (m) | סוס |

32.3   VERB DRILLS

(a) /hexlif/ "he exchanged"   החליף

A. Substitution Drill

Change your clothes.

.החלף את הבגדים
החליפי
החליפו
החלפנה

B. Substitution-Agreement Drill

Sara will change her job.

<u>.שרה תחליף את מקום העבודה</u>

אנו – הם – אתם – את – אתן

יוסף – אתה – הן – אני – שרה

C. Substitution-Agreement Drill

He replaces me in the evening.

<u>.הוא מחליף אותי בערב</u>

את – הם – משה – אתן

המזכירה – מי

D. Substitution-Agreement Drill

We exchanged the books this morning.

<u>.החלפנו את הספרים הבוקר</u>

התלמידים – בעלה – אני – אתה

אתם – אמי – את – אנחנו

(b) /siyem/ "he finished"   סיים

E.   Substitution-Agreement Drill

     Moshe! Finish the work already.

משה! סיים כבר את העבודה.

עטרה – תלמידים – חברות – רב

F.   Transformation Drill

     Instructor: We'll finish our studies next month.
     Student: We finished our studies last month.

סיימנו את הלימודים בחודש שעבר.	נסיים את הלימודים בחודש הבא.
סיימתי את הלימודים בחודש שעבר.	אסיים את הלימודים בחודש הבא.
סיימתם את הלימודים בחודש שעבר.	תסיימו את הלימודים בחודש הבא.
אחי סיים את הלימודים בחודש שעבר.	אחי יסיים את הלימודים בחודש הבא.
חנה סיימה את הלימודים בחודש שעבר.	חנה תסיים את הלימודים בחודש הבא.
אתן סיימתן את הלימודים בחודש שעבר.	אתן תסיימנה את הלימודים בחודש הבא.
סיימת את הלימודים בחודש שעבר.	את תסיימי את הלימודים בחודש הבא.
הן סיימו את הלימודים בחודש שעבר.	הן תסיימנה את הלימודים בחודש הבא.
אתה סיימת את הלימודים בחודש שעבר.	אתה תסיים את הלימודים בחודש הבא.

Do this drill in reverse, also.

G.   Substitution-Agreement Drill

     I finish work at 3:00 on Friday.

אני מסיים את העבודה ביום ששי ב-3.

הם – אנו – המזכירות – אשתי – הוא

GRAMMAR NOTES

32.4   The Prepositions /ke-/, /kmo/

        Students should note very carefully the usage of prepositions /ke-/ and
/kmo/.

(a) /ke-/

(1)   Before numbers /ke-/ means "approximately, about".

        /lex kearbaa rexovot./ "Go about four blocks."

        /lifney kexaci šana"/   "About a half year ago."

        /hu oved kexameš šanim baxevra./ "He's been working about 5 years in the
                                                company."

This may be paraphrased with /beérex/.

        /hu oved beérex xameš šanim baxevra./

        /hu gar xamiša rexovot mikan beérex./ "He lives about 5 blocks from here."

Both forms may be used.

        /hu gar beérex kexamiša rexovot mikan./

(2)   Before other words it means "as".

        /hi ovédet kemazkira./   "She works as a secretary."

This may be paraphrased with /betor/.

        /hi ovédet betor mazkira./

(b) /kmo/

        /kmo/ means "like, similar to, etc."   It may be used before the
conjunction /še-/.

        /ata medaber ivrit kmo israeli./ "You speak Hebrew like an Israeli."

        /ata medaber ivrit kmo šemedabrim baárec./ "You speak Hebrew like they do
                                                        in Israel."

        Traditional English grammar prescribes the use of as in the last sentence
above. However, this does not accord with actual English usage, and some
confusion may arise in the use of /ke-/ and /kmo/ by speakers of English. The
following examples illustrate possible mistakes and absurdities which may be
caused by this confusion.

        /hi ovédet kemazkira/ means (paraphrased) "She is employed as a secretary."

        /hi ovédet kmo mazkira/ means "Her working habits, schedule, manner of
operation, etc., are those of a secretary; but her real job is something else."

Two English translations are:

"She works like a secretary."
"She works as a secretary does."

but <u>not</u>   "She works as a secretary."

/hi ovédet <u>kmo</u> sus/ means (figuratively, of course)   "She works like
                                                                    a horse."

/hi ovédet <u>kesus</u>/ would mean that she is doing the actual work of a
horse, pulling a wagon, etc. That is, "She works as a horse."

(c) <u>Suffixed forms of /kmo/</u>

The suffixed forms of /kmo/ are:

1 s.	/kamóni/	"like me"	כמוני
2 m.s.	/kamóxa/	"like you"	כמוך
2 f.s.	/kamox/	"like you"	כמוך
3 m.s.	/kamóhu/	"like him"	כמוהו
3 f.s.	/kamóha/	"like her"	כמוה
1 pl.	/kamónu/	"like us"	כמונו
2 m.pl.	/kamóxem, kmoxem/	"like you"	כמוכם
2 f.pl.	/kamóxen, kmoxen/	"like you"	כמוכן
3 m.pl.	/kamóhem, kmohem/	"like them"	כמוהם
3 f.pl.	/kamóhen, kmohen/	"like them"	כמוהן

A. Transformation Drill

Instructor: He is a waiter.
Student: He works as a waiter.

הוא עובד כמלצר.	הוא מלצר.
היא עובדת כשחקנית.	היא שחקנית.
הוא עובד כמורה.	הוא מורה.
הוא עובד כחנווני.	הוא חנווני.
הוא עובד כיועץ.	הוא יועץ.
היא עובדת כפקידה.	היא פקידה.
הוא עובד כמנהל מחלקה.	הוא מנהל מחלקה.

B. Transformation Drill

Instructor: She works as a secretary.
Student: She works as a secretary.

היא עובדת בתור מזכירה.	היא עובדת כמזכירה.
הוא עובד בתור מנהל מחלקה.	הוא עובד כמנהל מחלקה.
היא עובדת בתור מורה.	היא עובדת כמורה.
הוא עובד בתור יועץ.	הוא עובד כיועץ.
הוא עובד בתור מלצר.	הוא עובד כמלצר.
הוא עובד בתור חנווני.	הוא עובד כחנווני.
הוא עובד בתור פקיד.	הוא עובד כפקיד.

Do this drill in reverse, also.

C. Transformation Drill

Instructor: I live about three blocks from here.
Student: I live about three blocks from here.

אני גר כשלושה רחובות מכאן.	אני גר שלושה רחובות מכאן בערך.
חכיתי בנמל התעופה כשעה.	חכיתי בנמל התעופה שעה בערך.
גמרתי את העבודה לפני כשעתיים.	גמרתי את העבודה לפני שעתיים בערך.
זה יעלה לך כשלושים לירות.	זה יעלה לך שלושים לירות בערך.
קנינו את הבית לפני כשנה.	קנינו את הבית לפני שנה בערך.
המשפחה שלי תגיע בעוד כחודש ימים.	המשפחה שלי תגיע בעוד חודש ימים בערך.

D. Expansion Drill

Instructor: I speak Hebrew like an Israeli.
Student: I speak Hebrew like an Israeli, and David speaks like me.

אני מדבר עברית כמו ישראלי	ודוד מדבר כמוני.
אתה מדבר עברית כמו ישראלי	ודוד מדבר כמוך.
היא מדברת עברית כמו ישראלית	ודוד מדבר כמוה.
אתם מדברים עברית כמו ישראלים	ודוד מדבר כמוכם.
אנחנו מדברים עברית כמו ישראלים	ודוד מדבר כמונו.
הן מדברות עברית כמו ישראליות	ודוד מדבר כמוהן.
אתן מדברות עברית כמו ישראליות	ודוד מדבר כמוכן.
את מדברת עברית כמו ישראלית	ודוד מדבר כמוך.
הוא מדבר עברית כמו ישראלי	ודוד מדבר כמוהו.
הם מדברים עברית כמו ישראלים	ודוד מדבר כמוהם.

RAPID RESPONSE DRILL

1. ?היכן עבד דב

2. ?היכן עובד דב עכשיו

3. ?בתור מה עבד דב בחברת החשמל

4. ?מה תפקידו בחברה המסחרית

5. ?מתי הוא סיים את הלימודים

386

REVIEW CONVERSATIONS

א: מי מנהל הפנקסים שלכם?

ב: מר זהבי.

א: חשבתי שמר זהבי כבר רואה חשבון מוסמך.

ב: לא. איפה? הוא עוד לא סיים את הלימודים.

א: מה אתה שח! הוא לומד כבר חמש שנים.

ב: אני חושב שיקח לו עוד חמש שנים עד שיגמור.

ג: סוף סוף סיימת את הלימודים.

ד: כן, בקושי.

ג: למה בקושי?

ד: כי לקח לי הרבה זמן לגמור.

ה: החלפתי את מקום העבודה.

ו: באמת? ואיפה אתה עובד עכשיו?

ה: אני עובד בחברת "הדר".

ו: איך העבודה החדשה? מעניינת?

ה: כן. העבודה מעניינת מאד.

ז: יש לי קשיים לדבר עברית.

ח: מדוע, הרי דברת טוב כשראיתי אותך.

ז: כן. זה היה לפני שנה.

ח: אתה לא מדבר עברית בבית?

ז: לא. אין לי עם מי לדבר.

ח: חבל.

ט: אתה יודע, משה? אני רואה חשבון מוסמך.

י: יופי, כמוני. גם אני רואה חשבון מוסמך.

ט: מתי סיימת את הלימודים?

י: הקיץ.

ט: מזל טוב.

י: תודה רבה. גם לך.

כ: יעקב עובד כמנהל פנקסים.

ל: באמת, ממתי?

כ: מלפֿני כחורש.

ל: איפה הוא עובד? באותו המקום?

כ: לא. הוא החליף את מקום העבודה.

אני רואה השכון מוסמך...

33.1 <u>Friends Meet at an Office</u> (contd.)

<u>MEṆAHEM</u>

How is the salary?	ex hamaskóret?	?איך המשכורת
salary	maskóret (f)	משכורת

<u>DOV</u>

Very good.	tova meod.	.טובה מאד
I'm earning	ani marvíax	אני מרוויח
almost double.	kim'at kifláim.	.כמעט כפליים
he earned	hirvíax	הרוויח
double	kifláim	כפליים

<u>MEṆAHEM</u>

You're exaggerating a bit.	ata magzim kcat.	.אתה מגזים קצת
Double?!	kifláim? !	!?כפליים

<u>DOV</u>

No.	lo.	.לא
In all seriousness.	bexol harecinut.	.בכל הרצינות
Almost double.	kim'at kifláim.	.כמעט כפליים
seriousness	recinut (f)	רצינות

<u>MENAHEM</u>

Soon you'll be rich,	bekarov tihye ašir,	בקרוב תהיה עשיר
and you won't speak to me.	velo tedaber iti.	.ולא תדבר אתי
rich	ašir (m.s.)	עשיר

<u>ḌOV</u>

If you would be working	lu haíta oved	לו היית עובד
in a private firm	bexevra pratit	בחברה פרטית
you, too, would be	gam ata haíta	גם אתה היית
earning more.	marvíax yoter.	.מרוויח יותר
if only	lu	לו
private	prati (m.s.)	פרטי

<u>MEṆAHEM</u>

Possibly. But here	yaxol lihyot. ax kan	יכול להיות. אך כאן
I have tenure	yeš li vétek	יש לי ותק
of ten years.	šel éser šanim.	.של עשר שנים
tenure		
length of service	vétek (m)	ותק

389

<u>DOV</u>

Yes, tenure is an important thing.	ken. vétek ze davar xašuv.	כן. ותק זה דבר חשוב.
important	xašuv (m.s.)	חשוב

33.2 ADDITIONAL VOCABULARY

He's not a poor man.	hu lo iš ani.	הוא לא איש עני.
poor	ani (m.s.)	עני
He has a high salary.	yeš lo maskóret gvoha.	יש לו משכורת גבוהה.
high, tall	gavóa (m.s.)	גבוה
He makes a good living.	hu marvíax maspik lemixya.	הוא מרויח מספיק למחיה.
sustenance	mixya (f)	מחיה
He earns three times as much. (as he earned before)	hu marvíax pi šaloš. (mima šehirvíax kódem)	הוא מרויח פי שלוש. (ממה שהרויח קודם)
times	pi	פי
<u>vetek</u> gives rights.	vétek makne zxuyot.	ותק מקנה זכויות.
he transferred ownership	hikna	הקנה
right, privilege	zxut (f)	זכות

33.3 VOCABULARY DRILLS

A.   Substitution-Agreement Drill   /ašir/   "rich"   עשיר

He's richer than I am.   <u>הוא יותר עשיר ממני.</u>

את – מנחם ורב – משפחת זהבי
הן – הוא

B.   Substitution-Agreement Drill   /ani/   "poor"   עני

He's not so poor.   <u>הוא לא כל כך עני.</u>

גב' כספי – הפקידים – המזכירה הזאת
החברות הפרטיות – משפחת הכלה – הוא

C.   Substitution-Agreement Drill /xašuv/ "important" חשוב

He's important to the company.   <u>הוא חשוב לחברה.</u>

המזכירות – הפקידים – גב' כהן – משה

D.   Substitution-Agreement Drill /gavóa/ "high, tall" גבוה

(The third consonant of this word is <u>h</u> . At the end of a word it is not
pronounced, but the vowel /a/ must precede it as before a word-final ' ע .)

The building is very tall.   <u>הבנין גבוה מאד.</u>

המחירים – המשכורת שלה – החיילות

החלונות – מלון רן – בנין מאיר

33.4   VERB DRILLS

/hirvíax/   "he earned"   הרויח

A.   Substitution-Agreement Drill

David will earn more in the new job.   <u>דוד ירויח יותר בעבודה החדשה.</u>

אני – אתה – המזכירה – אתן – אנחנו

הפקידים – את – הן – אתם – דוד

B.   Substitution-Agreement Drill

Yaakov earns enough.   <u>יעקב מרויח מספיק.</u>

אני – הפועלים – המורות – אחותי – יצחק

C.   Transformation Drill - Future to Past

Instructor: I'll earn more next year.
Student: I earned less last year.

הרווחתי פחות בשנה שעברה.	אני ארויח יותר בשנה הבאה.
הוא הרויח פחות בשנה שעברה.	הוא ירויח יותר בשנה הבאה.
הרווחנו פחות בשנה שעברה.	נרויח יותר בשנה הבאה.
אתן הרווחתן פחות בשנה שעברה.	אתן תרווחנה יותר בשנה הבאה.
הרווחנו פחות בשנה שעברה.	נרויח יותר בשנה הבאה.
כתו הרווחתם פחות בשנה שעברה.	כתו תרויח יותר בשנה הבאה.
הפקידים הרוויחו פחות בשנה שעברה.	הפקידים ירוויחו יותר בשנה הבאה.
את הרווחת פחות בשנה שעברה.	את תרויחי יותר בשנה הבאה.
הן הרוויחו פחות בשנה שעברה.	הן תרווחנה יותר בשנה הבאה.
אתה הרווחת פחות בשנה שעברה.	אתה תרויח יותר בשנה הבאה.

Do this drill in reverse, also.

GRAMMAR NOTES

33.5 Suppositions and Conditional Sentences

Examine the following sentences from the Basic Conversations:

/ani batúax šehahorim šelxa hayu nehenim meod mehahacaga./ "I am sure that your parents would have enjoyed the show very much."

/lu haíta oved bexevra pratit, gam ata haíta marvíax yoter./ "If you would be working in a private firm, you, too, would be earning more."

Note that the verb phrase consists of an auxiliary and a main verb. The auxiliary is the past tense of /haya/, and it agrees in person, gender, and number with the subject. The main verb is in the present tense form, and it agrees in gender and number with the subject.

The supposition may refer to a past contrary-to-fact situation or to a future situation:

"Your parents <u>would have enjoyed</u> the show."

or

"If you <u>would be working</u> in a private firm..."

The second example above could also be translated "If you <u>had been working</u> in a private firm, you, too, <u>would have earned</u> more."

The context conveys the tense of the situation.

The construction is the same in both clauses of an "if... then" sentence. However, if the supposition is about the past, then the past tense may be used in the if-clause.

/lu avádeta bexevra pratit, gam ata haíta marvíax yoter./

The future tense may be used in a supposition about the future.

/im taavod bexevra pratit, gam ata tarvíax yoter./

In the following drills the instructor states a fact, either affirmative or negative. The student responds with a supposition about a situation contrary to the fact.

A.   Transformation Drill

Instructor: You didn't work in a private firm, and you didn't earn much money.
Student: If you had worked in a private firm, you would have earned a lot of money.

1. ‏לא עבדת בחברה פרטית, ולא הרווחת הרבה כסף.‏

‏לו היית עובד בחברה פרטית, היית מרוויח הרבה כסף.‏

2. ‏מרים לא קיבלה משכורת היום, ואין לה כסף.‏

‏לו מרים היתה מקבלת משכורת היום, היה לה כסף.‏

3. ‏לא ישבנו באמצע האולם, ולא ראינו טוב את התפאורה.‏

‏לו היינו יושבים באמצע האולם, היינו רואים טוב את התפאורה.‏

4. ‏לא ירד גשם, ונסענו לטיול.‏

‏לו היה יורד גשם, לא היינו נוסעים לטיול.‏

5. ‏לא עברוני על יד ביתך ולא קראתי לך.‏

‏לו הייתי עובר על יד ביתך, הייתי קורא לך.‏

6. לא לקחת את הבגרים לניקוי אתמול, והם לא יהיו מוכנים למחר.

לו היית לוקחת את הבגרים לניקוי אתמול, הם היו מוכנים למחר.

7. לא נתת לי הזדמנות לדבר ולא אמרתי לך קודם.

לו היית נותן לי הזדמנות לדבר הייתי אומר לך קודם.

B. Transformation Drill

Instructor: She worked in a government office, and she earned a small salary.
Student: If she hadn't worked in a government office, she wouldn't have earned a small salary.

1. היא עבדה במשרד ממשלתי, והרוויחה מעט.

לולא היא היתה עובדת במשרד ממשלתי, היא לא היתה מרוויחה מעט.

2. המברק נשלח מוקדם הבוקר, וקבלתי אותו היום.

לולא היה המברק נשלח מוקדם הבוקר, לא הייתי מקבל אותו היום.

3. משה אכל דג מלוח והוא צמא.

לולא היה משה אוכל דג מלוח, הוא לא היה צמא.

4. הרופא רשם לי רפואה ואני מרגיש יותר טוב עכשיו.

לולא היה הרופא רושם לי רפואה, לא הייתי מרגיש יותר טוב עכשיו.

5. סיימת את הלימודים וראה מרוויח טוב.

לולא היית מסיים את הלימודים לא היית מרוויח טוב.

6. היא נתנה לנו את הכתובת ומצאנו את הבית בקלות.

לולא היתה נותנת לנו את הכתובת לא היינו מוצאים את הבית בקלות.

7. מרים נרקיס הציגה ונהניתי מהההצגה.

לולא מרים נרקיס היתה מציגה לא הייתי נהנה מהההצגה.

C. Transformation Drill

Instructor: I won't send the letter by air mail, and it won't arrive tomorrow.
Student: If I would send the letter by air mail, it would arrive tomorrow.

1. לא אשלח את המכתב בדואר אוויר והוא לא יגיע מחר.

לו הייתי שולח את המכתב בדואר אוויר הוא היה מגיע מחר.

2. הוא לא גר בתל אביב ואני לא רואה אותו.

לו הוא היה גר בתל אביב הייתי רואה אותו.

3. לא אלך למשרד היום ולא אכתיב את המכתב.

לו הייתי הולך למשרד היום הייתי מכתיב את המכתב.

4. משה לא ישאר בירושלים ולא תראו אותו כשתגיעו לשם.

לו היה משה נשאר בירושלים הייתם רואים אותו כשתגיעו לשם.

5. לא אבוא לכיתנו ביום שני ולא תאכלי דגים ממולאים.

לו היית באה לכיתנו ביום שישי, היית אוכלת דגים ממולאים.

D. Transformation Drill

Instructor: I'll send the letter by air mail and it will arrive tomorrow.
Student: If I didn't send the letter by air mail it wouldn't arrive tomorrow.

1. אשלח את המכתב בדואר אוויר והוא יגיע מחר.

   לולא הייתי שולח את המכתב בדואר אוויר הוא לא היה מגיע מחר.

2. אני עייף ולא יכול לטייל אתך עכשיו.

   לולא הייתי עייף הייתי יכול לטייל אתך עכשיו.

3. הוא עובד באותו המקום ושומע את כל החדשות.

   לולא הוא היה עובד באותו המקום לא היה שומע את כל החדשות.

4. משה יישאר בבית הים ותראינה אותו כשתחזורנה.

   לולא היה משה נשאר בבית הים לא הייתן רואות אותו כשתחזורנה.

5. אשתי מבינה עברית והיא תלך אתנו להצגה בבית הבימה.

   לולא היתה אשתי מבינה עברית לא היתה הולכת אתנו להצגה בבית

            הבימה.

RAPID RESPONSE DRILL

1. איך המשכורת של דב?

2. כמה הוא מרוויח?

3. מה אמר מנחם לדב על כך?

4. מה ענה דב למנחם?

5. למה נשאר מנחם במקום העבודה שלו?

REVIEW CONVERSATIONS

א: איך המשכורת שלך מדים, טובה?
ב: כן. טובה מאד. ושלך?
א: שלי לא כל כך טובה.
ב: כמה זמן את עובדת בחברה?
א: שנתיים.
ב: לא נורא. תרוויחי יותר בשנה הבאה.
א: אני מקווה.

ג: לו היית עובד בחברה פרטית גם אתה היית מרויח טוב.
ד: למה לי לעבוד בחברה פרטית? אני מרויח טוב בעבודה ממשלתית.
ג: זה דבר אחר.

ה: אתה יודע, משה לא איש עני.
ו: הוא גם לא עשיר.
ה: יש לו הרבה כסף בבנק.
ו: מאין אתה יודע?
ה: הוא הראה לי את החשבון שלו בבנק.

ז: אני לא יכול להסתדר עם המשכורת שלי.
ח: מדוע? אתה מרויח מספיק למחייה.
ז: המשכורת מספיקה לי בדיוק לשלושה שבועות.
ח: חבל שמשלמים רק פעם בחודש.

ט: יעקב שבע רצון מהעבודה שלו.
י: אני שמח מאד. איך הוא מרויח?
ט: הוא מרויח פי שלוש ממה שהרויח כאן.
י: לא. לא יכול להיות. אתה מגזים.
ט: אני לא מגזים. הוא מרויח בדיוק פי שלוש.

ואת היתרה מכניסים לבנק...

34.1 Friends Meet at an Office (concluded)

DOV

Tell me, Menahem.	tagid li, menáxem.	.תגיד לי, מנחם
How do you manage	ex ata mistader	איך אתה מסתדר
on your salary?	bamaskóret šelxa?	במשכורת שלך?
he told	higid	הגיד
he managed himself	histader	הסתדר

MENAHEM

We manage.	mistadrim.	.מסתדרים
We live on a budget.	ánu xayim betakciv.	.אנו חיים בתקציב
live, alive	xay	חי
budget	takciv (m)	תקציב

DOV

What do you mean,	ma zot oméret	מה זאת אומרת
you live on a budget?	atem xayim betakciv?	אתם חיים בתקציב?

MENAHEM

Very simple.	pašut meod.	.פשוט מאד
We list all the expenses,	rošmim et kol hahocaot,	רושמים את כל ההוצאות
divide the income	mexalkim et hahaxnasa	מחלקים את ההכנסה
according to the expenses	behet'em lahocaot,	בהתאם להוצאות
and the balance	veet hayitra	ואת היתרה
we put in the bank.	maxnisim labank.	.מכניסים לבנק
he listed	rašam	רשם
he divided	xilek	חילק
balance, remainder	yitra (f)	יתרה
bank	bank (m)	בנק

DOV

I can't save	ani lo maclíax laxsox	אני לא מצליח לחסוך
even a penny.	afílu pruta.	.אפילו פרוטה
he succeeded	hiclíax	הצליח
he saved	xasax	חסך
even	afílu	אפילו
penny	pruta	פרוטה
	(1000 pruta = IL 1)	

MENAHEM

No wonder. You've just	lo péle. harey rak	לא פלא. הרי רק
finished your studies.	siyámta et halimudim.	.סיימת את הלימודים
wonder	péle (m)	פלא

DOV

Nevertheless, I don't	ani bexol zot lo	אני בכל זאת לא
understand how you manage.	mevin ex ata mistader.	.מבין איך אתה מסתדר

MENAHEM

Nothing strange.	lo péle.	.לא פלא
My wife works, too.	gam išti ovédet.	.גם אשתי עובדת

34.2 ADDITIONAL VOCABULARY

I opened a bank account.	patáxti xešbon bankai.	.פתחתי חשבון בנקאי
I have a new check book.	yeš li pinkas čékim xadaš.	.יש לי פנקס צ'יקים חדש
check	čék	צ'ק
I borrowed 1000 pounds.	lavíti élef lírot.	.לוויתי אלף לירות
he borrowed	lava	לווה
The bank lent me 1000 pounds.	habank hilva li élef lírot.	הבנק הלווה לי .אלף לירות
he lent	hilva	הלווה
I got a loan in the amount of 1000 pounds.	kibálti halvaa besax šel élef lírot.	קבלתי הלוואה .בסך של אלף לירות
loan	halvaa (f)	הלוואה
amount	sax	סך
The interest is high.	haribit gvoha.	.הרבית גבוהה
interest	ribit (f)	רבית
I paid off the note.	paráti et haštar.	.פרעתי את השטר
he paid (a debt)	para	פרע
debt note, bill	štar	שטר

34.3 VOCABULARY DRILLS

A.　Substitution-Agreement Drill　/xay/ "live, alive"　חי

We live on a budget.

.אנו חיים בחשבון

הוא – רחל – המורות – אני – אנו

34.4 VERB DRILLS

(a)　/higid/　"he told"　הגיד

The past and present tenses of this verb are not used in spoken modern Hebrew. The verb /amar/　אמר　is used instead. In the infinitive, imperative, and future tense both verbs are used.

A. Substitution-Agreement Drill

Tell me, Menahem, How do you manage?

הגד לי, מנחם, איך אתה מסתדר?

שרה - תלמידים - גבירותי - מנחם

B. Substitution-Agreement Drill

I'll tell him the whole truth.

אני אגיד לו את כל האמת.

את - אתה - יונתן - אחם - הן
החיילים - עטרה - אנו - אתן - אני

C. Transformation Drill — Future to Past

Instructor: I'll tell him where we live.
Student: I told him where we live.

אמרתי לו היכן אנו גרים.	אגיד לו היכן אנו גרים.
אמרת לו היכן אנו גרים.	תגיד לו היכן אנו גרים.
דב אמר לו היכן אנו גרים.	דב יגיד לו היכן אנו גרים.
אמרנו לו היכן אנו גרים.	נגיד לו היכן אנו גרים.
אמרתם לו היכן אנו גרים.	תגידו לו היכן אנו גרים.
אשתי אמרה לו היכן אנו גרים.	אשתי תגיד לו היכן אנו גרים.
הבנות אמרו לו היכן אנו גרים.	הבנות תגדנה לו היכן אנו גרים.
הילדים אמרו לו היכן אנו גרים.	הילדים יגידו לו היכן אנו גרים.
אמרת לו היכן אנו גרים.	תגידי לו היכן אנו גרים.
אמרתן לו היכן אנו גרים.	תגדנה לו היכן אנו גרים.

(b) /histader/ "he managed" הסתדר

The /t/ of the prefix follows the /s/ of the root.

D. Substitution Drill

Get in line.

הסתדר בתור.
הסתדרי
הסתדרו
הסתדרנה

E. Transformation Drill

Instructor: I'll get along with the new boss.
Student: I got along with the new boss.

הסתדרתי עם הבוס החדש.	אסתדר עם הבוס החדש.
הסתדרנו עם הבוס החדש.	נסתדר עם הבוס החדש.
הסתדרתן עם הבוס החדש.	תסתדרנה עם הבוס החדש.
הסתדרת עם הבוס החדש.	תסתדר עם הבוס החדש.
הסתדרת עם הבוס החדש.	תסתדרי עם הבוס החדש.
הפועלים הסתדרו עם הבוס החדש.	הפועלים יסתדרו עם הבוס החדש.
המזכירות הסתדרו עם הבוס החדש.	המזכירות תסתדרנה עם הבוס החדש.
הסתדרתם עם הבוס החדש.	תסתדרו עם הבוס החדש.
הסתדרתן עם הבוס החדש.	אתן תסתדרנה עם הבוס החדש.
היא הסתדרה עם הבוס החדש.	היא תסתדר עם הבוס החדש.

Do this drill in reverse, also.

399

F. Substitution-Agreement Drill

He's managing with the money he has.

הוא מסתדר עם הכסף שיש לו.

אנו – אתן – היא – אני – הוא

(c) /rašam/   "he listed"   רשם

G. Substitution Drill

Write down all the numbers.

רשום את כל המספרים.

רשמי

רשמו

רשומנה

H. Transformation Drill - Future to Past

Instructor: He'll write down the correct numbers.
Student: He wrote down the correct numbers.

הוא רשם את המספרים הנכונים.	הוא ירשום את המספרים הנכונים.
את רשמת את המספרים הנכונים.	את תרשמי את המספרים הנכונים.
רשמנו את המספרים הנכונים.	נרשום את המספרים הנכונים.
הם רשמו את המספרים הנכונים.	הם ירשמו את המספרים הנכונים.
אתן רשמתן את המספרים הנכונים.	אתן תרשומנה את המספרים הנכונים.
המזכירה רשמה את המספרים הנכונים.	המזכירה תרשום את המספרים הנכונים.
אתה רשמת את המספרים הנכונים.	אתה תרשום את המספרים הנכונים.
הבנות רשמו את המספרים הנכונים.	הבנות תרשומנה את המספרים הנכונים.
רשמתם את המספרים הנכונים.	תרשמו את המספרים הנכונים.
רשמתי את המספרים הנכונים.	אני ארשום את המספרים הנכונים.

Do this drill in reverse, also.

I. Substitution-Agreement Drill

We list all the expenses.

אנו רושמים את כל ההוצאות.

אני – אשתי – המזכירות

המנהל – אנו

(d)   /xilek/   "he divided"   חילק

J. Substitution Drill

Distribute the mail.

חלק את הדואר.

חלקי

חלקו

חלקנה

K. Transformation Drill - Future to Past

    Instructor: We'll divide up the work.
    Student: We divided up the work.

חילקנו את העבודה.	נחלק את העבודה.
חילקתם את העבודה.	תחלקו את העבודה.
החיילים חילקו את העבודה.	החיילים יחלקו את העבודה.
הקצין חילק את העבודה.	הקצין יחלק את העבודה.
המנהלת חילקה את העבודה.	המנהלת תחלק את העבודה.
חילקתן את העבודה.	תחלקנה את העבודה.
המורות חילקו את העבודה.	המורות תחלקנה את העבודה.
אתה חילקת את העבודה.	אתה תחלק את העבודה.
חילקתי את העבודה.	אחלק את העבודה.
חילקת את העבודה.	תחלקי את העבודה.

Do this drill in reverse, also.

L. Substitution-Agreement Drill

    The waitress serves the food.

<u>המלצרית מחלקת את האוכל.</u>

אנו – הנשים – המלצרים

בני – המלצרית

(e)   /hiclíax/   "he succeeded"   הצליח

M. Substitution-Agreement Drill

    Go and succeed !

עלה והצלח !

עלי (והצליחי)

עלו (והצליחו)

עלינה (והצלחנה)

N. Transformation Drill - Future to Past

    Instructor: He'll succeed in his new job.
    Student: He succeeded in his new job.

הוא הצליח במקום החדש.	הוא יצליח במקום החדש.
הן הצליחו במקום החדש.	הן תצלחנה במקום החדש.
הצלחתי במקום החדש.	תצליחי במקום החדש.
היא הצליחה במקום החדש.	היא תצליח במקום החדש.
הצלחנו במקום החדש.	נצליח במקום החדש.
הצלחתם במקום החדש.	תצליחו במקום החדש.
הצלחת במקום החדש.	אתה תצליח במקום החדש.
הצלחתן במקום החדש.	אתן תצלחנה במקום החדש.
הצלחתי במקום החדש.	אצליח במקום החדש.
הם הצליחו במקום החדש.	הם יצליחו במקום החדש.

Do this drill in reverse, also.

O.   Substitution-Agreement Drill

     He succeeds in everything.   .הוא מצליח בכל דבר

                                 כתו – החיילים – הנשים – את – הוא

(f)   /xasax/   "he saved"   חסך

P.   Substitution Drill

     Save the money.   .חסוך את הכסף

                                                    חסכי

                                                    חסכו

                                           חסוכנה

Q.   Transformation Drill   –   Future to Past

     Instructor: I'll save what's left over.
     Student: I saved what was left over.

.חסכתי את היתרה	.אחסוך את היתרה
.חסכת את היתרה	.תחסוך את היתרה
.חסכת את היתרה	.תחסכי את היתרה
.חסכנו את היתרה	.נחסוך את היתרה
.חסכתם את היתרה	.תחסכו את היתרה
.חסכתן את היתרה	.תחסוכנה את היתרה
.מנחם חסך את היתרה	.מנחם יחסוך את היתרה
.אביכה חסכה את היתרה	.אביבה תחסוך את היתרה
.הם חסכו את היתרה	.הם יחסכו את היתרה
.הן חסכו את היתרה	.הן תחסוכנה את היתרה

Do this drill in reverse, also.

R.   Substitution-Agreement Drill

     She saves every penny.   .היא חוסכת כל פרוטה

                         הפועלים – מנחם – הילדות – המזכירה

(g) /lava/ "he borrowed" לווה

S. Transformation Drill   -   Future to Past

    Instructor: We'll borrow the money.
    Student: We borrowed the money.

לווינו את הכסף.	נלווה את הכסף.
לוויתי את הכסף.	אלווה את הכסף.
לווית את הכסף.	תלווי את הכסף.
בעלה לווה את הכסף.	בעלה ילווה את הכסף.
לוויתם את הכסף.	תלוו את הכסף.
הן לוו את הכסף.	הן תלווינה את הכסף.
היא לוותה את הכסף.	היא תלווה את הכסף.
אתן לוויתן את הכסף.	אתן תלווינה את הכסף.
הם לוו את הכסף.	הם ילוו את הכסף.

Do this drill in reverse, also.

T. Substitution-Agreement Drill

    He borrowed too much.

הוא לווה יותר מדי.

את – אתם – הן – אנו – היא

(h) /hilva/ "he lent" הלווה

U. Substitution Drill
    Lend me five pounds.

הלווה לי חמש לירות.

הלווי

הלוו

הלווינה

V. Transformation Drill   -   Future to Past

    Instructor: They'll lend him the money.
    Student: They lent him the money.

הם הילוו לו את הכסף.	הם ילוו לו את הכסף.
הלוויתי לו את הכסף.	אלווה לו את הכסף.
הלוותם לו את הכסף.	תלוו לו את הכסף.
אבי הילווה לו את הכסף.	אבי ילווה לו את הכסף.
המשפחה הלוותה לו את הכסף.	המשפחה תלווה לו את הכסף.
אנו הלווינו לו את הכסף.	אנו נלווה לו את הכסף.
אתה הלוות לו את הכסף.	אתה תלווה לו את הכסף.
הלוויתן לו את הכסף.	תלווינה לו את הכסף.

Do this drill in reverse, also.

W. Substitution-Agreement Drill

The banks lend at a high interest rate. .הבנקים מלווים בריבית גבוהה

החברה – הבנק הזה – החברות – הבנקים

X. Transformation Drill – <u>hif'il</u> to <u>kal</u>

Instructor: The bank lent me a thousand pounds.
Student: I borrowed a thousands pounds from the bank.

.לוויתי אלף לירות מהבנק	.הבנק הלווה לי אלף לירות 1.
.אחותי לוותה כסף ממרים	.מרים הלוותה כסף לאחותי 2.
.החנוונים לוו כסף מהאחים שלי	.האחים שלי הלוו כסף לחנוונים 3.
.לוויתם מאתנו הרבה כסף	.הלווינו לכם הרבה כסף 4.
.לווית כסף מהמנהל	.המנהל הלווה לך כסף 5.
.חברי לווה ממני חמש לירות	.הלוויתי חמש לירות לחברי 6.
.לווית כסף מבעלי	.בעלי הלווה לך כסף 7.
.לוויתן כסף מהמשרד	.המשרד הלווה לכן כסף 8.
.החברות לוו כסף מהממשלה	.הממשלה הלוותה לחברות כסף 9.

Note: Many speakers use the <u>hif'il</u> for both meanings "to lend" and "to borrow".
Context and the difference of prepositions, /le-/ and /mi-/, relieve any
ambiguity.

GRAMMAR NOTES

34.5 Nouns with Pronominal Suffixes - Singular Set

Many nouns have an alternant form before the pronominal suffixes. For example:

/šalom/	"peace"	/šlomi/	"my peace"
/báit /	"house"	/beyti/	"my house"
/érec /	"country"	/arci/	"my country"

The following is a general description of the alternations. In general they are similar to the alternations of absolute and construct state forms. See Grammar Note 9.4 (b).

(1) Nouns of the pattern /CaCVC/ have an alternant without the /a/:

/šalom/	"peace"	/šlomi/	"my peace"
/davar/	"saying"	/dvari/	"my saying"
/garon/	"throat"	/groni/	"my throat"

If the resulting initial cluster is non-permissible, then /e/ is inserted:

/racon/	"wish"	/reconi/	"my wish"
/makom/	"place"	/mekomi/	"my place

If the first consonant is /x/ or /'/ then /a/ is inserted:

/xaver/	"friend"	/xaveri/	"my friend"
/'adon/	"lord"	/'adoni/	"my lord"

Exceptions to this rule usually reflect a classical Hebrew form of a different type:

/rayon / "idea"   /rayoni / "my idea"

In classical Hebrew the form was /ra'yon/. Note the spelling רעיון .

(2) Feminine nouns ending in /-a/ have an alternant form with /-at-/:

/gisa/	"sister-in-law"	/gisati/	"my sister-in-law"
/avoda/	"work"	/avodati/	"my work"
/halvaa/	"loan"	/halvaati/	"my loan"

Sometimes there are other changes in addition to the /-t-/:

/braxa/	"blessing"	/birkati/	"my blessing"
/safa/	"lip"	/sfati/	"my lip"
/mišpaxa/	"family"	/mišpaxti/	"my family"

(3) In nouns of the pattern /CVCvC/ the second vowel is dropped.

If the first vowel is /e/ it changes to /i/ or /a/. The student must memorize which vowel is substituted.

/'ózen/	"ear"	/'ozni/	"my ear"
/béged/	"garment"	/bigdi/	"my garment"
/'érec/	"country"	/'arci/	"my country"
/yéled/	"boy"	/yaldi/	"my boy"
/séfer/	"book"	/sifri/	"my book"

Exceptions to this change of vowel are /néxed/ "grandson" /nexdi/ "my grandson"; /xélek/ "part" /xelki/ "my part".

The use of pronominal suffixes with nouns to show possession is more literary or formal. The usual spoken Hebrew construction is /ha ---- šeli/.

A.   Transformation Drill

     I washed my garment.

נקיתי את בגדי.	נקיתי את הבגד שלי.
נקיתי את בגדך.	נקיתי את הבגד שלך.
נקיתי את בגדך.	נקיתי את הבגד שלך.
נקיתי את בגדו.	נקיתי את הבגד שלו.
נקיתי את בגדה.	נקיתי את הבגד שלה.
נקיתי את בגדנו.	נקיתי את הבגד שלנו.
נקיתי את בגדכם.	נקיתי את הבגד שלכם.
נקיתי את בגדכן.	נקיתי את הבגד שלכן.
נקיתי את בגדם.	נקיתי את הבגד שלהם.
נקיתי את בגדן.	נקיתי את הבגד שלהן.

B.   Transformation Drill

     I read your book.

קראתי את ספרך.	קראתי את הספר שלך.
קראתי את ספרך.	קראתי את הספר שלך.
קראתי את ספרו.	קראתי את הספר שלו.
קראתי את ספרנו.	קראתי את הספר שלנו.
קראתי את ספרכן.	קראתי את הספר שלכן.
קראתי את ספרה.	קראתי את הספר שלה.
קראתי את ספרכם.	קראתי את הספר שלכם.
קראתי את ספרי.	קראתי את הספר שלי.

C.   Transformation Drill

     I met your daughter.

פגשתי את בתך.	פגשתי את הבת שלך.
פגשתי את בתו.	פגשתי את הבת שלו.
פגשתי את בתכם.	פגשתי את הבת שלכם.
פגשתי את בתם.	פגשתי את הבת שלהם.
פגשתי את בתה.	פגשתי את הבת שלה.
פגשתי את בתך.	פגשתי את הבת שלך.

D.   Transformation Drill

I am satisfied with his work.

אני *שבע* רצון מעבודתו.	אני *שבע* רצון מהעבודה *שלו.*
אני *שבע* רצון מעבודתנו.	אני *שבע* רצון מהעבודה *שלנו.*
אני *שבע* רצון מעבודתם.	אני *שבע* רצון מהעבודה *שלהם.*
אני *שבע* רצון מעבודתה.	אני *שבע* רצון מהעבודה *שלה.*
אני *שבע* רצון מעבודתך.	אני *שבע* רצון מהעבודה *שלך.*
אני *שבע* רצון מעבודתכם.	אני *שבע* רצון מהעבודה *שלכם.*
אני *שבע* רצון מעבודתן.	אני *שבע* רצון מהעבודה *שלהן.*
אני *שבע* רצון מעבודתי.	אני *שבע* רצון מהעבודה *שלי.*

RAPID RESPONSE DRILL

1. איך מסתדרים מנחם ואשתו במשכורת *שלו?*

2. מה זאת אומרת: הם חיים בתקציב?

3. כמה חוסך דב כל חודש?

4. למה הוא לא מצליח לחסוך?

5. מה הפלא *שמנחם* מצליח לחסוך כסף?

REVIEW CONVERSATIONS

א: איך אתם מסתדרים במשכורת?
ב: אנו חיים בתקציב.
א: מה זאת אומרת, חיים בתקציב?
ב: פשוט מאד. רושמים את ההוצאות ומחלקים את ההכנסות.
א: טוב מאד.

ג: אשתי התחילה לעבוד.
ד: טוב מאד. יהיה לך יותר קל.
ג: כן. היא מרוויחה די טוב.
ד: היא עובדת יום שלם?
ג: לא. רק חצי יום.

ה: לוויתי כסף בבנק.
ו: מדוע?
ה: הייתי צריך לשלם חוב.
ו: איך הרבית, גבוהה?
ה: לא. לא נורא.

ז: פרעתי את השטר האחרון.
ח: כמה שטרות היו לך?
ז: היו לי 6 שטרות.

35.1 Getting Up in the Morning

DOV

Tell me, Menaḥem,	emor li, menáxem,	אמור לי, מנחם,
What time do you	beéyze šaa ata	באיזה שעה אתה
get up every morning?	kam kol bóker?	קם כל בוקר?

MENAHEM

I get up	ani kam	אני קם
at 6:30.	bešaa šeš vaxéci.	בשעה שש וחצי.
And you?	veata?	ואתה?

DOV

Six-thirty !	šeš vaxéci !	שש וחצי !
So early?	kol kax mukdam?	כל כך מוקדם?
I just about	ani bekóši	אני בקושי
jump out of bed	kofec mehamita	קופץ מהמיטה
at 7:15.	bešéva varéva.	בשבע ורבע.
he jumped	kafac	קפץ
bed	mita (f)	מיטה

MENAHEM

What time	beéyze šaa	באיזה שעה
do you start working?	ata matxil laavod?	אתה מתחיל לעבוד?

DOV

I start work	ani matxil laavod	אני מתחיל לעבוד
at 8:00	bešaa šmóne.	בשעה שמונה
but I	ax ani	אך אני
always come late.	tamid meaxer.	תמיד מאחר.
always	tamid	תמיד
he was late	ixer	איחר

35.2 ADDITIONAL VOCABULARY

I shower	ani mitkaléax	אני מתקלח
every evening.	kol érev.	כל ערב.
he showered		hitkaléax	התקלח

I got dressed	hitlabášti	התלבשתי
in a hurry.	bimhirut.	במהירות.
he got dressed		hitlabeš	התלבש
hurry		mehirut (f)	מהירות

I didn't have a chance	lo hispákti	לא הספקתי
to comb my hair.	lehistarek.	להסתרק.
he combed his hair		histarek	הסתרק

35.3 VERB DRILLS

(a) /kafac/ "he jumped"   קפץ

A.   Substitution-Agreement Drill

I'll drop over to see you.

אֲנִי אֶקְפֹּץ לִרְאוֹת אֶתְכֶם.

אשתי – אנחנו – הם – אחי
הבנות – מר ווילאמס – אני

B.   Substitution-Agreement Drill

He jumped out of bed.

הוּא קָפַץ מֵהַמִּטָּה.

הילדים – אנו – אני – בתי
רב – אתה – אתן – הוא

(b) /ixer/ "he was late"   איחר

C.   Substitution-Agreement Drill

Don't worry, we won't be late.

אַל תִּדְאַג, לֹא נְאַחֵר.

אתה – הוא – התלמידים –
אני – היא – הן – אנו

D.   Substitution-Agreement Drill

Miriam was late this morning.

מִרְיָם אִיחֲרָה הַבּוֹקֶר.

אני – אתם – המנהל – אתן – את
אנחנו – אתה – כל התלמידים – בתך

(c) /hitkaléax/   "he showered"   התקלח
    /hitlabeš/   "he got dressed"   התלבש
    /histarek/   "he combed his hair"   הסתרק

E.   Substitution-Agreement Drill

He showered, got dressed, combed his hair,
and left the house in a hurry.

הוּא הִתְקַלַּח, הִתְלַבֵּשׁ, הִסְתָּרֵק
וְיָצָא בִּמְהִירוּת מֵהַבַּיִת.

אני – חנה – הן – אתה
אנו – הם – את – רב

410

GRAMMAR NOTES

35.4 Nouns with Pronominal Suffixes - Plural Set

Plural nouns have alternant forms before the plural set of pronominal suffixes.

There are usually two such alternant forms - one occurs before the singular suffixes and first person plural, and the other occurs before the second and third person plural suffixes.

In more formal pronunciation the stress is on the second syllable of the suffixes of the latter group. The other suffixes have either one syllable or the stress on the first of two syllables. In ordinary spoken style the stress is on the first syllable of all suffixes: /-éyxem, -éyxen, -éyhem, -éyhen/.

1 s.		/-ay/
2 m.s.		/-éxa/
2 f.s.		/-áix/
3 m.s.		/-av/
3 f.s.		/-éha/
1 pl.		/-éynu/
2 m.pl.		/-eyxem/
2 f.pl.		/-eyxen/
3 m.pl.		/-eyhem/
3 f.pl.		/-eyhen/

All suffixes of the plural set are spelled with a <u>yud</u> ＇ . Thus, for example, /-o/ and /-av/ "his" are distinguished in the spelling by ﬥ and ﬥ＇.

(a) /-im/ Plural Nouns

Before the singular suffixes and the first person plural suffix the /-im/ is dropped and the suffix added.

	/banim/"sons"	/sfarim/"books"	/binyanim/"buildings"	/avironim/"airplanes"
1s.	banay	sfaray	binyanay	avironay
2m.s.	banéxa	sfaréxa	binyanéxa	avironéxa
2f.s.	banáix	sfaráix	binyanáix	avironáix
3m.s.	banav	sfarav	binyanav	avironav
3f.s.	banéha	sfaréha	binyanéha	avironéha
1pl.	banéynu	sfaréynu	binyanéynu	avironéynu

If the vowel preceding the suffix is /a/ then it is dropped before the second and third person plural suffixes.

	/banim/
2 m.pl.	bneyxem
2 f.pl.	bneyxen
3 m.pl.	bneyhem
3 f.pl.	bneyhen

If an <u>initial</u> three-consonant cluster results, then /i/ or /a/ is inserted between the first two consonants. The student must memorize which vowel is inserted.

	/sfarim/	/yeladim/
2 m.pl.	sifreyxem	yaldeyxem
2 f.pl.	sifreyxen	yaldeyxen
3 m.pl.	sifreyhem	yaldeyhem
3 f.pl.	sifreyhen	yaldeyhen

/The /e/ of /yeladim/ was originially inserted to break up the non-permissible initial two-consonant cluster /yl-/. In the form /yaldeyhem/ the /a/ breaks up an initial <u>three</u>-consonant cluster /yld-/.)

There are exceptions to these rules:

	/batim/ "houses"	/rašim/ "heads"
2 m.pl.	bateyxem	rašeyxem
2 f.pl.	bateyxen	rašeyxen
3 m.pl.	bateyhem	rašeyhem
3 f.pl.	bateyhen	rašeyhen

In informal spoken Hebrew the /a/ preceding these suffixes is usually retained in a number of noun patterns:

	/miršamim/ "recipes"	/binyanim/ "buildings'
2 m.pl.	miršaméyxem	binyanéyxem
2 f.pl.	miršaméyxen	binyanéyxen
3 m.pl.	miršaméyhem	binyanéyhem
3 f.pl.	miršaméyhen	binyanéyhen

Note that the /-éy-/ is usually stressed in these forms, also.

(b)   <u>/-ot/ Plural Nouns</u>

The plural set of suffixes is added to the plural noun after the /-ot/:

	/aruxot/ "meals"	/pgišot/ "appointments"	/raayonot/ "ideas"
1 s.	aruxotay	pgišotay	raayonotay
2 m.s.	aruxotéxa	pgišotéxa	raayonotéxa
2 f.s.	aruxotáix	pgišotáix	raayonotáix
3 m.s.	aruxotav	pgišotav	raayonotav
3 f.s.	aruxotéha	pgišotéha	raayonotéha
1 pl.	aruxotéynu	pgišotéynu	raayonotéynu
2 m.pl.	aruxotéyxem	pgišotéyxem	raayonotéyxem
2 f.pl.	aruxotéyxen	pgišotéyxen	raayonotéyxen
3 m.pl.	aruxotéyhem	pgišotéyhem	raayonotéyhem
3 f.pl.	aruxotéyhen	pgišotéyhen	raayonotéyhen

If the vowel in the syllable immediately preceding the /-ot/ is /a/, then it is often dropped. Any resulting non-permissible clusters are broken up according to the rules for the /-im/ plurals.

	/banot/ "daughters"		/smalot/ "dresses'
1 s.	bnotay		simlotay
2 m.s.	bnotéxa		simlotéxa
2 f.s.	bnotáix		simlotáix
3 m.s.	bnotav		simlotav
3 f.s.	bnotéha		simlotéha
1 pl.	bnotéynu		simlotéynu
2 m.pl.	bnotéyxem		simlotéyxem
2 f.pl.	bnotéyxen		simlotéyxen
3 m.pl.	bnotéyhem		simlotéyhem
3 f.pl.	bnotéyhen		simlotéyhen

(In the form /simlotay/ the vowel /i/ breaks up the resulting initial three-consonant cluster /sml-/.)

The /a/ is not always dropped. There are classes of nouns in which it is retained in all styles of speech and other nouns in which it is retained in informal spoken style.

(c) /-áim/ Dual Nouns

The pattern of the dual nouns is similar to /-im/ plural nouns before suffixes. The /-áim/ is dropped and the suffixes are added. Before the second and third person plural suffixes a preceding /a/ is usually dropped. Resulting consonant clusters are broken up according to the same rules as for /-im/ plural nouns.

	/ragláim/ "feet"		/yadáim/ "hands"
1 s.	raglay		yaday
2 m.s.	ragléxa		yadéxa
2 f.s.	ragláix		yadáix
3 m.s.	raglav		yadav
3 f.s.	ragléha		yadéha
1 pl.	ragléynu		yadéynu
2 m.pl.	ragleyxem		yedeyxem
2 f.pl.	ragleyxen		yedeyxen
3 m.pl.	ragleyhem		yedeyhem
3 f.pl.	ragleyhen		yedeyhen

As with /-im/ and /-ot/ plural nouns, the entire paradigm is often regularized in informal speech. Thus, for example, /yadéyxem/ will be heard as well as /yedeyxem/.

A. Transformation Drill

These are my books.

Response	Prompt
אלו הם ספרי.	אלו הם הספרים שלי.
אלו הם ספריך.	אלו הם הספרים שלך.
אלו הם ספריך.	אלו הם הספרים שלך.
אלו הם ספריו.	אלו הם הספרים שלו.
אלו הם ספריה.	אלו הם הספרים שלה.
אלו הם ספרינו.	אלו הם הספרים שלנו.
אלו הם ספריכם.	אלו הם הספרים שלכם.
אלו הם ספריכן.	אלו הם הספרים שלכן.
אלו הם ספריהם.	אלו הם הספרים שלהם.
אלו הם ספריהן.	אלו הם הספרים שלהן.

B. Transformation Drill

My children study well.

Response	Prompt
ילדי לומדים טוב.	הילדים שלי לומדים טוב.
ילדיך לומדים טוב.	הילדים שלך לומדים טוב.
ילדיך לומדים טוב.	הילדים שלך לומדים טוב.
ילדיו לומדים טוב.	הילדים שלו לומדים טוב.
ילדיה לומדים טוב.	הילדים שלה לומדים טוב.
ילדינו לומדים טוב.	הילדים שלנו לומדים טוב.
ילדיכם לומדים טוב.	הילדים שלכם לומדים טוב.
ילדיכן לומדים טוב.	הילדים שלכן לומדים טוב.
ילדיהם לומדים טוב.	הילדים שלהם לומדים טוב.
ילדיהן לומדים טוב.	הילדים שלהן לומדים טוב.

C. Transformation Drill

My brothers live in Tel Aviv.

Response	Prompt
אחי גרים בתל אביב.	האחים שלי גרים בתל אביב.
אחיה גרים בתל אביב	האחים שלה גרים בתל אביב.
אחינו גרים בתל אביב.	האחים שלנו גרים בתל אביב.
אחיכם גרים בתל אביב.	האחים שלכם גרים בתל אביב.
אחיו גרים בתל אביב.	האחים שלו גרים בתל אביב.
אחיך גרים בתל אביב.	האחים שלך גרים בתל אביב.
אחיהן גרים בתל אביב.	האחים שלהן גרים בתל אביב.
אחיך גרים בתל אביב.	האחים שלך גרים בתל אביב.
אחיהם גרים בתל אביב.	האחים שלהם גרים בתל אביב.
אחיכן גרים בתל אביב.	האחים שלכן גרים בתל אביב.

D.   Transformation Drill

My friends are going to Israel.

חברי נוסעים לישראל.	החברים שלי נוסעים לישראל.
חבריכם נוסעים לישראל.	החברים שלכם נוסעים לישראל.
חברינו נוסעים לישראל.	החברים שלנו נוסעים לישראל.
חבריהם נוסעים לישראל.	החברים שלהם נוסעים לישראל.
חבריו נוסעים לישראל.	החברים שלו נוסעים לישראל.
חבריהן נוסעים לישראל.	החברים שלהן נוסעים לישראל.
חבריה נוסעים לישראל.	החברים שלה נוסעים לישראל.
חבריכן נוסעים לישראל.	החברים שלכן נוסעים לישראל.
חבריך נוסעים לישראל.	החברים שלך נוסעים לישראל.

E.   Transformation Drill

Your ideas are excellent.

רעיונותיכם מצויינים.	הרעיונות שלכם מצויינים.
רעיונותיו מצויינים.	הרעיונות שלו מצויינים.
רעיונותיהם מצויינים.	הרעיונות שלהם מצויינים.
רעיונותיכן מצויינים.	הרעיונות שלכן מצויינים.
רעיונותינו מצויינים.	הרעיונות שלנו מצויינים.
רעיונותי מצויינים.	הרעיונות שלי מצויינים.
רעיונותיה מצויינים.	הרעיונות שלה מצויינים.
רעיונותיך מצויינים.	הרעיונות שלך מצויינים.
רעיונותיהן מצויינים.	הרעיונות שלהן מצויינים.
רעיונותיך מצויינים.	הרעיונות שלך מצויינים.

F.   Transformation Drill

Her cakes are delicious.

עוגותיה טעימות מאד.	העוגות שלה טעימות מאד.
עוגותיהן טעימות מאד.	העוגות שלהן טעימות מאד.
עוגותיך טעימות מאד.	העוגות שלך טעימות מאד.
עוגותינו טעימות מאד.	העוגות שלנו טעימות מאד.
עוגותיכם טעימות מאד.	העוגות שלכם טעימות מאד.
עוגותיו טעימות מאד.	העוגות שלו טעימות מאד.
עוגותיכן טעימות מאד.	העוגות שלכן טעימות מאד.
עוגותי טעימות מאד.	העוגות שלי טעימות מאד.
עוגותיהם טעימות מאד.	העוגות שלהם טעימות מאד.
עוגותיך טעימות מאד.	העוגות שלך טעימות מאד.

G.   Transformation Drill

They cleaned our clothes.

הם ניקו את בגדינו.	הם ניקו את הבגדים שלנו.
הם ניקו את בגדיהן.	הם ניקו את הבגדים שלהן.
הם ניקו את בגדיו.	הם ניקו את הבגדים שלו.
הם ניקו את בגדיה.	הם ניקו את הבגדים שלה.
הם ניקו את בגדיהם.	הם ניקו את הבגדים שלהם.
הם ניקו את בגדיכם.	הם ניקו את הבגדים שלכם.
הם ניקו את בגדי.	הם ניקו את הבגדים שלי.
הם ניקו את בגדיכן.	הם ניקו את הבגדים שלכן.
הם ניקו את בגדיך.	הם ניקו את הבגדים שלך.
הם ניקו את בגדיך.	הם ניקו את הבגדים שלך.

H.   Transformation Drill

My feet hurt.

רגלי כואבות.	הרגליים שלי כואבות.
רגלינו כואבות.	הרגליים שלנו כואבות.
רגליו כואבות.	הרגליים שלו כואבות.
רגליהם כואבות.	הרגליים שלהם כואבות.
רגליה כואבות.	הרגליים שלה כואבות.
רגליהן כואבות.	הרגליים שלהן כואבות.
רגליך כואבות.	הרגליים שלך כואבות.
רגליכן כואבות.	הרגליים שלכן כואבות.

I.   Transformation Drill

How are your children?

מה שלום בניך?	מה שלום הבנים שלך?
מה שלום בניכם?	מה שלום הבנים שלכם?
מה שלום בניו?	מה שלום הבנים שלו?
מה שלום בניהן?	מה שלום הבנים שלהן?
מה שלום בניה?	מה שלום הבנים שלה?
מה שלום בניכן?	מה שלום הבנים שלכן?
מה שלום בניך?	מה שלום הבנים שלך?
מה שלום בניהם?	מה שלום הבנים שלהם?
מה שלום בני?	מה שלום הבנים שלי?
מה שלום בנינו?	מה שלום הבנים שלנו?

J.   Transformation Drill

Moshe hasn't seen our houses.

משה לא ראה את בתינו.	משה לא ראה את הבתים שלנו.
משה לא ראה את בתיכם.	משה לא ראה את הבתים שלכם.
משה לא ראה את בתיכן.	משה לא ראה את הבתים שלכן.
משה לא ראה את בתיה.	משה לא ראה את הבתים שלה.
משה לא ראה את בתיך.	משה לא ראה את הבתים שלך.
משה לא ראה את בתיו.	משה לא ראה את הבתים שלו.
משה לא ראה את בתי.	משה לא ראה את הבתים שלי.
משה לא ראה את בתיהם.	משה לא ראה את הבתים שלהם.
משה לא ראה את בתיך.	משה לא ראה את הבתים שלך.

35.5 Prepositions with Pronominal Suffixes

Prepositions occurring with the plural set of pronominal suffixes alternate in the same way as nouns.

	/lefaním/	"formerly"	/odot/	"about"
1 s.	lefanay	"before me"	odotay	"about me"
2 m.s.	lefanéxa	"before you"	odotéxa	"about you"
2 f.s.	lefanáix	etc.,	odotáix	etc.,
3 m.s.	lefanav		odotav	
3 f.s.	lefanéha		odotéha	
1 pl.	lefanéynu		odotéynu	
2 m.pl.	lifneyxem		odoteyxem	
2 f.pl.	lifneyxen		odoteyxen	
3 m.pl.	lifneyhem		odoteyhem	
3 f.pl.	lifneyhen		odoteyhen	

A.   Expansion Drill

Instructor: I'm standing in line.
Student: I'm standing in line, and Moshe is standing in front of me.

ומשה עומד לפני.	אני עומד בשורה
ומשה עומד לפניך.	אתה עומד בשורה
ומשה עומד לפניך.	את עומדת בשורה
ומשה עומד לפניו.	הוא עומד בשורה
ומשה עומד לפניה.	היא עומדת בשורה
ומשה עומד לפנינו.	אנו עומדים בשורה
ומשה עומד לפניכם.	אתם עומדים בשורה
ומשה עומד לפניכן.	אתן עומדות בשורה
ומשה עומד לפניהם.	הם עומדים בשורה
ומשה עומד לפניהן.	הן עומדות בשורה

B. Expansion Drill

Instructor: I stood in line.
Student: I stood in line and Miriam stood behind me.

ומרים עמדה אחרי.	עמדתי בשורה
ומרים עמדה אחריך.	עמדת בשורה
ומרים עמדה אחרינו.	עמדנו בשורה
ומרים עמדה אחריהן.	הבנות עמדו בשורה
ומרים עמדה אחריך.	עמדת בשורה
ומרים עמדה אחריהם.	התלמידים עמדו בשורה
ומרים עמדה אחריו.	דוד עמד בשורה
ומרים עמדה אחריכם.	עמדתם בשורה
ומרים עמדה אחריה.	היא עמדה בשורה
ומרים עמדה אחריכן.	עמדתן בשורה

RAPID RESPONSE DRILL

1. באיזה שעה מנחם קם כל בוקר?

2. באיזה שעה דב קם כל בוקר?

3. האם דב אוהב לישון?

4. באיזה שעה מתחיל דב לעבוד?

5. האם דב מגיע לעבודה בזמן?

REVIEW CONVERSATIONS

א: באיזה שעה אתה קם בבוקר?

ב: בשבע ורבע, ואתה?

א: אני קם ברבע לשבע.

ב: באיזה שעה אתה מתחיל לעבוד?

א: בשמונה.

ב: אה, אני מתחיל בתשע.

ג: מה אתה עושה בבוקר?

ד: או, מתרחץ, מתגלח, מתלבש.

ג: כמה זמן זה לוקח לך?

ד: חצי שעה בערך.

ג: אתה אוכל ארוחת בוקר בבית?

ד: לא. את זה אני לא מספיק.

ה: שוב אחרת. מה יהיה הסוף?

ו: הסוף יהיה שאצטרך לקום יותר מוקדם.

ה: כן. וללכת לישון יותר מוקדם.

ו: שמע, איך שלא יהיה אני בקושי מתעורר.

ה: קנה לך שעון מעורר חדש.

ו: זה רעיון טוב. אעשה זאת.

ז: מה אתה מתעטש?

ח: או, התקלחתי במים קרים הבוקר.

ז: למה? לא היו לך מים חמים?

ח: לא. יש לנו מים חמים רק פעמיים בשבוע.

ז: אתה נשמע די מצונן.

ט: למה אחרת היום?

י: התקלחתי הבוקר וזה לקח זמן.

ט: אז תתקלח בערב לפני שאתה הולך לישון.

י: אני לא יכול. בני מתקלחים בערב ואין מספיק מים חמים.

כ: איפה קנית את הספרים האלה?

ל: לא קניתי אותם. אינם ספרי. הם של אחי.

כ: חשבתי שהם ספריך. אתה תמיד קונה ספרים חדשים.

אני בקושי קופץ מהמיטה בשבע ורבע...

36.1 Getting Up in the Morning (contd.)

MENAHEM

Listen, Dov,	šma, dov.	.שמע, דב
it makes a bad impression	ze ose róšem ra	זה עושה רושם רע
when you're late every day.	šeata meaxer kol yom.	.שאתה מאחר כל יום
impression, mark	róšem (m)	רושם

DOV

I'll tell you, Menahem.	omar lexa menáxem.	.אומר לך, מנחם
Even when I	afílu kšeani	אפילו כשאני
get up early	kam mukdam	– קם מוקדם
I'm late.	ani meaxer.	.אני מאחר

MENAHEM

How is that possible?	eyx ze yaxol lihyot?	?איך זה יכול להיות

DOV

I'll give you an example.	eten lexa dugma.	.אתן לך דוגמה
Last week	bešavúa šeavar	בשבוע שעבר
I left the house at seven,	yacáti mehabáit bešéva	יצאתי מהבית בשבע
and I thought	vexašávti	וחשבתי
this time I'll get there	hine agía	הנה אגיע
early.	mukdam.	.מוקדם
example	dugma (f)	דוגמה
look (conjunction	hine	הנה
calling attention		
to what follows)		

MENAHEM

And what happened?	uma kara?	?ומה קרה
it happened	kara	קרה

DOV

I couldn't	lo yaxólti	לא יכולתי
start	lehadlik et	להדליק את
my car.	hamexonit šeli.	.המכונית שלי
he kindled, ignited	hidlik	הדליק
automobile	mexonit	מכונית

MENAHEM

What was wrong?	ma haya hakilkul?	?מה היה הקלקול

<u>DOV</u>

I didn't have any gasoline.	lo haya li délek.	לא היה לי דלק.
gasoline	délek (m)	דלק

<u>MENAHEM</u>

Dov, you have to watch the amount of fuel in the car.	dov, ata carix lišmor al kamut hadélek bamexona.	דב, אתה צריך לשמור על כמות הדלק במכונה.
he watched	šamar	שמר
quantity	kamut (f)	כמות
machine, car	mexona (f)	מכונה

<u>DOV</u>

Yes, I know but for some reason I forget.	ken, ani yodea. ax mišum ma ani šoxéax.	כן. אני יודע. אך משום מה אני שוכח.
because of	mišum	משום
because of something	mišum ma	משום מה

<u>MENAHEM</u>

You're an absent-minded fellow.	ata baxur mefuzar.	אתה בחור מפוזר.
young man	baxur (m)	בחור
absent-minded, scattered	mefuzar (m.s.)	מפוזר

36.2 ADDITIONAL VOCABULARY

I had a flat.	haya li téker.	היה לי תקר.
puncture	téker (m)	תקר
I had to change the tire.	hayíti carix lehaxlif et hacamig.	הייתי צריך להחליף את הצמיג.
tire	camig (m)	צמיג
I had an accident.	karta li teunat draxim.	קרתה לי תאונת דרכים.
accident	teuna (f)	תאונה
I collided with a truck.	hitnagášti im óto masa.	התנגשתי עם אוטו משא.
he collided	hitnageš	התנגש
auto	oto (m)	אוטו
load, burden	masa (m)	משא
They're fixing the car in the repair shop.	metaknim et haóto basadna.	מתקנים את האוטו בסדנה.
repair shop, garage	sadna (f)	סדנה

36.3 VERB DRILLS

(a) /kara/ "it happened"   קרה

A. Transformation Drill - Future to Past

    Instructor: What will happen?
    Student: What happened?

מה קרה?	מה יקרה?
לא קרתה לו תאונה.	לא תקרה לו תאונה.
אני יודע שקרו לך דברים מעניינים.	אני יודע שיקרו לך דברים מעניינים.
הרבה תאונות קרו בסוף השבוע.	הרבה תאונות תקרינה בסוף השבוע.

Do this drill in reverse, also.

(b) /hidlik/ "he lit"   הדליק

B. Substitution Drill

    Turn on the light.

הדלק את האורות.
הדליקי
הדליקו
הדלקנה

C. Transformation Drill - Future to Past

    Instructor: He'll start the car.
    Student: He started the car.

הוא הדליק את המכונית.	הוא ידליק את המכונית.
הדלקתי את המכונית.	אדליק את המכונית.
הדלקת את המכונית.	תדליקי את המכונית.
הדלקנו את המכונית.	נדליק את המכונית.
הדלקתם את המכונית.	תדליקו את המכונית.
הדלקת את המכונית.	תדליק את המכונית.
היא הדליקה את המכונית.	היא תדליק את המכונית.
הם הדליקו את המכונית.	הם ידליקו את המכונית.

Do this drill in reverse, also.

(c) /šamar/ "he guarded"   שמר

D. Substitution Drill

    Watch the children.

שמור על הילדים.
שמרי
שמרו
שמורנה

E. Substitution-Agreement Drill

I watch my diet.   אני שומר על הדיאטה שלי.

אשתי – הרופאים – הן – הוא

(/šeli/ may be varied or not.)

F. Transformation Drill - Past to Future

Instructor: The soldiers guarded the plane.
Student: The soldiers will guard the plane.

החיילים ישמרו על האוירון.	החיילים שמרו על האוירון.
נשמור על האוירון.	שמרנו על האוירון.
אשמור על האוירון.	שמרתי על האוירון.
השומר ישמור על האוירון.	השומר שמר על האוירון.
תשמרו על האוירון.	שמרתם על האוירון.
תשמורנה על האוירון.	שמרתן על האוירון.
החיילת תשמור על האוירון.	החיילת שמרה על האוירון.
את תשמרי על האוירון.	את שמרת על האוירון.
הבנות תשמורנה על האוירון.	הבנות שמרו על האוירון.

GRAMMAR NOTES

36.4 Construct State of Plural Nouns

(a) /-im/- Plural nouns and dual nouns

An /-im/-plural noun or dual noun in the construct state has the same form
as the noun with a third person plural pronoun suffix but minus the /-hem/.

/bateyhem/	"their houses"	/batey/	"houses of"
/bneyhem /	"their sons"	/bney /	"sons of"
/yaldeyhem/	"their children"	/yaldey/	"children of"
/sifreyhem/	"their books"	/sifrey/	"books of"
/yedeyhem/	"their hands"	/yedey/	"hands of"
/ozneyhem/	"their ears"	/ozney/	"ears of"
/ragleyhem/	"their feet"	/ragley/	"feet of"

(b) /-ot/ Plural Nouns

An /-ot/ - plural noun in the construct state has the same form as it does
before a pronoun suffix.

/bnotay/	"my daughters"	/bnot/	"daughters of"
/mišpexotéynu/	"our families"	/mišpexot/	"families of"

Most /-ot/ plural nouns will have a construct state form identical with the
absolute state form.

/ugot/	"cakes"	/ugot gvina/	"cheesecakes"
/aruxot/	"meals"	/aruxot érev/	"evening meals"

424

A. Transformation Drill - Singular to Plural

    Instructor: They work in a post office.
    Student: They work in post offices.

הם עובדים במשרדי דואר.	הם עובדים במשרד הדואר.
הם מגיעים באווירוני אל על.	הם מגיעים באווירון אל על.
בתי הספר נמצאים ברחוב הזה.	בית הספר נמצא ברחוב הזה.
נמלי התעופה הדשים מאד.	נמל התעופה חדש מאד.
קניתי ספרי לימוד חדשים.	קניתי ספר לימוד חדש.
הם רואי חשבון מוסמכים.	הוא רואה חשבון מוסמך.
הם בני שבע.	הוא בן שבע.
תן לי את עתוני הבוקר.	תן לי את עתון הבוקר.
הם בעלי מלונות גדולים.	הוא בעל מלונות גדולים.

Do this drill in reverse, also.

B. Transformation Drill - Singular to Plural

    Instructor: We ate an apple cake.
    Student: We ate apple cakes.

אכלנו עוגות תפוחים.	אכלנו עוגת תפוחים.
נתתי לחנה קופסאות שוקולד.	נתתי לחנה קופסת שוקולד.
הוא מכר לה צנצנות ריבה.	הוא מכר לה צנצנת ריבה.
היא הכינה ארוחות ערב.	היא הכינה ארוחת ערב.
שמו את החבילות במכוניות משא.	שמו את החבילות במכונית משא.
גמרנו את תוכניות הלימודים.	גמרנו את תוכנית הלימורים.
הן בנות שמונה.	היא בת שמונה.
הם מכרו לי זוגות נעליים.	הם מכרו לי זוג נעליים.

RAPID RESPONSE DRILL

1. מה עושה רושם רע על מנחם?

2. מה הדוגמה שדב נתן למנחם?

3. מדוע לא יכול היה דב להדליק את המכונה?

4. מה שוכח דב לעשות?

5. על מה צריך דב לשמור.

6. האם לדעתו של מנחם דב הוא בחור מסודר?

א: מה קרה למכונה שלך?

ב: כלום. קלקול קטן.

א: איפה המכונה?

ב: בסדנה. מתקנים אותה.

א: היא תהיה מוכנה הערב?

ב: אני מקווה כך.

ג: או - או - אין לי דלק.

ד: אין לך דלק? רק הבקר מלאת!

ג: לא הבוקר. אתמול.

ד: אז מה יהיה?

ג: כלום. נגש לתחנת הדלק.

ד: אתה חושב שיהיה לך מספיק דלק עד שם?

ג: ננסה ונראה.

ה: שוב שכחתי.

ו: מה שכחת?

ה: שכחתי להחליף את השמן במכונה.

ו: ואת המים בדקת?

ה: לא. גם את זה שכחתי.

ו: אתה בחור מפוזר.

ה: זה לא דבר חדש.

ז: אשתי הכינה עוגת תפוחים טובה.

ח: מתי, היום?

ז: לא. לשבת.

ח: חשבתי שהיום, הייתי בא לאכול.

ז: כבר לא נשאר כלום. גמרנו אותה.

ח: אז למה אתה מספר לי?

ז: רציתי שתדע שאשתי אופה טוב.

ט: אנו שמחים מאד. גמרנו את תוכניות הלימודים.

י: כמה תלמידים יהיו לכם בכתה?

ט: אני חושב שבע.

י: וכמה מורים?

ט: מורה אחד.

י: מורה אחד לשבעה תלמידים? בדרך כלל יש שנה תלמידים.

ט: כן. אין כלל בלי יוצא מהכלל.

כ: הם מכרו לי זוג נעליים.

ל: איך הן? טובות?

כ: לא. קצת קטנות.

ל: אז למה קנית אותם?

כ: זה היה הזוג האחרון בחנות.

לא היה לי דלק...

37.1 Getting Up in the Morning (concluded)

MENAHEM

Keep coming late to work, the boss will fire you.	tamšix leaxer laavoda hamenahel yefater otxa.	– חמשיך לאחר לעבודה המנהל יפטר אותך.
he fired (an employee)	piter	פיטר

DOV

Of this I'm not afraid. He needs me.	mize ani lo mefaxed. hu carix oti.	מזה אני לא מפחד. הוא צריך אותי.
he feared	paxad	פחד

MENAHEM

I believe that he needs you, but there's a limit to everything.	ani maamin šehu carix otxa. ax lekol davar yeš gvul.	אני מאמין שהוא צריך אותך. אך לכל דבר יש גבול.
he believed boundary, limit	heemin gvul (m)	האמין גבול

DOV

Listen, Menahem. There are many things more serious in life than coming late to work, right?	šma menáxem. yešnam harbe dvarim yoter reciniim baxaim meašer ixurim laavoda, naxon?	שמע, מנחם. ישנם הרבה דברים יותר רציניים בחיים מאשר איחורים לעבודה. נכון?
there are (m.pl.) serious	yešnam recini	ישנם רציני

MENAHEM

Right. But you don't have to cross the boundary.	naxon. ax lo carix laavor et hagvul.	נכון. אך לא צריך לעבור את הגבול.

DOV

I know. I'm like that, and that's it.	ani yodéa. ani kaze, vezéhu ze.	אני יודע. אני כזה. וזהו זה.
that, this (m.s.)	zéhu	זהו

37.2 ADDITIONAL VOCABULARY

(Let it remain)   šeyišaer   שֶׁיִּשָּׁאֵר
between us he won't   beynéynu - hu lo yuxal   בֵּינֵינוּ – הוא לא יוכל
be able to manage   lehistader   לְהִסְתַּדֵּר
without me.   bil'aday.   בִּלְעָדַי.

      without, except   bil'adey   בִּלְעָדֵי

37.3 VOCABULARY DRILLS

(a) /yeš ~ yešn-/   "there is, there are"

     The particle /yeš/ has the suffixed variant /yešn-/ is used only with a third person subject, and the suffix agrees with it in gender and number - /yešno, yešna, yešnam, yešnan./

     Only /yeš/ is used with /le-/ in the meaning "to have".

A. Transformation Drill

     There are many offices in this building.

יֶשְׁנָם הרבה משרדים בכנין הזה.   יש הרבה מִשְׂרדים בבניין הזה.

יֶשְׁנוֹ ספר מצויין על יד המלון.   על יד המלון יש סֵפֶר מצויין.

יֶשְׁנָה מלצרית יפה בבית הקפה.   יש מלצרית יפה בבית הקפֶה.

יֶשְׁנָן הצגות טובות בבית "הבימה".   יֵש הצגות טובות בבית "הבימה".

(b) /recini/   "serious"   רְצִינִי

B. Substitution-Agreement Drill

     The students are very serious.   הַתַּלְמִידִים רְצִינִיים מאד.

ההצגה בבית "הבימה" – החיילות – המורה החדש

החיים – המנהלת – התלמידים

(c) /beyn/   "between, among"   בֵּין

     The preposition /beyn/ is used with the singular set of pronominal suffixes - /beyni/, etc.,   The construction "between... and ..." is rendered /beyn... leveyn.../ or /beyn... le.../.

C. Expansion Drill

Instructor: I'll tell you something.
Student: I'll tell you something. Let it remain between me and you.

שׁיישאר ביני לבינך.	אומר לך דבר-מה
שׁיישאר ביני לבינו.	אומר לו דבר-מה
שׁיישאר ביני לבינם.	אומר להם דבר-מה
שׁיישאר ביני לבינכן.	אומר לכן דבר-מה
שׁיישאר ביני לבינך.	אומר לך דבר-מה
שׁיישאר ביני לבינכם.	אומר לכם דבר-מה
שׁיישאר ביני לבינה.	אומר לה דבר-מה
שׁיישאר ביני לבינן.	אומר להן דבר-מה

(d) /bil'adey/ "without, except"   בלעדי

The preposition /bli/ "without" has the alternant form /bil'ad-/ before
pronoun suffixes. The plural set of suffixes is used with this form. The "plural
construct" form /bil'adey/ occurs in formal style before nouns.

D. Transformation Drill

Instructor: I won't go with Moshe.
Student: Moshe will go without me.

משה ילך בלעדי.	לא אלך עם משה.
משה ילך בלעדיך.	לא תלך עם משה.
משה ילך בלעדינו.	לא נלך עם משה.
משה ילך בלעדיכם.	לא תלכו עם משה.
משה ילך בלעדיכן.	לא תלכנה עם משה.
משה ילך בלעדיך.	לא תלכי עם משה.
משה ילך בלעדיה.	היא לא תלך עם משה.
משה ילך בלעדיו.	הוא לא ילך עם משה.
משה ילך בלעדיהן.	הן לא תלכנה עם משה.
משה ילך בלעדיהם.	הם לא ילכו עם משה.

37.4 VERB DRILLS

(a) /piter/ "he fired"   פיטר

A. Transformation Drill - Future to Past

Instructor: The boss will fire you.
Student: The boss fired you.

המנהל פיטר אותך.	המנהל יפטר אותך.
פיטרתי את המזכירה.	אני אפטר את המזכירה.
פיטרנו את הפועלים.	נפטר את הפועלים.
הם לא פיטרו אותי.	הם לא יפטרו אותי.

Do this drill in reverse, also.

B. Transformation Drill - <u>pi'el</u> to <u>hitpa'el</u>

Instructor: The boss will fire her from the job.
Student: She will resign from the job.

היא תתפטר מהעבודה.	המנהל יפטר אותה.
נתפטר מהעבודה.	המנהל יפטר אותנו.
אחיו יתפטר מהעבודה.	המנהל יפטר את אחיו.
אתפטר מהעבודה.	המנהל יפטר אותי.
תתפטרו מהעבודה.	המנהל יפטר אתכם.
המזכירות תתפטרנה מהעבודה.	המנהל יפטר את המזכירות.

Do this drill in reverse, also.

C. Expansion Drill

Instructor: They didn't fire me.
Student: They didn't fire me. I quit.

אני התפטרתי.	לא פיטרו אותי.
אנחנו התפטרנו.	לא פיטרו אותנו.
הוא התפטר.	לא פיטרו את בעלה.
היא התפטרה.	לא פיטרו את אשתי.
הן התפטרו.	לא פיטרו את המזכירות.

(b) /paxad/ "he feared" פחד

The verb /paxad/ is unusual. In the past tense it is conjugated in the <u>kal</u>,
in the future it is conjugated in the <u>pi'el</u> - /yefaxed/; in the present tense
it is conjugated in either - /poxed/, /mefaxed/.

D. Substitution-Agreement Drill

I won't be afraid of the dog.   <u>אני לא אפחד מהכלב.</u>

אתה - הם - הילדות - אנו - אתם

את - אתן - מנחם - בתו - אני

E. Substitution-Agreement Drill

(The conjugations should be drilled separately.)

I'm not afraid of that.   <u>אני לא פוחד מזה.</u> (or) <u>אני לא מפחד מזה.</u>

אנו - הילדים - אתם - החיילות - את

אתה - היא - אתן - משה - אני

F. Substitution-Agreement Drill

I was afraid he'd be late.

פחדתי שהוא יאחר.

אתה – המורה – הקצינים – המנהלת

אנו – את – אתם – אני

(c) /he'emin/ "he believed"   האמין

G. Substitution Drill

Don't believe what he tells you.

אל תאמין מה שהוא אומר לך.

תאמיני

תאמינו

תאמנה

H. Substitution-Agreement Drill

I believe that this is correct.

אני מאמין שזה נכון.

אנו – היא – הנשים – המנהל

37.5 Abstract Nouns in /-ut/ "-ness"

Abstract nouns may be derived from many nouns and adjectives by adding the suffix /-ut/.

These nouns are feminine.

/mahir/	"quick"	/mehirut/	"quickness"
/recini/	"serious"	/recinut/	"seriousness"
/gadol/	"great"	/gadlut/	"greatness"
/efšari/	"possible"	/efšarut/	"possibility"
/naim/	"pleasant"	/neimut/	"pleasantness"

37.6 Hortatives

A wish or desire on the part of the speaker that someone else should do something or that something should happen is expressed by the construction /še-/ followed by the future tense of the verb.

/šeyišaer beynéynu/ "Let it remain between us."

/šeyavo maxar/ "Let him come tomorrow."

The English "let" in the above sentences simply expresses the speaker's wish. It does _not_ mean "permit, allow". This would be rendered in Hebrew /ten lo lavo maxar./

The construction with /še-/ may be considered an elliptical sentence with a preceding clause deleted such as /ani roce/ or /ani mekave/.

/ani roce šeyavo maxar./ "I want him to come tomorrow."

433

A. Transformation Drill

Instructor: I hope Moshe will come earlier.
Student: Let Moshe come earlier.

שמשה יבוא יותר מוקדם.	אני מקווה שמשה יבוא יותר מוקדם.
שיגיעו בשש.	אני רוצה שיגיעו בשש.
שתיסענה לחיפה.	אני רוצה שהן תיסענה לחיפה.
שתכין דגים.	אני מקווה שהיא תכין דגים.
שיהיה בריא.	אני מקווה שיהיה בריא.
שילמד עברית.	אני רוצה שילמד עברית.

RAPID RESPONSE DRILL

1. מה יעשה המנהל אם דב ימשיך לאחר לעבודה?

2. ממה דב לא מפחד?

3. האם איחור לעבודה זה דבר רציני?

4. מדוע לא יוצא לדב להגיע לעבודה בזמן?

434

REVIEW CONVERSATIONS

א: תמשיך לאחד –
ב: אז מה יהיה?
א: אז מר זהבי יפטר אותך.
ב: שיפטר אותי. אני בטוח שאמצא עבודה אחדת.

ג: המנהל צריך אותי.
ד: בשביל מה הוא צריך אותך?
ג: אני המזכירה היחידה בחברה.
ד: ומה עושה מרים?
ג: מרים כבר לא עובדת כאן.
ד: למה?
ג: המנהל פיטר אותה השבוע.

ה: שמע, אתה עובר את הגבול.
ו: במה אני עובר את הגבול?
ה: באיחורים שלך.
ו: ידידי היקר, ישנם הרבה דברים יותר חשובים.
ה: ממה?
ו: מאיחורים כמובן.

מעניין מאד. ראה את הכובות היפות...

38.1 <u>Purim Parade</u>

MR. WILLIAMS

What is	ma ze	מה זה
this noise	haráaš haze	הרעש הזה
in the street?	barexov.	ברחוב?
noise	ráaš (m)	רעש

MR. CARMI

It's the <u>Adloyada</u>.	zu adloyáda.	זו עדלאידע.
Today is Purim.	xag purim hayom.	חג פורים היום.
Purim festival	adloyáda(f) עדלאידע	
Purim, Feast of Lots	purim פורים	

MR. WILLIAMS

What is Purim?	ma ze xag purim?	מה זה חג פורים?
What kind of holiday	éyze xag ze.	איזה חג זה?
is it?		

MR. CARMI

Purim is	xag purim hu	חג פורים הוא
the happiest holiday.	haxag hasaméax beyoter	החג השמח ביותר
and especially	ubemeyuxad	ובמיוחד
for the children.	layeladim.	לילדים.
special	meyuxad מיוחד	

MR. WILLIAMS

Why just	láma dávka	למה דווקא
for children?	layeladim?	לילדים?

MR. CARMI

They put on costumes,	mitxapsim,	מתחפשים,
go to parties,	holxim lenešafim	הולכים לנשפים,
and eat poppy-seed cakes.	veoxlim ozney haman.	ואוכלים אוזני המן.
he disguised himself	hitxapes התחפש	
party, ball	néšef (m) נשף	
(special Purim cake)	ozen haman(f) אוזן המן	

MR. WILLIAMS

This morning I saw	raíti habóker	ראיתי הבוקר
children dressed	yeladim levušim	ילדים לבושים
in masks,	masexot	מסכות
and I didn't know why.	velo yadáti madúa.	ולא ידעתי מדוע.
dressed	lavuš לבוש	
mask	masexá (f) מסכה	

MR. CARMI

Mr. Williams,	mar Williams,	מר ווילאמס,
look at	habet al	הבט על
the parade.	hatahaluxa.	התהלוכה.
he looked	hibit הביט	
parade, procession	tahaluxa(f) תהלוכה	

437

MR. WILLIAMS

Very interesting.	meanyen meod.	‏מעניין מאד.‏
Look at	ree et	‏ראה את‏
the beautiful floats.	habubot hayafot.	‏הבובות היפות.‏
I've never seen	meolam lo raíti	‏מעולם לא ראיתי‏
a parade like this.	tahaluxa kazo.	‏תהלוכה כזו.‏
doll, mannekin	búba (f)	‏בובה‏
never	meolam...lo	‏מעולם לא‏

38.2 Additional Vocabulary

Have you ever seen	haim raíta ey páam	‏האם ראית אי-פעם‏
a parade like this?	tahaluxa kazo?	‏תהלוכה כזו?‏
ever	ey páam	‏אי-פעם‏
I've never seen	af páam lo raíti	‏אף פעם לא ראיתי‏
such a parade.	tahaluxa kazo.	‏תהלוכה כזו.‏
never	af páam...lo	‏אף פעם לא‏
This year no one	hašana af exad	‏השנה אף אחד‏
was dressed as a clown.	lo hitxapes leleycan.	‏לא התחפש לליצן.‏
no one	af exad...lo	‏אף אחד לא‏
I'll never learn	leolam lo elmad	‏לעולם לא אלמד‏
to bake ozney haman.	leefot ozney haman.	‏לאפות אוזני המן.‏
never	leolam...lo	‏לעולם לא‏
he baked	afa	‏אפה‏

38.3 VOCABULARY DRILLS

(a) /meyuxad/ "special"   ‏מיוחד‏

A. Substitution-Agreement Drill

This plane is specially for tourists.   ‏האוירון הזה מיוחד לתיירים.‏

‏האוניה – בית המלון – המשרדים ההם‏
‏בית הספר – החנויות – התוכנית‏

(b) /lavuš/ "dressed"   ‏לבוש‏

B. Substitution-Agreement Drill

She was dressed in a brown suit.   ‏היא היתה לבושה בחליפה חומה.‏

‏אני – התיירים – התלמידרות‏
‏אשתו – החייל – המנהלים‏

38.4 VERB DRILLS

(a) /hitxapes/ "he disguised himself" התחפש

A. Substitution-Agreement Drill

What are you going to be dressed as on Purim?

למה תתחפש בפורים?

כתך – הכנים שלכם – המורה
המורות – את – אנו

B. Substitution-Agreement Drill

He disguised himself as a movie actor.

הוא התחפש לשחקן קולנוע.

אני – אשתי – הכנות של משה
כעלה – אנו – הוא

(b) /hibit/ "he looked" הביט

C. Substitution Drill

Look at the costumes.

הבט על התחפשות.
הביטי
הביטו
הבטנה

D. Transformation Drill - Past to Future

Instructor: Moshe looked out the window.
Student: Moshe will look out the window.

משה יכיט דרך החלון.	משה הביט דרך החלון.
הם יכיטו דרך החלון.	הם הגיטו דרך החלון.
אנו נכיט דרך החלון.	הבטנו דרך החלון.
תכיט דרך החלון.	הבטת דרך החלון.
תכיטי דרך החלון.	הבטת דרך החלון.
הילדות תכטנה דרך החלון.	הילדות הגיטו דרך החלון.

Do this drill in reverse, also.

(c) /afa/ "he baked" אפה

The future forms of this verb are /yofe / etc. A frequent variant is
/yeefe/.

439

E. Transformation Drill - Future to Past

    Instructor: My mother will bake a cake for the holiday.
    Student: My mother baked a cake for the holiday.

אמי אפתה עוגה לחג.	אמי תאפה עוגה לחג.
אפינו לחם לשבת.	נאפה לחם לשבת.
מה אפית בשביל הילדים?	מה תאפי בשביל הילדים?
הנשים אפו אוזני המן.	הנשים תאפנה אוזני המן.

GRAMMAR NOTES

38.5 <u>Negative Adverbials</u>

    The negative adverbials /meolam, leolam, af paam, af exad, klum, šum davar/
are used with /lo/ when the verb occurs in the sentence.

            /<u>meolam lo</u> raíti tahaluxa kazo./
            "I've never seen such a parade."

In equational sentences /eyn/ may be used.

            /eyn klum bacincénet./
            "There is nothing in the jar."

    In response to a question they may be used without /lo/ or /eyn/, but they
still are negative.

         /ma šamáta meaxíxa./ "What did you hear from your brother."

         /šum davar/   "Nothing"

    The adverbials /meolam/ and /leolam/ "never" are used with past, and future
tense forms, respectively.

         /meolam lo raíti oto./ "I've never seen him."

         /leolam lo er'e oto./ "I'll never see him."

/af páam/ "never" may be used with any tense.

         /af páam lo dibárti ito./ "I've never spoken to him."

         /ani af páam lo medaber ito./ "I never speak to him."

         /af páam lo adaber ito./ "I'll never speak to him."

A. Response Drill

Instructor: have you ever eaten a pomegranate?
Student: Never.

אף פעם.	1. האם אכלת אי פעם רימון?
אף פעם.	2. האם למדת אי פעם צרפתית?
אף פעם.	3. האם היית אי פעם באילת?
אף פעם.	4. האם אתה אוכל גבינה?
אף פעם לא.	5. האם אתה אופה עוגות?
לעולם לא.	6. האם תהיה שחקן בהצגה?

The responses may be varied with /meolam/ etc.

B. Response Drill

Instructor: What did you hear from him?
Student: Nothing.

שום דבר.	1. מה שמעת ממנו?
שום דבר.	2. מה הוא סיפר לך?
שום דבר.	3. מה כתבת לדב?
שום דבר.	4. מה אתה אוכל עכשיו?
שום דבר.	5. מה שלח לדוד?

The responses may be varied with /klum/.

C. Response Drill

Instructor: Who are you talking to?
Student: Nobody.

עם אף אחד.	1. עם מי את מדברת?
אף אחד.	2. מי הקדים?
אף אחד.	3. מי בכיתה?
עם אף אחד.	4. עם מי אתה הולך לקולנוע?
אף אחד.	5. מי יגיע הערב?

RAPID RESPONSE DRILL

1. מה היה הרעש ברחוב?

2. איזה חג הוא חג פורים?

3. מה עושים הילדים בפורים?

4. מה ראה מר וויליאמס בבוקר?

5. על מה הביט מר וויליאמס?

6. האם מר וויליאמס ראה אי-פעם תהלוכה כזו?

REVIEW CONVERSATIONS

א: למה הילדים לובשים מסכות?

ב: היום חג פורים.

א: או כן. שכחתי.

ב: לך יש מסכה?

א: לא. אבל עד הערב תהיה לי.

ג: אתה הולך לנשף הערב?

ד: כן בטח. ואת ?

ג: גם אני מוזמנת לנשף מסכות.

ד: למה את מתחפשת?

ג: אני מתחפשת לחיילת.

ה: שלום חיים. מה שלומך? מה שמעת מאחותך?

ו: שום דבר.

ה: כבר הרבה זמן?

ו: כן.

ז: האם ראית את מרים נרקיס?

ח: מעולם לא.

ז: האם אתה חולה לראות אותה?

ח: לעולם לא.

ט: האם זה נכון שאתה לא מדבר עם יעקב?

י: לא. זה לא נכון.

ט: האם הוא הפריע במשהו?

י: בכלום.

כ: האם מישהו כאן צריך אותי?

ל: אף אחד.

כ: האם יהיו צדיקים אותי אי פעם?

ל: לעולם לא.

מ: האם מנחם יגוא הנה אי פעם?

נ: אף פעם.

מ: האם מישהו הפריע לו?

נ: בכלל לא. הוא לא אורג את מזג האוויר פה.

39.1 Buying Clothes

YONATAN

David, listen.	david. šma.	דוד, שמע.
I need	ani carix	אני צריך
a new suit	xalifa xadaša	חליפה חדשה
for the holidays.	laxagim.	לחגים.

DAVID

Do you want	ata roce		אתה רוצה
a ready-made suit	xalifa muxana		חליפה מוכנה
or custom made?	o lefi mida?		או לפי מידה?
according to		lefi	לפי
measure, size		mida (f)	מידה

YONATAN

I don't know.	ani lo yodéa.		אני לא יודע.
Do you know	ata makir		אתה מכיר
a good tailor	xayat tov		חייט טוב
in the neighborhood?	basviva?		בסביבה?
tailor		xayat (m)	חייט
neighborhood		sviva (f)	סביבה

DAVID

You can order	ata yaxol lehazmin		אתה יכול להזמין
a custom-made suit,	xalifa lefi mida		חליפה לפי מידה
In the men's clothing store.	baxanut lebigdey gvarim.		בחנות לבגדי גברים.
man		géver (m)	גבר

YONATAN

Really?	beemet?	באמת?
I didn't know.	lo yadáti.	לא ידעתי.

DAVID

If you wish,	im ata roce	אם אתה רוצה
I'm ready	ani muxan	אני מוכן
to go with you	laléxet itxa	ללכת אתך
there.	lešam.	לשם.

YONATAN

I'd be very grateful.	ode lexa meod.	אודה לך מאד.

DAVID

You'll need a tie	tictarex aniva	תצטרך עניבה
to match the suit.	mat'ima laxalifa.	מתאימה לחליפה.

<u>YONATAN</u>

Yes. We'll see	ken. nir'e		כן. נראה
what selection	eyze mivxar		איזה מכחר
they have.	yeš lahem.		יש להם.
selection		mivxar (m)	מכחר

<u>DAVID</u>

It's a big store.	zu xanut gdola.	זו חנות גדולה
They have	yeš lahem	יש להם
everything.	hakol.	הכל.

<u>YONATAN</u>

By the way,	agav,		אגב,
I also need	ani carix gam		אני צריך גם
a pair of shoes.	zug naaláim.		זוג נעליים.
incidentally		agav	אגב

<u>DAVID</u>

Oh, very good.	o - tov meod.	או - טוב מאד.
At the same time	beota hahizdamnut	באותה ההזדמנות
I'll get	ani ekne	אני אקנה
new slippers.	naaley báit xadašot.	נעלי בית חדשות.

39.2 Additional Vocabulary

I need...	ani carix...	אני צריך...
a new briefcase.	tik xadaš.	תיק חדש.
a new coat.	meil xadaš.	מעיל חדש.
a new hat.	kóva xadaš.	כובע חדש.
a new raincoat.	meil géšem xadaš.	מעיל גשם חדש.
a new robe.	xaluk xadaš.	חלוק חדש.
a new wallet.	arnak xadaš.	ארנק חדש.
a new sweater.	svéder xadaš.	סודר חדש.
a new belt.	xagora xadaša.	חגורה חדשה.
a new shirt.	kutónet xadaša.	כותונת חדשה.
a new handkerchief.	mimxata xadaša.	ממחטה חדשה.
a new undershirt.	gufia xadaša.	גופיה חדשה.
new pajamas.	pijáma xadaša.	פיג'מה חדשה.
new undershorts.	taxtonim xadašim.	תחתונים חדשים.
new shoelaces.	sroxim xadašim.	שרוכים חדשים.

I need...	ani crixa...	אני צריכה...
a new dress.	simla xadaša.	שמלה חדשה.
a new skirt.	xacait xadaša.	חצאית חדשה.
a new blouse.	xulca xadaša.	חולצה חדשה.
a new bra.	xazia xadaša.	חזיה חדשה.
a new slip.	taxtonit xadaša.	תחתונית חדשה.
a new umbrella.	mitria xadaša.	מטריה חדשה.
new stockings.	garbáim xadašot.	גרביים חדשות.

I know	ani makira	אני מכירה
a good seamstress.	toféret tova.	תופרת טובה.
he sewed	tafar	תפר

444

GRAMMAR NOTES

39.3 /kvar/ and /od/

/kvar/ generally stresses the fact that the action has been completed or **is**
to be completed. It is often translated as "already".

/kvar meuxar/   "It's late already."

With expressions of time it is equivalent to the English "has been."

/hu oved kan kvar xodšáim/ "He has been working here for two months."

In questions it is equivalent to "yet". /od/ is not used.

/kvar axálta?/ "Have you eaten yet?"

With verbs /od/ is usually translatable as "yet" or "still".

/od lo axálti/ "I haven't eaten yet"
/od mukdam/ "It's still early."

With nouns /od/ means "another, more".

/od davar exad/ "one more thing."

/ani ešaer kan od švuáim./ "I'm staying another two weeks here."

With certain time expressions /od/ means "no later than", "as early as".

/od hayom/ "before today is over"

In negative sentences /od/ may be ambiguous.

/eyn od xadašot./ "There is no news as yet."

or possibly "There is no more news."

On the other hand - /od eyn xadašot./ "There is no news as yet."

RAPID RESPONSE DRILL

1. ‏מה רוצה יונתן לקנות?‏

2. ‏איזו חליפה הוא רוצה – מוכנה או לפי מידה?‏

3. ‏איפה אפשר לקנות חליפה לפי מידה.‏

4. ‏מה עוד צריך יונתן לקנות?‏

5. ‏מה יקנה דוד?‏

REVIEW CONVERSATIONS

א: מרים, אני צריך חליפה חדשה.
ב: כן. אתה צריך את החליפה לחגים.
א: איזה צבע חליפה לקנות?
ב: אני חושבת שחליפה כחולה תהאים לך.
א: כן. אני מסכים אתך.

ג: אתה רוצה חליפה מוכנה?
ד: הייתי רוצה חליפה לפי מידה.
ג: אני מכיר חייט טוב.
ד: איפה גר החייט?
ג: כאן בסביבה.

ה: מה אתם עושים בעיר?
ו: אנו צריכים לקנות כמה דברים.
ה: מה אתם צריכים?
ו: פיג׳מות, ארנק, מטריה.
ה: אנו גם כן הולכים לעשות קניות.
ו: יופי. נלך ביחד.

ז: קנית נעליים?
ח: עוד לא.
ז: למה?
ח: לא היו בחנות נעליים יפות.
ז: וארנק יפה ראית?
ח: גם ארנק לא מצאתי.

ט: האם יש לך מעילים חדשים?
י: אין עוד מעילים לחורף.
ט: למה? כבר קר בחוץ.
י: לא, עוד לא קר.
ט: מתי יהיו לך מעילים?
י: המעילים החדשים יגיעו עוד השבוע.

40.1 Going to the Irrigation Project

MR. WILLIAMS

Hello, Mr. Carmi. I'm Mr. Williams from the American Embassy.	šalom mar kármi. ani mar Williams mehašagrirut haamerikáit.	שלום מר כרמי. אני מר ווילאמס מהשגרירות האמריקאית.
I heard about you in America.	šamáti odotéxa od beamérika.	שמעתי אודותיך עוד באמריקה.
about	odot	אודות
You're the director of the bureau of development.	ata menahel misrad hapitúax.	אתה מנהל משרד הפיתוח.
development	pitúax (m)	פיתוח

MR. CARMI

Oh - Mr. Williams! I've heard about you, too.	o- mar Williams! gam ani šamáti odotéxa.	אה - מר ווילאמס! גם אני שמעתי אודותיך.
Are you interested in seeing the new irrigation project in the Negev?	haim ata meunyan lir'ot et mif'al hamáim haxadaš banégev?	האם אתה מעוניין לראות את מפעל המים החדש בנגב?
project	mif'al (m)	מפעל
southern part of Israel	négev	נגב

MR. WILLIAMS

Yes, certainly. My wife and I would be very happy to visit there.	ken. bevaday. išti veani nismax meod levaker šam.	כן. בוודאי. אשתי ואני נשמח מאוד לבקר שם.
certain	vaday	וודאי
he visited	biker	ביקר

MR. CARMI

Tell me when it's convenient for you to go, and I'll take you for a tour.	tagid li matay šenóax laxem linsóa, veekax otxem lesiyur.	תגיד לי מתי שנוח לכם לנסוע, ואקח אתכם לסיור.
he told	higid	הגיד
convenient, comfortable	nóax (m.s.)	נוח
tour	siyur (m)	סיור

MR. WILLIAMS

Next Tuesday I have free time.	beyom šliši haba yeš li zman panuy.	ביום שלישי הבא יש לי זמן פנוי.
vacant	panuy (m.s.)	פנוי

MR. CARMI

Very good. Then I'll come to get you in the morning.	tov meod. az avo lakáxat otxem babóker.	טוב מאוד. אז אבוא לקחת אתכם בבוקר.
At six o'clock in the evening, You'll be back at home.	bešaa šeš baérev tiyu šuv babáit.	בשעה שש בערב תהיו שוב בבית.

447

MR. WILLIAMS

Thank you.	toda raba.	תודה רבה.
I'm sure that	ani batúax	אני בטוח
we'll enjoy it very much.	šenehene ِmeod.	שנהנה מאד.

40.2 At the Irrigation Project

MR. CARMI

Look Mr. Williams.	histakel, mar Williams.	הסתכל מר ווילייאמס,
Here is the pumping station.	hine taxanat haše'iva.	הנה תחנת השאיבה.
he looked at	histakel	הסתכל
station	taxana (f)	תחנה
he drew (water)	ša'av	שאב

MR. WILLIAMS

What ! We're there already?	ma ! kvar higánu?	מה, כבר הגענו?
Where are we?	éyfo ánu nimcaim.	איפה אנו נמצאים?

MR. CARMI

We're in	ánu nimcaim	אנו נמצאים
Upper Galilee.	bagalil haelyon.	בגליל העליון
There is Lake Kineret.	hine agam hakinéret.	הנה אגם הכנרת.
Galilee	galil	גליל
top, highest	elyon (m.s.)	עליון
lake, pond	agam (m)	אגם

MR. WILLIAMS

I see	ani roe	אני רואה
the pipes.	et hacinorot.	את הצנורות.
pipe	cinor (m)	צנור

MR. CARMI

The pipes	hacinorot	הצנורות
take the water	movilim et hamáim	מובילים את המים
to the main reservoir	lamaagar hamerkazi	למאגר המרכזי
in the south.	badarom.	בדרום.
he transported	hovil	הוביל
reservoir	maagar (m)	מאגר
South	darom	דרום

MR. WILLIAMS

How is the water?	eyx hamáim?	איך המים?
Sweet?	metukim?	מתוקים?

MR. CARMI

Yes. The waters of Kineret	ken. mey hakinéret	כן. מי הכנרת
are sweet.	metukim.	מתוקים.

MR. WILLIAMS

What is the length of the water carrier, Mr. Carmi?	ma órex movil hamáim, mar kármi.	מה אורך מוביל המים, מר כרמי?
length	órex (m)	אורך

MR. CARMI

The length of the water line is about 65 miles, and it passes along the coastline.	orko šel kav hamáim kešišim vexamiša mil vehu over leórex haxof.	אורכו של קו המים כשׁשׁים וחמשׁה מיל והוא עובר לאורך החוף.
mile	mil	מיל

MR. WILLIAMS

We want to thank you again for the interesting tour.	ánu rocim lehodot lexa šuv avur hasiyur hameanyen.	אנו רוצים להודות לך שׁוב עבור הסיור המעניין.

MR. CARMI

I'm happy you enjoyed it. Let's start home.	ani saméax šenehenétem. natxil laxzor habáyta.	אני שׂמח שׁנהניתם. נחחיל לחזור הביתה.

40.3 ADDITIONAL VOCABULARY

Galilee is in the north of Israel.	hagalil nimca bicfon haárec.	הגליל נמצא בצפון הארץ.
north	cafon	צפון

The Jordan is in the east.	hayarden nimca bamizrax.	הירדן נמצא במזרח.
east	mizrax	מזרח

The Mediterranean is in the west.	hayam hatixon nimca bamaarav.	הים התיכון נמצא במערב.
middle west	tixon (m.s.) maarav	תיכון מערב

Have a good time.	tevalu beneimim.	תבלו בנעימים.
he spent (time)	bila	בילה

GRAMMAR NOTES

40.4 Derived Nouns - mif'al

A frequently occurring noun derivation is the pattern /miCCaC/. Such nouns usually designate a concrete result of the action of the verb. These nouns are masculine.

/rašam/	"he listed"	/miršam/	"recipe"	i.e. list of ingredients
/pa'al/	"he worked"	/mif'al/	"project"	
/safar/	"he counted"	/mispar/	"number"	
/saxar/	"he traded"	/misxar/	"commerce"	
/katav/	"he wrote"	/mixtav/	"letter"	
/baxar/	"he chose"	/mivxar/	"selection"	

The prefix may be /ma-/ or /me-/ before /'/, /r/, /x/.

/'asa/	"he did"	/ma'ase/	"deed"
/'agar/	"he collected"	/ma'agar/	"reservoir"
/ra'a/	"he saw"	/mar'e/	"sight"
/xala/	"he got sick"	/maxala/	"sickness"
/raxok/	"distant"	/merxak/	"distance"

Occasionally a feminine derivation with /-a/ is used.

/se'uda/	"meal/	/mis'ada/	"restaurant"
/mivrak/	"telegram"	/mivraka/	"telegraph office"

40.5 Derived Adjectives - pa'il

A frequently occurring adjective derivation is /CaCiC/. These adjectives express qualities such as expressed in English with "-able".

/šavar/	"he broke"	/šavir/	"breakable, fragile"
/miher/	"he hurried"	/mahir/	"quick"
/xideš/	"he renewed"	/xadiš/	"modern"
/bxor/	"eldest son"	/baxir/	"senior"

RAPID RESPONSE DRILL

1. היכן שמע מר וויל|אמס אודות מר כרמי?

2. באיזה תפקיד עובד מר כרמי?

3. מה מעוניין מר ווילאמס לראות?

4. מתי נוח למר ווילאמס לנסוע?

5. את מה מראה מר כרמי למר ווילאמס?

6. איפה הם נמצאים?

7. מה רואה מר ווילאמס?

8. לאן מובילים הצנורות?

9. האם המים מתוקים או מלוחים?

10. מה אורכו של קו המים?

TESTS

        In addition to the Review Conversations the following two types of tests
are suggested for measuring the <u>overall</u> ability of the students in speaking
Hebrew. In both of them the student is required to convey a message accurately.
Tests on specific points of grammar or vocabulary are not given. Instead, the
instructor must sort any particular deficiencies out of the total conversation
and review the drills on these points to correct them. The instructor should
make notes during these tests so as not to interrupt a free-flowing conversation.
He should, of course, use his judgment in case there is any real difficulty or
the conversation goes too far from the main message.

Interpreter Situations

        The instructor pretends to know no English and engages in a conversation
with some one who, ideally, knows no Hebrew. The student acts as the interpreter.

        The following are suggested situations. The Hebrew is for the instructor
and the English for his conversation partner. The student does not use the
book.

        Before starting, the instructor and his partner should read through the
conversation to get the gist of it. During the conversation the student's
translations determine the course of the conversation. If he mis-translates, the
instructor should not correct him but should continue the conversation. The
corrections are made afterwards, and the student then tries again.

        In many cases the correct message will be conveyed even if there are errors
in the grammar or vocabulary of the translation. The instructor should
definitely not interrupt at such points. Continuing the conversation will build
confidence on the part of the student. It also illustrates how seemingly
insignificant errors turn out to be crucial while other seemingly gross errors
are comparatively minor.

        Suggested situations are given for use after Unit 4 and Unit 10. The
instructor should make up additional ones for the rest of the units. Ad-libbing,
within limits, will enliven the situation.

        Occasionally the student will encounter forms which he could not possibly
know at the particular stage of the course. He should make an intelligent guess
and continue the conversation. Results of such guesses often provide humorous
relief from the intensity of the course.

Interpreting Technique

        While most people learn informally how to work with interpreters and how
to function as an interpreter, the following guiding principles will be of
help to both the student acting as the interpreter and to the instructor and
his partner who are conversing with each other through the interpreter. The
remarks are intended only as rules of thumb for informal interpreting situations
such as those suggested here. In official or more serious situations the
student should not attempt to act as interpreter until he is considerably more
fluent in Hebrew. Indeed, he should not use an interpreter himself until he has
had some experience working with one in ordinary conversations.

(a) The interpreter is not a party to the conversation. He is, in a sense,
only a machine through which the others talk. The two people should address
each other as though they understood every word that the other was saying.
They do not address each other in the third person through the interpreter.
Thus, rather than saying "Ask him where he lives", one should simply say
directly, "Where do you live?".

In the use of interpreting situations as tests, the two persons holding
the conversation may understand each other without the student's translations.
In such case, they will have no difficulty addressing each other directly, but
they must resist the temptation to correct the translations.

(b) One should not lapse into side comments to the interpreter which he is not
expected to translate or which one assumes that the foreign national will not
understand. For one thing, it is impolite. For another, it is easy to be
misunderstood. In addition, almost all native Israelis speak at least some
English, and such asides may create the wrong atmosphere for communication.

(c) The interpreter translates directly what the others say. Thus, when one
asks the other, "/heyxan ata gar/", the interpreter says "Where do you live?"
and not "He wants to know where you live."

Prohibiting such third-person paraphrases will enable the instructor to
test the student's competence on specific points much more directly. For example,
if the instructor wishes to test the student's knowledge of pronominal suffixes,
he may "load" the conversation with suffixed forms for the student to translate.
Or conversely, he may have his conversation partner use a number of English
constructions which will require suffixed forms in Hebrew. Any deficiencies
on the part of the student will be revealed immediately and without subjecting
him to the tension or artificiality of a formal test.

Occasional informal interpreting is not a primary goal of this course,
but students should achieve the minimal skill for it as an incidental result.

Professional interpreting requires a great deal of training, a prodigious
memory, familiarity with the subjects of the conversation or text being translated, in addition to a degree of fluency which is not expected to be achieved
from a basic course such as this.

Unit 4.

A:	Good morning, Mr. Oren.	בקר טוב, מר אורן. :א
B:	Hello, how are you?	שלום, מה שלומך. :ב
A:	Fine, thanks. How's the wife and the family?	טוב תודה. מה שלום אשתך והמשפחה? :א
B:	Fine, thanks. Where do you live?	טוב, תודה. היכן אתה גר? :ד
A:	I live in Tel Aviv. Where are you staying?	אני גר בתל אביב. והיכן אתה גר? :א
B:	I'm staying at the Dan Hotel in the meantime.	אני גר במלון "דן" בינתיים. :ב
A:	The Dan Hotel is very nice.	מלון "דן" יפה מאד. :א
B:	I plan to live in Ramat Gan in about a month.	אני מתכונן לגור ברמת-גן בעוד כחודש ימים. :ב
A:	Very good. I hope you like Ramat Gan.	טוב מאד. אני מקוה שרמת גן תמצא חן בעיניך. :א
B:	Thank you. I heard that the house is very nice.	תודה רבה. שמעתי שהבית יפה מאד. :ב
A:	So long.	שלום. :א
B:	So long. Be seeing you.	שלום. להתראות. :ב

Unit 10. Situation 1

A: Excuse me, Sir.
I'm new in Tel Aviv.
I want to get to the post office.

א: סליחה אדוני.
אני חדש בתל אביב.
אני רוצה להגיע למשרד הדואר.

B: OK. You're now
on Hayarkon Street
The Post Office is
on Allenby Street.

ב: טוב. אתה נמצא עכשיו
ברחוב הירקון.
משרד הדואר נמצא
ברחוב אלנבי.

A: Yes.

א: כן.

B: Turn left at
the first corner
and go straight
to the Post Office building.

ב: אז פנה כאן
בפינה הראשונה
שמאלה, ולך ישר
עד לבנין הדואר.

A: Is it far from here?

א: האם זה רחוק מכאן?

B: No. It's very close.

ב: לא. זה קרוב מאד.

A: Thank you very much.

א: תודה רבה.

B: Don't mention it.

ב: על לא דבר.

Unit 10. Situation 2

A: Hello, Mr. Oren.

א: שלום, מר אורן.

B: Hello, Mr. Levi. How are you?

ב: שלום, מר לוי. מה שלומך?

A: Fine. Thanks. What's
new with you?

א: טוב תודה. מה חדש אצלכם?
מה חדש אצלכם?

B: Everything's fine.

ב: הכל בסדר, תודה רבה.

A: Do you want
to eat ice cream?

א: האם אתה רוצה
לאכול גלידה?

B: No why?

ב: לא. למה?

A: My wife is making
ice cream.

א: אשתי מכינה
גלידה.

B: Oh, really?

ב: או – באמת?

A: Yes. indeed.

א: כן. באמת.

B: That's different.
I'm coming now.
I'd like to eat her ice cream.

ב: זה דבר אחר.
אני בא עכשיו.
אני רוצה לאכול את הגלידה שלה.

Unit 10. Situation 3

B:	Hello, Mrs. Levi. How are you?	שלום גב' לוי. מה שלומך?	:ב
Mrs. A:	Fine, thanks. You've come to eat my ice cream?	טוב. תודה. אתה באת לאכול את הגלידה שלי?	גב' א:
B:	Why didn't you tell me before that you're making ice cream?	כן. למה לא אמרת לי קודם שאת מכינה גלידה?	:ב
Mrs. A:	You didn't give me a chance. I hope you like the ice cream.	לא נתת לי הזדמנות. אני מקוה שהגלידה חמצא חן בעיניך.	גב' א:
B:	From what I've eaten the ice cream is very good.	ממה שהספקתי לאכול הגלידה טובה מאד.	:ב
Mrs. A:	Thank you. Does your wife make ice cream?	תודה רבה. האם אשתך מכינה גלידה?	גב' א:
B:	No.	לא.	:ב
Mrs. A:	Why not?	למה לא?	גב' א:
B:	She doesn't know how.	היא לא יודעת.	:ב

<u>Taped Tests</u>

The following tests require the use of a tape recorder for the student to record his responses. Each test takes only a few minutes to administer. They are kept short since the instructor must listen to each tape individually in order to mark it.

The purpose of these tests is to judge the students' <u>functional</u> ability in the language, not necessarily his ability to translate a specific word or construction or sentence. The student is told to convey a particular message in a particular situation.   Thus, for example, the following instruction may be given:

> Mr. Caspi and you have just finished eating lunch, but you
> do not have to be back to the office for another half hour.
> Ask him if he would like to go for a little walk with you.

The student reads this instruction and responds with something like this: (recording his response)

> /haim ata roce letayel kcat?/

Note that the student is <u>not</u> told: Translate the following sentence - "Do you want to stroll a little bit?"

Sample tests are given for use after Units 11 through 15.   In preparing additional tests the supervising linguist and instructor must make sure that the given situation is not far-fetched and that the expected response is within the capability of the student at the particular stage of the course.   An easy way to prepare such tests is to compose the responses first, and then fashion a situation for them.   Students will often be amazed at the wide range of possibilities that exist even at an early stage of the course.   It is also advisable to include vocabulary that has not been used for several units.

<u>Numerical Grades</u>

Numerical grades are given for these tests.   Letter grades should be based on a distribution curve of the numerical grades achieved.

The following system should be used in marking the responses:

(1)   The prime criterion is the <u>correctness of the message</u>. If the response is perfectly correct grammatically and the pronunciation is very good, but the message is wrong, then the student gets a <u>zero</u> for that question.   For example, if the instructions are "Ask Mr. Caspi what he is doing on Tuesday", and the student responds with /ma ata ose beyom šeni/, then he gets a zero. This is very important.   There is no appeal from an incorrect message.

(2)   If the response is grammatically correct, the pronunciation is good, and the message is correct, then the student gets four (4) points for the response.

(3)   A grade of one, two, or three points is given on a more-or-less subjective basis determined by the completeness of the message, correctness of grammar and vocabulary, intelligibility of pronunciation, and lack of hesitation in respond- ing.   A combination of deficinencies should be given a lower mark, and if the response is really garbled then a zero should be given.   For example, the following responses to "Ask Mr. Caspi what he is doing on Tuesday evening" should be marked as noted.

(a)   /ma ata ose beyom šliši/ - 2 points.   The message is incomplete since /baerev/ was left out.

(b)   /ma ata ose bayom šliši beérev/ - 3 points.   The message is complete and correct except for the grammatical errors of /ba-/ and /be-/.

(c)   /ma at osa beyom šliši baérev/ - 2 points.   The mistake in gender is more crucial than the errors in response (b).

(d)   /ma ose beyom šliši érev/ - 1 point. The message is intelligible in context, but the construction is poor.

Occasionally certain pronunciation errors produce incorrect messages, such as the possible confusion of /šelaxem/ and /šelahem/.   In general, the instructor should hold to the rule that an incorrect message receives a zero.

The score is then totalled and a percentage grade given based on what a perfect score for the particular test would have been.   For example, if there are ten questions (or instructions) a perfect score would be 40.   A total score of 30 would give the student a grade of 75.

Some instructors may prefer, for mathematical simplicity, to give a grade of 5 points for a perfect response. However, it is recommended that the range be kept small.   The number 4 will give enough leeway for the instructor's judgment and still prevent wide discrepancies in marking different students. It will be found that with only a little experience different instructors will give similar grades for the same test.

These tests are not intended to give the student a series of grades from which a final grade for the course may be computed. They are intended as "bench marks" for the student so that he may have some idea how he is doing relative to the other members of the class and to a satisfactory rate of progress during the course.

Unit 11. Taped Test A

Situation: You are talking to Mr. Caspi in your office.

1.   Find out if he is free Wednesday evening.

2.   Invite him and his wife for dinner.

3.   Find out if 7:00 is convenient.

4.   Mr. Caspi says that seven o'clock is too early.   Suggest a later time.

5.   Give him your address: Mozkin Street, No. 5.

6.   Tell him it's about six blocks from your office.

7.   Tell him it's not far from the Embassy.

8.   Tell him it's in the vicinity of the Dan Hotel.

Unit 12. Taped Test A

You are dinner guests of the Caspis.

1. It is Friday night. What do you say to Mr. and Mrs. Caspi as you enter?

2. Mrs. Caspi says that she is happy you were able to come. What do you say?

3. You arrived a little late. Tell Mr. Caspi that you were not able to get there early.

4. Mrs. Caspi mentions that their daughter has just become engaged. What do you say?

5. Mr. Caspi asks you about your plans for touring Israel. Tell him that you and your wife plan to visit three big cities this week.

6. Mrs. Caspi mentions that she was in your neighborhood the other day but couldn't find your house. Tell her that it's the fourth house from the corner.

7. Mrs. Caspi asks you how to get to your house from her husband's office. Tell her to go seven blocks on Herzl St. and turn left at the seventh intersection.

Unit 12. Taped Test B

Mr. and Mrs. Caspi are your guests for dinner.

1. It is a holiday. What do you say to them as they enter your house?

2. Mr. Caspi tells you that he saw five new American planes at the airport that morning. Tell him that you saw the five planes the day before yesterday.

3. Mrs. Caspi says that she saw two new Israeli ships in the harbor. Tell her that you saw the two ships in New York harbor.

4. Tell them that you think the third new ship will arrive in Haifa in two weeks. Then correct yourself to say, 'No, I'm sorry. In three weeks.'

5. In answer to your questions Mr. Caspi says he will have a drink. Tell your wife to pour some cognac for Mr. Caspi.

6. Mr. Caspi asks you why you didn't stop by his office yesterday. Tell him that you didn't come because you couldn't get there before 5:00.

7. Mr. and Mrs. Caspi are leaving. Tell them good night and that you'll see them tomorrow.

Unit 12. Taped Test C

The Zahavis are your dinner guests .

1. It is Wednesday evening. What do you say to them as they enter?

2. The food is ready. Invite them to sit down at the table.

3. In answer to Mr. Zahavi's question tell him that you came
   to Israel on an American ship.

4. Mrs. Zahavi asks you which of the two ships she has seen in the harbor
   is American. Tell her both ships are American.

5. Mr. Zahavi wants to give you directions to the tourist office.
   Tell him, thank you, but that you know where it is.

6. Mr. Zahavi asks you what happened to some furniture and books that
   used to be in the office you are using. Tell him that you gave the
   three tables to Mr. Smith.

7. Tell him that you gave twelve books to Mr. Caspi and the rest of the books
   to Mr. Cohen.

Unit 13. Taped Test A

You are guests of the Caspis.

1. Mrs. Caspi asks you how you like the food. Tell her that you are enjoying
   it very much.

2. Ask Mrs. Caspi if she would tell you how to make gefilte fish.

3. Ask Mr. Caspi if they have gefilte fish every Friday evening.

4. You are trying to lose weight. Mrs. Caspi is offering you more to eat.
   Refuse it and explain why.

5. Mrs. Caspi asks you what you like best about Israel. Tell her that you
   find the people to be very nice.

6. She asks you what part of Tel Aviv you find most beautiful. Tell her that
   Dizengoff Street is very nice.

Unit 13. Taped Test B

You meet Mr. Caspi during the morning .

1. Tell Mr. Caspi that you haven't had your ten o'clock break yet.

2. Ask him if he has a mid-morning snack.

3. Invite him to lunch.

4. As you leave the office, tell your secretary that you'll finish lunch by two o'clock.

5. Mr. Caspi asks you how you like your house. Tell him you expect to be very happy there.

6. Ask Mr. Caspi what time he will close his office today.

7. Mr. Caspi asks you if your wife will be coming to meet you this afternoon. Tell him that she will come by the office at 4:00.

8. Tell him that your wife and his wife are going to the movies this evening.

9. Mr. Caspi tells you that he and his wife are meeting some foreign visitors tomorrow. Ask him in what language they will address them.

Unit 14. Tapes Test A

You enter a grocery store to buy some things.

1. Ask the grocer for half a kilo of yellow cheese.

2. Find out when the grocer got in the eggs.

3. Tell him you want a dozen eggs and a kilo of fresh apples.

4. Ask the grocer why the vegetables are so expensive today.

5. You see cans of ripe olives. Find out if he has green olives, also.

6. You want to be sure that the olives stay moist. Tell him you want them in a jar, not in a box.

7. Ask him how much all of it costs.

You are working in the embassy.

8. A man and a woman come into your office. Offer your services.

9. The woman needs help filling out an application. Ask her for her date and place of birth.

10. Ask her for her address and telephone number.

Unit 15. Taped Test A

1. You are walking along Allenby Road and meet two friends that you
    haven't seen for some time. Greet them and find out what's new
    with them.

2. They say that a lot has happened since you last met. Suggest that you
    all go to a coffe house.

3. The waiter asks you for your order. Order two cups of tea for them
    and an espresso for yourself.

4. The waiter asks if you want any cake with it. Your friends would like
    cheese cake, but you are on a diet. Order two servings of cheese cake for
    them and tell the waiter that you don't want anything for yourself.

5. Your espresso is very hot. Ask your friends if the tea is hot, too.

6. They say that the tea is very hot. Tell them to wait a bit until the tea
    cools.

7. You are now sitting relaxed. Ask your friends to tell you all the news.

8. They mention that they were in Haifa last week. Tell them that your wife
    was there with the whole family, also.

9. Your friends want to visit you Saturday morning. Tell them not to come
    in the morning but to come in the afternoon.

10. Tell them to come early and that you'll go for a walk on the beach.

11. Ask them if the cheese cake was sweet.

12. Tell the waiter that the espresso is very bitter and that you want some
    sugar.

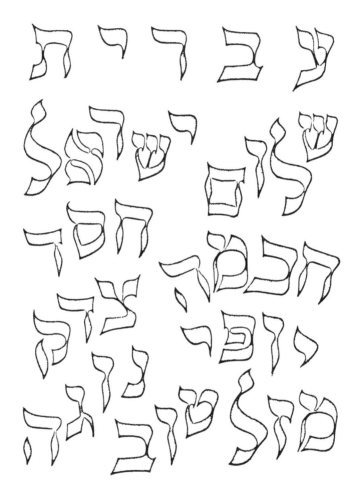

THE HEBREW ALPHABET

    Hebrew is written from right to left with an alphabet of twenty-two letters. Five of these letters have an alternant form when they are the last letter of a word.

    The names of the letters, the consonant sounds they represent, and their printed forms are as follows: (Two sizes of type are used in this book)

1.	álef	/'/	א	א
2.	bet (vet)	/b, v/	ב	בּ
3.	gímel	/g/	ג	ג
4.	dálet	/d/	ד	ד
5.	hey	/h/	ה	ה
6.	vav	/v/	ו	ו
7.	záin	/z/	ז	ז
8.	xet	/x/	ח	ח
9.	tet	/t/	ט	ט
10.	yud or yod	/y/	י	י
11.	kaf (xaf)	/k, x/	כ	כ
	kaf sofit		ך	ך
12.	lámed	/l/	ל	ל
13.	mem	/m/	מ	מ
	mem sofit		ם	ם
14.	nun	/n/	נ	נ
	nun sofit		ן	ן
15.	sámex	/s/	ס	ס
16.	áin	/'/	ע	ע
17.	pey (fey)	/p, f/	פ	פ
	fey sofit	/f/	ף	ף
18.	cádi	/c/	צ	צ
	cadi sofit		ץ	ץ
19.	kof or kuf	/k/	ק	ק
20.	reš	/r/	ר	ר
21.	šin, sin	/š/ /s/	ש	ש
22.	tav	/t/	ת	ת

The infrequent consonants /j/, /ž/, and /č/ are written with the following letters plus an apostrophe:

/č/	with /cádi/	'צ
/j/	with /gímel/	'ג
/ž/	with /záin/	'ז

Be careful not to confuse the following:

(a) bet and kaf   כ ב .
The bet has a slight projection in the lower right hand corner. The kaf is a smooth curve.

(b) gímel and nun   נ ג .
The gímel has a notch in the bottom.

(c) dálet, reš and kaf sofit   ך ר ד
The dálet has a slight projection in the upper right. The kaf sofit extends below the line.

(d) hey, xet, and tav   ת ח ה .
The hey and xet are the same except that the left vertical of the hey is not connected to the top, but the left vertical of the xet is. The left vertical of the tav has a foot projecting to the left.

(e) vav, záin, nun sofit   ן ז ו
The vertical stroke of the vav descends from the right hand edge of the top, and the vertical stroke of the záin descends from the center of the top. The vertical stroke of the zain also has a wiggle to it. The nun sofit extends below the line.

(f) tet and mem   מ ט
The tet is open at the top, and the mem is open at the bottom.

(g) mem sofit and sámex   ס ם
The lower half of the mem sofit is box-shaped, and the lower half of the sámex is elliptical.

(h) áin and cádi   צ ע
The right vertical of the áin curves down to the left, and the left vertical slants down and connects to it.

The left vertical of the cádi slants down to the bottom right corner and forms a sharp angle with the bottom horizontal. The right vertical slants down to the left and connects to the middle of the left vertical.

(i) šin and sin   ש
In fully punctuated texts the šin has a dot on the right שׁ and the sin a dot on the left שׂ . In most publications, though, there is no way to differentiate, and the reader must know what the particular word is. However, it is extremely rare that both possibilities could occur in the same context.

464

A.   Memorize and recite the letters of the /álef bet/ in order.   Do not
include the final letters or /<u>sin</u>/.

B.   Read off the following letters <u>from right to left</u>.

ע י נ י ך .11	י ו ר ץ .6	ש ל ו ם.1
ק ו ף .12	ש ג ר י ר ו ת .7	י ש ר א ל.2
ת ג ז י ם .13	מ ל ו ן ד ן .8	כ ס ד ר.3
כ ס פ י .14	ל א כ ו ל .9	מ ש פ ח ה.4
ה צ ט ל ב ו ת .15	מ ו ק ד ם .10	ס ו ב ה ב מ א ד.5

<u>Vowel Points</u>

The above list gives the consonantal values of the letters.   There is a
system of dots, "points", which are used in the Old Testament, poetry, dictionaries,
etc., to indicate the vowels.

They are as follows:
/The letter <u>álef</u> is used to illustrate.)

/i/			אִי	אִ
/e/	אֶ	אֵ	אֵי	אֶי
/a/		אָ	אַ	אֲ
/o/	אֳ	אֹ	אוֹ	אֺ
/u/			אוּ	אֻ

These vowel points represented different vowel qualities or lengths in
Classical Hebrew.   In modern Hebrew these distinctions have been reduced to
the five phonemes /i, e, a, o, u/, and therefore, there are several ways to
represent some of these vowels.

The "points" are used today mainly in editions of the Old Testament, poetry,
dictionaries, text books, and children's publications. School children are
taught to read them, but most adult native Israelis do not use them and even
have difficulty punctuating a text correctly. They are provided here only for
reference.   Students will find that they can learn to read unpointed Hebrew
fairly easily, and there is no need to detour by practicing first with pointed
texts.

The remarks on spelling in the next section apply to unpointed texts.

Spelling

There are two varieties of spelling in common use, /xaser/ "lacking" חסר
and /male/ "full" מלא . The /xaser/ spelling is used in older and more
conservative publications. It is basically the classical or Biblical spellings
but without the vowel points. Thus, the following are spelled the same way:

/axal/	"he ate"	אכל
/óxel/	"food"	אכל

but compare /oxél/   "is eating"   אוכל

/xadaš/	"new"	חדש
/xideš/	"he renewed"	חדש
/xódeš/	"month"	חדש

/diber/	"he spoke"	דבר
/daber/	"speak"	דבר
/davar/	"thing"	דבר

The /male/ spelling is used in most newspapers, periodicals, official
publications, etc. In the /male/ spelling almost all /o/ and /u/ vowels are
written with the letter vav ו , and almost all /i/ vowels with the letter
yod י . Exceptions are short, common words like /kol/ "all"כל,/im/ "if" אם ,
/im/ "with"עם , etc. A y between two vowels or after a consonant may be
written with two yod's יי . A vav pronounced /v/ will be written with two
vav's וו .   Thus, for example, the following forms will be distinguished:

/axal/	"he ate"	אכל
/óxel/	"food"	אוכל

/xadaš/	"new"	חדש
/xideš/	"he renewed"	חידש
/xódeš/	"month"	חודש

/diber/	"he spoke"	דיבר
/daber	"speak"	דבר
/davar/	"thing"	דבר

The following will be spelled the same:

/óxel/	"food"	אוכל
/oxél/	"is eating"	אוכל

Examples of the use of two yod's and vav's for /y/ and /v/ are:

/meanyen/	"interesting"	מעניין
/dávka/	"only thus"	דווקא

In this course the /male/ spelling is generally used.   Random words are in
the /xaser/ spelling to illustrate the possibilities.

The basic principle of Hebrew spelling is that all consonants are written
and that vowels are to be supplied by the reader after the consonants.   An
English sentence written in a comparable fashion would look like this:
"'nglsh 's mr dffclt thn Hbrw t lrn t rd."

Almost all educated speakers of English will have no trouble supplying
the vowels for this sentence.

With the use of <u>vav</u> and <u>yod</u> in the /male/ spelling Hebrew is just as easy to read -- provided the student has a good basis in spoken Hebrew.

The following drills and explanatory notes will introduce the student to the writing system. For a rapid exercise in recognition of letters and words the Basic Conversations of the first ten units may be used. Students should know them so thoroughly that reading them will be no problem at all.

The instructor should have the students cover the transcription or he may copy the words from the following drills on to flash cards for use in class. In using the book by himself the student can prepare a notched card such as this ⌐‾‾┐ . By moving the card down the columns he will expose the next word and the transcription of the preceding word for checking his own reading.

A. The vowel /a/ is supplied in the following words.   <u>alef</u>,   <u>hey</u>, and <u>ain</u> at the end of a word are not pronounced.

báal	בעל .11	ba	בא .1
sax	שח .12	ma	מה .2
xadaš	חדש .13	ba'a	באה .3
mar	מר .14	matay	מתי .4
gam	גם .15	arba'a	ארבעה .5
sfat hayam	שפת הים .16	raba	רבה .6
kvar	כבר .17	kcat	קצת .7
láma	למה .18	natáta	נתת .8
at	את .19	ata	אתה .9
yašar	ישר .20	mamaš	ממש .10

B. Supply the vowels /i/ and /a/.

higáta	הגעת .8	mišpaxa	משפחה .1
hitrašámta	התרשמת .9	binyan	בנין .2
tislax	תסלח .10	misrad	משרד .3
nimca	נמצא .11	ivrit	עברית .4
habáit	הכית .12	iša	אשה .5
david	דוד .13	miryam	מרים .6
yicxak	יצחק .14	rivka	רבקה .7

C. Supply the vowel /e/.

ken	כן	.11	šéket	שקט	.1
écel	אצל	.12	séfer	ספר	.2
pne	פנה	.13	gvéret	גברת	.3
telex	תלך	.14	érec	ארץ	.4
tešev	תשב	.15	beséder	בסדר	.5
eyx	איך	.16	et	את	.6
eyneyxem	עיניכם	.17	beemet	באמת	.7
eyneyhem	עיניהם	.18	ze	זה	.8
behexlet	בהחלט	.19	éyze	איזה	.9
dérex	דרך	.20	yeš	יש	10.

D. The <u>yud</u> indicates the vowel /i/. Supply /e/ or /a/ elsewhere.

tagzim	תגזים	.11	na'im	נעים	.1
pina	פינה	.12	yamim	ימים	.2
garim	גרים	.13	glida	גלידה	.3
yamína	ימינה	.14	lehakir	להכיר	.4
lehikanes	להיכנס	.15	dabri	דברי	.5
mexinim	מכינים	.16	mevin	מבין	.6
hi	היא	.17	šagrir	שגריר	.7
ra'íti	ראיתי	.18	xadiš	חדיש	.8
memaharim	ממהרים	.19	ani	אני	.9
memšalti	ממשלתי	.20	slixa	סליחה	10.

E. The <u>vav</u> indicates either /o/ or /u/. Supply /e/ or /a/ elsewhere.

xódeš	חודש	.11	šalom	שלום	.1
yoec	יועץ	.12	toda	תודה	.2
kódem	קודם	.13	šloma	שלומה	.3
rexov	רחוב	.14	me'uxar	מאוחר	.4
yaxol	יכול	.15	mukdam	מוקדם	.5
hu	הוא	.16	muxrax	מוכרח	.6
eclo	אצלו	.17	etmol	אתמול	.7
avurénu	עבורנו	.18	éyzo	איזו	.8
gadol	גדול	.19	kmo	כמו	.9
xošev	חושב	.20	malon	מלון	10.

F. The definite article is always written ה . In formal style it is
sometimes pronounced /he-/ but for the purpose of this course the student
may use /ha-/ will all words.

Read first the word without /ha-/ and then the same word with /ha-/.
Example: /iš/ - /haiš/. This drill is practice in recognition and not a
test. The transcription is given only for the first word on each line.

iš	האיש	-	איש .1
yoec	היועץ	-	יועץ .2
séfer	הספר	-	ספר .3
délet	הדלת	-	דלת .4
šagrirut	השגרירות	-	שגרירות .5
dóar	הדואר	-	דואר .6
misrad	המשרד	-	משרד .7
binyan	הבנין	-	בנין .8
memšalti	הממשלתי	-	ממשלתי .9
bet séfer	בית הספר	-	בית ספר .10
sfat yam	שפת הים	-	שפת ים .11
nemal teufa	נמל התעופה	-	נמל תעופה .12

G. The /-t/ feminine singular is always spelled ת . The rest of the word
is identical with the masculine singular in spelling except that the masculine
singular may have one of the final letters. If the student makes a mistake on
the feminine form after reading the masculine form correctly then he should
review the grammar drills of Unit 7.

medaber	-	medabéret	מדברת	-	מדבר .1
omer	-	oméret	אומרת	-	אומר .2
xošev	-	xošévet	חושבת	-	חושב .3
mitkonen	-	mitkonénet	מתכוננת	-	מתכונן .4
yodéa	-	yodáat	יודעת	-	יודע .5
moce	-	mocet	מוצאת	-	מוצא .6
nimca	-	nimcet	נמצאת	-	נמצא .7
amerikái	-	amerikáit	אמריקאית	-	אמריקאי .8
axer	-	axéret	אחרת	-	אחר .9
memaher	-	memahéret	ממהרת	-	ממהר .10

H. The /-a/ feminine singular is always spelled ה . The rest of the word is identical in spelling with the masculine singular except that the latter may have a final letter. If the masculine singular is a <u>lamed hey</u> form ending in /-e/ then the two forms will be identical in spelling.

If the student makes a mistake on the feminine form after reading the masculine form correctly then he should review the grammar drills of Unit 8.

muxrax	—	muxraxa	מוכרחה — מוכרח	1.
mevin	—	mevina	מכינה — מכין	2.
yaxol	—	yexola	יכולה — יכול	3.
gar	—	gára	גרה — גר	4.
saméax	—	smexa	שמחה — שמח	5.
xadaš	—	xadaša	חדשה — חדש	6.
mekave	—	mekava	מקורה — מקורה	7.
roe	—	roa	רואה — רואה	8.
roce	—	roca	רוצה — רוצה	9.
yafe	—	yafa	יפה — יפה	10.

I. The plural endings /-im/ and /-ot/ are spelled ים and ות . Many plurals have completely different vowels from the singular, but the consonants are generally the same, and the meaning can be gotten by sight.

séfer	—	sfarim	ספרים — ספר	1.
érec	—	aracot	ארצות — ארץ	2.
malon	—	melonot	מלונות — מלון	3.
misrad	—	misradim	משרדים — משרד	4.
mišpaxa	—	mišpaxot	משפחות — משפחה	5.
davar	—	dvarim	דברים — דבר	6.
binyan	—	binyanim	בנינים — בנין	7.
xadaš	—	xadašim	חדשים — חדש	8.
xadaša	—	xadašot	חדשות — חדשה	9.
yodéa	—	yod'im	יורעים — יורע	10.
rexov	—	rexovot	רחובות — רחוב	11.
roce	—	rocim	רוצים — רוצה	12.
xódeš	—	xodašim	חודשים — חודש	13.
yodáat	—	yod'ot	יורעות — יורעת	14.
aviron	—	avironim	אוירונים — אוירון	15.
safa	—	safot	שפות — שפה	16.
báit	—	batim	בתים — בית	17.
iš	—	anašim	אנשים — איש	18.
iša	—	našim	נשים — אשה	19.

J. The letters ב,כ,ל, מ at the beginning of a word may represent the prepositions /be-/, /ke-/, /le-/, and /mi-/. The first three may also represent the contraction of preposition and definite article /ba-/, /ka-/, /la-/.

malon dan	– bemalon dan	במלון דן –	מלון דן	1.
nemal hateufa	– lenemal hateufa	לנמל התעופה –	נמל התעופה	2.
arba'a	– kearba'a	כארבעה –	ארבעה	3.
amérika	– meamérika	מאמריקה –	אמריקה	4.
hamisrad	– bamisrad	במשרד –	המשרד	5.
hayam	– layam	לים –	הים	6.
habinyan	– mehabinyan	מהבנין –	הבנין	7.
habáit	– babáit	בבית –	הבית	8.
séder	– beséder	בסדר –	סדר	9.
kol	– bekol	בקול –	קול	10.
hakivun haze	– bakivun haze	בכיוון הזה –	הכיוון הזה	11.
hair	– lair	לעיר –	העיר	12.
hatocaot	– mehatocaot	מהתוצאות –	התוצאות	13.
bet haséfer	– mibet haséfer	מבית הספר –	בית הספר	14.
hahictalvut	– ad lahictalvut	עד להצטלבות –	ההצטלבות	15.
hadóar hamerkazi	– ladóar hamerkazi	לדואר המרכזי –	הדואר המרכזי	16.
israel	– beisrael	בישראל –	ישראל	17.
misrad hatayarut	– lemisrad hatayarut	למשרד התיירות –	משרד התיירות	18.
hapina harišona	– bapina harišona	בפינה הראשונה –	הפינה הראשונה	19.
rexov hayarkon	– lerexov hayarkon	לרחוב הירקון –	רחוב הירקון	20.

K. The letters ב ,כ and פ may represent b/v, k/x, p/f respectively.

pni	–	tifni	תפני – פני	1.
ken	–	vexen	וכן – כן	2.
bo	–	tavo	תבוא – בוא	3.
ptax	–	tiftax	תפתח – פתח	4.
bevakaša			בבקשה	5.

The root consonant structure of the language is transparent in the
spelling. Alternate forms of nouns before suffixes or in construct state
sequences are usually spelled the same way.

1. שלום – שלומי – שלומך
2. בית – בית ספר
3. מוקדם – קודם
4. מאוחר – אחרי
5. מוצא – נמצא
6. שמע – שמעי – שמעתי
7. יתר – יותר
8. אמור – אמדי – תאמר – אומרת – אמרת
9. אדון – אדוני
10. גברת – גברתי

The /-t/ alternant of feminine nouns before suffixes or in the construct
state has a ת replacing the ה .

1. אשה – אשתך
2. שפה – שפת הים
3. פינה – פינת מנדלי
4. משפחה – משפחת זהבי

The unstressed /a/ which is inserted before a ח or ע at the end of a
word is not spelled:

/samé(a)x/   שמח   :   /yodé(a)'/   יורע

A similar rule applies to a root consonantal /h/ ה at the end of a word:
/gavó(a)h/   גבוה . In modern Hebrew this /h/ is not pronounced at the end
of a word, but it functions as a consonant when suffixed: /gvoha/ גבוהה
Such roots are few in number and are not to be confused with the lamed hey
roots discussed in the Grammar Notes.

IMPORTANT NOTE ON PROCEDURE

The material in the following sections is not a substitute for the
regular conversational units. It is intended only as supplemental material
for introduction to reading.

In this section the Basic Conversations are written without transcription.
They are followed by narratives of the conversations. New words are underlined
and translated at the end of the narrative. The student will have to guess a
bit at the exact meaning of some forms, particularly third-person verb forms
which have not yet been drilled.

שיחה 11. הזמנה לארוחת ערב

מר כספי: מר ווילאמס, מה אתם עושים בליל שישי?

מר ווילאמס: בליל שישי הקרוב?

מר כ: כן.

מר וו: אני חושב שאין לנו כל תוכנית.

מר כ: אנו רוצים להזמין אתכם לארוחת ערב.

מר וו: תורה רבה. נשמח מאד.

מר כ: האם שבע ושלושים מתאים?

מר וו: כן. תן לי את הכתובת שלכם.

מר כ: אנו גרים ברחוב מוצקין מספר 3.

מר וו: אני חושב שנמצא את המקום ללא קושי.

1. מר כספי שאל את מר ווילאמס מה הוא ואשתו עושים בליל שישי הקרוב.
2. מר ווילאמס אמר שאין להם תוכנית. מר כספי רוצה להזמין אותם לארוחת
3. ערב. מר ווילאמס אומר שהם ישמחו מאד לבוא. מר ווילאמס קיבל
4. את הכתובת ממר כספי. הכתובת היא רחוב מוצקין מספר 3. מר ווילאמס
5. חושב שהוא ימצא את המקום ללא קושי.

| he asked | /šaál/ | שאל |
| he received | /kibél/ | קיבל |

שיחה 12. ארוחת ערב

גב' כספי: שלום גברת ווילאמס, שלום מר ווילאמס, מה שלומכם?

מר וו: שלום, שבת שלום.

גב' כ: אני שמחה מאד שבאתם.

גב' וו: איך יכולנו לסרב?

גב' כ: הכה ניגש לשולחן. משה, מזוג בבקשה את היין לקידוש.

1. גב' כספי שמחה מאד שהווילאמסים באו לארוחת ערב.
2. הווילאמסים אמרו שלא יכלו לסרב. גב' כספי הזמינה לשולחן,
3. ומר כספי מזג את היין לקידוש.

473

שיחה 13. • אֲרוּחַת עֶרֶב

גב' ור: הדגים נהדרים וכן החלה.

גב' כ: תודה רבה.

גב' ור: גברת כספי, את מוכרחה לתת לי את המרשם לדגים.

גב' כ: ברצון אתן לך את המרשם גב' ווילאמס.
           זו מסורת אצלנו בבית, לאכול בליל שישי דגים ממולאים.

גב' ור: גברת כספי, בבקשה, אל תתני לי יותר אוכל.

גב' כ: הרי לא אכלתם כלום.

גב' ור: אני בדיאטה.
           האוכל היה טעים מאד.

גב' כ: תודה רבה.

גב' ור: אתחיל בדיאטה שלי מחר.

1. גב' ווילאמס אמרה שהדגים נהדרים והחלה נהדרת, והיא

2. רוצה את המרשם לדגים. גב' כספי אמרה שהיא תתן לה את

3. המרשם ברצון. גב' ווילאמס בקשה מגברת כספי שלא תתן לה

4. יותר אוכל, כי היא בדיאטה. גב' כספי אמרה שהם לא אכלו

5. כלום. גברת ווילאמס אמרה שהאוכל היה טעים מאד, והיא

6. תתחיל בדיאטה שלה ממחר.

שיחה 14. בַּחֲנוּת מַכּוֹלֶת

חנווני: בוקר טוב, גברת זהבי. מה אני יכול לעשות בשבילך?

גב' זהבי: תן לי בבקשה מאתיים גרם גבינה.

ח: גבינה צהובה או גבינה לבנה?

גב' ז: גבינה צהובה. הביצים טריות?

ח: כן קבלתי אותן הבוקר.

גב' ז: אז תן לי תריסר.

ח: את צריכה ירקות? פירות?

גב' ז: לא תודה. זה הכל. כמה אני חייבת לך?

ח: זה יעלה לך שמונים ושלוש אגורות.

גב' ז: תן לי עודף מלירה.

1. החנווני שואל את גב' זהבי מה הוא יכול לעשות בשבילה.

2. היא אומרת שהיא רוצה מאתיים גרם גבינה. הוא שואל אם היא

3. רוצה גבינה צהובה או לבנה והיא <u>ענתה</u> שהיא רוצה גבינה צהובה.

4. גב' זהבי שואלת אם הביצים טריות והחנווני <u>ענה</u> שהוא קיבל

5. אותן <u>באותו היום</u>. גב' זהבי מזמינה תריסר ביצים. היא לא

6. רוצה ירקות או פירות והיא שואלת כמה זה עולה. הכל עלה לה

7. שמונים ושלוש אגורות והיא נותנת לו לירה והחנווני נותן לה את
8. העודף של שבע-עשרה אגורות.

עונה /oné, oná/   answers (present tense)

באותו היום /beotó hayóm/   on the same day

שיחה 15.   <u>בבית קפה</u>

עטרה: שלום דוד. מה נשמע?

דוד: בואי לשתות כוס קפה ואספר לך את הכל.

ע: רעיון טוב. איפה בית קפה?

ר: פה בפינה.

(בבית הקפה)

דוד: מלצר, פעמיים קפה, בבקשה.

מלצר: עם או בלי חלב?

עטרה: בשבילי אספרסו עם חלב.

ר: ובשבילי קפה הפוך.

מ: אתם רוצים עוגות?

ע: איזה עוגות יש לכם?

מ: יש לנו עוגת תפוחים ועוגת גבינה.

ע: עוגת תפוחים, בבקשה.

ר: גם בשבילי.

ע: הקפה חם. הזהר.

ר: אחכה קצת, והקפה יתקרר.

1. עטרה פגשה את דוד ברחוב ושאלה אותו מה נשמע.   דוד <u>הציע</u>
2. לה שילכו לשתות כוס קפה והוא יספר לה את הכל.   עטרה אמרה
3. שזה רעיון טוב ושאלה איפה בית הקפה.   דוד ענה לה שבית הקפה
4. נמצא בפינה.   בבית הקפה הזמין דוד קפה לשניהם.   המלצר שאל
5. אם הם רוצים את הקפה עם או בלי חלב.   עטרה הזמינה אספרסו
6. ודוד הזמין קפה הפוך.   (בשביל לעשות קפה הפוך מוזגים קודם
7. את החלב לכוס <u>ואחר כך</u> את הקפה.)   המלצר שאל אם הם רוצים
8. לאכול עוגות עם הקפה ואמר שיש לו עוגת תפוחים ועוגת גבינה.
9. שניהם הזמינו עוגת תפוחים.   אחרי שהמלצר <u>הביא</u> את הקפה
10. עטרה ראתה שזה חם מאד ואמרה לדוד להיזהר.   דוד חיכה עד
11. שהקפה התקרר.

הציע /hicía/   he suggested

אחר כך /axár kax/   afterwards

הביא /heví/   he brought

שיחה 16.   שׂיחה בבית הקפֶה

דוד: פגשתי את משה הבוקר.

עטרה: באמת? מה הוא סיפר לך?

ר: הוא סיפר לי שהוא קבל מכתב ממר וויל'יאמס.

ע: מאין הוא שלח את המכתב, מאמריקה?

ר: לא. מתל אביב.

ע: מתל אביב? מה הוא עושה שם?

ר: הוא נתמנה ליועץ השגרירות האמריקאית.

ע: מתי הוא הגיע?

ר: בשבוע שעבר. משה נסע לתל אביב וראה אותו.

ע: איך הוא נראה?

ר: משה אומר שהוא נראה טוב.

ע: הוא עוד מדבר עברית?

ר: כן. הוא דיבר עברית עם משה.

1.   עטרה ודוד יושבים בבית הקפה ודוד מספר לה שפגש את משה בבוקר.
2.   משה סיפר לו על מכתב שקבל ממר וויל'יאמס. עטרה שאלה מאין נשלח
3.   המכתב, ודוד ענה שמר וויל'יאמס שלח את המכתב מתל אביב. דוד המשיך
4.   לספר שמר וויל'יאמס נתמנה ליועץ השגרירות האמריקאית בישראל, והגיע
5.   לארץ בשבוע שעבר. משה נסע לתל אביב וראה אותו שם. עטרה שאלה
6.   איך נראה מר וויל'יאמס ודוד אמר שהוא נראה טוב. עטרה שאלה
7.   אם מר וויל'יאמס זוכר עדיין לדבר עברית. דוד ענה לה שכנראה כן
8.   כי הוא דבר עברית עם משה.

זוכר /zoxér/   remembers
כנראה /kanir'é/   apparently

476

שיחה 17.   <u>במשרד הדואר</u>

מר ווילימס: אני רוצה לשלוח את המכתב הזה לאמריקה.

פקיד: דואר רגיל או בדואר אויר?

מר וו: בדואר אויר.

פ: זה יעלה לך שלושים וחמש אגורות.

מר וו: כמה זמן זה יקח?

פ: אני לא יודע. אולי שבוע.

מר וו: שבוע? זה הרבה זמן.

פ: באם זה כל כך דחוף, שלח מברק.

מר וו: זה רעיון טוב. היכן המברקה?

פ: כאן, בקומה השניה.

מר וו: תודה רבה.

1. מר ווילימס רוצה לשלוח מכתב לאמריקה.   הפקיד שואל

2. אותו אם הוא רוצה לשלוח את המברק בדואר רגיל או בדואר אויר.

3. מר ווילימס עונה שהוא רוצה לשלוח את המכתב בדואר אויר והפקיד

4. אומר לו שזה יעלה שלושים וחמש אגורות.   מר ווילימס שואל כמה

5. זמן יקח עד שהמכתב יגיע לאמריקה.   הפקיד לא <u>בטוח</u> אך חושב שזה

6. יקח שבוע.   מר ווילימס חושב ששבוע זה הרבה זמן.   הפקיד מציע

7. לו לשלוח מברק אם הדבר דחוף כל כך.   הרעיון מוצא חן בעיני

8. מר ווילימס ושואל היכן המברקה.   הפקיד עונה לו שהמברקה נמצאת

9. בקומה השניה.

sure, certain   /batúax/   בטוח

שיחה 18.   <u>השעון</u>

רב: מה השעה?

אביכה: השעה רבע לשבע.

ר: מתי עומדים ההורים להגיע?

א: אני לא יודעת בדיוק. נדמה לי שבשמונה וחצי.

ר: ברקי בבקשה מתי שהמטוס יגיע. הייתי רוצה להגיע
           חצי שעה לפני הזמן.

א: ברצון. גם אני רוצה לנסוע אתך.

ר: טוב. אקח אותך.   נצטרך לחכות עד שהם יעברו
           את המכס.

א: יש לנו מספיק זמן.

ר: אני מקווה כך. התקשרי מיד.

1.   השעה רבע לשבע. ההורים של רב עומדים להגיע לנמל התעופה.
2.   הוא שואל את אביכה באיזה שעה בדיוק יגיעו.   אביכה חשבה שבשמונה
3.   וחצי אך היא לא היתה בטוחה.   רב אמר לה לבדוק מתי המטוס מגיע
4.   כי הוא רוצה להיות בנמל התעופה חצי שעה לפני הזמן.   אביכה רוצה
5.   לנסוע אתו.   רב אומר לה שיצטרכו לחכות עד שההורים יעברו את
6.   המכס.   אביכה אומרת שיש להם מספיק זמן להגיע ואינם מוכרחים למהר.

שיחה 19.   <u>שיחת חוץ</u>

יונתן: גטרה, את יודעת את מספר הטלפון של הדוד ראובן?

עטרה: לא. התקשר עם מודיעין. חייג אפס.

י: הלו, מודיעין? תני לי בבקשה מספר בחיפה.
               השם הוא ראובן דובדבני, רחוב יפו שבעים ושש.

מודיעין: המספר הוא שתיים שבע שש ארבע אפס. אתה יכול
               לחייג ישירות או דרך שיחות-חוץ, מספר תשע-עשרה.

י: תודה רבה. אזמין את השיחה במספר תשע-עשרה.

שיחות-חוץ: שיחות-חוץ. שלום.

י: תני לי בבקשה חיפה שתיים שבע שש ארבע אפס.

ש"ח: מה המספר שלך?

י: שש אפס שבע שמונה שלוש.

ש"ח: חכה רגע. הקו תפוס.

               הלו, חיפה שתיים שבע שש ארבע אפס?
               תל אביב קוראת. דברו בבקשה.

478

1. יונתן רוצה להתקשר עם הדוד ראובן ולא יודע את מספר הטלפון
2. שלו. הוא שואל את עטרה וגם היא לא יודעת. אך היא מציעה לו
3. לחייג אפס ולהתקשר עם מודיעין כדי לברר את המספר. יונתן מתקשר
4. עם מודיעין ומבקש את המספר של דודו בחיפה. מודיעין נותן לו
5. את מספר הטלפון ואומר לו שהוא יכול לחייג ישירות או להזמין את
6. השיחה דרך שיחות-חוץ מספר 19. יונתן מחליט להזמין את השיחה.
7. הוא מחייג 19 ומבקש מספר בחיפה. המרכזנית שואלת את המספר שלו.
8. הקו בחיפה תפוס והוא צריך לחכות רגע.

decides /maxlit/   מחליט
operator /merkazanit/   מרכזנית

שיחה 20.1   חום.

דוד: איזה חום.
יונתן: כן. זה לבטח חמסין.
ד: בוא נלך להתרחץ בים.
י: זה רעיון מצויין.
ד: אתה יורע לשחות?
י: כן. קצת. ואתה?
ד: כן. אני שחיין טוב.
י: מה דעתך שניסע להרצליה?
ד: ברצון. החוף שם יפה מאד.

1. דוד אומר שחם היום. יונתן מסכים ומוסיף שזה לבטח
2. חמסין. דוד מציע שילכו להתרחץ בים. יונתן אומר שזה
3. רעיון מצויין. דוד שואל את יונתן אם הוא יורע לשחות.
4. יונתן אומר שקצת ושואל את דוד אם הוא יורע לשחות.
5. דוד אומר שהוא שחיין טוב. יונתן מציע שיסעו להרצליה.
6. דוד אומר שהוא ישמח מאד כי החוף שם יפה מאד.

agrees /maskim/   מסכים
adds /mosif/   מוסיף

שיחה 20.2   <u>קור.</u>

רות:	קר היום.
יוסף:	כן. החורף כבר הגיע.
ר:	האם יורד כאן שלג?
י:	לעתים. כשקר מאד.
ר:	אני מאד אוהבת שלג.
י:	כן. זה מראה נחמד.
ר:	האם ראית שלג?
י:	בטח. פעם אחת. בירושלים.

1. רות אומרת שקר היום. יוסף מסכים ואומר שהחורף
2. כבר הגיע. רות היא אמריקאית שבאה לטיול בארץ. היא
3. שואלת את יוסף אם יורד שלג בישראל. יוסף עונה שלעתים
4. רחוקות, כשקר מאד. רות אומרת שהיא מאד אוהבת שלג.
5. יוסף אומר שזה מראה נחמד. היא שואלת את יוסף אם הוא
6. ראה שלג והוא עונה שראה שלג פעם אחת בירושלים.

In the following section only the narratives of the Basic Conversation are
given. Units 21 to 25, and 31 to 37 are continuous conversations and may
be read as single selections when final sections are completed.

21.   <u>תוכנית למוצאי שבת</u>

1. יונתן פגש את עטרה ואת דוד ברחוב ושאל אותם איזה
2. תוכניות יש להם למוצאי שבת. הם עוד לא החליטו כי דוד
3. רצה ללכת לקולנוע מוגרבי לראות סרט, ועטרה רוקקא רצתה
4. לראות את ההצגה בבית הבימה. יונתן ביקש מהם שיודיעו
5. לו אחרי שיחליטו כי הוא רצה להצטרף, ושיעברו על יד ביתו
6. ויקראו לו. דוד אמר טוב ושיעברו על יד ביתו בשעה שמונה
7. בערך. יונתן ביקש שלא ישכחו לקרוא לו והם <u>נפרדו</u>.

they parted /nifredu/   נפרדו

480

22. בַּקֻפָּה.

1. דוד הלך לקופה של בית הבימה לקנות כרטיסים למוצאי שבת.
2. הוא ביקש שלושה מקומות טובים. הקופאי אמר שיש לו שלושה
3. מקומות ביציע אבל קצת קצר בצד – לא באמצע. דוד שאל באיזה שורה
4. הם והקופאי ענה שהם בשורה השביעית ושהם הכרטיסים האחרונים.
5. דוד ידע שהוא לא יכול לשנות את דעתה של עטרה ואז אין לו
6. ברירה. הוא שילם 18 לירות לקופאי ולקח את הכרטיסים.

23. לִפְנֵי ההצגה.

1. יונתן התלוצץ ואמר לעטרה שהיא שוב ניצחה. היא ענתה
2. שהיא בדרך כלל מנצחת כי דוד הוא בעל טוב. דוד שאל אותם
3. אם הם רוצים לשתות משהו לפני שההצגה מתחילה. עטרה אמרה
4. שהיא לא צמאה. בין כה וכה לא היה זמן לשתות כי הפעמון צלצל
5. והם ניגשו למקומות שלהם. דוד הראה להם את המקומות ביציע
6. ועטרה אמרה שהם די טובים. דוד התפלא קצת ושאל אותה אם היא
7. קירותה לקבל בשש לירות כרטיסים בשורה הראשונה. עטרה לא ענתה
8. וביקשה ממנו שלא יפריע כי המסך עולה.

he joked /hitlocec/	התלוצץ
anyway /beyn kó vaxo/	בין כה וכה
he showed /her'a/	הראה
he was surprised /hitpale/	התפלא
from him /miménu/	ממנו

24. בַּ"כַּסִית".

1. אחרי ההצגה עטרה הציעה שיגשו לכסית לשתות כוס קפה.
2. דוד הסכים שזה רעיון טוב, ושהם יראו שם את השחקנים. יונתן
3. שאל את עטרה איך היא נהנתה מההצגה. עטרה אמרה שהיא נהנתה
4. מאד. לדעתה התפאורה היתה מקסימה, והשחקנים היו טובים.
5. יונתן הוסיף שגם הוא נהנה מאד ובפרט ממרים נרקיס. דוד אמר
6. שהוא לא משתגע אחריה ושלדעתו היא זקנה והקול שלה נמוך.
7. עטרה שאלה את דוד אם הוא מחרמט שהלך להצגה. דוד ענה שהוא
8. לא מחרמט, אך הוא היה נהנה יותר מסרט טוב.
9. עטרה פנתה ליונתן ואמרה שהיא בטוחה שההורים שלו היו
10. נהנים לראות את ההצגה. יונתן השיב שכן, אך חבל שזו היתה
    ההצגה האחרונה.

481

25. <u>יציאה משירות הקבע.</u>

1. עטרה <u>האיצה</u> בדוד שילכו כבר הביתה כי מאוחר.
2. דוד ביקש ממנה לחכות רגע, כי הוא רוצה לשתות עוד כוס קפה.
3. עטרה לא הסכימה ואמרה שילכו הביתה כי צריך לקום מוקדם.
4. ונתן <u>ציין</u> שעור מוקדם, ושאל את עטרה ודוד אם הם כבר
5. הולכים. עטרה <u>השיבה</u> שכבר חצות. יונתן אמר שהוא ישאר עוד
6. קצת. אולי יפגוש חברים. דוד רצה לשלם את החשבון ויונתן לא
7. נתן לו לשלם. דוד הודה לו והם נפרדו.

> she urged /heíca/ האיצה
> he pointed out /ciyen/ ציין
> she answered /heší̇va/ השיבה

26. <u>בצבא.</u>

1. מר וויליאמס פוגש את אביגדור ושואל אותו היכן הוא
2. מתחבא, כי הוא לא ראה אותו הרבה זמן. אביגדור אומר שהוא
3. משרת כבר שנה בחיל האוויר. מר וויליאמס שואל לשלומה של
4. מרים, ואביגדור עונה ששלומה טוב ושהיא גמרה את הגמנסיה
5. הקיץ ומחכה לצו גיוס. מר וויליאמס <u>צחק</u> ואמר: "יופי !
6. כל המשפחה תהיה בצבא." הוא שאל את אביגדור כמה זמן הוא
7. צריך עוד לשרת. אביגדור אמר שהוא צריך לשרת עוד שנה וחצי,
8. ומרים תשרת שנתחיים כי בנות משרתות חצי שנה פחות.

> he laughed /caxak/ צחק

27. <u>במספרה.</u>

1. מר וויליאמס נכנס למספרה ואומר לספר שהוא רוצה להסתפר
2. ולהתגלח. הספר מבקש ממנו לשבת ואומר שיחפנה אליו מיד. מר
3. וויליאמס רוצה תספורת קצרה. הוא לא רוצה חפיפה. מר וויליאמס
4. שבע רצון מהתספורת ומשלם לספר שתי לירות עבור התספורת ולירה
5. אחת עבור הגילוח.

28. בַּמְכַבֶּסֶה.

1. גב' וויל יאמס מביאה בגדים לניקוי יבש.
2. בעלת המכבסה שואלת אותה כמה חתיכות יש לה. גב' ווילי אמס
3. נותנת לה שתי חליפות ושני זוגות מכנסיים. יש כתמים על
4. הבגדים וגב' ווילי אמס מבקשת ממנה לשים לב לכתמים. הגברת
5. שואלת ממה הכתמים, כי יותר קל להוריד אותם כשיודעים ממה הם.
6. גב' ווילי אמס אומרת שהיא חושבת שהכתמים על המכנסיים הם משומן,
7. והכתמים על הז'קט הם ממיץ רימון. בעלת המכבסה אומרת
8. שכתמים מרימון לא יורדים בקלות. גב' ווילי אמס אומרת שהיא
9. יודעת, ומבקשת את בעלת המכבסה לנסות ולהוריד אותם כמיטב
10. יכולתה. בעלת המכבסה אומרת שהיא תשתדל. גב' ווילי אמס
11. מבקשת שהבגדים יהיו מוכנים לסוף השבוע. בעלת המכבסה מבטיחה
12. שהם יהיו מוכנים ונקיים.

promises /mavtixa/ מבטיחה

29. בַּסַנדְלַרִיַה.

1. מר ווילי אמס מוסר זוג נעליים שחורות וזוג סנדלים
2. לתיקון. הסנדלר שואל מה צריך לתקן. מר ווילי אמס אומר
3. שצריך לשים סוליות חדשות בנעליים השחורות, ועקבים לסנדלים.
4. הסנדלר שואל איזה עקבים לשים בסנדלים. עקבי עור, או גומי.
5. מר ווילי אמס מחליט על עקבי גומי. התיקון עולה שש לירות
6. ביחד ומר ווילי אמס מתלונן שזה הרבה כסף. הסנדלר לא רוצה
7. להוריד את המחיר ואומר למר ווילי אמס שאצלו מחיר אחיד.
8. מר ווילי אמס מסכים ומבקש ממנו להוציא את המסמר באותו הכסף.

complains /mitlonen/ מתלונן

30. הָעִיקָר הַבְּרִיאוּת.

1. משה כספי נכנס למשרד ורואה שמרים נראית לא טוב.
2. הוא שואל אותה מה שלומה. מרים אומרת שהיא חולה.
3. משה שואל אותה מה כואב לה, והיא אומרת שכואב לה כל
4. הגוף. היא היתה אצל הרופא, והרופא אמר לה שיש לה
5. שפעת בלי חום. משה אומר שגם הוא מרגיש לא טוב.
6. שניהם צחקו ואמרו שלא נורא, הם ישארו בחיים.

פגישה במשרד.   שיחות 31 - 37.

1. מנחם ורב נפגשו במשרד האוצר ושמחו מאד לראות אחד את השני.
2. רב התעניין לדעת מה מנחם עושה במשרד האוצר והתפלא לשמוע שהוא
3. עובד במשרד האוצר כבר כמעט שנה.   רב המשיך לשאול באיזה מחלקה
4. מנחם עובד ואם הוא שבע רצון מהעבודה.   מנחם השיב שהוא עובד
5. במחלקה הכלכלית והעבודה די מעניינת שם.   הוא שבע רצון.   אחר
6. כך התחיל מנחם לשאול את רב שאלות.   הוא התעניין לדעת אם רב
7. עובד עדיין בחברת החשמל.   רב ענה שהוא החליף את מקום עבודתו
8. והוא עובד עכשיו בחברה מסחרית בתפקיד של רואה חשבון מוסמך.
9. מנחם נהנה לשמוע שרב סיים סוף סוף את הלימודים על אף שהיו
10. לו קצת קשיים כפי שסיפר.

11. מנחם שאל את רב איך המשכורת שלו.   רב ענה שהמשכורת
12. שלו טובה מאד.   הוא מרוויח כמעט כפליים יותר ממה שהרוויח קודם.
13. למנחם היה קשה להאמין ואמר לרב שהוא בוודאי מגזים.   רב
14. הבטיח לו שאינו מגזים וכי זאת האמת.   מנחם חייך ואמר לרב
15. שעם משכורת כפולה הוא יתעשר בקרוב ולא ירצה אפילו לדבר אתו.
16. רב השיב למנחם שאילו היה גם הוא עובד בחברה פרטית היה גם הוא
17. מרוויח יותר.   גם מנחם חשב כך, אך ציין שיש לו בממשלה רותק
18. של עשר שנים, ושניהם הסכימו שגם רותק זה דבר חשוב.

19. רב התעניין לדעת איך באמת מסתדר מנחם עם המשכורת שלו.
20. מנחם סיפר שהם חיים לפי תקציב ובדרך זו מסתדרים פחות או יותר.
21. רב שאל איך הם עושים תקציב, ומנחם ענה שהם רושמים את כל
22. ההוצאות, מחלקים את ההכנסה כהתאם להוצאות ואת העודף מפקידים
23. בבנק.   רב התלונן שהוא אינו מצליח לחסוך אף פרוטה אחת.   מנחם
24. אמר שאין פלא כי רב הרי סיים את הלימודים רק לפני זמן קצר.
25. כשהמשיך רב ואמר שהוא בכל זאת מתפלא איך הם יכולים גם לחסוך וגם
26. להסתדר במשכורת ממשלתית, ענה לו מנחם שאין כל פלא כדבר.   גם
27. אשתו עובדת ומרוויחה.

28. רב שאל את מנחם באיזה שעה הוא מתעורר כל בוקר.   מנחם
29. ענה שהוא קם בשעה שש וחצי.   רב קרא בהתפעלות: "בשש וחצי?
30. כל כך מוקדם!?"   והוסיף שהוא בקושי רב מאד יוצא מהמיטה בשבע
31. ורבע.   מנחם שאל אותו באיזה שעה הוא מתחיל לעבוד, ורב ענה
32. שמתחילים בשמונה, אך הוא תמיד מאחר. מנחם אמר לו שהוא מתנהג
33. כמו רווק טיפוסי והציע לו שילך לישון יותר מוקדם ואז יוכל
34. לקום יותר מוקדם.   אך רב ענה לו שאינו מסוגל לקום יותר מוקדם -
35. הוא אינו מסודר כמו מנחם.

מנחם אמר לרב שלדעתו זה לא עושה רושם טוב כשמאחרים 36.

לעבודה כל יום.   רב ענה לו שזה לא <u>תלוי</u> מתי שהוא קם בבוקר, 37.

בכל זאת <u>יוצא לו</u> לאחר.   הוא נתן דוגמה שלפני כשבוע, החליט 38.

בכל זאת לקום מוקדם כדי להגיע לעבודה בזמן וכשניגש להדליק את 39.

המכונית, <u>נוכח לדעת</u> שאין בה דלק.   מנחם אמר לרב   שתמיד 40.

הוא חייב לשים לב לכמות הדלק במכונית.   רב ירע שמנחם <u>צודק</u>, 41.

וענה <u>בהתנצלות</u> שזה נכון, אך הוא בכל זאת שכח. 42.

מנחם המשיך לנסות <u>להשפיע</u> על רב ואמר לו שאם היה קורה 43.

במשרד ממשלתי דבר כזה, היה המנהל מפטר אותו מזמן, וחוץ מזה 44.

הוא חושב שרב כחור יותר מרי מפוזר.   רב ענה <u>בבטחון</u> שאינו 45.

מפחד מפיטורים.   המנהל שלו צריך אותו בעבודה.   מנחם ענה לו 46.

שאפילו אם המנהל צריך אותו, לכל דבר יש גבול ולא כדאי לעבור 47.

את הגבול.   רב ענה לו שיש בעולם דברים יותר חשובים מאשר 48.

איחור לעבודה והוא טיפוס כזה שלא יוכל להשתנות. 49.

Line

English	Transliteration	Hebrew	Line
Finance Ministry	misrad haocar	משרד האוצר	1.
despite	al af	על אף	9.
according to	kfi	כפי	10.
to believe	lehaamin	להאמין	13.
certainly	bevaday	בודאי	14.
he smiled	xiyex	חייך	14.
doubled	kfula	כפולה	15.
if	ílu	אילו	16.
according to	lefi	לפי	20.
deposit	mafkidim	מפקידים	22.
even	af	אף	23.
amazement	hitpaalut	התפעלות	29.
conducts himself	mitnaheg	מתנהג	32.
typical	tipusi	טיפוסי	33.
dependent	taluy	תלוי	37.
it turns out for him	yoce lo	יוצא לו	38.
he realized	noxax ladáat	נוכח לדעת	40.
is correct	codek	צודק	41.
apologetically	behitnaclut	בהתנצלות	42.
to influence	lehašpía	להשפיע	43.
confidence	bitaxon	בטחון	45.

The following section of the Reader is designed as a means of developing
the students' ability to proceed from a fixed text to free conversation.
The techniques supplement those of the conversational units. The conversational
units provide the drills which are necessary for fluent handling of the
pronunciation, grammar, and basic vocabulary of the language. The material
is deliberately limited in scope in order to provide the maximum amount of
practice in manipulating the structure of Hebrew.

The core of each unit in the course is the Basic Conversation. In contrast
to this, the core of each lesson in the following section is non-dialogue
material - an anecdote, a news article, a descriptive paragraph, or the like.

The first part consists of presenting the anecdote so that the students
can understand it easily.   The second part consists of conducting a conversation around the anecdote.   The students should go away from the class each
time feeling that they have used Hebrew freely and naturally in a significant
communication.   The general techniques for presenting the story and conducting
the conversation are described below.

(a) Presenting the story

The basic story of each lesson is presented in two versions. They are
called /núsax álef/ "Style A" and /núsax bet/ "Style B".   Version B is the
original story. Version A is a simplification for learning purposes.

In version A the facts or elements of the story are given in short, simple
sentences.   Only one new word or construction is introduced in each sentence.
Many sentences contain no new items, but are included so as to give the
complete story.

In version B the story is presented with the elements and constructions
which had been removed in order to simplify it for Style A . These elements
include such things as and, or, when, after, before, because etc.   The
constructions include relative clauses, nominalizations, and other transformations.

Version A is presented orally first. Students' books are closed. The
sentences are printed with a cue-word to the right.   This cue-word is generally
a new word or construction, but it may serve simply to recall a point of the
story.

1.   The instructor reads one sentence from A at a time.   Students repeat first
in unison and then individually.   Some of the sentences may be too long for
the students to comprehend and repeat as a whole the first time.   The instructor
should then present them in the same "reverse partial" manner of the Basic
Sentences of the conversational units.   There are double spaces between some
words to aid the instructor in breaking the sentences into parts.

2.   The instructor should make sure that the students understand each sentence
before proceeding to the next. If necessary, he may ask for a translation, but
the use of English should be kept to a minimum.

3.   After presenting several sentences the instructor should review them.   He
gives the cue-word, and a student responds with the entire sentence.   The
sentences should be reviewed in order first, but after the students are able to
respond easily he may select cue-words at random.

The instructor is not restricted to the cue-words given here but may give
any part of a particular sentence as a cue.   He may also call on different
students one after the other for the same sentence but with different cues.

4.   When all the sentences of A have been presented and reviewed, each student should be asked to recite all of them in order. The student will thus be giving a description or telling an anecdote, albeit in a very simplified manner.

5.   With the student's books still closed, the instructor then reads Version B . Students should comprehend the whole story. If there is any difficulty, the instructor should read the story slowly until the students can understand completely at normal speed.

6.   The students read Version B from the text.

With a very quick class or with one which has had previous training in reading Hebrew, step 6 may be omitted. In any case, the students need not "overlearn" it as with the sentences of the Basic Conversations. The conversation about the stories, as explained in (b), will enable the students to enlarge on the original anecdote with ease and enjoyment.

(b) Conducting the Conversation

1.   The basic technique is the use of different types of questions of varying difficulty and relative interest. The simplest type is the "yes-no" question. In this type the student replies simply "Yes" or "No", or, if asked to give a complete sentence, he will find the vocabulary and phrasing in the question itself.

> Example: Is Avigdor in the air force?
> Answer: Yes. or Yes, Avigdor is in the air force.

2.   The next easiest are "alternative" questions in which the student replies by selecting one of two answers suggested in the question.

> Example: Is Avigdor in the air force or the navy?
> Answer: Avigdor is in the air force.

"Alternative" questions are effective in expanding vocabulary since the student can learn antonyms in a conversational context.

> Example: Is Avigdor tall or short?

3.   The most difficult questions are those which begin with an interrogative word or phrase. In these the answer is not contained in the wording of the question, and the student often has to make certain grammatical transformations in the reply.

> Example: In which branch is Avigdor serving?
> Answer: Avigdor is in the air force.

Questions are also classified according to their closeness to the basic fixed text. These are divided into stages, labeled /šlavim/ "rungs" שלבים Questions in Stage 1, /šlav alef/, ask for answers contained within the wording of the basic story. Questions in Stage 2, /šlav bet/, ask for answers that must be inferred from the story. Questions in Stage 3, /šlav gímel), ask about the student's own life and experiences.

Below is a chart which shows samples of the three types of questions in each of the three stages. Note that in general the difficulty and also the interest of these questions increases from·/šlav álef/ to /šlav gímel/ and from top to bottom. The story on which these questions are based is the Basic Conversation of Unit 26.

Stage 1 שלב א   Stage 2 שלב ב   Stage 3 שלב ג

	Stage 1 שלב א	Stage 2 שלב ב	Stage 3 שלב ג
Yes-No	Is Avigdor in the air force?	Does Avigdor like the service?	Were you ever in the service?
Alternative	Is Avigdor in the air force or navy?	Was Avigdor in uniform or in civilian clothes?	Were you an officer or an enlisted man?
Interrogative word	How much longer does Avigdor have to serve?	What is the draft age in Israel?	Where did you serve while in the Army?

The instructor should proceed to ask the questions in the order given here, at least for the first time with each story. This will enable the students to learn the new vocabulary and to control the range of the discussion. Afterwards, the instructor may ask the questions in random order or in random order of students depending on what each student has to contribute to the discussion.

CAUTION:
The instructor should not give the students a lot of new vocabulary. This will bog down the class in lists of words instead of enabling the class to maintain a lively pace. This temptation is especially strong at Stage 3, שלב ג, when students often want to relate involved experiences.

Story 1.

המזכירה הנהדרת

נוסח "א".

1. מזכירה	אסתר עובדת כמזכירה בחברה גדולה.
2. מדפיסה	היא מדפיסה מכתבים.
3. הכתבות	היא לוקחת הכתבות.
4. עונה	היא עונה לטלפון.
5. חרוצה	היא בחורה חרוצה ואנטלגנטית.
6. עבור	אסתר עובדת עבור מר אלון.
7. מחלקה	הוא מנהל המחלקה הכלכלית של החברה.
8. עבורתה	מר אלון שבע רצון מעבורתה של אסתר.
9. הטובה ביותר	היא המזכירה הטובה ביותר בחברה.

נוסח "ב".

אסתר עובדת כמזכירה בחברה גדולה. היא מדפיסה
מכתבים, לוקחת הכתבות, ועונה לטלפון. היא בחורה
חרוצה ואינטלגנטית. אסתר עובדת עבור מר אלון שהוא
מנהל המחלקה הכלכלית של החברה. מר אלון שבע רצון
מעבודתה של אסתר, ולדעתו היא המזכירה הטובה ביותר
בחברה.

שלב "א"

1. האם אסתר עובדת כמזכירה?
2. האם החברה הזאת קטנה?
3. האם היא מדפיסה מכתבים?
4. האם היא מכתיבה הכתבות?
5. האם אסתר בחורה חרוצה?
6. האם היא עובדת עבור מר בן-דורי?
7. האם מר אלון מנהל המחלקה הכלכלית?
8. האם הוא שבע רצון מעבודתה?
9. האם יש מזכירה בחברה יותר טובה מאסתר?
10. האם אסתר עובדת כמזכירה או כספרית?
11. האם החברה הזאת קטנה או גדולה?
12. האם אסתר מדפיסה מכתבים או מנהלת פנקסים?
13. האם אסתר מכתיבה הכתבות או לוקחת הכתבות?
14. האם אסתר בחורה חרוצה או עצלה?
15. האם אסתר עובדת עבור מר בן-דורי או עבור מר אלון?
16. האם מר אלון מנהל המחלקה הכלכלית או נשיא החברה?
17. האם הוא שבע רצון או בלתי שבע רצון מעבודתה?

18. מה היא עבודתה של אסתר?
19. באיזה חברה עובדת אסתר?
20. מה תפקידה של אסתר?
21. מה לוקחת אסתר?
22. באיזה אופן עובדת אסתר?

489

שלב "יב"

1. האם אסתר נהנית לעבוד בחברה גדולה?
2. האם יש לאסתר הרבה עבודה?
3. האם אסתר היא מזכירה פרטית של מר אלון?
4. האם אסתר מקבלת משכורת גבוהה?

5. האם אסתר נהנית לעבוד בחברה גדולה או היתה נהנית יותר
   לעבוד בחברה קטנה?
6. האם יש לאסתר הרבה עבודה או מעט עבודה?
7. האם אסתר היא מזכירה פרטית של מר אלון או היא גם עובדת
   עבור אחרים?
8. האם אסתר מקבלת משכורת גבוהה או אותה המשכורת כיתר
   המזכירות?

9. מדוע לדעתך נהנית אסתר לעבוד בחברה גדולה?
10. מדוע לדעתך יש לאסתר הרבה עבודה?
11. מדוע לדעתך בחר מר אלון אותה למזכירתו הפרטית?
12. מדוע לדעתך מקבלת אסתר משכורת גבוהה?

שלב "יג"

1. האם יש לך מזכירה?
2. האם החברה שאתה עובד עבורה היא חברה גדולה?
3. האם המזכירה שלך עובדת הרבה זמן בחברה?
4. האם ישנן הרבה מזכירות בחברה שאתה עובד?
5. האם היית רוצה להיות מנהל מחלקה כלכלית?
6. האם אתה אוהב מזכירות יפות?

7. האם יש לך מזכירה או אתה עונה בעצמך לטלפון?
8. האם החברה שאתה עובד עבורה גדולה או קטנה?
9. האם המזכירה שלך עובדת הרבה או מעט זמן בחברה?
10. האם ישנן הרבה או מעט מזכירות בחברה שאתה עובד?
11. האם היית רוצה להיות מנהל מחלקה כלכלית או נשיא חברה?
12. האם אתה אוהב מזכירות יפות או לא אכפת לך?

13. למה היית רוצה שתהיה לך מזכירה?
14. מה גודל החברה שאתה עובד עבורה?
15. כמה זמן עובדת המזכירה שלך בחברה?
16. כמה מזכירות עובדות בחברה שאתה עובד?
17. באיזה תפקיד היית רוצה לעבוד?
18. איזה מזכירות אתה אוהב?

Story 2.

עקרת הבית

נוסח "א"

מרים היא עקרת בית.	1. עקרת בית
הבית שלה תמיד נקי ומסודר.	2. תמיד
היא טבחית טובה.	3. טבחית
היא מבשלת מצויין.	4. מבשלת
היא אופה מצויין.	5. אופה
לרגים הממולאים שהיא מכינה יש טעם גן-ערן.	6. טעם גן-ערן
מרים אוהבת את עבודת הבית.	7. עבודת בית
הכנת ארוחות טובות זה אצלה תחכיב.	8. תחכיב

נוסח "ב"

מרים היא עקרת בית למופת. הבית שלה תמיד נקי
ומסודר. נוסף לכך היא טבחית טובה. היא מבשלת ואופה
מצויין.
לרגים הממולאים שהיא מכינה יש טעם גן-ערן, ועוגת
התפוחים שלה מצויינת. מרים אוהבת את עבודת הבית, והכנת
ארוחות טובות, זה אצלה תחכיב.

שלב "א"

האם מרים עקרת בית?	1.
האם הבית שלה תמיד נקי ומסודר?	2.
האם היא טבחית טובה?	3.
האם היא מבשלת ואופה מצויין?	4.
האם לרגים שהיא מכינה יש טעם טוב?	5.
האם עוגת התפוחים שלה טעימה?	6.
האם מרים איננה אוהבת את עבודת הבית?	7.
האם מרים עקרת בית או מורה?	8.
האם הבית שלה תמיד נקי ומסודר או הפוך?	9.
האם היא טבחית טובה או רעה?	10.
האם היא מבשלת ואופה מצויין או לא כל כך טוב?	11.
האם לרגים שהיא מכינה יש טעם טוב או הם לא טעימים?	12.
האם עוגת התפוחים שלה מצויינת או גרועה?	13.
האם מרים אוהבת את עבודת הבית או את עבודת המשרד?	14.
מה עושה מרים?	15.
באיזה מצב נמצא הבית שלה?	16.
איזו טבחית מרים?	17.
איך מרים מבשלת ואופה?	18.
איזה טעם יש לרגים שהיא מכינה?	19.
איך עוגת התפוחים של מרים?	20.

491

שָׁלָב "כ"

1. האם מרים מעיינת בספרי בישול?
2. האם יש למרים הרבה עבודה בכיח?
3. האם כל המאכלים שמרים מבשלת טעימים?
4. האם היא עסוקה כל היום בעבודות הבית?

5. האם מרים מעיינת בכל ספרי הבישול שלה או רק בחלק מהם?
6. האם יש למרים הרבה עבודה בכיח או מעט עבודה?
7. האם כל המאכלים שמרים מבשלת טעימים או רק חלק מהם?
8. האם הכנת ארוחות טובות זו טרחה עבור מרים או תענוג?

שָׁלָב "ג"

1. האם אשתך עקרת בית טובה?
2. האם אתה מכין את הארוחות בבית?
3. האם אתה אוהב את עוגת התפוחים שאשתך מכינה?
4. האם הכנת ארוחות טובות זה תחביב אצל אשתך?

5. האם אשתך עקרת בית טובה או לא כל כך טובה?
6. האם אשתך או אתה מכינים את הארוחות בבית?
7. האם אתה אוהב את עוגת התפוחים שאשתך מכינה או
   אתה אוהב יותר עוגת תפוחים קנויה?
8. האם הכנת ארוחות טובות זה תחביב או טרחה אצל אשתך?

9. איזו עקרת בית אשתך?
10. מי מכין את הארוחות אצלכם בבית?
11. איזה עוגת תפוחים אתה אוהב?

Story 3.

המעשן הסרבן

נוסח "א"

תושב תל אביב נקנס אתמול.	1. נקנס
בית המשפט קנס אותו.	2. בית המשפט
הקנס היה בסך של 25 לירות.	3. קנס
הוא עישן סיגריה באוטובוס.	4. עישן
הנהג ביקש ממנו שלא יעשן.	5. נהג
הוא סרב להענות לבקשת הנהג.	6. להענות
הוא סרב לכבות את הסיגריה.	7. לכבות

נוסח "ב"

תושב תל אביב נקנס אתמול על ידי בית משפט
השלום לקנס של 25 לירות, על אשר סירב להענות
לבקשת נהג האוטובוס לכבות את הסיגריה שעישן בעת
נסיעה באוטובוס.

שלב "א"

האם תושב תל אביב נקנס?	1.
האם התושב נקנס ב-25 לירות?	2.
האם הוא נקנס על ידי בית משפט השלום?	3.
האם הוא רצה לכבות את הסיגריה?	4.
האם הוא עישן את הסיגריה בתחנת האוטובוסים?	5.
האם הוא עישן את הסיגריה בעת נסיעה?	6.
האם תושב תל אביב או תושב חיפה נקנס?	7.
האם התושב נקנס ב-25 לירות או ב-50 לירות?	8.
האם הוא נקנס על ידי בית משפט השלום או המחוזי?	9.
האם הוא עישן את הסיגריה בתחנת האוטובוסים או באוטובוס?	10.
האם הוא עישן את הסיגריה בעת נסיעה או כעת חניה?	11.
מה קרה לתושב תל אביב?	12.
בכמה נקנס התושב?	13.
על ידי איזה בית משפט הוא נקנס?	14.
מרוע הוא נקנס?	15.
היכן הוא עישן את הסיגריה?	16.

שלב ‏"ב"‏

1. האם מותר לעשן באוטובוס בזמן הנסיעה?
2. האם הרבה אנשים נקנסים על עישון באוטובוס?
3. האם קנס של 25 לירות הוא קנס גבוה ?

4. האם מותר או אסור לעשן באוטובוס בזמן נסיעה?
5. האם הרבה או מעט אנשים נקנסים על עישון באוטובוס?
6. האם קנס של 25 לירות הוא קנס גבוה או נמוך?

7. מדוע לדעתך אסור לעשן באוטובוס בזמן הנסיעה?
8. כמה אנשים לדעתך נקנסים על עישון באוטובוס?
9. מדוע לדעתך קנס של 25 לירות הוא קנס גבוה?
10. מדוע לדעתך ביקש הנהג ממנו לכבות את הסיגריה?

שלב ‏"ג"‏

1. האם אתה מעשן?
2. האם מותר לעשן באוטובוסים באמריקה?
3. האם אי פעם נקנסת על ידי בית משפט?
4. האם היית קונס בקנס גבו אדם שמעשן באוטובוס?
5. האם אתה בדרך כלל סרבן?

6. ‏אם ‏’ותה מעשן סיגרים, סיגריות או מקטרת?
7. ‏אם היית קונס אדם שמעשן באוטובוס, או זה לא מפריע לך?
8. האם אתה סרבן, או אדם נוח?

9. איזה סוג טבק אתה מעשן?
10. על איזו עבירה נקנסת?
11. באיזה קנס היית קונס אדם שמעשן באוטובוס?
12. איזה סוג אדם אתה?

Story 4.

כחירת משה לנשיא החברה

נוסח "א"

משה עומד להיבחר לנשיא החברה.	להיבחר	.1
זה עדיין סוד.	סוד	.2
הוא רוצה להפתיע את החברים.	להפתיע	.3
הכטחתי לו שלא אספר לאיש.	הכטחתי	.4
איחלתי לו הצלחה רבה.	הצלחה	.5
משה נבחר לנשיא חברת "לביא".	נבחר	.6
כל החברים היו מופתעים.	מופתעים	.7
הוא בחור צעיר.	צעיר	.8
הוא עובד בחברה שנתיים.	שנתיים	.9
החברה היתה במצב כספי רע.	מצב	.10
משה הכניס סכום כסף.	סכו י	.11

נוסח "יב"

בשכר שעבר פגשתי את משה כרחוב. הוא סיפר לי
שהוא עומד להיבחר לנשיא חברת "לביא", אך זה עדיין
סוד. הוא ביקש ממני לא לספר לאף אחד אודות זה, כי
הוא רוצה להפתיע את החברים. הכטחתי לו שלא אספר לאיש,
ואיחלתי לו הצלחה רבה.

משה נבחר לנשיא חברת "לביא", וכל החברים ה ו
מופתעים, שדורקא הוא נבחר, כי היה בחור צעיר ועוכד
בחברה רק שנתיים. מאוחר יותר החברר שחברת "לביא"
היתה במצב כספי רע. משה הכניס סכום כסף גדול לוכרה
ולכן בחרו אותו לנשיא.

שלב "א"

האם פגשתי את משה כרחוב?	.1
האם הוא סיפר לי שהוא עומד להיבחר לנשיא חברת "לביא"?	.2
האם משה רוצה להפתיע את החברים?	.3
האם הכטחתי למשה שלא אספר לאיש?	.4
האם משה נבחר לנשיא חברת "לביא"?	.5
האם החברים היו מופתעים?	.6
האם משה בחור צעיר?	.7
האם משה עובד בחברה שנתיים?	.8
האם חברת "לביא" היתה במצב כספי רע?	.9
האם משה הכניס סכום כסף גדול לחברה?	.10

495

11. האם פגשתי את משה ברחוב או במשרד?
12. האם משה עומד להיכחר לנשיא החברה או למנהל כללי?
13. האם משה רוצה להפתיע את החברים או לספר להם?
14. האם הבטחתי למשה שלא אספר לאיש או רק שאספר למשפחתי?
15. משה נכחר לנשיא חברת "לכיא" או לנשיא חברת "ירקון"?
16. האם החברים היו מופתעים או ידעו כבר?
17. האם משה בחור צעיר או אדם זקן?
18. האם משה עוכד בחברה שנתיים או חמש שנים?
19. האם חברת "לכיא" היתה במצב כספי רע או טוב?
20. האם משה הכניס סכום כסף גדול או קטן לחברה?

21. למה עומד משה להכחר?
22. מה רוצה משה לעשות?
23. מה הבטחתי למשה?
24. לאיזה חברה משה נכחר לנשיא?
25. איך הרגישו החברים?
26. כמה זמן עוכד משה בחברה?
27. באיזה מצב כספי היתה חברת לכיא?
28. מה הכניס משה לחברה?

שלב "כ"

1. האם אני חבר טוב של משה?
2. האם אני עוכד בחברת "לכיא"?
3. האם זה דבר רגיל לבחור כחור צעיר לנשיא חברה?
4. האם שמחתי לשמוע שמשה נתמנה לנשיא חברת "לכיא"?
5. האם זה דבר רגיל שחברה נמצאת במצב רע?
6. האם אני חבר טוב של משה או רק מכיר שלו?
7. האם אני עוכד בחברת "לכיא" או במקום אחר?
8. האם זה דבר רגיל לבחור כחור צעיר או אדם מכוגר?
9. האם שמחתי או הצטערתי לשמוע על זאת?
10. האם זה דבר רגיל שחברה נמצאת במצב כספי רע או בדרך
    כלל חברות נמצאות במצב כספי טוב?
11. ממה אתה יורע שאני חבר טוב למשה?
12. מרוע לדעתך אינני עוכד בחברת "לביא"?
13. למה לדעתך זה דבר כלתי רגיל לבחור כחור צעיר?
14. איך הרגשתי כששמעתי על התמנותו של משה?
15. מרוע לדעתך הכניס משה כסף לחברה?

496

שֶׁלֶב "ג"

1. האם אתה אוהב לשמור סוד?
2. האם אתה מופתע לעתים קרובות?
3. האם היית רוצה להיות נשיא חברה?
4. האם אתה עובד במקום עבודתך שנתיים?
5. האם החברה שאתה עובד עבורה נמצאת במצב כספי טוב?
6. כשמספרים לך סוד האם אתה שומר אותו לעצמך, או מספר לכולם?
7. האם אתה אוהב הפתעות או שאינך מתרגש מהן?
8. האם היית רוצה להיות נשיא חברה, או דיפלומט?
9. האם אתה עובד במקום עבודתך פחות או יותר משנתיים?
10. האם החברה שאתה עובד עבורה נמצאת במצב כספי טוב או רע?
11. מי מספר לך סודות?
12. את מי אתה אוהב להפתיע?
13. מה היית רוצה להיות?
14. כמה זמן אתה עובד במקום עבודתך?
15. לו היתה החברה שעבורה אתה עובד נמצאת במצב כספי רע –
    מה היית עושה?

Story 5.

הַאוֹפְנוֹעַן הָאַלְמוֹנִי

נוּסַח "א"

1. רכב	איש אחד רכב ברחוב.
2. אופנוע	הוא רכב על אופנוע.
3. פגע	הוא פגע בילד בן חמש.
4. ברח	רוכב האופנוע ברח.
5. תאונה	הוא ברח ממקום התאונה.
6. אלמוני	הרוכב היה אלמוני.
7. נפצע	הילד נפצע קשה.
8. טיפול	הוא הועבר לטיפול בבית חולים.

נוּסַח "ב"

רוכב אופנוע אלמוני פגע אמש בילד בן חמש ברחוב
נתן שבשכונת התקוה וברח ממקום התאונה. הילד נפצע
קשה והועבר לטיפול בבית החולים "איכילוב".

<u>שלב "א"</u>

1. האם האיש רכב על אופנוע?
2. האם הוא פגע בילד?
3. האם רוכב האופנוע ברח ממקום התאונה?
4. האם רוכב האופנוע היה אלמוני?
5. האם התאונה קרתה ברחוב?
6. האם הילד נפצע קשה?
7. האם הילד הועבר לבית חולים?
8. האם הילד הועבר לטיפול?

9. האם האיש רכב על אופנוע או אופניים?
10. האם הוא פגע בילד או בילדה?
11. האם רוכב האופנוע ברח או נשאר במקום?
12. האם רוכב האופנוע היה אלמוני או ידוע?
13. האם התאונה קרתה ברחוב או על שפת הים?
14. האם הילד נפצע קשה או קל?
15. האם הילד הועבר לביתו או לבית החולים?
16. האם הילד הועבר לטיפול או לבדיקות?

17. על מה רכב האיש?
18. במי פגע האופנוען?
19. מה עשה רוכב האופנוע אחרי התאונה?
20. מי היה רוכב האופנוע?
21. היכן קרתה התאונה?
22. מה היה מצבו של הילד?
23. לאן הועבר הילד?
24. לאיזה מטרה הועבר הילד לבית חולים?

<u>שלב "ב"</u>

1. האם רוכב האופנוע נסע במהירות רגילה?
2. האם הילד שיחק ברחוב?
3. האם הילד שם לב לרמזורים?
4. האם רוכב האופנוע אדם טוב?
5. האם האופנוען הרגיש שהוא פגע בילד?
6. האם האופנוען היה פחדן?
7. האם רוכב האופנוע עבר עבירה חמורה?
8. האם הילד ראה את האופנוע לפני התאונה?
9. האם היו הרבה אנשים ברחוב בזמן התאונה?

‏.10   האם רוכב האופנוע נסע במהירות רגילה או מופרזת?
‏.11   האם הילד שיחק ברחוב או עבר את הכביש?
‏.12   האם הילד שם לב או רק שיחק?
‏.13   האם רוכב האופנוע היה אדם טוב או רע?
‏.14   האם האופנוען היה פחדן או אמיץ?
‏.15   האם רוכב האופנוע עבר עבירה חמורה אֶו קֶלֶה?
‏.16   האם היו הרבה אנשים ברחוב או הרחוב ה ה ר ק מאדם?

‏.17   באיזה מהירות לדעתך ־־רע רוכב האופנוע?
‏.18   מה לדעתך עשה הילד.
‏.19   מדוע לדעתך הילד לא שם לב לרמזורים?
‏.20   איזה בן-אדם לדעתך היה רוכב האופנוע?
‏.21   מדוע לדעתך הרגיש האופנוען שהוא פגע בילד?
‏.22   מדוע לדעתך ברח רוכב האופנוע?
‏23   מדוע לדעתך רוכב האופנוע עבר עבירה חמורה
‏.24   מדוע לדעתך הילד לא ראה את האופנוע לפני התאונה?
‏.25   כמה אנשים היו לדעתך ברחוב בזמן התאונה?

‏שֶׁלֶב "ג"

‏.1   האם אתה רוכב על אופנוע?
‏.2   האם אתה נהג זהיר?
‏.3   האם קרתה לך אי פעם תאונה?
‏.4   האם אי פעם נפצעת בתאונה?
‏.5   האם הועברת לבית חולים?
‏.6   האם התאונה היתה באשמתך?

‏.7   האם אתה רוכב על אופנוע או רק נוהג מכונית?
‏.8   האם אתה נהג זהיר או פזיז?
‏.9   האם קרתה לך תאונה רצינית, או קלה?
‏.10   האם נפצעת קשה או קל?
‏.11   האם הועברת לבית חולים או נשלחת הכיתה?
‏.12   האם התאונה היתה באשמתך או באשמת מישהו אחר?

‏.13   מה אתה נוהג?
‏.14   איזה סוג נהג אתה?
‏.15   איזה סוג תאונה קרתה לך?
‏.16   באיזו צורה נפצעת?
‏.17   לאן הועברת לאחר שנפצעת?
‏.18   באשמת מי היתה התאונה?

Story 6.

תקלות בקשר הטלפוני

נוסח "א"

תקלות	.1
קשר	.2
להתקשר	.3
מספרים	.4
מקולקלים	.5
יתוקנו	.6

1. תקלות   היו תקלות בתל אביב.
2. קשר   התקלות היו בקשר הטלפוני.
3. להתקשר   אמש אי אפשר היה להתקשר בטלפון.
4. מספרים   הקושי היה במספרים המתחילים ב-61 וב-62.
5. מקולקלים   המספרים האלה היו מקולקלים.
6. יתוקנו   לא היה ידוע מתי המספרים יתוקנו.

נוסח "ב"

אמש אי אפשר היה להתקשר בטלפון בתל אביב
עם המספרים המתחילים ב-61 וב-62. לשאלה השיבו
ממספר 16 – שכל המספרים האלה מקולקלים ולא ידוע
מתי יתוקנו.

שלב "א"

1   האם היו תקלות בקשר הטלפוני בתל אביב?
2.   האם המספרים שמתחילים ב-61 וב-62 היו מקולקלים?
3.   האם השיבו ממספר 16 שהמספרים מקולקלים?
4.   האם היה ידוע מתי המספרים יתוקנו?

5   האם אפשר היה או אי אפשר היה להתקשר טלפונית בתל אביב?
6.   האם המספרים שמתחילים ב-61 וב-62 היו מקולקלים או
      במצב תקין?
7.   האם השיבו ממספר 16 שהם עובדים על הקווים או שלא
      ידוע מתי הקווים יתוקנו?

8.   מתי קרו התקלות בקשר הטלפוני?
9.   איזה מספרי טלפון היו מקולקלים?
10.   מה השיבו ממספר 16?
11.   מתי יתוקנו מספרי הטלפון המקולקלים?

שֶׁלָב "ב"

1. האם תקלות בקשר טלפוני קורות לעתים קרובות?
2. האם לדעתך ישנם הרבה טלפונים בישראל?
3. האם המרכזיות הן במצב תקין?
4. האם לדעתך עובדות הרבה מרכזניות בחברת הטלפון?
5. האם לדעתך עובדים הרבה קונים בחברת הטלפון?
6. האם מכשיר טלפון הוא מכשיר חשוב?
7. האם מחייגים מספר 16 כדי להודיע שהטלפון מקולקל?

8. האם תקלות בקשר טלפוני קורות לעתים תכופות או נדירות?
9. האם לדעתך ישנם הרבה, או מעט מכשירי טלפון בישראל?
10. האם המרכזיות נמצאות בדרך כלל במצב תקין, או מקולקלות?
11. האם הרבה או מעט מרכזניות עובדות בחברת הטלפונים?
12. האם הרבה או מעט קונים עובדים בחברת הטלפונים?

13. מי אחראי על שמירת קשר טלפוני תקין?
14. מדוע לדעתך צריכות מרכזיות הטלפון להיות תמיר במצב תקין?
15. מדוע לדעתך עובדות הרבה מרכזניות בחברת הטלפון?
16. מדוע לדעתך עובדים הרבה קונים בחברת הטלפון?
17. מדוע לדעתך קשר טלפוני הוא דבר חשוב?

שֶׁלָב "ג"

1. האם יש לך טלפון בבית?
2. האם ישנם הרבה טלפונים במקום עבודתך?
3. האם אתה מנהל הרבה שיחות חוץ?
4. האם אשתך מרברת הרבה בטלפון?
5. האם הטלפון בביתך תמיר במצב תקין?
6. האם ישנה מרכזיה גדולה במקום עבודתך?
7. האם יש לך חיוג ישיר במשרדך?
8. כמה שיחות טלפון אתה מנהל במשך היום?
9. האם אתה אוהב לרבר בטלפון?

10. האם אשתך או אתה מרברים הרבה בטלפון בבית?
11. האם יש לך חיוג ישיר במשרד או דרך המרכזיה?
12. האם אתה אוהב או שונא לרבר בטלפון?

13. ‏כמה מכשירי טלפון יש לך בבית?‏
14. ‏כמה שיחות אתה מנהל במשך היום?‏
15. ‏מה אתה עושה כשהטלפון שלך מקולקל?‏
16. ‏מה מספר הטלפון שלך בבית?‏
17. ‏כמה זמן מדברת אשתך בטלפון במשך היום?‏
18. ‏מה צבע מכשירי הטלפון בביתך?‏

Story 7.

‏פְּגִיעָה בָּרָצִיף‏

‏נֻסַח "אַ"‏

1. ‏מַשָּׂא   רחל היא אונית משא.‏
2. ‏רָצִיף   האוניה פגעה ברציף.‏
3. ‏חַרְטוֹם   היא פגעה בחרטומה   ברציף.‏
4. ‏עֲגִינָה   היא פגעה ברציף העגינה.‏
5. ‏תִּמְרוּן   היא פגעה ברציף   כעת תמרון.‏
6. ‏נִקְשְׁרָה   האוניה נקשרה למעגן.‏
7. ‏אֵירַע   המקרה אירע אור ליום ו'.‏
8. ‏נֶזֶק   נזק קטן   נגרם לרציף.‏

‏נֻסַח "בּ"‏

‏אניית המשא "רחל" של "צים" פגעה בחרטומה‏
‏ברציף העגינה בנמל הקישון, כעת תמרון ההתקשרות‏
‏למעגן.‏

‏המקרה אירע אור ליום ו' בשבוע שעבר. הנזק‏
‏שנגרם לרציף הוא קטן. לאניה לא נגרם נזק.‏

‏שָׁלָב "אַ"‏

1. ‏האם רחל היא אנית משא?‏
2. ‏האם האניה שייכת לחברת "צים"?‏
3. ‏האם האניה פגעה ברציף נמל הירקון?‏
4. ‏האם האניה פגעה בחרטומה ברציף?‏
5. ‏האם המקרה אירע אחרי הצהריים?‏
6. ‏האם הנזק שנגרם לרציף היה קטן?‏
7. ‏האם נגרם נזק לאנייה?‏

8. האם "רחל" היא אניה משא או אניה נוסעים?
9. האם האניה שייכת לחברת "צים" או לחברת "עוגן"?
10. האם האניה פגעה ברציף או במעגן?
11. האם האניה פגעה בחרטום או בצד?
12. האם האניה פגעה ברציף בעת תמרון או בעת טיול?
13. האם המקרה אירע אור ליום ה' או אור ליום ו'?
14. האם הנזק שנגרם לרציף היה גדול או קטן?

15. איזה אניה היא "רחל"?
16. למי שייכת האניה?
17. במה פגעה האניה?
18. ברציף של איזה נמל היא פגעה?
19. איזה תמרון התקיים בזמן פגיעת האנייה?
20. מתי קרה המקרה?
21. איזה נזק נגרם לרציף?
22. איזה נזק נגרם לאניה?

שָׁלָב "ב"

1. האם האניה "רחל" היא אניה גדולה?
2. האם הרבה מלחים משרתים על אנית משא?
3. האם זה דבר רגיל שאניה פוגעת ברציף?
4. האם תמרוני התקשרות מתקיימים לעתים תכופות?
5. האם בדרך כלל נגרם נזק לאניה כתוצאה מפגיעה?

6. האם הרבה או מעט מלחים משרתים על אנית משא?
7. האם זה דבר רגיל או דבר נדיר שאניה פוגעת ברציף?
8. האם בדרך כלל נגרם נזק לאניה או רק לעתים רחוקות?
9. מה היה הגורם לפגיעה?
10. היכן נמצא נמל הקישון?

שָׁלָב "ג"

1. האם שרתת פעם על אניית משא?
2. האם נסעת פעם באניית משא?
3. האם ראית פעם פגיעה?

503

4. האם האנייה שעליה אתה משרת היא אניית משא או
אניית מלחמה?

5. האם הרבה או מעט מלחים משרתים באנייה שלך?

6. האם השתתפת בתמרון התקשרות?

7. איזה אנייה היא האנייה שאתה משרת בה?

8. למה לדעתך תמרוני התקשרות הם תמרונים קשים?

9. איך לדעתך אפשר למנוע פגיעה ברציף?

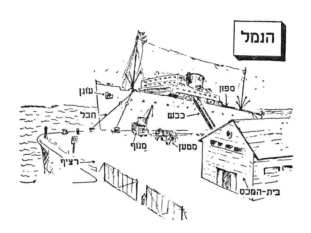

customs house	bet méxes	(m)	בית-מכס
rope	xével	(m)	חבל
gangplank	kéveš	(m)	כבש
cargo	mit'an	(m)	מטען
crane	manof	(m)	מנוף
deck	sipun	(m)	סיפון
anchor	ógen	(m)	עוגן
pier	racif	(m)	רציף

Story 8.

הנוכל המבוקש

נוסח "א"

1. משטרה	המשטרה מחפשת איש.
2. נוכל	האיש הוא נוכל.
3. סחורות	הוא הוציא סחורות.
4. מרמה	הוא הוציא את הסחורות במרמה.
5. שילם	הוא שילם בצ'קים.
6. כיסוי	לצ'קים לא היה כיסוי.
7. חשוד	החשוד היה בן 37.
8. נהג	הוא נהג להכנס לחנויות שונות.
9. הציג	הוא הציג את עצמו כבעל חנות.
10. קבלן	הוא הציג את עצמו כקבלן.

נוסח "ב"

המשטרה מחפשת אחרי נוכל, שהצליח להוציא
מבעלי חנויות בתל-אביב סחורות באלפי לירות
כשלמו בצ'קים ללא כיסוי.
החשוד, בן 37, נהג להכנס לחנויות שונות
בתל-אביב והציג עצמו חליפות, כקבלן, כבעל חנות
לצרכי חשמל, פקיד סוכנות ועוד. הוא רכש סחורות
שונות ושילם תמורתן בצ'קים שנמצאו ללא כיסוי.

שלב "א"

1.	האם המשטרה מחפשת אשה?
2.	האם האיש שהמשטרה מחפשת אחריו הוא נוכל?
3.	האם האיש הצליח להוציא סחורות מבעלי חנויות?
4.	האם הוא שילם בצ'קים?
5.	האם לצ'קים היה כיסוי?
6.	האם החשוד בן 35?
7.	האם הוא נהג להיכנס לחנויות שונות בתל אביב?
8.	האם הוא היה מציג את עצמו כבעל חנות?
9.	האם הוא רכש סחורות שונות?

505

10. ‏האם המשטרה מחפשת איש או אשה?‏
11. ‏האם האיש שהמשטרה מחפשת אחריו הוא נוכל או אדם ישר?‏
12. ‏האם שווי הסחורות היה של אלפי לירות או רק מאות לירות?‏
13. ‏האם המבוקש יותר צעיר מבן 35 או יותר מבוגר?‏
14. ‏האם הוא היה נוהג להיכנס לחנויות שונות או רק לחנות אחת?‏
15. ‏האם הוא רכש סחורות שונות או סחורות מסוג אחד?‏

16. ‏מה הצליח האיש להוציא מבעלי חנויות?‏
17. ‏באיזה שווי היו הסחורות שהאיש הוציא?‏
18. ‏במה הוא שילם?‏
19. ‏בן כמה החשוד?‏
20. ‏מה הוא נהג לעשות?‏
21. ‏איך הוא הציג את עצמו?‏
22. ‏איזה סוג סחורות הוא רכש?‏

‏שלב "ב"‏

1. ‏האם זה דבר רגיל שהמשטרה מחפשת אחרי נוכלים?‏
2. ‏האם ישנם הרבה נוכלים בעולם?‏
3. ‏האם זה דבר רגיל לשלם בצ'קים ללא כיסוי?‏
4. ‏האם אדם כגיל 37 הוא אדם צעיר?‏
5. ‏האם בדרך כלל נוכל נכנס לחנויות שונות?‏
6. ‏האם בדרך כלל נוכלים מציגים את עצמם כבעלי עסקים?‏
7. ‏האם נוכלים רוכשים בדרך כלל סחורות שונות?‏

8. ‏האם זה דבר רגיל או נדיר שהמשטרה תופסת נוכלים?‏
9. ‏האם ישנם מעט או הרבה נוכלים בעולם?‏
10. ‏האם זה דבר רגיל או בלתי רגיל לשלם בצ'קים ללא כיסוי?‏
11. ‏האם נוכלים מציגים את עצמם בדרך כלל כבעלי עסקים או
כמורים?‏

12. ‏איך יודעים שהחשוד בן 37?‏
13. ‏מה עושה הנוכל עם הסחורות שהוא רוכש?‏

שֶׁלַב "ג"

1. האם המשטרה חפשה אי-פעם אחריך?
2. האם נפגשת אי-פעם עם נוכל?
3. האם שלמת אי-פעם בצ׳ק ללא כיסוי?
4. האם היית חושד באדם שמציג את עצמו כתפקידים שונים?
5. האם לדעתך תשלום בצ׳קים ללא כיסוי זו עבירה חמורה?
6. האם היית קונס אדם שמשלם בצ׳קים ללא כיסוי?

7. האם לדעתך תשלום בצ׳קים ללא כיסוי זו עבירה חמורה או קלה?

8. מדוע המשטרה חפשה אחריך?
9. באיזה הזדמנות נפגשת עם נוכל?
10. מה היתה הסיבה ששילמת בצ׳ק ללא כיסוי?
11. כמה היית קונס אדם שמשלם בצ׳ק ללא כיסוי?

Story 9.

הקלפָן המֹיֹראש.

נוֹסח "א"

1. ישיש	הישיש הוא בן 92.
2. קלפן	הישיש הוא קלפן.
3. להתאבד	הוא רצה להתאבד.
4. זעק	הוא זעק בתחנת המשטרה.
5. מדוכא	האיש נראה מדוכא.
6. הפסיד	האיש הפסיד את כל כספו.
7. ירוד	מצבו הכלכלי והנפשי היה ירוד.
8. רחף	מצבו רחף אותו למעשה יאוש.
9. ותיק	האיש הוא ותיק בארץ.
10. גורש	הוא גורש מביתו על ידי אשתו.
11. בחוסר כל	הוא מסתובב ברחובות בחוסר כל.
12. יובא	הוא יובא היום בפני רופא פסיכיאטור.
13. חקירה	הוא יובא לרופא לשם חקירה.

נוסח "ב"

חיפה. – – "עצרו אותי, אני רוצה להתאבד" זעק
בשבת ישיש כבן 92 בתחנת המשטרה, בחיפה.
האיש שנראה מרוכא סיפר ליומנאי, כי הפסיד את כל
כספו במשחקי קלפים וכי מצבו הכלכלי והנפשי הירוד
דוחף אותו למעשה יאוש.
הישיש, שהוא ותיק בארץ, מסר עוד כי לפני חורש
גורש מביתו על ידי אשתו, ומסתובב ברחובות בחוסר כל.
"הקלפן המיואש" נשאר בינתיים בתחנת המשטרה
והיום הוא יובא בפני רופא-פסיכיאטור לשם חקירה.

שלב "א"

1.	האם הישיש גר בחיפה?
2.	האם הישיש הוא קלפן?
3.	האם הישיש רצה להתאבד?
4.	האם הוא זעק בתחנת המשטרה?
5.	האם האיש נראה מרוכא?
6.	האם האיש הפסיד את כל כספו?
7.	האם מצבו הנפשי ירוד?
8.	האם מצבו הרע דחף אותו למעשה יאוש?
9.	האם הישיש הוא ותיק בארץ?
10.	האם הוא גורש מביתו על ידי בנו?
11.	האם הוא מסתובב ברחובות בחוסר כל?
12.	האם הוא נמצא בתחנת האוטובוסים?
13.	האם הוא יובא לרופא פסיכיאטור לחקירה?
14.	האם הישיש הוא בן 92 או בן 120?
15.	האם הישיש גר בחיפה או בתל אביב?
16.	האם הישיש הוא קלפן או מנהל פנקסים?
17.	האם הישיש רצה לחיות או רצה להתאבד?
18.	האם הוא שחק או זעק בתחנת המשטרה?
19.	האם הישיש הרוויח או הפסיד את כספו בקלפים?
20.	האם מצבו הנפשי טוב או ירוד?
21.	האם הישיש ותיק בארץ או עולה חדש?
22.	האם הוא גורש מהבית על ידי בנו, או על ידי אשתו?
23.	האם הוא מסתובב ברחובות כאדם עשיר או בחוסר כל?
24.	האם הוא נמצא במשטרה או בבית מלון?
25.	האם הוא יובא לחקירה בפני רופא פסיכיאטור או כפני שופט?

26. בן כמה הישיש?
27. באיזה עיר הוא גר?
28. מה הוא עשה בתחנת המשטרה?
29. איך נראה האיש?
30. מה דחף אותו למעשה היאוש?
31. מי גרש את הישיש מביתו?
32. איך הוא הסתובב ברחובות?
33. היכן הוא נמצא ברגע זה?
34. למי הוא יובא לחקירה?

שלב "ב"

1. האם הישיש היה קלפן מקצועי?
2. האם בגדיו היו קרועים?
3. האם הוא היה רעב?
4. האם הוא הפסיד הרבה כסף?
5. האם השוטרים חקרו אותו?

6. האם האיש היה לבוש בבגדים שלמים או קרועים?
7. האם הוא היה רעב או שבע?
8. האם הוא הפסיד הרבה או מעט כסף בקלפים?

9. מה הביא את האיש למשחקי קלפים?
10. באיזה צורה ניסה הישיש להתאבד?
11. מה גרם לדכאון הנפשי שלו?
12. מה דחף את אשתו לגרש אותו מהכית?
13. היכן הוא התגורר עד זמן מעצרו?
14. למה הוא יובא בפני רופא פסיכיאטור?

שלב "ג"

1. האם אתה משחק בקלפים באופן קבוע?
2. האם אתה נהנה ממשחקי קלפים?
3. האם הפסדת את כל כספך בקלפים?
4. האם אי פעם רצית להתאבד?
5. האם גורשת אי פעם מביתך?
6. האם משחק קלפים מרגיע אותך?
7. האם קרה לך שהיית במצב נפשי ירוד?
8. האם אתה מיואש לפעמים?
9. האם הסתובבת אי פעם בחוסר כל?
10. האם נחקרת אי פעם על ידי חוקר משטרה?

האם אתה משחק בקלפים באופן קבוע או רק לעתים?   .11
הٰאם אתה מפסיד או מרויח כסף בקלפים?   .12
האם משחק קלפים מרגיע, או מרגיז אותך?   .13
האם אתה מיואש לפעמים, או תמיד במצב רוח טוב?   .14
האם נחקרת אי פעם על ידי מישהו, או אתה היית החוקר?   .15

למה אתה משחק בקלפים?   .16
מה עושה עבורך משחק קלפים?   .17
באיזה סכומי כסף אתה משחק?   .18
מה אתה עושה כשאתה במצב רוח ירוד?   .19
למה החוקר חקר אותך?   .20

Story 10.

<u>שוטד הציל חיי נוסעים</u>

נוסח "א"

חיים לוי הוא   סמל   במשטרת באר שבע.   סמל   .1
הוא הציל חמישה נוסעים.   הציל   .2
הנוסעים נתקעו במי שטפון.   נתקעו   .3
המקרה קרה ב-2.30 לפנות בקר.   לפנות בקר   .4
הנהג התקשר עם משטרת באר שבע.   התקשר   .5
הנהג לא יכול להתניע את המכונית.   להתניע   .6
הנוסעים לא יכלו לצאת   מהמכונית בגלל הגשם.   לצאת   .7
הגשם היה שוטף.   שוטף   .8
ניידת משטרה הגיעה למקום.   ניידת   .9
הנוסעים היו לכודים במכונית.   לכודים   .10
הסמל לוי כיצע הערכת מצב מהירה.   הערכת מצב   .11
הסמל פשט את בגריו.   פשט   .12
הוא חצה את האגם.   חצה   .13
הוא חילץ את הנוסעים אחד אחד.   חילץ   .14
בין החמישה שחולצו היתה תינוקת בת שנתיים.   תינוקת   .15
הנוסעים חזרו ממסיבת חתונה.   חזרו   .16

510

נוסח "ב"

סמל ממשטרת באר שבע, חיים לוי, הציל חיי
חמישה נוסעי מונית, שנתקעו במי השטפון.

ביום ו' בשעה 2:30 לפנות בוקר התקשר נהג
מונית עם משטרת באר שבע והודיע, כי מכוניתו
נתקעה בגשם ואינו יכול להתניעה. הוא הוסיף כי
במכונית נמצאים חמישה נוסעים שאינם יכולים לצאת
בגלל הגשם השוטף.

ניידת שהגיעה למקום מצאה, כי גובה המים עלה
בינתיים והנוסעים לכורים במונית בלי יכולת לצאת.
סמל לוי ניצע הערכח מצב מהירה, פשט את בגדיו וכשהוא
חוצה את אגם המים חילץ את הנוסעים אחד אחר. בין
החמישה שחולצו היתה תינוקת בת שנתחיים, שלוש נשים
ונער שכולם חזרו ממסיבת חתונה.

שלב "א"

האם חיים לוי הוא סמל נמשטרת באר שבע?	1.
האם הוא הציל חיי ארבעה נוסעים?	2.
האם הנוסעים נתקעו במי השטפון?	3.
האם המקרה קרה ב-3:30 לפנות בוקר?	4.
האם נהג המונית התקשר עם משטרת באר שבע?	5.
האם הנהג הודיע שהוא לא יכול להתניע את המונית?	6.
האם ירד גשם שוטף?	7.
האם ניידת המשטרה הגיעה לעזרת הנוסעים?	8.
האם הנוסעים היו לכורים במונית?	9.
האם הסמל פשט את בגדיו?	10.
האם הסמל חצה את האגם?	11.
האם הסמל חילץ את הנוסעים אחד אחד?	12.
האם בין הנוסעים היתה תינוקת בת שנתחיים?	13.
האם הנוסעים חזרו ממסיבת חתונה?	14.
האם חיים לוי הוא סמל או קצין?	15.
האם הוא הציל חיי 4 אנשים או 5 אנשים?	16.
האם המקרה קרה לפנות בקר או בשעות הערב?	17.
האם הנוסעים היו בתוך המונית או על ידה?	18.
האם הסמל חילץ את הנוסעים אחד אחד או כולם ביחד?	19.
האם הנוסעים חזרו ממסיבת חתונה או מנשף פורים?	20.

‫21.‬ ‫מי הוא חיים לוי?‬

‫22.‬ ‫מה עשה הסמל?‬

‫23.‬ ‫מה קרה לנוסעים?‬

‫24.‬ ‫מתי קרה המקרה?‬

‫25.‬ ‫מה עשה נהג המונית?‬

‫26.‬ ‫באיזה מצב היו הנוסעים?‬

‫27.‬ ‫כמה נוסעים היו במונית?‬

‫28.‬ ‫מאין חזרו הנוסעים?‬

‫שלב "ב"‬

‫1.‬ ‫האם תפקידו של שוטר הוא לעזור לבני אדם?‬

‫2.‬ ‫האם זה דבר רגיל שמונית מתקלקלת בזמן נסיעה?‬

‫3.‬ ‫האם הרבה מכוניות נתקעות במי שטפון?‬

‫4.‬ ‫האם זה דבר רגיל שגשם גורם לשטפון?‬

‫5.‬ ‫האם זה דבר רגיל לקחת תינוקת למסיבת חתונה?‬

‫6.‬ ‫האם זה דבר רגיל או נדיר שמכונית מתקלקלת בזמן נסיעה?‬

‫7.‬ ‫האם הרבה או מעט מכוניות נתקעות במי שטפון?‬

‫8.‬ ‫האם זה דבר רגיל או דבר נדיר שגשם גורם לשטפון?‬

‫9.‬ ‫מדוע לדעתך תפקידו של שוטר הוא לעזור לבני אדם?‬

‫10.‬ ‫מדוע מתקלקלות מכוניות בזמן נסיעה?‬

‫11.‬ ‫איך גורם גשם לשטפונות?‬

‫12.‬ ‫מדוע צריכים שוטרים לדעת לשחות?‬

‫13.‬ ‫מדוע לא יכלו הנוסעים לצאת מהמכונית?‬

‫14.‬ ‫מדוע התקשר הנהג עם משטרת באר שבע?‬

‫שלב "ג"‬

‫1.‬ ‫האם אתה שוטר?‬

‫2.‬ ‫האם קרה לך שהצלת חיי אדם?‬

‫3.‬ ‫האם קרה לך שלא יכולת להתניע את מכוניתך?‬

‫4.‬ ‫האם קרה לך שנתקעת בשטפון?‬

‫5.‬ ‫האם אתה יודע לשחות?‬

‫5.‬ ‫האם אתה שוטר או חייל?‬

‫6.‬ ‫האם קרה לך שהצלת חיי אדם או אף פעם לא?‬

‫7.‬ ‫האם קרה לך שלא יכולת להתניע את המכונית שלך,‬
‫או אף פעם לא?‬

‫8.‬ ‫האם אתה שחיין טוב או לא כל כך?‬

9. איזה חפקיד אחה ממלא?

10. איזה מכונית אחה נוהג?

11. איזה שחיין אתה?

12. באיזה מצב המכונית שלך?

The following section of the Reader contains selections from newspapers
and periodicals. New vocabulary is given with illustrative sentences. These
sentences do not necessarily reflect the content of the story itself. Occasionally these sentences use forms of the new words which are different from the
forms occurring in the story. Many words which seem new or strange at first
glance are simply different forms of words or roots familiar from the preceding
parts of the course. Only the more unusual abbreviations are explained.

The selections are not presented in any particular order of subject
matter. Comparative difficulty has been taken into account, the shorter, easier
articles being presented first, but the judgment is subjective.

Selections were made mainly from 1965 publications, but many articles were
selected specifically because they would not become dated.

Story 11.

הדירה שלנו קטנה אך חדישה מאד.	apartment /dira/ (f)	דירה
בעל הבית השכיר את הדירה לעולים חדשים.	he rented out /hiskir/	השכיר
הצבעי רצה יותר מדי כסף לצבוע את הדירה.	painter /cabai/ (m)	צבעי
החדר שלו מלא קופסאות ריקות.	empty /reyk/ (m.s.)	ריק
נוכחתי שהשעה מאוחרת מאד.	he realized /noxax/	נוכח
למה אתם מתלוננים כל כך?	he complained /hitlonen/	התלונן
באיזה מדור של החברה את עובדת?	section, department /mador/ (m)	מדור
זו לא היתה רמאות - הוא לא הכין מה שאמרנו לו.	deception, swindle /ramaut/(f)	רמאות
לא יכולתי למצוא את המפתח למזוודה.	key /maftéax/ (m)	מפתח
בעל הבית גבתה את שכר דירה מהם.	he collected /gava/	גבה

קיבל דירה לצביעה -
והשכיר אותה ל-3 חדשים

- מאת סופר "מעריב" -

צבעי, שקיבל על עצמו צביעת דירה ריקה ברמת-יצחק
ברמת-גן, נעצר אתמול על ידי המשטרה, אחר שבעל
הדירה, שמסר לו את העבודה, נוכח להפתעתו, כי
דירתו הושכרה על-ידי הצבעי לדיירים חדשים.
אתמול אחר הצהריים התלונן במדור הרמאויות במחוז
תל-אביב מר שלמה ברשקובסקי מחל-אביב, בעל דירה
ריקה ברחוב הרא"ה ברמת-גן. לפי דבריו, הוא מסר לפני
כשבועיים דירה בת שני חדרים לצביעה ומסר את המפתחות
לצבעי. אתמול בבוקר, כאשר ביקר בדירה, מצא בה ...
דיירים. הם סיפרו לו, כי הדירה הושכרה להם על-ידי הצבעי
שסיפר להם כי בעלי הדירה נסעו לארה"ב, וגבה מהם 600 ל"י
שכר דירה בעד 3 חדשים.

Story 12.

חדיר וכשאינו תדיר – תדיר קודם.	frequent	/tadir/ (m.s.)	תדיר
שרות המכוניות הוגבר בערב החג.	it was strengthened	/hugbar/	הוגבר
הוא יעבור בחברת החשמל החל מיום שני.	beginning from, as of	/haxel mi/–מ החל	
המשכורת שלי גבוהה השנה לעומת השנה שעברה.	against, opposite	/leumat/	לעומת
התנועה בשעות 4 – 6 חזקה מאד.	traffic, movement	/tnua/(f)	תנועה
השירות הסדיר יתחיל בשבוע הבא.	regular	/sadir/ (m.s.)	סדיר
המכוניות החדשות פחות מרווחות מהמכוניות הישנות.	spacious	/meruvax/ (m.s.)	מרווח

"אגד" יוסיף מכוניות
בקו אילת – תל-אביב

חדירות שרותי "אגד" לאילת הוגבר החל מיום
א' הקרוב ע"י הוספת מכונית ששית לקו תל-אביב –
אילת וחזרה.
שלוש מכוניות כיום תסענה לאילת דרך מעלה
העצמאות ומכחש רמון ו-3 תסענה דרך הערבה
ככביש החדש. לעומת זאת, התנועה מאילת לתל-אביב
תתנהל 4 פעמים ביום דרך מעלה העצמאות ורק פעמיים
ביום דרך הערבה.
השירות הסדיר של "אגד" לאילת מתנהל במכוניות
תיירים מרווחות.

– מאת "מעריב" –

515

Story 13.

שיפ״ר	/šiper/	he improved	הממשלה שיפרה את הרחובות במרכז העיר.
רכש	/raxaš/	he acquired	רכשנו הרבה חברים בארץ.
אפיק	/afik/ (m)	channel	עכשיו יש שני אפיקים בכבל הטלפוני.
תת-ימי	/tatyami/ (m.s.)	undersea	הכבל התת-ימי הונח לפני עשר שנים.
יבשה (f)/	/yabaša/	continent, dry land	כמה יבשות יש בעולם?
בוסס	/busas/	it was based	הקשר מבוסס על קו ישיר.
קרקע	/karka/ (m)	land, ground	קנינו קרקע קרוב למרכז העיר.
רשת	/réšet/ (f)	network	רשת הטלפונים באמריקה היא הגדולה בעולם.
משא ומתן	/masa umatan/	negotiations	המו״מ נמשך עד שהגענו להסכם.
קיים	/kayam/ (m.s.)	existing, lasting	דוד מלך ישראל חי וקיים.
צמצם	/cimcem/	he reduced	צמצמנו את הוצאות העבודה.

דואר ישראל ישפר הקשר
הטלפוני עם ארצות אמריקה
מאת צבי לביא

דואר ישראל הקציב 2.5 מליון ל"י, כדי לרכוש זכויות
שימוש בשני אפיקים של הכבל הטלפוני התת-ימי והטראנס-אטלנטי,
המחבר את אירופה עם יבשת אמריקה.

הדבר נעשה, כדי לשפר את איכות הקשר הטלפוני בין ישראל
לארה"ב ושאר מדינות אמריקה, המבוסס עתה על קשר ראדיו ישיר.

הזכויות יירכשו בכביל חדש, שיונח בקרוב על קרקע האוקיאנוס
האטלנטי ויתווסף לרשת הכבילים המונחת שם מכבר. המו"מ על הרכישה
מתנהל עתה עם הדואר הבריטי וחברת טלפון אמריקנית.

הקשר הקיים סובל מהפרעות אטמוספיריריות וקוסמיות, אשר יצומצמו
עד מאוד לאחר שתהיה בידי דואר ישראל הזכות להעביר שיחות טלפון דרך
הכביל התת-ימי. אז חועברנה שיחות טלפון ברדיו רק עד צרפת, ומשם
בכביל לאמריקה.

Story 14.

הילדים לא מצייתים להוריהם.	he obeyed	/ciyet/	ציית
הנהג לא ציית לתמרור "עצור".	signpost	/tamrur/ (m)	תמרור
התאונה אירעה בצומת דרכים ליד בית החולים.	juncture	/cómet/ (m)	צומת
האופנוע התנגש באוטובוס ברחוב הירקון.	he collided	/hitnageš/	התנגש
אני מפחד לנסוע על קטנוע.	motor scooter	/katnóa/ (m)	קטנוע
צריכים להזהר כשחוצים כביש.	he crossed	/xaca/	חצה

פצועים בתאונות דרכים 3

אוטובוס "דן", שהיה נהוג בידי אברהם כהן,
שלא ציית לתמרור "עצור" בצומת הרחובות ברון הירש
ופינסקר בפ"ת, התנגש בקטנוע שהיה נהוג בידי שמעון
לוי בן 24 מראש העין ופצעו קשה.

בתאונת דרכים אחרת, שארעה בצומת כביש השרון
וכפר סבא, נפצע קשה דוד בן ישראל, בן 47 משיכון
נווה עמל בהרצליה כאשר נפגע על-ידי רוכב קטנוע
בעת שחצה את הכביש.

בתאונת דרכים שארעה אמש ברחוב הרצל, כרמת גן,
נפצע קשה ישיש בן 70, שמואל אברהם מנחלת גנים
כאשר נפגע על-ידי רוכב קטנוע בעת שחצה את הכביש.
הוא הועבר לבית החולים בתל-השומר.

— מאת "מעריב" —

517

Story 15.

מנחם בא מאוחר על אף שם מוקדם הבוקר.	in spite of	/al af/	על אף
הם החליטו לחת את הכסף בלי התנגדות.	opposition	/hitnagdut/ (f)	התנגרות(f)
הנציגים מארה"ב יגיעו מחרתיים.	representative	/nacig/ (m)	נציג
הוא חבר בסיעה השמאלית.	party, group	/sia/ (f)	סיעה
שלושה אנשים התפטרו מהמועצה אחרי הישיבה.	council	/moaca/ (f)	מועצה
מועצת העיריה מתאספת כל שבועיים.	municipality	/iria/ (f)	עיריה
עוד לא שלמנו את מס ההכנסה.	tax	/mas/ (m)	מס
המסים העירוניים הועלו בשנה שעברה.	municipal	/ironi/ (m.s.)	עירוני
חברי המועצה מדברים על השאילתא שהוצגה.	official query	/šeilta/ (f)	שאילתא
הסיבות שהביא לא מחקבלות על הרעת.	reason	/siba/ (f)	סיבה
הסיעה הדתית התפטרה מהמועצה.	religious	/dati/ (m.s.)	דתי

הועלה מחיר המים ברמת-גן
מאת סופר "למרחב" כגוש דן

רמת גן. — על אף התנגדות נציגי סיעת מפא"י החליטה אמש
מועצת עירית רמת-גן, ברוב קולות, להעלות את מחיר המים
לתושבים. גובה ההעלאה הוא 17 אחוז, לפי קביעת ההנהלה.
המתנגדים טוענים שההעלאה הממשית מגיעה ל-70 אחוז.

בישיבה הוחלט לא להעלות השנה את המסים העירוניים.
בראשית הישיבה הציג א. אלקס, מ.יעת מפא"י, שאילתא לראש העיר,
לפיה נתבקש קרינוצי להודיע מה היו הסיבות, שהניאו השבוע להתפטרות
ראש המועצה הדתית בעיר מתפקידו.

518

Story 16.

המים בבאר הזאת קרים ומתוקים.	well	/be'er/ (f)	בְּאֵר
בית כנסת בצפת ישוחזר ע"י העיריה.	it was restored	/šuxzar/	שׁוּחֲזַר
נולדתי בירושלים בעיר העתיקה.	ancient	/atik/ (m.s.)	עַתִיק
החנות חשופץ ע"י הבעלים החדשים.	it was renovated	/šupac/	שׁוּפַּץ
הם השיגו את המטרה בלי שום קושי.	purpose, target	/matara/ (f)	מַטָרָה
ייחסו את ההצלחה לעבודה הקשה שלו.	he attributed	/yixes/	יִחֵס
הוא עלה לארץ בתקופת המנדט הבריטי.	period, era	/tkufa/ (f)	תְקוּפָה
התיקונים עלו לו הרבה כי הבית היה מוזנח.	it was neglected	/huznax/	הוּזְנַח
השגרירות הוקפה ע"י שוטרים.	it was surrounded	/hukaf/	הוּקַף
העיריה תקים את ההריסות בעיר העתיקה.	ruin	/harisa/ (f)	הֲרִיסָה
הפועלים יתחילו מחר בהכשרת הקרקע.	making fit	/haxšara/ (f)	הַכְשָׁרָה
בתי דירות יוקמו בשטח הזה.	area	/šetax/ (m)	שֶׁטַח
התלמידים יעזרו בנטיעת העצים.	planting	/netia/ (f)	נְטִיעָה

תשוחזר באר אברהם

מאת סופר "למרחב" בנגב

באר שבע. – באר אברהם אבינו שבעיר העתיקה
בבאר שבע חשופץ ותשוחזר ע"י העיריה במטרה להפכה
לאטרקציה לתיירים.

הבאר שמייחסים אותה לתקופת האבות, היתה עד כה
מוזנחת ומוקפת הריסות ומבנים ישנים. בימים אלה
החלה העיריה בפינוי ההריסות והכשרת השטח לנטיעת
פארק עירוני.

Story 17.

מַסָע	/masa/ (m)	journey	במסעו האפריקני הוא יבקר בשמונה ארצות.
חניך	/xanix/ (m)	apprentice	חניכי בית הספר לומדים שש שעות ביום.
ערך	/arax/	he arranged	הנשים תערוכנה את התוכנית לסוף השבוע.
תחפשֹׁת	/taxpóset/ (f)	masquerade	היתה להם תחפושת מוצלחת בחג הפורים.
התלווה	/hitlava/	he joined	אחי התלווה אלי בנסיעה.
כלי	/kli/ (m)	instrument, dish	אני לא אוהב לרחוץ כלים.
איכר	/ikar/ (m)	farmer	האיכרים העלו את מחירי הירקות.
חצר	/xacer/ (f)	yard	לבית הספר חצר גדולה למשחקים.

מסע עדלאידע בקריית ביאליק
מאת סופר "למרחב"

חיפה. – מאות תלמידי ביה"ס הממלכתי בקרית
ביאליק ועמם חניכי ביה"ס הטכני של חיל האוויר, יערכו
היום אחה"צ, ברחובות הקרייה מסע עדלאידע.

למסע התחפושות יתלוו טרקטורים וכלים חקלאיים
אחרים של איכרי כפר ביאליק. בחצר ביה"ס יפתח בשעות
הערב "לונה פארק" לילדי הקריה.

Story 18.

יוֹשֵׁב ראש	/yóševroš/ (m)	chairman	.חברי המועצה בחרו אותו ליושב-ראש
הִמְרִיא	/himri/	he took off (by plane)	היועץ החדש המריא היום מניו יורק בדרכו לארץ.
בירה	/bira/ (f)	capital	.ירושלים היא בירת ישראל
שֶׁנהב	/šenhav/ (m)	ivory	.רוב השנהב בא מארצות אפריקה והודו
תוֹם	/tom/ (m)	end	.הוא המריא מלוד בתום ביקורו בישראל
נוֹעַד	/no'ad/	he met	.הנשיא נועד אתמול עם ראש הממשלה
תחום	/txum/ (m)	area, boundary	.הוא יצא מתחום העיר
משוּתף	/mešutaf/	shared, cooperative	.הם הצליחו בעבודה המשותפת
מִשְׁלחת	/mišláxat/ (f)	delegation	.היו"ר קבל את פני המשלחת

קדיש לוז בקמרון

אבידג'אן, 18 (ע"צ) – יו"ר הכנסת, קדיש לוז,
המריא היום מאבידג'אן, בירת חוף-השנהב, בתום ביקור
של 48 שעות, אל התחנה הבאה במסעו האפריקני – יאונדה,
בירת קמרון.

אתמול נועד קריש לוז עם נשיא חוף-השנהב, הופואה-
בואני, והיום, לפני שהמריא לדרכו, אמר לעתונאים, כי
לישראל ולחוף-השנהב תחומי התעניינות משותפים רבים.

יו"ר הכנסת הבטיח קבלת-פנים חמה כיותר למשלחת
של חברי פרלמנט מחוף-השנהב, אשר תבקר בישראל.

521

Story 19.

.מגדל השידור יוקם בחודש הבא	tower	/migdal/ (m)	מגדל
.חפרו יסודות למגדל השידור	foundation	/yesod/ (m)	יסוד
.גובה המגדל יגיע ל-100 מטרים	height	/góva/ (m)	גובה
.המגדל ישא על פיסגתו את אנטנת הטלביזיה	peak	/pisga/ (f)	פיסגה
.אנטנת הטלביזיה תתנשא לגובה של 18 מטרים	he reached up	/hitnase/	התנשא
.אנשי שירות ההנדסה יקימו את המגדל	engineering	/handasa/ (f)	הנדסה
.עברנו לגור במחוז הדרום	district, region	/maxoz/ (m)	מחוז
.קניתי שולחן להרכבה עצמית	putting together	/harkava/ (f)	הרכבה
.השולחן היה מפורק	unassembled	/meforak/	מפורק
.הקליטה כרדיו טובה מאד	reception	/klita/ (f)	קליטה
.האוכלוסיה בישראל גדלה בשנה האחרונה	population	/uxlusia/	אוכלוסיה
.הכבישים החדשים רחבים מאד	wide	/raxav/ (m.s.)	רחב
.בית הדין העליון נמצא בירושלים	uppermost, supreme	/elyon/ (m.s.)	עליון
.הוא מחוסן נגד שפעת	protected	/mexusan/ (m.s.)	מחוסן
.שיטת הלימודים בבית הספר היא קלה	system, method	/šita/ (f)	שיטה
.המשדר החדש יהיה בעל עוצמה חזקה	power, strength	/ocma/ (f)	עוצמה
.עוצמת השידור היתה זעירה	small, low	/zair/ (m.s.)	זעיר

היום יוחל בהקמת מגדל השידור לטלביזיה
מאת סופר "מעריב"

ירושלים. - הבוקר יחל הדואר ישראל בחפירת היסודות למגדל השידור
לטלביזיה בהרי-יהודה - על כך מסר דובר משרד הדואר.

המגדל, שיגיע לגובה של 100 מטרים, ישא על פסגתו את אנטנת הטלביזיה,
שתתנשא לגובה של 18 מטרים נוספים.   עם השלמת היסודות יחלו אנשי שירות

הנדסת הראדיו של משרד הדואר במחוז ירושלים והדרום, בהרכבת המגדל עצמו, אשר חלקיו
המפורקים כבר מצויים במקום. ליד המגדל חיבכה תחנת השידור לטלביזיה. משדר זה
יאפשר קליטת שידוריו לאוכלוסיה במרכז הארץ. אנטנת הטלביזיה עומדת להגיע מחוץ לארץ
בחודשיים הקרובים. מגדל זה ישמש גם להפעלת שידורי רדיו בשיטת ה"אף אם", לצורכי
הקהל הרחב. שיטה זו מאפשרת שידורי רדיו באיכות עליונה ומחוסנת מפני הפרעות. דואר
ישראל מפעיל כיום שידורים בשטה זו לצרכיו הטכניים, בשלוש הערים הגדולות, בעוצמות
זעירות. משדר זה, שיופעל תוך שנה, לערך, הוא שלב ראשון בהקמת רשת של משדרי
"אף אם", בכל רחבי הארץ.

Story 20.

בעונת החורף ירדו שלגים רבים.	season	/ona/ (f)	עונה
בחפירות האחרונות נתגלו כלים עתיקים מאד.	digging	/xafira/ (f)	חפירה
באיזור ההרים קריר בקיץ.	district	/eyzor/ (m)	איזור
המטיילים חשפו דרכים חדשות.	he uncovered	/xasaf/	חשף
אתר עתיק נתגלה בחפירות.	site	/atar/ (m)	אתר
מי הנחל נשפכים אל הים.	brook, stream	/náxal/ (m)	נחל
נערכה מסיבה לחברי המשלחת.	gathering, party	/mesiba/ (f)	מסיבה
המסיבה נערכה במועדון.	club, meeting hall	/moadon/ (m)	מועדון
היו"ר הטעים את חשיבות הפעולה.	he stressed	/hit'im/	הטעים
החברים סיירו במכרה זהב.	mine	/mixre/ (m)	מכרה
עקב הגשמים נסגר הכביש לתנועה.	because of	/ékev/	עקב
ייצור המכוניות הוגבר השנה.	manufacturing	/yicur/ (m)	ייצור
בחפירות נמצאו מטבעות נחושת עתיקים.	copper	/nexóšet/ (f)	נחושת
הסיור נדחה בגלל מחלת מורה-הדרך.	on account of	/biglal/	בגלל
הממשלה ערכה סקר על כמות מי הגשמים.	survey	/séker/ (m)	סקר
הצוללנים הם שחיינים מצויינים.	frogman	/colelan/ (m)	צוללן
שרידי הכלים שנמצאו הועברו למוזיאון.	remnant	/sarid/ (m)	שריד

מנהל המוזיאון העריך את התגליות החדשות.	discovery	/taglit/ (f)	תגלית
בסיכום דבריו ציין המנהל את חשיבות העבודה.	summary	/sikum/ (m)	סיכום
השוטר מסר עדות בבית המשפט.	evidence	/edut/ (f)	עדות

עונת החפירות השניה בזמנע
תיפתח ב-28 במארס

תל אביב. – עונת החפירות השניה באיזור תמנע תיפתח ב-28
במארס, על-ידי משלחת הערבה הארכיאולוגית, בראשותו של ד"ר
בנו רוטנברג.

החפירות – מטעם מוזיאון הארץ והטכניון, בשיתוף עם
האוניברסיטה של תל-אביב תנוהל ע"י אפי יכין מהאוניברסיטה
של תל-אביב ומטרתן לחשוף אתר פרהיסטורי בכניסה לנחל תמנע,
שהוא מהתקופה הכלקוליתית.

ד"ר רוטנברג, שמסר על כך אתמול במסיבה השבועית של
מועדון רוטרי, ב"בית ציוני אמריקה", הטעים כי עוד בשנת
1960 גילתה המשלחת מכרה מאותה תקופה וגם מחנה עבורה, שנהרסו
עקב עבודות הפיתוח של מפעל תמנע החדש. האתר שאותו עומדים לחשוף
עתה, הוא כנראה מחנה העבורה והייצור של נחושת, ואף הוא נמצא
בסכנה בגלל עבודות הפיתוח במקום.

ד"ר רוטנברג הוסיף, כי משלחת הערבה תפתח גם בסקר תת-ימי של
חוף ים-סוף בעזרת צוללנים-מתנדבים, במטרה למצוא שרידים של
אניות או כלים. הסקר קשור בתגליות אחרות שנמצאו בסביכה בזמן
האחרון.

סיכום העונה הראשונה של החפירות, מראה כי תעשיית הנחושת
בערבה הוקמה, כנראה, ע"י ממלכת אדום. בתקופה שלפני המלוכה
הישראלית. לא נמצאה כל עדות לקיום של מכרות מתקופת שלמה
המלך – ציין ד"ר רוטנברג.

Story 21.

אנו עומדים על סף תקופה חדשה.	threshold	/saf/ (m)	סַף
סוף סוף נמצא הפתרון לשאלות.	solution	/pitaron/ (m)	פִּתְרוֹן
החומרים מיובאים מארה"ב.	material	/xómer/ (m)	חוֹמֶר
המלצר הגיש את הארוחה.	he offered	/higiš/	הִגִּישׁ
הכניסה מותרת לכל הגילים.	permitted	/mutar/ (m.s.)	מוּתָּר
אין תחליף לקפה טוב.	substitute	/taxlif/ (m)	תַּחְלִיף
בגנה זאת צמחים נהדרים.	plant, vegetation	/cémax/ (m)	צֶמַח
מסרתי את הבגדים לניקוי חימי.	chemical	/ximi/ (m.s.)	חִימִי
הועדה החליטה לצרף את משה.	committee	/vaada/ (f)	וְעָדָה
הפקיד קבל הכשר לעבודה סורית.	fitness decree	/hexšer/ (m)	הֶכְשֵׁר
החום בימים אלה פשוט בלתי נסבל.	insufferable	/bilti nisbal/	בִּלְתִּי נִסְבָּל
החיירים סבלו מתלאות הדרך.	hardship	/tlaa/ (f)	תְּלָאָה
התייר הביע את כעסו על התלאות.	he expressed	/hibía/	הִבִּיעַ
אורחי המלון נהנים מבריכת השחייה.	guest	/oréax/ (m)	אוֹרֵחַ
קץ התלאות הגיע כשבאנו למלון.	end	/kec/ (m)	קֵץ
שלג ירד השנה לעתים די תכופות.	often	/txufot/	תְּכוּפוֹת
משה מלא מרירות על משכורתו הנמוכה.	bitterness	/merirut/ (f)	מְרִירוּת
הוא דיבר ברוגז רב עם המנהל.	anger	/rógez/ (m)	רוֹגֶז

חלב מאפשר לשמותו אחרי אכילת בשר

מאת סופר "מעריב" לעניני תיירות

אחת הבעיות הקשות ביותר של התיירות בישראל עומדת על סף פתרון:
באחד מבתי-המלון הגדולים ייכנס לשימוש חלב – שאין בו שום חמרי חלב – שניתן
להגישו יחד עם ארוחות-בשר. כן מותר "תחליף החלב" לשימוש בבישול, בהכנת
גלידה ודברי-מאפה וכו'.

בחלב זה, המיוצר בארה"ב מצמחים וחמרים כימיים, נעשה מבחן ע"י
"ועדת הטעימה" של מלון "שרתון" בתל-אביב וחברי הוועדה טוענים, כי רובם לא
הצליחו להבחין בין "חלב" זה לבין חלב אמיתי. החלב "פארווה" – קיבל הכשר
מטעם פקחי-הכשרות של המלון ויוגש לאורחי "שרתון" החל בשבוע הבא.   כך יושם
קץ למצב כלתי-נסבל ולתלאות אין-קץ מצד תיירים, המכיעים תכופות מרירות ורוגז
על שאינם יכולים לשתות קפה או תה בחלב לאחר ארוחתם.

הנהלת "שרתון" כבר הביאה כמות "חלב" אשר תספיק לחדשיים ועל
אף מחירו הגבוה כבר עומד המלון להזמין כמויות נוספות.

Story 22.

עסקתי כעבודה כל היום.	he was busy	/asak/	עסק
בכל בית יש מכשיר כיבוי.	extinguishing	/kibuy/ (m)	כיבוי
הכבאים כיבו את הדליקה.	fire, conflagration	/dleka/ (f)	דליקה
הדליקה פרצה בקומה השביעית.	it burst, broke out	/parac/	פרץ
המזבלה המרכזית נמצאת רחוק מהעיר.	dump	/mizbala/(f)	מזבלה
הדליקה פרצה סמוך לחצות.	nearby, close to	/samux/ (m.s.)	סמוך
עבדתי הקיץ במשק.	farm	/méšek/(m)	משק
הדליקה פשטה במהירות רבה.	it spread, stretched	/pašat/	פשט
האש השחיתה עצים רבים.	he destroyed	/hišxit/	השחית
התבואה היתה יבשה.	harvest	/tvua/ (f)	תבואה
שני הרחובות מקבילים זה לזה.	parallel	/makbil/	מקביל
הדליקה פשטה בצד השני של החצר.	side	/cad/ (m)	צד

האש כובתה במהירות, אולם נזק כבל זאת נגרם.   however   /ulam/   אולם

מנחם הסתפק במשכורת נמוכה.   he was satisfied   /histapek/   הסתפק

מנהל הפנקסים אחראי כלפי רואה החשבון.   opposite, against   /klapey/   כלפי

אנשי משמר מישראל וירדן
עסקו בכיבוי דליקה בשדה

מאת סופר "מעריב"

אנשי משמר הגבול הישראליים ולגיונרים ירדניים
עסקו אתמול בשעות הצהריים בכיבוי דליקת שדה גדולה, שפרצה
במזבלה הסמוכה למשק מבוא-ביתר ופשטה אל שטח ירדן בהשחיתה
שרות תבואה שם.

פעולות הכיבוי נמשכו שעות אחדות והתנהלו במקביל
בשני צידי הגבול, אולם, לא הורגש שיתוף פעולה בין שני
הצדדים, אשר הסתפקו בהחלפת קריאות אלה כלפי אלה.

527

Story 23.

הוא התייצב לשירות צבאי.	he was present	/hityacev/	התייצב
אליזבת היא מלכת אנגליה.	queen	/malka/	מלכה
כל שגריר חדש מגיש כתב-האמנה.	credentials	/ktav haamana/	כתב-האמנה
השגריר היה לבוש בהתאם להוראות.	instruction	/horaa/ (f)	הוראה
הוא חבש צילינדר.	top hat	/cilinder/	צילינדר
רעיית השגריר נלוותה אליו.	wife	/raaya/	רעייה
טקס מסירת כתב-האמנה נערך בשעה 1 בצהריים.	ceremony	/tékes/ (m)	טקס
הציר הישראלי הגיע לוועידה.	minister	/cir/ (m)	ציר
הנספח הצבאי החדש הגיע לשגרירות.	attaché	/nispax/ (m)	נספח
ארמון המלכה הוא מבנה עתיק ביותר.	palace	/armon/ (m)	ארמון
השגריר הגיע לטקס במרכבה.	chariot	/merkava/ (f)	מרכבה
השגריר נתקבל בטקס מלכותי.	royal	/malxuti/ (m.s.)	מלכותי

השגריר רמז יתייצב בפני המלכה אליזבת ביום ה'

מאת סופר "מעריב" בלונדון

טלגרפית.

שגרירה החדש של ישראל בבריטניה, מר אהרון רמז, ימסור
את כתב-האמנתו למלכה אליזבת ביום ה'.

מר רמז ילבש בהזדמנות זו - בהתאם להוראות חצר סנט ג'יימס -
פראק וצילינדר, רעייתו תלבש שמלת ערב, אף כי הטקס ייערך בשעה
1 בצהריים.

השגריר החדש ורעייתו, בלוויית הציר אפריים עברון, הציר הכללי,
מר שמחה סורוקר, הנספח הצבאי, אלוף משה גורן, ונספח העתונות, מר
מתתיהו שרון, יצעו מן השגרירות לארמון באקינגהם, בשלוש מרכבות
מלכותיו ז.

Story 24.

אדם שאינו אוכל בשר הוא אדם צמחוני.	vegetarian	/cimxoni/(m)	צמחוני
אמירים הוא כפר של טבעונים.	naturalist	/tiv'oni/(m)	טבעוני
נערכה מסיבה לרגל פתיחת העונה.	for the purpose of	/lerégel/	לרגל
הרבה אנשים יוצאים לקייט לגליל.	summer vacation	/káit/ (m)	קייט
שאר האנשים יושבים בבית.	remainder	/šear/ (m)	שאר
רוב המושבים נמצאים בצפון הארץ.	settlement	/mošav/ (m)	מושב
מזון קונים בחנות המכולת.	food	/mazon/ (m)	מזון
טעמו של הסוכר החום גס יותר מטעמו של הסוכר הלבן.	coarse, plain	/gas/ (m.s.)	גס
חלב הוא משקה מזין.	nutritious	/mezin/ (m.s.)	מזין
אדם שאוכל מאכלי בשר הוא אדם בשרני.	meat eater	/basrani/(m)	בשרני
הצמחונים מתנזרים מבשר.	he abstained	/hitnazer/	התנזר
האיש הלה אינו אוכל בשר.	that one	/hala/	הלה
האורח הסיט את כוס התה.	he pushed aside	/hesit/	הסיט
אמנם האיש אוהב תה, אך עם סוכר לבן.	indeed	/omnam/	אמנם
הוא לגם מהקפה והסיט את הכוס.	he sipped	/lagam/	לגם
האיש מחבב לשתות בורשט קר.	he liked	/xibev/	חיבב
הוא אוהב לשתות כל דבר לחוד.	separately	/lexud/	לחוד

זה וכורשט...

במסיבת עתונאים שנערכה כפר הצמחונים והטבעונים
אמירים, לרגל פתיחת עונת הקייט הראשונה במקום, סיפר בין השאר
חבר המושב, מר יהושע רובן, כי את מזונם ממתיקים תושבי "אמירים"
בסוכר חום, אשר טעמו גס יותר ומזכיר את טעם הלחם, ובכל זאת
הוא מזין ובריא יותר.

בקשר לכך הוסיף מר רונן, המשמע גם כמזכיר המועצה האזורית
מרום-הגליל: "כאשר ביקר נכבדי אורח בשרבי (כלומר, שאינו מתנזר
ממאכלי בשר) הגשתי לפניו תה ממותק בסוכר חום. טעם הלה מן התה,
אך מיד הסיט את הכוס הצידה ואמר: 'ישעיהו, אני אמנם אוהב ללגום
תה ומחבב לשתות כורשט - אך כל אחד לחוד ולא כשהם ממוזגים יחדיו'..."

Story 25.

אש נפתחה ממוצב סורי.	position	/mucav/(m)	מוצב
הסורים פתחו באש מנשק אוטומטי.	weapons	/nések/(m)	נשק
הם פתחו באש לעבר המשק.	across	/leéver/	לעבר
החציר עלה באש.	hay	/xacir/ (m)	חציר
הגשם ירד לסירוגין.	intermittently	/leserugin/	לסירוגין
האש נמשכה כמחצית השעה.	half	/maxcit/(f)	מחצית
הטרקטוריסט תפס מקום מחבוא.	he seized	/tafas/	תפס
הילדים הוכנסו למקום מחסה.	refuge, shelter	/maxse/(m)	מחסה
המשטרה ערכה חקירה.	investigation	/xakira/(f)	חקירה
המשקיפים יצאו למקום.	observer	/maškif/(m.s.)	משקיף
משקיפי האו"ם הפסיקו את האש.	United Nations /umot meuxadot/		אומות מאוחדות
הטרקטוריסט חולץ מאיזור האש.	he was rescued	/xulac/	חולץ

הסורים ירהו באש על טרקטוריסט

כתבריה. - מוצבים סוריים פתחו באש מנשק אוטומאטי לעבר טרקטוריסט
של קיבוץ תל-קציר אשר עבד בשדרות המשק אתמול אחה"צ.

האש נפתחה בשעה 17.20, כאשר הטרקטוריסט עבר כחלקת החציר.
האש נמשכה לסירוגין כמחצית השעה.

הטרקטוריסט הצליח לתפוס מחסה, אולם נשאר בשטח כשטח עד ליאחר גמר
חקירת משקיפי האו"ם, ירק אז חולץ, יחד עם הטרקטור.

Story 26.

צה"ל הוא צבא ההגנה לישראל.	defense	/hagana/ (f)	הגנה
השיעור עובר בקצב מהיר.	rhythm, tempo	/kécev/ (m)	קצב
קנדה עורכת מצוד על טרוריסטים.	hunting	/macod/ (m)	מצוד
ביצוע הפעולה נעשה ע"י המשטרה.	accomplishment	/bicúa/ (m)	ביצוע
ניסו להתנקש בחיי הנשיא.	assassination	/hitnakšut/	התנקשות
ההתנקשות בוצעה באמצעות הצבא.	means	/emcaut/ (f)	אמצעות
הפצצה נשלחה בחבילה.	bomb	/pcaca/ (f)	פצצה
החייל הטיל את הפצצה.	he dropped	/hitil/	הטיל
כנופית הטרוריסטים נעצרה ע"י המשטרה.	gang	/knufya/ (f)	כנופיה
הכתובת של משה שונה מהכתובת של רחל.	different	/šone/ (m.s.)	שונה
הטרוריסט הטמין את הפצצה בבית.	he hid, buried	/hitmin/	הטמין
אדם זקן נעזר במקל.	stick, rod	/makel/ (m)	מקל
הדינמיט הוטמן בתיבה.	box	/teyva/ (f)	תיבה
המשטרה והצבא נקטו באמצעי בטחון.	he took, held	/nakat/	נקט

ועידת שרי נאט"ו נפתחת היום

אוטאבה, 21 (ע"ר) - ועידת שרי החוץ וההגנה של מדינות נאט"ו
עומדת להיפתח כאן ביום ד' (היום), וכינתיים הגבירה ממשלת
קנדה את קצב המצוד שהיא עורכת על טירוריסטים קנדרים דוברי
צרפתית, החתורים בביצוע שורת התנקשויות באמצעות פצצות.

בארבעת הימים האחרונים הטילו כנופיות אלמוניות פצצות בשש
מקומות שונים בעיר מונטריאל, וכן הטמינו 18 מקלות דינמיט
בתינוק דואר ברחבי העיר קוויבק. המשטרה והצבא נקטו אמצעי
בטחון יוצאים מן הכלל, כדי להגן על שלחות נאט"ו.

Story 27.

רכבת הנוסעים הגיעה מחיפה.	train	/rakévet/(f)	רכבת
לא היו לנו מכשולים בדרך.	obstacle	/mixšol/(m)	מכשול
מסילת הרכבת עוברת ע"י קיבוץ נען.	track	/mesila/(f)	מסילה
הרכבת לא התהפכה.	he turned over	/hithapex/	התהפכה
לרכבת קטר ריזל חרש.	locomotive	/katar/(m)	קטר
הנוסעים חשו בזעזוע חזק.	shaking	/zaazúa/(m)	זעזוע
מכשול הונח לרוחב המסילה.	width	/róxav/(m)	רוחב
המסילה בנויה מברזל.	iron	/barzel/(m)	ברזל
ברזל מעורגל הונח על המסילה.	rolled(metal)	/meurgal/	מעורגל
קוטר הברזל היה 2 ס"מ.	diameter	/kóter/	קוטר
השוטרים שחקרו את התאונה היו מנפת צפת.	district	/nafa/(f)	נפה
מאהלי הבדואים נמצאים במרכז הארץ.	encampment	/maahal/(m)	מאהל
לכל שבט בדואי מנהיג משלו.	tribe	/šévet/ (m)	שבט

ילד רצה לראות איך קופצת הרכבת
מאת אורי פורת – כתב "ידיעות אחרונות "

רכבת נוסעים שעשתה דרכה בערב יום העצמאות מחל-אביב לבאר-שבע, עלתה על
מכשול שהונח על המסילה ליד קיבוץ נען, אבל לא התהפכה – דבר זה נודע רק עתה.

נהג הקטר, שחש בזעזוע, עצר את הרכבת וגילה כי לרוחב המסילה הונח ברזל
מעורגל, המשמש לבנין, בקוטר של 2 ס"מ.

למקום הוזעקה משטרת רהובות. שוטרים בפיקודו של ראש מחלקת החקירות של
הנפה, פקד נתן קפלן, פשטו בסביבות המסילה וערכו חקירות במאהלי הבדואים בין
חולדה לנען.   לעת ערב נתגלה ילד בן 12, משבט אל עסאם, אשר הודה, כי הניח את
הברזל על המסילה, "משום שרציתי לראות איך הרכבת קופצת".

Story 28.

נשיא המדינה קבל את החיילים המצטיינים.	he excelled	/hictayen/	הצטיין
הנשיא רואה בעבודתו חובה נעימה.	duty, obligation	/xova/ (f)	חובה
הנשיא קיבל את החיילים בעונג.	pleasure	/óneg/ (m)	עונג
למעלה ממאה חיילים נתקבלו ע"י הנשיא.	more, above	/lemála/	למעלה
החיילים גרים בצריפים.	barrack	/carif/ (m)	צריף
בין המצטיינים היו חיילים מיחידות המיעוטים.	minority	/mi'ut/ (m)	מיעוט
הרמטכ"ל הוא ראש המטה הכללי של צה"ל.	chief of staff	/ramatkal/	רמטכ"ל
אחרי מעקב ממושך נבחרו החיילים המצטיינים.	following	/maakav/ (m)	מעקב
המפקדים עקבו באופן רצוף אחרי עבודת החיילים.	successive, constant	/racuf/	רצוף
קבלות פנים בבית הנשיא מתקיימות מידי פעם בפעם.	every(time)	/midey/	מידי
קבלות הפנים מתקיימות בפרוס יום העצמאות.	on the eve of	/bifros/	בפרוס
יחידות המיעוטים נמצאות במסגרת צה"ל.	framework	/misgéret/ (f)	מסגרת
קצינים בכירים השתתפו בטכס.	senior	/baxir/ (m.s.)	בכיר

חיילים מצטיינים נתקבלו ע"י הנשיא

"המדינה כולה רואה חובה וענוג לעצמה להביע לכם את ברכתה על אשר
פעלתם ועל אשר אתם עתידים לפעול" - במלים אלה בירך אתמול נשיא המדינה,
מר זלמן שזר, למעלה ממאה חיילי צה"ל מצטיינים, שנתקבלו בצריף הנשיא.

יחד עם ברכתו למצטיינים - ביניהם כמה מחיילי המיעוטים ואזרח אחד,
שצויין לשבח על ידי הרמטכ"ל - הגיע נשיא המדינה את תודתה לרמטכ"ל ולמפקדים על
אשר טרחו לקיים מעקב ער ורצוף אחרי התנהגותם, מעשיהם והישגיהם של החיילים ולבחור
מהם, כמרי שנה, בפרוס יום העצמאות את אלה הראויים להערכה. הנשיא הדגיש, כי
חיילים אלה הם בחזקת מופת חינוכי חשוב הן במסגרת צה"ל והן מחוצה לו. כל אחד
מהחיילים המצטיינים קינל תעודה מיוחדת. בטכס נכחו הרמטכ"ל ומפקדים בכירים בצה"ל.

Story 29.

נשיא המדינה מסר את הצהרת-האמונים.	oath of office	/hacharat emunim/	הצהרת-אמונים
משה צבר הרבה נקודות במשחק.	he piled up	/cavar/	צבר
107 קולות הוטלו לקלפי.	ballot box	/kálpey/(f)	קלפי
מר זהבי מועמד לנשיאות חברת זוהר.	candidate	/muamad/(m.s.)	מועמד
הוא נמנע מלהצטרף למפלגה.	he abstained	/nimna/	נמנע
ההצבעה עברה כלי הפרעות.	voting	/hacbaa/(f)	הצבעה
המנהל נעדר מהישיבה.	absent	/needar/(m.s.)	נעדר
ע. אסף המנוח מת ימים מספר לפני ההצבעה.	the late	/hamanóax/	המנוח
נשיא החברה תמך בבחירתו של מנהל חדש.	he supported	/tamax/	תמך
לא באתי עם אשתי. באתי לבד.	alone	/levad/	לבד
הורגש המתח הרב בקלפיות.	tension	/métax/(m)	מתח
בזמן ההצבעה שרר שקט באולם.	he prevailed	/sarar/	שרר
הוזמנתי לביתו לארוחת ערב חגיגית.	festive	/xagigi/(m.s.)	חגיגי
הנורה הגדולה נשרפה.	light bulb	/nura/(f)	נורה
הצלם מעתון "הארץ" נכח במקום.	photographer	/calam/(m)	צלם
אולם המליאה היה מלא אנשים.	plenary chamber	/ulam melia/	אולם מליאה
קהל רב הריע לנשיא המדינה.	he cheered	/hería/	הריע
הפתק הוטל לקלפי.	slip of paper	/pétek/	פתק

ש. ז. שזר נבחר לנשיא המדינה
ימשור היום הצהרת-אמונים

ירושלים – ש. ז. שזר נבחר אתמול לנשיא השלישי של מדינת ישראל, בצברו 67 קולות
מתוך 107 הקולות שהוטלו לקלפי. היום יגיש הנשיא את הצהרת-האמונים שלו לכנסת.

שמותיהם של שני מועמדים הוגשו לכנסת: ש.ז. שזר – שקיבל 67 קולות,
ופ. כרנשטיין שקבל 33 קולות. 7 חברי כנסת נמנעו מהצבעה ו-12 נעדרו. ע.אסף
המנוח מת ימים מספר לפני ההצבעה. ואמנם בחירתו של שזר היתה ידועה מראש.
מועמדותו נתמכה ע"י מפלגות הקואליציה ומפ"ם, ואילו בכרנשטיין תמכו "חרות"
וה"ליברלים" בלבד. כמו כן היה ידוע שמק"י ואגורת ישראל יימנעו מהצבעה.

קשה, אם כן, לדבר על מתח ששרר בעת ההצבעה או בעת ספירת הקולות, אך
חגיגיות היתה כה אתמול, בישיבת הכנסת. נורות נוספות הוצבו כדי לסייע לצלמים
ולהאיר את האולם; אולם המליאה היה מלא מן הרגיל. ובחוץ – עמדו מאות והריעו
לבאים וליוצאים.

בדיוק בשעה 4 פתח היו"ר את הישיבה המיוחדת של הכנסת. הוא מינה ועדת
קלפי (ר. הקטין מאחה"ע, א. כהן מה"ליברלים", נ. לוין מ"חרות" וש. שורש ממפא"י.)
חברי-הכנסת מלאו את פתקי ההצבעה אותם מצאו על שולחנותיהם וסגרו את המעטפות.

ברכות לנשיא – ראשון המצביעים היה יו"ר הכנסת ק. לוז. לאחר מכן הקריא
מזכיר הכנסת את שמות המצביעים. אחד אחד קמו חברי-הכנסת וניגשו לקלפי שהוצבה
ליד מושבו של היו"ר. בשעה 4.30 נסתיימה ההצבעה וב-4.40 הוקראו התוצאות: ש.ז.
שזר נבחר לנשיאה השלישי של המדינה.

עם היוודע התוצאות ערכו "מומהים" חשבון. הם הישוו את שמות המצביעים
לתוצאות וגילו, שלשזר "חסרים" שני קולות מאלה ש"הגיעו" לו על פי יחסי הכוחות
המפלגתיים בכנסת.

עם תום ההצבעה מיהרו חברי כנסת רבים אל ביתו של שזר כדי להודיע
לו על התוצאות ולברכו.

Story 30.

מרים עובדת כמזכירה בסוכנות נסיעות.	agency	/soxnut/ (f)	סוכנות
למר כהן יש הרבה ידידים בגולה.	Diaspora, exile	/gola/ (f)	גולה
דבר בקול רם !	high, loud	/ram/ (m.s.)	רם
מר אורן היה מלא חרדה לקראת התפקיד החדש.	anxiety, terror	/xarada/ (f)	חרדה
הם התפללו את תפילת השחרית בבית.	prayer	/tfila/ (f)	תפילה
קולות נסתרים אמרו לו שהוא יצליח.	hidden	/nistar/ (m.s.)	נסתר
הנאום של המורה החדש היה מעניין.	speech	/neum/ (m)	נאום
הסעודה היתה מפוארת.	meal, banquet	/seuda/ (f)	סעודה
מבקר המדינה גר בירושלים.	comptroller	/mevaker/ (m)	מבקר
עבדתי במחיצתו כעשר שנים.	partition	/mexica/ (f)	מחיצה
מר כהן הוא מארח למופת.	host	/mearéax/ (m.s.)	מארח
הילדה קבלה שי מהוריה.	gift	/šay/ (m)	שי
הבאנו הרבה מזכרות מהטיול.	souvenir	/mazkéret/ (f)	מזכרת
המנורה נותנת הרבה אור.	candelabrum, lamp	/menora/ (f)	מנורה
לסופר יש סגנון מיוחד בכתיבה.	style	/signon/ (m)	סגנון

שזר נפרד מחבריו בהנהלת הסוכנות

ירושלים - "אני נושא אתי את מטען השירות שלי בעבודתי בסוכנות היהודית, בארץ ובגולה, אל המקום הרם - מלא חרדה ותפילה, שכורות נסתרים של האומה יעמרו לי בתפקידי", - הצהיר נשיא המדינה הנבחר, זלמן שזר, בנאומו הראשון שנשא אמש לאחר בחירתו כנשיא המדינה ב"בית אלישבע", בירושלים.

שזר היה אורחה של הנהלת הסוכנות היהודית בירושלים, אשר חבריה נפררו ממנו לאחר 12 שנות עבודה.

בסעורת הערב החגיגית שנערכה לכבוד הנשיא הנבחר ורעייתו, השתתפו חברי הנהלת הסוכנות מכל המפלגות, ראשי המפלגות, מבקר הסוכנות וההסתדרות הציונית העולמית מ. כ. מאירי, אב בית הדין של הקונגרס הציוני ד"ר ש. אגרנט וכן ותיקי התנועה הציונית שעברו כמחיצתו של שזר.

שזר קיבל ממארחיו שי מזכרת - מנורת כסף עתיקה מליטא, בסגנון חסירי מתקופת הבעש"ט.

536

The following are common proverbs and expressions. They are fully
pointed in order to familiarize the student with the vowel points.

בְּרוּכִים הַבָּאִים.

כָּל הַהַתְחָלוֹת קָשׁוֹת.

אֵין חָכָם כְּבַעַל הַנִּסָיוֹן.

אֵין דָּבָר הָעוֹמֵד בִּפְנֵי הָרָצוֹן.

זֵכֶר צַדִּיק לִבְרָכָה.

בְּשָׁעָה טוֹבָה וּמָצְלַחַת.

הִנֵּה מַה טּוֹב וּמַה נָּעִים שֶׁבֶת אַחִים. גַּם יָחַד.

אִם תִּרְצוּ אֵין זוֹ אַגָּדָה.

אִם אֵין אֲנִי לִי מִי לִי?

אַל תָּדִין אֶת חֲבֵרָךָ עַד שֶׁתַּגִּיעַ לִמְקוֹמוֹ.

אַחֲרוֹן אַחֲרוֹן חָבִיב.

הַתִּקְוָה

עוֹד לֹא אָבְדָה תִקְוָתֵנוּ	כָּל עוֹד בַּלֵּבָב פְּנִימָה
הַתִּקְוָה בַּת שְׁנוֹת אַלְפַּיִם	נֶפֶשׁ יְהוּדִי הוֹמִיָּה,
לִהְיוֹת עַם חָפְשִׁי בְּאַרְצֵנוּ	וּלְפַאֲתֵי מִזְרָח קָדִימָה
אֶרֶץ צִיּוֹן וִירוּשָׁלַיִם.	עַיִן לְצִיּוֹן צוֹפִיָּה.

חם ונשלם שבח לאל בורא עולם

GLOSSARY

The glossary lists words as they appear in the breakdown following the
sentences of the Basic Conversations and Additional Vocabulary. Certain words
appear in more than one form, such as masculine and feminine, when the
grammatical explanation for the differences has not yet been given in the units
up to the point where the word first occurs. In later units verbs are listed
only in the 3 m.s. past tense form and adjectives only in the m.s. form regardless of the form which occurs in the Basic Sentence itself.

Words are listed alphabetically in transcription. /š/ follows /s/, and
/'/ is disregarded. The unit in which the word first occurs is also given.

The words introduced in the Reader are not listed here. There are several
good dictionaries available which will serve the student's purposes well. One
of the handiest for general use is Ben-Yehuda's Pocket English-Hebrew-Hebrew-
English Dictionary, edited by Ehud Ben-Yehuda and David Weinstein, Washington
Square Press, Inc., New York, 1961, 90¢ (paperback).

-a	1	her	ה–
ad	6	until, up to	עד
adáin	5	as yet	עדיין
adloyáda (f)	38	Purim celebration	עדלאידע
adom (m.s.)	14	red	אדום
adoni	6	sir	אדוני
af exad...lo	38	no one	לא ...אף אחר
af páam...lo	38	never	לא ...אף פעם
afa	38	he baked	אפה
afarsek (m)	14	peach	אפרסק
afílu	9	even	אפילו
afor (m.s.)	20	gray	אפור
afuna (f)	14	peas	אפונה
agam (m)	40	lake, pond	אגם
agas (m)	14	pear	אגס
agav	39	by the way	אגב
agora (f)	14	agora (1/100 lira)	אגורה
agvania (f)	14	tomato	עגבניה
ahav	20	he liked, loved	אהב
áin (f)	3	eye	עין
akev (m)	29	heel	עקב
al (neg. part.)	5	don't	אל
al	6	on	על
al yad	7	next to, alongside	על יד
amad	18	he stood	עמד
amar	16	he said	אמר
amárta (m.s.)	7	you said	אמרת
amerikái (m.s.)	2	American	אמריקאי
anan (m)	20	cloud	ענן
anavim (m.pl.)	14	grapes	ענבים
anáxnu	26	we	אנחנו
ani	1	I	אני
ani (m.s.)	33	poor	עני
arba (f)	11	four	ארבע
arbaa (m)	5	four	ארבעה
arbaasar (m	11	fourteen	ארבעה–עשר
arbaesre (f)	11	fourteen	ארבע–עשרה
arim (f.pl.)	8	cities	ערים
arnak (m)	39	wallet, purse	ארנק
aruxa (f)	11	meal	ארוחה
asaper	15	I will tell	אספר
asara (m)	11	ten	עשרה
asimon (m)	19	token	אסימון
asit (f.s.)	5	you did	עשית

asíta (m.s.)	5	you did	עשית
asur (m.s.)	23	forbidden	אסור
ašir (m.s.)	33	rich	עשיר
at (f.s.)	4	you	את
ata (m.s.)	4	you	אתה
avad	31	he worked	עבד
aval	22	but	אבל
avar	16	he passed	עבר
avatíax (m)	14	watermelon	אבטיח
avir (m)	17	air	אויר
aviron (m)	3	airplane	אוירון
avor (m.s.imv.)	6	pass, cross	עבור
avur	4	for, on behalf of	עבור
ax	4	but	אך
axad'asar (m)	11	eleven	אחר-עשר
axake	15	I will wait	אחכה
axálti	13	I ate	אכלתי
axaray	24	after me	אחרי
axarey	10	after, behind	אחרי
axaron (m.s.)	22	last	אחרון
axat (f)	11	one	אחת
axát'esre (f)	11	eleven	אחת-עשרה
axer (m.s.)	7	other	אחר
axid (m.s.)	29	uniform	אחיד
axot (f)	26	sister	אחות
axšav	7	now	עכשיו
ayef (m.s.)	25	tired	עיף
az	7	then, so	אז
ba (m.s.pres.)	7	come	בא
báa (f.s.pres.)	7	come	באה
báal (m)	1	husband	בעל
bacal (m)	14	onion	בצל
bacal yarok (m)	14	scallion	בצל ירוק
badak	18	he examined	בדק
báit (m)	4	house	בית
bakbuk (m)	14	bottle	בקבוק
bama (f)	22	stage, platform	במה
bank (m)	34	bank	בנק
banot (f.pl.)	26	girls, daughters	בנות
bari (m.s.)	30	healthy	בריא
bat (f.s.)	5	you came	באת
bat (f)	26	daughter	בת
báta (m.s.)	5	you came	באת
batúax (m.s.)	14	sure, certain	בטוח
baxur (m)	36	young man	בחור
be-	1	in, at	ב-
bediyuk	10	exactly	בדיוק
beérex	21	approximately	בערך
béged (m)	28	garment	בגד
behexlet	10	definitely	בהחלט
beim	17	if	באם
beracon	13	willingly	ברצון
bérex (f)	30	knee	ברך
bet séfer (m)	5	school	בית ספר
bétax	20	sure	בטח
béten (f)	30	stomach, abdomen	בטן
beyca (f)	14	egg	ביצה
beynatáim	4	meanwhile	בינתיים
bifrat	24	especially	בפרט
biker	40	he visited	ביקר
bil'adey	37	without, except	בלעדי
binyan (m)	6	building	בנין
birer	19	he found out	בירר

bišvil	14	for	כשביל
bli	15	without	בלי
bo (m.s.imv.)	15	come	בוא
braxa (f)	10	blessing	ברכה
brera (f)	22	choice	ברירה
briut (f)	30	health	בריאות
búba (f)	38	doll	בובה
cad (m)	22	side	צד
cafon	40	north	צפון
cahov (m.s.)	14	yellow	צהוב
came (m.s.)	23	thirsty	צמא
camig (m)	36	tire	צמיג
carix (m.s.)	14	need, must, have to	צריך
cav (m)	26	order, command	צו
cava (m)	26	military services	צבא
cava	27	he dyed	צבע
ček (m)	34	check	צ'ק
céva (m)	14	color	צבע
cilcel	23	it rang	צילצל
cincénet (f)	14	jar	צנצנת
cinor (m)	40	pipe	צינור
cixcéax	29	he polished	צחצח
cnon (m)	14	turnip	צנון
cnonit (f)	14	radish	צנונית
da'ag	25	he worried	דאג
daatxa	21	your opinion	דעתך
dag (m)	13	fish	דג
daka (f)	18	minute	דקה
darom	40	south	דרום
davak	20	he was attached	דבק
davar (m)	6	thing	דבר
dávka	21	just, it so happens	דווקא
daxuf (m.s.)	17	urgent	דחוף
day	23	enough	די
dea (f)	21	opinion	דעה
délek (m)	36	gasoline	דלק
dérex (f)	10	way, path, through	דרך
diéta (f)	13	diet	דיאטה
diber	16	he spoke	דיבר
dóar (m)	6	mail, post office	דואר
dod (m)	19	uncle	דוד
dóda (f)	19	aunt	דודה
dugma (f)	36	example	דוגמה
duvdevanim (m.pl.)	14	cherries	דובדבנים
écba (f)	30	finger	אצבע
écel	9	at	אצל
éfes (m)	19	zero	אפס
efšar	10	possible	אפשר
élef	14	thousand	אלף
élu	22	these	אלו
elyon (m.s.)	40	top, highest, supreme	עליון
émca (m)	22	middle, center	אמצע
emet (f)	9	truth	אמת
emor (m.s.imv.)	5	tell, say	אמור
érec (f)	2	country	ארץ
érev (m)	11	evening	ערב
érex (m)	21	value	ערך
éser (f)	11	ten	עשר
esrim	11	twenty	עשרים

eškolit (f)	14	grapefruit	אשכולית
et	2	(prep. indicating object)	את
et (f)	20	time	עת
eten	13	I will give	אתן
ex	3	how	איך
-ex	1	you, your (f.s.)	־ך
exad (m)	11	one	אחד
ey páam	38	ever	אי פעם
eyfo	4	where	איפה
eyn (neg. part.)	5	not	אין
eynáim (f.du.)	3	eyes	עיניים
eynáix	3	your (f.s.) eyes	עיניך
eynéni	5	I don't, I'm not	אינני
eynéxa	3	your (m.s.) eyes	עיניך
eyx	3	how	איך
éyze (m)	5	which	איזה
éyzo (f)	9	which	איזו
gadol (m.s.)	4	big, large, great	גדול
gam	1	too, also	גם
gar (m.s.)	4	live, stay	גר
gára (f.s.)	4	live, stay	גרה
garbáim (f.du.)	39	stockings	גרביים
garon (m)	30	throat	גרון
gavóa (m.s.)	33	high, tall	גבוה
géšem (m)	20	rain	גשם
géver (m)	39	man	גבר
gézer (m)	14	carrot	גזר
gihec	28	he pressed	גיהץ
gimnásia (f)	26	high school	גימנסיה
giyus (m)	26	conscription	גיוס
glída (f)	9	ice cream	גלידה
gram (m)	14	gram	גרם
gruš (m)	19	agora (old name)	גרוש
guf (m)	30	body	גוף
gufia (f)	39	undershirt	גופיה
gúmi (m)	29	rubber	גומי
gvina (f)	14	cheese	גבינה
gvirtí	6	ma'am	גברתי
gvul (m)	37	boundary, limit	גבול
ha-	1	the	־ה
habáyta	25	(to) home	הביתה
hacaga (f)	21	show, presentation	הצגה
hafsaka (f)	23	interruption, intermission	הפסקה
hafux (m.s.)	15	reversed, inverted	הפוך
haim	4	yes-or-no question word	האם
hakol	14	everything	הכל
halvaa (f)	34	loan	הלוואה
hamšex (m.s.imv.)	6	continue	המשך
hamšíxi (f.s.imv.)	6	continue	המשיכי
harbe	17	much, many	הרבה
harey	8	(interjection)	הרי
hasbara (f)	31	information	הסברה
háva	12	let's	הבה
heemin	37	he believed	האמין
héna	5	hither, (to) here	הנה
hexlif	32	he exchanged	החליף
hexlit	21	he decided	החליט
heyxan	4	where	היכן
hi (f.s.)	2	she	היא
hibit	38	he looked	הביט
hicig	21	he showed, presented	הציג

hiclíax	34	he succeeded	הצליח
hictalvut (f)	6	intersection	הצטלבות
hictaref	21	he joined	הצטרף
hictarex	18	he needed	הצטרך
hidlik	36	he ignited, kindled	הדליק
hifría	22	he disturbed	הפריע
hifsik	23	he interrupted	הפסיק
higat (f.s.)	2	you arrived	הגעת
higáta (m.s.)	2	you arrived	הגעת
higáti	2	I arrived	הגעתי
higía	16	he arrived	הגיע
higid	34	he told	הגיד
hikna	33	he transferred ownership	היקנה
hilva	34	he lent	הלווה
hine	36	look!	הנה
hirgiš	30	he felt	הרגיש
hirvíax	33	he earned	הרויח
hispik	18	he made it in time	הספיק
histader	34	he managed himself	הסתדר
histakel	40	he looked at	הסתכל
histaper	27	he got a haircut	הסתפר
histarek	35	he combed his hair	הסתרק
hištaamem	24	he became bored	השתעמם
hištadel	28	he strove	השתדל
hišta'el	30	he coughed	השתעל
hištagéa	24	he went crazy	השתגע
hit'anyen	24	he became interested	התעניין
hit'ateš	30	he sneezed	התעטש
hitgaléax	27	he shaved (himself)	התגלח
hitkaléax	35	he showered	התקלח
hitkarev	24	he approached	התקרב
hitkašer	18	he got in touch	התקשר
hitlabeš	35	he got dressed	התלבש
hitnageš	36	he collided	התנגש
hit'orer	25	he woke up	התעורר
hitpana	27	he became unoccupied	התפנה
hitrašamt (f.s.)	3	you were impressed	התרשמת
hitrašámta (m.s.)	3	you were impressed	התרשמת
hitraxec	20	he bathed	התרחץ
hitraxek	24	he withdrew	התרחק
hitxapes	38	he disguised himself	התחפש
hitxaret	24	he regretted	התחרט
hizaher (m.s.imv.)	15	be careful	הזהר
hizdamnut (f)	8	opportunity	הזדמנות
hoci	29	he took out	הוציא
hodía	21	he informed	הודיע
horid	28	he brought down	הוריד
horim (m.pl.)	18	parents	הורים
hovil	40	he transported	הוביל
hu	2	he, it	הוא
-i	1	my, me	־י
ikar (m)	30	principle	עיקר
im	8	if	אם
im	15	with	עם
imri (f.s.imv.)	5	tell, say	אמרי
ir (f)	8	city	עיר
israeli (m.s.)	5	Israeli	ישראלי
iša (f)	1	wife, woman	אשה
išen	23	he smoked	עישן
iti	18	with me	אתי
itim (f.pl.)	20	times	עתים
iton (m)	31	newspaper	עתון
itonut (f)	31	press	עתונות

ivri	(f.s.imv.)	6	cross, pass	עברי
ivrit	(f)	5	Hebrew	עברית
íxer		35	he was late	איחר
ka'av		30	it hurt	כאב
kacar	(m.s.)	27	short	קצר
kacin	(m)	26	officer	קצין
kafac		35	he jumped	קפץ
kafe	(m)	15	coffee	קפה
káic	(m)	20	summer	קיץ
kalkali	(m.s.)	31	economic	כלכלי
kalut	(f)	28	ease	קלות
káma		14	how much, how many	כמה
kan		6	here	כאן
kara		21	he called, read	קרא
kara		36	it happened	קרה
karov	(m.s.)	4	near, close	קרוב
kartis	(m)	22	ticket, card	כרטיס
kaspi	(m.s.)	31	financial	כספי
katom		14	orange	כתום
kav	(m)	19	line	קו
kaxol	(m.s.)	14	blue	כחול
kcat		7	a little, some	קצת
kdey		19	in order to	כדי
ke-		4	approximately	כ-
keev	(m)	30	pain	כאב
kéfel	(m)	28	pleat	קפל
kélev	(m)	20	dog	כלב
kémax	(m)	14	flour	קמח
ken		1	yes	כן
késef	(m)	29	money, silver	כסף
kétem	(m)	28	stain, spot	כתם
ki		21	because, that	כי
kibálti		14	I received	קבלתי
kibel		16	he received	קיבל
kibes		28	he laundered	כיבס
kicer		27	he shortened	קיצר
kiduš	(m)	12	Sabbath ceremony	קידוש
kifláim		33	double	כפליים
kilkel		19	he damaged	קלקל
kim'at		31	almost, approximately	כמעט
kišuim	(m.pl.)	14	squash	קשואים
kivun	(m)	8	direction	כיוון
klal	(m)	23	generalization	כלל
klum		13	nothing	כלום
kmo		5	like	כמו
knisa	(f)	22	entrance	כניסה
kódem		7	before	קודם
kol		5	all	כל
kol kax		5	so, as much	כל כך
kol	(m)	1	voice	קול
kolerábi	(m)	14	kohlrabi	קולרבי
kolnóa	(m)	7	movie theater	קולנוע
koma	(f)	17	story, floor	קומה
kor	(m)	20	cold	קור
kore	(m.s.pres.)	21	call, read	קורא
konsul	(m)	31	consul	קונסול
konsulári	(m.s.)	31	consular	קונסולרי
kos	(f)	15	drinking glass	כוס
kóši	(m)	11	difficulty	קושי
kóva	(m)	39	hat	כובע
kruv	(m)	14	cabbage	כרוב
kruvit	(f)	14	cauliflower	כרובית
kše-		10	when (conj.)	כש-
któvet	(f)	11	address	כתובת

kufsa (f)	14	box, can	קופסה
kufsaót (f.pl.)	14	boxes, cans	קופסאות
kutónet (f)	39	shirt	כותנת
kvisa (f)	28	laundry	כביסה
la-	1	to	‏-ל
laasot	14	to do	לעשות
lagur	4	to reside	לגור
laléxet	10	to go	ללכת
láma	7	why	למה
lamádet (f.s.)	5	you learned	למרת
lamádeta (m.s.)	5	you learned	למרת
lamádeti	5	I learned	למרתי
lánu	11	to us	לנו
latet	13	to give	לתת
lava	34	he borrowed	לווה
lavan (m.s.)	14	white	לבן
lavétax	21	for sure	לבטח
lavuš	38	dressed	לבוש
láyla (m)	11	night	לילה
ledaber	5	to speak	לדבר
leexol	9	to eat	לאכול
lefi	39	according to	לפי
lehagia	6	to arrive	להגיע
lehakir	2	to know (a person)	להכיר
lehazmin	11	to invite	להזמין
lehikanes	9	to enter	להכנס
lehitraot	1	to see again	להתראות
leolam ... lo	38	never	לעולם לא
lesarev	12	to refuse	לסרב
letayel	8	to stroll, hike	לטייל
lev	28	heart	לב
levanim	28	sheets, underwear etc.	לבנים
lex (m.s. imv)	6	go	לך
lexi (f.s. imv)	6	go	לכי
li	2	to me	לי
lifney	2	before, ago	לפני
lifnot	15	near, before	לפנות
liknot	14	to buy	לקנות
limonim (m.pl.)	14	lemons	לימון
linsóa	18	to travel	לנסוע
líra (f)	14	Israeli pound	לירה
lir'ot	8	to see	לראות
lisxot	21	to swim	לשחות
lišlóax	17	to send	לשלוח
lištot	15	to drink	לשתות
lu	33	if only	לו
lud, lod	3	Lydda (place name)	לוד
ma	1	what	מה
maafera (f)	23	ashtray	מאפרה
maagar (m)	40	reservoir	מאגר
maala (f)	30	degree, a virtue	מעלה
maarav	40	west	מערב
maaraxa (f)	23	act	מערכה
maavar (m)	22	aisle	מעבר
madxom (m)	30	thermometer	מרחום
máim (m.pl.)	15	water	מים
makom (m)	11	place	מקום
maksim (m.s.)	24	wonderful, fascinating	מקסים
malon	4	hotel	מלון
mamaš	5	really	ממש
manganon (m)	31	administration	מנגנון
mar (m.s.)	15	bitter	מר

mar'e	20	sight, vision	מראה
masa (m)	36	load, burden	משא
masar	28	he delivered	מסר
masax (m)	23	curtain	מסך
masexa (f)	38	mask	מסכה
maskóret (f)	33	salary	משכורת
masmer (m)	29	nail	מסמר
masóret (f)	13	tradition	מסורת
maspik	18	enough	מספיק
máSehu (m)	23	something	משהו
matáim	14	two hundred	מאתיים
matay	2	when (interrogative)	מתי
mat'im (m.s. pres)	11	is suitable	מתאים
matok	15	sweet	מתוק
matos (m)	18	airplane	מטוס
mávet (m)	24	death	מות
maxar	19	he sold	מחר
maxlaka (f)	31	department, division	מחלקה
mazal (m)	12	luck	מזל
mazkir	32	secretary	מזכיר
mea	14	hundred	מאה
meat	20	a little, few	מעט
mecig (m.s. pres)	21	show	מציג
mecuyan (m.s.)	21	excellent	מצויין
medaber (m.s. pres)	5	speak	מדבר
medabéret (f.s. pres)	5	speak	מדברת
medini (m.s.)	31	political	מדיני
mefuzar (m.s.)	36	absent-minded, scattered	מפוזר
mehirut (f)	35	hurry	מהירות
meil (m)	39	coat	מעיל
mekava (f.s. pres)	3	hope	מקוה
mekave (m.s. pres)	3	hope	מקוה
mekulkal (m.s.)	19	out of order	מקולקל
melafefonim (m.pl.)	14	cucumbers	מלפפונים
melcar (m)	15	waiter	מלצר
melcarit (f)	15	waitress	מלצרית
melon (m)	14	canteloupe	מלון
mélax (m)	14	salt	מלה
memaher (m.s. pres)	8	hurry	ממהר
memSalti (m.s.)	7	governmental	ממשלתי
memula	13	filled	ממולא
menuxa (f)	25	rest	מנוחה
meod	2	very	מאד
meolam ... lo	38	never	מעולם לא
merkazi (m.s.)	6	central	מרכזי
meSune (m.s.)	20	odd, strange	משונה
meunyan (m.s.)	23	interested	מעונין
méxes (m)	18	customs	מכס
mexin (m.s.)	9	prepare	מכין
mexir	29	price	מחיר
mexona (f)	36	machine, car	מכונה
mexonit	36	automobile	מכונית
méyle	29	so be it	מילא
meytav	28	the best	מיטב
meyuxad (m.s.)	38	special	מיוחד
mézeg (m)	20	temperament	מזג
mézeg avir	20	weather	מזג-אויר
mezog (m.s. imv)	12	pour	מזוג
mi-, me-	3	from, by	-מ
mic	14	juice	מיץ
mic tapuzim	14	orange juice	מיץ תפוזים
mida (f)	39	measure	מידה
mif'al (m)	40	project	מפעל
mil	40	mile	מיל
miménu	30	from him	ממנו
mimxata (f)	39	handkerchief	ממחטה

miršam (m)	13	recipe	מירשם
mis'ada (f)	15	restaurant	מסעדה
misderon (m)	23	lobby	מסדרון
mispar (m)	11	number	מספר
misrad (m)	7	office	משרד
misxari (m.s.)	31	commercial	מסחרי
mišpaxa (f)	1	family	משפחה
mišum	36	because of	משום
mišxa (f)	29	ointment	משחה
mita (f)	35	bed	מיטה
mitkonen (m.s. pres)	4	plan	מתכונן
mitkonénet (f.s. pres)	4	plan	מתכוננת
mitria (f)	39	umbrella	מטריה
mitxabe	26	he hid (himself)	מתחבא
mivrak (m)	17	telegram, cable	מברק
mivraka (f)	12	telegram office	מברקה
mivxar (m)	39	selection	מבחר
mixnasáim (m. du.)	28	trousers, slacks	מכנסיים
mixtav (m)	17	letter	מכתב
mixya (f)	33	sustenance	מחיה
miyad	18	immediately	מיד
miznon (m)	23	luncheonette	מזנון
mizrax	40	east	מזרח
mocet (f.s. pres)	3	find	מוצאת
modiin (m.s.)	19	information (service)	מודיעין
mul	30	opposite	מול
musmax (m.s.)	32	certified, ordained, authorized	מוסמך
muxrax (m.s.)	1	have to, must	מוכרח
muxraxa (f.s.)	1	have to, must	מוכרחה
náal (f)	29	shoe	נעל
naim (m.s.)	2	pleasant	נעים
naki (m.s.)	28	clean	נקי
namal, namel	3	port	נמל
namux (m.s.)	24	low, short(height)	נמוך
nasa (3 m.s. past)	16	he travelled	נסע
našva (3 f.s.)	20	(it)blew	נשבה
natáta (2 m.s.)	7	you gave	נתת
naxon (m.s.)	4	correct	נכון
nazélet (f)	30	head cold	נזלת
nehedar (m.s.)	13	wonderful	נהדר
nehena	24	he enjoyed, derived benefit	נהנה
néšef (m)	38	party, ball	נשף
nexmad	20	lovely, nice	נחמד
nicéax	23	he won	נצח
nidme (m.s. pres)	18	seems	נדמה
nigaš	12	we will	ניגש
nika	28	he cleaned	ניקה
nimcet (f.s.)	7	situated, found	נמצאת
nimca (m.s.)	7	situated, found	נמצא
nimca (1 pl. fut.)	11	we will find	נמצא
nimkar (m.s.)	19	is sold	נמכר
nimnem	25	he dozed	נמנם
nirdam	25	he fell asleep	נרדם
nir'e (m.s. pres)	16	is seen, appears	נראה
nisa	28	he tried	ניסה
nisa	21	we will go (by vehicle)	ניסע
nismax (1 pl. fut.)	11	we will be happy	נשמח
niš'ar	25	he stayed	נשאר
nišma (m.s.)	15	is heard	נשמע
nitmana (3 m.s. past)	16	he was appointed	נתמנה
nóax (m.s.)	40	convenient, comfortable	נוח
noládeta	14	you were born	נולדת
nora (m)	30	terrible	נורא

o	3	or	או
-o	1	him, his	־ו
od	4	still, yet	עוד
ódef (m)	14	surplus	עודף
odot	40	about	אודות
ole (m.s. pres)	14	cost	עולה
oméret (f.s. pres)	7	say	אומרת
onia (f)	3	ship	אוניה
or (m)	29	leather, skin	עור
órex (m)	40	length	אורך
ose (m.s. pres)	11	do	עושה
otax (f.s. obj)	2	you	אותך
óto (m)	36	auto	אוטו
otxa (m.s. obj)	2	you	אותך
óxel (m)	13	food	אוכל
ózen	30	ear	אוזן
ózen haman (f)	38	special Purim cake	אוזן המן
páam (f)	15	time (occurrence)	פעם
paamon (m)	23	bell	פעמון
pagášti	16	I met	פגשתי
panuy (m.s.)	40	vacant	פנוי
para	34	he paid (a debt)	פרע
pašut (m.s.)	31	simple	פשוט
paxad	37	he feared	פחד
paxot	18	less	פחות
péle (m)	34	wonder	פלא
petruzília (f)	14	parsley	פטרוזיליה
pi	33	time	פי
pijáma (f)	39	pajamas	פיג׳מה
pina (f(	6	corner	פינה
pinkas	32	notebook, ledger	פינקס
piter	37	he fired (an employee)	פיטר
pkida	28	clerk	פקידה
pne (m.s. imv)	6	turn	פנה
pni (f.s. imv)	6	turn	פני
pnim (m)	23	interior	פנים
po	15	here	פה
prat (m)	24	detail	פרט
prati (m.s.)	33	private	פרטי
pri (m)	14	fruit	פרי
pruta	34	penny (1000 pruta - IL. 1)	פרוטה
raa (3 m.s. past)	16	he saw	ראה
ráaš (m)	38	noise	רעש
raba (f.s.)	1	much	רכה
racon (m)	13	desire	רצון
raev (m.s.)	23	hungry	רעב
ragil	17	regular	רגיל
rait (f.s.)	4	you saw	ראית
ráita (m.s.)	4	you saw	ראית
rak	26	only	רק
ramzor (m)	6	traffic light	רמזור
rašam	30	he listed	רשם
raxok (m.s.)	6	far	רחוק
rayon, raayon	15	idea	רעיון
recini	37	serious	רציני
recinut (f)	33	seriousness	רצינות
recua (f)	29	strap	רצועה
refua (f)	30	medicine	רפואה
réga (m)	18	minute, moment	רגע
régel (f)	30	foot, leg	רגל
réva (m)	18	quarter	רבע

rexov (m)	6	street	רחוב
riba (f)	14	jelly	ריבה
ribit	34	interest	ריבית
rimonim (m.pl.)	14	pomegranates	רימונים
rišona (f.s.)	6	first	ראשונה
roca (f.s. pres)	6	want	רוצה
roce (m.s. pres)	7	want	רוצה
roa (f.s. pres)	7	see	רואה
roe (m.s. pres)	7	see	רואה
roe xešbon (m)	32	accountant	רואה חשבון
rofe (m)	30	doctor	רופא
roš (m)	30	head	ראש
róšem (m)	36	impression	רושם
rúax (f)	20	wind	רוח
ruc	1	run	רוץ
saara (f.s.)	27	a hair	שערה
saarot (f.pl.)	27	hair, hairs	שערות
sabon (m)	28	soap	סבון
sadna (f)	36	repair shop, garage	סדנא
safa (f)	5	shore, language, lip	שפה
safam (m)	27	mustache	שפם
safot (f.pl.)	5	languages	שפות
saméax	5	happy	שמח
sam	28	he put	שם
sandal	29	sandal	סנדל
sandlar	29	shoemaker	סנדלר
sapar	27	barber	ספר
sax	34	amount	סך
sax (m.s. pres)	8	say	שח
saxa	21	he swam	שחה
saxkan (m)	24	player, actor	שחקן
saxkanit (f)	24	player, actress	שחקנית
saxyan (m)	21	swimmer	שחיין
saxyanit (f)	21	swimmer	שחיינית
sear (m.s.)	27	hair	שער
séder (m)	1	order	סדר
séfer (m)	5	book	ספר
segol	14	purple	סגול
sélek (m)	14	beet	סלק
seret (m)	21	film, ribbon	סרט
seva (f)	27	gray hair	שיבה
sfat yam	8	seashore	שפתיים
silsul (m)	27	curling	סילסול
simla (f)	28	dress	שמלה
siper	16	he told	סיפר
sixa (f)	19	conversation	שיחה
siyem	32	he finished	סיים
siyur (m)	40	tour	סיור
slixa (f)	1	pardon	סליחה
smali (m.s.)	22	left	שמאלי
smexa (f.s.)	5	happy	שמחה
smóla	6	to the left	שמאלה
sóda (f)	15	club soda	סודה
sof (m)	28	end	סוף
srox (m)	29	lace	שרוך
sukar (m)	14	sugar	סוכר
sulia (f)	29	sole	סוליה
sus (m)	32	horse	סוס
sva racon (m.s.)	27	satisfied	שבע רצון
svéder (m)	39	sweater	סוודר
sviva (f)	39	neighborhood	סביבה

šaa (f)	18	hour	שעה
ša'av	40	he drew	שאב
šagrirut (f)	2	Embassy	שגרירות
šalax	15	he sent	שלח
šalom (m)	1	peace, welfare	שלום
šaloš	11	three	שלוש
šam	6	there	שם
šamar	36	he watched	שמר
šamáti	4	I heard	שמעתי
šaménet (f)	14	sour cream	שמנת
šamir (m)	14	dill	שמיר
šana (f)	12	year	שנה
šapáat (f)	30	influenza, grippe	שפעת
šata	23	he drank	שתה
šavúa (m)	2	week	שבוע
šaxar (m)	25	dawn	שחר
šaxax	21	he forget	שכח
šaxor	14	black	שחור
še-	3	that (conjunction)	-ש
šéleg	22	snow	שלג
šel	4	of	של
šelax (f.s.)	4	of you, yours	שלך
šeli	4	of me, mine	שלי
šelxa (m.s.)	4	of you, yours	שלך
šem (m)	19	name	שם
šémen (m)	14	oil	שמן
šémeš (f)	20	sun	שמש
šemot (m.pl.)	19	names	שמות
šen (f)	30	tooth	שן
šeret	26	he served	שרת
šéš'esre (f)	11	sixteen	שש-עשרה
šeš (f)	11	six	שש
ševa	11	seven	שבע
šeuit (f)	14	beans	שעועית
šezifim (m.pl.)	14	plums	שזיפים
šiamem	24	he bored	שיעמם
šiša (m)	6	six	שישה
šiša'asar (m)	11	sixteen	שישה-עשר
šiši (m.s.)	11	sixth	שישי
šiv'a (m)	11	seven	שבעה
šivaasar (m)	11	seventeen	שבעה-עשר
šlax	17	send	שלח
šlom	1	the welfare of	שלום
šlošáasar (m)	11	thirteen	שלושה-עשר
šloša (m)	11	three	שלושה
šlóš'esre (f)	11	thirteen	שלוש-עשרה
šlošim	11	thirty	שלושים
šma (m.s. imv)	8	listen	שמע
šmona (m)	11	eight	שמונה
šmoná'asar (m)	11	eighteen	שמונה-עשר
šmóne (f)	11	eight	שמונה
šmoné'esre (f)	11	eighteen	שמונה-עשרה
šmonim	14	eighty	שמונים
šnáim (m)	11	two	שנים
šnatáim (f)	26	two years	שנתיים
šnéym'asar (m)	11	twelve	שנים-עשר
šokolad (m)	23	chocolate	שוקולד
štáim (f)	11	two	שתים
štar	34	debt note, bill	שטר
štéym'esre (f)	11	twelve	שתים-עשרה
šulxan (m)	12	table	שולחן
šum (m)	14	garlic	שום
šuman (m)	28	grease	שומן
šura (f)	22	row	שורה
šuv	23	again	שוב

ta	19	booth	חא
tafar	29	he sewed	תפר
tafkid (m)	32	duty, function	תפקיד
tafus (m.s.)	4	occupied	תפוס
tagía (m.s.)	4	you will arrive	תגיע
tagía (3 f.s.)	4	she will arrive	תגיע
tagzim	5	you will exaggerate	תגזים
tagzími (f.s.)	5	you will exaggerate	תגזימי
tahaluxa (f)	38	parade, procession	תהלוכה
takciv	34	budget	תקציב
takir	2	you will know	תכיר
takíri (f.s.)	2	you will know	תכירי
tamšix (m.s.)	6	you will continue	תמשיך
tamšíxi (f.s.)	6	you will continue	תמשיכי
tamid	35	always	תמיד
tapúax (m)	14	apple	תפוח
tapuxey adama (m.pl.)	14	potatoes	תפוחי אדמה
tapuzim (m.pl.)	14	oranges	תפוזים
tari (m.s.)	14	fresh	טרי
tašlum (m)	22	fee, payment	תשלום
taxana (f)	40	station	תחנה
taxtonim (m.pl.)	39	undershorts	תחתונים
taxtonit (f)	39	slip	תחתונית
tayarut (f)	7	tourism	תיירות
teena (f)	14	fig	תאנה
teenim (f.pl.)	14	figs	תאנים
téker (m)	36	puncture	תקר
ten (m.s. imv)	11	give	תן
téred (m)	14	spinach	תרד
téša (f)	11	nine	תשע
teufa (f)	3	flight	תעופה
teuna (f)	36	accident	תאונה
tifne (m.s.)	6	you will turn	תפנה
tifni (f.s.)	6	you will turn	תפני
tif'ora (f)	24	stage setting	תפאורה
tigmor (m.s.)	10	you will finish	תגמור
tik (m)	39	brief case, file folder	תיק
tiken	29	he repaired	תיקן
tíras (m)	14	corn	תירס
tislax (m.s.)	7	you will pardon	תסלח
tispóret (f)	27	haircut, hairdo	תספורת
tisróket (f)	27	hair do	תסרוקת
tiš'a (m)	11	nine	תשעה
tiša'asar (m)	11	nineteen	תשעה-עשר
tixon (m.s.)	40	middle	תיכון
tmarim (m.pl.)	14	dates	תמרים
tmidi (m.s.)	27	permanent	תמידי
tocaa (f)	5	result	תוצאה
tocaot (f.pl.)	5	results	תוצאות
toda (f)	1	thanks	תודה
tor	32	line, turn	תור
toxnit	11	plan, program	תוכנית
treysar (m)	14	dozen	תריסר
tša'esre (f)	11	nineteen	תשע-עשרה
turai (m)	26	private (military rank)	טוראי
u-	1	and	ר-
uga (f)	15	cake	עוגה
ulam (m)	22	hall, orchestra	אולם
ulay	17	maybe, perhaps	אולי
vaday	40	certain	וודאי
ve-	3	and	ר-
vétek	33	length of service	וותק
vexen	13	and so	וכן

-xa (m.s.)	1	you, your	־ךָ
xacait (f)	28	skirt	חצאית
xaci (construct)	14	half of	חצי
xacilim (m.pl.)	14	eggplants	חצילים
xacot	18	midnight	חצות
xadaš (m.s.)	7	new	חדש
xadaša (f.s.)	7	new	חדשה
xadiš (m.s.)	3	modern	חריש
xafifa (f)	27	shampoo	חפיפה
xag (m)	12	holiday	חג
xagora (f)	39	belt	חגורה
xáil (m)	26	branch of service	חיל
xaklai (m.s.)	31	agricultural	חקלאי
xaklaut (f)	31	agriculture	חקלאות
xala (f)	13	chala, twist bread	חלה
xala	31	he got sick	חלה
xalav (m)	14	milk	חלב
xalifa (f)	28	suit	חליפה
xaluk (m)	39	robe	חלוק
xam (m.s.)	15	hot, warm	חם
xameš (f)	11	five	חמש
xaméš'esre (f)	11	fifteen	חמש-עשרה
xamiša (m)	11	five	חמישה
xamišáasar (m)	11	fifteen	חמישה-עשר
xamsin (m)	21	desert heat wave	חמסין
xamuc	15	sour	חמוץ
xanaya (f)	22	parking	חניה
xardal (m)	14	mustard	חרדל
xása (f)	14	lettuce	חסה
xasax	34	he saved	חסך
xašmal	32	electricity	חשמל
xašuv (m.s.)	33	important	חשוב
xatixa (f)	28	piece	חתיכה
xaval	24	it's too bad	חבל
xaver (m)	25	friend	חבר
xavila (f)	14	package	חבילה
xay	34	live, alive	חי
xayav	14	owe	חייב
xayal	26	soldier	חייל
xayat (m)	39	tailor	חייט
xayim (m.pl.)	24	life	חיים
xazak (m.s.)	30	strong	חזק
xaze (m)	30	chest	חזה
xazia (f)	39	bra	חזיה
xéci (m)	14	half	חצי
xem'a (f)	14	butter	חמאה
xen	3	favor, charm	חן
xešbon (m)	25	bill, account	חשבון
xevra (f)	25	company	חברה
xilek	34	he divided	חילק
xiyeg	19	he dialed	חייג
xódeš (m)	2	month	חודש
xof	21	beach, shore, coast	חוף
xofši (m.s.)		free	חופשי
xom (m)	20	heat	חום
xóref (m)	22	winter	חורף
xošev (m.s. pres)	7	think	חושב
xošévet (f.s. pres)	7	think	חושבת
xuc	5	outside	חוץ
xulca (f)	39	blouse	חולצה
xum	14	brown	חום
xupim (m.pl.)	21	beaches, shores, coasts	חופים

yaale (3 m.s.)	14	will cost, go up	יעלה
yabaša (f)	26	dry land, continent	יבשה
yacía (m)	22	balcony	יציע
yad (f)	30	hand	יד
yafa (f.s.)	3	beautiful, pretty	יפה
yafe (m.s.)	3	beautiful, pretty	יפה
yáin (m)	12	wine	יין
yakar (m.s.)	14	expensive, dear	יקר
yam (m)	4	sea	ים
yamim	4	days	ימים
yarad	22	he descended	ירד
yarok	14	green	ירוק
yašan	25	he slept	ישן
yašar (m.s.)	19	straight	ישר
yašir (m.s.)	19	direct	ישיר
yaveš	28	dry	יבש
yaxol (m.s.)	6	is able	יכול
yaxólnu	12	we were able	יכולנו
yecia (f)	22	exit	יציאה
yemama	18	24 hour period	יממה
yemína	6	to the right	ימינה
yemini (m.s.)	22	right	ימיני
yérek	14	vegetable	ירק
yesudar (s m.s.)	4	will be arranged	יסודר
yeš	9	there is, there are	יש
yešnam	37	there are	ישנם
yéter	4	rest, remainder	יתר
yexola (f.s.)	6	can	יכולה
yexólet (f)	28	ability	יכולת
yikax	17	will take	יקח
yitkarer (3 m.s.)	15	it will cool	יתקרר
yitra (f)	34	balance, remainder	יתרה
yoec (m)	2	counsellor, adviser	יועץ
yófi (m)	26	beauty	יופי
yom (m)	2	day	יום
yomáim	2	two days	יומיים
yoter	13	more	יותר
zaken (m.s.)	24	old	זקן
žaket (m)	28	jacket	ז'קט
zarax	20	it shined	זרח
ze	4	it, this	זה
zehu	37	that, this	זהו
zeytim (m.pl.)	14	olives	זיתים
zman	18	time	זמן
zol (m.s.)	14	cheap	זול
zot (f)	7	it, this	זאת
zu (f)	13	it, this	זו
zug (m)	28	pair	זוג
zxut (f)	23	right, privilege	זכות